FOUNDATIONS OF CLINICAL AND COUNSELING PSYCHOLOGY

FOUNDATIONS OF CLINICAL AND COUNSELING PSYCHOLOGY

Arthur C. Bohart
Judith Todd
California State University, Dominguez Hills

HARPER & ROW, PUBLISHERS, New York
Cambridge, Philadelphia, San Francisco, Washington,
London, Mexico City, São Paulo, Singapore, Sydney

Sponsoring Editor: Leslie Carr
Text Design Adaptation: Barbara Bert, North 7 Atelier Ltd.
Cover Design: Brenda Booth
Production Manager: Willie Lane
Compositor: ComCom Division of Haddon Craftsmen, Inc.
Printer and Binder: R. R. Donnelley & Sons Company
Cover Printer: NEBC

FOUNDATIONS OF CLINICAL AND COUNSELING PSYCHOLOGY

Library of Congress Cataloging-in-Publication Data

Bohart, Arthur C.
Foundations of clinical and counseling psychology.

Includes bibliographies and index.
1. Clinical psychology. 2. Psychotherapy.
3. Counseling. I. Todd, Judith. II. Title. [DNLM:
1. Counseling. 2. Psychology, Clinical. 3. Psychotherapy. WM 105 B676f]
RC467.B64 1988 616.89 87–26965
ISBN 0–06–046672–3

88 89 90 91 9 8 7 6 5 4 3 2 1

To Our Parents

Brief Contents

Detailed Contents

Preface

Our first goal in writing this text was to design an introductory clinical psychology text that emphasizes psychotherapy while still retaining coverage of other important topics, such as assessment, history and new directions, and professional, legal, and ethical issues. A large portion of the book is devoted to the major theoretical models for doing psychotherapy: psychoanalytic, object relations, client-centered, existential and gestalt, behavioral, cognitive, and family systems models. In addition we cover types of group therapy, sex therapy, specific techniques such as hypnosis, and relatively new fields such as behavioral medicine. Rather than simply summarizing the psychotherapy theories, we wanted to give students a sense of the important intellectual issues raised by each approach and to help them investigate areas of difference and commonality among the theories.

A second goal was to present not only the accepted models, but also the the *latest* major theoretical developments, such as object relations theory and self psychology. These are certainly the most exciting and influential developments in the psychoanalytic area in recent years, stimulating a healthy rebirth of interest in psychoanalytic views. Similarly, we present recent developments in cognitive therapy, such as Beck's work with anxiety disorders, and in family systems views. Finally, we cover recent relevant research findings. However, we must acknowledge that any attempt to be comprehensive and up-to-date would be doomed before it started. There is simply too much to know and too much to read, and knowledge explodes and develops too fast. Thus it is inevitable that we may have been unable to include all important references and developments. We must apologize in advance for this.

Our third goal was to write a *useful* book—a stimulating and engaging text that would be pedagogically sound and flexible enough to fit the needs of different instructors. The use of both clinical cases and everyday examples engages students' interest, stimulates critical thinking, and encourages students to consider the relation between application and theory. Clear headings and subheadings and a detailed table of contents help students organize their reading and learning. Boxes highlight specific points and issues in each chapter.

In keeping with our third goal, we have prepared an accompanying *Instructor's*

Resource Guide, which contains suggestions for different ways of using the text and additional lecture and discussion topics, as well as an extensive text bank of multiple-choice and essay examination questions.

When we started writing this book, we believed we were trying to write it from a theoretically unbiased perspective. However, it is apparent that we do have a bias: toward an eclectic, "open" view of doing clinical and counseling psychology. We do not believe that any one perspective has demonstrated that it contains more "truth" about human behavior and the remediation of psychological problems than any other. Because we believe each viewpoint is limited and incomplete, a fourth goal was to provide critiques of each perspective. We hope we have done this in an evenhanded manner and that individuals committed to each perspective will feel our criticisms are fair. We hope we have not put ourselves in the position of the comedian Mort Sahl, who used to end his comedy monologues by wondering if there was anyone left in the audience that he hadn't offended.

Generally the critical evaluation of each approach comes at the end of the chapter on that approach, and includes a brief review of relevant research, especially on the effectiveness of that approach to therapy. While some instructors may wish to delete the evaluation sections or have students make their own evaluations first, we believe that evaluating each theory and comparing it to others increases students' intellectual grasp of each approach and enhances their ability to reason about theory and practice.

In keeping with our eclectic bias we have included two chapters that are not often found in introductory clinical or counseling psychology texts. The first is a chapter on research on psychotherapy. We believe it is important that students be aware of the great difficulties involved in sorting out belief and opinion from knowledge about psychotherapy. We are dismayed whenever a student is dogmatically sure that the behavioral approach or the humanistic approach or the systems approach is best. We hope that the research chapter will introduce students to the complexities of empirical studies of psychotherapy, provide them with an overview of the current (but rapidly changing) state of knowledge, and increase their critical reasoning skills about research and the nature of knowledge.

The second special feature is the chapter on areas of convergence among differing approaches to psychotherapy. Eclecticism in psychotherapy seems to be the "wave of the future." There is now a Society for Psychotherapy Integration, a journal of eclectic psychotherapy, and a *Handbook of Eclectic Therapy.* The chapter on convergences among psychotherapies pulls together the threads running through the previous chapters and critcally examines crucial differences and commonalities among all approaches. Again, the inclusion should enhance both students' basic knowledge and their ability to reason critically about important issues in theory and practice. We hope that this presentation of our views on areas of convergence will be, as has been suggested by some of our reviewers, a theoretical contribution to this new area in the field of psychotherapy.

To deal with the problem of sexist language, we have tried to balance our usage of male and female pronouns. If male pronouns are used in one section of a chapter, female pronouns may be used in another. If we refer to the client as "he," we may refer to the therapist as "she." We also use plural pronouns to avoid the problem altogether.

This book could not have been completed without the invaluable assistance of many people. We would like to thank our editor, Leslie Carr. We want to thank Gene Kalland and the other members of the California State University Dominguez Hills Professional Development Committee who supported the book's fledgling development. We wish to thank our supportive colleagues in the psychology department, especially Lisa Gray-Shellberg, Diane Henschel, and Beverly Palmer. We would like to thank Hope Todd, Joanne Uno, and Barbara Hazelleaf, who did much of the initial typing on the manuscript. We wish to extend special thanks to those persistent and brave souls who reviewed our writings and gave us helpful feedback: Franz R. Epting, University of Florida; Ruthellen Josselson, Towson State University; Joseph Lyons, University of California, Davis; Beverly L. Palmer, California State University, Dominguez Hills; Lyle Schmidt, Ohio State University; T. Gale Thompson, Bethany College; Donald H. Voss, Slippery Rock University of Pennsylvania; and Rudolph L. Zlody, College of the Holy Cross; and Michael J. Moore, Fran Miller, and Peter Hoon. These reviewers made many valuable suggestions, and, as it is customary to point out, any deficiencies in the book are solely our own. We would also like to thank several individuals who did research or editing for us: Louise Jackson, Debi Shapiro, Rose Lopez, and Hope Todd. Finally, we would like to thank our respective children, Kelly and Emily (Judy) and Maura (Art), for actually being able to survive on their own at various times while we worked.

Arthur C. Bohart
Judith Todd

Chapter 1

Professional Psychology in Context

Clinical psychology and counseling psychology are helping professions, specifically mental health professions. In the United States today many individuals, groups, and institutions offer to help others in many ways. These groups overlap to a surprising degree with clinical and counseling psychology in terms of their goals, methods, and clientele. With this degree of overlap and with the diversity of types of help available, it may seem difficult to distinguish clinical and counseling psychology from other mental health and helping professions.

If the general goal of the mental health professions is to help individuals reduce their suffering and improve their life effectiveness, then many other institutions, individuals, and groups share the same goal. Schools and churches, for instance, attempt to improve and help members of the community by teaching academic skills and moral behavior. Many groups, from weight clinics to seminars on how to become rich and famous, are in the business of changing the behavior of others.

In addition to sharing goals clinical psychology, counseling psychology, and the other mental health professions share helping methods with other groups. The helping methods of counseling and psychotherapy include many techniques used by others, such as advice ("You should give up drinking," "You need to raise your consciousness"), suggestion ("You Higher Self will appear to help you," "You will not feel like smoking"), and interpretation ("You feel life is meaningless because you haven't accepted Jesus," "You aren't earning riches because of your underlying belief that you don't deserve them"). Weight clinics and smoking cessation centers employ behavior modification techniques that were developed and researched by clinical psychologists, and many ministers, priests, and rabbis engage in individual and couples counseling.

Finally, it has been found that there is a great deal of overlap in clientele among these different helping approaches (Katz & Rolde, 1981). Often the unhappy person who goes to a professional psychologist has already been to seminars and groups, seen one or more physicians, learned meditation, or tried to obtain help in other ways. It appears that people who feel in need of help are often willing to try many different approaches. However, it is clear that not all helping approaches are of equal value for all problems.

While clinical psychology and counseling psychology exist in a social matrix with other helping groups, they can nevertheless be distinguished from others in several important ways. Professional psychologists are just that—professional. They have attended recognized universities where they have received extensive postgraduate education and training in research, evaluation, and implementation of helping methods, and they are often licensed or certified by the state to engage in specific kinds of helping practice.

Educated in the graduate departments of universities, professional psychologists are unique in the emphasis on research in their training. Clinical psychology as a field is based on what is known as the scientist-practitioner model (discussed below), a model that incorporates both academic research and applied helping skills as necessary for the profession. This emphasis on research means that the clinical and counseling psychologists are trained to assess and evaluate what they do more rigorously than other helpers. The therapeutic approaches they use are likely to be based on the most researched theories and methods in the helping field. Thus, clinical and counseling psychologists employ helping methods that are more likely to have been subjected to empirical research than those of other helpers.

The questions of who needs professional help and what kind of help are answered differently by different individuals involved. Let us take excessive drinking of alcohol as an example. An excessive drinker's neighbors may regard him as willfully rebellious, needing prison; the drinker's minister may see him as weak, needing spiritual help; the drinker's wife may see him as sick, needing medical help; and the drinker may well deny the need for any help at all.

Helpers may recommend different types of help. Even professional helpers may disagree on what is needed. Physicians may believe that excessive drinking is a physical disease requiring medical help, while psychologists may believe that excessive drinking is a psychological or behavior problem requiring psychological help. The answers to the question of who needs what sort of help, then, will partly reflect competition between helping professions.

The question of who should receive professional help also reflects society's attitudes toward problem behavior. These attitudes change with time. In the eighteenth century in the United States public drunkenness was considered normal, socially acceptable behavior. In the nineteenth century excessive drinking came to be regarded as a sin railed against by ministers and temperance workers. By the twentieth century public drunkenness was a crime, to be controlled through laws and imprisonment. In recent decades excessive drinking has been regarded as a disorder requiring professional help.

When public drunkenness was socially accepted, it was not defined as a problem. Once excessive drinking came to be viewed as a problem of concern to the whole community, how best to prevent and control it raised the difficult issue of balancing traditional values of individual liberty and the need to control the behavior of certain individuals. Our society is comfortable with depriving of their liberty individuals who engage in behaviors with serious consequences to others, such as murder or assault. Our society seems to prefer trying to use medical treatment or psychological help to control individuals who engage in behaviors with less serious or more ambiguous consequences. Clinical and counseling psychology allow us to treat social problems while preserving our value of individualism.

Because our society constantly redefines social problems and the types of behaviors that require professional help, the roles of clinical and counseling psychologists are constantly changing. Furthermore, many individuals define *themselves* as in need of help or treatment. As increasing numbers of problematic behaviors are defined as suitable for psychological treatment, the diversity of roles for professional psychologists has also increased in recent years. The goals, methods, and clientele of professional psychology will continue to change, as will be discussed in Chapter 12. However, let us first try to define and describe the fields of clinical psychology, counseling psychology, and the other mental health professions as they exist in the United States today.

THE MENTAL HEALTH PROFESSIONS

Besides clinical psychology and counseling psychology, there are several other mental health professions that help individuals whose thoughts, feelings, or behaviors are problematic to themselves or to others. The differences among these professions can be examined in terms of education and training requirements, licensing and certification requirements, specific areas of expertise, typical activities, and levels of pay and prestige. The type of education required for psychiatrists and psychologists is standard across the United States, but the licensing and certification requirements vary from state to state. The education and certification requirements for the other professional groups vary to a large degree from state to state. The professional duties of the different mental health professionals (MHPs) also vary, but in most cases, they overlap.

Clinical Psychology

Historically, the existence of clinical psychology as a separate professional field has been tenuous, with special competition between psychiatry and clinical psychology. Just a few years ago there was heated controversy over the right of clinical psychologists to do anything besides psychological assessment and counseling with children. In 1954 the American Medical Association (AMA) declared that psychotherapy was a medical treatment, with the implication that psychotherapy by a psychologist constituted practicing medicine without a license and was therefore illegal. In 1958 the American Psychiatric Association adopted the AMA position and opposed the legal certification of psychologists. The American Psychological Association (APA) threatened to sue the AMA and "the other APA" over these issues. However, these conflicts were worked out by the 1960s. With the liberal funding of mental health programs in that prosperous decade, there was business enough for everyone, and the competition between psychology and psychiatry was reduced. When funds for mental health were greatly reduced in the 1980s, the competition between MHPs again intensified, with many threats to psychology as an independent profession.

Education and Training According to the APA, the term *psychologist* should be used only for individuals with a doctoral degree in psychology. However, increasing numbers of people are earning master's degrees in psychology. What are they to be called? Master's level psychologists almost always find appropriate employment, and even individuals with a bachelor's degree may hold jobs in agencies or companies that require performing some of the functions of a psychologist. However, their status remains highly controversial within the APA, which still holds to the necessity of the doctoral degree.

There are two educational models for the profession of clinical psychology. The scientist-practitioner training model incorporates both academic research skills and applied helping skills. Clinical psychologists trained according to the scientist-practitioner model are unique among mental health professionals in their knowledge of assessment, evaluation, and the empirical basis for their methods. The professional model, while still requiring a doctoral degree, eliminates the academic research requirement for clinical psychology. In the 1960s schools of professional psychology were established. Following the professional training model, these graduate schools emphasize clinical training, not research.

At present there are two types of doctoral degrees in clinical psychology. The Ph.D., or Doctor of Philosophy, is awarded by academic departments of psychology in universities upon the completion of a research dissertation. For a Ph.D. in clinical psychology, a year of internship in an APA-approved clinical setting is required in addition to three years of related course work and the research dissertation, for a total of five postgraduate years. (A Ph.D. in other areas of psychology, such as social or experimental psychology, usually requires three years, since there is less course work and no clinical internship.) Professional schools offer the Psy.D., or Doctor of Psychology, and their programs take from four to six years after the bachelor's degree.

Licensing and Certification At present all states regulate the practice of clinical psychology through licensing, certification, and registration. Licensing of psychologists is a fairly recent phenomenon. Most laws regarding licensure where enacted in the 1950s and 1960s. As psychotherapy became acceptable and even popular, some unscrupulous and untrained individuals were offering to treat the public. Many people believe that individuals seeking psychological help are exceptionally vulnerable and liable to be harmed by inept or exploitative practitioners. At the same time, organized medicine was trying to ensure that only medical doctors treated the public with psychotherapy, and psychologists wanted to legitimize their right to offer psychotherapeutic services to the public. Desires to protect the public and for professional recognition led the psychological community to urge their state governments to enact laws to license psychologists.

A license is issued to professionals who have demonstrated competence in their field, and it permits them to practice in the state. Regulations vary, but we can use California licensing law, which is similar to that of many states, as an example. California law requires 2,000 hours of supervised clinical practice in a multidisciplinary setting to be obtained within a 24-month period after acquiring a doctoral degree. After candidates apply for a license and verify their education and training, they must take a national multiple-choice examination relating to all areas of psychology, such as statistics, research design, and clinical practice. If they pass the written exam, candidates must submit to a one-hour oral examination by two licensed psychologists, in which they are asked about ethics, the law, and clinical practice. This procedure is supposed to ensure that only ethical, competent people are licensed as psychologists and allowed to offer psychological services to the public.

Certification is a weaker form of control than licensure. The state certifies that the person claiming to be a psychologist has indeed completed all the educational and training requirements for the profession, but issuing a certificate does not include evaluating the candidate for competence.

Registration is a still weaker form of control. Practicing psychologists merely register their practice with the state.

In addition to licensing or certification, experienced psychologists may seek to become diplomates of the American Board of Professional Psychology (ABPP). To qualify for this diploma, a psychologist must have five years of professional experience, be a member of the APA, hold a Ph.D. from an APA-approved program, submit copies of his or her work, see an unknown patient under observation, and pass an oral examination. Being an ABPP diplomate implies additional competence and professional status for the psychologist.

Roles of Clinical Psychologists The licensing and certification laws of most states explicitly state what psychologists may do. In 1987 the APA approved a revised Model Act for State Licensure of Psychologists, which serves as a model for state laws. This act's definition of the practice of psychology gives a fairly complete description of the roles of psychologists:

> The practice of psychology is defined as the observation, description, evaluation, interpretation and modification of human behavior by the application of psychological principles, methods and procedures, for the purpose of preventing or eliminating symptomatic, maladaptive, or undesired behavior and of enhancing interpersonal relationships, work and life adjustment, personal effectiveness, behavioral health, and mental health. The practice of psychology includes, but is not limited to, psychological testing and the evaluation or assessment of personal characteristics such as intelligence, personality, abilities, interests, aptitudes, and neuropsychological functioning; counseling, psychoanalysis, psychotherapy, hypnosis, biofeedback, and behavior analysis and therapy; diagnosis and treatment of mental and emotional disorder or disability, alcoholism and substance abuse, disorders of habit or conduct, as well as of the psychological aspects of physical illness, accident, injury or disability; and psychoeducational evaluation, therapy, remediation and consultation. Psychological services may be rendered to individuals, families, groups, and the public. The practice of psychology shall be construed within the meaning of this definition without regard to whether payment is received for services rendered.

There are many different types of employment available to psychologists. Clinical psychologists work in private practice and in mental health agencies. They also work in universities, hospitals, prisons, schools, health organizations, halfway houses, nursing homes, police departments, and private companies and businesses. Recently psychologists have been involved in Employee Assistance Programs (EAPs), in which businesses retain mental health professionals to provide treatment of disturbed or troublesome employees, as a way to improve company functioning and profits.

In both private and institutional practice, psychologists engage in a variety of types of psychotherapy (which are discussed in most of the rest of this book). In addition to individual, group, marriage, and family therapy, some clinicians treat sexual dysfunctions, some do behavior modification, some use biofeedback, and others perform hypnosis, according to their training and expertise. Besides therapy, clinical psychologists are qualified to administer, score, and interpret a variety of tests designed to assess psychopathology, personality development, and intellectual functioning. Psychologists are the only MHPs qualified to administer and interpret individual psychological tests. One major difference between the practice of clinical psychology and that of psychiatry is that only psychologists may administer and interpret psychological tests and only psychiatrists may prescribe drugs and hospital treatments. Some clinical psychologists engage in university teaching and research, as well as or instead of assessment and treatment.

Because of the doctoral degree and the extensive training requirements, and because of years of struggle to obtain public recognition and parity with medical doctors, clinical psychologists are the second most prestigious group of MHPs, and they command, on average, the second highest fees. Their average salary remains about 40 percent of that of psychiatrists (Cattell, 1983).

Counseling Psychology

Although similar in many ways to clinical psychology, counseling psychology is distinguished by requiring a doctoral degree in counseling psychology or counselor education, by stressing certain theories of therapy (such as client-centered therapy, discussed in Chapter 5), and by working with a relatively nondisturbed clientele. Counseling psychologists may assess and counsel individuals or groups regarding their life problems, career plans, relationship issues, academic choices, and the like. They may teach in counseling psychology programs at universities and conduct research on communication, relationships, and the counseling process. Some counseling psychologists obtain the psychologists' license and work in private practice, clinics, hospitals, student counseling services, and business in as many diverse roles as clinical psychologists.

Educational Psychology

Overlapping with clinical and counseling psychology is educational psychology, which requires an Ed.D., Doctor of Education, degree. Educational psychologists stress research, assessment, and counseling relevant to the educational process, such as learning, motivation, or disability. They often obtain the psychologists' license and work in schools, universities, private practice, and mental health agencies, again in a variety of roles similar to those of clinical psychologists.

School Psychology

The requirements and roles of school psychologists vary from state to state and from school district to school district. Generally, school psychologists have had teaching experience and hold at least a master's degree in school psychology, pupil personnel, or other areas. As the name implies, they work in schools and participate in evaluating and treating children. They may assess children for giftedness, as well as trying to discover causes and remedies for difficulties in school.

Psychiatry

The most prestigious and powerful mental health profession is psychiatry. Psychiatrists are physicians who have specialized in psychiatry, and they tend to view mental disorders as having a chemical or biological basis. They must first acquire an M.D., or Medical Doctor, degree (or other medical degree) from an accredited medical school. They must then complete a three-year residency in psychiatry, during which they provide psychiatric services under the supervision of one or more psychiatrists. Critics of this admittedly rigorous and demanding regimen complain that the majority of it is irrelevant to the practice of psychiatry. Others argue that because organic processes and physical diseases may be part of or must be distinguished from mental disorders, the extensive medical training is necessary.

Psychiatrists are licensed by state medical boards, and they are thus qualified to work in hospitals and agencies and to engage in private practice. In most states only psychiatrists may commit people to mental hospitals against their will. In California a psychiatric nurse, clinical social worker, or psychologist on a hospital staff may sign commitment papers, but only with the additional signature of a psychiatrist. Until recently a psychologist's clients who required hospitalization had to admit themselves or the psychologist had to find a psychiatrist willing to treat them. The clients' treatment was taken over by a psychiatrist and the psychologist usually stopped seeing them during their hospital stay. This situation may be changing (this and related issues will be discussed in Chapter 12).

In addition to hospitalizing their patients, psychiatrists are by law permitted to engage in a variety of forms of psychotherapy, including individual, group, and family therapy. Psychiatrists also diagnose patients, usually through a diagnostic interview known as the mental status exam. They are the only MHP allowed to prescribe drugs, including the psychotropic drugs. They may prescribe electroconvulsive shock therapy, occupational therapy, and other forms of hospital treatment.

Many psychiatrists work in private practice and are affiliated with a hospital, while some work exclusively in mental hospitals and hospitals with psychiatric wards. Psychiatrists also work in outpatient mental health clinics, and the director of such community facilities is often a psychiatrist.

Psychiatrists have the highest status and highest rate of pay of all the MHPs.

Psychoanalysis

At the present time in the United States a psychoanalyst must hold a medical degree and must have received special psychoanalytic training at a psychoanalytic institute, including taking special courses, seeing patients under a training analyst, and undergoing a long and intensive analysis with an experienced psychoanalyst. The psychoanalytic institutes are independent of medical schools. In other countries MHPs other than physicians may seek psychoanalytic training and become psychoanalysts. In the United States social workers and psychologists may take analytic training at certain institutes, and they may engage in analytically oriented psychotherapy, although it remains controversial whether they may call themselves psychoanalysts.

Since psychoanalysis is a long and expensive procedure, psychoanalysts almost always work in private practice. They typically see patients individually several times a week for one to several years. (Psychoanalytic therapy is described in Chapter 3.) Since they hold medical degrees, psychoanalysts may prescribe drugs and hospitalize patients if necessary.

Their fees are equivalent to those of psychiatrists.

Social Work

Social work is a fairly old mental health profession, older than professional psychology. The practice of social work has changed in recent years. In the early years of the profession social workers provided direct services to the disadvantaged portions of the population as part of the services of charities. Often politically liberal or radical social workers organized communities and lobbied for social change. They helped the needy obtain charitable services, find jobs, get training, get medical treatment, deal with crises, and the like. Now they rarely do this type of work. Their profession has evolved to resemble clinical psychology.

The master's degree in social work, or M.S.W., requires two years of course work and supervised experience after the bachelor's degree. Licensing (for the LCSW, Licensed Clinical Social Worker) and certification requirements vary greatly from state to state. In some states and in some jobs social workers need only the bachelor's degree.

Like psychologists, social workers work in a variety of settings, including private practice and hospitals and agencies, and they provide several types of psychotherapy. Some decades ago many social workers became analysts, and many still remain psychodynamically oriented in theory and practice. Today most social workers spend most of their time doing intake interviews, treatment plans, and, most of all, individual and group therapy and counseling.

In terms of power, prestige, and pay, social workers generally rank somewhat lower than psychologists. However, fees for social workers in private practice vary greatly.

Marriage, Family, and Child Counseling

Some states now license or certify a relatively new group of MHPs called marriage, family, and child counselors (MFCCs). In California, for example, the MFCC license requires 3,000 hours of supervised training and a master's degree in MFCC or its equivalent. An equivalent degree is presently open to interpretation and controversy, so that people with master's degrees in several different subjects, such as clinical psychology or pastoral counseling, may be allowed to take the MFCC examination. The MFCC examination has written and oral components that test for knowledge, ethics, and clinical competence.

MFCCs are supposed to engage in group or marriage, family, and child counseling, according to their expertise. They work in a variety of settings, as well as in private practice.

Since MFCCs have less training and a lower level degree, they are usually paid less than psychologists and often less than social workers. Some agencies prefer to hire MFCCs as a way to cut the cost of providing counseling and therapy to the public. While MFCC fees are usually lower than those of psychologists, some energetic and successful MFCCs in private practice command higher fees.

Other Mental Health Professionals

Mental Health Counselors Some states offer an optional certificate for mental health counselors. These individuals may hold bachelor's or master's degrees with various types of training and experience required for the certificate. They engage in a variety of types of group and individual counseling in a variety of service settings.

Psychological Assistants Some states allow unlicensed persons to work under the supervision of licensed psychologists as psychological assistants, so they may gain necessary experience. A psychological assistant is employed by a licensed psychologist or psychiatrist to perform limited psychological functions within the assistant's area of competence. The assistant must perform his or her work only while the supervisor is on the premises, and the supervising psychologist must provide a certain number of hours of face-to-face supervision for every so many hours of work. In addition, the assistant must be making progress toward an advanced degree in psychology. Supervising psychologists must verify annually to the licensing board that their assistants meet all of the above requirements.

Typically, psychological assistants perform limited services, such as administering psychological tests (which are perhaps scored and interpreted by the supervising psychologist), some forms of behavior modification, intake interviews, or play therapy with a child while the employing psychologist sees the parents. Some experienced assistants do individual psychotherapy, in a way similar to private practice, although they are not technically independent practitioners.

Bachelor's Level Professions There are several bachelor's level mental health professions, which do limited forms of counseling rather than psychotherapy. A recently developed college major is human services. These students do course work in topics like clinical psychology, psychopathology, social work, agency administration, and counseling skills, and they do many hours of fieldwork in many different settings. Human services workers work in agencies providing services for children, the disabled, the elderly, and other disadvantaged portions of the population. In many ways the human services worker resembles the social worker of old.

Other bachelor's level graduates work in hospitals, clinics, and community agencies under a variety of job titles: counselor, alcoholism counselor, intake worker, community worker, recreation leader, group leader, welfare officer, evaluation officer, drug rehabilitation leader, and many other titles. The job requirements, skill level, and services performed in these positions vary, but often resemble the work of psychologists and other therapists.

There are even jobs in the mental health field for people without a bachelor's degree. For example, the position of psychiatric technician in a hospital requires two years of college. Psych techs, as they are called, usually perform protective or custodial services in hospital wards, but some engage in individual and group counseling with patients.

Psychiatric Nurses The profession of psychiatric nursing requires a bachelor's degree in nursing and usually some type of postgraduate course work or training. Psychiatric nurses generally work in mental hospitals and on psychiatric wards, performing nursing duties, such as overseeing the administration of prescribed medications and the daily care of patients. Psychiatric nurses may also conduct individual or group counseling and participate in behavior modification programs in the hospital, and some engage in private practice.

Paraprofessional Counselors Paraprofessional counselors, also called nonprofessional counselors or peer counselors, may have little formal education, but they receive special training in counseling skills to enhance their natural helping abilities. Paraprofessionals generally work in community agencies that treat special populations that are underserved or poorly served by the usual mental health institutions. Often a paraprofessional counselor is a member of the underserved group. For example, ex-drug addicts may assist drug abusers, and a minority group member may counsel minorities. The use of paraprofessional counselors was encouraged by research in the 1960s that showed that naturally helpful nonprofessionals were as effective in counseling certain groups as psychiatrists and psychologists.

Trainees and Volunteers Many undergraduate and graduate students in psychology and related fields volunteer to work in mental health and community agencies in order to obtain training and experience in their chosen fields and to be of service to the community. (Nonstudent citizens also volunteer to be of service.) If there are formal ties between the agencies accepting volunteers and the university sending out students, the volunteers may have a formal role with a title such as trainee or intern. In return for giving their time, the trainees receive supervision and in-service training, which help the students to obtain future employment, to get into graduate school, and to explore how well they like the mental health field. Trainees take part in many mental health services, including many activities similar to those undertaken by professional psychologists.

PROFESSIONAL PSYCHOLOGY IN ITS PRESENT-DAY CONTEXT

As all the mental health professions have grown, the overlap in functions and populations served and, to some degree, the competition among the professions have also grown. Clinical psychology is constantly expanding into new areas, both as research suggests new applications and as society comes to view psychological intervention as the solution to more and more of its problems. For example, research discovered that people could learn to control their own brain waves and other autonomic responses thought to be outside of conscious control; this discovery led to behavioral treatments involving biofeedback for migraine headaches, high blood pressure, and other disorders. An example of turning to psychology for a solution to a social problem can be seen in Siegel's (1983) argument that the United States should shift the focus of its handling of the crime problem from capturing and punishing the criminals to providing psychological treatment for the inevitable victims.

Along with growth has come increased contact between professional psychology and the other mental health professions. Often this contact is cooperative and fruitful, but as has long been the case between psychiatry and clinical psychology, there may be competition and conflict over expertise, methods of treatment, and the right to treat certain groups. Some people, including many MHPs, have come to believe that a system that involves many specialist groups, each with its own methods, training, and regulations, has outlived its usefulness. The time and money spent on competition, legal battles, and replication of services could be better spent on cooperating to solve society's problems. Cattell (1983) argues for greater cooperation between psychiatry and psychology and for an end to the battle for "control of the booming $17 billion a year mental health business." In actual practice the similarities among the various MHPs appear to be greater than their differences.

As stated before, often various MHPs work effectively together. In the decade before World War II the team approach to the treatment of mental illness was developed. The psychiatrist was the head of the team, made most of the treatment decisions, prescribed medication, and was responsible for the physical well-being of the patients. The clinical psychologist assessed patients for their intellectual and personality functioning. The social worker coordinated the cases, often did the intake interviews, and worked with the family members of the patients. The provider of actual psychotherapy, if any, varied. In some hospitals the psychiatric nurse was part of the team, overseeing daily care of patients and in some cases providing therapy.

The team approach survives today in many agencies and in mental hospitals. Decisions may be made in a more egalitarian fashion today, and psychologists and social workers may be more involved in providing psychotherapy and counseling than in earlier years. More members have been added to the team, including MFCCs, speech therapists, occupational therapists, and paraprofessional counselors. Today clinical psychologists in mental hospitals and in community agencies generally work in departments of psychology, rather than in departments of psychiatry, and therefore have more independence and status than in earlier years.

Even in private practice cooperation among the different professions is common. A psychologist in private practice may work with a psychiatrist in order to obtain medication or hospitalization for clients when necessary. A psychiatrist may make referrals to a psychologist when patients need assessment or a special kind of treatment. Psychologists, social workers, and MFCCs may refer clients to each other when the clients are outside their areas of expertise or are unable to afford their fees.

As new psychological techniques are developed and as people increasingly seek psychological solutions for their problems, the diversity of psychotherapy and other psychological services offered by MHPs should increase. However, Albee (1970) argues that professional psychology should be working to put itself out of business by focusing on the prevention of psychological disorders. He believes that psychologists should stop wasting their expertise providing inefficient and costly psychotherapy to a few individuals, but should focus instead on "giving psychology away" by teaching the public how to help themselves. Levy (1984) also argues that psychologists should no longer focus on the treatment of mental illness, but must expand into wide areas of service, prevention, health enhancement, and evaluation. Weiss (1983) urges psychology to move into the field of behavioral toxicology and environmental health science, including research, assessment, treatment, prevention, and education related to environmental hazards that affect behavior.

One limit to psychology's expansion is the apparently increasing reluctance of taxpayers and insurance companies to pay for such services. Demonstrating the cost effectiveness of psychological treatments in terms of prevention of more serious problems or reduction in the use of other types of services is becoming highly important for the future of the mental health professions. Clinical psychologists are the MHPs best trained to do research and provide such evidence.

While professional psychologists have always been concerned with ethical practice, their expanding roles and issues of cost and payment will lead to increased concern and possibly controversy over laws and ethics as they apply to psychology. Much heated discussion has already been generated over how best to preserve the ethical obligation of client confidentiality while still providing necessary information to third party payers. It is only to be expected that controversies over what constitutes ethical practice will increase as psychologists develop new methods and move into new fields. Laws, ethics, and the future of clinical psychology are discussed in Chapter 12.

Now that we have tried to define clinical and counseling psychology in their present-day context, let us turn to the history of psychology as an applied profession. Clinical psychology is not a very old profession, and it evolved to its present state because of specific social and professional forces. A review of its historical development may explain some of the current controversies in the field and predict its future development. In fact, we believe, only an understanding of the history of the field will complete the discussion of professional psychology in context.

A SHORT HISTORY OF PSYCHOLOGY

Modern professional psychology evolved as the synthesis of two distinct trends in history. Its current theories and practices, its controversial issues, and its status as a field of endeavor can be more easily understood by examining those two historical forces. One trend is the development of psychology as an independent academic discipline within universities. The other is the failure of other disciplines to deal adequately with deviant members of society. These two forces came together in the individualistic, pragmatic United States of the twentieth century to develop a unique scientific and applied field, professional psychology.

Academic Psychology

The kinds of questions that the academic discipline of psychology studies have interested individuals and scholars since ancient times. "What is the relation between the pure immortal soul and the corrupt mortal body?" became in recent centuries "What is the relation between the mind and the body?" This fascinating question is still studied in fields such as psychosomatic medicine and biofeedback. How does the mind work? What motivates people to behave the way they do? How can we explain deviant behavior? What can we do about it? How can we all get along together? These are ancient questions of interest to modern psychology and to most people.

Among the ancient Chinese, Egyptians, Hebrews, Greeks, and Romans, gods and demons were believed to cause everything and provided the answers to the above questions. In the early Christian era the conflict between God and Satan and the concept of sin provided answers. After universities were founded in Europe in the fifteenth and sixteenth centuries, secular scholars as well as priests began to study these ancient questions, and academic departments of philosophy were formed.

After the Renaissance the world entered a period of rapid social change brought on by the expansion of knowledge, increases in the population, urbanization, and the Industrial Revolution. Religion was no longer adequate to provide the guideposts needed. Science emerged with what seemed to be more adequate explanations for many phenomena through the scientific method of careful observation, measurement, and experimentation. There was hope that the method would eventually solve all of the questions that have long perplexed humankind.

In the nineteenth century these ancient questions were still in the province of philosophy departments of universities. In the last part of that century a new discipline, psychology, broke away from philosophy to become a separate academic specialty. It charged itself with studying the same types of problems as philosophers, but by applying the new scientific method. Some scholars in the new field viewed humans as just another natural phenomenon, not special creations in God's image, and others saw them as machines, but psychologists agreed that the nature of humanity and the nature of the mind could be discovered through measurement and experimentation.

The year 1879 is the generally accepted date for the birth of academic psychology. In that year Wilhelm Wundt established the first independent psychology laboratory in Leipzig, Germany. Wundt argued that the subject matter of psychology was experience, not the relation of the body and soul, and that the mind alone was a legitimate object of scientific study. While Wundt is considered the first "Great Mind" in psychology, other scholars at that time were also doing work that became part of psychology. In 1869 Galton in England began his study and measurement of individual differences in attributes and abilities. And in 1875 William James, considered the first American psychologist, equipped part of a small laboratory at Harvard for the study of mental associations.

Even though James began his work before Wundt opened his laboratory, psychology became established as an academic discipline in the United States somewhat later than in Europe. Most early American psychologists traveled to Europe in order to study psychology. In 1883 G. Stanley Hall set up the first full-scale psychology laboratory in the United States at Johns Hopkins University. In 1888 James M. Cattell at the University of Pennsylvania held the first professorship in psychology. In 1890 William James published the first psychology book, *The Principles of Psychology.* In 1892 the American Psychological Association (APA) was formed with 26 members. By 1900 the APA had 127 members. The field of psychology has expanded ever since, with about 1,100 APA members by 1930, 37,000 by 1975, 60,000 in 1980, and 70,000 in 1985.

Psychology as an academic discipline has experienced several major shifts in the focus of its subject matter over the years. Early psychology was concerned with the structure and contents of the mind. The method of study was individual introspection to report mental associations. This method was abandoned fairly early, and the focus of psychology became the functions of the mind, what it does and how. About 1913 the approach called behaviorism broke with previous positions. John B. Watson, a major proponent of this view, argued that the proper study of psychology was observable behavior, that the mind cannot be observed. Pavlov's studies on the conditioned reflex bolstered Watson's position. Like the times in the United States, Watson's behaviorism was mechanistic, materialistic, and positivistic. By the 1920s behaviorism had largely replaced the study of the mind and individual experience in academic psychology in the United States. B. F. Skinner carried behaviorism further from the 1940s into the 1980s with his arguments for strict empiricism and the objective, atheoretical description of behavior without any reference to a "mind."

In recent years the mind has crept back into academic psychology. Albert Bandura, a prominent psychologist, developed social learning theory in the 1960s, which added the concept of imitation and the influence of other people to behavioristic learning theory. In the 1970s Bandura began to write about possible internal, or cognitive, variables that affect behavior and learning. He contributed to the development of a currently important body of theory and research called cognitive behaviorism. Swiss biologist Jean Piaget's influential research on cognitive development in infants and children also contributed to the new emphasis on cognition, which is a process of the mind. The long conflict over whether the proper study of psychology is the mind or behavior appears to be reaching a synthesis that psychology studies both.

Society's Treatment of Its Deviant Members

For far longer than academic departments of psychology have existed in universities, society has had to deal with its deviant members. The history of how society has treated its deviants coincided with the developments in academic psychology to produce a new applied profession, clinical psychology, the twentieth century in the United States, where the individualistic science fit in well with the individualistic values of the culture.

Who Is Deviant? People who do not conform to the behavior or beliefs of the majority of the members of society have always existed. For the sake of discussion, let us divide such deviant or nonconforming members of society into two types, the disturbed and the disturbing. Disturbing people are bothersome to other people. They may hold politically radical views and foment revolution; they may get drunk and fail to work; they may steal. The way our society is organized in the United States today, extremely bothersome people are handled by the legal system and are often incarcerated. Other societies in other times handled them by different means: The medieval community stoned them; the Roman Senate ordered them to commit suicide; the feudal lord had them executed or thrown in the dungeon; the sultan sold them into slavery.

There are also disturbed people. Other people or they themselves think that there is "something wrong" with them, but through the ages no one has been quite sure what it is. They suffer from uncontrollable urges to kill themselves; they are severely anxious for no reason; they see or hear things that others say are not real; they suffer paralysis or weakness when others say they are well; they are troubled by intrusive thoughts; they feel compelled to perform certain acts over and over. In the United States today such individuals are viewed as being psychologically disordered and in need of treatment by various mental health professionals. In previous ages disturbed people were sometimes tolerated or even venerated as "seers," but often they were killed, tortured, and locked away, although without doubt many such individuals were protected and cared for by their families, just as many are today.

A complex legal system has evolved in our society to deal with highly disturbing people. These laws are supposed to protect the life, well-being, and property of all the members of the community from the harmful acts of the criminal few. The most common method of social control of such people is imprisonment as a form of punishment, isolation, or rehabilitation. Our society has developed a number of ways of dealing with the disturbed, including voluntary or involuntary hospitalization, antidepressant drugs, electroconvulsive shock treatments, group therapy, individual psychotherapy, cognitive behavior modification, psychoanalysis, counseling, pastoral counseling, medical consultation, and other possibilities.

Perhaps, the most difficult cases for society are the disturbed disturbing people who don't do anything bad enough to merit prison and yet resist or seem unsuitable for mental treatment. What of the schizophrenic who stands in the middle of the freeway trying to direct traffic because God told him to? What of the alcoholic executive who functions well in the morning, but is drunk all evening? What of the psychopathic person who continually exploits, deceives, and abandons those who love him or her? How is society to help or control the behavior of such individuals, especially if they deny any problems? As other institutions, such as the churches, the schools, the family, the work place, and even the prison system, fail to help or change these people, the community may turn to the mental health professions for solutions. In recent decades it seems that such social control problems are increasingly defined as being suitable for treatment by the mental health professions.

In addition to people that others view as deviant, individuals may define themselves as needing professional help, although others may view them as well adjusted. Examples include the successful businessperson who experiences life as meaningless, the beautiful and wealthy actress with painfully low self-esteem, and the respected scientist who thinks her work is useless. When such people do not find the help they need from their families and other institutions in the community, they may turn to the mental health professions. Again, it seems in recent decades that individuals are increasingly likely to define their problems as psychological and suitable for treatment by mental health professionals.

From Supernatural to Medical Model The history of how society has arrived at ways of dealing with disturbed and disturbing people is fascinating. We can safely assume that what we call mental illness or emotional disturbance today has always existed. Although described in different terminology according to the times, examples of mentally disturbed individuals abound in history. King Saul of Israel suffered terrible bouts of depression and tried to kill his own son. The Roman emperor Caligula was grandiose and delusional, claimed to be a god, and slaughtered hundreds of people, including the beloved sister he married. King George III was depressed and manic in cycles, and his erratic behavior lost Britain the American colonies. Their behavior as described in whatever terms by their contemporaries would clearly be called symptomatic of mental disorder today.

The presence of holes in the skulls of some ancient individuals indicates that trephining or trepanning (to cut out a circular section of bone) was a Stone Age practice. From this and other evidence modern scholars conclude that ancient people used this technique to treat disturbed, or disturbing, people because they viewed the disturbance as an invasion of spirits which would leave through the skull holes. If the disturbance were caused by pressure on the brain due to infection, the buildup of fluid, or a tumor, then trephining may have helped. Evidence of healing around some of the holes indicates that some individuals survived the operation, and we can make the assumption that the survivors were better adapted to their environment than they had been before the operation, or at least that they were no longer as disturbing. It is also assumed that this treatment was administered by the shamans or priests, the experts on invading spirits.

Many early peoples, including the early Greeks and Romans, believed that disturbance was caused by the invasion of spirits, gods, or demons, and priests were viewed as the appropriate professionals to treat disturbed individuals. Hippocrates, the so-called father of medicine, disagreed with the prevailing view and argued that disturbance was due to natural, not supernatural causes. He believed that most disorders were due to brain pathology and hysteria in women was due to the wandering of the womb to other parts of the body. He recommended humane treatment for the victims of brain pathology and marriage for the victims of wandering wombs.

Plato wrote that mental disturbance was partly organic, partly moral, and partly divine. Anticipating a modern idea, he believed that dreams represented denied desires. Aristotle raised the possibility that disturbance was due to purely psychological causes, but rejected this hypothesis in favor of organic causes.

Greek scholars also studied the causes of disturbance. Asclepiades distinguished between acute and chronic mental disorders, and he differentiated among illusions, delusions, and hallucinations. He also believed in humane treatment and was opposed to the common practices of bleeding, restraints, and locking people in dungeons. Aretaeus described bipolar depression (also called manic-depressive disorder), and he was the first to attach importance to the prepsychotic personality in determining the course of the disorder. Galen, the accepted authority in Greek, Roman, and Arabic medicine for several centuries, believed that the causes of disturbance were either physical or mental, and he organized the available knowledge about physical and mental disorders, before the onset of the Dark Ages. Although the Romans treated some disturbed people with bleeding and incarceration, they also developed pleasant sanitariums for the mentally disordered, with exercise, rest, and entertainment as the forms of treatment.

Although the belief in natural causes of mental disturbance persisted, many Europeans returned to the model of demonology in the Dark Ages. They believed that the causes of mental disturbance and some other forms of deviance were wickedness, possession by a devil, and witchcraft, and they returned dealing with such problems to the province of religious experts. In the early Middle Ages the clergy treated disturbed individuals by prayer, the laying on of hands, and other relatively benign measures. The monastaries were refuges for the mentally ill, who were usually treated kindly. In the later part of the Middle Ages the treatment of disturbed people often involved cruelty, torture, and execution.

We may wonder how anyone could conceive of torturing an unfortunate disturbed person. If it is unquestionably believed by the religious experts and all the members of the community that the disordered person is possessed by an evil demon, and if helpful and concerned people want to save that individual's immortal soul, then it becomes logical to make the body such an uncomfortable and miserable place that the demon will want to leave. The person was tortured for his or her own good, and the disturbed individual may have welcomed the treatment, for it is common for severely depressed people to believe that they are guilty, worthless, and deserving of punishment. Even the ultimate treatment of death by drowning or burning may have been viewed positively by both the community and the victim as finally releasing that person from suffering at the hands of the devil.

The end of the Middle Ages was a chaotic period in European history. Natural and manmade disasters abounded—war, plague, the breakup of the feudal system. People were confused and fearful, and they needed explanations for the distressing events around them. Witchcraft and demonology at least provided explanations and guidelines for what to do. If members of the community were disturbed or disturbing, it was natural to suspect them of practicing witchcraft or of being victims of witchcraft. The suspected persons were then tortured until they confessed to whatever the community expected to hear, usually implicating other members of the community, who were then tortured and confessed and so on.

Certainly not all victims of witchcraft trials and accusations were mentally disturbed, and certainly not all mentally disturbed individuals became victims of the witch hunt. Many were kept at home and helped by their families, and some received other forms of treatment based on the perceived organic causes.

From the sixteenth through the nineteenth centuries the care of the mentally disturbed was transferred from the monastaries and dungeons to asylums run by charities and local governments. The conditions in the asylums were not much better than in the dungeons. Inmates were chained, poorly fed, exhibited to the public for a fee, and subjected to various "treatments" such as hot pokers, cold baths, and straitjackets. Care and treatment in asylums were provided by wardens or stewards. It seems that the majority of asylum inmates were poor, violent, or unwanted but undivorceable wives. More fortunate disturbed individuals were cared for at home.

By the eighteenth century some priests and scholars began to argue openly against the prevailing views and to advocate more humane treatment for disturbed persons. At the end of the century French physician Philippe Pinel was able to convince important people to allow him to try an experiment at the large asylum in Paris: to release the inmates from restraints and to treat them with kindness and decent food and conditions. These changes worked wonders, and most inmates improved dramatically. At the same time in England William Tuke established a country house where disturbed individuals lived, worked, and rested in a kindly religious atmosphere. As word of the success of these humane treatments spread, others tried to implement reforms.

In the United States reformer Benjamin Rush (1745–1813) encouraged humane treatment of the mentally disordered, although he continued to consider bleeding and purging to be appropriate treatment for some cases. Dorothea Dix (1802–1887) was another important reformer. Through extensive traveling and zealous campaigning between 1841 and 1881, she improved conditions in prisons, almshouses, and asylums throughout the United States and also in Europe. Single-handedly, she convinced charities and state governments to build at least 32 new mental hospitals in the United States. Another contribution to efforts to reform asylums was made by Clifford Beers. Beers was forcibly hospitalized near the turn of the century, and in 1908 he published a book, *A Mind That Found Itself,* in which he described his terrible experiences. He helped form the National Committee for Mental Hygiene and served as its secretary for 30 years.

During the early and middle nineteenth century in the United States "moral treatment" was used in some mental hospitals, led by the Rev. Dr. Woodward of Worcester State Hospital. The advocates of moral treatment believed that the mentally disturbed were normal people with temporary problems who would benefit from a favorable environment, emotional support, and being involved in work. Similar to milieu therapy today, treatment involved activities similar to group therapy, occupational therapy, and supportive individual counseling. Treatment and care were provided by wardens or stewards. Recovery rates for moral treatment were reported to be between 70 and 90 percent in the early part of the century, although these figures were later disputed.

In the latter part of the century the effectiveness of moral treatment and other treatments in mental hospitals declined because of a number of factors. A major factor was overcrowding, as funds were cut and large numbers of poor immigrants were consigned to the hospitals. The influx of immigrants and the disruptions that accompanied industrialization and expansion also contributed to the difficult social conditions that increased the numbers of individuals who were dealt with by hospitalization. The growing evidence of the lack of success of moral treatment and the old wardens and stewards of the mental hospitals set the stage for a new set of authorities to claim the ability to solve the problems of the disturbed, and the medical model of mental illness gained credence at the end of the nineteenth century.

The medical profession became part of the reform of the treatment of the disturbed. In the eighteenth and nineteenth century several European physicians argued that organic brain disease caused some, if not all, mental disorders. Redefining the disturbed as ill was certainly an improvement over seeing them as evil or possessed. Mental illness was supposed to carry no more social or moral stigma than a broken leg or measles, and it, like other illnesses, was deserving of humane treatment.

The model of scientific medicine also appeared to be a useful way to define and discover cures for the illnesses afflicting the disturbed. The medical model first takes note of symptoms, such as fever or red spots. The study of symptoms reveals that certain symptoms often appear together in syndromes, such as red spots appearing just after the onset of fever. The study of syndromes may reveal a specific disease process, such as measles. Once a disease can be diagnosed, then its cause may be investigated and discovered, such as a measles virus. Once the cause is known, a prevention or treatment can be developed, such as measles vaccine. Accurate diagnosis must precede treatment. The success of this model in defeating numerous diseases that long plagued humankind is well known.

Physician Emil Kraepelin (1856–1926) used the medical model to develop the first classification system for mental disorders. Kraepelin believed that each type of mental illness was a separate and distinct disorder with an organic cause and that the course and outcome of each mental illness were as predetermined as those of measles. The medical model requires diagnostic classification before causes and cures can be discovered, and Kraepelin provided this first step for mental illnesses. Using only his own keen powers of observation and organization, he developed a precise and comprehensive system of diagnostic categories that is still used with some modifications today.

The medical model of mental illness is probably the most widely accepted view of disturbed people today. Its wide acceptance is due both to the credibility and power of the medical profession and to the tendency to define increasing numbers of human problems as medical disorders. To return to an example we have already discussed, at various points in our history excessive drinking has been viewed as acceptable, a sin, a crime, and a disease. When moral exhortation and Prohibition failed to control excessive drinkers, people began to view alcoholism as a disease and to turn to the medical profession to control drinking through medical "treatment." In a similar manner, previous views of disturbed people were not successful in helping or changing them, and a disease model led to hopes for a "cure."

However, the medical model has not been as successful as it was with physical disease in discovering causes, preventions, and cures for mental illness, all of which remain extremely controversial. In fact, when medicine took over the mental hospitals in the latter part of the nineteenth century, recovery rates rapidly declined from the levels reported under moral treatment. Another explanation for the wide acceptance of the medical model of mental illness can be found in the tremendous impact of Sigmund Freud, who was a medical doctor, although he himself believed that his form of psychotherapy should be practiced independently of medicine.

From Medical to Psychological Model: Sigmund Freud Sigmund Freud (1856–1939) developed the first comprehensive theory of personality development and psychopathology. His influence on the twentieth century has been equated with that of Marx. The impact of his ideas and extensive writings can be seen in the widespread acceptance of some of his ideas today, ideas that are almost taken for granted, such as that childhood experiences affect adult personality or that we defend ourselves against certain thoughts and feelings. He developed the theory and therapeutic techniques of psychoanalysis (described in Chapter 3), a therapy that survives today in both its original form and in numerous variations.

Early in his medical career Freud intended to become a neurologist and pursue research. He went to Paris to study with the famous neurologist Jean Charcot and his student Pierre Janet. Charcot treated the hysterical disorders of his time, such as women with paralyzed healthy limbs or inexplicable yet disabling pains, through hypnosis and suggestion, with impressive success. Back in Vienna, Freud watched his friend and colleague Josef Breuer treat a patient diagnosed as a hysteric with daily sessions of talking and hypnosis, again with impressively successful results. After some time this patient, known as Anna O., began to talk of sexual fantasies regarding Dr. Breuer during her hypnotic trances. At this point Breuer abruptly terminated treatment, which Freud thought was a mistake. Freud was able to see the significance of the patient's expression of feelings for the doctor as being a necessary part of psychotherapy. In 1895 Breuer and Freud published *Studies in Hysteria,* in which the concept of transference in the therapist-patient relationship was described.

Soon most of Freud's medical practice was composed of neurotic women seeking relief. He began by using hypnosis, but soon abandoned it in favor of having the patient just talk while in a relaxed state on a couch. He directed patients to free associate, that is, to say freely whatever entered their mind. He found that childhood memories and sexual thoughts were invariably reported. (The sexual content is perhaps unsurprising, given that his women clients were lying on a couch talking intimately to a man!) Freud discovered that when the patient could not free associate, some especially painful memory was later reported. He noticed that patients were helped to free associate and to uncover important material when they discussed their dreams. In 1900 he published his classic *The Interpretation of Dreams.* In this book he presented his theory of neurosis, his concept of the unconscious, and his belief that dreams symbolize repressed desire—conclusions he had deduced from the data of his clinical cases.

At first Freud thought that neurosis was due to a genuine sexual trauma early in childhood, such as viewing the primal scene of parental intercourse or being sexually molested. These ideas met with considerable resistance and scorn from the medical community, and Freud himself was horrified by them. After a long period of self-analysis, he arrived at the insight that the sexual traumas and memories of his patients might be fantasies. Although somewhat relieved, he was at first distraught that his theory of neurosis was destroyed. However, he soon came to the conclusion that fantasy can have just as much impact, possibly more, on the small child's developing psyche as real events, and he elaborated his theory of neurosis to include the effect of unconscious conflicts as expressed in fantasies, dreams, and imaginary "screen memories." At present some psychoanalytic writers and other scholars are going back to Freud's original idea and believe that Freud's patients' difficulties were due to genuine sexual traumas. Particularly in the case of Anna O., many now believe that she was actually molested by her father (Masson, 1984).

In 1909 American psychologist G. Stanley Hall invited Freud to speak at Clark University in Massachusetts. He gave five highly influential lectures, now considered classics, which were published in 1910 in the *American Journal of Psychology.* In the United States at that time only academic psychology was interested in Freud's ideas; medicine ignored him or held him and his theories in disdain. In the two decades from 1919 until his death in London from painful cancer of the jaw in 1939, Freud's prominence increased, and there was widespread acceptance of psychoanalytic theory. By 1920 over 200 books on psychoanalysis had been published in the United States alone.

Psychoanalytic theory was a historical turning point from the late nineteenth-century medical view that the cause of disturbance was organic malfunction of the body to the twentieth-century psychological view that at least some of the causes were to be found in the mind. Academic psychology and psychoanalysis developed during the same time, but they were unrelated in aims, methods, and subject matter. The aim of early academic psychology was the scientific study of the normal mind; that of psychoanalysis was the treatment of disturbed individuals. The method of psychology was scientific experimentation; that of psychoanalysis was observation of clinical cases. The subject matter of psychology was normal experience and behavior; that of psychoanalysis was abnormal psychology. The two different disciplines, psychology and psychoanalysis, interacted with the social forces of the times and with previous models of mental illness to find expression in the evolution of clinical psychology.

Clinical Psychology

Psychology as an academic discipline began in Europe, and the majority of early American psychologists studied there. But psychology fit the times in the United States, and it rapidly expanded in influence there, while remaining a relatively minor area of study in Europe. Clinical psychology developed in the United States, remained an American specialty for decades, and is now exported to Europe and other countries. The popularity of clinical psychology in the United States is partly due to its ability to address certain social problems while preserving the American value of individualism and without necessitating social change.

The end of the nineteenth century found the United States a diverse and prosperous country in certain areas and among certain classes. It had experienced three decades of official peace after the Civil War. A rapid expansion of the population and a large influx of immigrants allowed the country to be settled from coast to coast. Urbanization and industrialization were under way in all sections of the country. Tendencies toward social reform that had begun with abolitionist, feminist, and temperance movements in the early part of the century had been dissipated in the violence of the Civil War. The cultural values tended toward rugged individualism, competition, and individual achievement. Academic psychology and its scientific study of the individual fit the times well. It only remained for individualistic scientific psychology to be applied to help the casualties of the social forces of the era for clinical psychology to develop as a field.

In 1896 Lightner Witmer established the first psychological clinic at the University of Pennsylvania for the evaluation and treatment of children and young people. The founding of this first clinic for psychological services in a university setting established the combined academic and applied approach that is characteristic of clinical psychology. In 1907 Witmer established and edited a journal called *Psychological Clinic.* The *Journal of Abnormal Psychology* also began in 1907, so professional psychologists had two journals for the communication of their ideas and research. About 20 psychological clinics had been established at American universities by 1915. Some included counseling services for students at the universities, but the emphasis was on services for children.

Although clinical psychology began in the United States, work in Europe influenced its practice. In 1904 Carl Jung in Switzerland was experimenting with a word association test for the assessment of personality. In 1905 Alfred Binet and Theodore Simon in Paris developed the first intelligence test for children. The test was designed to predict which children would do well in school. It sampled school-related skills in a standardized manner, and a child's score could be compared to the scores of other children. The intelligence test worked well for what it was designed to do. It was psychology's first great public success.

World War I provided another opportunity for applied psychology to prove itself.

The U.S. Army needed a way to predict which soldiers would do well and which would not, so that the costs of training and shipping a soldier who would fail could be saved. Psychologists developed the Army Alpha test, the first group test of intelligence. It did a fairly good job of screening recruits. The Army Beta was a nonverbal test for illiterates. At the same time Robert Woodworth developed the Personal Data Sheet, a pencil-and-paper personality test also useful for screening recruits. By the end of the war the statistical procedures and standards for establishing the norms, reliability, and validity of psychological tests had been formulated. Also by the end of the war clinical psychology was recognized as a discipline, as reflected in the formation of a clinical division within the American Psychological Association in 1919.

Between the world wars psychology as a science and a profession developed steadily. Like all mental health professions, applied psychology was then dominated by the psychoanalytic model. Academic psychology, on the other hand, was dominated by behaviorism. Watson wrote that disturbance was not due to conflicts over sex as Freud said, but due to faulty conditioning. However, his ideas were not reflected in behavior therapy until decades later.

In the 1920s and 1930s professional psychology was associated with the child guidance movement. Clinical psychologists worked in child guidance clinics as members of a team. The team approach involved a psychiatrist, a psychologist, and a social worker working together on a case under the direction of the psychiatrist. The main job of the psychologist was testing and school relations. During these decades most professional and clinical psychologists held master's degrees.

World War II provided a major impetus to the profession of clinical psychology. The war created an enormous demand for assessment and psychotherapy services for hundreds of thousands of soldiers. There was so much demand that clinical psychology was able to move rapidly into providing psychotherapy for adults, not just assessment for children, without encountering much resistance from medicine or other groups. In 1946 the Veterans Administration, the National Institute of Mental Health, and the U.S. Public Health Service began to fund training programs in clinical psychology at universities. They supported training programs in order to produce more psychologists to provide the many services that returning soldiers would require for years to come. This financial support contributed greatly to the expansion of clinical psychology as a field.

During the 1940s several events besides the war influenced the course of clinical psychology. A little earlier, in 1939, a major new individual intelligence test, the Wechsler-Bellevue for adults, was published. In 1942 Carl Rogers published his book *Counseling and Psychotherapy,* in which the tenets of client-centered therapy were described. It was the first new clinical theory to challenge the analytic view, for behaviorism was not incorporated into clinical psychology until much later. In 1943 the first major empirically derived, pencil-and-paper personality test, the Minnesota Multiphasic Personality Inventory (MMPI), was published. In 1947 the National Training Laboratory at Bethel, Maine, held its first summer workshop. This event saw the birth of the T-group or sensitivity training group. For the first time therapy-like services were offered to nondisturbed individuals.

In 1944 the American Psychological Association was reorganized to establish Division 12 as the Division of Clinical Psychology. Seeing the increased demand and increased training opportunities brought on by the flow of funds from the Veterans Administration, the APA held a special conference on the training of clinical psychologists. The Boulder Conference of 1949 established the scientist-practitioner model of clinical psychology, which reflects the early academic-applied roots of clinical psychology. It established the Ph.D. as the degree required for clinical psychology. The Ph.D. is a research degree, but it would be awarded in an applied field. The Boulder model set standards for training both in academic knowledge, principles, and research and in applied skills by establishing course and internship training requirements for graduate schools in clinical psychology. At the end of training a clinical psychologist was supposed to be competent in assessment, psychotherapy, and research.

During the 1950s clinical psychology expanded into new research and treatment areas. For example, in 1958 Joseph Wolpe published *Psychotherapy by Reciprocal Inhibition,* which helped establish behavior therapy as a major opponent of the psychoanalytic view. The 1960s saw an explosion of diverse theories and techniques. Psychoanalysis was no longer the dominant view. Important therapies included client-centered, humanistic, Gestalt, and behavior therapy. Clinical psychologists were conducting individual, group, marriage, and family therapy. They were involved in the human potential movement, which offered psychological services to nondisturbed people in order to help them reach their full potential. In short, many new ideas were tried.

The phenomenal postwar growth of clinical psychology was due to several factors. The scientist-practitioner model bore fruit, for academic research frequently provided new applications of psychological principles and developed new techniques of behavior change. By the early 1960s the majority of people in the United States were prosperous to a degree never before seen in history, and they could afford a sense of social responsibility for less fortunate individuals. The public turned to psychology for solutions to social problems, because psychology had proved so successful in the two world wars. Psychology also fit in with the still treasured value of individualism. It was essentially a conservative approach in that problems were defined as being within individuals or, at most, their families. Solutions could be found that did not require change in anyone else, the community, or society. Social problems were addressed solely through the treatment of individuals.

In 1963 President Kennedy signed the Community Mental Health Act, which provided funding for many community-based mental health agencies. The goal of this act was to reduce the population warehoused in large mental hospitals and to allow the mentally disturbed to be treated in their own communities. Psychologists found extensive employment in the agencies and programs funded by the act. The federal government and the Veterans Administration continued to be generous with funds for training psychologists, and research was also liberally funded. This steady flow of money coupled with positive public attitudes contributed to the growth of clinical psychology.

With the growth of the field came increasing diversity. In 1973 the American Psychological Association held the Vail Conference to reevaluate the training requirements for clinical psychology. Critics of the Boulder model argued that research skills were irrelevant to the practice of most clinical psychologists and that assessment and therapy skills should be emphasized. The Vail Conference developed the professional training model. Shortly after the conference, many professional schools of psychology were established, to offer the Psy.D. degree.

The decades since the 1960s have not been as positive for the field of clinical psychology. Although the numbers of psychologists continue to increase, the rate of growth of the field has slowed and employment opportunities are fewer. Public acceptance of clinical psychology has decreased and controversy in the field has increased due to a number of factors. The political and economic state of the entire country has been tumultuous since the 1960s: Leaders were assassinated, Vietnam intensified dissension, Watergate was a shocking revelation, the energy crisis contributed to a declining economy and periods of recession. The poor economy meant that government had less funds for psychological research and services and that the public no longer felt the sense of social responsibility necessary to fund such programs.

Perhaps the optimism of the 1960s created expectations for solutions to social problems that psychology could not provide. Even during the most prosperous decade the poor were never provided with services adequate to help them. The community mental health agencies were also inadequately financed, yet the big state mental hospitals closed, forcing many disturbed people into prisons, streets, and cheap hotels.

Some psychological research may have contributed to the dashing of high expectations for psychology. Research from the late 1960s revealed that the result of psychotherapy was not always improvement, that nonprofessional counselors were just as effective as professionals with some groups, and that complex clinical interpretations of psychological tests made no better predictions than simple statistical formulas (see Chapters 2 and 10).

The result of such apparently negative research findings coupled with the effects of a poor economy has been severe criticism and fund cuts for clinical psychology and other mental health professions. Reduced funding has led to increased competition among professional groups for the few remaining dollars. The 1980s became a period of unease over the future of professional psychology and over the future of human life itself. Professional psychology must continue to evaluate itself, to reorder its priorities, and to develop in new areas in order to survive and improve its position, as well as its services.

IN CONCLUSION

We trust that by now you have a good idea of the scope of modern clinical and counseling psychology. We also hope that we have increased your awareness of the historical and societal forces that have shaped professional psychology. These forces will be evident in the controversies over theory and practice described in the following chapters. We believe that professional psychology is an exciting field precisely because it is constantly changing in response to important social issues. It is the quintessential human activity of asking essential questions and seeking ultimate answers. It is part of the process by which we as a people at this point in history are determining the meaning and direction of our lives.

REFERENCES

Adams, H. B. (1964). "Mental illness" or interpersonal behavior? *American Psychologist, 19,* 191–197.

Albee, G. W. (1970). The uncertain future of clinical psychology. *American Psychologist, 25,* 1071–1080.

Alexander, F. G., & Selesnick, S. T. (1966). *The history of psychiatry.* New York: Harper & Row.

Beers, Clifford W. (1908). *A mind that found itself.* New York: Longmans.

Benjamin, L. T. (1986). Why don't they understand us? A history of psychology's public image. *American Psychologist, 41,* 941–946.

Braginsky, B., Braginsky, D., & King, K. L. (1969). *Methods of madness: The mental hospital as the last resort.* New York: Holt, Rinehart & Winston.

Cattell, Raymond B. (1983). Let's end the duel. *American Psychologist, 38,* 769–776.

DeLeon, P., VandenBos, G., & Cummings, N. (1983). Psychotherapy—Is it safe, effective, and appropriate? The beginning of an evolutionary dialogue. *American Psychologist, 38,* 907–911.

Deutch, A. (1952). *The mentally ill in America,* (2nd ed.). New York: Columbia University Press.

Fagan, T. K. (1986). School psychology's dilemma: Reappraising solutions and directing attention to the future. *American Psychologist, 41,* 851–861.

Fitzgerald, L. F., & Osipow, S. H. (1986). An occupational analysis of counseling psychology: How special is the specialty? *American Psychologist, 41,* 535–544.

Guthrie, D. J. (1946). *A history of medicine.* Philadelphia: Lippincott.

Katz, R., & Rolde, E. (1981). Community alternatives to psychotherapy. *Psychotherapy: Theory, Research and Practice, 18,* 365–374.

Knesper, D. J., Pagnucco, D. J., & Wheeler, J. R. C. (1985). Similarities and differences across mental health services providers and practice settings in the United States. *American Psychologist, 40,* 1352–1369.

Levy, L. H. (1984). The metamorphosis of clinical psychology: Toward a new charter as Human Services Psychology. *American Psychologist, 39,* 486–494.

Lewis, N. D. C. (1941). *A short history of psychiatric achievement.* New York: Norton.

Masson, Jeffrey M. (1984). *The assault on truth: Freud's suppression of the seduction theory.* New York: Farrar, Straus & Giroux.

Rosen, G. (1962). *Madness in society.* New York: Harper & Row.

Russell, W. L. (1941). A psychopathic department of an American general hospital in 1808. *American Journal of Psychiatry, 98,* 229–237.

Schoeneman, T. J. (1982). Criticisms of the psychopathological interpretation of witch hunts: A review. *American Journal of Psychiatry, 139,* 1028–1032.

Siegel, M. (1983). Crime and violence in America: The victims. *American Psychologist, 38,* 1267–1273.

Stone, S. (1937). Psychiatry through the ages. *Journal of Abnormal and Social Psychology, 32,* 131–160.

Szasz, T. (1961). *The myth of mental illness.* New York: Harper & Row.

Taube, C. A., Burns, B. J., & Kessler, L. (1984). Patients of psychiatrists and psychologists in office-based practice: 1980. *American Psychologist, 39,* 1435–1447.

Tourney, G. (1967). A history of therapeutic fashions in psychiatry, 1800–1966. *American Journal of Psychiatry, 124,* 784–794.

Watkins, C. W., Lopez, F. G., Campbell, V. L., & Himmell, C. D. (1986). Counseling psychology and clinical psychology: Some preliminary comparative data. *American Psychologist, 41,* 581–582.

Watson, R. I. (1963) *The great psychologists.* Philadelphia: Lippincott.

Weiss, B. (1983). Behavioral toxicology and environmental health science: Opportunity and challenge for psychology. *American Psychologist, 38,* 1174–1187.

Zilboorg, G., & Henry, G. W. (1941). *A history of medical psychology.* New York: Norton.

Chapter 2

Diagnosis and Assessment

All people engage in diagnosis and assessment every day of their lives. A young woman meets a young man, looks him over, asks him questions, and observes his reactions to her. On the basis of this assessment, she may diagnose him as a "nerd," a "hunk," or a "nice guy" and then try to predict whether she should go out with him. A parent observes that his 3-year-old doesn't throw a ball well, cries easily when frustrated, and says things like "Listen! The birds are waking the sun up!" On the basis of these observations, he concludes that his child is "stupid" and "slow" and predicts that she will have trouble in school. Another parent, making the same observations, concludes that her child is a "creative" and "clever" person who will do well in school. We all need to observe others, categorize them, and make predictions about their behavior so we can understand them and guide our behavior toward them.

In the examples above the observations are informal and haphazard, the categories used contain value judgments ("nerd" and "stupid"), and the predictions may well be wrong. Assessment in clinical psychology, on the other hand, is supposed to be systematic, objective, and accurate. Clinical psychology has applied the scientific method of empirical observation and measurement to these very human activities of trying to assess others. Their training in measurement, statistics, and research methods helps clinical psychologists to collect accurate psychological information about individuals.

Clinical psychology's scientific approach to assessment has resulted in the development of psychological tests. These tests vary in how they are constructed, administered, scored, and interpreted and in what they are supposed to measure. There are group and individual intelligence tests, which may be short or long, with sections that test vocabulary, arithmetic, logical reasoning, and other abilities. Personality tests may involve simply true or false responses to a series of statements about life, or they may require making up stories about pictures or supplying the endings to incomplete sentences. Whatever their form, psychological assessment procedures have certain characteristics in common. They are designed to serve specific purposes and to measure specific aspects of people, they attempt to be as objective as possible, and they are subject to empirical verification.

The purpose of using psychological tests is to obtain accurate, objective information about an individual's psychological functioning so that predictions and decisions about that person can be made. Parents may need to know a child's current level of intellectual functioning so they can decide what type of special education, if any, they should obtain for their child. A behavior therapist may need to assess the frequency, intensity, and precipitating events of a target behavior like smoking in order to plan a treatment program. A court may order an assessment of a prisoner's personality to determine whether that person is competent to stand trial. These examples are just a few of the purposes of psychological assessment, as we shall see.

We can define psychological assessment as the process of collecting information in a systematic, objective, empirical way about individuals' intellectual functioning, behavior, or personality so that predictions and decisions about them can be made. A psychological test is any procedure or method that can be used to obtain such information. And now let us turn to one of the major reasons for psychological assessment, diagnosis.

DIAGNOSIS

One of the traditional goals of psychological and psychiatric assessment is to reach a diagnosis of the patient's disorder. As discussed in Chapter 1, the medical model holds that the first step in dealing with a disorder is to diagnose what it is, so its cause can be discovered and a treatment can be scientifically developed. In this model the type of treatment prescribed for a specific disorder is directly related to the diagnosis, but, as we shall see, this does not necessarily happen with psychological disturbance. Diagnosis may also be useful for research, including demographic research, research into the causes of mental illness, and research on the effectiveness of therapy. Finally, in the "real world," diagnosis is required by health insurance programs, which will pay for the treatment of only certain disorders. Controversies over diagnosis reflect the economic factor of health insurance requirements as well as scientific disagreements and competition between psychology and psychiatry (Gorenstein, 1984).

The German physician Emil Kraepelin developed the first modern classification system for mental illnesses in 1896. He carefully observed which symptoms tended to go together and gave a label to each set of symptoms. He believed that each designated disorder had a separate cause and a definite, predictable course and outcome. He invented the term schizophrenia, which referred to the split between affect (emotions) and cognition (thoughts) typically seen in such patients, not to a "split personality." He also described five types of schizophrenia: undifferentiated (or simple), catatonic, hebephrenic, paranoid, and residual. The differences between psychosis and neurosis and between different types of neuroses were already known, but he systematized these categories.

Kraepelin's original nosology, or system of classification, has held up well over time. The first Diagnostic and Statistical Manual of Mental Disorders (DSM-I), published by the American Psychiatric Association in 1952, was basically an expanded version of Kraepelin's categories. DSM-I contained 60 types and subtypes of mental illness. DSM-II, published in 1968, listed 145 categories. Both DSM-I and II leaned heavily on the traditional medical categories of mental illness. Due to criticism of DSM-II's reliance on psychiatric jargon and subjective judgments of patients' internal states, the American Psychiatric Association made major changes in DSM-III, published in 1980. DSM-III lists approximately 205 separate conditions, including such "disorders" as tobacco dependence, binge eating, sexual dysfunctions, and adjustment reactions. Albee (1985) noted, "Clearly the more human problems that we label mental illnesses, the more people that we can say suffer from them. And, a cynic might add, the more conditions therapists can treat and collect health-insurance payments for." More discussion about DSM-III follows later.

Reliability and Validity

We must always ask about the reliability and validity of any system of classification or measurement. Reliability refers to the "trustworthiness" or consistency of the measuring device, that is, is the same result obtained every time one measures and when different people measure? If you measure your desk with a yardstick and find that it is 38 inches wide, you will find that it is still 38 inches wide when you measure it the next day or if someone else measures it—the yardstick is very reliable.

Validity refers, not to the measuring system itself, but to the appropriateness of the interpretation of the results of the measurements, that is, does the measuring device "really" measure what the person using it says it is measuring. If you use a yardstick to measure your desk, most people will agree that your conclusion that it is 38 inches wide is appropriate and accurate. It is, however, possible for a method of measurement to be reliable, but not valid. For example, suppose that you measure your desk with a plastic tape measure that over years of use has stretched. When you or anyone else uses this tape to measure your desk several times, it gives consistent results—it is reliable. However, concluding that your desk is 38 inches wide on the basis of this reliable measurement is not appropriate or valid.

Diagnosis can be looked at as a nominal scale of measurement, that is, a measuring scale that names items or puts them into categories (sorting eggs into medium, large, and extra large categories is an example of a nominal scale). Thus, we can try to assess the reliability and validity of any system of diagnosis, and there are serious problems with the reliability of diagnosis of mental disorders. Many studies have documented that different diagnosticians often reach different diagnoses on the same patients. The inadequate reliability of DSM-II has been documented (Zubin, 1967). Sufficient studies of DSM-III have not been done to draw a conclusion about its reliability (Nobins &

Helzer, 1986), but it may not fare much better. For one thing, the more categories there are, the more room for disagreement there is. For example, how does a diagnostician distinguish between agoraphobia with panic attacks, social phobia, panic disorder, and generalized anxiety disorder? Or between cyclothymic disorder; major depression, recurrent; and bipolar disorder, mixed? Or between schizophreniform disorder and schizoaffective disorder? Agreement between diagnosticians tends to be high for broad categories, such as neurosis versus psychosis or schizophrenia versus organic brain damage, but tends to be low for narrow categories such as those just mentioned. Another difficulty for diagnostic reliability is that patients change. While we may be glad they improve, patients may look like one category of disturbance when they are first seen, and then look like something else later, thus resulting in different labels at different times, thereby reducing reliability.

The validity of diagnosis may be even more important and more controversial than reliability. Validity refers to the "truth" or "reality" of the results of the measurement, that is, the appropriateness or accuracy of the interpretation of those results. If you want to measure the width of your desk, the yardstick is fairly obviously a valid device. However, what is "really" being measured in diagnosis? The medical model implies that diagnosis is tapping "real" underlying organic disorders. But there is a great deal of debate about the existence of mental illnesses (Szasz, 1961; Gorenstein, 1984). Some argue that there is no such thing, that what are being labeled in diagnosis are problems in living, reactions to high levels of stress, poor social competence, faulty social learning, communication disorders, and the casualties of poor parenting, abuse, exploitation, and poverty. Albee (1985) has noted that political ideology is implicated in this debate. As he said, "Conservatives strongly favor a constitutional-organic disease explanation, largely because no major social change is called for if the problems are all inside the skin." Liberals favor an environmental view of psychological disorders, because helping the disturbed by changing social conditions can justify their goal of increasing social justice. A "scientific" resolution to the debate over the validity of diagnosis and the medical model of mental illness is probably unlikely.

DSM-III

DSM-III was developed partly as an attempt to solve the problems with the reliability and validity of DSM-II. DSM-II contained much psychiatric and psychoanalytic jargon, such as "poorly developed ego strength" and "superego lacunae." It frequently depended on the diagnostician's ability to make inferences about the patient's internal state, such as "hears voices and holds grandiose beliefs." DSM-III attempted to correct these defects by basing categories on "objective" criteria and observable behavior, so that all observers would be able to agree whether or not a given person exhibited a specific behavior or not. A diagnosis is reached when a given person exhibits so many of the listed behaviors for a specific category.

In addition, DSM-III tried to take into account the complexity of psychological disorders by including more variables in each diagnosis. It is based on what is called a multiaxial model. Any single patient can be evaluated and categorized along five independent dimensions, or axes. Axis I contains the clinical syndromes, or typical diagnostic labels for mental disorders, such as adjustment reaction of adolescence, bipolar depression, and schizophrenia. Axis II deals with personality disorders, such as narcissistic and borderline personality disorder, and specific developmental disorders, such as dyslexia and mental retardation. Axis I diagnoses are supposed to be relatively temporary disorders, while Axis II covers those that are present early and are relatively enduring characteristics that are more difficult to change. Axis III assesses physical disorders and conditions, such as injuries or chronic illnesses that may affect the course of a mental disorder. Axis IV is designed to measure the severity of psychosocial stressors, and Axis V estimates highest level of adaptive functioning the past year. Patients are categorized on all five axes, which are supposed to be independent of each other. For example, a person may exhibit both a phobia (Axis I) and a dependent personality disorder (Axis II). DSM-III attempts to take into account the patient's physical and social context, coping skills, and level of previous functioning.

While an improvement over DSM-II, DSM-III has no clear or consistent theoretical or empirical basis. In fact, the manual states that "DSM-III is generally atheoretical with regard to etiology" and that disorders "are described at the lowest order of inference necessary to describe the characteristic features of the disorder" (American Psychiatric Association, 1980, p. 7). While many professionals criticize DSM-III's atheoretical stand, others regard it as a strength, as an attempt to remain as objective and behavioral as possible. Nevertheless, an implicit medical model is still evident in many categories (such as amnestic syndrome or alcohol hallucinosis), while others seem to be more behavioral or environmental (such as conduct disorder or reactive attachment disorder of infancy).

Furthermore, in the guise of being "objective," many DSM-III labels contain latent and not so latent value judgments (such as histrionic or narcissistic personality disorder). Many critics claim that DSM-III is biased toward seeing all behavior as symptomatic of some disorder or other (see Box 2.1). Others (Kaplan, 1983) have argued that it is biased in a sexist direction in that certain male behavior is seen as normal or "human," while certain female behavior is viewed as deviant (see Box 2.2).

Smith and Kraft (1983) surveyed over 500 American Psychological Association psychologists for their opinions of DSM-III. The majority clearly disavowed DSM-III, saying they would prefer a new nosology based on better empirical research than that cited in DSM-III. Most psychologists believe that categories of behavior derived from good empirical evidence free of the medical model would lead to a more valid and reliable diagnostic system than DSM-III. There is little or no research on DSM-III to assess the validity and utility of its rules for categorization (Nobins & Helzer, 1986). In addition, the political process of revising DSM-III has been very controversial, as described in Box 2.2.

Criticisms of Diagnosis

Some people criticize the whole notion of diagnosis, regardless of the system, because diagnosis or classifying various disorders often leads to labeling. These critics argue that labeling people gives us a false sense of doing something helpful and useful, that labels always contain hidden value judgments, that labels are a way of controlling or devaluing others by objectifying them and making them "different," and that there is no mental illness or "disorder" to label anyway (Szasz, 1961).

Others believe that labels or diagnoses stigmatize a person, who may then be affected by a "self-fulfilling prophecy," that is, once people know that someone has been diagnosed as "schizophrenic" or "paranoid," they may act differently toward that person and induce the very behavior the label leads them to expect. Indeed, Farina and his colleagues have demonstrated that people both expect mental patients to be highly unpredictable (Farina & Fisher, 1982) and behave differently around them (Farina, Holland, & Ring, 1966). Rosenhan's (1973) study of "sane" graduate students admitted to mental hospitals demonstrated how others then construed all their behavior as evidence of abnormality.

Labeling is also criticized as being a mechanism of social control. The medical model and its attendant system of diagnosis is perceived by some critics to be a way for society to allow mental health professionals to become the social control agents of various irritating deviant members of society. If an irritating deviant, such as a loud drunk, is labeled as having the "illness" of "alcohol dependence," then doctors and psychiatrists are the proper authorities for controlling that behavior.

It can be argued that diagnosis by itself is neither totally desirable nor totally undesirable. The question is do the benefits of diagnosis outweigh the drawbacks? Some medical labels, such as venereal disease or AIDS, carry a social stigma, but a correct diagnosis of such diseases has positive benefits, such as correct treatment and possible cure. Much research (some of it cited in the paragraph above) demonstrates the social stigma attached to mental illness labels. Is there any evidence that diagnosis has positive consequences, such as determining the type of treatment to be administered?

Unfortunately, it often appears that in practice individuals receive the form of treatment that is available, regardless of their diagnosis. In hospitals with group therapy and occupational therapy, most patients receive group therapy and occupational therapy whether they are schizophrenic or manic-depressive, whether they are a character disorder or a neurotic. In clinics with individual psychotherapy, family therapy, and behavior modification, clients get one or more of these forms of treatment regardless of diagnosis. Often what type of treatment they receive depends on such factors as whether other family members can make the appointment times, whether a certain kind of therapist has any free patient hours, or whether someone at the clinic wants to try a new kind of therapy on certain problems.

Setting aside the usefulness or harmfulness of diagnosis, let us ask *how* a diagnosis is made. One way is to interview individuals, ask them all sorts of questions about their symptoms, and then find the DSM-III description that they fit most closely. Another way is to give them psychological tests. This way is far more complicated and requires additional professional skill on the part of the diagnostician. So let us now turn to the topic of psychological assessment.

ASSESSMENT

Psychological assessment is used for many different purposes: to make a diagnosis, to make a differential diagnosis, to determine intellectual functioning, to detect personality dynamics, to reveal family dynamics, to evaluate psychotherapy outcomes, to screen candidates for jobs, to help individuals decide on a vocation. The clinical psychologist has training and expertise in theories of measurement, test construction, test validity

BOX 2.1
20 Years After DSM-III: DSM-X

DSM-III made a useful start in demystifying psychiatric jargon. Instead of vague, abstract, esoteric descriptions understandable only to the most well-trained of mental health professionals, it substituted simple lists of observable symptoms. We predict that this trend will continue and that eventually diagnosis will be freed from jargon completely. Below is a draft of what we expect DSM-X to look like. Note that not only has everyday language replaced esoteric medical terminology, but the trend in DSM-III toward finding a label for every possible human condition has been continued so that the following set of labels should be applicable to *everyone.* Note also that the negative, stigmatic connotations of the labels have been strengthened.

Annotated DSM-X

I. Psychosis
- **A.** Out to lunch
- **B.** Not pulling with both oars (differential diagnosis between this and out to lunch may be difficult)
- **C.** Just plain bonkers
- **D.** Wired (bipolar disorder, manic in DSM-III)
- **E.** Big crybaby (major depression in DSM-III)

II. Neurosis
- **A.** Real pain in the neck
- **B.** Scared of own shadow
    - **1.** Sleeps with lights on
    - **2.** Wears suits of armor
- **C.** Doesn't have act together
- **D.** Kiss-up
    - **1.** Acute
    - **2.** Chronic
    - **3.** Transient, situational
- **E.** Forget his/her head if not attached to shoulders
- **F.** Uptight (compulsive personality disorder in DSM-III)
- **G.** Stressed-out
- **H.** Looks good, but Isn't

III. Personality disorders
- **A.** Spacey
- **B.** Redneck
- **C.** Effete intellectual/nattering nabob of negativism
- **D.** Real loser
- **E.** Sniveler

IV. Disorders of childhood
  A. Spoiled brat
  B. Little monster
  C. Momma's boy
  D. Fraidy-cat

V. Any other behavior, not listed elsewhere

and reliability, and administration, scoring, and interpretation of individual and group psychological tests. An important aspect of the expertise of a clinical psychologist is knowing what tests to use for what purposes. Appropriate requests for assessment from psychiatrists, schools, and courts ask one or more questions about the client and leave the choice of assessment instruments to the professional judgment of the psychologist. Psychological tests are generally administered along with other relevant tests in a test battery.

Clinical psychologists have certain ethical obligations when engaged in psychological assessment. As in all situations, including psychotherapy and teaching, psychologists must serve the best interests of the client. This ethical principle includes fully explaining the purposes of psychological assessment procedures to clients and revealing the results of such assessments to them in a helpful way. Like all psychological information, the information obtained by psychological assessment must be protected and kept confidential, except under special circumstances such as when the client is a danger to others. In addition, clients should be informed of their right *not* to be tested or to discontinue at any time and of the limits to confidentiality.

Most practicing clinical psychologists use tests to help determine a diagnosis or a differential diagnosis, to make a prognosis, to assess intellectual and personality functioning in order to make educational or treatment recommendations, or to evaluate treatment. Often a pencil-and-paper test, the MMPI (described later), is routinely given to patients entering a psychiatric hospital or ward or to clinic clients on intake. It is used to determine a preliminary diagnosis and sometimes to screen out clients for whom the agency may be inappropriate. Psychological tests are also used extensively in research.

In a differential diagnosis, the psychologist is being asked to determine which of two or more possible things is wrong with a client when the client's symptoms present a confusing or conflicting picture. One of us tested a young man several years ago at a Veterans Administration hospital. He looked psychotic, but not all of his symptoms fit a diagnosis of schizophrenia, so a psychological assessment was requested. The psychological tests indicated organicity, that is, a physical disorder of the brain. There was no other evidence of a brain problem, no evidence of an injury, nothing indicating a tumor. The admitting psychiatrist was about to prescribe Thorazine, but on the basis of the results of the psychological tests ordered a brain scan instead. An unsuspected hematoma was discovered. The appropriate medication for this condition is blood thinning drugs, not Thorazine, which might have made him much worse. Within a few weeks this young man was discharged as "cured."

BOX 2.2
Controversies Over DSM-III-R

The professional and political conflicts involved in developing a system of diagnosis of mental disorders became quite public during the 1987 revision of DSM-III, known as DSM-III-R. The Diagnostic and Statistical Manual of Mental Disorders is published by the American Psychiatric Association, and critics charge that it is biased toward the therapeutic theories and professional needs of psychiatry. For decades psychologists, social workers, and others have complained that they are not sufficiently consulted in the process of developing the diagnostic categories for the DSM, even though they are forced to use it in order to receive reimbursement for their services from third party payers (private and government health insurance). They argue that psychiatrists are favored by third party payers, because the diagnoses used as a basis for reimbursement fit the theories and treatment methods of psychiatrists.

At least three categories proposed for DSM-III-R aroused particularly strong opposition from psychologists, social workers, feminists, and others. These three were originally called masochistic personality disorder, premenstrual dysphoric disorder, and paraphilic rapism. Feminist critics called the original language for these categories "antifemale" and argued that they could easily be used to reinforce negative attitudes toward and discrimination against women.

Along with other groups, the Committee on Women in Psychology of the American Psychological Association charged that the psychoanalytic term masochistic personality disorder would be disproportionately applied to women in a blame-the-victim process. This diagnosis would be applied to persons who engaged in apparently self-defeating behaviors and who stayed in situations that appeared to be harmful to them. For example, women who stay with husbands who beat them would be considered to have a psychopathological condition, rather than being a victim of abuse. The APA Committee on Women stated,

> A large and well-developed body of research in the area of victimization would suggest that many of the critria of this proposed diagnosis are, in fact, normative responses to the experience of having been victimized.

The committee was also concerned about the potential uses of the diagnosis.

> In a worst-case scenario, it is possible to imagine a battered woman with children who leaves her batterer and files for custody of the children, but loses it because she is diagnosed as having *Masochistic Personality Disorder,* while her batterer (for whom there exists no corollary diagnosis) appears more "normal" and functional.

The National Association for Social Workers issued a statement declaring,

> We feel that the diagnostic criteria . . . describe what social workers know to be the transient effects of battering or sexual assault on women's functioning. Describing it as a personality disorder implies grave and unchangeable psychopathology and it could be used against women in custody battles, self-defense murder cases and sexual harassment litigation.

In response to such criticisms the name of this category was changed to "self-defeating personality disorder" in order to make it equally applicable to men. Many groups continued to oppose its inclusion, but it ended up being included in the appendix.

The proposed category of premenstrual dysphoric disorder would obviously be applied only to women, and critics charged that it attempted to create a mental disorder for the known gynecological disorder of PMS, or premenstrual syndrome. The American Psychiatric Association Committee on Women, the Committee on Women of the American Psychological Association, the National Association of Social Workers, and others opposed this category, which was changed to "periluteal dysphoric disorder" in order to separate it more clearly from PMS. Defenders of the category argued that it would help women by legitimizing the monthly depression of those who have it and by allowing them to receive reimbursable treatment for it. However, critics continued to oppose the inclusion of this category, because it creates a gender-specific mental disorder, it reinforces stereotypical views of women as victims of "raging hormones," it can be used as a "scientific excuse" against women in the work place, there is not sufficient evidence for it, and many other objections. It was also placed in the DSM-III-R appendix.

The category of paraphilic rapism would appear likely to be used to diagnose mostly men, yet feminists objected strongly to it. In addition to citing research that did not support the creation of such a category, the Committee on Women of the American Psychological Association stated, "It appears to add little to the understanding of individuals who engage in sexual assault. Additionally, it would seem to provide an instant insanity plea for anyone charged with rape." At one point the name was changed to "paraphilic coercive disorder," but finally the category was dropped from DSM-III-R.

Some people argue that paraphilic coercive disorder was dropped to placate feminist critics so that self-defeating personality disorder could be retained. At one point a category of sadistic personality disorder was suggested to balance self-defeating personality disorder, so that there would be a label for the abusers as well as the victims of abuse, and this category was also added to the appendix.

Defenders of DSM-III-R stated that they created and changed and kept and eliminated various categories based on "scientific evidence," but critics still contend that "science" is being used to cover up a very political process. What do you think?

In addition to diagnosis, clinical psychologists are often requested to do intellectual assessments, usually of children who are having some kind of problem in school. The intellectual level of adults may be assessed for vocational counseling purposes, if it is suspected that an organic process is lowering their competence or if it is important to know their current level of functioning during or after a mental illness. As stated before, a particular type of psychological test is generally administered along with other relevant tests in a test battery. For example, children may do poorly in school because of organic problems (such as difficulty with perceptual-motor coordination) or because of emotional problems, as well as because of low intelligence. A typical test battery for such a case would include the Wechsler Intelligence Scale for Children, Revised, an achievement test (to assess current grade level performance), the Bender-Gestalt Visual-Motor Test (to assess organicity), and one or more personality tests (to assess emotional factors).

Clinical psychologists may do personality assessments for a variety of reasons, and the reason will determine the type(s) of tests used. The use of personality tests for diagnosis and in conjunction with intelligence testing has already been mentioned. Typically, however, personality tests are used to help develop treatment plans for clients, to indicate the direction psychotherapy should take or issues to cover, or

Table 2.1 10 MOST FREQUENTLY USED PSYCHOLOGICAL TESTS

1. Wechsler Adult Intelligence Scale, Revised (WAIS-R)
2. Minnesota Multiphasic Personality Inventory (MMPI)
3. Bender-Gestalt Visual-Motor Test
4. Rorschach test
5. Thematic Apperception Test (TAT)
6. Wechsler Intelligence Scale for Children, Revised (WISC-R)
7. Peabody Picture Vocabulary Test (PPVT)
8. Sentence completion test (all kinds)
9. House-Tree-Person Test (HTP)
10. Draw-a-Person Test (DAP)

Source: Lubin, B., Larsen, R., & Matarazzo, J. (1984). Patterns of psychological test usage in the United States: 1935–1982. *American Psychologist, 39,* 451–454.

perhaps to determine the effectiveness of therapy. A typical personality test battery may include an objective test such as the Minnesota Multiphasic Personality Inventory, a projective test such as the Rorschach or the Thematic Apperception Test, and perhaps a drawing technique such as the Draw-a-Person.

Lubin, Larsen, and Matarazzo (1984) surveyed over 200 clinical psychologists as to which psychological tests they used most frequently. Table 2.1 shows the 10 most frequently used tests, and this chapter will cover each in detail. Although not in the top 10, certain other tests will be discussed as well: the Stanford-Binet intelligence test (ranked fifteenth, but historically important), the Edwards Personal Preference Test (ranked seventeenth, but often used in research), the Eysenck Personality Inventory (ranked below thirtieth, but also used in research), and the Strong Vocational Interest Blank (ranked eighteenth) and the Kuder Preference Record (ranked twenty-second), which are examples of vocational interest tests. Most of the frequently used tests are quite old, but new psychological tests are constantly being developed and marketed, such as the Kaufman Assessment Battery for Children (Kaufman & Kaufman, 1983) and the Millon tests for psychopathology (Millon, 1981). In fact, the market is so flooded with new tests that some psychologists may feel unable to evaluate them adequately, and so they stick with the old standbys.

After a test battery is administered, the tests must be scored and interpreted. While we will describe the major psychological tests and how they are used, the procedures for scoring and interpreting the tests are beyond the scope of this book. Postgraduate course work and hundreds of hours of supervised experience are necessary to become competent in these tasks. After scoring and interpreting the tests, the psychologist generally writes a psychological assessment report. The report integrates the test findings, attempts to answer the diagnostic or referral questions, and makes appropriate recommendations. (See Box 2.4 for a sample psychological assessment report.)

Intellectual Assessment

Zimmerman and Woo-Sam (1984, p. 57) define individual intellectual assessment as "the process by which a trained professional collects information about an individual that allows for the identification of skills or disabilities that enhance or interfere with the subject's functioning in his/her environment." Although they avoid the use of the words intelligence and test, the way the trained professional collects this information is by administering one of the so-called intelligence tests.

When the new field of psychology began to apply the scientific method to philosophical questions about the nature of the human mind, an important step was to try to measure it. As a complex method of measurement, the intelligence tests have been psychology's big success, and their success contributed to the development of the field. Designed to predict school performance, intelligence tests do predict school grades well, but school grades do not predict much of anything else in life. At present there is much controversy over the nature of intelligence and whether intelligence tests "really" measure intelligence at all.

At the turn of the century the Paris public school system asked Alfred Binet and his colleagues to develop a test that would predict which children would do well in school and which children would not, so it could save the money that would have been spent on children who would fail anyway. Note the assumption that if children fail to benefit from schooling, it must be because of some (measurable) defect in the children, not because of any inadequacy in the educational system. Even today many psychologists assume that "schools adhere to the basic premise that education must be tailored to the individual intellectual needs of the child" (Zimmerman & Woo-Sam, 1984, p. 57) and that intelligence tests can identify those needs. However, many critics think that the tests are still used to label and discriminate against children, rather than to "tailor" or change education.

Binet did as he was asked, and he did it brilliantly. The first intelligence scale was published in 1905 (Binet & Simon, 1905). He developed tests that directly sampled the skills needed in school, such as verbal comprehension, numerical skills, logical reasoning, visual discrimination, and the like. He developed standardized tests of these skills and administered them in standardized ways to many children. Because of this standardization, the performance of different children could be compared directly. In addition, he developed the concept of age norms. He noted how many children of a particular age passed specific test items. Test items that half of 6-year-olds passed were called 6-year items. By this means the scores of children could be directly compared across ages. A 9-year-old who passed the 6-year items and failed the 7-year items was considered to be the intellectual equal of an average 6-year-old.

Many psychological assessment instruments use the concept of norms. When a psychological test is constructed, it is given to a large number of representative people. The scores of this standardization group become the test norms, that is, how most people perform on the test. The score of an individual who later takes the test can then be compared to the test norms. It is possible to say that a particular individual scores so much higher or so much lower than most people, and thus the person's score is placed in an empirical context.

Binet's test was modified in the United States by psychologists at Stanford University (Terman, 1916). It is still in use today as the Stanford-Binet, Form LM (Terman & Merrill, 1973) and the more recent Stanford-Binet Fourth Edition, published in 1986. It can be used to test individuals from age 2 years to adult. The age norms are now statistically transformed into IQ (intelligence quotient) scores; an IQ of 100 represents the average or mean score for an age group. The test samples school-related skills by asking children to define words, solve math problems, tell what a saying means, and the like.

The Wechsler intelligence scales are now used more often than the Stanford-Binet. Beginning in the 1940s and making later revisions, David Wechsler and his colleagues have developed an intelligence test for children age 5 to 15, the Wechsler Intelligence Scale for Children, Revised, or WISC-R (Wechsler, 1974); one for adults, the Wechsler Adult Intelligence Scale, Revised, or WAIS-R (Wechsler, 1981); and another for children age 4 to 6, the Wechsler Preschool and Primary Scale of Intelligence or WPPSI (Wechsler, 1967).

The structure of all the Wechsler is alike. They are divided into two parts: verbal subtests, which assess verbal skills such as vocabulary and comprehension, and performance subtests, which tap nonverbal skills such as putting puzzles together and copying designs. Unlike the Stanford-Binet, which contains different subtests for different ages, all individuals are tested on the same subtests.

The IQ for the Wechsler tests, like the Stanford-Binet IQ, is a statistically transformed score with the mean for each age group set at 100. Thus, the IQ score is still an age norm, for it is derived from the scores of a representative sample of 100 or 200 people in each age group. Three IQ scores are calculated for an individual: the verbal IQ, the performance IQ, and the full scale IQ. The three IQs and the scores on each subtest provide a great deal of information about an individual's relative strengths and weaknesses, more information than the Stanford-Binet's single IQ score.

There are many other intelligence scales, some with special uses. For example, the Peabody Picture Vocabulary Test or PPVT (Dunn, 1959) can be used to test children and adults who have a problem speaking English, perhaps because they are not native English speakers or because they have a speech disorder. Test-takers are presented with four pictures and asked to point to the picture that represents a certain word. The vocabulary is different for different age groups. For example, children may be asked to point to a "car," while adults may be asked to point to "imbibe" or "bovine." The raw scores are converted to IQ scores, which compare fairly well to the IQs from other tests. This test is short and easy to administer, and it may provide a better estimate of a speech-disordered person's intellectual functioning than a Wechsler test.

One of the latest additions to the field of intellectual assessment of children is the Kaufman Assessment Battery for Children or K-ABC (Kaufman & Kaufman, 1983). It is suitable for children age 2 to 12. This test has two unique features. It tries to assess the functions of the right and left hemispheres of the brain, and it tries to separate the measurement of skills or "intelligence" from that of fact-oriented or acquired knowledge. The separation of measurements is an attempt to answer the frequent criticism that intelligence tests really measure cultural and acquired knowledge and are therefore biased in favor of middle-class, white people. The test has three sections. The Sequential Processing scale involves the solution of problems presented in a serial or temporal order (a left hemisphere function); the Simultaneous Processing scale requires the integration and synthesis of problem materials (a right hemisphere function); and the Achievement scale assesses scholastic achievement or grade-level performance.

Although not an intelligence test, the Bender-Gestalt Visual-Motor Test (Bender,

1938) is often given along with intelligence tests as a part of a test battery. It is designed to assess whether there is impairment in an individual's visual-motor coordination, which would be due to some organic factor, such as a brain tumor, brain damage, or minimal brain dysfunction. It consists of a series of geometric designs on small cards. The test-taker is given a blank sheet of paper and a pencil and asked to copy the designs as they are presented one at a time. The test-taker must be able to perceive the design and then draw it, hence a measure of visual-motor coordination. The copied designs are scored for their accuracy and their preservation of the gestalt, or overall form, of the designs.

Achievement tests are also frequently given with intelligence tests. It is often important to know how the level of global functioning measured by the intelligence tests compares to the level of academic achievement. Discrepancies, such as a child with a high IQ and low achievement, require explanation. There are many group and individual achievement tests, but the Wide Range Achievement Test or WRAT (Jastak & Jastak, 1965) is a nice example. It is short and straightforward in administration and scoring. It assesses three areas of achievement: reading, spelling, and arithmetic. An individual's scores in the three areas are transformed into grade equivalents, which are based on the norms for representative samples of children in each grade.

Reliability and Validity of Intelligence Tests Intelligence tests are among the most reliable psychological tests. Recall that reliability refers to the consistency of a measuring device: Does it make the same measurement time after time? There are several statistical procedures for determining test reliability, including test-retest and split-half reliability. Test-retest is the type of reliability we have discussed so far, and it is determined by giving the same test to the same group of people at different times. Split-half reliability is determined by comparing the scores of a group of people on one half of a test administered once to their scores on the other half.

It is generally agreed that properly administered intelligence tests are highly reliable, by both split-half and test-retest measures of reliability, except for young children, whose motivation and cooperation may change greatly. A 12-year-old's IQ will generally be quite similar to his or her IQ at 13; the IQs at ages 12 and 20 will be less similar but still close. Careful standardization and using the same subtests for all ages contribute to the these tests' reliability.

The validity of intelligence tests is much more debatable. (The controversy over validity is discussed in the section on criticisms of psychological testing later in this chapter.) Recall that validity refers to the accuracy or appropriateness of the interpretation of the results of a test: Do IQ tests really measure intelligence as they are often interpreted to do? Naturally, the answer to this question depends on the definition of intelligence.

Like many subsequent psychologists, Binet developed a pragmatic definition of intelligence—it was whatever the tests he was constructing measured. Spearman (1904) originated the theoretical definition of intelligence as a unitary factor, which became known as *general intelligence* or *g factor.* He considered intelligence to be an innate, global capacity that runs through and accounts for all the different skills and abilities a person may have. Although Wechsler's tests divide verbal and performance skills, he, like Spearman, defined intelligence as "the aggregate or global capacity of the individual to act purposefully, to think rationally, and to deal effectively with his environment" (Wechsler, 1974, p. 3).

Other researchers have refuted the idea of intelligence as a unitary factor. Gardner (1983) identified at least seven different kinds of intelligence: linguistic skills, logical and mathematical skills, visual and spatial conceptualization, musical skills, bodily kinesthetic skills, interpersonal skills, and intrapersonal knowledge. Each kind of intelligence functions semiautonomously and has its own form of memory, learning, and perception. Gardner argued that our culture values only the first two kinds of intelligence and they are what intelligence tests measure, not "true" intelligence.

One type of evidence used to assess the validity of intelligence tests is called *predictive validity.* What do the tests predict? Career success? Happiness? Income potential? No, they predict school grades, because they sample school-related tasks and skills. And what do school grades predict? College grades. And college grades predict graduate school grades. Do these grades predict anything like success or income? Of course not. Neither IQ scores nor academic grades appear to be related to any form of definable life success or achievement.

The question of the validity of intelligence tests is important because of the social uses to which the tests are put. Although IQ tests are often used to help children receive the most appropriate and helpful educational experiences they can, they are at times used to label certain people, to lay the fault of their failure in school on them rather than on the educational system, and to assign minority group children disproportionately to special education classes, as will be discussed later in this chapter. If these tests do not really measure intelligence, if there are indeed many types of intelligence that people could use if the culture valued them, then these uses of intelligence tests represent a social injustice. Test validity is more than a theoretical issue of interest to psychologists; it has real life consequences for some people and for society.

Personality Assessment

Two major types of personality tests have developed in the United States. The oldest type is the projective test. The test-taker is given an ambiguous stimulus, such as a picture of a scene, an ink blot, or an unfinished sentence, and is asked to tell a story about the scene, say what the ink blot looks like, or finish the sentence. There are no objectively right or wrong answers to guide them. Clients must "project" their own thoughts, beliefs, and feelings onto the stimulus in order to make sense out of it. This is known as the projective hypothesis. The projective hypothesis also assumes that test-takers will reveal their unconscious personality dynamics in their projected responses, because the ambiguity of the test and the test directions make it impossible to fake or become guarded or defensive in their responses.

The other type of personality tests is the objective or structured tests. These tests usually require subjects' answers to written questions with a pencil, hence their other name, pencil-and-paper tests. The answers required are usually short, such as true or false or agree or disagree, so that objective tests may take less time to administer than projective tests. The answers generally can be scored by machine, so scoring also takes less time.

Projective tests are somewhat like essay examinations, in which test-takers must create their own answers from what they have in their minds, while objective tests are like multiple-choice examinations, in which test-takers chose from among a limited number of given answers.

Projective Tests As might be guessed from the projective hypothesis, projective tests grew out of the psychoanalytic tradition (see Chapter 3). Carl Jung first experimented with this idea in 1904, when he developed a word association test to detect patients' unconscious conflicts and personality dynamics. The most famous projective test, the Rorschach ink blot test, was developed by Herman Rorschach, a Swiss psychoanalyst, in the 1910s (Rorschach, 1921). The second most popular projective test, the Thematic Apperception Test (TAT), was created in the 1930s (Murray, 1938). The Draw-a-Person (DAP) was developed in the 1940s (Machover, 1949); the House-Tree-Person (HTP) was a later extension. Sentence completion tests were constructed in the 1940s and 1950s (Rohde, 1957). It is apparent that the most frequently used projective tests are quite old.

The Rorschach test consists of 10 ink blots printed on cards. Rorschach chose ink blots because they do not depict anything realistic, and he made them just the way one usually makes ink blots—by dropping some ink in the middle of a piece of paper and folding it in half, thereby spreading the ink in a symmetrical pattern. Rorschach had specific theoretical reasons for choosing the shape, color, and order of presentation of his ink blots. For example, he started with an all black, fairly easy ink blot, one which is often seen as a bat or a butterfly. His second card contained the addition of some red ink parts, which he supposed would throw test-takers off guard and stimulate deep emotional responses. How they handled this stress and integrated the parts of the blot would indicate their coping abilities and degree of personality integration or disintegration.

The Rorschach is administered by psychologists to clients individually. The psychologist presents the ten ink blot cards in the designated order one by one, asks the client to tell what each looks like, and then inquires as to what aspect of the blot, such as its shape, color, or texture, made it look like that.

After the Rorschach is administered, it is scored and interpreted according to a complex system. There is much controversy among competing systems as to the best way to score and interpret. In addition to Rorschach's original methods, Beck (1945), Klopfer (Klopfer & Kelley, 1942), Exner (1974, 1978), and others have developed scoring methods and interpretation rules, with Exner's system apparently the most popular at present. Even though the scoring and interpretation of the Rorschach is complex and beyond the scope of this book, you can easily imagine how a person whose response to the first card is "A raging witch with her intestines hanging out" differs in important ways from someone whose response is "It looks like a bat."

The TAT consists of 31 cards each with a rather realistic drawing of people in various scenes. Because the TAT is supposed to be a projective test, the pictures are not drawn with photographic realism, but are in fact quite vague in many details, although certain pictures are supposed to elicit certain themes or important issues. In practice today a subset of 10 cards is generally given to individuals in a traditional order. Some psychologists develop preferences for certain cards over others, or they may vary the cards according to the nature of the test-taker or the diagnostic question. For example, there is a card depicting a person alone at a window in a darkened room.

This card is not often used, but psychologists may choose to use it if they are testing depressed and possibly suicidal individuals, for it tends to "pull" themes of loneliness, sadness, and sometimes suicide.

Like the Rorschach, the TAT is administered by psychologists to clients individually. Clients are directed to make up a story about each picture, to tell how the story begins, what is going on in the picture, what the characters are thinking and feeling, and how the story ends.

After the TAT is administered, it is analyzed for recurring themes, how the issues of aggression or nurturance or achievement are handled in certain cards which pull these motives, degree of social appropriateness or maturity, how well organized and coherent the stories are, adequacy of reality testing, quality of family dynamics reflected in the stories, and other variables.

The DAP is generally administered individually, but it may be given in groups. The administration of this test is simplicity in itself. The psychologist gives clients a blank piece of paper and a pencil and asks them to draw a whole person. If clients express doubt, the psychologist may explain that this is not a test of artistic ability and any kind of whole person will do. They are then given another piece of paper and asked to draw a whole person of the opposite sex. Most people draw a person of their own gender first. Some psychologists ask their clients to describe the personalities of the persons they drew and to indicate their age, occupation, and other details.

While the administration is simple, the interpretation of the DAP is complex and subject to controversy. Nevertheless, it is an interesting test, and you might want to try it yourself. Draw a person and see if you can figure out what it says about you. For example, common sense would suggest that if you draw a smiling person it indicates something different about you at this time than if you drew a crying person.

The HTP is similar in many ways to the DAP. Clients are given a blank sheet of paper and a pencil and told to draw a picture with a house, a tree, and a person in it. The relations between the house, tree, and person are supposed to indicate how people view their world and themselves in it. A variation of this test, often used with children, is to ask clients to draw a picture of their family. The way the family members are depicted, their relative sizes, their facial expressions, and the relations between them may be quite revealing of how clients see their families. For example, a child who draws her mother, father, and brothers all together in one room, with herself to the side, may feel left out or rejected by her family.

There are several sentence completion tests available, the Rotter Sentence Completion Test (Rotter & Rafferty, 1950) being perhaps the best known. Clients are asked to finish series of incomplete sentences, such as "Mothers are . . . ," "I hate . . . ," "I am very good at . . . ," "Girls are best because . . . ," or "Life can be very . . ." The tests may be administered individually in oral form, in which the psychologist reads the sentence beginning to the client, or they may be administered in written form, with the test-takers writing down the completions. You can easily imagine how a child who says "I am very good at nothing" differs in important ways from a child who says "I am very good at school and baseball."

Objective Tests There are many objective pencil-and-paper tests used in research and personality assessment, and they generally have a strong empirical or theoretical basis.

These tests are an economical use of the psychologist's time. Clients can answer the test questions by themselves, without any interaction with the psychologist after initial instructions are given, and they can be answered on machine-scorable answer sheets, which lend themselves to computer analysis, as described later.

Burisch (1984) distinguishes three major approaches to objective personality scale construction: external, inductive, and deductive. In the external approach, also known as the empirical approach, the test constructors know that people differ, but not how, so they determine the difference(s) empirically. They invent a lot of test items, give them to people who are known to differ in some way (say, anxious people and relaxed people), and then make their test up from items the two groups answer differently. In the inductive approach the constructors "discover" laws or personality structure by giving many people many test items and then subjecting their responses to mathematical analyses that determine which items go together. In the deductive approach constructors have a theory or definition of what they want to measure before they begin, and their theory or definition guides the choice of test items. They choose test items because they look like they fit, or they may ask the opinions of experts as to what items they should use. The differences in these three ways of constructing psychological tests will become clear as specific tests are discussed.

External approach The Minnesota Multiphasic Personality Inventory (MMPI), the personality test most frequently used by clinical psychologists and researchers alike, is an example of the empirical or external approach. The MMPI has a scale called Depression. People who were known to be depressed were compared to people who were not. Since it was not known how they were different, both groups answered hundreds of items, and the items that depressed people answered differently from undepressed people were put in the Depression scale. There was no theoretical reason why depressed people should answer the items differently from the undepressed—it was just an empirical observation that they did. Therefore, the items must measure something about depressed people, whatever it is, and they were put together in a Depression scale.

The MMPI was developed by Hathaway and McKinley in the late 1930s and early 1940s (Hathaway and McKinley, 1943). It was originally developed to diagnose psychopathology in psychiatric and medical settings, but it is now used for many other purposes. It consists of several hundred statements about life, opinions, likes and dislikes, family events, and similar things, about which people must make a forced choice between agree and disagree, as the items apply to them. MMPI items range from statements like "I like mechanics magazines" and "I am happy most of the time" to "I am worried about sex matters" and "At times I have a strong urge to do something harmful or shocking." Students (and psychologists, too) often have fun making up MMPI-like test items. See Box 2.3 and try to make up a few yourself.

The test is divided into 10 empirically derived scales: (1) Hypochondriasis (somatic problems and physical complaints); (2) Depression (sadness, hopelessness, depression), (3) Hysteria (using repression and denial as defenses), (4) Psychopathic Deviate (antisocial behavior, such as impulsivity, poor judgment, disregard for authority), (5) Masculine-Feminine (sex role attitudes and behavior), (6) Paranoia (suspiciousness, hostility, and aloofness), (7) Psychasthenia (anxiety, phobias, obsessiveness), (8)

BOX 2.3
New, Improved MMPI Items

A favorite pastime of psychologists is developing new MMPI items. Over the years we have collected quite a few from various sources, including our students. The wording of these items is quite similar to many genuine MMPI items. Here are a few.

I like mechanics.

I am attracted by opposite sexes.

Cauliflower makes me sad.

I am not troubled by thoughts of housework.

I am sure most people would pick their noses if they thought they could get away with it.

I am excited by committee meetings.

As a child I was often an imaginary companion.

I feel like jumping off low places.

I think I would like the work of a chicken plucker.

I am bored by thoughts of death.

Sometimes I have difficulty remembering what I have done after hours of watching television.

I am not afraid to wash clothes.

My mother's third cousin was a good man.

I have used floor wax to excess.

Pedestrians are not to be trusted.

I cannot read or write.

My navel is always cold.

I like to kill gnats.

Some people never smell me.

Sometimes I find it hard to know what to say at an orgy.

Piercing screams make me nervous.

I am afraid of finding my self.

Schizophrenia (being unconventional, withdrawn, confused, unusual in one's thinking); (9) Mania (impulsivity, optimism, high energy, impatience), and (Scale 0) Social Introversion (sociability). In recent years many new scales have been constructed empirically from the original MMPI test, such as the Ego Strength and Anxiety scales. Because the MMPI was originally designed to detect psychopathology, the titles of the original 10 scales, as you can see, have negative connotations which are not appropriate for the many uses to which the MMPI is now put. Psychologists generally try to avoid the titles and refer to the scales by number when using the MMPI for career counseling and other assessment of "normals."

In addition to the 10 personality scales, the test has 4 validity scales: ? (the number of omitted items); L, Lie scale; F, Faking scale, and K, Defensiveness scale. These scales represent an attempt to build checks for validity into the assessment device itself. Obviously, if individuals fail to answer many items, it reduces the validity of their answers. The L scale is composed of socially desirable items that no one ever does, such as "I read all of the editorials in the newspaper every day." People who endorse many of these items are apparently trying to present themselves in a socially favorable way. This tendency to lie may reduce the validity of their answers. The F scale is composed of unusual items that are rarely marked by anyone. People who endorse many of these items may be faking, confused, or unable to read. The K scale is supposed to measure the personality trait of defensiveness. It is added to the scores of some of the other scales as a corrective factor.

Since the MMPI scales were developed by comparing "abnormal" groups to "normal" Minnesotans from the 1930s, some people believe that the norms for what is considered a "high" score are out of date. For example, a 1930s, Minnesota farmer was not likely to have a high score on the Schizophrenia scale unless there was actually something seriously wrong with him. A high score for a drug-using college student today might not indicate any serious disorder. Although the standardized norms are out of date, both "clinical lore" and computer programs have come to take this kind of variation into account.

In addition to the scores on individual scales, psychologists interpret the *profile* of the MMPI scores. The clients' scores on all the scales are drawn on a graph so that the peaks and valleys of the high and low scores can be seen. This profile can then be interpreted according to clinical inferences or according to empirically derived rules. Controversies over the appropriate interpretation of the MMPI are discussed further in the sections below on clinical versus statistical prediction and on the uses of computers in assessment.

The Million tests are recent competitors of the MMPI. The Million Clinical Multiaxial Inventory (MCMI) is similar to the MMPI in its construction and purpose. The MCMI is shorter, with 175 items compared to over 550 for the MMPI. The scores and profiles on 20 scales are designed to give diagnoses that are similar to those in DSM-III. While the 20 MCMI scales are empirically derived, as are the MMPI scales, the comparison group for each scale was not "normals," but the general psychiatric population. Thus, the MCMI is appropriate only for diagnosing psychopathology.

In addition to the MCMI, there are the Million Adolescent Personality Inventory (MAPI) and the Million Behavioral Health Inventory (MBHI). Each test is designed for use with specific patient populations in clinical settings, and so the Millon tests may be more useful than the MMPI in certain cases.

The Millon tests continue to be researched by Millon and others. Some researchers (Widiger et al., 1985) argue that the MCMI does not validly assess DSM-III categories on Axis II, while others (Millon, 1985) claim that the body of evidence supports its validity. The tests are constantly revised according to Millon's research results. For example, the MCMI-II has two new personality disorder scales and revised versions of several test items that proved insufficiently discriminating.

The Millon tests are best scored and interpreted by computer. The computer-generated report gives the clinician a list of possible diagnoses on Axes I and II of DSM-III, a personality description based on both Millon's personality theory and empirical factors, and recommendations for treatment and therapy.

Inductive approach In the second type of approach to personality scale construction, the inductive approach, a personality structure and its test are "discovered" by giving huge numbers of people huge numbers of test items and subjecting the responses to a statistical procedure called factor analysis. Factor analysis discovers responses that consistently go together and therefore presumably measure some "real" aspect or dimension of personality. What that dimension is may be inferred by examining the content of the items that statistically go together. The Eysenck Personality Inventory (EPI) was developed using just this method. It is supposed to measure three fundamental dimensions of personality, which Eysenck labeled extraversion-introversion, neuroticism, and psychoticism. While a fairly important research questionnaire, the EPI is not frequently used by clinical psychologists in the United States.

Deductive approach The deductive approach to personality scale construction assumes that a great deal is already known from theory and possibly other research about the personality construct to be measured. This knowledge and how the construct is defined govern the formulation of the test items.

A good example of this type of test is the Edwards Personal Preference Schedule or EPPS (Edwards, 1954, 1959). Edwards started with Murray's (1938) theory that certain essential human motives or "presses" account for individual differences in behavior. Edwards chose to measure 15 of these motives, such as achievement, dominance, dependency, aggression, and nurturance. From his knowledge about how these motives work, Edwards made up items that he thought would tap each motive, and he also asked experts for their opinions as to what items would measure the motives. For example, "I like to work toward some goal I have set for myself" seems to measure achievement motivation, and "I like to order people around" seems to tap dominance. Statements that tap different motives were paired (a total of 225 pairs). Test-takers must choose which of the two statements they prefer or is more true of them. This procedure results in a hierarchy of motives, which can be drawn on a graph and interpreted.

The EPPS is a long, complicated, and, let's face it, boring test. However, Burisch (1984) argues that a good deductive test can be short and easily constructed in a couple of hours. For example, try to make up a test to measure procrastination. What items do you think would tap that motive? Think of your own tendencies to procrastinate and think of your procrastinating friends. Surely "I like to put things off to the last minute," "I rarely complete tasks ahead of time," and "I would rather enjoy life and think about chores later" immediately come to mind. You can probably develop a 12-item personality scale in little time, And according to most research, it will probably do a pretty good job of measuring procrastination! Even more simply, you could just ask people to rate themselves on how much they procrastinate, for such self-rating scales also do a fairly good job of assessment.

Burisch (1984) reviewed 15 studies that directly compared the validity and effectiveness of the three approaches to personality test construction. In all cases the different approaches were found to produce personality tests with similar levels of validity and effectiveness. However, it is obviously cheaper and quicker to make up short deductive and self-rating tests, which are also simpler to administer and score. Despite these conclusions, such research findings do not stop the long, complicated MMPI from being the most frequently used personality test in the world.

Reliability and Validity of Personality Tests The reliability of personality tests ranges from low to moderately high, depending on the type of test and method of scoring. For example, the reliability of the computer-scored MMPI may be quite high. Although individuals change, it is not unusual for a person to show a certain MMPI profile one year and to have almost the same profile the next. On the other hand, the reliability of a complex test like the Rorschach may be quite low, even among psychologists using the same scoring system, because there is so much room for judgment in scoring projective responses. Some researchers believe that the test-retest reliability of a personality test may be irrelevant. They assume it is human nature to change both over time and from situation to situation, so it is not reasonable to expect measures of human nature (i.e., personality) to stay the same (i.e., be reliable).

As with intelligence tests, the greater controversy is over the validity of the interpretation of personality tests and how they are used (see the section on criticisms of psychological tests). It is difficult to decide how to assess the validity of personality tests. What are these tests "really" measuring anyhow? Are they measuring enduring traits, temporary states, actual mental disorders, unconscious impulses, motives, emotions, or what? How psychologists answer this question depends on their theoretical orientation, as well as on the type of test under consideration. As you might expect, there is no universally accepted personality theory and therefore no general agreement on what the tests are supposed to measure.

As stated before, there are several types of evidence in evaluating validity. One way to try to validate the interpretation of personality test scores is to see how they correlate with other personality tests, a potentially circular process. The MMPI is the most researched test in the world, and it is the most frequently used to validate other tests. Predictive validity might also be used. Can MMPI profiles predict which alcoholics will recover or which chronic pain sufferers will benefit from surgery? The MMPI is often used to make these kinds of predictions with a fair degree of success. Several hundred new studies on the MMPI are published every year, so it would appear to have acceptable validity, at least for a substantial number of researchers.

Clinical Versus Statistical Prediction In the 1950s Paul Meehl (Meehl, 1954, 1956) started a controversy that threatened to tear clinical psychology apart when he presented convincing evidence that statistical interpretation of test results is better than clinical interpretation. *Clinical prediction* refers to the complicated, intuitive process in which professional psychologists use their extensive training and clinical experience to interpret the results of psychological tests. Clinical interpretation is a special skill and art of clinical psychologists. *Statistical prediction* refers to the application of empirically derived arithmetic rules or actuarial tables. According to Meehl, a statistical table, or today a computer, can do the same thing as a trained clinical psychologist and do it better. If there is empirical evidence that certain test scores predict certain behaviors, then the "interpretation" of test results does not take any particular skill other than looking up in a table what a score means. Many clinicians find this idea unacceptable (Matarazzo, 1986).

Over the years there have been many studies to try to decide this controversy. A typical study gives a group of clinical psychologists some test results, say, several MMPI profiles, and asks them to make certain predictions about the individuals based on their clinical interpretation of the test results. The same set of MMPI profiles is subjected to statistical interpretation—predictions based on empirical data about what scores predict what behaviors. Then the two types of predictions are compared as to which is most accurate. After years of such studies, Meehl's original conclusion still stands: Where appropriate statistical information exists, clinical interpretation cannot improve on it. The key phrase is "where appropriate statistical information exists," since statistical predictions will be only as good as the empirical evidence on which they are based.

Meehl and others argue that psychologists' efforts should be directed toward collecting the empirical evidence necessary to create "cookbooks" for psychological tests so as to make good statistical interpretations and predictions and that training in clinical interpretation should be dropped. However, at present, most psychologists seem to agree that it is still best to use both statistical and clinical interpretation of psychological tests.

Other Forms of Assessment

For almost every possible situation where people want to understand what is going on, psychologists have developed some kind of assessment procedure. There are methods for measuring organization dynamics, group dynamics, interpersonal interactions, unconscious physiological responses, vocational interests, achievement, and much more. This section will cover a few representative forms of assessment, forms that are not measures of personality or intelligence, but that may be used in conjunction with personality or intellectual assessment.

Neuropsychological Assessment Neuropsychological assessment involves a set of procedures designed to detect the presence, extent, and type of organic brain damage or neurological impairment in individuals. Typically, it is used to assess stroke patients, head injury victims, amnesia sufferers, and people with brain tumors, epilepsy, senility, or learning disabilities. In addition to use in medical research, neuropsychological tests are used for diagnosis, prognosis, and planning of patient care and rehabilitation, and they are especially useful in assessing the specific neurological deficit involved in learning disabilities in children so that individually tailored treatment plans can be made. As researchers learn more about the brain and its contribution to behavior, physiological and neurological factors must be taken into account in all forms of assessment, and we can expect that neuropsychological assessment will become an increasingly important part of the occupation of psychologists.

The oldest neuropsychological test is the Bender-Gestalt, already discussed in the section on intellectual assessment. Short and easy to administer, it involves copying geometric designs, a task commonly incorporated into modern tests. While good at detecting organic brain disorders that affect visual-motor coordination, the Bender-Gestalt does not give as comprehensive a diagnosis as modern tests. Another figure copying test, the Rey-Osterrieth Complex Figure (Osterrieth, 1944) is now used frequently. The client copies one very complicated geometric drawing with different colored pens so that the client's strategy for copying the design can be analyzed for specific types of neurological deficit.

The Halstead-Reitan Battery is a complicated, but comprehensive test developed and continually revised by Reitan and his colleagues (Reitan, 1966; Reitan & Davison, 1974). To give you an idea of just how comprehensive it is, Reitan recommends allowing 8 hours to give the test! It includes several procedures: the WAIS-R; aphasia tests; copying tasks; tactile, visual, and auditory discrimination tests; speech, rhythm, and form board problems; and more. The Reitan is criticized because it lacks a specific test for memory. It also lacks a published manual with directions for administration, scoring, and interpretation. Directions and research on the test are published in a variety of papers, and Reitan training workshops are offered to psychologists and physicians.

The Luria-Nebraska Neuropsychological Battery does have a manual (Golden, Hammeke, & Purisch, 1980), but like the Reitan, the tests in the battery undergo constant alteration. The battery consists of over 250 items divided into 11 content scales, from which 3 overall scales are derived. For example, the Tactile scale, a content scale, measures touch localization and tactile recognition by asking patients to do things such as tell where they are being touched with a pencil. Another content scale, the Memory scale, measures types of memory deficits by asking patients to do things such as repeat back a short story. The three derived scales are the Pathognomonic, which contains items from throughout the battery that detect the presence or absence of brain damage; the Left Hemisphere, which contains items from parts of the battery that reflect left brain function; and the Right Hemisphere, which contains items that reflect right brain function. The Luria-Nebraska has been criticized for its theoretical foundations and for methodological flaws in its standardization. Not as old or as well established as the Reitan, it needs further research to establish its value.

Assessment of children with learning disabilities almost always includes the WISC-R, and researchers are finding ways to analyze WISC-R subtest scores for what they indicate about specific forms of neurological impairment.

Neurological assessment may also include asking children to perform difficult motor tasks, such as walking on the sides of the feet. How well children perform such tasks for their age and what sorts of behaviors are elicited by the tasks can provide trained observers with much information about the children's neurological functioning.

As many of the recent advances in clinical psychological research are in neuropsychology, the tests and procedures involved in neuropsychological assessment will continue to change.

Interviews and the Mental Status Examination In spite of the growing use of computers and personality tests, interviewing as a method of assessment is showing a resurgence in popularity. Professionals have made the apparently surprising discovery that clients will tell them all they want to know if they simply ask them, so many psychologists and psychiatrists do diagnostic interviews.

Intake interviews, conducted when a client first appears at a hospital or agency for services, usually take 45 to 90 minutes and can follow a structured, question-and-answer format or be relatively unstructured. There are many outlines available for structured interviews. Most professionals seem to prefer a semistructured interview that follows an outline they prefer or is required by their agency while allowing for variation as determined by the particular case and their theoretical orientation. For example, all interviewers must obtain information about the patient's symptoms, but a psychoanalyst might want information on defenses and ego structure and a behaviorist would want information on environmental circumstances.

The characteristics of a good psychological interview are probably the same as for any kind of interview. Questions should be asked matter-of-factly with a nonjudgmental attitude, and the questioner should listen and observe carefully. The results of the interview will be utilized to make a diagnosis, prognosis, and treatment plans, so a sufficient amount of relevant information must be elicited to meet these purposes. Besides identifying data such as name, age, and the like, the gathered information should include what the patient's problems and symptoms are, when they began, and what brought them on. The patient's past psychological history, medical history, and personal history is typically also asked. Any information from psychological tests, if available, will be included in the report of the results of a diagnostic interview. The goal is to obtain as much information as possible in order to be able to help the client.

The mental status examination is the formal part of an interview that assesses the client's current mental functioning. Usually fairly structured, this interview may include clinical tests such as asking the patient to repeat a series of digits backwards, to answer questions about current events, or to subtract 7 from 100 serially. The typical mental status exam tries to cover the following areas:

1. General appearance and behavior. Is the person neat or disheveled, walking straight or not, alert or stuporous, avoidant of eye contact, slow moving or agitated?
2. Speech and thought. Is the person's speech coherent, understandable, excessive, nonexistent? Is thinking logical, peculiar, confused, grandiose?
3. Consciousness. Is the person conscious, clear, confused?
4. Mood and affect. Is the person's prevailing mood sad, elated, irritable, appropriate, inappropriate?
5. Perception. Is the person hallucinating and when?
6. Obsessions and compulsions. Does the person engage in repetitive behavior or reveal intrusive thoughts? If so, are they seen as real or symptomatic?
7. Orientation. Does the person know what time, day, year it is?
8. Memory. How are the person's long-term and short-term memory?
9. Attention and concentration. Is the person distracted, preoccupied, able to concentrate?
10. General information. Can the person name the president, six large states, the capitals of a few countries?
11. Intelligence. What level of education has the person attained? Are the questions in #10 answered well?

12. Insight and judgment. Does the person seem to have insight into his or her current situation? (Judgment often seems to be assessed by whether persons agree that they are in need of treatment!)

Behavioral Assessment Although the techniques of behavioral assessment are quite old, its recognition as a separate type of assessment is recent. No books on the subject were published before the mid-1970s, but now there are many. Two journals in the field, *Behavioral Assessment* and *Journal of Behavioral Assessment,* were begun only in 1979. Since then, research and applications of behavioral assessment have proliferated, and the field continues to expand and change.

Behavioral assessment is derived from the empirical and theoretical foundations of behaviorism and behavior therapy (covered in Chapter 7). It shares with them the assumptions that behavior has multiple causes, that the environment and the person interact to cause behavior (reciprocal determinism), that individuals have behavioral skills as well as deficits, and that mediational variables such as social support systems, cognitive coping strategies, past experiences, and physiological responses or disorders are important in determining behavior. The functional analysis of behavior attempts to study all these factors, because the assessment of any one in isolation will result in an inadequate or wrong conclusion. Because of its ties to academic behaviorism and its empirical hypothesis-testing paradigm, behavioral assessment also values quantification of variables, objective observation, and assessment and intervention within controlled conditions. Therefore, behavioral assessors obtain information about the rate, duration, and intensity of target behaviors and the conditions under which they occur.

In clinical psychology behavioral assessment is used most often in conjunction with behavior therapy. A general list of purposes, in addition to empirical research, would include to identify target behaviors to modify, to identify alternative (desirable) behaviors to replace or reduce undesirable ones, to identify causal variables so interventions can be made at that point, to develop a functional analysis of the entire environmental and social situation in which the client is embedded, to design intervention strategies, and to evaluate and modify the intervention(s).

Most behaviorists would agree that methods of behavioral assessment include interviews, naturalistic observation, analogue observation, participant observation, self-monitoring, psychophysiological measures, and behavioral questionnaires. Although more controversial, neuropsychological assessment, projective methods, intelligence tests, computer-assisted assessment, and other techniques may also be included in behavioral assessment. Because behavioral assessment is a rapidly growing and changing field, any attempt to list all its methods would soon be outdated, but we can describe some of the techniques most widely used today.

Behavioral assessment interviews All behavioral interventions require some form of interview before they are attempted. The behavior therapist must first ask clients the nature of their problems and when and where they occur. Interviews are necessary to define the problem(s), target the behavior(s), and set therapy goals. Compared to nonbehavioral interviews, behavioral interviews tend to be more structured, more focused on overt behavior, more oriented to environmental causes of behavior, less interested in the past, and more quantitative.

Naturalistic observation In this method two or more trained observers enter the client's natural environment (home, classroom, hospital ward) and systematically record the occurrence or nonoccurrence of predefined behaviors. Behaviors to be sampled in this way are carefully selected and defined prior to observation. They may be undesirable behaviors to be decreased, desirable behaviors to be increased, or behaviors with causal significance to be analyzed. For example, observers may go into the homes of obese individuals to observe their eating patterns or into bars to observe the drinking behavior of alcoholics.

Analogue observation Observations of behavior are made in a controlled environment that is different from, but similar or analogous to the client's natural environment. Role playing is a form of analogue observation often used to assess social skills. A shy client may role play a scenario of being more assertive with the therapist role playing the client's boss or date. The behavior avoidance test (BAT) is another type of analogue assessment. Clients are asked to approach a feared object, such as a snake or hypodermic needle, and their behavior is carefully observed and recorded.

Participant observation A family member or other involved person who is not a professional is asked to monitor the target behavior. For example, parents may be asked to keep a record of all instances of tantrums thrown by their difficult child.

Self-monitoring Clients are asked to observe and record the occurrence or nonoccurrence of their own predefined behaviors. Smokers may be asked to record all cigarettes smoked, when, where, what they were doing as they smoked, how much they did or did not enjoy it, and what they were thinking about when they decided to smoke.

Psychophysiological measures The increasing popularity of biofeedback and behavioral medicine has contributed to the development of psychophysiological techniques in behavioral assessment. Measures of brain waves, eye movements, skin temperature, pulse, muscle tension, respiration, penile erections, skin conductance, and blood pressure have been used in the behavioral assessment of headaches, phobias, high blood pressure, pain, anxiety, smoking, sexual dysfunctions, compulsions, and many other problems.

Behavioral questionnaires Written questionnaires, checklists, and rating scales are often used in behavioral assessment. For example, a questionnaire could be used to collect information on what, when, where, how much, and how often someone eats. Or a rating scale could ask clients to rate their levels of anxiety under different example conditions. Compared to personality questionnaires, behavioral questionnaires tend to be shorter, more specific, and more focused on the occurrence and frequency of behaviors than on enduring traits. They are a quick and inexpensive way to screen clients and to obtain preinterview and preintervention data.

Product-of-behavior measures Product-of-behavior measures are records of data generated by the target behaviors themselves. For example, weight is often used as a product-of-behavior measure of eating behavior. Such assessments have the advantage of being objectively measurable and easily obtained as a by-product of the intervention procedures.

Vocational, Aptitude, and Interest Tests Professional psychologists are involved in many other forms of assessment. This chapter cannot cover them all, but we will cover one final area. Assessment of vocational skills and potentials, aptitudes, and vocational and life interests is often done by counseling and educational psychologists.

Vocational, aptitude, and interest tests are used to help parents, schools, and individuals make educational and vocational decisions. They are supposed to measure people's talents, interests, and potentials, characteristics that should be related to what sorts of education and careers they would do well in. They are not intelligence tests, which supposedly measure a global ability to do well in school (some view this as "scholastic aptitude"). And they are not achievement tests, which are supposed to measure level of performance already achieved in various subjects. Rather, these tests attempt to identify specific talents or unknown potential or patterns of interests to predict how individuals will "fit" in certain careers or educational programs.

There are many group and individual aptitude and interest tests. Among the best known—and the ones most often used by professional psychologists—are the Strong and the Kuder. First developed in the 1920s, the Strong Vocational Interest Blank is now known as the Strong-Campbell Interest Inventory (Campbell & Hansen, 1981). It was constructed using the empirical method of contrast groups, like the MMPI. It includes over 300 items, such as "Watching an open-heart operation," "Sports pages in the newspaper," and "Outspoken people with new ideas," for which test-takers indicate their interest by marking "Like," "Indifferent," or "Dislike." These items were administered to national samples of 200 to 300 women and 200 to 300 men in nearly 100 different occupations. The contrast sample consisted of several hundred women and men not identified by occupation. Their answers were compared to the answers of those in different occupational groups to identify those test items that statistically distinguished each occupational group from the general group. It is assumed that if an individual's answers on the Strong inventory match the interest patterns of certain occupational groups, then that person would be likely to find satisfaction in that vocation. There are also 23 Basic Interest scales on the Strong, and these scales indicate low, moderate, and high interest in categories such as nature, science, art, religious activities, and sales.

Begun in the 1930s and published in several different forms, the Kuder test in its latest form is known as the Kuder Occupation Interest Survey—Form DD (Kuder, 1966). It is composed of 100 triads of work-related activities, such as "Read lessons to a blind student," "Keep records of experimental results," and "Interview people in a survey of public opinion." For each triad of activities, the test-taker indicates the most preferred and least preferred activity. This procedure results in a rank ordering of preference for the different kinds of activities, and the individual's pattern of ranked interests can be related to occupational scales and college major scales to indicate possible educational and career goals.

Reliability and Validity of These Other Forms of Assessment In general, the more structured and objective the assessment procedure, the higher its reliability and consequent validity will be. Thus, more structured interviews result in higher reliability than unstructured ones. The validity of interviewing will have to do with the correctness of the diagnosis reached through an interview and the success of the treatment plans it leads to. Interviews are probably the most frequently used assessment procedure of all. They appear to be as effective as test batteries in diagnosis and assessment, and they are cheaper and quicker. Although some evidence questions their validity, in actual practice numerous treatment decisions and diagnoses are reached with interviews, so it would appear that many people think that interviewing does have adequate reliability and validity.

There are special problems in determining test-retest reliability of neuropsychological tests. Organic patients may be deteriorating or (preferably) improving, so that their performance will differ on subsequent tests. Also, their performance may improve due to practice. In spite of these problems, some studies (Boll, 1981; Golden, Hammeke, and Purisch, 1980) indicate that reliability is adequate. Validity of such tests will depend on their ability to pinpoint the location of brain lesions, as determined by brain scans, the results of neurosurgery, or autopsy, as well as their ability to predict treatment outcomes. Studies (reviewed by Goldstein, 1984) indicate fairly good validity for the Reitan, while that of the Luria-Nebraska remains severely criticized (Adams, 1984).

As you might expect, the reliability and validity of the empirically derived behavioral assessment methods are mostly well researched. Furthermore, the results of such research lead to changes in the methods in order to improve reliability and validity. Many studies (reviewed by Ciminero, Calhoun, & Adams, 1984; Haynes & Wilson, 1979; Nelson & Hayes, 1979) indicate good reliability and validity for behavioral assessment, while others (Haynes, 1984) suggest that at least some methods have not been adequately researched for reliability and validity.

According to the research done for their manuals, the reliability of both the Strong and the Kuder tests is high—in fact, close to the reliability of intelligence tests. Because aptitude and interest tests are used to make long-term decisions about education and careers, it is important that their predictive validity be high. According to several studies, between one-half and three-fourths of subjects in studies on predictive validity choose college majors (Hansen & Swanson, 1983) or enter careers (Campbell, 1966; Spokane, 1979) which would be predicted by their scores on the Strong. The Kuder predicts careers accurately about half the time (Zytowski, 1976). While a 50 percent correct prediction rate may not seem high to you, it does, in fact, represent good predictive validity for a psychological test.

THE PSYCHOLOGICAL ASSESSMENT REPORT

Recall that psychological assessments are generally done only because someone (the referral source, which in some cases is the tester) needs information or has a question about a client that psychological tests can answer. Thus, to be of any use, the results of psychological assessment must be reported both to the client who took the tests and to the referral source. Most frequently test results are communicated to other professionals or the referral source in a formal written report. The test results must be described, discussed, and integrated into conclusions regarding diagnosis, treatment recommendations, personality analysis, or whatever the purpose of the testing was.

Like all information obtained in the course of psychologists' professional activities, test results and test reports should be kept confidential. The client owns the information, and it may be released to another professional, the courts, an agency, or a school only with the written consent of the client or the client's parent or guardian. Clients should be tested only after they have given their informed consent, again in writing. Informed consent means they have consented to testing (or treatment) only after all the possible benefits and harmful effects of it have been fully explained to them. They should also give informed consent to the release of information obtained from testing. In some cases, it may not be in the client's best interests to release the test findings. For example, a father suing for custody of his children may request psychological assessment of the family to support his suit in court, but the results of the assessment may indicate that he is psychologically unstable and inadequate to parent at that time. The psychologist may be in an ethical dilemma here, because it may be in the best interests of the children that this information be made available to the court, but it would not be in the best interests of the father, who is the client. The ethical issues involved in confidentiality will be discussed in Chapter 12.

In addition to reporting the results of psychological assessment to other professionals and referral sources, the results of testing must be given to the client. It is not the general practice for psychologists to give clients written reports, but rather to discuss the results with the client. Ethical psychologists are concerned with the well-being of their clients, and this concern translates into efforts to ensure that all clients clearly understand the results of the psychological tests they took and what they mean. To accomplish this, it may be necessary to educate clients about the nature of psychological tests and to explain the meaning of their particular responses or scores to them.

Most psychologists develop a standardized way of writing their assessment reports. Sometimes the agencies where they work require the report to be in a certain form. Psychological assessment reports vary greatly, because they must be tailored to the needs of the client, the nature of the information sought, and the person who will read and use the report. (Box 2.4 contains a sample assessment report.) Nevertheless, most reports begin with basic identifying information: client's name, address, gender, age, marital status, educational or occupational status, date and place of testing, date of the test report, tester's name and title, reason for testing or the referral question, and tests administered.

The identifying information is usually followed by a section called "Behavioral Observations" or "Test Behavior." This section should include observations of the client's appearance, attitude, and behavior during the testing—anything that might affect the interpretation of the test results. For example, a client's arriving disheveled and smelling of alcohol would affect the scores on an intelligence test.

The next section of the test report, which may precede the behavioral observations or which may be left out, is commonly called "Social History" or "Personal History." This section would contain a summary of what the tester knows about the client's family background and current situation. This information may be obtained by interviewing the client or from the referral source. Only history that might affect the test results should be reported. For example, the fact that a client's child was hospitalized with a grave illness at the time of testing might affect scores on the MMPI, but the fact that the family owns a restaurant may be irrelevant.

BOX 2.4
Psychological Assessment Report

Leya N. Couch, Ph.D.
Licensed Clinical Psychologist
111 First Street
Beverly Hills, CA 91000

NAME:	Laura T.
ADDRESS:	222 Main Street Long Beach, CA 90000
DATE OF BIRTH:	September 30, 1969
GENDER:	Female
OCCUPATION:	Student
DATES OF TESTING:	May 11, 1986; May 18, 1986
PLACE OF TESTING:	Office
DATE OF REPORT:	June 5, 1986
TESTS ADMINISTERED:	Wechsler Adult Intelligence Scale, Revised (WAIS-R), Thematic Apperception Test (TAT), Draw-a-Person (DAP), Rotter Sentence Completion, Strong-Campbell Interest Inventory, Minnesota Multiphasic Personality Inventory (MMMPI)
REASON FOR REFERRAL:	Parents requested evaluation to explain recent low grades in high school and to obtain career guidance for Laura

BEHAVIORAL OBSERVATIONS:

Laura T., an attractively dressed 17-year-old woman, was friendly, cooperative, and sociable during most of the testing. She maintained good eye contact with the examiner, and she smiled and conversed appropriately. During the administration of the WAIS-R, she seemed motivated to do her best by concentrating well on the test items and thoughtfully considering her answers. Her approach to the performance subtests was methodical and efficient in that she first examined the task, appeared to think about her response, and then quickly executed her plan. She made frequent remarks about her own good performance, such as "That was easy" or "Not too bad."

Laura became somewhat more anxious and resistant during the administration of the personality tests. She became somewhat agitated, squirming in her chair and pulling at her hair, when presented with the more emotion-laden TAT cards. She complained several times about the difficulty of drawing the DAP, although she produced detailed and complex drawings. She also complained vociferously about the length of the MMPI and groaned over several of the items, but she completed it quickly nevertheless. She took the Strong-Campbell Interest Inventory home to complete, and she reported that she found that test interesting and enjoyable.

SOCIAL HISTORY:

An interview with Laura's mother revealed the following information. At present Laura lives at home with her mother, an elementary school teacher, her stepfather, a computer professional, and her younger half brother. Her father, an architect, resides in San Diego with his wife, and Laura occasionally visits them there. Laura is a senior at Long Beach High School, where she is involved in drama, choir, and several clubs. Last year she received an award for outstanding achievement in the performing arts, and this year she is rehearsing for her role in the senior play.

Laura was a planned baby, and her parents had greatly looked forward to the birth of their first child. There were no problems in the pregnancy, and she was born healthy after an uneventful delivery. Her mother reported that her developmental milestones were all early, with Laura walking at 9 months and toilet trained at 15 months, for example. She was a happy baby, and all the relatives remarked on how sociable she was.

Laura's parents divorced when she was 2 years old, and her mother remarried when she was 4. Her mother stated that Laura seemed to adjust well to the divorce and to the birth of her half brother when she was 5. Now the family get along together about as well as most families, according to the mother, with Laura calling her stepfather "Dad" and having occasional fights with her brother.

Laura had always done well in school, the mother reported, until the last couple of years. She started reading when she was 3, and she received high grades throughout school. Her mother thought that Laura performed much better when she was challenged and that she had a tendency to give up easily on a task that either frustrated or did not interest her. In the last couple of years Laura has received either A or F grades. She apparently did well only in classes that interested her. Recently, because of talks with the school counselors and because she wants to attend college, she has been working to raise all of her grades to A or B.

Laura stated that she realizes she was wrong to let her grades drop and that she plans to attend community college for a year in order to raise her grades so she can attend the state university. Her long-range plans are to become a singer and an actress.

EVALUATION RESULTS:

WECHSLER ADULT INTELLIGENCE SCALE, REVISED

Verbal tests	Scaled score	Performance tests	Scaled score
Information	14	Picture Completion	14
Digit Span	12	Picture Arrangement	17
Vocabulary	17	Block Design	19
Arithmetic	11	Object Assembly	13
Comprehension	19	Digit Symbol	11
Similarities	16		

Verbal score:	148
Performance score:	143
Full scale score:	149

A WAIS-R verbal score of 148, a performance score of 143, and a full scale score of 149 place 17-year-old Laura T. in the very superior range of intellectual functioning. While clearly capable of superior school work in all subjects, Laura showed some relative strengths and weaknesses in her subtest scaled scores. Her lowest scores, 11 on both Arithmetic and Digit Symbol and 12 on Digit Span, occurred on subtests that tap short-term memory and numerical ability. Her highest scores revealed several strengths. Laura has a well-developed vocabulary (17 on Vocabulary), good abstract verbal reasoning (16 on Similarities), and excellent spatial relations ability (19 on Block Design). Her sense of what is socially appropriate and her sequential reasoning skills are also well developed, as shown in her high scores on Comprehension (19) and Picture Arrangement (17).

The personality tests indicated that Laura is basically a healthy, well-balanced, creative, assertive teenager. All of her MMPI scores were near the mean, except for a somewhat elevated score (71) on scale 4 (Pd), which would suggest some degree of family conflict and rebelliousness, as might be expected in teenagers. Laura's sentence completions tended to be optimistic, devoid of negative feelings, with themes of achievement, family support, and dreams of success.

Laura's TAT stories were coherent and imaginative, with themes of family conflict and needs for love, acceptance, achievement, and self-actualization. In several stories the character's need for achievement and actualization was in conflict with his or her need for love and acceptance from family, as in Story 2: "Mother and daughter had a disagreement. Daughter is feeling guilty because she is going to school, leaving the family to work, and she's afraid she'll grow different and they won't love her any more. But of course they do, and she does well in school." In most of the stories the characters care for one another and there is a happy ending, perhaps indicating some use of denial as a defense. Laura may be experiencing some inner conflict between her need for independence and her dependence on her family for love and acceptance, and she may be denying or trying to look on the bright side in order to deal with it.

Laura's DAP drawings were artistic and elaborate, with much shading, erasing, and detail. She drew the female first, then the male about the same size. The young woman she drew was dressed glamorously in pearls and a long gown. The head was of moderate size, held high, with a straightforward and cheerful expression on the face. The shoulders and torso were large, suggesting strength, while the hands were hidden behind the back, suggesting passivity and helplessness. Slim legs with small feet peeping out from a slit in the long skirt suggest conflict about sexuality and uncertainty or lack of grounding. The male figure looked sturdy, with large shoulders and torso, hands on hips, and large feet firmly on the ground. Laura may be experiencing some conflict between her inner strength and assertiveness and her feelings of passivity and uncertainty. The glamorous drawing fits in with her aspirations to be an actress.

On the Strong-Campbell Interest Inventory, Laura indicated that she was most interested in the artistic (A) and social (S) general occupational themes, with a high interest in music and dramatics. Her interest patterns were most similar to people in the occupations of musician, advertising executive, beautician, flight attendant, broadcaster, florist, fine artist, photographer, and chef. With her high intelligence, she may be better suited to some occupations (musician, advertising executive) than others (beautician). Her interest in and sensitivity to people appears through all the tests in this evaluation, and her interest in music and dramatics has been stated in her career aspirations to be a singer and actress.

Laura T. appears to be a highly intelligent, well-balanced teenager. There is nothing in the testing to suggest a reason for her low grades. She is independent, assertive, and creative, and she may have allowed these qualities to stop her from trying her best in unchallenging, uninteresting courses. She appears to have realized that better grades will be instrumental in allowing her to attend university, and she is working to improve them. As is developmentally appropriate for a teenager, Laura appears to exhibit some rebelliousness and family conflict. She may also be experiencing some inner doubt and uncertainty over the conflict between her desires for independence and achievement and her dependence on her family for love and acceptance. She appears to be experiencing some inner conflict and some conflict between her own desires and those of her family over her career aspirations to be a singer and actress. She seems to be handling these feelings well through the use of denial as a defense and trying to think positively.

DIAGNOSTIC IMPRESSION: None.

SUMMARY AND RECOMMENDATIONS:

Seventeen-year-old Laura T. scored in the very superior range of intellectual functioning on the WAIS-R, with her greatest strengths in the areas of social sense, sequential and abstract reasoning, spatial relations, and vocabulary and with relative weakness in the areas of short-term memory and numerical ability. Personality assessment suggested a well-balanced, socially sensitive teenager who is experiencing some inner conflict between her desires for dependence and independence and some family conflict possibly over her career aspirations. She handles these feelings with denial and a positive outlook. She is achievement motivated, wants to attend college, and dreams of success as a singer and actress. Both her interest patterns on the Strong-Campbell and her intellectual ability fit with those aspirations. Laura has the motivation and ability to do very well in college. I recommend that while in college she pursue personal or career counseling to help her further clarify her career choices, develop her identity, and fulfill her high potential.

The major portion of a test report will be devoted to discussion and interpretation of the test results. Usually called "Test Results," "Results of Assessment," or "Evaluation Results," this section may summarize WAIS-R scores in a chart or table or discuss each test administered one at a time or present results in a number of different ways. A single test result in isolation is meaningless, and only when it is substantiated by other results can a meaningful conclusion be drawn. For example, a single bizarre story on the TAT is not evidence of schizophrenia, but coupled with certain signs on the Rorschach and elevated scores on the F and Schizophrenia scales of the MMPI, it can be seen as part of the evidence for a diagnosis of schizophrenia. Consistent and inconsistent findings must be pointed out and explained. A good report generally pulls together the findings of different tests in some meaningful way. That will be determined by the nature of the findings, the theoretical biases of the tester, the intended audience and use(s) of the report, and the nature of the referral question(s). You can see that a report written by a psychoanalytically oriented psychologist to be sent to a psychiatrist for the purposes of determining the direction of a client's individual therapy will be different in many ways from a report written by a behaviorist to be sent to a rehabilitation center for determining a client's day treatment or from a school psychologist's report on a student's intelligence to be used to determine classroom placement.

The assessment report should conclude with a diagnostic impression, treatment recommendations, or a brief answer to whatever question was asked by the referral source and possibly a summary. A brilliant synthesis of all the test findings is also nice. As is true of the rest of the report, this section should be worded carefully to help and not harm the client. Obviously, pejorative labels such as "psychopathic deviant" or "inadequately humorous character disorder" should be avoided. Strengths, as well as any deficits or difficulties, should be noted. In addition to being careful to help the client, care should be taken to help the reader of the report, and it should be written in plain English, rather than psychological jargon.

USE OF COMPUTERS IN ASSESSMENT

Like every other field, clinical psychology makes increasing use of computers in its work. While still extremely experimental, there are even computer programs to conduct psychotherapy or counseling; the computer is programmed to ask questions, make comments, and even give interpretations, and the client types what he or she wants to say directly into the computer (Weizenbaum, 1966). There is some evidence that certain individuals are more comfortable communicating with the completely nonjudgmental computer than with humans (Canoune & Leyhe, 1985) and that some people find this type of "therapy" helpful (O'Dell & Dickson, 1984; Zarr, 1984). However, the computer is used mainly in the administration, scoring, interpretation, and reporting of psychological tests.

There are computer programs to administer a variety of psychological tests, even one to administer the Rorschach! The most widely used program administers the MMPI, and the Millon tests are also available on computer. In a computerized administration of the MMPI, the directions for taking the test appear on the screen first; then as each item appears, the client presses T for true and F for false.

Computer administration of psychological tests clearly saves time for psychologists, who don't have to be present at all while clients take the tests. Some psychologists argue that it also results in more valid scores, first because when using the keyboard, clients are less likely to become confused or make mistakes than when marking their answers on a form, and second because they may be more likely to be honest with the impersonal machine. One drawback is that clients, especially upset or disturbed ones, may be intimidated by having to use a computer. However, computer administration is so clear and simple that most people lose their discomfort quickly (Moore, Summer, & Bloor, 1984) and many even start to enjoy themselves.

Probably the earliest use of computers or computer-like machines in psychology was scoring test answers. A great time-saver, computer or machine scoring is a natural for tests like the MMPI. Machines can quickly scan answer sheets and print out both scale scores and profiles. A program that administers the MMPI can also automatically score it and print out the profile for immediate inspection by the psychologist. Recent developments in this area include a program to score the Rorschach.

Over the years such programs have been developed to interpret the results of tests, particularly the MMPI. These programs are supposed to be based on extensive research by the program author and possibly others and to use empirically derived rules to interpret individual test results and to "correct" out-of-date MMPI norms.

The evidence on clinical versus statistical prediction suggests that computer interpretations of tests are in general more accurate than those of individual psychologists, because computers can store and integrate far more empirical data than most people can learn and remember. Nevertheless, because clients are individuals and may be exceptions to empirical rules, all computerized reports carry the caution that they are only to be used by psychologists who know the client being evaluated and who have the expertise to evaluate the reported results.

Computers are also used to compose and print psychological assessment reports. Some programs score the test, interpret the scores according to built-in empirical rules, and then compose and print out the report. Psychologists may use word processors to write their reports themselves. A word processor can make short work of composing, editing, changing, and printing assessment reports. Many psychologists develop an all-purpose report framework and then simply fill in the individual information for each report. They can then print as many copies as they need and store the report permanently on computer disks. For a psychologist whose practice is devoted to assessment, this use of computers is an incredible time-saver. In addition, human services agencies and psychologists in private practice, like many businesses, use computers to keep files, bill clients, and keep accounts.

Not everyone is enthusiastic about the increasing use of computers in psychology. Some critics fear that psychological "interpretations" printed out by a computer will appear to have greater "scientific value" than they truly have or that such printouts might be misused by nonprofessionals. Some believe that the computerized assessments have not been sufficiently validated (Matarazzo, 1986). Others fear that the increasing use of computers in psychology will increase risks to the confidentiality of psychological information. However, methods of safeguarding computer data are constantly being developed, and we can assume that psychologists will make use of them to keep the information obtained in the course of their professional duties as confidential as they have in the past. Like labeling and psychological testing, computers cannot be good or bad, but how they are used may be.

CRITICISMS OF PSYCHOLOGICAL TESTING

Psychological tests and assessment procedures have been criticized since they were first developed. Criticisms can be grouped into three major areas: validity of interpretation of test results, cost-effectiveness, and purposes for which assessments are used.

The validity of intelligence tests is now quite controversial. Many researchers, among them Gardner (1983) and Piaget and his colleagues (Flavell, 1963), have argued that there are types of intelligence that are not being measured by current intelligence tests. This theoretical argument becomes important outside of academia when the lives of individuals are affected by decisions based on intelligence test scores.

It is relatively easy to criticize the validity of projective tests, because their interpretation depends on the theoretical framework of the tester. For example, a psychologist with a psychoanalytic orientation may try to use the Rorschach to reach conclusions about a patient's ego strength or unconscious defenses. Behaviorists would reject the validity of such an interpretation, because they do not accept the existence of the ego or the unconscious. They would not accept this interpretation even if empirical research demonstrated that people with poor ego strength could be differentiated from people with good ego strength. Even psychologists within similar theoretical frameworks may disagree with each other's interpretations of projective tests.

Nevertheless, many studies by Exner and his colleagues (reviewed by Erdberg & Exner, 1984) have demonstrated the validity of specific sorts of Rorschach interpretations, such as quality of reality testing.

Arguments over the validity of objective tests like the MMPI are open to settlement by empirical studies. While it may remain forever debatable whether the MMPI is really measuring "hypochrondriasis" or "psychasthenia" (whatever that is), there are literally thousands of studies demonstrating that the MMPI can accurately detect many different things, such as neurosis versus psychosis or whether someone will benefit from a certain kind of treatment. If you accept this kind of evidence, then, the MMPI may be said to have adequate validity.

Even if it is generally agreed that psychological tests are valid, they can still be criticized as not cost-effective if a simpler, cheaper way of doing the same thing exists. We have already discussed the clinical versus statistical prediction controversy and the evidence that appears to show that empirically derived statistical rules for pencil-and-paper test results are just as good, if not better, at making clinical predictions as interpretation by individual psychologists. Using computers to interpret tests may be more cost-effective than using expensive psychologists.

Some critics have pointed out that the old statistical versus clinical judgment controversy is irrelevant because neither process is very accurate. It is argued that the most accurate predictions can be made using only a person's past behavior as a basis. For example, an experimental study may demonstrate that several clinical psychologists can examine *x* number of MMPI profiles of prisoners and predict which ones will return to crime on release with about 30 percent accuracy. A statistical rule applied to the same profiles may be able to hit about 40 percent accuracy. This finding may be interesting to academicians engaged in the statistical versus clinical judgment controversy, but it is not exciting when we realize that released prisoners return to crime about 60 to 80 percent of the time. Simply predicting that all prisoners will return to crime will result in an accuracy rate of 60 percent. And it is a lot cheaper and quicker than either clinical judgment or statistical methods.

However, it is often more important to be able to make certain decisions about a specific individual than it is to make an accurate prediction. Let us take the example of suicide. Only about 2 percent of callers to a suicide prevention hot line actually make a suicide attempt (Farberow & Schneidman, 1961). If all we were interested in was accurate prediction, we could simply predict that all callers would not attempt suicide and hang up on them. After all, we would be right 98 percent of the time, an incredibly high level of predictive validity. Obviously, though, the consequences of the 2 percent error are not acceptable in the case of suicide. Thus, questions and procedures have been developed to identify callers at high risk for suicide, so preventive actions can be taken. This assessment procedure results in a high rate of errors by incorrectly identifying persons who would not attempt suicide as suicide-attempters. In this case it is preferable to make certain kinds of incorrect predictions, and we can conclude that the assessment procedure to make these predictions is cost-effective.

This brings us to the final area of criticism of psychological assessment. As we have pointed out before, psychological tests in and of themselves cannot be good or bad. But many have argued that they have been misused. Most will agree that an assessment procedure that identifies potential suicides, even if not accurate because it overestimates suicide attempters, is both cost-effective and of positive value to society. That is an easy example. Other uses of psychological tests are more controversial.

The most well-known controversy over the use of psychological tests has to do with intelligence tests. Here the use of the test is directly related to its validity. Intelligence tests have been used to place certain students in institutions or special education classes. If the tests do not really measure intelligence, then it is possible that at least some individuals so placed do not belong there. If the tests in fact measure acquired knowledge or level of education or cultural values, then minority group members in particular may be discriminated against if the tests are used to make such decisions about them, because they may not have had equal education and their culture may be different.

The controversy over the validity of intelligence tests was "settled" by the California State Supreme Court in 1979 in the cae of *Larry P.* v. *Wilson Riles and the Board of Education,* in which it ruled that intelligence tests were biased in favor of middle-class white children and against minority groups. Larry P. was a black child assigned to special education classes on the basis of his score on an intelligence test. Special education classes contain far more minority group students than their proportion in the population. Larry P.'s parents argued that this disproportionate assignment of minority students to special education classes constituted discrimination and denied Larry P. an equal education. The California State Supreme Court agreed and ruled that schools could no longer assign students to special education classes on the basis of their intelligence test scores alone, that they had to take into account other information as well. While the Court and many others believe that this case represents a misuse of psychological tests, others (such as Lambert, 1981) believe that the Court was wrong and that intelligence tests are a valid way to make such educational decisions. It is clear that something is wrong when so many minority students have difficulty in our educational system, but we will leave it to you to consider what it is, only noting that the use of intelligence tests here may perpetuate a tendency to blame the victim.

The most frequently used psychological test of all, the MMPI, is also a frequent target of criticism. Its very success and popularity may lead to its misuse, as people try to apply it in situations for which it was not designed. For example, it was useless in predicting success in the Peace Corps. The MMPI was (and sometimes still is) used to make employment and personnel decisions without adequate research to test its validity for those kinds of decisions. Individuals applying for jobs or promotions may rightfully complain that they cannot see the relevance of MMPI test items to either the job they want or their competence to do it. Employers may respond that they do not want to hire and train a disturbed or unstable individual who will quit or cause other problems. The job may require personal stability, such as one involving national security or secret work. Insurance companies may want companies to hire only the healthy to reduce health benefit payments. Nevertheless, the use of the MMPI to deny employment or promotions to certain kinds of individuals would appear to be open to the criticism of misuse and to be an issue of concern of civil libertarians.

New applications of the MMPI are being researched all the time. Many of them appear to be valuable and useful extensions of the test and psychological knowledge. For example, using the MMPI to predict which chronic pain sufferers would benefit from back surgery (Turner, Herron, and Weiner, 1986) would save medical expenses and unnecessary suffering from surgery that won't help. Predicting which form of treatment will best help clients is another example of a beneficial use of the MMPI. While recognizing the benefits of psychological testing, both ethical psychologists and concerned citizens should remain aware of the potential for the misuse of tests and the need to take appropriate action through psychological organizations, the courts, or the legislature to prevent and remedy such misuse.

IN CONCLUSION

This chapter described intelligence tests, projective and objective personality tests, and other forms of psychological assessment. It also discussed the reliability and validity, cost-effectiveness, and social uses or misuses of tests. Because clinical psychologists are trained to research, develop, administer, score, and interpret psychological tests, they will remain an important part of professional psychology. Through constant research and the help of computers to analyze and integrate this research, psychological tests will continue to improve and find new applications. Because people have always wanted to be able to predict human behavior in many situations, the tests will continue to be used and possibly misused. Educating the public, as well as students of clinical psychology, about the nature and meaning of psychological tests may become an important ethical obligation of psychologists.

REFERENCES

Adams, K. M. (1984). Luria left in the lurch: Unfulfilled promises are not valid tests. *Journal of Clinical Neuropsychology, 6,* 455–458.

Albee, G. (1985, February). The answer is prevention. *Psychology Today,* pp. 60–64.

American Psychiatric Association. (1980). *Diagnostic and Statistical Manual of Mental Disorders (3rd ed.).* Washington, DC: Author.

Beck, S. (1945). *Rorschach's test.* New York: Grune & Stratton.

Bender, L. (1938). A visual motor gestalt test and its clinical use. *American Orthopsychiatric Association, Research Monographs,* No. 3.

Binet, A., & Simon, T. (1905). Methodes nouvelles pour de diagnostic du niveau intellectuel des anormaus. *L'Anee Psychologique, 11,* 191–244.

Boll, T. J. (1981). The Halstead-Reitan neuropsychology battery. In S. B. Filskov & T. J. Bolls (Eds.), *Handbook of clinical neuropsychology.* New York: Wiley-Interscience.

Burisch, M. (1984). Approaches to personality inventory construction: A comparison of merits. *American Psychologist, 39,* 214–227.

Campbell, D. P. (1966). Occupations ten years later of high school seniors with high scores on the SVIB life insurance salesman scale. *Journal of Applied Psychology, 50,* 369–372.

Campbell, D. P., & Hansen, J. C. (1981). *Manual for the SVIB-SCII* (3rd ed.). Palo Alto, CA: Stanford University Press.

Ciminero, A. R., Calhoun, K. S., & Adams, H. E. (Eds.). 1984. *Handbook of behavioral assessment* (2nd ed.). New York: Wiley.

Canoune, H., & Leyhe, E. (1985). Human versus computer interviewing. *Journal of Personality Assessment, 49,* 103–106.

Dahlstrom, W. G., & Welsh, G. S. (1960). *An MMPI handbook: A guide to use in clinical practice and research.* Minneapolis: University of Minnesota Press.

Dunn, L. M. (1959). *Peabody Picture Vocabulary Test.* Minneapolis: American Guidance Service.

Edwards, A. L. (1954). *Manual for EPPS.* New York: Psychological Corporation.

Edwards, A. L. (1959). *Edwards Personal Preference Schedule.* New York: Psychological Corporation.

Erdberg, P., & Exner, J. E. (1984). Rorschach assessment. In G. Goldstein & M. Hersen (Eds.), *Handbook of psychological assessment.* New York: Pergamon Press.

Exner, J. E. (1974). *The Rorschach: A comprehensive system* (Vol. 1). New York: Wiley.

Exner, J. E. (1978). *The Rorschach: A comprehensive system* (Vol. 2). New York: Wiley.

Farberow, N. L., & Schneidman, E. S. (1961). *The cry for help.* New York: McGraw-Hill.

Farina, A., & Fisher, J. D. (1982). Beliefs about mental disorders: Findings and implications. In G. Weary & H. Mirels (Eds.), *Integrations of clinical and social psychology.* New York: Oxford University Press.

Farina, A., Holland, C. H., & Ring, K. (1966). The role of stigma and set in interpersonal interaction. *Journal of Abnormal Psychology, 70,* 421–428.

Flavell, J. A. (1963). *The developmental psychology of Jean Piaget.* Princeton, NJ: Van Nostrand.

Gardner, H. (1983). *Frames of mind: The theory of multiple intelligences.* New York: Basic Books.

Golden, C. J., Hammeke, T., & Purisch, A. (1980). *The Luria-Nebraska battery manual.* Los Angeles: Western Psychological Services.

Goldstein, G. (1984). Comprehensive neuropsychological assessment batteries. In G. Goldstein & M. Hersen (Eds.), *Handbook of psychological assessment.* New York: Pergamon Press.

Goldstein, G., & Hersen, M. (Eds.). (1984). *Handbook of psychological assessment.* New York: Pergamon Press.

Gorenstein, E. E. (1984). Debating mental illness: Implications for science, medicine, and social policy. *American Psychologist, 39,* 50–56.

Gould, S. J. (1981). *The mismeasure of man.* New York: Norton.

Hansen, J. C., & Swanson, J. L. (1983). Stability of interests and the predictive and concurrent validity of the 1981 Strong-Campbell Interest Inventory. *Journal of Consulting Psychology, 30,* 194–201.

Hathaway, S., & McKinley, J. (1943). *The Minnesota Multiphasic Personality Inventory.* New York: Psychological Corporation.

Haynes, S. M., and Wilson, C. C. (1979). *Behavioral assessment.* San Francisco: Jossey-Bass.

Haynes, S. N. (1984). Behavioral assessment of adults. In G. Goldstein & M. Hersen (Eds.), *Handbook of psychological assessment.* New York: Pergamon Press.

Herman, S. (1977). New dimensions in psychodiagnostics. *American Psychologist, 32,* 784–785.

Hersen, M., Kazdin, A. E., & Bellack, A. S. (Eds.). (1983). *The clinical psychology handbook.* New York: Pergamon Press.

Jastak, J. F., & Jastak, S. P. (1965). *The Wide Range Achievement Test: Manual of instructions.* Wilmington, DE: Guidance Associates.

Kaplan, M. (1983). A woman's view of DSM-III. *American Psychologist, 38,* 786–792.

Kaufman, A. S., & Kaufman, N. L. (1983). *K-ABC: Kaufman Assessment Battery for Children.* Circles Pines, MN: Guidance Services.

Klopfer, B., & Kelley, D. (1942). *The Rorschach technique.* Yonkers, NY: World Book.

Kuder, G. F. (1966). *General manual: Occupation Interest Survey—Form DD.* Chicago: Science Research Associates.

Lambert, N. M. (1981). Psychological evidence in *Larry P.* v. *Wilson Riles:* An evaluation of the evidence by a witness for the defense. *American Psychologist, 36,* 937–952.

Lubin, B., Larsen, R., & Matarazzo, J. (1984). Patterns of psychological test usage in the United States: 1935–1982. *American Psychologist, 39,* 451–454.

Machover, K. (1949). *Personality projection in the drawing of the human figure: A method of personality investigation.* Springfield, IL: C. C. Thomas.

Mackenzie, B. (1984). Explaining race differences in IQ: The logic, the methodology, and the evidence. *American Psychologist, 39,* 1214–1233.

Matarazzo, J. D. (1986). Computerized clinical psychological test interpretations: Unvalidated plus all mean and no sigma. *American Psychologist, 41,* 14–24.

Meehl, P. E. (1954). *Clinical versus statistical prediction: A theoretical analysis and review of the evidence.* Minneapolis: University of Minnesota Press.

Meehl, P. E. (1956). Wanted—A good cookbook. *American Psychologist, 11,* 263–272.

Meehl, P. E. (1965). Seer over sign: The first good example. *Journal of Experimental Research in Personality, 1,* 27–32.

Millon, T. (1981). *Disorders of personality: DSM III, Axis II.* New York: Wiley.

Millon, T. (1983). *Millon Clinical Multiaxial Inventory Manual.* Minneapolis, MN: National Computer systems.

Millon, T. (1985). The MCMI provides a good assessment of DSM-III disorders: The MCMI-II will prove even better. *Journal of Personality Assessment, 49,* 379–391.

Millon, T., Green, C. J., & Meagher, R. B. (1982). *Millon Adolescent Personality Inventory.* Minneapolis, MN: National Computer Systems.

Millon, T., Green, C. J., & Meagher, R. B. (1982). *Millon Behavioral Health Inventory Manual.* Minneapolis, MN: National Computer Systems.

Moore, N. C., Summer, K. R., & Bloor, R. N. (1984). Do patients like psychometric testing by computer? *Journal of Clinical Psychology, 40,* 875–877.

Murray, H. A. (1938). *Explorations in personality.* New York: Oxford University Press.

Nelson, R. O., & Hayes, S. C. (1979). Some current dimensions of behavioral assessment. *Behavioral Assessment, 1,* 1–16.

Nobins, L. N., & Helzer, J. E. (1986). Diagnosis and clinical assessment: The current state of psychiatric diagnosis. In M. R. Rosenzweig & L. W. Porter (Eds.), *Annual review of psychology.* Palo Alto, CA: Annual Reviews.

O'Dell, J., & Dickson, J. (1984). ELIZA as a "therapeutic" tool. *Journal of Clinical Psychology, 40,* 942–945.

Osterrieth, P. A. (1944). Le test de copie d'une figure complex. *Archives de psychologie, 30,* 206–356.

Reitan, R. M. (1966). A research program on the psychological effects of brain lesions in human beings. In N. R. Ellis (Ed.), *International review of research in mental retardation.* New York: Academic Press.

Reitan, R. M., & Davison, L. A. (1974). *Clinical neuropsychology: Current status and applications.* Washington, DC: Winston.

Rohde, A. R. (1957). *The sentence completion method.* New York: Ronald Press.

Rorschach, H. (1921). *Psychodiagnostik.* Bern: Bircher. (English translation 1942)

Rosenhan, D. (1973). On being sane in insane places. *Science, 179,* 250–258; *180,* 365–369.

Rotter, J. B., & Rafferty, J. E. (1950). *The Rotter Incomplete Sentences Blank.* New York: Psychological Corporation.

Smith, D., & Kraft, W. A. (1983). DSM-III: Do psychologists really want an alternative? *American Psychologist, 38,* 777–785.

Snyderman, M., & Herrnstein, R. J. (1983). Intelligence tests and the Immigration Act of 1924. *American Psychologist, 38,* 986–995.

Spearman, C. (1904). "General intelligence," objectively determined and measured. *American Journal of Psychology, 15,* 201–293.

Spokane, A. R. (1979). Occupational preferences and the validity of the Strong-Campbell Interest Inventory for college women and men. *Journal of Counseling Psychology, 26,* 312–318.

Szasz, T. (1961). *The myth of mental illness: Foundations of a theory of personal conduct.* New York: Harper & Row.

Terman, L. M. (1916). *The measurement of intelligence.* Boston: Houghton Mifflin.

Terman, L. M., & Merrill, M. A. (1973). *Stanford-Binet Intelligence Scale, 1972 Norms Edition.* Boston: Houghton Mifflin.

Turner, J., Herron, L., & Weiner, P. (1986). Utility of the MMPI Pain Assessment Index in predicting outcome after lumbar surgery. *Journal of Clinical Psychology, 42,* 764–769.

Wechsler, D. (1967). *Manual for the WPPSI.* New York: Psychological Corporation.

Wechsler, D. (1974). *Manual for the WISC-R.* New York: Psychological Corporation.

Wechsler, D. (1981). *Manual for the WAIS-R.* New York: Psychological Corporation.

Weizenbaum, J. (1966). ELIZA—A computer program for the study of natural language communication between man and machine. *Communication Associates Computing Machinery, 9,* 36–45.

Widiger, T. A., Williams, J. B., Spitzer, R. L., & Frances, A. (1985). The MCMI as a measure of DSM-III. *Journal of Personality Assessment, 49,* 366–378.

Zarr, M. (1984). Computer-mediated psychotherapy: Toward patient-selection guidelines. *American Journal of Psychotherapy, 38,* 47–62.

Zimmerman, I. L., & Woo-Sam, J. M. (1984). Intellectual assessment of children. In G. Goldstein & M. Hersen (Eds.), *Handbook of psychological assessment.* New York: Pergamon Press.

Zubin, J. (1967). Classification of the behavior disorders. *Annual Review of Psychology, 18,* 373–406.

Zytowski, D. G. (1976). Predictive validity of the Kuder Occupational Interest Survey: A 12- to 19-year follow-up. *Journal of Counseling Psychology, 3,* 221–233.

Chapter 3

Sigmund Freud and Psychoanalysis

I treated a young lady who suffered for six years from an intolerable and protracted nervous cough. . . . Every other remedy had long since shown itself powerless, and I, therefore, attempted to remove the symptom by psychic analysis. All that she could remember was that the nervous cough began at the age of fourteen while she boarded with her aunt. She remembered absolutely no psychic excitement during that time, and *did not believe there was a motive for her suffering* [italics added]. Under the pressure of my hand, she at first recalled a large dog. She then recognized the memory picture; it was her aunt's dog which was attached to her, and used to accompany her everywhere, and without any further aid it occurred to her that this dog died and that the children buried it solemnly; and on the return from this funeral her cough appeared. I asked her why she began to cough, and the following thought occurred to her: "Now I am all alone in this world; no one loves me here; this animal was my only friend, and now I have lost it. . . ." That was, therefore, the pathogenic idea: People do not love her, everybody else is preferred; she really does not deserve to be loved, etc. (Freud, 1895/1937, pp. 204–205)

. . . one analysand with marked obsessive-compulsive problems, based as is usually the case on an unconsciously maintained anal orientation to himself and his world, would at times grunt, groan, and writhe on the analytic couch in his efforts to force

> out some of his thoughts and feelings; finally he would appeal to the analyst explicitely for help in "getting it out." Upon analysis, this conduct proved to be a reenactment of his ambivalence during and after toilet training with respect to holding on to or letting go of his stools; it was also a reenactment of his conflictual retentive-expulsive actions in other areas of his life. In his childhood he often had ended up requiring help from his mother in completing his evacuations. It also emerged that he derived some secret masturbatory pleasure from the considerable and prolonged anal stimulation occasioned by his intermediate "paralysis." (Schafer, 1978, pp. 36–37)

> The idea that a neurotic is suffering from a sort of ignorance, and that if one removes this ignorance by telling him facts (about the causal connection of his illness with his life, about his experiences in childhood, and so on) he must recover, is an idea that has long been superceded, and one derived from superficial appearances. . . . if knowledge about his unconscious were as important for the patient as the inexperienced in psychoanalysis imagine, it would be sufficient to cure him for him to go to lectures or read books. . . . (Freud, 1910/1963, p. 93)

The most influential approach to psychotherapy has been that of psychoanalysis. Developed originally by Sigmund Freud, psychoanalysis has provided many insights into both the process of psychotherapy and the nature of psychopathology. Many of Freud's insights have been incorporated into other approaches to psychotherapy that may diverge widely from psychoanalysis in other respects.

Psychoanalysis has spawned a host of creative offshoots. Taken all together these are called the "psychodynamic" view. The dynamic view of the person holds that the personality is an organized system of forces and counterforces. Different dynamic theorists may disagree on what forces in the personality are important, but all usually include the need to protect against pain as one of the major forces that drives the human. One of the major ways this is done is to deny painful aspects of the self or personality and keep them from awareness. Some of the dynamic theorists who have developed out of psychoanalysis are Jung, Adler, Rank, Reich, Sullivan, Horney, Fromm, Erickson, and Hartmann. More recent developments are object relations theory and Kohut's self psychology. In this chapter we will look at Freud's view of psychopathology and psychotherapy ("classical" psychoanalysis) and review Jung and Adler. Unfortunately, because of space limitations these latter theorists will be given only brief consideration. In the next chapter we will consider in some detail the contributions of object relations theory and Kohut and evaluate the psychodynamic approach in general.

THEORY OF PSYCHOANALYSIS AND PERSONALITY

Hidden Meaning and the Concept of Repression

The core idea in Freudian psychoanalysis can be seen in the first two quotations at the start of the chapter. In both cases the client's overt symptomatology (the cough in the first case and the difficulty in "getting it out" in the second) is actually not the problem. Rather, the symptoms are expressions of meanings hidden deep in the personality structure. The hidden meaning of the cough has to do with feelings of loss, of being alone, and of being unlovable. The second client's difficulty in getting his feelings and thoughts out is an expression of underlying conflicts over the act of defecation. The idea that overt behavior contains hidden meanings (Cameron & Rychlak, 1985) means that there is a kind of "secret code" to overt behavior that must be deciphered if we are to help the client modify his or her actions. It is not sufficient to treat the symptoms themselves. Treating the overt behavior will be useless unless the hidden meanings are dealt with. In order to deal with them the client must become aware of them, and that is the ultimate goal of Freud's psychoanalysis. However, as the last quote at the start of the chapter indicates, intellectual knowledge about hidden meanings is not sufficient for therapeutic change to occur. Therapy must include the reexperiencing of the feelings and affects that accompany the hidden meanings. For instance, it would not be enough for the woman to know intellectually that conflicts about being lonely and being unlovable were underlying her cough. She would have to experience the feeling of being alone and unlovable for her awareness of these hidden meanings to be therapeutic. We will discuss why this is so later. We point out now that object relations theory and Kohut's self psychology place an even greater emphasis on emotional reexperiencing in therapy than Freud did.

Most of Freud's original work was done with patients who used to be diagnosed as suffering from the neurotic disorder of conversion hysteria. In the current edition of the Diagnostic and Statistical Manual of the American Psychiatric Association (DSM-III), the terms neurotic and conversion hysteria no longer appear. Conversion hysteria is now called conversion disorder. Because for Freud (and, indeed, many modern psychoanalysts) the concept of the neurotic disorders was so important, we will briefly describe it. Basically *neurotic disorders* are disorders in which the individual has one or two symptoms that interfere with his functioning, but otherwise he is in touch with reality. This differs from psychosis, in which the individual is "out of touch" with reality, and personality disorders, in which the individual has pervasive characterological difficulties in the personality. Neurotic disorders include the following categories listed in DSM-III: general anxiety disorder, phobias, obsessive-compulsive disorder, conversion disorder, and dissociative disorders.

In *conversion disorders* clients suffer from one or more physical symptoms that mimic physical illnesses. For instance, a client may lose sight or hearing or speech, with no detectable physical cause for the loss. In fact, tests will often reveal that the client's eyes respond to light, ears to sound, and so on. Breuer and Freud (Freud, 1895/1937) originally treated conversion disorders with hypnosis. Under hypnosis the client was asked to recall when the particular symptom began. It was found that the symptom was associated with an emotionally charged, forgotten memory. When this memory was recovered, the symptom would vanish. For instance, Anna O., Breuer's most famous client, developed the symptom of being unable to drink out of a glass and swallow water. The incident she had forgotten was one in which she had unexpectedly discovered her maid allowing a dog to drink out of a glass. Anna O. recalled feeling repulsed and disgusted. With the recovery of the memory, and her disgust, the symptom vanished, and she was able to drink easily from a glass.

One of us had a similar experience with a client, although in this case it was not a physical symptom as such but anxiety that appeared. Dana came to therapy one day feeling quite anxious, but she could not figure out why. We reviewed the events of the day, but all we managed to discover was that her anxiety had appeared sometime after she had gone to an office party. However no concrete incident that might have caused her anxiety could be located. Dana was then put into a light hypnotic trance and instructed to remember back to the party. As she reviewed the events of the party she recalled that she had been talking with a group of women. One of the women made an offhand comment that sounded vaguely like a critical remark directed at Dana. However, because the statement was not clear and it was only an offhand remark, it was passed over by both Dana and the others as the conversation flowed on. Yet it was at this point that Dana's anxiety had begun. When she recalled this incident (and incidentally expressed some anger toward this woman, with whom she had previously had some conflict), the anxiety vanished.

It was such experiences with clients that led to Freud's view of psychopathology and then to his theory of personality. The client suffers from a symptom that disrupts the client's life. The symptom seems irrational and inexplicable; it does not appear to make sense. For instance, Dana's anxiety did not make sense to her, nor did Anna O.'s difficulty in swallowing liquids. Furthermore, the client is unable to control the symptom consciously. However, there is a reason for the symptom at another, nonconscious level. Thus, the overt symptom is a disguised manifestation of a hidden meaning. In particular, the underlying meaning involves an emotional conflict of some sort. Though the emotional conflict is not in consciousness, it nevertheless manifests itself in overt behavior.

We may now ask why is this memory forgotten? Why was Anna O. unable to recall the dog's drinking out of the glass? Freud's answer was that such things are forgotten because they are painful and thus are blocked out of consciousness. Freud arrived at this conclusion by finding that some clients seemed to resist remembering the feelings that had been forgotten. From this Freud ultimately developed the concept of *repression,* that is, some emotionally conflictual material is excluded from consciousness because of its painful nature.

But why did the excluded material continue to influence behavior? Why was it not simply hidden and forgotten? After all, most of us have drawers, boxes, or closetsful of things we have stuffed away and forgotten, without their coming back to haunt us. Freud's answer was that it remains active because it is emotionally charged. It "clamors" for expression. Breuer and Freud used the term *strangulated affect* to capture this idea. The method of cure was to make these emotions available to consciousness, thereby allowing them expression and discharge. This idea is usually called *emotional catharsis.* Freud later abandoned the idea that catharsis is what makes therapy work, but he retained the idea that unconscious material remains active because it has a kind of "charge" (or "energy") attached to it.

We now have the basics of Freud's view of psychopathology and personality. Certain conflictual material is excluded from consciousness because it is too painful. However, because it is emotionally charged, it remains active in the personality, and overt behavioral symptoms result from it. Full awareness (including allowing oneself to experience the emotions consciously) results in alleviation of the symptoms. These are Freud's theoretical hypotheses to explain the observations that recovery of forgotten, emotionally tinged memories seemed to be related to the disappearance of hysterical symptoms. We mention this because other theorists have other ways of explaining these observations. For instance, while the idea that unconscious material is forgotten because it is painful is still retained by modern psychoanalytic theorists, not all retain the idea that repressed material remains active because it is charged with some kind of energy.

Metapsychology

With this in mind we will now look at how Freud extended the above ideas to a whole theory of personality and psychopathology. We will be discussing Freud's *metapsychology,* which is what is most disputed by many modern psychoanalytic theorists and practitioners. The metapsychology consists of Freud's belief that the personality is fundamentally an energy system whose business is the regulation and discharge of both sexual and aggressive energy and his belief that the mind consists of three structures: the id, the ego, and the superego.

As Freud extended his work, he began to find that the removal of symptoms in his hysterical clients did not effect a total cure. Other symptoms would pop up. This led Freud to believe that the ultimate causes of the person's problems lay deeply buried in the personality. In the second quote at the start of the chapter the man's problems in "getting it out" are not based on a single, emotionally charged memory, but on the repression of a whole set of experiences with toilet training when he was a child. As Freud continued to delve into the buried memories of his clients, he came to believe that psychological problems were not usually the result of a few highly charged emotional memories (traumatic memories), but rather the result of *patterns* of repression of meanings and associated experiences in early childhood.

In addition Freud believed that many of the buried memories revolved around sexual themes. It is now unclear to what extent Freud actually *found* these themes in his client's repressed memories and to what extent he went *looking* for them (see Masson, 1985). It is known that theorists both prior to and at the time of Freud (including Freud's friend Wilhelm Fleiss) were speculating that many psychological problems had their origins in sexual repression (Ellenberger, 1970). Freud was working during the Victorian era, a time of sexual repression, and it would not be surprising if sexual conflicts figured prominently among the emotional difficulties people had. Further, it was also about this time that Freud began his own self-analysis and began to uncover themes of repressed sexuality in himself. As a result Freud began to believe that repressed sexuality lay at the core of psychopathological behavior. His clients' reports of early childhood sexual experiences with adults led to the formulation of his *seduction theory.* This theory held that it was the repression of actual traumatic memories of childhood seductions that caused neurotic behavior. However, Freud began to suspect that many of these seductions had in fact not taken place. This led to the crucial idea that what had been repressed were not memories of actual experiences, but memories of *primitive sexual wishes and fantasies* that were too painful for the individual to acknowledge consciously.

Freud later developed the idea of the regulation of aggressive energy in the form of what he called the death instinct. He believed we each have competing "life" (or sexual) instincts and "death" instincts. The death instinct is supposedly an impulse to die or to return to inert matter. It is turned outward as aggression, as a defense to keep us from killing ourselves. Many analytic theorists do not accept the concept of the death instinct, though they may believe in an aggressive instinct. For our purposes we will mainly talk about the development and regulation of sex and aggression, not the death instinct.

If, during development, various infantile sexual or aggressive wishes and fantasies are unacceptable to consciousness, they will be repressed (pushed out of consciousness). Repression leads to *fixation,* that is, if some wish is repressed, the developmental "stream" is arrested at that point. The infantile wish, with its accompanying energy, remains alive and active. The "trick" for the personality is to find an outlet for the repressed wish and simultaneously to keep it unconscious and hidden. The way to do this is to let the wish out in a disguised form. Much of personality—overt behaviors, values, beliefs, goals, job and mate choices, recreational choices—consists of disguised outlets for primitive, childhood repressed wishes and conflicts. It is not only people with psychological problems who have repressed wishes and fantasies, but all of us. For Freud, personality was the system of controls and restraints we develop in the first five or six years of life to regulate and channel our repressed primitive wishes, fantasies, and conflicts. Our early childhood experiences are the primary determinant of our current personality functioning. To quote a recent psychodynamic viewpoint,

> [Psychoanalysis] holds that in truly important moments of one's life one is unwittingly held captive by the past. Whom we marry and how the marriage fares; the work we choose and how well we do it; whether we have children and when and how we raise them and feel about them; when we become ill and how we survive or fail to—all these and other vital events of the life course can be understood in depth only after we have a sufficient understanding of the personal past. (Adelson & Doehrman, 1980, p. 100)

Defense Mechanisms

Although all of us have repressed wishes, most of us, while we may have our troubles, do not develop persistent neurotic symptoms. Nor do we develop psychotic delusions and hallucinations. Nor do we become alcoholics or consistently act in impulsive or self-destructive ways. Whether or not we end up relatively "symptom free" depends on how our personalities regulate our repressed wishes and fantasies. For Freudians, that ultimately depends on the crucial, formative experiences with one's family in early childhood.

Perhaps the most socially adaptive way of handling repressed wishes and conflicts is *sublimation.* In sublimation the repressed desire is channeled into some socially acceptable outlet. For instance, aggressive feelings may be channeled into being a highly competitive athlete. Sexual wishes associated with defecation and the anal stage of development (discussed below) may be channeled into creative activity, such as painting and sculpting. Or, early childhood wishes and conflicts may get channeled into founding the most influential of all theories of personality and psychopathology (see Box 3.1).

But sometimes we are unable to sublimate. Then we must rely on *defense mechanisms* that distort reality to some slight degree. The concept of defense is a pervasive one in psychoanalytic theory. Psychoanalysis holds that the most fundamental factor

BOX 3.1
Freud's Defenses

> Freud's wish to restore and preserve an early idealized image of his mother ran through his life like a red thread, influencing his reconstruction of his early childhood history, his choice of a field of study, his important adult relationships, and his theoretical ideas. The defensive operations which Freud employed to protect the idealized version of his mother from invasion by a deep unconscious ambivalence conflict fatefully left their mark on his theory of psychosexual development and its central metapsychological reifications, in which the sources of evil were internalized, hostility was displaced onto the father, and the split-off bad maternal image was relegated largely to the psychology of the girl (Stolorow & Atwood, 1979)

Stolorow and Atwood are not "classical" psychoanalysts, who see everything in terms of sex and aggression. Nevertheless, they do use Freudian concepts of how early childhood conflicts may determine adaptive adult behavior to analyze Freud's life and work.

in psychic development is avoidance of painful or threatening information. Repression is the fundamental way we have of avoiding painful information. In order to maintain repression, and to try to protect the ego from anxiety, we utilize the defense mechanisms.

Denial is the simplest of these. Denial is the refusal to recognize the real nature of one's behavior. A person may act quite seductively, for instance, but deny there is any sexual intent to his behavior. Another person may exhibit symptoms of anger, such as a flushed face, angry expression, and angry tone of voice, yet deny that she is angry. Denial is the mechanism most commonly used by alcoholics. Long past the time when friends, neighbors, employers, and doctors have told an alcoholic that he has a drinking problem, the alcoholic will deny that he has a problem. He may do this even after drunk driving arrests, numerous blackouts, or signs of cirrhosis of the liver. Denial is a relatively primitive defense mechanism and can be seen in children. For instance, a child may deny being tired when all the behavioral signs point to fatigue. Denial conceals painful material from consciousness by simply denying the true meaning of one's behavior, even while one engages in it.

Rationalization is giving a plausible and acceptable reason for one's behavior and feelings in order to hide one's real motives. A rationalization we frequently heard in college was from male students who would claim that they bought *Playboy* magazine "for the articles" (but, of course, they never bought any other magazine with similar articles and stories). Alcoholics often combine rationalization with denial. For each lapse into excessive drinking the alcoholic will have an excuse. It was because she was depressed or she had to join the office party and so on.

With *projection* the individual projects onto others the wishes, aims, and motives he cannot accept in himself. If I have a lot of repressed hostility, I may see other people as dangerous and hostile. I may adopt a defensive, suspicious view of other people and be constantly on the lookout to protect myself from their malicious intentions and purposes. If I have repressed my sexual impulses, I may angrily criticize what I see as everyone else's preoccupation with sex. Projection allows some gratification of the repressed impulses by allowing them into consciousness, but protects the individual by ascribing the impulses to other people.

Most of us are familiar with *displacement.* In displacement we deflect our feelings onto another target. Often we do this consciously. We get angry at our boss and come home and yell at our kids. With true displacement, however, this is done unconsciously. We actually believe we are angry at our kids and deny our anger is toward our boss.

In *reaction formation* the individual acts in a way that is diametrically opposite to what she unconsciously wants. Thus, if a person has a good deal of unconscious hostility, she may act like an uncompromising pacifist on the surface or she may strongly condemn contact sports or violence on television. Conversely, a person with strong repressed dependency needs may intensely value toughness, physical violence, and contact sports. It should be pointed out that neither being a lover of violent sports nor being a pacifist is *necessarily* a reaction formation against unconscious impulses. Perhaps a better index of reaction formation would be the rigidity with which beliefs are held, an unwillingness to tolerate or even consider different points of view. For psychoanalysis, rigidity of belief systems is usually a sign of defensiveness. A conflict area can often be identified by the degree of emotion invested in surface issues associated with it. The person cannot be flexible because she is protecting herself in that area. A fully functioning person is able to consider other points of view, even though she may come to identify strongly with one particular perspective.

With *intellectualization* the individual "understands" and acknowledges that he "must have" certain repressed impulses. Knowledge of the impulses is thereby allowed into consciousness, but not the impulses themselves. For instance, a client may intellectually accept that she had incestuous feelings toward her father, while still repressing the actual feelings and impulses themselves.

With *compensation* the individual deals with frustration and inadequacy in one area by investing in another area. Thus an individual who has underlying feelings of physical inadequacy as a male (he is not athletic or handsome) may compensate by becoming highly competent at intellectual pursuits. Conversely, an athlete who feels intellectually inferior may overinvest in his athletic skills.

According to psychoanalytic theory, defense mechanisms involve mild distortions of reality, but they are functional and necessary. However, if the defenses become too rigid or are overused, they may unduly constrict the individual's functioning. And, what happens when an individual's defenses fail, when they fail either to provide a sufficient outlet for unconscious impulses or when the unconscious impulses begin to break into consciousness? It is at this point that neurotic symptoms appear.

Psychopathology and Anxiety

For Freud neurotic anxiety appears when one's defenses begin to break down. It is a signal that forbidden unconscious impulses are breaking into consciousness. Generalized anxiety disorder and panic disorder, in which free-floating anxiety is experienced, are examples. The person is overwhelmed by anxiety and cannot pin down any particular cause because the cause is unconscious: The anxiety is a signal of danger from within.

Other neurotic disorders also develop when unconscious impulses get intensified and threaten to break into consciousness. Symptoms develop that, like the defense mechanisms, allow some expression of the unconscious impulses, but disguise their nature. But because more extreme measures are now needed, the symptoms that develop are likely to be socially dysfunctional. For example, in order to control unconscious conflicts over sexuality, an individual may develop a phobia about being outside in crowds (where he is afraid he might unconsciously "lose control"). If unconscious hostile and rebellious impulses are threatening to break through, a person might carry "rule following" to the extreme or develop elaborate obsessive-compulsive rituals to control the impulses. She may wash her hands 200 times a day in order to quell anxiety by washing away those "dirty" unconscious hostile, rule-breaking impulses.

Why does this happen? Usually it happens because some event happens to intensify one's unconscious conflicts. If I have strong unconscious hostility, I may shy away from situations in which I might be tempted to lose control. I may avoid, as an example, being in situations where I have the power to take out my hostility on others. Being in such a situation may provide so much unconscious temptation that I need to develop some neurotic symptomatology to keep my defenses in order. For instance, suppose I am a lawyer who is made a judge with the power to impose sentences. The possibility that my unconscious hostility may now come out in harsh, punitive judgments may be so threatening that I break down.

Suppose I am harboring unconscious sexual desires to steal mommy away from daddy (and in the process violate the marital norm of faithfulness) and suddenly I am confronted with temptation in the form of a neighbor's wife who is making advances toward me. Suddenly I develop a conversion reaction in the form of paralysis of my legs. Or I am a famous prince of Denmark (Hamlet) and I am supposed to avenge my father's murder. My uncle has murdered him and married my mother. Yet I am overcome with a chronic paralysis of will and cannot act. Why? Possibly because my uncle did what I unconsciously had wanted to do myself (see Jones, 1954).

What happens if neurotic symptoms don't work as defenses? What happens if even they fail in keeping unconscious material out of consciousness? The person may then experience a psychotic episode, which can essentially be seen as a disintegration of the ego (the ego is discussed in the next section). Unconscious material now floods into consciousness. As an example, one of us was working with a paranoid schizophrenic who said that people were drugging him at work (he worked as a janitor in an airline firm) and accusing him of wanting to sleep with his mother. While Freudian psychoanalysis attempts to help the average neurotic to gain insight into his defenses, with psychotics the Freudian approach is the opposite. It tries to shore up defenses and restore the ego.

Developmental Stages and Id, Ego, and Superego

We have now seen how repression and other defense mechanisms function to keep material unconscious and how psychopathology develops when they do not work. Now we wish to look at personality development both in terms of Freud's concept of the mind and various stages of development.

Freud held that there are three "structures" or components to the mind, the ego, the id, and the superego. At birth the person is all *id.* The id is the biological storehouse of primitive impulses. It is all "want." Since it is pure desire, it has no concept of reality—others don't exist, reality doesn't exist, and time doesn't exist. The only thing that does exist is the desire for pure gratification. At birth the infant has no concept of itself as a separate human being, of others as human beings, of itself and the world as separate, of time, or of the difference between reality and fantasy.

The first stage of personality development, which lasts from birth to about 1½ or 2 years, is the *oral* stage. It is called oral because during this stage the mouth is the primary erogenous zone, that is, sexual gratification is gained primarily through oral stimulation. This is why the infant not only nurses, but is constantly putting things into its mouth.

The most crucial thing that happens at the oral stage is the beginning of the development of the *ego.* At birth the infant is all id, but soon learns that its needs will not automatically be met whenever it wants. As a result the infant begins to develop a concept of reality. It must learn to develop a concept of itself as separate from the world. It must develop concepts of external "objects" that will help it gain gratification. Objects are any things that populate the external world. Among the objects that one must form concepts of to view reality accurately are chairs, tables, floors, cribs, bottles, spoons, and so on. Among the most important object concepts the child needs to form are concepts of other people. In forming concepts of objects and of the external world, the child needs to realize that fantasies and reality are separate. The ego can be thought of as the "executive" part of the personality. It is the part that learns to perceive reality accurately in order to help the id get its demands met as effectively as possible. If at this stage (through severe neglect, extreme overindulgence, inconsistent experience) a strong ego does not begin to develop, the person will be predisposed to having psychotic experiences under stress in later life. Other oral fixations (the stopping of the developmental process in the oral stage) may lead to dependency, alcoholism, overeating, or a constant need to be loved and "nourished" by others.

The ego continues to develop during the *anal* stage, which lasts from about age 1½ to 3. In this stage of personality development the anus becomes the primary erogenous zone, and the child gains sexual gratification through the act of defecation. The child will be fascinated by its feces at this age. Parents' attempts at toilet training will be interpreted as infringements on the child's freedom to indulge in instinctual gratification. As such the anal stage is when the issue of socialization becomes prominent. The developing ego must learn to control and regulate impulses. The child is confronted with the need to regulate its bodily activities in order to follow societal rules and will experience anger at the parents for imposing restrictions on gratification of its bodily pleasures.

If the anger is repressed, the child may become on the surface a rigid, orderly, rule-following person, concerned with cleanliness. Underneath is a great deal of "dirty" anger. This is the *anal-retentive* pattern. For the anal-retentive, rules and rituals become defense mechanisms for binding and controlling unconscious hostility. In addition the individual may engage in *undoing* rituals to overcome unconscious guilt over the buried anger and rebellion. Undoing rituals are like atonements. For instance, undoing can be used to overcome unconscious guilt over sexuality as well. One may need to shower or wash one's hands after making love. The ritualistic nature of defenses developed at this developmental stage lay the basis for obsessive-compulsive neurosis, in which individuals may have to shower for hours a day or engage in other extreme undoing rituals.

If the anger is not repressed, the person may repetitively act out his anger, constantly trying to prove his independence. In effect he is "defecating all over everyone," and this is the *anal-expulsive* pattern.

The *phallic* stage is the most important one according to Freud. It is the stage during which the third component of mental functioning—the *superego*—develops. It occurs between the ages of 4 and 6. Though most of Freud's clients were women, the phallic stage is named after the male and is one example of why Freud has often been accused of being a sexist. During the phallic stage sexuality becomes localized in the genitals. Problems with sexuality usually have some component deriving from the phallic stage. Of particular importance during this stage is the *Oedipus complex.* The male child presumably begins to develop sexual feelings toward his mother and wants some kind of sexual contact with her. As a result of this he views his father as a rival and may harbor primitive fantasies of wanting to murder his father and take his place. However, the male child becomes afraid that if the father finds out about these feelings and wishes, the father will castrate him. This *castration anxiety* leads the child to repress both his rivalrous feelings toward his father and his lustful feelings toward his mother.

The way the male child resolves the oedipal crisis is to *identify* with his father (and be able to possess his mother vicariously as a result). This identification leads both to an adoption of the male sex role and to the development of the superego. The superego is formed out of the internalized (or "introjected") values of the parent. It consists of both the parent's moral values (essentially the "conscience") and a perfectionistic standard of what a good person should be like (the "ego-ideal"). If the values of the superego are harsh or unrealistic, the individual will be constantly plagued with feelings of guilt and failure. The individual may have a need to punish himself and may set up situations where others are rejecting or punitive. The individual may unconsciously cause painful accidents to happen and in the extreme may have unconscious suicidal wishes that get expressed in self-destructive acts (for instance, through reckless driving).

The "female Oedipus complex" is similar in its general outlines to that of the male. However, there are some important differences. According to Freud, little girls note that they are missing something that little boys have. This is called *penis envy.* The girl's desire for her father is not only sexual, but is based on the desire to obtain a penis as well. Because girls do not fear being castrated, there is less fear to lead to repression. As a result girls develop less strong superegos than boys (Freud, 1925/1961).

For Freud the phallic stage was the major source of neurotic psychopathology. According to Kaplan (1984), it is during the phallic stage that the child finds that desire is not merely restricted as in the anal stage (when defecation was not completely forbidden, but merely regulated), but completely forbidden. Kaplan sees this as the "humiliation" of oedipal defeat. It makes the child feel small and puny compared to the parents. The oedipal situation becomes a fundamental issue in the establishment of adult personality in adolescence.

Between age 6 and adolescence is the *latency* period, during which the child is busy regulating the repressed impulses from the oedipal period. That period was so tumultuous that the child spends the next few years mastering and taming them.

Psychoanalytically, this is why children at this age are often so fascinated with rules and the establishment of order in their lives. At adolescence, the *genital* period, the upsurge of sexuality reawakens oedipal conflicts. The adolescent's task is to not allow incestuous oedipal feelings to surface into consciousness. Rebelliousness against the parents and intense love affairs with peers are ways of distancing and redirecting the incestuous wishes so that they do not become conscious. If handled effectively, these desires will be tamed and sublimated, and adult personality established.

With the phallic stage the three major mental structures are all established. The mind can almost be thought of as a kind of stage with three actors on it. The three voices are in constant contention, and psychopathology can be seen as the conflict among them. The ego bears the brunt of coordinating the primitive wishes of the id, the limitations imposed by reality, and the moral restrictions of the superego. Repression complicates matters. Primitive wishes and impulses are repressed and kept out of conscious awareness, partly to satisfy the moral values of the superego. Repression weakens the ability of the ego to deal realistically with the world. A particularly harsh superego may lead to extreme and debilitating repression. On the other hand, a particularly weak superego may lead to psychopathic behavior.

Not only are primitive wishes and fantasies repressed, but parts of the ego itself are unconscious. This is necessary for repression to occur. After all, repression is a kind of unconsciously "deliberate" avoidance of painful material. If this avoidance were done consciously, it would not work, so the act of avoiding itself must be performed unconsciously. As one of our children said about something she was trying to forget, "I have to forget that I've forgotten, too. Otherwise I'll remember it." Therefore, repression means that forces unknown to the ego may be controlling behavior. As a result, the person will engage in behavior for reasons unknown to the conscious ego. Such behavior will be consciously experienced as "irrational" or "ego-alien." It is such an experience that often propels a person to seek therapy.

To sum up, the Freudian view of both personality and psychopathology is that both ultimately rest on unconscious self-deception. Behavior is under the control of hidden meanings that are hidden because they are too painful to consciousness to be acknowledged and known. For Freud, these hidden meanings revolve around primitive sexual and aggressive impulses. As part of this self-deception we must of necessity distort external reality also, via mechanisms such as projection and displacement. Thus most of us live in a world where objective reality is obscured by shadows from our past. These shadows also distort our perception of our own inner reality of feelings, thoughts, and motives. We live in a reality of our own construction, contrived to protect us from painful self-knowledge. Therefore, none of us lives fully in touch with external or internal reality. For most of us the distortions are compatible enough with social reality that we are generally functional. For some of us the distortions are discrepant enough, and the resulting behavior deviant enough, that our behavior is dysfunctional and in need of treatment.

PSYCHOTHERAPY

The goal of classical Freudian psychoanalysis is to "lift repression" (Freud, 1937/1963). Freud said, "Where id was shall ego be" (1932/1964). However, it is rarely the case that all repression is lifted. Often some repression is lifted and some is reworked so that it is not so incapacitating (Freud, 1937/1963). Following from this, the goal of psychoanalysis is insight into and conscious awareness of the hidden meanings influencing behavior. This involves overcoming resistance, which is the main work of therapy.

How does awareness and the lifting of repression cure? Before therapy the ego is not able to control behavior effectively because it is being guided by forces of which the ego is unaware. When the ego becomes aware of these forces, they can be controlled consciously and channeled into suitable outlets. It is important to note that insight does not eliminate the previously unconscious primitive impulses. A man's awareness that he has primitive wishes to kill his father and sleep with his mother does not relieve him of these impulses, but it does allow him to control them, rather than being controlled by them. Luborsky (1984) said that what changes in psychoanalysis is the function that controls and regulates a wish or need, but "the wish, need or intention . . . change[s] relatively little" (p. 20). (In the next chapter we will look at some recent psychoanalytic theorists' views of what happens when one gains insight.)

While the impulses themselves may change relatively little, learning that these impulses are there helps one *discriminate* between reality and one's primitive wishes, fantasies, and feelings. I may come to therapy because I feel people in authority are always putting me down. In therapy I may find that I am displacing onto authority figures unconscious perceptions of my father. I may discover that I could never face up to perceiving my father as critical because I would then have to face up to all the buried anger I have toward him. I now can separate what people in authority are really saying and thinking from what I am displacing onto them. Thus an important consequence of lifting repression is the ability to see reality more clearly.

The ultimate goal of therapy for Freud is to facilitate the individual's ability to love and work (Ekstein, 1974). Freud did not believe that the goal of therapy is to make a person "happy." In fact, he saw therapy as "replacing neurotic misery with common unhappiness" (1918/1955). One of the major achievements of therapy is an increase in the person's capacity to tolerate ambivalence and conflict or to live with "uneasiness" (Bettelheim, 1982). In relegating happiness to a secondary place among goals for healthy functioning, Freud's thought is compatible with many other theorists, including Rogers, Perls, and Beck.

Free Association

So how does classical psychoanalysis go about facilitating insight? Originally Freud used hypnosis. However, he abandoned hypnosis early in his work. For a while he used a technique where he placed his hand on the client's head to "suggest" that they remember (see the second quote at the start of the chapter). Eventually he abandoned this, too, in favor of the method of free association.

You might be thinking that hypnosis seems like the answer. Hypnotize patients, ask them to recover memories from early childhood, and therapy should be easy and quick. This logic is similar to that of those who once advocated the use of LSD in therapy or nonstop 36-hour marathon encounters. Wouldn't it be nice if we could take a drug or encounter for 36 hours, overcome all our defenses, and dig up all the hidden truths about ourselves? Why spend years in psychoanalysis? But Freud would not have approved of the use of drugs or marathon group therapy any more than he did of hypnosis. And the reason is crucial.

The reason is that finding the buried memories is but a part of the therapeutic process. It would be like someone's giving you a drug that would enable you to answer a complicated mathematics problem. You may know that answer, but will you have to take a drug every time you want to know some other answer? Or, is the process of finding the answer as important as the answer itself? For Freud it is. Using the easy magic of hypnosis or drugs or marathon encounters to leapfrog defenses and resistances to get to "the truth" is bad therapy. You might be able to leapfrog these obstacles, but Freud wants you to clear the roads of them, so to speak. Thus, psychoanalysis needs to be a process done with relatively full awareness. After all, what you want is to be able to relate to yourself in a fully conscious way. So you have to learn to do it while being fully conscious. You need to learn to do it by slowly and painstakingly confronting obstacles to full awareness as they arise. As you work through and discard or modify each obstacle or defense, you do indeed get closer to the buried childhood memories. But in addition you have already become less defensive and more flexible and better able to tolerate painful self-knowledge. In some sense, learning how one defends oneself, and that one can live with more flexible defenses, is as important as recovery of memories.

Freud devised a technique to allow the person to stay conscious. This was *free association.* He believed that nothing psychological happens by chance. This is called "psychic determinism." Any thought that appears in consciousness is there for some reason. No matter how trivial or irrelevant, it is likely to be connected to some unconscious dynamic material. Normally people control their stream of thoughts. For example, in conversations with others we focus our thoughts and what we say on the conversation. We screen out, ignore, or do not give verbal expression to irrelevant thoughts and to thoughts that we judge to be socially inappropriate because they are hostile, sexual, or embarrassing. Freud wanted to relax the censoring activity that accompanies normal consciousness, so that deeper dynamic associations to surface thoughts could become conscious. So he instructed his patients to say whatever came to mind, regardless of how apparently irrelevant or inappropriate it was. In order to facilitate this, the client would lie on a couch, and Freud would sit behind him. This was presumed to reduce the demands of a normal social situation, where one converses face to face and does not let one's mind wander to whatever associated thoughts come up.

Suppose a client is discussing how loving his wife is and what an ungrateful wretch he is for not being more attentive to her. Suddenly he thinks of something that seems totally irrelevant—how much he hates spinach. It may turn out, through subsequent exploration, that it is no mere chance that this thought surfaced at that point. There may be an unconscious link between "spinach" and "wife." Perhaps the wife is *so* "loving" that he feels she treats him like a child. Since "being made to eat your spinach" is a fairly common image associated with being a child, the thought of spinach at that point makes sense. After this link is established, further exploration might uncover feelings of being smothered, and still further exploration feelings of anger, and finally feelings of being castrated. The unconscious is seen to follow a kind of emotional logic in how one thought flows into another. Topics are organized together based on their emotional associations, and it is this organization that the analyst hopes to tap into. But what does the analyst do while the client free associates?

Therapist Interventions

Psychoanalytic interventions are largely a matter of timing. Good analytic interventions first prepare a context for insight to develop and then facilitate the development of that insight. At first the therapist will do relatively little other than listen. She may ask questions like "What does spinach remind you of?" or "What else comes to mind?" Such questions will help the client explore his experience, and eventually certain aspects of the client's experience will become more crystallized and focused.

When the context is sufficiently crystallized and developed, then the analyst may broach an *interpretation.* For the context to be sufficiently crystallized the topic under discussion must have been explored enough for certain themes to be nearly apparent to consciousness. In addition, at the moment an interpretation is made, the context must be "affectively" alive, that is, the emotions associated with the underlying themes must be present or nearly present in consciousness. Put another way, a good interpretation works when it relates to something that is currently "on your mind," something you are currently "working on." Most of us have had the experience of being emotionally involved in talking about a problem (say, with our boss). At that moment, if a friend makes a response like "He sounds like a real idiot" or "I bet you feel you can't show your real stuff around him," it will very likely *feel* relevant at that moment and help us crystallize our feelings about the boss. But if the same comments are made an hour later, when we are thinking about something completely unrelated, they will feel pallid, flat, and useless.

An interpretation is a response designed to increase client insight. It attempts to bring into consciousness some thematic material that is unconscious.

There are two general kinds of interpretations, vertical and horizontal (Bellack, 1954). A *horizontal interpretation* identifies common themes in apparently unrelated aspects of the client's experience. A *vertical interpretation* relates aspects of current experience to "deeper" childhood experiences. For instance, suppose several experiences surface in which the spinach-hating client reports that his wife and secretary are constantly "taking care of him." The analyst might make a horizontal interpretation: "You seem to feel uneasy about all these situations in which women 'take care of you,' and I wonder if it is because they make you feel a little like a child." A vertical interpretation (usually made much later in therapy after the affective context has been prepared) might relate the client's dislike of being treated like a child to feelings of having been overmothered (and thus demasculinized or "castrated") as a child.

Interpretations are supposed to be short and couched in concrete, vivid everyday language. Both of these requirements relate to the need for an interpretation to have a concrete emotional impact (we will discuss this below). In addition, interpretations are supposed to address themselves to material that is near the surface of consciousness. We have already mentioned that interpretations are made only when sufficient material has been examined by client and therapist so that the common underlying theme is apparent. After the client has related several instances of feeling disgruntled at his wife's taking care of him, the theme that he feels he is being treated like a child almost pops out, and it is at this point that interpreting this to the client will facilitate therapeutic insight.

Interpretations need to deal with material that is already nearly in consciousness so that therapy proceeds gradually. One cannot simply jump to deep vertical interpretations, for instance, that our client is suffering from castration anxiety. There are three reasons for this. First, we have already seen that one goal of psychoanalysis is the gradually working through the blockades the person has constructed against awareness of the unconscious impulses. Deeper material is presumably more anxiety provoking and better defended. It is easier and less anxiety provoking to recognize that "I feel my wife treats me like a child" than it is to realize that "I felt overmothered and castrated as a child." As the client gradually confronts deeper and deeper material, the ability to tolerate the anxiety associated with deeply buried memories increases (this process is not unlike that of systematic desensitization, discussed in Chapter 7).

The second reason for proceeding gradually has to do with the *plausibility* of the interpretation (Fisher, 1956). After only one example of feeling disgruntled at his wife's taking care of him, it might not seem plausible to the client if the analyst were to jump in with, "You feel angry with your wife because she always treats you like a child." It would be even more implausible to say, "Your disgruntlement with your wife is based on feeling castrated as a child." The context for interpretation must be prepared. Going gradually is a matter of bringing sufficient material into consciousness so that the next interpretation will seem plausible. Once the client accepts that he dislikes feeling treated like a child by his wife, it might seem more plausible to him that he may have felt overmothered as a child. Once that is accepted it may seem more plausible that he felt emasculated by his mother's overattention.

The third reason insights must be acquired gradually is that insight is therapeutic only if it is affectively meaningful. (We will discuss this in the next section when we discuss the therapeutic conditions of change.)

What happens if interpretations are badly done? (We hope this section will discourage you from playing amateur psychoanalyst with yourself, friends, or relations.) We have said that the affective context for an interpretation must be carefully prepared. If our client, for instance, were to say to his wife, "Don't tell me to eat my spinach!" it would do no good for her to retort, "You are rebelling against me only because you didn't feel like a man when your mother told you what to do." Not only is the interpersonal atmosphere a very unsafe one for our client to consider the truth of such a remark, but the careful exploration needed to make such an interpretation therapeutically useful has not been done. Such an interpretation, *even if true* (and, of course, without the exploration you don't know it's true—you're only guessing) will not be therapeutic. All the intervening resistances to insight have not been worked through, and the result of such an interpretation might be only to make the client more defensive.

Breaching defenses too quickly may make the client feel bad about himself. Our client has presumably been overmothered as a child. This may make him unusually sensitive to criticism from mother-figures. But, of course, all he knows is that he feels bad about himself when his wife criticizes him. His conscious context, then, is to take comments about himself as criticisms. So when a mother-figure (his wife) tells him he was overmothered as a child, he will not take this as an insight-gaining, repression-lifting interpretation, but as a criticism. While this might be especially true if the interpretation is done by someone close to the person, the same thing can happen with inappropriately timed interpretations done by analysts. Thus, interpretations that go too deep too fast will not be therapeutic. They may actually be harmful, may lead to overwhelming anxiety, and possibly could result in disintegration of the ego and increased psychopathology.

Therapeutic Conditions of Change

It is possible for people to have knowledge about themselves that is totally useless to them in terms of therapeutic change. Such knowledge, even if accurate, may actually shore up defenses, rather than lead to their disappearance. This happens if the knowledge is in the form of an intellectual insight. Freud found early (see the third quote at the beginning of this chapter) that the knowledge that transforms is knowledge that is affectively meaningful. Put another way, insights that are acquired without an accompanying emotional experience will not be therapeutic. For instance, somewhere at the basis of your character, according to psychoanalytic theory, are oedipal feelings. If you are a male, somewhere deep inside you is primitive lust toward your mother and hatred toward your father. If you are a female, you harbor hidden feelings of lust toward your father and hatred toward your mother. Yet we venture to guess that most of you have no awareness of such feelings. Presuming that analytic theory is true, such buried feelings play a role in whatever personal failings you may have. Now, we have just told you that those feelings are there in you. You have acquired (if you believe us) intellectual insight. Have you noticed any magical transformations in yourself? Have you suddenly found all your conflicts or self-doubts vanishing? Probably not.

The reason is that your knowledge is purely intellectual, abstract, and hypothetical. What you know is that you must have hated your father or mother. That is different from experientially knowing that you hated your father or mother. To think that you must have hated your father or your mother is to deduce from your current behavior, and from psychoanalytic theory, that these feelings must be there somewhere in you. You have no direct awareness of them, no direct personal memories of hating your father or mother (or lusting after one or the other). To acquire therapeutic insight is to relive the emotion of hating. To remember your personal experience of the feelings will be to reexperience them in the therapeutic context. It is one thing, for instance, to remember that you must have been happy at your high school graduation. It is another to remember suddenly some concrete instances that happened, and feel a rush of that feeling of happiness, and say, "Oh yeah! I *was* happy!" Thus you must recover the deepest and most personal part of your memories—your feelings—in order for insight to be therapeutic.

Even after a person achieves early childhood insights that are accompanied by emotional reexperiencing, there is no magical change. But how can this be so, since we said that the goal of psychoanalysis is to lift repression? We have already partially answered this in our discussion of why Freud abandoned hypnosis. Basically, a process of working through feelings and behavior must be engaged in. The working through phase of therapy is the longest. Clients must learn how derivatives of early childhood feelings have been woven into the fabric of their whole life. They need to examine specific events to find where the unconscious feelings are coloring and distorting their perceptions of situations and relationships. For example, you might examine an instance of anger at your boss to see if unconscious hatred of a parent is coloring your reactions. Insight does not magically lead to change. It is rather a precondition to change, because change actually occurs through the working through process.

Television and movie portrayals of instantaneous and magical therapeutic change are seriously distorted. A client has a hysterical symptom, such as blindness. The doctor discovers the reason—the client saw his wife in the arms of another and became hysterically blind to deny what he saw. The doctor confronts the client with the truth. The patient resists: "No! No!" But finally the patient faces up to it: "You're right! . . . I can see!" Most therapists agree that change is slow and gradual. In a small survey of over 30 therapists of all persuasions done by one of us (Bohart, 1979) there was only one therapist who reported a case in which change was sudden and instantaneous as a result of an insight.

Dreams, Resistance, and Transference

We have now seen that the major therapeutic tool of psychoanalysis is interpretation. We have also seen that insight must be accompanied by emotional reliving and working through in order to be therapeutic. We now wish to discuss three sources of data that the analyst uses in facilitating therapeutic change.

For Freud, *dreams* were the "royal road to the unconscious." Freud believed that dreams express unconscious wishes and conflicts in symbolic form. Therefore, they can be used to acquire insight. The client is asked to free associate to the dream symbols in order to discover their unconscious meaning. More recent theories of what dreams are and of what fantasy is in general (see Klinger, 1971) question the idea that dreams are primarily symbolic representations of unconscious wishes. However, free associating to one's dreams still can be therapeutically useful in helping to uncover unconscious material.

Resistance provides another general source of data about repression. The basic phenomenon is that no matter how much people may consciously wish to change (especially if their symptoms are painful), unconsciously they do *not* wish to change. To change is to undo the repression that protects them from painful unconscious memories, and therefore, they will unconsciously resist treatment.

Resistance manifests itself in many ways in therapy. It may show up in difficulties in free association ("I can't think of anything at all to say"), in missing or being late for appointments, or in wasting most of the appointment talking about trivia. A client may try to seduce the therapist, literally or figuratively, to keep the therapist from forcing confrontation with the unconscious. Aside from literal sexual seduction, a person may try flattering the therapist, buying her gifts, or wanting to be "friends" outside of therapy. The client may resist by belittling or berating the therapist or by deciding therapy is a waste of time or through a temporary "flight into health," insisting that problems are solved after a few sessions.

The phenomenon of resistance to change is noted by therapists of most persuasions. However, there are different ways of interpreting the cause of resistance, as you shall see later on in this book. The psychoanalytic interpretation of resistance is that it occurs because the client is unconsciously avoiding the pain of facing unpleasant buried memories.

Resistance may be confronted by the analyst. *Confrontation* is essentially a kind of interpretation in which the therapist attempts to make the client aware of what the client is really doing and the consequences of the behavior. For example, the therapist may present the possibility that there is some underlying motive to the client's repeated missed appointments. Good confrontation, as with good interpretation in general, does not force insight. The client may be confronted with the idea that something underlies the missed appointments, but then the client and therapist will *explore* to find out what it is.

Confrontation is a response that is especially susceptible to misuse. It is too easy for the therapist to use confrontations as punishments or manipulations. For instance, a client may really feel therapy is not working. For the therapist to say, "You only feel that because unconsciously you don't want to get well" could be a dangerous response. It may manipulate the client into staying in therapy when it indeed isn't working. It would be more appropriate in such a situation for the therapist to be more open-minded and help the client explore the possibility that resistance underlies the desire to terminate, rather than to assume that is the reason.

We have saved the *transference* relationship for last because it is actually the most important part of psychoanalysis. If you remember, overt relationships to people and to the world are derivatives of unconscious conflicts. In particular, the way adults perceive and relate to significant other people is almost invariably tinged by unconscious feelings and wishes they had toward the significant others in their early childhood. Thus people transfer onto others feelings and reactions they had toward their parents. This is done not only to use other people as outlets for disguised wishes, feelings, and fantasies, but also as a defense against recognition of these wishes and fantasies. I may sublimate my lustful feelings toward my mother by transferring them onto other women in my adult life. The women I get involved with allow me to express in various disguised ways my repressed feelings concerning my mother. And by having an outlet for these feelings, I am able to maintain the repression so that I never have to face up to their true nature. This partly explains why people often get involved in the same kind of destructive relationship time and again. For instance, our client who was overmothered may continually seek out women who dominate him and with whom he can feel simultaneously protected and rebellious.

The therapist, as a significant relationship, becomes a target for transference of significant emotional themes from childhood. Our client, for instance, may see any friendly, helpful gestures by the analyst as signs that the analyst will "mother" and protect him. Certainly he will *wish* for the analyst to mother and protect him. To the extent that he initially sees the analyst as fulfilling these infantile wishes, he will see the analyst as wonderful and therapy as wonderful. This is *positive transference.* However, as soon as the analyst does not act in accord with his unconscious wishes and fantasies, he may begin to feel lost, frightened, and even angry. If the client begins to feel angry toward the analyst, this will be *negative transference.* Even if he unconsciously is able to see the analyst as the all-protective mother, he may exhibit negative transference toward the analyst. After all, unconsciously he both likes the safety of being overmothered and resents feeling emasculated. So he may begin to see the analyst as trying to belittle him. Resistance is another reason for positive and negative transference. By lauding or criticizing the therapist, the client unconsciously resists facing himself.

In order to use the transference therapeutically the analyst attempts to remain relatively anonymous and neutral in demeanor. It is often said that the analyst attempts to act like a "blank screen" onto which the client can transfer images of childhood relationships. This does not mean that the analyst acts like a personality-less robot. It simply means that she does not share her *personal* reactions to things. She will keep back her own opinions, her own views, and, to some degree, her own emotional reactions. She may nevertheless convey warmth and empathy to the client and not be phony or assume a false facade. If the client reports some unusual behavior (for example, "I had sex with my sister"), the analyst does not give approval or disapproval. If the client says, "What do you think of that?" the analyst's reply would be, "It's more important to discover what you think of it." By remaining relatively neutral in expressing opinions and judgments, the analyst allows the transference to become clear. If the client accuses the analyst of being critical of him, this must be a transference since the analyst has not expressed judgments.

The transference relationship is so important therapeutically because the client acts out the core of his neurotic problems right in therapy. Insight into the unconscious dynamics of these problems can be acquired *as the problems are lived out and experienced directly.* We have already seen that interpretations are most effective if timed to coincide with an affectively alive context, and the transference relationship is certainly that. The client feels treated like a child by experiencing the analyst as treating him like a child, and in this affective context he may gain insight into how he constructs reality.

In order to handle the transference relationship well, the analyst must be careful not to let her personal reactions intrude. However, in order to do this the therapist must be aware of her own *countertransference.* Remember that all people have unconscious memories that color their current experiences. If therapists are to react clearly and objectively to their clients, they must be aware of what kind of unconscious transference relationships they are projecting onto their clients. If I have an unconscious need for approval, for instance, I may be devastated by a client's negative transference and may react in a way that has no therapeutic benefit or even impedes the process. There are many other unconscious conflicts or needs that a therapist might transfer onto the client, such as the need to be respected or looked up to or the need to be loved. If a therapist has unconscious conflicts over sex, he may "see" his clients as conflicted over sex. If a therapist is afraid of her anger, she may unconsciously try to work this out by assuming that her client must learn to deal with his anger. In order to be aware of countertransference, the psychoanalyst must undergo a training analysis herself.

Mechanics of Psychoanalysis

Classical Freudian psychoanalysis is a lengthy affair. Freud himself often saw clients six days a week and complained that the one-day break would set the analysis back. Modern analysts usually see clients three to five times a week. A full-fledged analysis usually lasts several years. Furthermore, since analysis is never complete, clients often return periodically to analysis (Malcolm, 1981).

Because it is believed that making too many concessions to the client, such as allowing sessions to run long or going for walks, may increase resistance, the client is seen in a fairly rigid format. He is usually billed for missed appointments, rarely allowed more than the traditional "50 minute hour," and rarely seen in settings other than the therapist's office.

At approximately $100 an hour several times a week over a period of years classical psychoanalysis is obviously expensive. Its high cost is part of the reason for the development of modern shortened versions. We will discuss these short-term approaches to psychoanalytic therapy in the next chapter.

THE NEO-FREUDIANS

There have been so many creative offshoots from traditional Freudian psychoanalysis that we cannot consider them all here. In this chapter we will briefly review the contributions of Jung and Adler, perhaps the two most famous theorists to develop out of psychoanalysis. We will mention the achievements of the group of theorists collectively known as the neo-Freudians. Then we will consider one offshoot—bioenergetics—that is quite distinctive in its differences not only from psychoanalysis, but also from other approaches to therapy. (The most recent developments in the psychoanalytic movement are considered in the next chapter.)

Adler

Alfred Adler (1929/1964) was Freud's contemporary and a respected psychiatrist in his own right when he studied with Freud. He subsequently rejected many of Freud's ideas. Like many others, Adler rejected Freud's emphasis on sexuality and the unconscious as crucial forces in personality development. He called the system he developed "individual psychology."

Adler emphasized the unique individuality of each personality. In contrast to Freud, who viewed the personality as fundamentally split into conflicting components, Adler saw the personality as unified. Adler also focused on the conscious side of the personality. Like later ego analysts, Adler believed that the strivings of a rather rational, organized self accounted for much behavior. He felt that the relation of this self to other people ("social interest") and the striving of this self toward future goals ("fictional finalism") were also important. Adler stressed the ongoing social environment as a cause of behavior more than Freud did. For this reason some have seen Adler as one of the forerunners of the community psychology movement (see Chapter 12).

Adler is perhaps best known for his concepts of the inferiority complex and striving for superiority. He began with the idea of "organ inferiority." He argued that people born with certain physical defects (inferior organs, such as deafness, poor vision, lameness) would organize their personalities around compensating for the feelings of inferiority engendered by the defect. Later he came to believe that feelings of inferiority as a result of being a small, weak child are universal. Some individuals would successfully compensate for their feelings of inferiority and achieve a great deal, while others would fail to do so and would develop feelings of insecurity or grandiosity or other symptoms. The negative personality characteristics surrounding the attempt to deal with these feelings were called an *inferiority complex.*

For Adler, the basic dynamic motivating force within the personality is *striving for superiority.* This basic force is normal and inborn and continues throughout life. All people strive for self-esteem, perfection, and completion in all their behaviors. This dynamic force results in achievement and fulfillment in most individuals, although each expresses these strivings in different ways. Some strive for superiority by being successful in their occupations, others by being loving or creative. Disturbed individuals may express their strivings for superiority in less desirable ways, such as becoming tyrannical at home or being viciously competitive. Unlike Freud, Adler was an optimist, and he believed that the normal, inborn motivation for humans is a prosocial striving for accomplishment and achievement.

Adler's approach to therapy was active, kindly, and "commonsensical." He appealed to his patients' rationality and supported their general strivings and goals. Part of his treatment of neurotic behavior was to help his patients choose more socially effective means of pursuing their general goals. He often worked with children, and he would invite family members, teachers, and other involved adults to attend therapy sessions. He would support the child and explain the child's view to the surrounding adults, somewhat like family therapists today. He also tried to make the child's and the family's goals explicit, so they could all agree to work together.

This brief summary cannot do justice to Adler's theory, which also included a personality typology and extensive discussion of people's styles of life. Style of life referred to the person's individuality, ways of handling problems, methods of compensation for feelings of inferiority, and specific goals and ways of achieving them. Like Freud, he believed the style of life was set in early childhood and continued in the same direction throughout adulthood. Adler began the notion that people's earliest memory indicates the basic direction of their life. (The earliest memory of one of us is taking a nap!)

Although Adler still has followers with their own journal, *The American Journal of Individual Psychology,* his system never became as famous and popular as Freud's. His theory is criticized as being shallow, simplistic, and contradictory. His emphasis on future goals determining present behavior seems to be teleological and antideterministic, yet he also believed that style of life was set by early childhood and that the current environment contributed to behavior, both certainly deterministic tenets. Nevertheless, his ideas of compensating for inferiority and his emphasis on the ego have become widely accepted.

Jung

Carl Jung (1933, 1956) studied under Freud when he was just beginning his psychiatric practice. Like Adler, he disagreed with Freud's emphasis on sexuality. His extensive theory of personality, called analytical psychology, was considerably more mystical and philosophical than Freud's. However, his therapeutic practices were generally similar to Freud's. Jung emphasized dreams even more than Freud. The kinds of interpretations he made also focused on symbolic and archetypal meanings underlying behavior, in addition to meanings from early childhood.

Like Freud, Jung believed that psychic energy coursing through personality structures causes behavior. However, while this energy derives from biological processes, it is not particularly sexual. This energy motivates behavior whose goal is the actualization and fulfillment of the self, an idea similar to Adler's striving for superiority. In this respect Jung's theory presaged both recent developments in psychoanalysis and humanistic approaches.

Like Freud and unlike Adler, Jung emphasized unconscious determinants of behavior. He divided the unconscious into two parts—the personal unconscious and the collective unconscious. The personal unconscious contains repressed and forgotten memories from infancy and childhood. It is unique to the individual, depending on the types of childhood experiences the individual had.

The collective unconscious is transpersonal and shared by all human beings. It is the foundation of the entire personality structure and contains inherited memory traces embedded in the brain. These include memories from humankind's ancestral past and prehuman nature. For example, humans are predisposed to know God, since the memory traces of countless preceding generations' experience of God are in the collective unconscious. Jung wrote that the collective unconscious contains centuries of wisdom and experience.

Archetypes are the "primordial images" or "universal thought forms" found in the collective unconscious. After centuries of experiencing similar issues, the human brain evolves archetypes to deal with each issue. Like all evolutionary structures, archetypes help us survive. Some archetypes are so important to our evolutionary survival that they have formed important subsystems within the personality structure. Jung wrote especially about the persona, shadow, anima-animus, and self archetypes. To simplify greatly, the persona is the socially conventional mask we all wear; the shadow is the darker, animal side of human nature; anima represents the feminine in men and animus represents the masculine in women; and the self is our striving for unity and wholeness. Jung wrote extensively about the self and its strivings for actualization.

Jung developed a complex personality typology of eight major types based on two major life orientations—extraversion and introversion—coupled with four psychological functions—thinking, feeling, sensing, and intuiting. Extraversion is an outer-directed orientation to life; introversion is inner directed. A person could be a thinking introvert, who spends all her time alone reading philosophical works; a feeling extravert, who constantly creates emotional scenes with other people; a feeling introvert; and so on.

Jung's impact has perhaps been greater in fields other than psychology. His importance to philosophy, art, literature, metaphysics, and history is acknowledged by many. His ideas are complex, unsystematic, and subjective. An idea such as the collective unconscious is untestable and in its pure form is not accepted as a scientific hypothesis today. However, many cognitive psychologists do believe there may be inborn ways of organizing information, somewhat like archetypes.

Neo-Freudians

Many highly creative therapists and theorists have arisen from the psychoanalytic perspective. These include Karen Horney (1945), Harry Stack Sullivan (Mullahy, 1952), and Erik Erikson (1968). What is common to all these theorists is a greater emphasis on the importance of relationships to others in determining personality and psychopathology than is found in classical Freudian theory. Horney's three orientations to life—moving toward people, moving away from people, moving against people—stress relationships. Erikson saw development in interpersonal terms. For instance, the key development at Freud's oral period is for Erikson the development of "basic trust." Furthermore, Erikson saw development as continuing throughout the life span, instead of being largely completed by age 5. His approach has become increasingly influential in the field of developmental psychology.

Harry Stack Sullivan believed that we develop a concept of the "good me" based on what is acceptable to our parents. Those aspects of ourselves that we consider to be the "bad me" are split off from consciousness. With his emphasis on the "good me" and the "bad me" and their development as a result of relationships to others, Sullivan was a precursor of object relations theory (discussed in the following chapter).

Along with a greater emphasis on the importance of interpersonal relations in the development of personality, these theorists also generally place greater emphasis on the ego than did Freud. For Freud, the ego developed out of the id, and its main function was to mediate between the id and reality. Erickson and Sullivan, as well as others such as Heinz Hartmann (1964), saw the ego as having greater autonomy. They saw humans as consisting of more than the management of sexual and aggressive instincts. In this respect these theorists were also precursors of the developments to be considered in the next chapter.

BIOENERGETIC THERAPY

Developed by Wilhelm Reich (1942, 1945, 1951), who was a student of Freud, and more recently by Alexander Lowen (1958, 1965, 1967), bioenergetic therapy takes Freud's ideas on psychic energy and repression a few steps farther. Although Reich fell into disrepute in the 1950s, his ideas are currently enjoying a positive reevaluation. Many of his ideas on character armor and personality development are now seen as major contributions to psychoanalytic theory. Reich believed all psychopathology is due to sexual repression. Lowen stressed that it is not just sexual, but repression of all bodily and biological pleasure that causes neurosis.

The theory behind bioenergetics is that the basic biological life energy of individuals can become blocked and distorted as a result of early learning and repeated experiences. Certain aspects of experience are learned to be painful and dangerous, and they are blocked from awareness by the action of the body's musculature. Libido, or life energy, is biological, and repression of life energy is biological and physical, not just psychological. For example, a child may learn that anger is not an acceptable feeling. She may be taught some general lesson; such as "Good girls are always nice," or she may be punished for expressing anger. As the child grows up, there are inevitably occasions when anger is the natural, biological response. In order to block the awareness of the dangerous feeling, she will deny the anger literally with the body. Muscles will be tensed to prevent expression of the anger. The jaw will be clenched, to hold back angry words, and the mouth may be forced into a smile; the arms will be held tightly to the sides, to deny the possibility of striking or pushing. Think of your own feelings and behavior when you are really angry, but pretending not to be, and you may be aware of having clenched your jaw or held your arms down. This behavior can become a problem when the person is not conscious of the denial of the feeling and the accompanying counteractive muscle tension.

The physical denial of certain feelings repeated over the years gradually distorts the development of the body. The constant, unconscious muscle tension actually makes the muscles and bones grow differently than they would have otherwise. The denied feelings are permanently embedded in the body. This rigidification of body and personality is called "character armor" by Reich and "neurotic character structure" by Lowen. The defense against certain feelings becomes like armor on the body. Like real armor, it prevents people from getting close to others, from being aware of their own bodily sensations, and from functioning as free, whole organisms. They have become literally crippled.

Bioenergeticists believe that each type of denied feeling leads to a different body type, a different form of character armor, which they can diagnose by looking at the person's physique. This belief has a certain amount of common sense. You can see that if you held your body in a certain way for years, it would grow differently. Perhaps you can also see how Reich placed Freud's ideas on defense mechanisms and psychic energy in the body. Reich's defense mechanisms work by blocking biological energy with the muscles, by denying dangerous feelings by activating the opposing muscles.

The bioenergetic treatment for psychological disorders is, as you might guess, quite physical. Through specific exercises and bodily manipulation, therapists try to increase clients' awareness both of their bodily processes and the blocked emotions. The physical and mental pain that clients' report as a result of forcing their muscles to move in new ways is interpreted by the therapist. The therapy also stresses emotional catharsis. The goal of therapy is to loosen the character armor so that life energy can flow freely. Then the client can function as a whole, integrated, free and responsive individual.

REFERENCES

Adelson, J., & Doehrman, M. J. (1980). The psychodynamic approach to adolescence. In J. Adelson (Ed.), *Handbook of adolescent psychology.* New York: Wiley.

Adler, A. (1964). *Social interest: A challenge to mankind.* New York: Capricorn Books. (Original work published 1929)

Bellack, L. (1954). *The TAT and CAT in clinical use.* New York: Grune & Stratton.

Bettelheim, B. (1982). *Freud and man's soul.* New York: Vintage.

Bohart, A. (1979). *Personal paradigms, resistance, and change in psychotherapy.* Paper presented at the Western Psychological Association Convention, San Diego, CA.

Breuer, J., & Freud, S. (Eds.). (1937). *Studies in hysteria.* Boston: Beacon Press. (Original work published in 1895)

Cameron, N., & Rychlak, J. F. (1985). *Personality development and psychopathology* (2nd ed.). Boston: Houghton Mifflin.

Ekstein, R. (1974). Psychoanalytic theory: Sigmund Freud. In A. Burton (Ed.), *Operational theories of personality.* New York: Brunner/Mazel.

Ellenberger, H. F. (1970). *The discovery of the unconscious.* New York: Basic Books.

Erikson, E. (1968). *Identity: Youth and crisis.* New York: Norton.

Fisher, S. (1956). Plausibility and depth of interpretation. *Journal of Consulting Psychology, 20,* 249–256.

Freud, S. (1937). Psychotherapy of hysteria. In J. Breuer & S. Freud (Eds.), *Studies in hysteria.* Boston: Beacon Press. (Original work published 1895)

Freud, S. (1955). Lines of advance in psycho-analytic theory. In J. Strachey (Ed.), *The standard edition of the complete psychological works of Sigmund Freud* (Vol. 17). London: Hogarth Press. (Original work published 1918)

Freud, S. (1961). Some psychical consequences of the anatomical distinction between the sexes. In J. Strachey (Ed.), *The standard edition of the complete psychological works of Sigmund Freud* (Vol. 19). London: Hogarth Press. (Original work published 1925)

Freud, S. (1963). Analysis terminable and interminable. In P. Rieff (Ed.), *Sigmund Freud: Therapy and technique.* New York: Crowell-Collier. (Original work published 1937)

Freud, S. (1963). Observations on "wild" psychoanalysis. In P. Rieff (Ed.), Sigmund *Freud: Therapy and technique.* New York: Crowell-Collier. (Original work published 1910)

Freud, S. (1964). The dissection of the psychical personality. In J. Strachey (Ed.), *The standard edition of the complete psychological works of Sigmund Freud* (Vol. 22). London: Hogarth Press. (Original work published 1924)

Hartmann, H. (1964). *Essays on ego psychology.* New York: International Universities Press.

Horney, K. (1945). *Our inner conflicts.* New York: Norton.

Jones, E. (1954). *Hamlet and Oedipus.* Garden City, NY: Doubleday.

Jung, C. G. (1933). *Modern man in search of a soul.* New York: Harcourt Brace Jovanovich.

Jung, C.G. (1956). *Two essays on analytical psychology.* New York: New American Library (Meridian Books).

Kaplan, L. J. (1984). *Adolescence: The farewell to childhood.* New York: Simon & Schuster.

Klinger, E. (1971). *Structure and function of fantasy.* New York: Wiley.

Lowen, A. (1958). *Physical dynamics of character structures.* New York: Grune & Stratton.

Lowen, A. (1965). *Love and orgasm.* New York: Macmillan.

Lowen, A. (1967). *The betrayal of the body.* New York: Crowell-Collier.

Luborsky, L. (1984). *Principles of psychoanalytic psychotherapy: A manual for supportive-expressive treatment.* New York: Basic Books.

Malcolm, J. (1981). *Psychoanalysis: The impossible profession.* New York: Vintage.

Masson, J. M. (1984). *The assault on truth: Freud's suppression of the seduction theory.* New York: Farrar, Straus & Giroux.

Masson, J. M. (Ed.). (1985). *The complete letters of Sigmund Freud to Wilhelm Fliess 1887–1904.* Cambridge, MA: Harvard University Press.

Mullahy, P. (1952). *The contributions of Harry Stack Sullivan.* New York: Hermitage Press.

Reich, W. (1942). *The function of the orgasm.* New York: Orgone Institute.

Reich, W. (1945). *Character analysis.* New York: Orgone Institute.

Reich, W. (1951). *Selected writings.* New York: Farrar, Straus & Giroux.

Schafer, R. (1978). *Language and insight.* New Haven: Yale University Press.

Stolorow, R. D., & Atwood, G. E. (1979). *Faces in a cloud: Subjectivity in personality theory.* New York: Aronson.

Chapter 4

Recent Developments in Psychoanalysis

In recent years there has been a resurgence of interest in psychoanalytic theory. Two recent approaches that have attracted attention are object relations theory and Kohut's self psychology. Both continue trends found in the work of Adler, Jung, Horney, Sullivan, Erikson, and others who came after Freud. Both view the development of a stable, cohesive self or identity as fundamental and relations with people as crucial in this development. Psychoanalytic therapeutic approaches that require considerably less time than classical analysis are another area of current interest.

OBJECT RELATIONS THEORY

According to Harry Guntrip (1973), important precursors of object relations theory were Melanie Klein (1932/1975) and Harry Stack Sullivan. Other important figures (see St. Clair, 1986) associated with this approach are D. W. Winnicot, W. R. D. Fairbairn, Otto Kernberg, Margaret Mahler, and James Masterson (1981; 1985). Object relations theorists generally reject in whole or in part Freud's metapsychology, that is, his concept of id, ego, and superego and the idea that the personality is an energy-regulating device. Some substitute a rather complex metapsychology of their own. But because it is difficult and not necessary in order to gain a general view of object relations theory, we will only briefly touch on it later.

Self-Structure and Integration of Aims

> A person is a whole self and so unique that it is impossible to find, among all the millions of human beings that have existed and do exist, any two who are exactly alike. When a baby is born, he contains a core of uniqueness that has never existed before. The parents' responsibility is not to mold, shape, pattern, or condition him, but to support him in such a way that his precious hidden uniqueness shall be able to emerge and guide his whole development. (Guntrip, 1973, p. 181)

It is apparent from this quote that we have come a long way from Freud. Whereas Freud saw development in terms of regulating and expressing sexuality (and later aggression), object relations theory focuses on the development of a separate, differentiated, integrated, cohesive self. Certainly the regulation of sexuality and aggression are important issues for the development of a differentiated cohesive self, but so are hunger, needs for closeness, attention, competence, mastery, and others.

Object relations theory is thus more comprehensive than Freud's psychoanalysis. Sex and aggression are important, but they are only a part of the whole story. A fully developed self is unique. It is also creative, flexible, and self-regulating. It is true to itself, and behavior flows from its own plans and schemes, rather than from some externalized image of how it should be (a "false self"). The most crucial factor in the development of a true self is relations to other people, particularly the mother. As we said in the previous chapter, relations with other people are seen by psychoanalysts as a subcategory of relations with objects in general. Hence, even though the object relations theorists are most interested in relations with people, they call them "object relations." Now read the following quote with the understanding that the word *"people"* can be substituted for *object,* and see what it means to you. "The entire process of growth, disturbance, and restoration of wholeness as an ego or personal self depends upon the ego's relations with objects, primarily in infancy, and thereafter in the unconscious . . . interacting with object-relations in real life" (Guntrip, 1973, p. 95).

Along with the emphasis on the development of the self in the context of relations to other people comes a deemphasis of Freud's view of the mind as composed of id, ego, and superego. For Freud the id was a biological repository of primitive sexual and aggressive energies. But, if sex and aggression are *energies* that build up and clamor for discharge, people have a need to act aggressively or sexually regardless of what is going on in their lives. For Freud relations with other people are based on their being sources of need gratification. It is important for an individual to be liked or loved by other people, because people are vehicles of sexual gratification. All motives, such as the need to achieve, to have power over others, to have positive self-esteem, to be loved, are all ultimately secondary to the basic needs of discharging and regulating sexuality and aggression.

Many object relations theorists reject the view that sexuality and aggression are instinctual energies that build up and clamor for discharge (Guntrip, 1973; Eagle, 1984). They believe that both sex and aggression have a biological component, but neither are instincts in the generally accepted meaning of the word, that is, they are not energies that build up and need to be discharged or reduced. In rejecting an energy model of motivation object relations theory is in accord with most modern views of needs and motivations (see Weiner, 1980). According to Guntrip, sex is better thought of as a biologically based *appetite.* An appetite may increase in intensity if a person is not able to engage in the desired activity, but there is no energy that builds up if the person does not engage in it. For example, if one has an interest or "appetite" for going to classical music concerts, one's desire to go may increase if one has not been for a while, but there is no buildup of "classical music energy." Freud's energy idea implies that one needs to *discharge* the energy in order for pleasure to occur. Such a view makes orgasm the ultimate goal of sexual activity and makes any sexual activity without orgasm appear to be ultimately incomplete. This is quite out of keeping with modern views of sexuality (see, for instance, Zilbergeld, 1978). In fact, this view is now seen as one of the *causes* of sexual problems. Sexual activity and becoming aroused may be experienced as pleasurable whether or not they lead to orgasm. If sex is an energy that needs to be discharged and dissipated, then this does not make sense. If sex is an appetite, then it does make sense.

Similarly, if aggression is an instinctual energy, then we as a species would periodically have to act aggressively in order to dissipate this energy. But while most modern theorists believe there is a biological basis to aggression, they hold that that basis is a response to threat rather than instinctual energy. We may learn to enjoy aggression for its own sake, but that is because aggression, like sex, can come to serve other needs in the personality. There is no aggressive energy that needs to be discharged.

If the self is the focus of development, and not sex and aggression, then what is the self? Morris Eagle (1984) defined the self as a

> biologically evolved adaptive hierarchical structure coordinating a wide range of subordinate functions. In as complex a system as a person, one would expect the evolution of a superordinate structure whose main functions would include the coordination and fulfillment of a wide range of the person's interests and needs.

Thus the self is an *organization* that attempts to coordinate a host of goals, desires, aims, and values. For instance, at any given moment I may have a host of conflicting aims and goals. I may feel hungry, tired, bored with my studies. Yet I may have the goal of passing the test tomorrow, which may relate to other goals of becoming a psychologist, pleasing my parents, maintaining my self-esteem. I may also have a desire to please my spouse, who wants to go out, or to pay attention to my children. The individual needs an organizational structure that can prioritize competing aims, desires, and feelings and bring some coherence to how the individual goes about meeting them. That is what the self is and what it does.

Eagle goes on to suggest that some of our aims are infantile and some are not available to conscious awareness, having been split off and disavowed, usually in early childhood. He sees persons as

> attempting to carry out a variety of aims—some in conflict with each other and others harmoniously, some infantile and others more mature, and all with varying degrees of conscious awareness and of acknowledgment as one's own aims, ranging from full conscious awareness and acknowledgment to total lack of awareness and disavowal. (p. 123)

Disowned or disavowed aims imperil adequate functioning of the self.

> A superordinate structure or self-organization which excludes and dissociates a wide range of strivings and aims does not adequately reflect one's welfare and is therefore carrying out its adaptive functions poorly. (p. 207)

Thus if persons have disavowed certain primitive wishes in early childhood, their self-organization cannot function adequately. These wishes still influence their behavior, but cannot be integrated and coordinated with other aspects of their personality because they are not available to awareness.

Sex and aggression, in this view, are aims or desires, not instincts. As such, they need to be integrated with other aims and desires. Sex, as an appetite, may become integrated with other aspects of the self so that it comes to serve a variety of other needs of the self. And it takes on many meanings. It becomes part of the functioning of the self and takes a place in the whole system of personal values and meanings. For Freud many of our "higher" aims, such as success, self-esteem, and closeness, are ultimately in the service of sexual discharge; for Guntrip, Eagle, George Klein, and others, it is just the reverse. Sexual activity may be a means of achieving closeness and intimacy, a way of proving attractiveness or self-worth, an "achievement" activity, or an act of rebellion. Klein (1976) says that sexual cravings are not the naggings of undischarged sexual tension, but represent the failure to actualize some self-value that has become symbolized by sexual activity. Thus sexual tension usually has more to do with an individual's needs for closeness, acceptance, or achievement than it does with some pure need for "sex." After all, if it were just a need for "sex" one could masturbate. The point is that in the human there really isn't something so simple as a need for sex. Rather, sex becomes an activity through which a whole range of other needs and values get expressed.

This way of looking at the self provides a better explanation of what happens in therapy than classical analytic theory. Classical analytic theory therapy makes repressed impulses conscious, but then what? You can't go have sex with your mother or father. All you can do is make sure these impulses don't distort your view of the world. But what do you do with them? In object relations theory aims are influenced by their place in the whole self-structure and take on different meanings depending on how they are integrated into the personality. The problem with repression is that certain primitive childhood aims are split off from the self-structure and therefore not given a chance to be integrated effectively. Conscious awareness in therapy allows these aims to be integrated in the adult self and therefore modified.

Consider a client who gets in touch with infantile rage toward his father, who often slighted him. In classical analytic therapy what does a person now do with this rage? We have had clients get in touch with such rage, only to feel worse, saying, "Now what do I do?" Our answer was that the rage needs to be worked through until the client can "let go" of it. This usually involves forgiving the father, which itself involves relinquishing demands that the father (or all people, including oneself) be perfect. It also involves recognizing the father's humanness. Finally, it involves the realization that the client is now an adult and no longer needs to feel so threatened by such slights. These learnings fundamentally alter the rage so that it either goes away or becomes considerably less intense.

We will now look at the most commonly accepted object relations views of the development of the self.

Mahler and Separation-Individuation

Margaret Mahler (Mahler, 1968; Mahler, Pine, & Bergman, 1975) conducted observational studies of mothers and children to arrive at her model of development. For her, development is primarily a matter of *separation* and *individuation,* that is, the child must separate herself from other objects and the external world and develop a sense of her own uniqueness as an individual. According to Mahler, the child in the first month of life is in the stage of *normal autism.* In this stage the infant is only fleetingly attentive to external reality, being more preoccupied with internal stimuli. The infant could be described at this stage as *narcissistic.* It has no interest in the external world; in fact, it does not even have a concept of the external world. External objects, such as the mother, are not seen as external objects, and their presence may only be dimly sensed as an accompaniment of need gratification. The infant may believe that her desires are all that is needed to make the mother magically appear to satisfy them. So the infant also believes itself to be *omnipotent* at this age. Most infants outgrow this fundamental autistic stage. Children who do not outgrow it suffer from the disorder of childhood autism.

From the second or third month the child begins to attend to the world. At this stage, known as *normal symbiosis,* the child cannot distinguish between its own efforts to get its needs met and the responses of the mother to its needs. The child may now be aware of external stimuli, particularly of those associated with the mother, but the child does not perceive the mother as an external object (a separate person). In effect the child experiences itself as fused with the mother, as sharing a common boundary with the mother. When the mother feeds the child, for instance, the child perceives the mother's arm and the bottle as part of its own body feeding itself. Thus, when the mother does not immediately gratify the infant's hunger, the child perceives its own self as inflicting pain and frustration.

Individuals who do not grow out of this stage, are predisposed to psychotic disorganization.

> The essential feature of symbiosis is hallucinatory or delusional . . . omnipotent fusion with the representation of the mother and, in particular, the delusion of a common boundary of the two actually and physically separate individuals. This is the mechanism to which the ego regresses in cases of the most severe disturbance of individuation and psychotic disorganization, which I have described as "symbiotic child psychosis." (Mahler, 1968, p. 9)

At about 4 months of age the separation-individuation process proper begins. The first phase of the process, from about 4 months to 10 months, involves the infant's development of a sense of *bodily separation* from the mother. Through its activities the child begins to realize that it and the mother are physically separate. This realization, however, is anxiety provoking, and the child will periodically "check back" with the mother in order to reassure itself of her presence.

The next phase, from about 10 to 14 months, is that of *practicing.* It is divided into early practicing and practicing proper. *Early practicing* involves gradual acquisition of motor skills that allow further separation from the mother. *Practicing proper* begins when the infant begins to walk. This is the peak period of the child's omnipotence. The child acts as if it is on top of the world, and can master anything, as a whole new world is opened up to it by its ability to move around. However, this sense of omnipotence is still linked to the psychological presence of the mother as the child's "security blanket."

Before we discuss the next phase, we should discuss the mother's activity during the whole maturation process. For development to be successful the child must experience "good enough mothering" (Winnicot, 1965). A good mother enjoys her child and is comfortable holding it. Mahler believes that how and when a mother holds her child conveys to the child a whole host of attitudes. As the child begins to separate and individuate, the mother is neither too distant nor too close. An overprotective, smothering mother holds a child when she needs comforting rather than when the child needs comforting. This behavior may stifle the child's initiative and moves toward autonomy. It inhibits the child's ability to develop a sense of itself as separate from the mother and to develop its capacity for independent judgment. A distant, rejecting mother may also be harmful because she does not provide a safe place of support to which the child can return after venturing out into the world. The child needs both a sense of support from the mother as it challenges the world and some freedom to explore. A distant, rejecting mother may allow freedom, but provide no support. Her child will never successfully separate and individuate because it will forever long for union with her. It will fantasize union with the mother because that is the only way it can control its own anxiety in response to its mother's abandonment or neglect.

It is particularly important that the mother effectively balance support and freedom in the next phase of separation-individuation, that of *rapprochement* from about 14 to 24 months. Some object relations theorists hypothesize that many different kinds of psychopathology, including borderline personality disorder and eating disorders such as bulimia, have their roots in this developmental phase. During rapprochement the child becomes more aware of its separateness from the mother. Its joyous sense of omnipotence vanishes as it begins to recognize its separateness. It begins to feel small, deflated, weak, and helpless. This is the beginning of the rapprochement crisis. The child must master the fact of its separateness from the mother. In addition, it is during this time that the child becomes aware of gender differences, and thus analytic theorists see it as the beginning of a person's identity as a male or female.

During rapprochement *splitting* is used as a defense mechanism. As the child begins to form a *representation* (or image) of the mother as a separate person, the child is confronted with some painfully contradictory information. Mother is good, a rewarding source of pleasure and support, but she is also bad, a frustrating source of criticism, punishment, and saying no. It is too painful for the child to perceive the "good" mother as having bad qualities, so the image of mother is split in two. When mommy is being nice, the child's image is of the "good mother"; when she is being critical, the image is of the "bad mother." In other words, the mother is perceived as all good or all bad, depending on how she is acting, and the two images are not integrated. Similarly, the child splits his own self-image into the "good me" and the "bad me." When the child is being praised by the mother, he feels good and sees himself as all good. When he is being criticized, he feels bad and sees himself as all bad, rotten through and through.

The point here is that the child's self-image is unfinished. First, the child judges himself completely in terms of how the mother is responding to him: *He* is bad if *she* is critical of him. Second, the child engages in global, either-or thinking: I cannot be both good and bad at the same time; I am either all bad or all good. Thus the child does not have an integrated image of a whole self, consisting of good and bad aspects. Similarly, the child does not have an integrated image of the mother or, by extension, of people in general.

All children use splitting as a defense mechanism at a certain point in development, but it is crucial that the child develop *whole object representations* and *emotional object constancy.* With good enough mothering, the child eventually overcomes his defensive need to separate good and bad images of the mother. He will be able to unify them into an image of a *whole person.* He will also be able to develop whole object representation of his self-image. Then, when his mother is critical of him, he will not see her as all bad nor will he see himself as all bad. By extension, as an adult he will not completely devalue people just because they do something that displeases him nor will he idealize them, just because he feels attracted to them, and expect them to be perfect in his terms and to meet all his needs. Because he is able to see people as having both good and bad qualities, he will develop emotional object constancy, that is, he will be able to maintain a constant emotional reaction toward someone. Being able to separate a person's actions from the person, he will be able to continue to love the person, even if the person engages in some behavior that displeases him.

In addition to being able to maintain positive feelings toward a person, it is sometimes necessary to be able to maintain negative feelings toward someone. For instance, battered women are often unable to maintain negative feelings toward their husbands. As soon as the husband apologizes and acts repentant, the wife "forgets" her negative reaction to him.

The achievement of emotional object constancy and whole object representations happens during the final phase of the separation-individuation process. This phase of *consolidation of individuality* occurs at 24 to 36 months. The person who achieves these goals can maintain self-esteem even in the face of failing at something, can continue to like and prize others even if they do not live up to expectations, can maintain a "good self" image without needing to please others continually. The person will be able to continue to develop his or her true self, that is, to separate his or her own intentions, perceptions, and goals from others.

We have already mentioned some of the things that can go wrong during this sequence of separation-individuation. A person may fail to establish whole object representations and emotional object constancy. The individual may be unable to form stable, enduring relationships, constantly fluctuating from intense love and involvement to intense disappointment. He or she may be unable to establish a stable, cohesive identity in terms of an integrated set of goals, values, and self-perceptions. This may lead to unstable vocational pursuits—frequent job changes and inability to settle on and pursue some career. The individual may exhibit a pattern of impulsiveness as the result of these instabilities. Because the individual has not developed a stable inner self, he may need constant emotional stimulation from outside to feel alive and involved. Thus he may invest himself in casual or promiscuous sex, use of drugs, and gambling. Because he has not learned emotional object constancy, his emotional responses may be intense but momentary. He may be afflicted with intense feelings of hostility which come and go. If he does not completely establish a sense of self as a separate object—if he feels fused with the mother—he will continually search for the "ecstasy" of the fusion experience. He may seek intense, immediate personal encounters (such as promiscuous or casual sex) in which he can temporarily experience that sense of fusion, but then when he is alone, he will feel depressed, empty, and abandoned.

An individual who exhibits a pattern of impulsive behavior, anger and depression, intolerance of being alone, and identity problems is likely to fit the criteria for borderline personality disorder in DSM-III. While there is controversy over both the definition and cause of this condition (Gunderson, 1979), it is the disorder on which recent object relations theorists have focused. Borderline personality involves the failure to establish a healthy identity. Object relations theory does not discount the importance of the oedipal phase, but believes that disorders arising from that stage of development, that is, the neurotic disorders, are less severe because a stable identity has at least been established by then.

Object relations theory, as do most psychoanalytic theories, seems to postulate a *structural* model of personality development. As part of ego development, stable core images of the self and of others must be formed early. This constitutes the foundation of later personality development. If this fundamental development is flawed, if development is arrested at an early stage before a stable ego can be formed, then every bit of personality built on top of it, so to speak, will be unstable. As a result of this view, psychoanalysis holds that more severe disorders occur earlier and represent more fundamental flaws in the structure of the personality.

KOHUT AND SELF PSYCHOLOGY

Another newer psychoanalytic theory that postulates a structural model of personality development is *self psychology.* For Heinz Kohut (1971, 1977), the growth of a stable, cohesive, unique self is the basic issue in personality development. Other issues, such as how the parents handle toilet training during the anal stage or how they react to the child during the phallic stage, make sense only if we see them in terms of this growth, and psychopathology is seen as a result of the thwarting of the growth. In focusing on this issue, Kohut's self psychology is similar to Rogers's client-centered therapy, discussed in Chapter 5 (Kahn, 1985; Stolorow, 1976; Rogers & Sanford, 1984).

Self-objects are crucial in the person's development of a cohesive self. A self-object is another person who supports the individual's sense of self. The most basic mode of such support is through empathy. People need the support of self-objects throughout their lives, but self-objects are most important in early childhood. Kohut subscribes to the idea that in early childhood the infant does not have a concept of itself as a completely separate individual from its mother. The mother supports the child's developing self by helping the child with tension regulation, that is, by providing for the child's basic needs. More importantly, the mother provides psychological support. In order to develop a cohesive self the child must develop mature ambitions, ideals, and positive self-esteem. It must develop the ability to support itself in the face of frustration and to nurture and empathize with itself.

Initially these functions are provided by the mother, if the child is lucky enough to have good mothering. Early in childhood, before the child has completely separated itself from the mother, it will have grandiose and exhibitionistic needs. In order for the child to develop a sense of its own self-worth, the mother must engage at this stage in *empathic mirroring,* that is, the mother must be able to experience and to respond to the child's "look at me" behavior with appreciation and joyfulness. If the child rarely or never gets empathic mirroring, then it never has the kind of appreciative support it needs to grow. Any one of you who has been around small children will have experienced their "look-at-me" behavior. One must be "properly appreciative" in order for the child to develop a sense of its own self-worth.

At the same time, mothers (and other self-objects, such as fathers) are not always available to provide empathic mirroring. Mother may be busy, or father may be tired. There will be inevitable failures in empathic mirroring. However, if a self-object always provided empathic mirroring, the child would never learn to take over this function itself. In optimal development the periodic failures of empathic mirroring allow the child to learn to provide its own self-support. At times of the mother's unavailability the child can model the mother's empathic response and "talk" internally to itself as the mother would. Put in Kohut's terms, a "transmuting internalization" occurs in which the function of self-support provided by the mother gets internalized and built into the individual's own self-structure. Optimal empathic mirroring from the mother leads to a modulating and softening of the grandiose and exhibitionistic tendencies of the child, and the development of healthy, mature self-esteem, ambitions, and assertiveness.

Somewhat later the child develops *idealizing needs.* It is reinforcing to the self-image and self-esteem of the child to be soothed and nurtured by someone who is idealized. Thus idealizing the mother helps the child feel good about itself. If the mother is empathic, the child will eventually develop the ability to soothe itself. It will also internalize the ideals of the parents. Further, it will grow out of the need to idealize the mother and, by extension, other individuals as well. As the child develops the ability to soothe itself, it no longer needs to see the person who soothes it as perfect.

The achievement of a cohesive nuclear self is the end product of development. This cohesive self includes the functions of both healthy self-assertiveness and an internalized image of parental goals and ideals. Kohut appears to view the self as a structure and therefore talks about functions' becoming internalized as a part of that structure. Kahn (1985), in presenting Kohut's views, says that transmuting internalizations lead "in gradual increments, to self-structuralization" (p. 897). He talks about psychological difficulties in terms of damage or weakness to the structure: "Normal structuralization is impeded, and the self begins to lose its inherent cohesion, becoming fragmented" (p. 897).

It is unclear how literally the term *structure* is to be taken. We have already pointed out a similar structural idea in object relations theory, which holds that personality development will be flawed if the early structure of identity is weak and unstable. The concept of a structure is consistent with the psychoanalytic tendency to see personality in relatively fixed terms and to assume that a kind of "fixed core" of personality gets built in early childhood.

The child who does not achieve a cohesive nuclear self may develop a *narcissistic personality disorder.* This disorder is characterized by incessant needs to be the center of attention and to be loved and admired. The person also has fantasies of unlimited success. Some narcissistic people, who have not successfully internalized an idealized image of their parents, may continually search for merger with people whom they can idealize. The self-esteem of narcissistic individuals depends on the availability of people who can admire them or of people they can identify with and idealize. When they do not have these things or when they engage in behaviors that are less than admirable, they respond with shame and rage rather than with the more mature emotion of guilt. Kohut assumes that all these characteristics are behaviors and responses that are "normal" in childhood. However, the narcissistic adult remains in those infantile modes of being.

The Oedipus Complex and Anxiety

Kohut's (1984) version of the Oedipus complex is different from Freud's. Kohut assumes that the child enters the oedipal stage joyfully if it has had a healthy environment until then. For Kohut the primary issues of the oedipal stage are not sex and aggression, but affection and assertiveness. The young male child begins to explore his affectional capacity in relation to his mother and his assertive capacity in relation to his father. The converse happens for the female child.

At this age assertion and aggression are often not sufficiently differentiated for the child, and neither are sex and affection. As a result, if the parents handle the situation badly, assertion degenerates into aggression and affection degenerates into sexual wishes. Thus, according to Kohut, the Oedipus complex as Freud portrayed it is actually not universal, but a product of poor parental management. If the mother has conflicts over sexuality herself, she may be put off or threatened by her child's affectional moves. Her sense of threat may inadvertently sexualize these affectional moves for the child. Similarly, if the father is threatened by the child's assertion, then the situation may become a competitive, rivalrous one, leading to feelings of hostility toward the father.

For Kohut, castration anxiety is actually a metaphor for *disintegration anxiety.* Anxiety is fear of the self's disintegration or a sense of the self as disintegrating, in contrast to Freud's view of anxiety as a signal that the repressed is about to break through into consciousness. Kohut's view of penis envy should also be mentioned. For Kohut, penis envy in the girl is a result of failure on the part of parents and culture to prize the uniqueness and individuality of the female. It is a metaphor for the girl's diminished sense of self due to her parents' and society's masculine bias.

Even if as children people receive adequate empathic responding from their parents, they continue to need self-objects throughout their lives. One of Kohut's interesting ideas is that anyone who supports a person's self-development can function as a self-object. For instance, you may find one theorist in this book that you really resonate with. That theorist will be a self-object for you. As you read about that theorist and find your developing ideas mirrored and supported in the theorist's work, that mirroring and support will further the development of your own ideas. Rock stars are often self-objects for teenagers, and for young adults it is often a respected teacher or supervisor. Of course, we all want self-objects in our romantic relationships—someone who "prizes" us and likes us for who we are.

PSYCHOTHERAPY

Kohut and Object Relations Theory

There are several similarities between object relations approaches to therapy and Kohut's approach. First, all the approaches stress the importance of therapist empathy. While empathy was always mentioned as an important quality in psychoanalysis, it is particularly emphasized by these newer approaches. In classical psychoanalysis the importance of empathy lay primarily in the ability of the therapist to tune into the client. In the newer approaches empathy itself is a major vehicle of therapeutic change. This is particularly true for Kohut, who postulates a failure of empathy in early childhood as the cause of pathology. The provision of empathy by the therapist actively institutes a condition for maturation and growth of the self.

Second, all the approaches place less emphasis on insight than classical psychoanalytic therapy. This does not mean that insight is not important. However, a greater premium is placed on *direct experiential learning* in therapy. Masterson (1981) calls therapy an "experiment in individuation." Change occurs through the experiential reliving of early childhood conflicts in therapy, and through that reliving the maturational process is freed for the individual to develop a more differentiated and cohesive self. He says the goal of therapy with borderline clients is "the reliving of old experiences by the more mature psyche, . . . thereby freeing the self-representation to separate from the object representation" (1981, p. 231). It is true that classical analytic theory also requires the emotional reexperiencing of infantile conflicts. However, the purpose in classical analytic theory is to acquire insight; emotionally reexperienced insights are seen as more therapeutic. For Kohut and object relations theory, the emotional reliving leads to an active, corrective, learning process in therapy. According to Kohut, when pathological early childhood experiences are revived and reworked in therapy, the therapist can provide the empathic conditions missing in childhood (including the occasional failures of empathy necessary for transmuting internalizations to occur). In these circumstances "The accretion of psychological structure that optimally should have occurred during normal development is now belatedly occurring in the therapeutic milieu" (Kahn, 1985, p. 900).

Guntrip (1973) has perhaps most forcefully expressed the idea that through the experiential quality of the therapy relationship growth can be achieved.

> I cannot think of psychotherapy as a technique but only as the provision of the possibility of a genuine, reliable, understanding, and respecting, caring personal rela-

> tionship in which a human being whose true self has been crushed by the manipulative techniques of those who only wanted to make him "not a nuisance" to them, can begin at last to feel his own true feelings, and think his own spontaneous thoughts, and find himself to be real. (p. 182)

Third, all these therapeutic approaches advocate the selective use of therapist self-disclosure. For instance, the therapist may reveal her feelings of ignorance or clumsiness in attempting to understand the client. Or the analyst may reveal her own occasional needs to use the client as a self-object (Wolf, 1983). For Kohut, a parent may have been unable to provide empathy because his or her own self-development was incomplete. As a result, he or she may have been more interested in gaining emotional support from the child, rather than in giving it to the child. Self-disclosure by the therapist may help the client realize that the therapist is not there to use the client for her own needs. This may help the client to overcome feelings of resistance and defensiveness and therefore, to grow: "Since in essence, resistance is nothing but fear of being traumatically injured again, the decisive event of its analysis is the moment when the analysand has gained courage from these self-revelations of the analyst to know that the analyst does not need to feed on the patient to achieve cohesion and harmony" (Wolf, 1983, pp. 500–501). Guntrip clearly believes that the therapist should be a real person in therapy, at least more so than in traditional analytic therapy. In a somewhat related fashion, Masterson (1981) will abandon therapeutic neutrality to confront clients with the destructiveness of some of their behavior.

Fourth, object relations and Kohut approach the transference relationship differently than classical psychoanalysis. For Freud, transference relationships were ultimately patterns of resistance. For Kohut, they may involve resistance, but they are also expressions of the self's needs from early childhood. Needs for mirroring and for idealizing will be expressed in therapy. In the mirroring transference the infantile, grandiose self demands continual empathic approval and attention from the therapist. In the idealizing transference the client wishes for the therapist to be the all-powerful person who can fix all the client's problems. While it is acceptable for the analyst to provide some mirroring, it is actually through failures in empathy that these two transferences get resolved. Through failures in empathy the patient is reminded of the unempathic parent. These experiences are then relived, but because they are relived in the context of an overall empathic relationship, growth of the self occurs.

Finally, the goal of both object relations therapy and Kohut's therapy is similar. As we have seen, the goal is the development of the self. For object relations theory this includes separation of the self from the mother and forming differentiated and integrated representations of both the self and of others. According to Masterson, this manifests itself in increased client autonomy and the ability of the client to take responsibility for himself and manage his life in a constructive manner. In addition it should lead to a capacity for creativity, intimacy, and flexibility. For Kohut the goal of therapy is the development of a cohesive self that has realistic ambitions and goals, is able to be creative, intimate, and flexible, and is able to make its own judgments and maintain its own self-esteem.

Brief Forms of Psychoanalytic Psychotherapy

We now turn our attention to another recent development in psychoanalysis, that of relatively brief forms of psychotherapy. Among the problems associated with classical psychoanalytic therapy are its lengthiness and its expense. This is also true to some extent of object relational treatment of borderline personality and of Kohut's treatment of narcissistic personality. In contrast, Luborsky (1984) has outlined his *supportive-expressive* approach to psychoanalytic psychotherapy. This relatively brief form of psychotherapy can be practiced on an open-ended basis or on a time-limited basis, in which case it usually lasts less than 25 sessions. Strupp and Binder (1984) have developed a time-limited dynamic therapy that lasts 25 to 30 sessions. There are other approaches to brief psychoanalytic psychotherapy (reviewed in Strupp and Binder), but we will focus on these two. Among the virtues of these approaches is that both have been presented as psychotherapy treatment manuals. This relatively recent innovation in writing about psychotherapy developed because of the need to standardize treatment for purposes of doing research on psychotherapy. The treatment manuals are somewhat more concrete and specific in describing treatment than many other writings on psychoanalysis.

Strupp and Binder's time-limited dynamic therapy is based on the assumption that

> earlier difficulties with significant others have given rise to patterns of interpersonal relatedness that originally served a self-protective function but are now anachronistic, self-defeating, and maladaptive. Central to these problems are deficiencies in self-esteem, inability to form satisfying interpersonal relationships that gratify the person's needs for closeness, and interferences with autonomous adult functioning. (Strupp & Binder, 1984, pp. xiii–xiv)

In childhood the person experiences a disturbed pattern of interpersonal relationships, from which he develops organizing themes that form a rigid, habitual way of construing and acting in current relationships. These patterns are hidden from the self because of "the ubiquitous human tendency to hide from oneself painful experiences and their aftermath" (p. 32). The client unconsciously believes these patterns will bring him security and nurturance in current relationships. Relationships are defensively distorted in order to protect the self as the person strives to achieve these primitive, unconscious forms of intimacy. Time-limited dynamic therapy attempts to identify and concentrate on these "focal issues."

Strupp and Binder believe that these central relationship issues will manifest themselves in the therapeutic relationship and that the reexperiencing of them in the transference relationship will be therapeutic. The therapist attempts to help the client become aware of the symbolic meanings of his or her behavior, but this needs to be done when "an appropriate affective context exists" (1984, p. 136). At the same time intellectual reconstruction of the past is deemphasized. In fact, Strupp and Binder assume that it is impossible to really recover the past. The most important quality of a therapeutic relationship is that it is a human one. Learning occurs not through acquisition of abstract knowledge, but "rather it is the result of a human *experience* in which he or she feels understood and in which this understanding is given new meanings" (1984, p. 45). While it is true that transference involves bringing past relationships into the current, therapeutic relationship, Strupp and Binder assume that the client's feelings toward the therapist also include some real aspects of the here and now relationship. The therapist is to use her own feelings as signals of how the client is attempting to structure their relationship. Empathic listening is important, and the therapist is encouraged to engage in honest self-disclosure, if necessary and appropriate.

Luborsky's supportive-expressive psychoanalytically oriented therapy is similar. It is based on the assumption that a *core conflictual relationship theme* (CCRT) is at the center of a person's problems. This relationship theme developed from early childhood experiences, but the client is unaware of it and its relation to childhood experiences. Therapy is oriented toward increasing the client's awareness of the theme. It is assumed that the client will have better control over behavior if he knows more about what he is doing at the unconscious level. This knowledge is acquired through reliving childhood experiences. Interpretations must be done only with strands of the CCRT that are close to awareness and not heavily defended against in the therapeutic moment. As we have said, knowledge alone does not change previously unconscious wishes and needs. However, it does lead to an increased ability to master and control them consciously. Luborsky says that the change "may be considered to have enabled the person to function at a higher level of organization" (1984, p. 21). The transference relationship is important in that the CCRT will probably be lived out and enacted in relationship to the therapist. A supportive, empathic relationship is considered crucial, and Luborsky speculates that compared to the acquisition of insight, the relationship may be the more potent therapeutic factor.

Luborsky's supportive-expressive psychotherapy begins with a "socialization interview" in which the client is told how psychotherapy proceeds, what is expected of the client, and what the therapist will do. In the initial, supportive phase of therapy the therapist attempts to listen nonjudgmentally, demonstrate acceptance and understanding, support defenses and activities that bolster positive functioning, and encourage a "we" feeling. In the expressive phase the therapist is more active: listening, responding, and listening further.

In general, the brief forms of psychoanalytic psychotherapy are appropriate for relatively "more healthy" clients, that is, clients who may have some significant symptoms, but whose functioning in general is relatively adequate.

Summing Up Recent Approaches

As we have pointed out, object relations therapy, Kohut's therapy, and the brief therapies have some common themes. We want to review these briefly. First, they place greater emphasis on the curative power of the therapeutic relationship itself than did classical psychoanalysis. Second, they place less emphasis on change through insight and reconstruction of the past and more emphasis on change through reliving significant early childhood relationship issues in the context of therapy. Third, they allow the therapist to be more flexible than in classical analysis and encourage the therapist to provide empathy as a vehicle of therapeutic change and to use self-disclosure, when therapeutically appropriate, to help overcome resistance.

EVALUATION OF PSYCHOANALYTIC APPROACHES

In the following sections we will offer a number of critical evaluations of the psychoanalytic approaches discussed in this and the previous chapter. We will look at the effectiveness of psychoanalysis as a psychotherapy and consider some aspects of psychoanalytic views of personality and psychopathology. We will also look at three criticisms launched at aspects of Freudian psychoanalysis from within psychoanalysis itself. These criticisms are Bettelheim's (1982) view that Freud has been mistranslated into English, Spence's (1982) view that Freud's "archeological" model of therapy, in which it is presumed that the "truth" about one's past is uncovered, is inadequate, and Masson's (1984) claim that Freud was unjustified in abandoning his seduction theory of neurosis.

Effectiveness of Psychotherapy

Because classical psychoanalysis, in which the client is seen three to five times a week for several years, is the most thorough and intensive of all approaches to psychotherapy, some have concluded that it is therefore the most effective. Fine (1973), for instance, says, "Psychoanalysis was the first psychotherapeutic system that had any value. Currently it is the most complete, the most highly developed, the one with the greatest theoretical sophistication and *by far the most effective*" (p. 30, italics ours). Arlow (1984) claims that "when properly applied to the appropriate condition, psychoanalysis remains the most effective mode of therapy yet devised" (p. 37). However, not all analysts are so confident of the superiority of intensive, long-term psychoanalysis, though they may generally have a psychoanalytic view of psychological problems. Among these was Freud himself, who in one of his last essays, entitled "Analysis: Terminable and Interminable" (1937/1963), was less than sanguine on the effectiveness of psychoanalysis as a therapy, wondering if it was more useful as a research technique.

How effective is long-term, intensive psychoanalysis? The answer is that there is no evidence that it is more effective than other therapies, including short-term psychoanalytic approaches. Erwin (1980) even argues there is no evidence for its effectiveness at all. A study of psychoanalysis at the Menninger Clinic (Kernberg et al., 1972) involved 42 clients over a 20-year period. Some were seen in regular analysis (an average of 835 hours), others in a shorter version of psychoanalytic therapy (average 289 hours). For the most part there was no evidence that clients who had regular analysis improved more than clients who had short-term analysis, though there were some clients for whom it did work better.

The fact there is no evidence currently available to support the claim that long-term, intensive psychoanalysis is more effective than other approaches does not mean that with subtler measures such evidence may not be found in the future. However, it must be pointed out that just because a therapy is long and involved does not mean it works better. Much of the historical exploration that occurs in psychoanalysis may be of theoretical use to the analyst who is interested in developing theories of personality, but it may be no more useful in helping a client change than a history of how a car was originally built and driven for years would help an auto mechanic fix something that is wrong now. Such information may simply not be relevant to the change process.

In this respect it could be that long-term psychoanalysis takes so long because it is inefficient at focusing on what is needed for change. That this may be so is illustrated by the recent brief psychoanalytic approaches, which work not by endless exploration of the past, but by a much more focused exploration of certain themes.

While there appears to be no evidence for the effectiveness of long-term psychoanalysis, there is evidence that psychoanalytically oriented psychotherapy is effective. From the results of their "meta-analysis" of many studies of psychotherapy, Smith, Glass, and Miller (1980) calculate an average "effect size" of 0.69 for psychoanalysis. They also find an effect size of 0.89 for dynamic-eclectic therapies, which are therapies based on dynamic principles, but more eclectic in techniques than psychoanalysis. Basically, the larger the effect size, the more substantial the amount of change. The highest effect sizes calculated have been around 1.0 for some of the behavior and cognitive therapeutic techniques. (We will explain an effect size in more detail in Chapter 10.) To date no therapy has demonstrated an effect size sufficiently higher than the others to conclude that it is superior. The effect sizes mentioned for psychoanalytic approaches are in the average range, meaning these approaches are indeed effective and about as effective as other approaches.

In a study considered by many to be one of the best empirical examinations of psychotherapy, Sloane and his colleagues (1975) compared four months of psychoanalytically oriented psychotherapy to four months of behavior therapy. It was concluded that psychoanalytically oriented therapy and behavior therapy were approximately equal in effectiveness, and clients in both exhibited significantly more positive change than a group of untreated control patients. (We will review this study in more detail in Chapter 10.) Finally, several other studies have suggested that short-term psychoanalytically oriented therapy is effective (see Luborsky, Singer & Luborsky, 1975).

Some psychoanalytic proponents claim that their therapy is superior because it cures the underlying disorder, while other approaches are superficial. This argument rests on the assumption that psychological problems are grounded in deep early childhood experiences that must be worked through in order for change to occur. However, evidence (see Nicholson & Berman, 1983) suggests that many so-called superficial treatments are quite effective and that their positive benefits persist long after therapy has been terminated. Long-term, in-depth therapy may have other positive benefits *in addition to* symptom removal, but therapy can remove symptoms without deep exploration.

There may be some disorders for which an in-depth approach is necessary. As yet there is relatively little evidence on the effectiveness of object relations therapy with borderline personality disorders or Kohut's therapy with narcissistic personality disorders. Proponents of these approaches claim that an in-depth method is necessary for these ingrained "characterological" or personality disorders. It is possible that research will sustain this claim.

Aside from the question of its effectiveness, is there any evidence for some of the key components of psychoanalytic therapy? Orlinsky and Howard (1986) summarize several studies and conclude that there is evidence that both interpretation and a focus on the patient's transference reactions are frequently, but not consistently, associated with therapy's being effective. Luborsky, Crits-Christoph, and Mellon (1986) have also studied transference reactions in therapy and find evidence to support several of Freud's formulations. For instance, a client's core conflictual relationship problems were found to manifest themselves in a variety of relationships in the client's life and in relationship to the therapist. There was also evidence that this relationship theme could be found in the client's memories of early childhood relationships.

Personality and Psychopathology

We now turn to a brief review and evaluation of psychoanalytic perspectives on personality and psychopathology. The concept of the unconscious is central to psychoanalytic formulations. Evidence for the existence of some kind of unconscious now seems convincing (it is reviewed in Chapter 11). However, psychoanalysis assumes that some things are unconscious because they have been repressed. Repression has not been extensively researched, partly because of the difficulty of studying things like repression in the laboratory (see Feshbach & Weiner, 1986). At the same time the possibility of something like repression is compatible with several modern cognitive versions of the unconscious (Shevrin & Dickman, 1980; Bowers & Meichenbaum, 1984). In studies in which words are presented to subjects at a very rapid exposure speed and the subjects are asked to report what they saw, subjects do not recognize certain emotionally charged words as rapidly as neutral words, even though the words can be shown to have been perceived unconsciously (Kostandov & Arzumanov, 1977; Shevrin, 1973).

For psychoanalysis the content of the unconscious includes material from early childhood. For instance, according to object relations theory, most people still harbor unconscious wishes to be fused with mother. Silverman and Weinberger (1985) report on research in which the sentence "Mommy and I are one" was presented to subjects at a speed so rapid that it was subliminal (not producing a sensation that is consciously perceived). In a series of studies this subliminal perception was found to reduce psychopathological symptoms and to improve performance on mathematics tests. In one study (Palmatier & Bornstein, 1980) smokers receiving behavior therapy were broken into two groups. One group received several subliminal exposures to the "Mommy and I are one" message in addition to the behavior therapy. This group had a much higher rate of maintaining abstinence from smoking than the group that did not receive this message. Similar results have been found with treatment of a variety of other disorders (see Silverman & Weinberger, 1985, p. 1301).

Another important idea of object relations theory is that the developing individual must separate and individuate from the mother. If this does not happen, the individual will not develop stable boundaries between herself and others. Blatt and Wild (1976) review studies suggesting that individuals with less well-developed boundary concepts exhibit more psychopathology. For instance, Blatt and Ritzler (1974) measured boundary disturbances with the Rorschach ink blot test. They found that schizophrenics with more severe disturbances exhibited greater difficulties in reality testing.

We have seen that many psychoanalytic thinkers consider childhood events to be the primary determinant of the most important aspects of adult functioning. Adelson and Doehrman (1980) say,

> [Psychoanalysis] holds that in truly important moments of one's life one is unwittingly held captive by the past. Whom we marry and how the marriage fares; the work we

> choose and how well we do it . . . all these and other vital events of the life course can be understood in depth only after we have a sufficient understanding of the personal past. (p. 100)

Writing on marriage, Meissner (1978) says,

> For any given husband and wife, the marital dyadic relationship is . . . inextricably bound to the parent-child relationship in their families of origin. . . . The capacity to successfully function as a spouse is largely a consequence of the spouse's childhood relationships to his own parents. . . . the relative success that the marital partners experience and the manner in which these developmental tasks are approached and accomplished are determined to a large extent by the residues of internalized objects and the organization of introjects which form the core of the sense of self. . . . (pp. 26–27, italics omitted)

There are two important points to this. First, both these quotes state that major aspects of adult functioning are largely determined by childhood events. Second, though neither of these quotes says so explicitly, many psychoanalytic theorists locate the determinants of adult functioning not merely in childhood, but in early childhood. For instance, object relations theorists presume that the process of introjection, which is thought to form the core of the sense of self, occurs within the first two to three years of life. They tend to explain key events in adult life in terms of events presumed to have happened in this time period. Advocates of Kohut's self psychology similarly focus on very early childhood. And for Freud, personality was largely formed by age 5 or 6.

Many theorists agree that adult personality is shaped in many respects by childhood events (for instance, Carl Rogers and Aaron Beck), but not all, including many analytically oriented theorists, agree that early childhood is of much greater importance than the rest of childhood, adolescence, or adulthood in forming personality and causing psychopathology. Many would argue that present events, such as stress, play a major role in creating adult psychopathology (see Bloom, 1984). They see Freud, self psychologists, and object relations theorists as overemphasizing early childhood. They argue, as do Chess and Thomas (1984), that behavior is determined by many factors and to place such a heavy emphasis on one developmental period is to oversimplify a complex process.

Can we resolve this issue? Are our personalities, adult behaviors and interactions, and psychopathological symptoms primarily determined in early childhood? If so, then factors in adulthood will play a relatively secondary role in causing psychopathology. In addition, there should be a good deal of stability and continuity from personality in childhood to personality in adulthood. Also, we would expect that aspects of personality formed in early childhood should be largely unmodifiable by events later on in life. Thus we might expect that early events, such as loss of a parent, abuse, other trauma, or poor parenting will have a direct impact on how the child will be as an adult.

In order to understand the issue we need to sketch two differing views of development. The one we are currently considering holds that certain times in childhood are critical periods in development. The first three years of life, and more specifically the rapprochement crisis (age 14 to 24 months), are seen as crucial in determining a separate and individuated self. Without such a separated and individuated self the person will have difficulties in adult relationships, regardless of the other persons involved. For instance, Wachtel (1984) describes a man who dreamed of being swallowed by his girl friend. Messer and Winokur (1984) suggest that this problem may be a fundamental ego boundary problem from early childhood, but Wachtel thinks that it more represents current problems with that particular girl friend.

Theorists that hold to these or similar views believe that certain intrapsychic structures (such as the ego or the self) are formed during these first three to five years of life. For Freud, the oedipal period (age 4 to 6) was critical, and personality was largely determined by the end of that period. Once the structures are formed defectively, later experiences will not modify them (except for psychotherapy). Furthermore, they see these structures as of fundamental importance in determining adult functioning in key areas.

A different view of the relationship of childhood to adulthood is held by psychoanalytic theorists like Bowlby (Hamilton, 1985) and Wachtel (1984), as well as by some nonanalytic theorists (for instance, Kagan, 1984). These theorists see development as a continuous process. Early childhood events may predispose the individual to develop in certain ways or to have certain types of problems as an adult, but these events do not irrevocably fix central aspects of the personality so that later events have only secondary importance in development. Instead, later events can undo directions in development established earlier, or they may interact in complex ways with earlier events to turn development in new directions. Furthermore, it is a continuous "envelope of events" (Kagan, 1984) that is important in creating stable patterns of behavior.

To give an example of this, some object relations theorists believe that what happens around 18 months is crucial for determining separation and individuation in a person. If the child at that age has an overprotective, smothering mother, this stage will not be successfully negotiated, and the child will be left with a fundamental impairment in his ability to tell himself apart from others. Even if the mother suddenly became a supporter of separation-individuation when the child was 3 or 4, it would be too late. In contrast, the envelope of events view holds that if a child has poor parenting until age 3, but good parenting thereafter, the damage from early childhood can largely be undone. Further, this view holds that to create an adult with separation-individuation problems you would most likely need a continuous envelope of dysfunctional parenting, not merely through the first three years of life, but perhaps even through adolescence. And even then the problem might not become manifest unless the person got involved with someone who is "smothering and engulfing."

This latter view would see early childhood experience as creating a predisposition to having certain kinds of adult problems, or as creating an increased probability of having problems as an adult. However, it would not see early childhood as primarily determining how we are as adults.

The issue is one of proportion. In both cases early childhood is seen as important; the question is how important. Much research suggests that there are significant factors in adulthood that seem to determine many kinds of psychopathology. For instance, Brown and Harris (1978) attribute 80 to 90 percent of the causes of depression in women to "provoking agents" such as loss, poor housing, and family alcoholism. Also, vulnerability to depression is greatly enhanced by the lack of a good social support network. This is not to say that childhood events are of no importance. Brown, Harris, and Bifulco (1986) found that death of a parent enhanced vulnerability to depression in these women. The stresses in adulthood appear to play a significant role, although a vulnerability may be created by a childhood event. As another example, Bloom (1984) cites research suggesting that divorce increases the likelihood of psychopathology in adult males ninefold.

There are many case histories that suggest that how the parents relate to the child plays an important role in determining psychopathology in adulthood. Masterson (1985) gives several cases to support his view that parents' inability to allow their children to separate and individuate results in personality problems in adolescence or adulthood. However, such case histories usually do not demonstrate that the *key* damage was done during these critical periods. For instance, in Masterson's cases most of the examples of bad parenting recalled by the client come from periods considerably later in childhood. It is only an assumption that the bad parenting was also present when the client was 18 months old and that it was then that the key damage was done. An alternative possibility is that it was the continuous presence of bad parenting throughout childhood and adolescence that created the client's difficulties.

To what extent is there stability and continuity between childhood behavior and adulthood? This is a complex issue, but there is some relevant research. We will not review the research itself, but cite conclusions drawn from it. Maccoby (1980) concludes "It is now widely accepted that developmental change is the rule rather than the exception. . . . The characteristics a child has at a given age will not be the same characteristics the same child has later on, even though the two may be connected" (p. 29, as quoted in Singer, 1984). Similarly, several researchers have looked at the issue of whether pathology in childhood portends pathology in adulthood. Their conclusion is that neurotic and adjustment disorders do not portend psychological difficulty in adulthood, whether or not the child has had therapy (Eme, 1979; Cass & Thomas, 1979; Dohrenwend et al., 1980). For instance, Dohrenwend and his colleagues conclude that "most neurotic children become normal adults" (p. 23). However, some disorders are continuous from childhood to adulthood, especially the more severe ones, such as schizophrenia. To quote Cicchetti and Schneider-Rosen (1986), in regards to depression,

> Maladaptation at one period of development may have very different consequences for depression from that at another developmental period. The resulting causal network will be very complex. Early incompetence will have a variety of effects, some of which will tend to perpetuate incompetence, others of which may constitute a vulnerability to depression, and still others of which may potentiate later adaptation. (p. 92)

Is development *fixed* in early childhood? Chess and Thomas (1984) followed 133 infants into adulthood. Some developed behavior disorders; some did not. Their conclusions are as follows.

> So many person and situation variables were influential in the development of a behavior disorder that the search for simple formulas and categorizations was totally unrealistic. (p. 216)

> We . . . cannot look to any single age period where life events are all-important determinants of future development. (p. 239)
>
> Striking has been the capacity for flexibility, adaptability and mastery in the face of all kinds of adverse and stressful life experiences. (p. 293)
>
> We now have to give up the illusion that once we know the young child's psychological history, subsequent personality and functioning are *ipso facto* predictable. On the other hand, we now have a much more optimistic vision of human development. The emotionally traumatized child is not doomed, the parents' early mistakes are not irrevocable. . . . (Chess, 1979, p. 112)

Similarly, Livson and Peskin (1980) conclude "neither past nor present, neither childhood nor adolescence, nor any era of adulthood is fixed in its effects or of higher priority in its contribution" (p. 84). This research suggests that while early childhood is one important time of life, it is not necessarily more important than any other. It also suggests that earlier effects on personality can be modified and even undone by later events.

Other research demonstrates that early childhood *can* be important. Bowlby (Hamilton, 1985) holds that the attachment between mother and infant is important in influencing later development and that insecurely attached infants are more likely to have behavior problems later on. However, Bowlby does not believe that insecure attachment *determines* later behavioral difficulty; rather it makes it *more probable.*

Similarly, in one study of girls raised in institutions, Rutter (1986) found that "adverse experiences in childhood were associated with substantially worse psychosocial outcomes in early adult life" (p. 8). However, Rutter also found that "marriage to . . . a well-functioning man who provided a supportive relationship was associated with a marked improvement in functioning. Good experiences in adult life can lead to important psychosocial gains" (p. 8). To quote Cicchetti and Schneider-Rosen (1986), "The failure to achieve adaptation at one period makes adaptation that much more difficult at the next . . . but early problems or deviations in the successful resolution of a developmental task may be countered by major changes in the child's experience that could result in the successful negotiation of subsequent developmental tasks" (pp. 87–88).

We mentioned previously that loss of a parent has been found to predispose the child to depression in adulthood. However, Rutter (1986) suggests that the long-term effects of a death on a child "probably stem as much from factors consequent upon the death as from the death itself. These other factors include such hazards as the break-up of the home, frequent changes of caretaker, changes in family roles, financial and material disadvantage, the effects of bereavement on the surviving parent, and the arrival of a stepparent." Furthermore, Garmazy (1986) suggests that parent loss will have a more significant effect on a child between the ages of 5 and 10 than on a younger child. Thus, while loss of a parent can have a significant effect on later development, the period of greatest vulnerability may be later rather than earlier childhood. Furthermore, the loss may affect development because it creates a continuous envelope of adverse experiences, such as family and financial instability.

Some research (Garmazy, 1986; Weintraub, Winters, & Neale, 1986) has found that depression in the parent affects the development of the child. More significantly, there are now a number of experts who believe that abuse in childhood, by parents or others, is often a precursor of adult psychopathology. Abuse seems to be highly associated with dissociative disorders, such as multiple personality (Summit, 1987). It also seems to be a precursor of depression, anxiety, and borderline personality disorder in many (Briere & Runtz, in press). Abuse significantly increases the probability of later disorder. Briere (1987) estimates that 40 percent of those abused in childhood will develop psychopathological symptoms in adulthood, while another 40 percent will develop transitory problems. Only 20 percent appear to escape relatively unscathed. Furthermore, many of the symptoms associated with having been abused as a child are compatible with object relations theory, such as splitting.

This brief review does not do full justice to the range and complexity of the issue of the relationship between childhood experiences and adult psychopathology. However, there is a good deal of convergence among findings. First, early childhood experiences can have a significantly negative impact on development. Second, an exposure to negative circumstances for a continuous period of time has a lasting impact, although this does not disprove the idea of critical periods for aspects of personality development. Third, early childhood is not necessarily the only or the most important period for the development of pathology, and in some cases later periods of childhood may be more important. Fourth, even though bad early childhood experiences may significantly bias development in a negative direction, later events can change this. Fifth, the relationship between adult dysfunction and childhood is complex.

Other criticisms of certain psychoanalytic views of early childhood have been made by some psychoanalytically oriented thinkers. Eagle (1984), for instance, points out that Margaret Mahler's view that the infant in the first month of life is autistic and unresponsive to the external world does not fit with research about infants. Infants from birth are highly responsive to the external world. Similarly, Eagle criticizes some psychoanalytic theorists for "adultomorphizing" children, that is, seeing children in terms of adult processes. For instance, adult narcissists are totally wrapped up in themselves. They are not concerned with others, and they want everyone to adore them. The same behavior is attributed to children, but is seen as normal then. But despite superficial similarities it is unlikely that the child's preoccupation with its own activities and its demands for attention have much in common with an adult male's desire for unlimited success or to be loved by all the attractive women in the world. In fact, object relations theorists and Kohut see children as normally being what would be pathological in adults. Children cannot tell themselves apart from another person and believe themselves and the other person to be the same. They live in a state of "primary hallucinatory disorientation" according to Margaret Mahler. When the mother is mean to a child, it believes it is actually hurting itself, and so on. If an adult presented these "symptoms," the adult would be seen as psychotic. Other psychoanalytic theorists, such as Bowlby (Hamilton, 1985) and Eagle (1984), believe that such negative views of children as "defective adults" are unwarranted.

Similarly, some object relations theorists talk as if the infant *believes* that it and the mother are "one." It may be that an infant doesn't think very much about the issue of whether it and its mother are separate. If it has no concept of "separate," then it has no concept of "being one with mother" either. In other words, although it may not have ideas of "me" and "mom" as separate entities, that does not mean it has the idea that "me and mom are one" either. To have that idea the infant would already have to have concepts of objects as separate and distinct and then somehow believe that while objects are separate and distinct, it and the mother are the same object. Again, seeing the infant as believing it is fused with the mother is often based on adults who seem to act as if they are seeking merger and fusion with a loved one. But as an adult my wanting merger or fusion with another adult can be something I seek only because I recognize (and perhaps dislike) my separateness. Splitting is still another idea Eagle labels as "adultomorphizing" when we attribute it to infants.

Finally, Kohut (1984) has argued that Freud's Oedipus complex is not universal. Instead, it only occurs when the parents handle things badly around age 5. The idea that the Oedipus complex is a reaction to poor parenting has been echoed by some research in developmental psychology (Brophy, 1977).

From our perspective some of the above problems appear to lie in the belief in a unitary character structure or ego that is fixed at an early age rather than in a multifaceted character structure, some parts of which are fixed, other parts of which are not. As we shall see when we talk about the trait-situation controversy in Chapter 8, behavior is characterized by a great deal of variability from one situation to a different situation (Mischel & Peake, 1982). If people have a relatively fixed character structure that determines behavior, why do they frequently act dominant in some situations but submissive in others or shy in some situations but outgoing in others, as seems to be the case? It may be more fruitful to see development in terms of a large number of different "strands" in behavior. Certain strands may remain quite immature and fixated in early childhood. These might be split off from consciousness. Other strands may change and mature as the person grows. Following Eagle's view of the self, the immature, fixated parts may be integrated to form a self-structure in different ways at different times during a person's life. At particularly crucial times the immature, fixated strands may become operative and play a disruptive role in behavior. For instance, repressed, split off feelings toward the mother may show up only when a person becomes intimate with another person. Other strands may have matured quite adequately, so that the person has mature relations to people in other respects.

Bettelheim and the Mistranslation of Freud

Bruno Bettelheim, himself an eminent psychoanalyst, has recently argued, "The English translations of Freud's writings are seriously defective in important respects and have led to erroneous conclusions, not only about Freud the man but also about psychoanalysis" (Bettelheim, 1982, p. vii). Bettelheim covers a number of what he sees as mistranslations, but we will focus on one set, the German words that became "ego" and "id" in English. Bettelheim points out that the terms Freud actually uses in German are "I" and "it" and that Freud really meant to talk about the "I" and the "it" rather than the "ego" and "id." Furthermore that is how they are translated into all other languages besides English. Bettelheim quotes Freud as saying, "You will probably object to our having chosen simple pronouns to denote our two institutions, or provinces, of the soul, instead of introducing for them sonorous Greek names. In psychoanalysis, however, we like to keep in contact with the popular mode of thinking . . ." (p. 60). He argues that Freud's English translators were attempting to make Freud sound more "scientific" and that is why they used the Latin equivalents *ego* and *id.* Those who disagree with Bettelheim point out that Freud had a fluent knowledge of English and approved the translation, which was done by a friend. Bettelheim's rejoinder is that Freud was once quoted as saying that he preferred having a good friend to a good translator.

Using Bettelheim's translations, the phrase "Where id was shall ego be" becomes "Where it was shall I be." According to Bettelheim this is precisely what Freud meant to convey about the process of therapy and what his clients were contending with. A client comes in experiencing his actions as not "of himself,": "It made me do it." Through therapy these disowned actions become part of himself, part of the "I." Such a translation puts Freud's thinking much closer to both object relations and Kohut's self psychology on the one hand and to humanistic theories, such as gestalt and client-centered therapy on the other. Therapy becomes a matter of bringing disowned parts into the self so that "I" can control and be responsible for the individual's actions. It seems more "human" and less mechanistic than viewing the personality in terms of ego and id. Bettelheim contends that the English translation of Freud dehumanizes his views.

Spence and Historical Truth Versus Narrative Truth

Freud likened his therapy to archeology. The therapist is like the archeologist who searches for ancient relics of lost civilizations, digging down through layer upon layer of ever more ancient civilizations until he reaches the bottom. The therapist engages in a kind of psychic excavation of the personality, seeking buried "truths" from the deepest layer of early childhood.

Based on this archeological model, analysts have believed that the memories clients ultimately uncover (often after years of analysis) represent *historical truth,* that is, they are actual memories of what really happened to the client or what the client really fantasized about as a child. Recently Spence (1982), himself a psychoanalyst, has challenged this view. We cannot reproduce all of Spence's argument here, but basically it is that psychoanalysis cannot be said to be uncovering historical truth. What is reported in therapy is often a verbal account of pictorial data, and Spence discusses how one can never completely reproduce the experience of seeing a picture in words. Thus all verbal reports of childhood are by their nature merely maps or translations of pictorial data. The implication of this is that all verbal reports are *interpretations.* That is, in focusing on the remembered pictorial data from my childhood I am interpreting it when I put it into words, just as I would be if I reported my observation of a crime scene to the police.

Most of us are aware by now that what we see in any particular scene is partially determined by how we are looking at it. Different observers can see the same scene quite differently and give differing accounts of it. In psychoanalysis a crucial change is the acquiring of a different *interpretive scheme.* Most of us do not have a view of the world that includes constructs such as "Children sexually lust after their parents." We *learn* in psychoanalysis to see the world through such an interpretive framework, and that interpretive framework is then brought to bear on our own memories. Do we actually "recover" memories of having lusted after our parents? Or, do we learn to see our behavior and interpret our feelings as meaning that we lusted after our parents?

Spence points out that this is simply undecidable. There is no way to verify empirically the "truth" or "falsity" of these memories. Among other things, Spence cites recent research and theory on memory that suggests that memories are usually reconstructions (for instance, most of the time when you remember an incident you "see" yourself in it, yet that is not how you actually experienced it at the time). Indeed, in some sense the question of truthfulness is meaningless. What is meaningful is the fact that the interpretive scheme we learn in psychoanalysis creates more of a sense of order in our experience.

Narrative truth has to do with how well an explanation makes an individual's "life story" a sensible coherent whole. But, what purpose does this kind of "truth" serve? Fingarette (1963) suggests that the development of a coherent explanation for symptoms reduces anxiety. Remember that Kohut defines anxiety as disintegration anxiety, the sense of being fragmented. A coherent explanation helps "make sense" of behavior. By itself the consequent reduction in anxiety helps the individual to manage behavior better. In other words, if a person is feeling fragmented and anxious (puzzled and confused about her symptoms), she is less able to manage them and get on with her life. Having a sensible explanation for a symptom robs it of its "power," so to speak. The person is not so frightened or mystified by it and therefore is more confident that she can control it without letting it disrupt her life. In addition, a good explanation will suggest ways of coping. In some sense, whether or not your overreaction to criticism is actually due to how your father treated you is beside the point, but having that explanation helps you cope. You might be able to say to yourself, "Oh, there I go again. Now remember. Part of this is my father, so let me just stop a minute and sort out what is real here."

The obvious problem with Spence's view is that one can wonder if any old explanatory system can work. In work with some rural clients who were not psychologically sophisticated, Kelly (see Chapter 8) made up interpretations, based on no particular theory, and found that they could be therapeutic. We do not believe, however, that any old explanation will do. The explanation has to be "plausible," and we take this to mean that it must "fit the facts." Psychoanalytic explanations, while perhaps not the only plausible explanation of a person's problems, work to the extent that they are compatible with the data. A theorist may never be able to prove that a client lusted after his mother at age five and that this caused his adult neurosis. But this explanation would not be therapeutic if clients were not able to recover memories that make it plausible that they lusted after their mothers at age 5 and make it plausible that these experiences caused the adult problems. The fact that we are dealing with alternate interpretive schemes is demonstrated by the fact that Kohut looking at the Oedipus complex sees something different from what Freud saw. But both interpretations are plausible only because something in clients' experience and memory is compatible with them, no matter which interpretation ultimately turns out to be "true." And, after all, which turns out to be true is a matter that may not be established for years. As long as an interpretation is plausible and fits a client's memories of experience, that may be all that is needed for therapy to occur.

Spence's way of looking at psychoanalysis is in keeping with other recent views of psychoanalysis as *hermeneutics*. Hermeneutics is essentially an interpretive discipline. For instance, in hermeneutics a historian may attempt to read the "hidden meanings" in ancient texts. It is an empathic discipline, where one attempts to imagine oneself into the text and then interpret what it is saying. Viewing psychoanalysis this way would lead to seeing it as an attempt to intuit the "hidden text" or hidden meanings in behavior. As an interpretive discipline, of course, there is no "one" absolutely true interpretation. Therefore, in keeping with Spence, psychoanalysis no longer becomes a quest for historical truth.

Masson and the Seduction Theory

Early in Freud's work he believed that his patients were suffering from repressed memories of actual traumatic events of having been sexually abused, or "seduced," as children. He later came to believe that most of his clients had not actually been abused, but that what had been repressed were infantile wishes and desires.

Recently, Masson (1984) has argued that the seduction theory was correct and that Freud's clients probably had been molested as children. Summit (1987) has argued that some of Freud's early work was a masterful description of the relationship of child abuse to psychopathology. However, Freud changed his mind. Summit says that during Freud's time it was taken as ridiculous on the face of it that adults did such things to children. Thus when Freud came out with his seduction theory, he was heavily criticized. Some time thereafter Freud revised his theory so that instead of presenting a "radical" view of adults as sexual molesters, he presented a "radical" view of children as having sexual lusts and fantasies. Freud then saw his patients not as suffering from real abuse, but from their own infantile wishes.

The importance of the controversy lies in how much one's problems are a response to real traumatic events, and how much they are simply a result of one's fantasies. In light of recent information about the prevalence of childhood sexual abuse, it does not seem improbable that many "Oedipal fantasies" were indeed memories based on actual childhood experiences. We have mentioned that some researchers believe that childhood abuse is at the heart of a variety of disorders, including some anxiety disorders, some depressions, borderline personality, and multiple personality. Furthermore, some of the symptoms described by object relations theorists, such as splitting and dissociation of parts of the self, are found in victims of abuse. Alice Miller (Conners, 1987) is still another analytic theorist who believes that child abuse is at the heart of many disorders.

Of course, as Masterson (1985) pointed out, it need not be an either-or issue. The key event in psychopathology from a Freudian standpoint is that in using mechanisms like repression or splitting, individuals cut off from conscious experience aspects of themselves. In some sense it may not matter whether these cut-off elements are fantasies or memories of actual events.

CONTRIBUTIONS OF PSYCHOANALYSIS

Psychoanalysis remains one of the most productive theoretical approaches to personality, psychopathology, and psychotherapy. Much of what was objected to in earlier analytic theory (such as the idea that practically everything we do is sex in disguise) has been abandoned by recent developments that focus on the self. One of Freud's major contributions is that he alerted us to the major role that unconscious forces play in determining behavior. We are only now beginning to realize the truthfulness of this and to explore it empirically (see Chapter 11).

Freud was among the first to question the ability of "pure rationality" to control behavior and to call attention to the influence of nonrational or irrational forces. This is an insight adopted by virtually every other therapeutic approach in one way or the other. Freud noticed that change occurs only if the emotional level of personality is involved, and this insight in one form or the other is also adopted by most other approaches.

The importance of early childhood and familial factors in understanding adult personality is another contribution, despite our feelings that psychoanalysis may sometimes focus too exclusively on early childhood.

Vivid, detailed descriptions of adult pathology are yet another contribution. Many find the concept of splitting useful in understanding the pathological behavior associated with borderline personality disorders. In fact, underlying all psychoanalytic formulations are attempts to outline the emotional conflicts and tempests involved in primary relationships with the self and others, and psychoanalytic accounts vividly capture these conflicts and tempests, regardless of whether they are literally repetitions of early childhood events or not (which is still being debated). In this sense psychoanalysis has developed the most complete taxonomy and "language" of wishes, fears, needs, and conflicts that play such a major role in human relationships. Whether or not I literally lusted after my mother and hated my father when I was age 5, this metaphor vividly captures feelings we can all identify with (jealousy, love, feelings of privilege, feelings of being rejected).

Psychoanalysis has also called our attention to the role of self-deception in the construction of personality and in behavior. The question of how much and why individuals deceive themselves is not yet resolved (see Martin, 1985), but it seems likely that concepts such as "repression" and "defense" will continue to play a major role in helping to understand behavior.

In addition, recent psychoanalytic approaches that focus on the development of the self have brought a new understanding to certain kinds of psychopathology. These approaches also bring psychoanalysis into greater alignment with both cognitive-behavioral and humanistic approaches, suggesting the possibility of some "grand synthesis" in the future. Eagle's (1984) view of the self as a hierarchical organizing structure—derived from object relations theory, Kohut's self psychology, and other recent analytic developments—is compatible with the cognitive-behavioral views of Mahoney and Beck, as well as with recent social psychological research on self-schemas.

Other contributions of psychoanalysis include the emphasis on "twilight phenomena" (imagery, fantasy, and dreams), the importance of which has only recently begun to be appreciated (see Singer, 1974), an early recognition that something in the therapeutic relationship may be a crucial therapeutic ingredient, and the recognition of the importance of the therapist's nonjudgmental attitude as part of the therapeutic process.

Finally, it would seem that many psychoanalytic insights are now being recognized by the recent development of cognitive perspectives. As we shall see in the cognitive-behavioral chapter, there is now talk of "core assumptions" learned in early childhood, resistant to modification because of a "protective zone" around them. These sound like nothing more than psychoanalytic insights rephrased in different theoretical terms.

REFERENCES

Adelson, J., & Doehrman, M. J. (1980). The psychodynamic approach to adolescence. In J. Adelson (Ed.), *Handbook of adolescent psychology.* New York: Wiley.

Arlow, J. A. (1984). Psychoanalysis. In R. J. Corsini (Ed.), *Current psychotherapies* (3rd ed.). Itasca, IL: Peacock.

Bettelheim, B. (1982). *Freud and man's soul.* New York: Random House.

Blatt, S. J., & Ritzler, B. A. (1974). Thought disorder and boundary disturbances in psychosis. *Journal of Consulting and Clinical Psychology, 42,* 370–381.

Blatt, S. J., & Wild, C. (1976). *Schizophrenia: A developmental analysis.* New York: Academic Press.

Bloom, B. L. (1984). *Community mental health: A general introduction* (2nd ed.). Monterey, CA: Brooks/Cole.

Bowers, K. S., & Meichenbaum, D. (1984). *The unconscious reconsidered.* New York: Wiley.

Briere, J. (1987). *Research findings on short and long term effects.* Presented at the Child Abuse Reporting Course, Harbor-UCLA Medical Center, Torrance, CA, January 16, 1987.

Briere, J., & Runtz, M. (In press). Post-sexual abuse trauma: Data and implications for clinical practice. *Journal of Interpersonal Violence.*

Brophy, J. (1977). *Child development and socialization.* Chicago: Science Research Associates.

Brown, G. W., & Harris, T. O. (1978). *Social origins of depression.* New York: Free Press.

Brown, G. W., Harris, T. O., & Bifulco, A. (1986). Long-term effects of early loss of parent. In M. Rutter, C. E. Izard, and P. B. Read (Eds.), *Depression in young people: Developmental and clinical perspectives.* New York: Guilford.

Cass, L. K., & Thomas, C. B. (1979). *Childhood psychopathology and later adjustment: The question of prediction.* New York: Wiley.

Chess, S. (1979). Developmental theory revisited. Findings of longitudinal study. *Canadian Journal of Psychiatry, 24,* 101–112.

Chess, S., & Thomas, A. (1984). *Origins and evolution of behavior disorders.* New York: Brunner/Mazel.

Cicchetti, D., & Schneider-Rosen, K. (1986). An organizational approach to childhood depression. In M. Rutter, C. E. Izard, & P. B. Read (Eds.), *Depression in young people: Developmental and clinical perspectives.* New York: Guilford.

Conners, D. (1987). Interview: Alice Miller. *Omni, 9* (6), 72–83.

Dohrenwend, B. P., Dohrenwend, B. S., Gould, M. A., Link, B., Neugebauer, R., & Wunsch-Hitzig, R. (1980). *Mental illness in the United States.* New York: Praeger.

Eagle, M. N. (1984). *Recent developments in psychoanalysis: A critical evaluation.* New York: McGraw-Hill.

Eme, R. F. (1979). Sex differences in childhood psychopathology: A review. *Psychological Bulletin, 86,* 574–595.

Erwin, E. (1980). Psychoanalytic therapy: The Eysenck argument. *American Psychologist, 35,* 435–443.

Feshbach, S., & Weiner, B. (1986). *Personality* (2nd ed.). Lexington, MA: Heath.

Fine, R. (1973). Psychoanalysis. In R. J. Corsini (Ed.), *Current psychotherapies.* Itasca, IL: Peacock.

Fingarette, H. (1963). *The self in transformation.* New York: Harper & Row.

Freud, S. (1963). Analysis terminable and interminable. In P. Rieff (Ed.), *Sigmund Freud: Therapy and technique.* New York: Collier. (Original work published 1937)

Garmazy, N. (1986). Developmental aspects of children's responses to the stress of separation and loss. In M. Rutter, C. E. Izard, & P. B. Read (Eds.), *Depression in young people: Developmental and clinical perspectives.* New York: Guilford.

Gunderson, J. G. (Ed.). (1979). Special issue: The borderline syndrome. *Schizophrenia Bulletin, 5* (1).

Guntrip, H. (1973). *Psychoanalytic theory, therapy, and the self.* New York: Basic Books.

Hamilton, V. (1985). John Bowlby: An ethological basis for psychoanalysis. In J. Reppen (Ed.), *Beyond Freud: A study of modern psychoanalytic theorists.* Hillsdale, NJ: Analytic Press.

Kagan, J. (1984). *The nature of the child.* New York: Basic Books.

Kahn, E. (1985). Heinz Kohut and Carl Rogers: A timely comparison. *American Psychologist, 40,* 893–904.

Kernberg, O. F., Burstein, E. D., Coyne, L., Appelbaum, A., Horwitz, L., & Voth, H. (1972). Psychotherapy and psychoanalysis: Final report of the Menninger Foundation's psychotherapy research project. *Bulletin of the Menninger Clinic, 36,* 1–276.

Klein, G. S. (1976). *Psychoanalytic theory: An exploration of essentials.* New York: International Universities Press.

Klein, M. (1975). *The psycho-analysis of children.* New York: Delta. (Original work published 1932)

Kohut, H. (1971). *The analysis of the self.* New York: International Universities Press.

Kohut, H. (1977). *The restoration of the self.* New York: International Universities Press.

Kohut, H. (1984). *How does analysis cure?* Chicago: University of Chicago Press.

Kostandov, E., & Arzumanov, Y. (1977). Averaged cortical evoked potentials to recognized and non-recognized verbal stimuli. *Acta Neurobiologiae Experimentalis, 37,* 311–324.

Livson, N., & Peskin, H. (1980). Perspectives on adolescence from longitudinal research. In J. Adelson (Ed.), *Handbook of adolescent psychology.* New York: Wiley.

Luborsky, L. (1984). *Principles of psychoanalytic psychotherapy: A manual for supportive-expressive treatment.* New York: Basic Books.

Luborsky, L., Singer, B., & Luborsky, L. (1975). Comparative studies of psychotherapies. *Archives of General Psychiatry, 29,* 719–729.

Luborsky, L., Crits-Cristoph, P., & Mellon, J. (1986). Advent of objective measures of the transference concept. *Journal of Consulting and Clinical Psychology, 54,* 39–47.

Maccoby, E. E. (1980). *Social development.* New York: Harcourt Brace Jovanovich.

Mahler, M. (1968). *On human symbiosis and the vicissitudes of individuation: Vol. 1. Infantile psychosis.* New York: International Universities Press.

Mahler, M., Pine, F., & Bergman, A. (1975). *The psychological birth of the human infant.* New York: Basic Books.

Martin, M. W. (Ed.). (1985). *Self-deception and self-understanding.* Lawrence: University Press of Kansas.

Masson, J. M. (1984). *The assault on truth: Freud's suppression of the seduction theory.* New York: Farrar, Straus & Giroux.

Masterson, J. F. (1981). *The narcissistic and borderline disorders: An integrated developmental approach.* New York: Brunner/Mazel.

Masterson, J. F. (1985). *The real self: A developmental, self, and object relations approach.* New York: Brunner/Mazel.

Meissner, W. W. (1978). The conceptualization of marriage and family dynamics from a psychoanalytic perspective. In T. J. Paolino & B. S. McCrady (Eds.), *Marriage and marital therapy: Psychoanalytic, behavioral and systems theory perspectives.* New York: Brunner/Mazel.

Messer, S. B., & Winokur, M. (1984). Psychoanalytic therapy versus psychodynamic therapy: Commentary on Paul L. Wachtel. In H. Arkowitz & S. B. Messer (Eds.), *Psychoanalytic therapy and behavior therapy: Is integration possible?* New York: Plenum Press.

Mischel, W., & Peake, P. K. (1982). Beyond *déjà vu* in the search for cross-situational consistency. *Psychological Review, 89,* 730–755.

Nicholson, R. A., & Berman, J. S. (1983). Is follow-up necessary in evaluating psychotherapy? *Psychological Bulletin, 93,* 261–278.

Orlinsky, D. E., & Howard, K. I. (1986). Process and outcome in psychotherapy. In S. L. Garfield & A. E. Bergin (Eds.), *Handbook of psychotherapy and behavior change* (3rd ed.). New York: Wiley.

Palmatier, J. R., & Bornstein, P. H. (1980). The effects of subliminal stimulation of symbiotic merging fantasies on behavioral treatment of smokers. *Journal of Nervous and Mental Disease, 168,* 715–720.

Rogers, C. R., & Sanford, R. C. (1984). Client-centered psychotherapy. In H. I. Kaplan & B. J. Sadock (Eds.), *Comprehensive textbook of psychiatry* (Vol. 4). Baltimore: Williams & Wilkins.

Rutter, M. (1986). The developmental psychopathology of depression: Issues and perspectives. In M. Rutter, C. E. Izard, & P. B. Read (Eds.), *Depression in young children: Developmental and clinical perspectives.* New York: Guilford.

Shevrin, H. (1973). Brain wave correlates of subliminal stimulation, unconscious attention, primary- and secondary-process thinking, and repressiveness (Monograph 30). *Psychological Issues, 8,* 56–87.

Shevrin, H., & Dickman, S. (1980). The psychological unconscious: A necessary assumption for all psychological theory? *American Psychologist, 35,* 421–434.

Silverman, L. H., & Weinberger, J. (1985). Mommy and I are one: Implications for psychotherapy. *American Psychologist, 40,* 1296–1308.

Singer, J. L. (1974). *Imagery and daydream methods in psychotherapy and behavior modification.* New York: Academic Press.

Singer, J. L. (1984). *The human personality.* New York: Harcourt Brace Jovanovich.

Sloane, R. B., Staples, F. R., Cristol, A. H., Yorkston, N. J., & Whipple, K. (1975). *Short-term analytically oriented psychotherapy vs. behavior therapy.* Cambridge, MA: Harvard University Press.

Smith, M. L., Glass, G. V., & Miller, T. I. (1980). *The benefits of psychotherapy.* Baltimore: Johns Hopkins University Press.

Spence, D. P. (1982). *Narrative truth and historical truth: Meaning and interpretation in psychoanalysis.* New York: Norton.

Sroufe, L. A. (1979). The coherence of individual development: Early care, attachment, and subsequent developmental issues. *American Psychologist, 34,* 834–841.

St. Clair, M. (1986). *Object relations and self psychology: An introduction.* Monterey, CA: Brooks/Cole.

Stolorow, R. D. (1976). Psychoanalytic reflections on client-centered therapy in the light of modern conceptions of narcissism. *Psychotherapy: Theory, Research and Practice, 13,* 26–29.

Strupp, H. H. (1982). The outcome problem in psychotherapy: Contemporary perspectives. In J. H. Harvey and M. M. Parks (Eds.), *Psychotherapy research and behavior change.* Washington, DC: American Psychological Association.

Strupp, H. H., & Binder, J. L. (1984). *Psychotherapy in a new key: A guide to time-limited dynamic psychotherapy.* New York: Basic Books.

Summit, R. (1987). *Introduction to the problem of child abuse.* Presented at the Child Abuse Reporting Course, Harbor-UCLA Medical Center, Torrance, CA, January 16, 1987.

Wachtel, P. L. (1984). On theory, practice, and the nature of integration. In H. Arkowitz & S. B. Messer (Eds.), *Psychoanalytic therapy and behavior therapy: Is integration possible?* New York: Plenum.

Weiner, B. (1980). *Human motivation.* New York: Holt, Rinehart and Winston.

Weintraub, S., Winters, K. C., & Neale, J. M. (1986). Competence and vulnerability in children with an affectively disordered parent. In M. Rutter, C. E. Izard, & P. B. Read (Eds.), *Depression in young people: Developmental and clinical perspectives.* New York: Guilford.

Winnicot, D. W. (1965). *The maturational processes and the facilitating environment.* New York: International Universities Press.

Wolf, E. S. (1983). Concluding statement. In A. Goldberg (Ed.), *The future of psychoanalysis: Essays in honor of Heinz Kohut.* New York: International Universities Press.

Zilbergeld, B. (1978). *Male sexuality.* New York: Bantam Books.

Chapter 5

Client-Centered Therapy

I had been working with a highly intelligent mother whose boy was something of a hellion. The problem was clearly her early rejection of the boy, but over many interviews I could not help her to this insight. I drew her out, I gently pulled together the evidence she had given, trying to help her see the pattern. But we got nowhere. Finally, I gave up. I told her that it seemed we had both tried, but we had failed, and that we might as well give up our contacts. She agreed. So we concluded the interview, shook hands, and she walked to the door of the office. Then she turned and asked, "Do you ever take adults for counseling here?" When I replied in the affirmative, she said, "Well then, I would like some help." She came to the chair she had left, and began to pour out her despair about her marriage, her troubled relationship with her husband, her sense of failure and confusion, all very different from the sterile "case history" she had given before. Real therapy began then, and *ultimately* it was very successful.

This incident was one of a number which helped me to experience the fact . . . that it is the client who knows what hurts, what directions to go, what problems are crucial, what experiences have been deeply buried. It began to occur to me that unless I had a need to demonstrate my own cleverness and learning, I would do better to rely upon the client for the direction of movement in the process. (Rogers, 1961, pp. 11–12)

> Roger's method brought it home that the decisions a person must make are inherently that person's own. No book knowledge enables another person to decide for anyone. That goes for life decisions and life-style as well as, moment by moment, what to talk about, feel into, struggle with. Another person might make a guess, but ultimately personal growth is from the inside outward. A process of change begins and moves in ways even the person's own mind cannot direct, let alone another person's mind. (Gendlin, 1984, p. 297)

These two quotes capture the "prime directive" of the client-centered approach to psychotherapy. The client-centered approach originated with Carl Rogers in the early 1940s, with the publication of his book *Counseling and Psychotherapy.* Eugene Gendlin made a major contribution to its development in the late 1950s and early 1960s. Since then he has continued to contribute with his work on "experiential psychotherapy" (Gendlin, 1973) and "focusing" (Gendlin, 1981). Rogers in recent years changed the name of his approach from "client-centered" to "person-centered" because he was applying it in many areas of life besides psychotherapy, such as education and the pursuit of world peace. However, he believed that the term client-centered was still accurate when talking about psychotherapy or counseling (Rogers, 1985, personal communication), and we have chosen to retain that label because it is the more commonly used term. We also include in this section the views of R. D. Laing on schizophrenia because they are compatible with the client-centered tradition, although Laing himself has not been associated with that approach.

MODEL OF THE PERSON

The fundamental concept of client-centered therapy is to respect and facilitate the *self-propelled* and *self-generated* growth process in the individual. Perhaps it is easier to explain this by describing some of the things a traditional client-centered therapist *does not* do. First, the therapist does not give specific advice about solving problems ("Why don't you try being honest with her?"). Second, the therapist does not give general advice on strategies for living ("You should live in the here and now"). Third, the therapist does not judge or condemn ("It is all right to get angry with your mother"; "You are a bad person for having gotten drunk"). Fourth, the therapist does not label ("You are a psychotic"). Fifth, the therapist does not develop a treatment plan for the client ("First we will work on your lack of assertiveness, then on your anxiety"). Sixth, the therapist does not direct the client to talk about certain things ("Does this remind you of something in your past?"). Seventh, the therapist does not interpret the meaning of the client's experience ("You are not really angry at me; you are really angry at your father").

The fundamental concept, that the therapist is to respect and facilitate the self-propelled growth process in the individual, is based on two premises. The first premise is that there are many possible personal realities. No one is in a position to judge someone else's reality as being less correct, more distorted, or less adequate than someone else's reality (Rogers, 1980). The second premise is that if the personal reality of an individual is respected by others and a basic trust is demonstrated toward that person, then a self-propelled growth process will move in a positive, life-affirming direction.

Multiple Realities

Most people believe that somewhere "out there" is "a" reality and ultimately there is one correct way of viewing it. For instance, most of us would agree with the Freudian view that people misperceive and distort reality from time to time. Certainly we would think that a person who thought that people on television talk shows were secretly talking about him or who saw things no one else did was distorting reality.

At the same time, most people are aware that there *are* different ways of experiencing reality. Is there, for instance, a "correct" way of experiencing anchovy pizza? We are personally convinced that those who *like* anchovy pizza are distorting reality, but they would probably say the same about us. It is clear that people accept differences in tastes in music, clothing, and food, preferences for hobbies, choice of careers, and so on.

However, different cultures have different ideas about how people should live. Although they may accept differences within limits, they do have ideas about what is appropriate, or correct, in different settings. For instance, there are very few settings in our culture in which it is correct, or even acceptable, to be nude. The list of "correct" and "incorrect" ways to live is quite extensive and includes both moral and legal rules.

Thus, while people recognize that there are variations in how individuals experience certain aspects of reality, they believe that everyone should experience some aspects the same way, the "correct" way. If someone does *not* experience one of these aspects in that way, it is said that they are "distorting" reality or are "out of touch." Many Freudian notions are based on this idea. For instance, the concept of transference assumes that patients distort their perceptions of the psychoanalyst by transferring onto the analyst feelings they had toward their parents. The defense mechanisms are other Freudian concepts that include the idea of distortion or misperception of reality. Transactional analysis (see Chapter 9) also includes a concept of distortion. It sees people as acting out "games" or "life scripts" of which they are unaware. Thus, a person's *conscious* perception of what is going on is a *misperception.*

Rogers argued that there are *multiple* realities. To believe that someone is out of touch with reality or is distorting it is to believe that there is a correct way of viewing reality. Rogers believed that reality is relative to each person's point of view and therefore there is no possible way for any human to determine which is "the correct" view, if indeed there is a "correct" view.

This premise sounds simple, but it can lead to disturbing questions. Must we respect the reality of a Hitler? What about a woman who believed her child was possessed by the devil and threw it out of a tenth-story window? To deal with this issue we will turn to Rogers' second premise, but first we will examine a theorist who has carried the idea of the acceptance of divergent views of reality to its logical extreme.

Laing on Schizophrenia

R. D. Laing's views on schizophrenia, as expressed in *The Politics of Experience* (1967), are compatible with Rogers's views on multiple realities. Laing quoted the following example from Kraepelin (1906).

> First of all, you see a servant-girl, aged twenty-four, upon whose features and frame traces of great emaciation can be plainly seen. In spite of this, the patient is in continual movement, going a few steps forward, then back again. . . . *Attempting to stop her movement,* we meet with unexpectedly strong resistance; *if I place myself in front of her with my arms spread out* in order to stop her, . . . she suddenly turns and slips through under my arms, so as to continue on her way. . . . We notice besides that she holds a crushed piece of bread spasmodically clasped in the fingers of the left hand, which she absolutely *will not allow to be forced from her. . . . If you prick her in the forehead with a needle,* she scarcely winces or turns away, and leaves the needle quietly sticking there. . . .

Laing commented:

> If we see the situation purely in terms of Kraepelin's point of view, it all immediately falls into place. He is sane, she is insane; he is rational, she is irrational. This entails looking at the patient's actions out of the context of the situation as she experienced it. But if we take Kraepelin's actions (in italics)—he tried to stop her movements, stands in front of her with arms outspread, tries to force a piece of bread out of her hand, sticks a needle in her forehead and so on—out of the context of the situation as experienced and defined by him, how extraordinary they are! (1967, p. 73)

Laing wrote that the schizophrenic's experience of the world makes sense if one could view it from the schizophrenic's context. Therefore, it is incorrect to say that the schizophrenic is "crazy" and that we are "normal." In fact, Laing even went so far as to suggest that what passes for normalcy is distorted, denied, and alienated functioning. The schizophrenic is someone who has broken through this "phony" way of living, and the schizophrenic experience is actually a growth experience. Instead of trying to "cure" schizophrenia, we should support and trust the experience of schizophrenics and help them explore it. By so doing they will eventually return to "reality," but with a more profound ability to experience and deal with it than most of us have.

Crucial, then, to Laing's view of schizophrenia is that the reality of the schizophrenic must be respected and that a therapist's task is not to try to judge that experience, alter it, or cure it, but rather to facilitate the client's accepting and exploring of that experience. In this sense Laing's views are a logical extension of Rogers's first premise.

The Meaning of Acceptance

But what about respecting the reality of a Hitler or the woman who killed her child? If we trust the experience of all clients, could the therapist not end up supporting and facilitating murder, child abuse, rape, robbery, or other acts most of us see as negative? Rogers's answer to this is that the self-actualization or growth process is positive: "I find it significant that when individuals are prized as persons, the values they select do not run the full gamut of possibilities. I do not find, in such a climate of freedom, that a person comes to value fraud and murder and thievery. . . ." (Rogers, 1967, p.26). Rogers asserted that individuals who are prized and trusted will naturally choose "prosocial" values.

But what does it mean to prize, trust, or accept another's experience? Does this mean the therapist should agree with the way clients view the world, or support and positively reinforce any behavior? What if the therapist disagrees with the clients views and sees their behavior as destructive?

For Rogers, to accept or trust another's reality does not mean to agree with it or approve of it. It means to acknowledge nonjudgmentally that it is what the other actually perceives. Put another way, an accepting attitude means to listen nonjudgmentally. A patient (labeled paranoid schizophrenic by the hospital) may say that the police are always following him around in helicopters and that he is planning to retaliate by blowing up the police station. Does acceptance mean saying "I agree with you. Go to it"? No. It means acknowledging that the client really does experience the police as out to get him. Wanting to blow up the police station is a logical (but not reasonable!) outcome of the way the client is experiencing the world. Either agreeing with the client or telling him that he is wrong or crazy would be making a judgment.

But as the therapist does not agree that the police are out to get him and certainly does not want him to blow up the police station, what does he or she do? Rogers distinguished between accepting another's way of experiencing the world and accepting his or her *behavior.* A parent can accept and understand a child's desire to stick her finger in a flame (it is bright, it is pretty, the child is curious), while certainly not allowing the child to go through with the act. Thus, one can respect and accept another's experience of the world while *not* supporting or encouraging certain behaviors that might flow from it. An example of a lack of acceptance would be a parent who not only stops a child from putting her finger in the flame, but tells the child she is wrong or bad for even wanting to do this.

A therapist might want to go further than restraining destructive behavior and express disagreement with the client's experiencing. How is this done? Eugene Gendlin (1967) suggests that therapists can express a viewpoint if they offer it as their own. They would not say, "You are wrong" or "You are crazy for seeing the police as dangerous," but they might say, "I don't agree with you. I don't see the police as out to get you." The latter way of expressing a viewpoint implies a respect for and acknowledgment of the client's perspective that the former does not.

In sum, the prime directive of client-centered therapy is to accept and respect the experience of the client. This means acknowledging there are multiple possible ways of viewing reality. Acceptance is neither approval of the client's perspective or actions nor agreement with them.

Because of his emphasis on respecting the world view of each individual client, Rogers was against labels. He preferred that the therapist relate to the client as another person rather than as a "schizophrenic" or an "obsessive compulsive." Psychiatric labels carry the implication that there is something "wrong" with the person. In addition to being judgmental, labels tend to pigeonhole and categorize. Therefore, they may blind the therapist to the uniqueness of the individual.

Personal Constructs and Values

Personal constructs is a term borrowed from George Kelly (1955). Kelly's idea was that people organize their lives in terms of their constructs, or concepts, about people, events, and even physical reality. Values can be considered a subset of constructs that have a positive or negative component. People have private values about what constitutes attractive physical appearance and how important physical appearance is, what constitutes a good romantic partner and and how important it is to have a romantic partner. They have moral values about killing, telling the truth, and stealing. They have conventional values about being a good member of society, driving on the right side of the road, and wearing clothes in public. Examples of personal constructs and values are (1) I tend to be a hardworking person (a construct about the self); (2) I believe Carl Rogers's ideas about human nature are wrong; (3) That person is a rat!; (4) People who don't look at you while they are talking are trying to hide something; (5) To live a good life one should get married, get a good job, work hard and make a lot of money; (6) Communism is evil; (7) Men don't cry; (8) It is wrong to feel angry toward one's parents.

Congruent with his belief in multiple realities, Rogers believed it is important that people hold their personal constructs and values *tentatively.* He said that in the early stages of therapy, "Personal constructs are rigid, and unrecognized as being constructs, but are thought of as facts" (1961, p. 134), but later, "The ways in which experience is construed are much loosened" (1961, p. 141). Finally, in the highest stage of development, "Personal constructs are tentatively reformulated, to be validated against further experience, but even then, to be held loosely" (1961, p. 153).

To put it another way, Rogers seemed to be advocating that people act like good scientists in regard to their personal beliefs and treat personal constructs as hypotheses, rather than as fixed, objective facts. Values and beliefs about themselves and others are all to be treated as imperfect formulations about reality. As with scientific theories, they may be mistaken, and people must be open to challenging even their most deeply held values if they run into experiences that call them into question. This does not mean one cannot be committed to a set of values or personal constructs. Scientists may be committed to a point of view, but still hold open the possibility that future experience may prove them wrong.

To hold personal constructs tentatively means to move away from rigid, absolute "shoulds" (Rogers, 1961, p. 168). If individuals see their values as fixed, unchanging facts, then they must follow them. They have no choice. Rogers wanted people to *choose* their values on the basis of what makes sense to them, not to adopt values because some authority said that is how one should be. He wanted individuals to challenge and test their values to see if they make sense. Chosen values lose their "should-like" quality, because they become something the person *wants* to do because they make sense to the person. Rogers believed values are meaningful only if so chosen.

Process Orientation

Rogers saw fully functioning individuals as process oriented. This has two meanings. To be process oriented means to see life as a process of becoming and to focus on doing. People are creatures whose nature is characterized by change and that means that the fully functioning person is continually open to the reevaluation of values, goals, and attitudes about life. In this regard the individual does not even have a fixed "self." As the individual grows and changes, so the self-concept will grow and change. In some important sense you are not the same person you were when you were fourteen years old, and your attitudes, values, and self-concept have probably altered to reflect this change.

A process orientation involves focusing attention on the *doing* of things rather than on their *outcomes* (Rogers, 1961, p. 171). Being overly focused on the outcome of actions can lead to excessive preoccupation with self-evaluation. People are inclined to evaluate themselves in terms of success or failure: "I am a good person" if I succeed; "I am a bad person" if I fail. This excessive preoccupation with evaluation draws attention away from the process of doing and prevents people from investing all their energies in the doing of the activity. Paradoxically, by focusing on how well they are succeeding, they may increase their odds of failure. This does not mean they do not have to try to do things well. For instance, to play a guitar, you have to hit the right notes. But if you are worried about the final outcome, that is, whether you will be judged a success or a failure, you are actually drawing attention away from the doing (from the moment-to-moment business of hitting the right notes), and as a result you may do poorly. From Rogers's perspective, people should focus on what they did "wrong" not to evaluate (I was bad), but only to learn how to improve.

People who are overly concerned about the outcome of their actions are probably concerned with whether they are good or bad people. To ask whether "I am good or bad" or whether "I have good traits or bad traits" is to treat oneself as if one had a fixed self. From a Rogerian perspective it is no better to have a fixed positive self-concept than to have a fixed negative self-concept. Fully functioning individuals would have no fixed beliefs about themselves at all and in this sense may not even think about their "self" at all. In other words, if I never worry about whether my successes or failures mean *I* am good or bad and if I focus on how I am doing this task at this moment, then I am concerned with learning from my success or failure, but not whether *I* am good or not.

Internality and Authority

Rogers's emphasis on individual views of reality leads to a rejection of authority. No one possesses "the correct" answers as to how others should live their lives. This includes parents, the school system, society at large, and religion. Does this mean people should not even listen to authority? No. But they should not accept what "authorities" say simply because they are the authority. People must always take the responsibility of listening to and evaluating any idea, no matter what its source, to see if it makes sense to them. Adopting an idea only because a teacher, parent, religious leader, or therapist says it is so may lead to conflict between the adopted value and what a person feels. Fully functioning individuals are autonomous, self-directed, and congruent, that is, their behavior arises from a chosen set of values that are congruent with their perceptions and experience.

EXPERIENCING

As we have seen, the fully functioning person holds constructs tentatively, does not adopt them just because they were offered by an authority, and continually evaluates them against his or her own experience to see if they make sense. But what is this "experience" against which values and constructs are checked?

You may have heard that it is good to "get in touch with feelings." Often client-centered therapy is seen as emphasizing this process, and one of the techniques of client-centered therapy is called "reflection of feelings." Yet actually it is more accurate to say that client-centered therapists want us to "listen to our experience."

Freud was the first to point out that an affective component seems to be necessary for psychotherapy to work. This is not surprising, since problems are frequently based on the fact that bodily or emotive responses are incongruent with perceptions or intellectual beliefs. You may feel like eating, though intellectually you decide you should lose weight. Or you intellectually decide it would be good for you to study, but you find yourself wanting to watch TV. Since the bodily or affective level seems to be so integrally involved in personal problems, it is not surprising that psychotherapy must involve it in some way. Clearly, if we were able to decide intellectually what was good for us and always and easily put it into operation, few therapists would be needed (see Chapter 11). But exactly how the emotive or bodily component plays a role in psychotherapy and mental health is open to debate. For Freud it was a matter of "getting in touch with" primitive childhood fantasies that carry an emotional charge. In other therapies, such as primal therapy (Janov, 1970), it is a matter of getting in touch with a buried reservoir of pain and then expressing and discharging it. In many existential or humanistic approaches it is a matter of "getting in touch with feelings," which means being willing to acknowledge and label one's anger, sadness, or fear.

Client-centered therapy based primarily on Gendlin's theory of experience (Gendlin, 1969) has a somewhat different view of the role of the affective component. Experiencing is a broader construct than "feelings." People are said to *experience* feelings. The goal of client-centered therapy is to help clients become able to experience feelings and to listen to their experience. In the process of experiencing a feeling it is more important to listen to the experience of the feeling than to the feeling itself.

Experiential Knowing

What is experience? That's a difficult question, and perhaps we can begin to answer it by appealing to your "experience." Let us break down "knowing," or acquiring of knowledge, into two components. The first is intellectual and verbal. This is the kind of knowing you are engaged in right now. You are reading words and thinking about what they mean. The second kind of knowing is experiential. This is knowing that seems more "visceral," "gut level," sensory, and nonverbal. The difference is not hard to illustrate. Reading a description of being kissed romantically is not the same as experiencing being kissed romantically. There is a kind of "knowing" about being kissed romantically that is beyond what can be conveyed in words. In fact, if one were to try to describe what it feels like to be kissed romantically, the words would *come from* the experience. They are attempts to verbally encode the experience and as such, they can never do more than convey *part* of it. What one knows about being kissed romantically at an experiential level will always be more than one can put into words.

The nonverbal, bodily way of knowing includes the processing of sensory and muscular information. Feelings are bodily events and may be particularly important guides to bodily ways of knowing. However, we know more things in an experiential or bodily way than feelings. We *can* know how we feel, but we also "know how things taste," "how some things feel when we touch them," and how it feels to "know how" to play the guitar.

If you were asked to describe what it feels like to be kissed romantically, you would probably try to describe the bodily sensations that are associated with the experience. You might use metaphors and analogies: "It feels like you were melting for a moment," "It feels like two parts being joined together," "There is a sense of quickening, or excitement, a sense of letting go." Similarly, in describing being rejected, you might say, "It feels like I was kicked in the gut" or "It feels like I was thrown out the door." Again, you are using metaphorical language to try to "capture" that set of bodily sensations that were your experience of being rejected.

"Getting in touch with feelings" for a client-centered therapist, then, means listening to and trying to capture the felt meanings of experience. It does not mean identifying emotions, though that may be a useful route into experiential knowing. More important is the nonverbal sense of what objects and events are felt as meaning. If you feel loved, that probably includes a whole set of experiences you have shared with the person who you feel loves you. If you feel anger, that is because you are experiencing the interaction with another person as anger provoking. Thus, paying attention to feelings is important because they are an indication of how you are experiencing a particular situation or relationship.

What is true for each individual is what that individual knows experientially. This does not mean it is objectively true or experientially true for other people. For instance, you may know that you experience eating anchovy pizza as unpleasant, even if it is judged good by others. Since there is little societal pressure to like anchovy pizza, you are allowed to "follow your own feelings" in the matter. But what happens when an individual's experiential sense disagrees with something society holds to be objectively true and seems to care about? For instance, what if your experiential sense is that you care little about financial success, but everyone tells you you should care about it and evaluates you on the basis of it? Rogers seemed to believe that people will be affected more by their experiential sense than by their intellectual perceptions. If they do not actually "follow" their experiential sense, they will still be influenced by it in experiencing conflict between it and what they *think* society says they ought to do.

Did Rogers believe that people should always follow their experiential sense? Remember, this is different from feelings. For instance, if I am feeling anger, does that mean I should express or act out my anger? No. To experience anger means to experience a situation as anger provoking. If I experience the situation as anger provoking, does that mean it is anger provoking? Again, the answer is no. That is certainly how I am construing the situation at an experiential level, but that does not necessarily mean my construction of the situation is objectively true. Yet at the same time I have little control over my experiencing the situation that way. The crucial thing is to listen to it. While it may be inaccurate in an objective sense, it is nevertheless how I am experiencing the situation at a gut level. Furthermore, it may be correct, because I may have picked up cues from the situation at a gut level of which I was not consciously aware.

Listening means to try to capture the meaning of experience. For instance, I might say, "I *feel* you dislike me." There are some psychologists who would say that such a statement is inaccurate. Rather, I should say, "I *think* you dislike me." However, to say "I feel you dislike me" is to say that my experience around you is like my experience around people who have later proven to dislike me. And I may experience this even though intellectually I have no evidence that you dislike me. I could express this as "I *think* you like me, but I *feel* as if you didn't."

It is against this experiential sense of things that the individual's personal constructs are to be checked to see if they "make sense." While Rogers did not claim that a person's experiential sense is always correct, he did believe there needs to be a congruence between the intellectual and experiential levels. If something is not true for a person at an experiential level, it does not matter if intellectually it seems it ought to be true. A person may be able to resolve incongruence by listening to the experiential level to try to grasp the meanings implicit in it. Gendlin suggests that such a process leads ultimately to an integration of the intellectual and experiential in regard to that particular issue.

PSYCHOPATHOLOGY

From the client-centered perspective psychopathology occurs when individuals do not hold constructs tentatively, do not listen to experience, and as a result are not able to act autonomously. Such people experience incongruence between what they think ought to be and what they experience. Ultimately, all forms of psychopathology—anxiety, depression, alcoholism, rigid behavior, psychotic episodes—result from such incongruence. Laing's (1967) description of how schizophrenia develops out of a "divided self" is a similar view. For Laing, schizophrenia develops because the split between the public facade the individual adopts to please others and the private, "true" self becomes too extreme, and the true self begins to "suffocate" inside. A psychotic episode occurs when the "good little boy or girl" facade cracks and the true self erupts in a disorganized and undifferentiated manner.

Thus, psychopathology results from not accepting, listening to, or being true to one's experienced sense of what is true. The case of Janet is an example. Janet appeared to be distant, unemotional, and unfriendly. She was planning to be a doctor. Then, one day she was completely changed. She was friendly and warm. She said that she had finally admitted to herself that she did not want to be a doctor and had changed her major to art. From a Rogerian perspective, Janet had adopted the ideal that she should be a doctor. In order to pursue this goal she had consistently denied her own feelings and her own experiential sense of what *she* enjoyed, what felt meaningful to her. It affected her whole personality. She could not allow herself to experience happy, warm, or outgoing feelings, because if she did she might also fully experience her disaffection with chemistry, biology, and other classes she was forcing herself to take.

The above should not be construed to mean that you should never take a class that you find boring. Even though a class may be boring, it might be experientially meaningful to take it anyway, because you know at a feeling level that the class fits your goals. Rather, you should pay attention to the experience of a class as boring to see what it means. Does it mean that it is *this* class that is boring, or is it that you are feeling bored with the whole field? If it is the latter, you may wish to reevaluate your career goals.

Why do people *not* listen to their experience? Rogers said that this occurs because in childhood people are taught that their acceptance or worth as individuals is dependent on their meeting someone else's standards. Children are born with a primitive and undifferentiated "organismic valuing process" through which they directly experience what is meaningful or life-enhancing for them. The valuing process will grow and differentiate if children are allowed to stay in touch with it. However, parents and school teach rules as to what children should be and think, and the question of whether those rules make sense to the children is never raised. In fact, if children protest that the rules do not make sense, they may well be punished.

For Rogers, emotional disturbance is caused by child-rearing practices that do not convey *positive regard* to the child. By putting *conditions of worth* on the child, the parent forces the child to ignore its organismic valuing and thereby creates incongruence. It is this incongruence that causes trouble in development.

Rogers thought that the organismic valuing process is the innate way that humans have to learn positive or prosocial behavior and that it is a reliable, valid, and important source of information and guide to action. Humans find it innately rewarding or reinforcing to be kind to each other, to relate to each other, to be affectionate and helpful, and so forth. It is only when the child learns to ignore organismic valuing that behavior goes awry.

Rogers did not advocate letting children follow only rules or perceptions that make sense to them. For instance, Rogers was not saying that the child has the right to stick her finger in a flame because the rule against doing it doesn't make sense to her. However, insisting that the child follow the rule should be done without telling her that she is bad or wrong or stupid for wanting to stick her hand in the flame. Conditions of worth are not imposed on the child. In other words, good parenting makes every effort to help children see the "sense" in a parental rule or point of view, rather than having the children adopt it simply because "It is right." Even if there are occasions when children have to conform to a rule that does not make sense to them, at the very least the parent tries to convey positive regard and not to invalidate the child's experience.

If children are told that their experiential sense is bad or wrong often enough, they will begin to distrust it, perhaps even to deny it. They will become "other-directed" and depend on authorities to tell them what is correct. They will adopt rules and perspectives in a rigid, either/or manner and lose the ability to be spontaneous, creative, and self-directed.

PSYCHOTHERAPY

Therapeutic Process

The process of psychotherapy for Rogers is the restoration of the individual's ability to refer directly to what is experienced as true or meaningful for the self. This occurs primarily through the process of self-acceptance. If clients can adopt a nonjudgmental, self-accepting attitude toward themselves, then they can learn to tune into their experiential sense of things. As this occurs, they hold constructs more tentatively and become more flexible, less structure-bound, and more autonomous.

This view of therapy does not mean that clients will automatically or magically find answers to all their questions. For Rogers, life is a continual growth process in which people are periodically challenged to develop and expand their skills in living. "Self-actualized" people are *not* perfect, are not always happy, are not even always congruent with themselves. Rather, they are people who accept the fact that they will be periodically challenged and at those times are willing to reevaluate their personal constructs. They are willing to face the anxiety and disorganization attendant on the struggle to solve a new life problem and move ahead. Rather than "self-actualized," it would be more accurate to call them "self-actualizing." Rogers said, "I believe they would consider themselves insulted if they were described as 'adjusted,' and they would regard it as false if they were described as 'happy' or 'contented,' or even 'actualized' " (Rogers, 1961, p. 186). They know they will not do everything perfectly and that there will be times of unhappiness. But because they view life as a process rather than expecting it to be some fixed state of bliss, they try to learn from the mistakes and to live with the unhappy times in order to move forward.

The ability to listen to their feelings, similarly, does not mean that they magically find the right answer to life dilemmas. Rogers said, "(One's) organism would not by any means be infallible. It would always give the best possible answer for the available data, but sometimes data would be missing . . ." (Rogers, 1961, p. 191). At the experiential level a person may feel confusion because a major life decision such as getting divorced must include many pros and cons. If the individual can experience the pros and cons (I enjoy being around her, but I enjoy not having to answer to someone), then he can have a direct experiential sense of the whole conflict. But that experiential sense will *not* be one clear feeling, like "leave" or "stay." Rather, it will include the whole experience of the situation and how one experiences one's goals. Gendlin says the person experiences the problem as a kind of "all that."

Tuning into the experiential sense of the problem, then, means focusing precisely on what *feels* unclear (Gendlin, 1984). As a person does this, different meanings separate out, and the person begins to get in touch with how he experientially *weighs* components of the dilemma (My enjoyment of her feels more important than my desire for freedom). In addition, as the person attends to how each component of the dilemma feels, a kind of constructive process takes place. According to Gendlin, as the person attempts to capture experiential meanings in words or images, there is a kind of momentary experiential resolution of some aspect of the problem and a "felt give" or sense of relief. Ultimate problem resolution is made up of many such momentary bits of integration, building on one another. Thus, for Gendlin and Rogers, one important aspect of therapy could be said to be "creative problem solving."

To sum up, the process of psychotherapy includes two elements. First, clients learn to listen and accept their experiential sense of things. As they do this, they become more flexible and more self-directed and begin to hold constructs tentatively. Second, the direct focusing on experience itself helps the clients to resolve the life problems they are facing.

Role of the Therapist

There has been an evolution in the role of the client-centered therapist (Hart, 1970). In the 1940s the therapist was to remain relatively anonymous and to create a warm, accepting climate in which the client would feel free to engage in self-exploration. In the 1950s therapist empathy was stressed. The therapist was not only to convey warmth, but also to make an active effort to understand the client's subjective experience. A technique called reflection of feelings was developed, in which the therapist "mirrors" back to the client the therapist's understanding of the client's subjective experience. The stereotypical picture of the client-centered therapist is based on this period.

In the late 1950s and early 1960s there was a further evolution. Rogers (1957) published a paper suggesting that it is the *therapeutic relationship* itself that is therapeutic. More important than the therapist's professional training, theoretical point of view, or techniques are certain personal qualities. Therapists who have these qualities will be effective; those who do not have them will not be. This bold and far-reaching statement implied that a person could be a psychiatrist, a psychologist, or a barber and be an effective therapist if the person had certain crucial personal qualities. It also implied that the crucial qualities were independent of whether the person was a Freudian, Rogerian, Jungian, or behaviorist.

What are these personal qualities? Rogers listed several in 1957, but they have generally been reduced to three major groups: nonpossessive warmth, accurate empathy, and genuineness (we use the names given them by Truax and Carkhuff, 1967). We will discuss each quality in turn and try to identify its therapeutic value.

Nonpossessive Warmth *Nonpossessive warmth* is a general name for a quality or set of qualities called, variously, *unconditional positive regard,* prizing, acceptance, respect, caring, or even *nonpossessive love* (Rogers, 1965). There actually seems to be three interrelated qualities. First, the therapist must positively prize or *care* for the client. Second, this caring must be *nonpossessive,* a quality related to the idea of acceptance. Third, the therapist must not only care for clients in a nonpossessive way, but also treat them with *respect* as autonomous individuals, equal in value to the therapist.

Caring is probably therapeutic because it builds trust and is a motivator. Clients are more likely to reveal themselves to, take chances with, and try hard for someone who they feel cares about them.

Nonpossessiveness seems to be related to acceptance. Possessive caring is caring with an attempt to control the other. Being nonpossessive in therapy means acknowledging clients' autonomy, accepting their choices, and not imposing one's will on them. As we have stated before, acceptance does not mean approval. It means responding to others nonevaluatively, acknowledging and listening to them nonjudgmentally. Possessive parents or lovers are always either approving or disapproving of the behavior of the child or of the romantic partner. Nonpossessiveness contributes to therapeutic effectiveness because most people are averse to feeling controlled or judged by another. Feeling controlled or judged may motivate clients to rebel or make them feel unsafe.

Respect for clients' individuality and autonomy goes hand in hand with nonpossessive acceptance. The therapist's attitude of respect reinforces clients' belief in themselves as autonomous individuals who are capable of making decisions for themselves. Some parents seem to care for their children in a way that does not include respect. For example, by being overprotective they convey the message that the children are incompetent to take care of themselves. Respect also implies trust in the client. An attitude of trust should increase the clients' trust in themselves and in the therapist, with a resultant lowering of defenses. As respect and trust increase, so will clients' openness to communications from the therapist.

Accurate Empathy *Accurate empathy* is the ability to enter clients' worlds and to see things from their point of view. This is more difficult than it may seem. To be accurately empathic, one must be able to *decenter,* a concept borrowed from the work of Piaget (Cowan, 1978). Decentering is the ability to step outside of one's own perspective and, through imagination and logic, guess at how things would look from someone else's perspective. For adults it is relatively easy to imagine how someone else is seeing the physical world. For instance, it is not hard for students to imagine what the classroom looks like physically to the professor as he or she lectures, even though the students are not on the podium. It is quite another thing to imagine how a teacher is experiencing the lecture material and the classroom situation. The experiencing of any given situation is based on how the person is construing that situation and that is based on that person's prior *experiences.* Since everyone's experiences are different to some extent, it may be difficult for one person to guess how another is construing a situation. It may be relatively easier if the two people are similar in many ways (Henschel & Bohart, 1984). The greater the difference in prior experience, the greater the difficulty in achieving empathy. Yet true empathic ability is probably demonstrated more in situations when a person is trying to grasp the experience of someone quite different (Henschel & Bohart, 1984).

The therapist must be careful not to mistake recalling his or her own experience for having an empathic response. Let us say clients are describing the breakup of their relationships to you. You have been "dumped" yourself, so you believe you know how it feels. In an attempt to be empathic, you say "I bet you feel rejected. I bet you're feeling abandoned also." What you have done is to recall how you felt in a situation that you are assuming is similar to the clients and you have imagined how *you* would feel if you were in the clients' shoes. But true empathy is not how you would feel if you were in the clients' shoes, but an attempt to guess at how they feel, that is, how you would feel if you were *they,* in their shoes. It is the ability to understand from their point of view why a client might feel depressed and sad at being given a big promotion at work, why parents might feel glad at the prospect of never seeing one of their children again, why a person might feel happy at the death of a parent. We have deliberately picked hard-to-understand examples to point out that true empathy is not imagining how you would feel in the situation (most of us would feel happy with the promotion, sad at the thought of never seeing our child again, and sad at the death of a parent). Rather, true empathy is the ability to guess at how others are experiencing the world so that they feel the way they do.

How does one be empathic? We have described empathy as an ability, but it is not something that one simply "has." Rather, empathy is an active process, a skill that must be practiced. Rarely will a person have a magical flash of insight in which the person just "knows" how another is experiencing the world. Usually a person can achieve that knowledge only through a laborious process of listening, adjusting guesses, and listening some more. Here is how it goes. The client has said that he has been dumped by his girl friend. You make a guess at what he is experiencing, based on your own experience in such situations and your general knowledge of the experience of others in such situations. You state your guess, and then you *listen* to see if you have guessed right. You will know from the client's *response.* This response will be not only what the client says, but his body language. If the client says, "Yes, that's it!" then you probably hit it. If the client hesitates and says, "Yes, that *must* be it," then you know you didn't. If your guess is accurate, the client will know right away. It will "feel right" to him. If the client has to hesitate, then at an experiential level what you have said did not *feel* right, even though at an intellectual level the client decides it "must be right." So you listen, and based on what cues the client gives back to you, you make another guess, and then you listen further.

Achieving accurate empathy can take time because it requires clarifying communication between the therapist and the client. When the client speaks to the therapist, in both words and nonverbal gestures, the therapist *interprets* the client's words and gestures based on the therapist's experience of what they mean. But the client may mean something different. Empathy involves learning the client's private language. For example, when the client says "My girl friend dumped me," you may take that to mean "I feel rejected," but perhaps the meaning the client attaches to that statement and wants to convey to you is "People always mistreat me." Therefore, empathy is normally achieved over a period of time in therapy. It is not usually something one magically "has" at the start of counseling. Empathy will develop more quickly if therapists are willing to suspend their own private way of interpreting words and behaviors, remember that clients may interpret them differently, and then look for cues as to what clients mean by them.

Reflection of feeling is a technique that was developed in the 1950s as a means for the therapist to convey empathic understanding of the client back to the client. A typical reflection starts out "It sounds like you feel . . ." or "You're saying that . . ." Reflection of *feeling* is actually a misnomer, because the therapist reflects not only feelings, but the *meanings* of what the client says. To give an example:

CLIENT: I failed the test! Boy, does that screw things up! I'm behind on my other classes, but now I'm going to have to devote extra time to this one.

REFLECTION (OF FEELING): You're sounding very frustrated and overwhelmed.

REFLECTION (OF MEANING): You're saying that failing the test means you're going to have to change your plans, and devote more time than you would have to that class.

REFLECTION (OF FEELING AND MEANING): It almost sounds like you're feeling a little desperate. How can I get caught up on my other classes, *and* devote extra time to this one?

Notice that the reflections do more than repeat what the client just said. Often people think of reflecting as nothing but parroting, as in the following parody:

CLIENT: I'm feeling depressed today.
COUNSELOR: You're feeling depressed today.
CLIENT: I think I'll kill myself.
COUNSELOR: You think you'll kill yourself.
CLIENT: I'm going to jump out the window.

COUNSELOR: You're going to jump out the window.
CLIENT: I'm jumping out the window.
COUNSELOR: You're jumping out the window.
SOUND FROM BELOW: Plop!
COUNSELOR: Plop!

Good reflections do not simply repeat back to the client what the client has already said. At the very minimum they paraphrase. For instance, a simple paraphrasing of the client's statement about being depressed might be, "You're feeling down today." Most reflections, however, go beyond what the client actually said to try to capture more of the flavor of the client's experience than the client put into words. The presumption is that the client's words summarize or convey a fraction of the client's total experience in the moment. Good reflections guess at what some related aspects of that experience might be. In the examples of reflections, each one goes beyond the client statement to make a guess at what the client is experiencing at the moment but did not say. For instance, the first reflection presents a guess that the client is feeling frustrated and overwhelmed, although this was not stated. The reflection is a step in the constructive activity of empathic understanding. If the client responds to the reflection with "Yes, I sure am!" the therapist guessed correctly and may have moved closer to the therapeutic goal of being able to guess what it feels like to be that client. If the client says, "No, it's more like I'm feeling picked on by life. I'm being treated unfairly," then the therapist has also moved forward in gaining an understanding of the client's subjective world.

Reflection differs from *interpretation* (see Chapter 3) in that while both guess at the meanings that underlie the client's statement, reflection tries to stay with meanings that are within the client's current awareness. Interpretation attempts to uncover hidden meanings of which the client is unaware. For instance, an interpretation to our client's statement about failing the test might be, "Is it possible that your failing the test means that you don't really like that class?"

Empathy and reflection are presumed to be therapeutic for the following reasons. First, empathy, along with warmth, creates a sense of trust. Second, feeling understood is often by itself therapeutic. Simply knowing that someone else can understand what they feel may make people feel less alone and more "normal." Third, empathy and reflection focus clients' attention on their experiential level. In effect, they train clients to listen to and to try to capture the meanings in their own experience. Thus empathy is directly training the skill Rogers believed is so important in living.

Genuineness The third important quality for therapists to possess is *genuineness.* Words associated with this quality include congruence, honesty, authenticity, openness, and self-disclosure. Genuine people are congruent. That means that their outer actions are congruent with some facet of their inner thoughts and feelings. Put another way, what they say and what they do is an accurate reflection of some aspect of what they are currently thinking and feeling. In this sense they can also be called honest and authentic. However, genuineness must be distinguished from the terms openness and self-disclosure, although they are related. Self-disclosure and openness are more like things people do. They disclose their problems to another; they are open about private thoughts and feelings to another. However, people can be genuine and not open or not self-disclosing. And people can self-disclose and be incongruent or phony. Suppose we asked you to tell us about your sexual fantasies. You might feel that it is none of our business. You might act congruently with that feeling and choose not to tell us. In that case you are being genuine, but you are not being open and self-disclosing about your sexual fantasies. Conversely, you might feel it is none of our business, but because some psychologist told you that the healthy person is open and self-disclosing, you go against your feelings and tell us. In this case you are being open, but you are being incongruent and ungenuine at the same time.

People never express or act on everything they are thinking and feeling. They always select. While a professor lectures to a class, she may be simultaneously experiencing (1) a desire to communicate ideas on the class topic, (2) a concern that the students understand what is being said, (3) hunger, (4) anger at her landlord, and (5) dislike of the awful shirt the man in the first row is wearing. If the professor were to try to express or act on all these things, her behavior would be confused and confusing. Instead, she selects those parts of her experience relevant to the situation to express in behavior. It is relevant to act on a desire to communicate and on a concern for the students. It is irrelevant to interject "I'm hungry" or "That darn landlord!" or "That's an awful shirt!" Is the professor being phony because she does not say these things? No. She is congruent because what she does say and do is an accurate reflection of the part of her that is relevant to that situation. As we said before, people always select. We never act on or verbalize everything we're thinking and feeling. If we did, we would engage in unending monologues and no one else would get a word in edgewise.

Therapeutic genuineness consists of being congruent with the aspects of experience relevant to the therapeutic relationship. Similarly, therapeutic self-disclosure is self-disclosure that is relevant to the purposes of the therapeutic relationship. It would be therapeutically inappropriate, therefore, for a therapist to start self-disclosing out of the blue about his sex life to the client. However, if enough trust was established and it was therapeutically useful, it might be appropriate for a therapist to share some of this kind of information.

Thus, while therapists should always be genuine, they should only selectively and judiciously self-disclose. Gendlin (1968) states that when the therapist does self-disclose, it must be done in a way that is more growth-producing than self-disclosures made by "the person on the street." Gendlin's point is that it is not enough to merely blurt out what one is feeling. For instance, if the therapist finds the client boring at any time in therapy, it is not therapeutically effective to say, "You're boring." This is the kind of response the person is liable to get from someone in everyday life. To make the self-disclosure more therapeutic, the therapist should "own" the feelings and say, "I feel bored," rather than "You are boring." The therapist should also try to be concrete and specific about what the client is doing to make her feel bored, for instance, "I feel bored because you are talking about your problems without sharing with me any of your feelings about them." Gendlin (1968) suggests it is useful to give a two-sided message, mentioning the negative, "I feel bored," but also giving something positive, for instance, ". . . and I don't like feeling bored because I am concerned about you and want to be involved in what you are saying."

Genuineness and self-disclosure appear to be therapeutic for several reasons.

First, there is a modeling effect. If the therapist wishes the client to open up, then some gesture of opening up on the therapist's part might provide a model. The therapist is also modeling the idea that one doesn't have to be perfect. Second, by being genuine and by selectively self-disclosing the therapist is demonstrating trust in the client ("Gee, the therapist trusts me enough to share some private things with me."). Third, self-disclosure can give immediate feedback to the client on the impact of his behavior. Fourth, self-disclosure can create a sense of empathy. Judiciously timed, selective self-disclosure about the therapist's own experiences can demonstrate empathy and understanding of the client's feelings. Fifth, if the therapist's self-disclosures are offered tentatively, this gives therapist and client the opportunity to explore together what is going on in the relationship and to clarify each other's perceptions.

Rogers's statement that therapy is a function of the quality of the relationship, the emphasis on the qualities of warmth, empathy, and genuineness, and Gendlin's theory of experiencing changed the client-centered approach from a specific set of therapeutic techniques to a philosophy of therapy. What this meant was that therapists could use any technique—behavioral, gestalt, analytic—as long as they maintained the qualities of a good therapeutic relationship and as long as the technique was used only when it was experientially meaningful for the client and was withdrawn if the client experienced it as meaningless or useless. With this change the client-centered approach became a model for the eclectic practice of therapy. Hart (1970) discusses an informal study in which tapes of various client-centered therapists were identified by expert listeners as being from a wide range of other therapies, such as Adlerian or rational emotive.

CURRENT STATUS AND NEW DIRECTIONS

While only a minority of therapists currently identify themselves as client centered in a pure sense, Carl Rogers has been rated as the most influential psychotherapist (Rogers & Sanford, 1984). This suggests that his ideas have influenced many therapists who are eclectic or of other theoretical orientations.

Rogers's emphasis on the importance of the therapeutic relationship has been almost universally adopted. For instance, Beck (Beck, Rush, Shaw, & Emery, 1979), a cognitive-behavioral therapist (see Chapter 8), believes that therapists must be warm, empathic, and genuine. However, although he believes this is the basis of a good therapeutic relationship, he does not believe it is *sufficient* for the relationship to be therapeutic and thinks certain procedures are necessary. This position is not incompatible with client-centered therapy, as long as therapists mold their interventions to fit each client. Of the basic therapeutic conditions, empathy is now seen as an important therapeutic quality in recent theoretical developments in psychoanalysis (see, for example, Kohut's approach, discussed in Chapter 4). Truax and Carkhuff (1967), Carkhuff and Berenson (1967), and Egan (1982) have developed eclectic models of doing therapy that include the contributions of different schools. Each of these models has Rogers's therapeutic conditions as its core.

Robert Carkhuff was among the first to believe that therapeutic skills could be taught, and he developed training programs to increase levels of warmth, empathy, and genuineness. These and related programs are now widespread, and basic listening and reflecting skills are included even in behavioral counselor training approaches (Brown & Brown, 1977). Many of these programs have been used to train paraprofessional counselors.

Gendlin (1984) has been primarily interested in "giving psychology away." He has developed techniques for training the ability to focus on and use one's experience to grow and change (Gendlin, 1981). The interest in giving psychology away can also be seen in Carkhuff's training programs for basic counselor skills, which have been taught to students, housewives, people looking for jobs, and hospitalized mental patients. Related to this are Goodman's (1984) SASHA tapes for teaching basic communication skills and Gordon's (1984) efforts to teach effective parenting, leadership, and teaching skills.

A new direction in terms of theory has been the work of Wexler and others (Wexler & Rice, 1974) to apply an information-processing interpretation to client-centered therapy. Despite Rogers's emphasis on feelings, there has always been a cognitive, information-processing flavor to his theorizing. For instance, getting in touch with feelings is seen informationally:

> Often I sense that the client is trying to listen to himself, is trying to hear the *messages* and *meanings* which are being communicated by his own physiological reactions. . . . He comes to realize that his own inner reactions and experiences, the *messages* of his sense and viscera, are friendly. He comes to want to be close to his *inner sources* of *information. . . .*" (Rogers, 1961, p. 174, italics ours)

This leads to the client's having

> access to all of the available data in the situation. . . . He could permit his total organism, his consciousness participating, to consider each stimulus, need, and demand, its relative intensity and importance, and out of this complex weighting and balancing, discover that course of action which would come closest to satisfying all his needs in the situation. (Rogers, 1961, p. 190)

Thus, the work of Wexler and his colleagues is an extension of an idea already implicit in Rogers's own work.

Wexler (1974) suggests that the therapist is a "surrogate information processor." What therapists do is direct clients' attention to ignored or neglected aspects of information (that is, feelings and experience), help clients sort out and differentiate relevant from irrelevant aspects of this and other information, and then help clients integrate the information into new and more effective cognitive structures for interacting with reality. Empathy responses are seen as active shapers and facilitators of information processing. They draw out the implications in what clients say, focus attention on selected aspects of client communication, and model and suggest ways of integrating or synthesizing differing themes in what clients say.

Wexler's view of the client-centered therapist as being quite active in helping clients process information appears to be accurate. In a famous film of Carl Rogers working with a woman named Gloria (Rogers, 1965), for instance, most of Rogers's responses did more than simply reflect what Gloria said. Instead they drew out implications, compared differing bits of information, and focused Gloria's attention on the parts of what she said that Rogers probably felt were important. In addition, Bohart (1982) has argued that the client-centered therapist may be indirectly shaping and molding clients' cognitions in a manner reminiscent of the goals of Beck and other cognitive therapists. In any case, Wexler's cognitive view of client-centered therapy makes it compatible with recent developments among some cognitive behaviorists, who now emphasize meaning (Mahoney, 1985) and "meaning structure" (Meichenbaum, Butler, & Gruson, 1981).

In the 1970s Rogers's attention turned to the use of encounter groups. Encounter groups are groups of individuals, in which openness, honesty, and feedback among participants is encouraged. They were highly popular in the 1960s and 1970s (Lieberman, Yalom, & Miles, 1973; Rogers, 1970a). From a client-centered perspective these groups have been used for therapy purposes, as well as for increasing communication and understanding among nonpatient populations.

Rogers's recent efforts involved utilizing encounter groups to increase understanding among blacks and whites in South Africa, Protestants and Roman Catholics in Northern Ireland, and other disparate groups (Rogers & Ryback, 1984). He also did work in the Soviet Union (Rogers, 1987). Rogers believed that if world leaders could communicate on a more personal level, chances for world peace and understanding would be increased. As an example he argued that the Camp David talks between Begin of Israel and Sadat of Egypt were going nowhere until President Carter began to share some personal reminiscences with Begin. It was shortly after that the stalemate in negotiations was broken (Rogers & Ryback, 1984).

EVALUATION OF CLIENT-CENTERED THERAPY

Research

Rogers was one of the pioneers of empirical research on psychotherapy. An early attempt to evaluate the effects of client-centered therapy on outpatients (Rogers & Dymond, 1954) found support for its effectiveness, but many have criticized the research design as flawed. A later attempt to evaluate its effects on hospitalized schizophrenics (Rogers, Gendlin, Kiesler, & Truax, 1967) produced equivocal results, with some evidence for effectiveness if the therapist was high in the therapeutic qualities. In general, research has supported the effectiveness of client-centered therapy (Smith, Glass, & Miller, 1980), with its average level being in the same range as psychoanalytic, transactional analytic, and many other approaches. However, it did not have as high an effect size as some of the cognitive and behavioral approaches.

Recently Rogers and Sanford (1984) have summarized research done in foreign countries on psychotherapy, the teacher-student relationship, and the use of encounter groups. These studies are reported as demonstrating the effectiveness of the person-centered approach. Specifically, teachers high in the facilitative (therapeutic) qualities were found to be more effective. The encounter groups were utilized with a variety of populations, from neurotic students to businesspersons to cancer patients. Generally these participants experienced positive benefits from their encounter experiences.

Therapeutic Conditions The hypothesis that high therapeutic conditions of warmth, empathy, and genuineness are both necessary and sufficient for therapy has been extensively explored. Originally it was believed that the evidence was strong that high levels of these therapist qualities were related to therapeutic effectiveness (Truax & Mitchell, 1971). However, more recent results were not supportive, and critical reanalyses of some of the earlier data have been done.

At present reviews of the research arrive at conflicting conclusions. Mitchell, Bozarth, & Krauft (1977) conclude that the evidence is mixed, though it "does seem to suggest that empathy, warmth, and genuineness are related in some way to client change but . . . their potency and generalizability are not as great as once thought" (p. 481). On the other hand, Gurman (1977) has concluded that "there exists substantial, if not overwhelming, evidence in support of the hypothesized relationship between patient-perceived therapeutic conditions and outcome in individual psychotherapy and counseling" (p. 523).

One of the research problems is that a stronger positive relationship is found if the conditions are measured by the clients' perceptions of them than if they are measured in other ways, such as rating the tapes of the therapist by independent observers. But, of course, if a client is getting better, he or she might feel more positively toward therapy and see the therapist as higher in these conditions. Two recent reviews both note that there are positive relationships between high levels of therapist conditions as perceived by the client and change. One (Patterson, 1984) generally concludes that the evidence is supportive. The other (Watson, 1984) does not believe the supportive evidence is a true test of Rogers's initial hypotheses. In sum, there is controversy over the relationship of these therapeutic conditions to change.

Experiencing One of the basic goals of client-centered therapy is to help the client "get in touch with his or her feelings," or, as we have seen, to learn to utilize the experiential level of his or her personality more fully. It was believed that therapy increased this ability and that an increase in this ability would relate to a positive therapeutic outcome. Gendlin and his colleagues (Gendlin, Beebe, Cassens, Klein, & Oberlander, 1968) found that high levels of this ability did relate to positive outcome, but that ability to relate to one's experience did not increase to any great extent over the course of therapy. Instead, it appeared that people high in this ability had entered therapy with high levels. Therapy then helped them to utilize this ability to change, but it did not teach the ability. Since these results, Gendlin has devoted his efforts to developing ways of teaching this ability (see Gendlin, 1981), which he now calls "focusing ability."

Gendlin and his colleagues noted an important distinction between two ways of having a "here and now" focus in therapy. Many existential and humanistically oriented therapists (see Chapter 6) believe the client should be discouraged from talking about past events (as in psychoanalysis) and that therapist and client should focus on the client's current feelings and perceptions of the therapist, herself, and other group members in group therapy. Yet when Gendlin and his colleagues attempted to measure here and now focus in this sense, it turned out not to relate to positive change. In other words, therapy that focused on issues and feelings arising from the therapy context was not more successful than therapy that allowed discussion of issues outside of that context, such as the client's past. Similarly, Lieberman, Yalom, & Miles (1973) found that encounter groups that allowed clients to "bring in outside material," rather than keep a here and now focus on interactions within the group, were more successful.

In contrast, Gendlin found that a different kind of here and now focus did relate to positive change. Clients who were experientially involved in the here and now in whatever they were talking about (for instance, the past) were more likely to experience positive change.

Other research on the ability to relate to oneself experientially (or to focus) has found that it relates to creativity (Gendlin, 1969) and even to longevity in elderly people (Gendlin, 1981). However, because client-centered therapy does not teach this ability, Gendlin has suggested that therapies that use more active or body-oriented techniques might be useful for people low in this ability.

Task Analysis A recent movement in psychotherapy research is to study the sequence of specific events in psychotherapy, using what is called a "task analytic" approach (Rice & Greenberg, 1984). Rice and Saperia (1984) studied "evocative unfolding," which is a more specific and well-defined approach to client-centered empathic responding. It is based on the belief that clients describe situations and their reactions to them in a highly condensed form.

Suppose a client brings in the following "problematic reaction: She was in a conversation with a friend, suddenly blurted out something hostile, then felt embarrassed afterwards. When she relates this incident to the therapist, she condenses it into a few sentences. Through evocative unfolding the therapist has the client try to vividly recapture the experience. With that as a basis, the client is led through an exploration of the experience, focusing both on her internal reactions and on what was going on in the situation.

During this process meanings implicit in the client's reaction to the situation become clear. In addition, the client usually realizes that her reaction to the situation represents a broader way she has of reacting to other situations as well. This leads to a reprocessing of the experience, and some therapeutic movement or gain. For example, the client, in vividly recalling the incident, might realize that she had been perceiving the other person in the situation as challenging her intellectual competence. She might become aware that this had led her to feel that she was being "put down," although she was not completely aware of her perception or her feeling at the time. Her blurting out an insult now no longer seems so unexpected and inexplicable. In addition, she might also realize that she has a tendency to perceive herself as being criticized or rejected whenever someone seems to be disagreeing with her.

Rice and Saperia studied the process of evocative unfolding by having undergraduate psychology students meet with therapists for two sessions. In one session they dealt with a problematic reaction that they had experienced. In the other the students met with the same therapist, but the therapist responded in a more traditional, unstructured, client-centered way. Some students had evocative unfolding first and the traditional approach second, while others had the reverse. The study found that evocative unfolding led to more therapeutic resolution than the traditional client-centered approach. In addition, by tape-recording the interactions and studying the sequence of therapeutic events that occurred, general support was found for the model of how evocative unfolding worked.

Theory

Client-centered therapy generally avoids diagnosis in the sense of labeling personality types and problems, and it has not developed a theory of how different types of personalities are organized or evolve. In contrast, object relations theory presents a specific model of how borderline personality develops and what the underlying psychological difficulty is (failure of separation-individuation). Similarly, while social learning theory does not have a general theory of personality types, it does have a theory of how individuals develop different kinds of behavior patterns in different situations.

There is a reason for the lack of such theoretical constructs in client-centered therapy. It is that the therapist wishes to encounter her client free of preconceptions in order to relate to the unique person that he is. There is a fear that psychiatric diagnosis or preconceived models of personality structure and development will predispose the therapist to relate to the client as a type rather than as an individual.

The virtue in this approach is that, if practiced, it does allow the therapist to be open to the configuration of experiences, talents, and characteristics of the client. However, there are a number of drawbacks. First, client-centered therapists do have theoretical preconceptions. Generally they believe that a client's problems are due to his lack of self-acceptance, resulting from the imposition of conditions of worth on his behavior and from not being receptive to his experiential life. Therefore, the therapist is likely to look for, and to find, signs of lack of self-acceptance and a distrust of feelings.

Another problem is that the client-centered therapist must virtually "start over" with each new client. Her perspective does not have a theory of how particular problem behaviors develop. All she has is a very general and vague notion that somehow a particular client's problems, no matter how they differ from some other client's problems, are due to a lack of self-acceptance and openness. This umbrella theory is supposed to account for alcoholism, schizophrenia, depression, phobias, adjustment disorders, borderline personality, narcissistic personality, and so on. In contrast, both psychoanalysis and social learning theory have some theoretical "machinery" to account for how different people develop different disorders. These accounts do lead to specific treatment recommendations for different disorders, but client-centered therapy does not.

One of the contributions of the client-centered approach is the eclectic model of therapy, where the therapist is free to borrow from psychoanalytic, behavioral, cognitive, systems, or other perspectives. However, the approach provides no guidelines for when to use aspects of these different therapies. The choice depends on the moment-to-moment intuition of the therapist. It is possible that as our knowledge progresses, we will be able to say, "If the person is depressed, generally do this," "If the person is anxious, generally this works," and so on. Yet the client-centered approach provides no basis for detecting differences between disorders or for formulating specific treatment plans.

The client-centered approach cannot make these differentiations partly because it has no model of personality organization. All that can be said about the functioning of an individual is whether he trusts his feelings, is congruent, holds constructs tentatively, and is self-accepting. Yet many psychologists believe there is more to the organization of personality than that. Even the concept of self in Rogerian theory is vague. Ironically, Rogers can be said to be one of the first to emphasize the development of a true, actualized, and separate self, predating to some degree the efforts of object relations theorists and self psychologists. Yet many have argued (see Kahn, 1985, for example) that Rogers's concept of self is less well-developed, deep, and complex than that of Kohut and the object relations theorists. According to Rogers individuals are supposed to self-actualize, to become their "real selves," but he does not present a clear concept of what the real self is. It seems to have to do with what the individual feels, but this is not explicated clearly. Rogers does talk about the self-concept, but that is presumably the image a person has of himself, not who the person really is. He talks of how people often try to live up to a concept of themselves, resulting in distrust of their "real selves." Does he mean that the "real self" they distrust is simply another term for feelings or experience? This is left unclear.

Because of the lack of personality theory and because of its intense focus on the uniqueness of the individual, client-centered therapy does not have a well-differentiated view of psychopathology. Rather than diagnose or categorize the client, the client-centered therapist prefers to relate empathically to the client's experiential view of the world. The belief in multiple realities means that the therapist does not try to judge the appropriateness of the client's experience of the world. This may be an effective approach when working with a client—creating a trusting atmosphere in which therapy can take place. The problem arises when we move away from therapy to attempts to devise theoretical models to understand personality and psychopathology.

The client-centered therapist's intense focus on the individual tends to result in a view that all psychopathology arises from the client's inability to trust himself. First, such a view ignores biological factors. Second, it ignores the possibility that social, ecological, and systems factors may create psychopathology, even in people who are congruent. In studies of "groupthink" in social psychology, Janis (1972) found that otherwise "normal" individuals can come to make risky and bizarre decisions under the influence of certain subtle dynamics of group interaction. Similarly, Haney, Banks, and Zimbardo (1973) found that some students who were otherwise free of any apparent signs of psychopathology became brutal or experienced psychological breakdowns when put in roles of guard or prisoner in a "mock" prison setup. It is difficult to attribute such pathological behavior to personal incongruences within the self. Finally, Watzlawick, a family systems theorist (see Chapter 9), has argued that often pathological behavior arises *from* being congruent. He suggests that pathological behavior is behavior that has worked in the past, but is dysfunctional in the current situation although the person does not recognize this. When things continue to go wrong, the person tries harder to make things go right by increasing the behaviors that worked in the past. Increasing the now dysfunctional behaviors simply makes matters worse. Yet the person is behaving in what appears to the person to be a congruent manner; he's doing what he believes.

In general there is an intense "self" orientation in client-centered therapy. Rogers (1977) believes that social changes do not result from attempts to change society at a collective level, but from creating personal change within individuals. Yet the individual and society are two parts of a balanced system. Elsewhere Rogers has argued that our school systems create a lack of self-trust and stifle self-actualization (Rogers, 1970b; Rogers, 1983). In order to create self-actualizing people it would seem that we must therefore change society (at least our school systems), not just try to foster actualization in individuals. But to change society we must understand all political, cultural, and social forces that are involved. Schools are the way they are because they are an intricate part of society. For instance, Rogers generally believes it is better for students to learn by pursuing their own interests than by studying what others (the teachers and the institution) think is important. While this may be true, the problem is that society has a stake in what any individual student learns. The sole goal of education is not only actualization of the individual. It is also, among other things, to prepare the student to play a role in society. Therefore, society dictates through the schools what it thinks needs to be learned. Some of this may be legitimate. Consider medical school. If Rogers's ideas were carried to an extreme, could we rely on surgeons who learned only what they felt interested in or is there a body of knowledge that they *ought* to learn if they want to be surgeons? We are sympathetic with Rogers's views that schools do not foster individual initiative, actualization, and creativity as much as they could. But in order to change this, we would argue, one has to do more than change individuals from within. One must understand how schools play an intricate role in society and understand the forces that keep them the way they are.

There are other problems with the Rogerian focus on the self. These are shared with other theories such as object relations theory, gestalt, and existentialism. All of these theories in one form or another see the fundamental event in the development of mental health as the development of an integrated, autonomous, separate, actualized self. It is assumed that only an autonomous, actualized self can maturely relate to others. Therefore, for all these theories, good relationships to other people follow self-actualization. However, it has been argued that the emphasis on individuation and development of selfhood is culture-specific and may reflect the high value Western cultures place on individualism. In contrast, Asian personality theories (Pederson, 1983) stress the development of the person through relationships. What Asian theories see as healthy, Western theories tend to see as unhealthy: an "other" orientation, the positive value of dependency, and so on. And the reverse is true; for some Asian theories "self" doesn't really even exist, and an emphasis on self-actualization is contrary to optimal development. Similarly, Gilligan (1982) has argued that the emphasis many theories place on development of separateness and autonomy over interdependence and connectedness to others reflects a masculine cultural bias. Whether there is a correct theory, we do not know. The important thing is to realize that emphasis on self-actualization and autonomy may reflect "actualization" of cultural values as much as it reflects "fundamental truth" about personality development.

CONTRIBUTIONS OF THE CLIENT-CENTERED APPROACH

One of Rogers's contributions has been his emphasis on the importance of the therapist-client relationship. This is now generally accepted by therapists of many differing orientations. In particular his emphasis on empathy is now incorporated into such diverse approaches as Beck's cognitive therapy of depression and Kohut's self psychology. The emphasis on the therapeutic conditions of warmth, empathy, and genuineness has been translated into communication skills training programs. And Rogers's belief that nonprofessionals high in these conditions can be effective counselors has contributed to the use of nonprofessional counselors in many ways by community psychologists.

Rogers was one of the first theorists to stress the importance of the self and of the person's being congruent. His focus on self-acceptance is similar to ideas put forward by cognitive theorists such as Beck and Ellis. His view of multiple realities is currently accepted by the constructivist viewpoint of theorists like Paul Watzlawick as well as the cognitive theorist Michael Mahoney.

Finally, Gendlin has contributed an integrative model for the underlying process of change in psychotherapy. In addition, he has done extensive research on experiencing, which currently is one of the most well-substantiated constructs in terms of relating to change in psychotherapy. In general, the client-centered tradition has had a heavy research orientation and has contributed substantially to the empirical investigation of psychotherapy process.

REFERENCES

Beck, A. T., Rush, A. J., Shaw, B. F., & Emery, G. (1979). *Cognitive therapy of depression.* New York: Guilford.

Bohart, A. (1982). Similarities between cognitive and humanistic approaches to psychotherapy. *Cognitive Therapy and Research, 6,* 245–250.

Brown, J. H., & Brown, C. S. (1977). *Systematic counseling: A guide for the practitioner.* Champaign, IL: Research Press.

Carkhuff, R. R., & Berenson, B. G. (1967). *Beyond counseling and therapy.* New York: Holt, Rinehart and Winston.

Cowan, P. A. (1978). *Piaget: With feeling.* New York: Holt, Rinehart and Winston.

Egan, G. (1982). *The skilled helper: A model for systematic helping and interpersonal relating* (2nd ed.). Monterey, CA: Brooks/Cole.

Ends, E. J., & Page, C. W. (1957). A study of three types of group psychotherapy with hospitalized male inebriates. *Quarterly Journal of Studies in Alcoholism, 18,* 263–277.

Gendlin, E. T. (1967). Therapeutic procedures in dealing with schizophrenics. In C. R. Rogers, E. T. Gendlin, D. J. Kiesler, & C. B. Truax (Eds.), *The therapeutic relationship and its impact: A study of psychotherapy with schizophrenics.* Madison: University of Wisconsin Press.

Gendlin, E. T. (1968). The experiential response. In E. Hammer (Ed.), *Use of interpretation in treatment.* New York: Grune & Stratton.

Gendlin, E. T. (1969). Focusing. *Psychotherapy: Theory, research and practice, 6,* 4–15.

Gendlin, E. T. (1973). Experiential psychotherapy. In R. Corsini (Ed.), *Current psychotherapies,* Itasca, IL: Peacock.

Gendlin, E. T. (1981). *Focusing.* New York: Bantam Books.

Gendlin, E. T. (1984). The politics of giving therapy away: Listening and focusing. In D. Larson (Ed.), *Teaching psychological skills: Models for giving psychology away.* Monterey, CA: Brooks/Cole.

Gendlin, E. T., Beebe, J., Cassens, J., Klein, M., & Oberlander, M. (1967). Focusing ability in psychotherapy, personality, and creativity. In J. M. Shlien (Ed.), *Research in psychotherapy* (Vol. 3). Washington, DC: American Psychological Association.

Gilligan, C. (1982). *In a different voice.* Cambridge, MA: Harvard University Press.

Goodman, G. (1984). SASHA tapes: Expanding options for help-intended communication. In D. Larson (Ed.), *Teaching psychological skills: Models for giving psychology away.* Monterey, CA: Brooks/Cole.

Gordon, T. (1984). Three decades of democratizing relationships through training. In D. Larson (Ed.), *Teaching psychological skills: Models for giving psychology away.* Monterey, CA: Brooks/Cole.

Gurman, A. S. (1977). The patient's perception of the therapeutic relationship. In A. S. Gurman & A. M. Razin (Eds.), *Effective psychotherapy: A handbook of research.* New York: Pergamon Press.

Haney, C., Banks, C., & Zimbardo, P. (1973). Interpersonal dynamics in a simulated prison. *International Journal of Criminology and Penology, 1,* 69–97.

Hart, J. T. (1970). The development of client-centered therapy. In J. T. Hart & T. M. Tomlinson (Eds.), *New directions in client-centered therapy.* New York: Houghton Mifflin.

Henschel, D. M., & Bohart, A. C. (1984). Egocentric versus decentered empathy (Summary of paper presentation). In G. I. Lubin & M. K. Poulsen (Eds.), *Piagetian theory and its implications for mental health. Proceedings: Ninth through twelfth Interdisciplinary Conference.* (Vol. 2). Los Angeles: University of Southern California.

Janis, I. L. (1972). *Victims of groupthink.* Boston: Houghton Mifflin.

Janov, A. (1970). *The primal scream.* New York: Dell.

Kahn, E. (1985). Heinz Kohut and Carl Rogers: A timely comparison. *American psychologist, 40,* 893–9045.

Kelly, G. A. (1955). *The psychology of personal constructs: A theory of personality* (2 vols.). New York: Norton.

Kraepelin, E. (1906). *Lectures on clinical psychiatry.* London: Bailliere, Tindall and Cox.

Laing, R. D. (1967). *The politics of experience.* New York: Pantheon Books.

Lieberman, M. A., Yalom, I. I., & Miles, M. B. (1973). *Encounter groups: First facts.* New York: Basic Books.

Mahoney, M. J. (1985). Psychotherapy and human change processes. In M. J. Mahoney & A. Freeman (Eds.), *Cognition and psychotherapy.* New York: Plenum.

Meichenbaum, D., Butler, L., & Gruson, L. (1981). Toward a conceptual model of social competence. In J. D. Wine & M. D. Smye (Eds.), *Social competence.* New York: Guilford.

Mitchell, K. M., Bozarth, J. D., & Krauft, C. C. (1977). A reappraisal of the therapeutic effectiveness of accurate empathy, nonpossessive warmth, and genuineness. In A. S. Gurman & A. M. Razin (Eds.), *Effective psychotherapy: A handbook of research.* New York: Pergamon Press.

Patterson, C. H. (1984). Empathy, warmth, and genuineness in psychotherapy: A review of reviews. *Psychotherapy, 21,* 431–444.

Pedersen, P. B. (1983). Asian personality theory. In R. J. Corsini & A. J. Marsella (Eds.), *Personality theories, research, and assessment.* Itasca, IL: Peacock.

Rice, L. N., & Greenberg, L. S. (Eds.). (1984). *Patterns of change: Intensive analysis of psychotherapy process.* New York: Guilford.

Rice, L. N. & Saperia, E. P. (1984). Task analysis of the resolution of problematic reactions. In L. N. Rice & L. S. Greenberg, (Eds.), *Patterns of change: Intensive analysis of psychotherapy process.* New York: Guilford.

Rogers, C. R. (1942). *Counseling and psychotherapy.* Boston: Houghton Mifflin.

Rogers, C. R. (1957). The necessary and sufficient conditions of therapeutic personality change. *Journal of Consulting Psychology, 21,* 95–103.

Rogers, C. R. (1961). *On becoming a person.* Boston: Houghton Mifflin.

Rogers, C. R. (1965). *Client-centered therapy* (Film No. 1). In E. Shostrom (Ed.), *Three ap-*

proaches to psychotherapy (Three 16 mm color motion pictures). Santa Ana, CA: Psychological Films.

Rogers, C. R. (1967). Toward a modern approach to values: The valuing process in the mature person. In C. R. Rogers & B. Stevens (Eds.), *Person to person: The problem of being human.* New York: Pocket Books.

Rogers, C. R. (1970a). *Carl Rogers on encounter groups.* New York: Harper & Row.

Rogers, C. R. (1970b). Current assumptions in graduate education: A passionate statement. In J. T. Hart & T. M. Tomlinson (Eds.), *New directions in client-centered therapy.* Boston: Houghton Mifflin.

Rogers, C. R. (1977). *Carl Rogers on personal power.* New York: Delacorte.

Rogers, C. R. (1980). Do we need "a" reality? In C. R. Rogers, *A way of being.* Boston: Houghton Mifflin.

Rogers, C. R. (1983). *Freedom to learn for the 80's.* Columbus OH: Merrill.

Rogers, C. R. (with R. Sanford). (1987). *Inside the world of the soviet professional.* Unpublished manuscript.

Rogers, C. R., & Dymond, R. F. (Eds.). (1954). *Psychotherapy and personality change.* Chicago: University of Chicago Press.

Rogers, C. R., Gendlin, E. T., Kiesler, D. J., & Truax, C. B. (1967). *The therapeutic relationship and its impact: A study of psychotherapy with schizophrenics.* Madison: University of Wisconsin Press.

Rogers, C. R., & Sanford, R. C. (1984). Client-centered psychotherapy. In H. I. Kaplan & B. J. Sadock (Eds.), *Comprehensive textbook of psychiatry* (Vol. 4). Baltimore: Williams & Wilkins.

Rogers, C. R., & Ryback, D. (1984). One alternative to nuclear planetary suicide. In R. F. Levant & J. M. Shlien (Eds.), *Client-centered therapy and the person-centered approach: New directions in theory, research, and practice.* New York: Praeger.

Smith, M. L., Glass, G. V., & Miller, T. I. (1980). *The benefits of psychotherapy.* Baltimore: Johns Hopkins University Press.

Truax, C. B., & Carkhuff, R. (1967). *Toward effective counseling and psychotherapy: Training and practice.* Chicago: Aldine.

Truax, C. B., & Mitchell, K. M. (1971). Research on certain therapist interpersonal skills in relation to process and outcome. In A. E. Bergin & S. L. Garfield (Eds.), *Handbook of psychotherapy and behavior change.* New York: Wiley.

Watson, N. (1984). The empirical status of Rogers's hypotheses of the necessary and sufficient conditions for effective psychotherapy. In R. F. Levant & J. M. Shlien (Eds.), *Client-centered therapy and the person-centered approach: New directions in theory, research, and practice.* New York: Praeger.

Wexler, D. A. (1974). A cognitive theory of experiencing, self-actualization, and therapeutic process. In D. A. Wexler & L. N. Rice (Eds.), *Innovations in client-centered therapy.* New York: Wiley.

Wexler, D. A., & Rice, L. N. (Eds.). (1974). *Innovations in client-centered therapy.* New York: Wiley.

Chapter 6

Existential, Gestalt, and Other Humanistic Approaches

> I have forsaken an earlier position . . . because even the earlier position was only a pause on the way. What lasts in thinking is the way. (Martin Heidegger, 1959, p. 98)
>
> Lose your mind and come to your senses. (Fritz Perls)

We have already considered one of the most important existential-humanistic approaches in the work of Carl Rogers. In this chapter we will look at the two other major approaches in this perspective, existential therapy and gestalt therapy, and briefly consider transpersonal psychology.

THE CONCEPT OF THE RIVER

Of all the major approaches, the existential-humanistic approach places the most emphasis on the person as the author of his or her own life. For this approach the very essence of the person is the freedom to shape and reshape his or her own life and identity. The personality is viewed as a continual process of growth and change. The individual never possesses a fixed self, or character structure, or identity. People are "open systems," continually interacting with the environment, taking in information, and growing and changing as they creatively deal with a continual influx of information. The metaphor most appropriate for the personality in the humanistic approaches is "the river." While the river can be said to have an identity, it is never the same from one moment to the next or one place to the next. Its nature at any given moment is influenced by where it has been, where it is going, and where it is now and what happens to it at any time in the past or present.

Humanists believe that if early childhood events are still influencing a person it is because the person, as the author of her own fate, is still allowing or choosing (often unconsciously) to let them do so. Personality is not so much something that is built up inside from experiences, as it is something that the person is actively maintaining through choices. The radical emphasis on growth, change, and choice means the humanistic approaches place a heavy emphasis on creativity and the individual's reaching his or her full potential.

Humanistic approaches also generally see the human being holistically. No part of the human is disowned or seen as somehow "lower" or "less human" than other parts. Humanists generally reject Freud's view of the person as split into relatively "higher" (ego) functions and relatively "lower" or more primitive (id) functions. Sex and aggression are not seen as primitive, selfish impulses in and of themselves. They are primitive and selfish only if the person chooses to express them that way. If owned and acknowledged, these parts can play creative, life-actualizing roles in personality development. By the same token the emotional and intuitive functions are not seen as things to be controlled. Subjectivity, fantasy, and intuition are all regarded as sources of growth and creativity.

Many of the approaches within the humanistic perspective either trace their roots to a philosophical movement called "existentialism" or reflect ideas compatible with it. For this reason, we will begin this chapter with a brief survey of ideas from the existential philosophical tradition, concentrating on the work of Edmund Husserl, Martin Heidegger, and Jean-Paul Sartre.

EXISTENTIAL THERAPY

Philosophical Background

Phenomenology is the philosophical approach associated with Edmund Husserl (1964). Husserl's goal was to suspend acceptance of all concepts about reality in order to get to things that could not be doubted about reality: pure phenomena. Imagine looking at all things that come into your consciousness as though they were images on a movie screen. Imagine examining them while suspending all judgment about what they are, what they mean, or what they consist of. To the extent that you can do this, you approximate what Husserl was striving for. For instance, you see someone acting "crazy." Can you suspend your judgment that he is acting "crazy"? Can you suspend your tendency to characterize his behavior at all? It is impossible to suspend all preconceptions, but the phenomenologists tried to approach this ideal. Their cry was "To the things themselves!"

One example of the phenomenological method in psychology is the work of R. D. Laing (see Chapter 5). Laing wished to study schizophrenia without any preconceptions. So he suspended the ideas that the schizophrenic is mentally ill, crazy, or incomprehensible. In trying to look at the schizophrenic without preconceptions, he arrived at a theory very different from the traditional view of schizophrenia as an illness or disorder. Recently, Carl Rogers (1985) discussed several attempts to use the phenomenological method scientifically. As we shall see in Chapter 11, the phenomenological method in various guises appears in most approaches to psychotherapy. Some meditational approaches are virtually identical in their goals to the phenomenological method.

Martin Heidegger's philosophy was based on Husserl's phenomenological approach, but went in a different direction (Frings, 1968; Schmitt, 1969). He held that humans, in contrast to objects, exist as interactive entities with reality. People are *activities* rather than fixed things, in constant dialogue with their surroundings. At any given moment the individual is a creative construction of both past history and current situation. As a result the individual is never the same from moment to moment. Heidegger would have considered the belief in a fixed personality structure, including the various labels such as borderline, passive, or narcissistic personality, to be an *inauthentic* way of relating to ourselves and others. People do not "have" personalities; they constantly create and recreate their personalities through their choices and actions.

Inauthenticity is an attempt to deny the existence of choice. Jean-Paul Sartre (1956) suggested that people become anxious when they face the fact that they are responsible for themselves and their choices. The concept of a fixed identity reduces anxiety. Thinking of myself as a "good" person becomes a substitute for examining my behavior and making choices on the basis of rightness or goodness. If I define myself as a borderline personality, then I no longer have to consider myself responsible for my impulsive acts. In order to avoid the anxiety of choice we all seek fixed identities, such as "being a doctor," or "being an honorable man." Yet what really counts is not who we are, but what we do, that is, how we choose to behave.

Every time a person makes a choice he opens up new possibilities in both himself and the world. For example, if I act cruelly toward someone, I "bring out" the negative in myself and perhaps in that person. If I act caringly, I may allow potential positive aspects to come forth.

As such, humans are the creatures through which reality "knows" itself. An individual's actions allow what has previously been only potential, or "hidden," in reality to be articulated. The most important kind of knowing is *knowing how.* Knowing how is the kind of knowing involved in acting. For instance, learning how to play the guitar brings forth potential in the player and musical potential in an object. Intellectual *knowing about* facts is less useful. For instance, therapy should be a learning *how* to be human, rather than a learning *about* oneself, that is, about one's past. One needs to learn how to listen to oneself, how to be in tune with one's nature as a creature in transition.

With this brief summary of its philosophical basis, we will now look at existential psychotherapy. We will not concentrate on different existential theorists by name, but we will list here some of the important names: Ludwig Binswanger (1963), Medard Boss (1963), Rollo May (May, Angel, & Ellenberger, 1958), J. F. T. Bugental (1976), Salvador Maddi (Kobasa & Maddi, 1983), and Irving Yalom (1981). A closely related approach is Victor Frankl's (1963) logotherapy.

Theory of Personality and Psychopathology

For the existential approach the primary fact of human existence is that people are free to create their own meaning and identity in life. But can anyone be *anything* he or she wants? The answer to that is obviously no. There are limits. People must accept *finiteness* as a fundamental fact of existence. Humans are finite in two senses. Reality imposes *limits* and everyone ultimately dies. Reality places limits on people in several ways. We are limited by our biology and by the time and place into which we are born. Being born with a handicap, into a starving Ethiopian family, or as a black slave in 1800 would all impose certain limitations.

But there are two ways of thinking about limits: To see them as restricting freedom or to see them as defining freedom. Limits and freedom are two sides of the same coin. There could be no freedom without limits. If I could choose to be anything I wanted at any time, then both freedom and choice would lose all meaning. If I could have anything I wanted at any given moment, then I would never really have to choose.

Thus freedom and choice are mutually interdependent. The individual is free within the limitations imposed by the facts of his existence to create life in any way he can. The individual is free to choose how he will deal with limits. He can view them as immutable barriers and give up, or accept them as challenges. If I lose the use of my legs in an automobile accident, I can withdraw from activities or I can learn to maneuver in a wheelchair and continue with my life. Some limitations cannot be transcended. If I am in prison sentenced to be executed, I may be unable to escape or get the sentence changed. However I can still choose how I spend my last days, and how I approach death. The trick is to do as much as possible with what one has. Each individual can be creative and forge something meaningful out of whatever life has given him. Existentialists call the courage to face up to adverse circumstances in life the "courage to be" (Tillich, 1952).

The individual's choices not only create the meaning of her life and being, but also influence the meaning of events surrounding her. The existential view can properly be considered a "field" or "systems" view of behavior. As the meaning of a word is determined by the rest of the sentence it is embedded in and the meaning of a sentence may change if one word is changed, the meaning of any event in an individual's life is determined by the whole web of meanings she has attributed to herself and the world. How the individual sees herself and the world may change if the meaning of some important event in her life changes.

Therefore people create the structure of their own life, and each choice moves them along their life path. But at any moment they can choose to alter the path. Right now your choice to continue to read this chapter is in some sense "creating" who you are. In reading this chapter you are acting on your perception of your interests and values at this moment. Perhaps you are a student planning a career in psychology, but perhaps you are not a good student. Perhaps you feel awkward around others and have low self-esteem. If, as you read, you grow more and more bored, you might toss the book away and go change your major the next day. Perhaps you change to dentistry. Pursuing dentistry, you associate with different people and take different courses. Now you may find new aspects of yourself opening up. Your values may change and your self-image may improve. You discover that you are so interested in dentistry that you do well academically. Instead of feeling stupid, you now see yourself as motivated and capable. Possibly before you saw yourself as awkward, dull, and romantically undesirable. Now you find yourself talking with enthusiasm to another person who is interested in dentistry, and romantic sparks begin to fly. Your self-image in that area begins to change also.

If people create their life structure and identity through their choices, why does anyone choose a miserable or self-defeating existence? One answer to this is that they are often unaware that they are choosing. They may not have had any experiences that allow them to realize that they have a choice in how they move through life. A woman who grows up in a family and community where the message is that a woman's place is in the home may accept that message as objectively true. She will not see the possibility of any choice over her role as a woman.

Many existential theorists also stress the denial of the possibility of choice. According to May and Yalom (1984), people deny choice because of anxiety. They point out that existentialism is a "depth psychology," similar to psychoanalysis, but what is hidden is the possibility of choice, rather than sexual and aggressive impulses. To avoid anxiety, people avoid their own potential. Often they try to actualize an image of what society says they ought to be. They ought to be a businessperson rather than an artist, married rather than single, heterosexual rather than homosexual, religious rather than nonreligious, or whatever. They deny the possibility of choosing to be anything other than what society says they should be. And, they become anxious if they sense that they may not fit these images. They deny to themselves knowledge of their true wants and goals, in order to try to fit these images.

But these attempts to avoid anxiety don't always work, and anxiety may be a signal that one is living an inauthentic existence. Two cases illustrate this point. A man was going for his doctorate because his parents strongly wanted a Ph.D. in the family. About three years into his graduate program, just about the time he had to pass three comprehensive exams to advance to his dissertation, he became anxious and depressed. The interesting thing was that he became anxious and depressed after passing the first two exams with outstanding performances. He found he could not even study for the third. An existential view would be that as the man approached completion of his degree, the lack of fit between that goal and his own feelings grew more and more pronounced. After a stormy period of depression, anxiety, and several suicide attempts, this man finally took an "existential leap" and dropped out of school. He got a job as a teacher of handicapped children, and his depression and anxiety vanished, and when last heard of, he was living a normal life. In this case anxiety and depression were signals of inauthencity, rather than from repressed instincts (psychoanalysis), dysfunctional cognitions (cognitive approaches), or conditioning (behavioral approaches).

Another case was a woman in an unfulfilling marriage. She was distant, cold, and reserved, seemed vaguely "out of touch" all the time, and was usually somewhat negative and depressed. Some friends described her as a basically negative person who "liked" to see the worst in the world. Finally, on facing up to the lack of fit between herself and her marriage, she left it. Literally overnight her "character" changed. The same person that had struck most of us for years as cold and reserved became open, warm, and vital.

For existentialists anxiety results from denial of one's authenticity and potential.

But we said earlier that it was to avoid anxiety that people denied their ability to choose in the first place. According to existentialists, people deny their ability to choose to avoid the basic anxiety associated with human finiteness. For existentialists, anxiety is unavoidable. To live is to have to choose. But to have to choose is to face up to the basic uncertainty of life. Whenever we make a choice we are literally betting our lives. By choosing to read this book and to pursue your college career, you are betting that a college degree will be good for you in some way. The problem is that you may bet on a career only to find there are no jobs available in the field you want when you graduate. Or there may be jobs, but you discover that you want to change fields or that you aren't as talented in your field as you would have liked. To live authentically is to face up to the fact that there are no "safe" choices in life. And, eventually you will die. If you happen to have made "wrong" choices, time may run out before you can rectify things. Thus death is the ultimate source of anxiety, and the ability to face up to one's own death is a precondition to authentic living.

Existentialists do not hold that one choice is necessarily superior to another. Any choice involves risk. One is taking a risk by leaving a marriage (you might be unhappier outside it; you might have been able to work things out), and one is taking a risk by staying in it (you might miss a happier existence; you might not be able to work things out). Telling oneself "I must get a Ph.D.," or "I must stay married," or "I must remain a full-time housewife" reduces anxiety. Then you do not have to make a choice either way. But even though you do not know it, you are making a choice, only the choice is to not face up to the reality of your situation. Other ways you might deny the reality of choice is by drinking too much, taking drugs, becoming paranoid, by trying to overcontrol your life, or you may become obsessive. You try to control every little detail of your life. You may want rigid agendas before you do anything. You may become obsessed with cleanliness or health. You could become hypochondriacal and run to the doctor to get every little bodily twinge checked out. Or you might become paranoid and suspicious, on the lookout for anyone who might do you in. You might become dependent, hoping others will make choices for them. You can pretend the future doesn't exist and become an impulsive creature of the moment, thereby denying that choice has some future impact. Or you may become psychotic. From an existential perspective, all these kinds of psychopathology result from an attempt to deny choice.

The inauthentic person does not integrate the past, present, and future in his or her choices. He may avoid choice by thinking in terms of the future: "I'll be myself as soon as I've gotten a good job" or "a good relationship." He may idealize others, thus denying the basic imperfection and uncertainty of life. Or, he may pursue happiness. Victor Frankl (as quoted in May & Yalom, 1984) said that happiness is something that cannot be pursued, it is something that can only ensue. In other words, happiness is a by-product of creative involvement in the world. The "more we deliberately search for self-satisfaction the more it eludes us, whereas the more we fulfill some self-transcendent meaning happiness will ensue" (May & Yalom, 1984, p. 380). Finally, the person living an inauthentic life will often have stereotyped and undifferentiated values, probably swallowed whole from others, rather than authentically chosen. As a result, inauthentic patterns of living often consist of attempts to force oneself and the world into rigid, preconceived patterns. Often the values are treated as objectively real, and the person does not even realize they are chosen.

Psychotherapy

The existential approach is really more of a point of view on psychotherapy than a specific psychotherapeutic approach. The existentially oriented therapist can use any technique or approach, as long as it is used in a way compatible with existential ideas. Some of the earlier existentialists, like Ludwig Binswanger, were psychoanalytic in many respects. Some modern existential therapists practice more like gestalt therapists, others more like client-centered therapists. Nevertheless, there are some general ideas and principles of existential therapy.

The ultimate goal of existential therapy is to get the client to become aware of his or her own goals in life and to make authentic choices. Therapy can be seen in all cases as helping a client "de-restrict" himself or herself, as helping the person to grow. In order to do this the client must confront himself and what he has been avoiding. This means confronting his own anxiety and ultimately his own finiteness. Often it is the deepest potentialities that are denied in order to control our anxiety. To choose potential is to risk, but there will be no richness in life, no joy, unless one confronts the possibility of loss, tragedy, and ultimately, death.

One of the first things a client needs to do is to expand awareness. That means to become aware of the potential she is denying, the means she is using to maintain the denial, the reality that she can choose, and the anxiety associated with choice. In order to do this the therapist uses the two basic tools of empathy and authenticity. Empathy is used as a form of the phenomenological method. The therapist attempts to respond to the client without preconceptions. An empathic and nonjudgmental attitude may allow the client's inner world to come to the surface.

The other important tool is the therapist's own authenticity. If the goal of therapy is for the client to be authentic, then it is important that the therapist model authenticity. To be authentic the client has to learn that he does not have to play roles, that he does not have to be perfect or what he is "supposed" to be, that he does not have to deny aspects of his own experience, and that he can take risks. Therefore, the therapist must model these qualities and try to be a "real" person in therapy. The therapist should not play the role of the all-knowing expert, should be willing to confront and accept aspects of herself, and should be willing to admit mistakes. The therapist should demonstrate flexibility. In this regard the therapist should not follow a rigid program, even if it is an existential one. Finally, the therapist should be willing to take risks, perhaps by trying out therapeutic responses to see if they might be helpful even if they may turn out to be incorrect.

But what does it mean for the therapist to be "real" in therapy? We considered this question in our discussion of genuineness in the chapter on client-centered therapy. It is important because we are aware of a number of instances in which, in our opinion, the concept of "realness" in therapy has been abused by individuals labeling themselves "existential therapists."

Some therapists seem to have a simplistic concept of "being real." They assume that social interaction is guided by a norm of "being polite" and that people do not express their feelings and thoughts about what they "really" feel toward one another. They believe the therapist should drop the "polite facade" and say what she "really" feels. In accord with this rationale some existentially oriented therapists will often confront clients with their personal reactions to them. They may say things like "You are a dumb shit!" (Lieberman, Yalom & Miles, 1973), "You're playing games," or "When are you going to start taking responsibility for yourself?"

While such responses may not occur in everyday "polite" social interaction with coworkers or friends, they are certainly not uncommon in more intimate relationships. Parents from time immemorial have harangued their children to "take more responsibility." Husbands and wives in conflict often accuse one another of "playing games." Therefore, when a therapist gives such responses, she is not saying anything different from what a person probably has already heard. Most people don't need to go to a therapist to be told that they are "full of it" or not up to snuff in some way or the other. Most people have someone in their life who is all too happy to tell them such things. Gendlin (1968) has stated that the therapist must be able to give feedback in a more effective way than the way the person on the street gives it. Confrontations such as the ones above fail by this criterion, since they are not unlike what clients are likely to encounter in everyday life.

Generally it is believed that confrontations are more effective if they are presented as "I" statements. For instance, one could say "I find it hard to get involved in what you are saying, when you only give dry facts and none of your feelings" instead of "You talk nothing but shit." One could say "I'm having a hard time figuring out what you really feel or really want" instead of "You're playing games." One might say, "I get frustrated when you talk only about what others have done to you and not about what you could do for yourself" instead of "When are you going to start taking responsibility for yourself?"

"I" statements have two advantages. First, they communicate concrete information in a nonjudgmental way about the impact the client is having on the therapist. "I" statements give the specific impact of the client's behavior on the therapist and more concrete information about what precisely the difficulty is. Second, "I" statements are actually more honest than a statement like "You talk nothing but shit," which we believe is dishonest. It is a judgment passed by one person on another, and as such it cannot be what the person passing the judgment actually experiences or feels. What that person is most likely to be experiencing is probably "I'm bored with what you're saying" or "I wish you would talk about something else." Yet the therapist says neither of these. Instead the therapist blames her reaction of boredom or dislike on the client: You say nothing that interests me. Therefore, we maintain that such communications are actually dishonest. "I" statements are more honest because they are more likely to mirror accurately what the therapist is actually experiencing.

Beyond empathy and authenticity there are few techniques that are specifically existential. However, Frankl's logotherapy, which is generally considered a form of existential therapy, has contributed two: paradoxical intention and de-reflection. Paradoxical intention is similar to paradoxical intervention, used by family therapists (see Chapter 9). The client is urged to wish for the very thing she fears or to engage in the behavior she fears. Thus a person with a fear of germs would be instructed to deliberately get herself dirty.

De-reflection, used in cognitive-behavioral approaches, is based on the premise that focusing too much on problems exacerbates them (as an example, think of the last time you tried to get a melody out of your head). The therapist tries to shift the client's attention. This is not to teach the client to deny or repress. Rather, if the client's attention can be directed to positive aspects of his or her life, the negative will not loom so large and may fade away. The best cure for shyness, for instance, is to get so involved in a social situation that one "forgets" to worry about how one is being seen by others.

We now turn our attention to a therapeutic approach that is closely related to both existential and client-centered approaches theoretically, but differs substantially in its practice.

GESTALT THERAPY

> In 1970 a terminally ill Fritz Perls was in bed in a hospital in Chicago. At about nine o'clock that evening he kind of half got up with all this paraphernalia attached. The nurse said, "Dr. Perls. You'll have to lie down." He sort of went back down and then almost sat up and swung his legs out a bit. Again she said, "You must lie down." He looked her right in the eye and he said, "Don't tell me what to do," fell back, and died. (Robert Shapiro, as quoted in Shepard, 1975, p. 192)

If there was ever an apostle of "doing your own thing" among the major theorists of psychotherapy, it was Fritz Perls. We have already seen that the existential approach values the individual's choosing his or her own values and life path. For Perls, this emphasis on individual self-determination and responsibility was central (see Box 6.1). Perls has been virtually synonymous with gestalt therapy and is considered by many to be its "founder" (or "finder," as Perls said). According to Martin Shepard's (1975) biography, gestalt was really the joint product of Perls, his wife, Laura Perls, and a philosopher, Paul Goodman. Perls, however, was the most visible figure and achieved almost "guru" status on the West Coast in the late 1960s. As such, for many years people thought of gestalt therapy in terms of Fritz Perls. Yet there is a good deal of diversity among therapists who identify themselves with the gestalt approach, and many do not have Perls's emphasis on "rugged individualism." In fact, Perls's individualistic emphasis actually contradicts other aspects of gestalt theory, as we shall see. In recent years gestalt has steadily become more interpersonal and "softer" (Kempler, 1973; Simkin & Yontef, 1984).

Theory of Personality

Gestalt therapy is a field theory (Kaplan & Kaplan, 1985) in that it holds that one must look at the total configuration of interrelationships in a person's life to understand his behavior. This configuration includes the person's past experiences, beliefs and values, expectations, current momentary desires and needs, current structure of life, including where he lives, his relationships, and work, and finally, the immediate situation he is in at the moment. The word *gestalt* (German, "shape" or "form") refers to this configuration of integrated parts.

The state of every element in a field is determined in part by its interaction with every other element in the field. A simple analogy would be a stew. Carrots in a stew made with lamb will taste differently from carrots in a stew made with beef. Beef in

BOX 6.1
Fritz Perls's
Gestalt Prayer

I do my thing, and you do your thing
I am not in this world to live up to your expectations
And you are not in this world to live up to mine.
You are you, and I am I,
And if by chance we find each other, it's beautiful.
If not, it can't be helped.

(Fritz Perls, as quoted in Shepard, 1975, p. 3)

a stew made with carrots will taste a little different from beef in a stew without carrots, and so on. Thus the nature of each element in the stew is partly determined by the whole configuration of the stew, and the whole configuration is determined by the interaction of the elements.

This is also true of people, according to gestalt. Psychologically, a person exists at each moment in a field consisting of past experiences, self-image, beliefs, values, and attitudes, hopes and fears for the future, significant relationships, career, neighborhood, material possession, and culture. It also includes the person's current biological state, momentary needs and desires, and immediate situation (the physical environment, the people present, what is going on). Behavior and experience will be determined at any given moment by the interaction of all these elements. Because there is always some change in some element of this field, the individual is never exactly the same person as he was at any time before. Every day I sit down to breakfast something will be different, if only that I have another day's experience to throw into the "stew." But in addition the people around me will have changed, and there may be some changes, however small, at work also.

Such a view is a *nonlinear* perspective on the causes of behavior, experience, and identity. It is the entire configuration that determines behavior, experience, and identity; they cannot be attributed to any one of the elements in the configuration. A *linear* view traces behavior directly to one or several elements. Suppose I am acting rebellious at work. Psychoanalysis might hold that my rebellion is caused by the childhood trauma of having an overcontrolling and domineering father. A cognitive view might hold that my rebellion is caused by my dysfunctional belief that "I must have my own way." A behavioral view might hold that it is caused by the situational factor of having coworkers who reinforce acting rebellious around the boss. According to gestalt theory, past experiences, beliefs, and the current situation influence and determine one another, and then the combination influences behavior. Thus my past experience with my father, my current beliefs, and the situation all interact and influence one another.

Let us look at another set of examples of how the person experiences the current situation in terms of all the other elements in the field. If I am hungry, I will be acutely aware of the presence or absence of food in the situation; if I am in class, my hunger may change my experience of the situation, so that the psychology professor's highly interesting lecture may seem boring and trivial. Or, if I believe psychology is irrelevant to my future plans, I may experience the lecture as boring and trivial. Or, if my past experience has included a large number of academic failures, I may believe that whether I listen in class or not is irrelevant to how well I will do on the test, and I may find it difficult to experience the lecture as involving.

But conversely, my hunger, which I experienced as pressing in the classroom situation, may fade completely into the background if the terribly attractive fellow student who I have had a secret crush on for weeks suddenly comes over and asks if I would help with today's lecture notes. Similarly, suppose I plan to be an engineer and therefore hold the belief that this required psychology class is irrelevant to my vocational pursuits. The ideas I have learned seem "cold" and "irrelevant." Now, a few years later, I am working as an engineer and am having difficulties with my staff. Suddenly the ideas about relating to people that had seemed cold and irrelevant seem immediate, vital, and alive.

The past will take on different roles in one's current behavior depending on the other elements present. There is no simple linear relationship between the past and the present. The same past experience may play a destructive, disintegrative role in one "stew" and a constructive, integrative role in another. One's past failure experiences in class may interact destructively with usual classroom situations. They may contribute to a configuration that leads you to behave self-destructively by not paying attention and by believing that you will probably fail anyway. But the same set of experiences may interact in a quite different manner with a different classroom situation. Suppose as part of the psychology class you are assigned to spend 10 hours at a child care center. While there, you notice a child who seems to be having trouble with the class material and who seems to have a negative self-image as a result. Your own experience leads you to establish an immediate empathy with the child. Through your support and empathy the child begins to change for the better, both in terms of his self-image and in terms of his performance. This, in turn, increases your own feelings of competence. You return to class with a more positive self-image, a greater sense of motivation, and perhaps now begin to do better yourself. The role played by the past, as with any other element, in the stew of one's current experience, changes as a function of all other elements present and how those elements blend together.

All the elements we have been discussing form a dynamic whole with each here and now situation. The situations individuals live in from moment to moment are, in some sense, part of them. Who they are at any given moment is partially determined by the situation. The "self," from this point of view, is not an internal structure existing somewhere within the person. Rather, it is an ever-shifting, ever-changing part of the ongoing organizational field of experience. The self is really a concept that is part of the stew. It is a concept that helps people to organize the field of their experience in an adaptive way. As with any other concept, its meaning will shift and change in response to other elements present. For instance, our bodies are usually incorporated as part of our self, but sometimes we experience our bodies as alien, particularly if "they" do things we don't like, such as eat or drink too much or get too emotional to function smoothly. Different events, situations, and sensations will be incorporated into the self at different times. Children, for instance, define themselves partially in terms of where they live, who their parents are, and what schools they attend (Montemayor & Eisen, 1977). At a football game I may function as if my self includes my team. If they win, I feel enhanced; if they lose, I feel defeated.

Therefore, the self exists at the *contact boundary* between the person and the current situation. An important part of healthy functioning is the ability to draw appropriate contact boundaries between the self and the world. For example, a person who includes too much as part of his self might take too much responsibility for others or feel guilty if things don't go well for others.

Organismic Self-regulation

The field of experience includes some parts that are figural, that is, that stand out and capture attention, and other parts that are background. According to gestalt, there is a constant flow of elements in the field as some parts become figural and then recede into the background. Things that become figural are called *incomplete gestalts,* or *unfinished business.* For instance, hunger is an incomplete or unfinished part of the field of experience, and it will have a tendency to become figural. However, it will become figural only if it is the most pressing incomplete gestalt present. In our earlier example, hunger became figural during a lecture, but if an attractive classmate asks for help with lecture notes, hunger may temporarily recede into the background as the less pressing of the incomplete gestalts in my current field.

Some incomplete gestalts come from the past. If I have a good deal of unresolved anger toward my father, this may "lurk" in the background until the proper situation brings it forth. Then, as I am dealing with a boss who reminds me of my father, that unfinished business may become figural, influencing my reactions to my boss.

In the fully functioning person there is a spontaneous, natural process of organismic self-regulation. This means that the total configuration of the field of experience will be organized in such a way that the incomplete gestalts that emerge and capture attention are the ones most important to overall organismic well-being. The most pressing incomplete gestalt may be relevant to my future goals, and it may take precedence over a more momentary need.

For instance, it is Sunday afternoon and you have a midterm on Wednesday. You should study, but there is a television show that sounds attractive. Most of us, because we are *not* fully functioning, will experience our attention's being drawn to the television show. If we have an experience of the prospects of studying at all, it will be aversive. We will struggle between what we should do (study) and what we would like to do (watch television). We may try to force ourselves to study. Or we may bargain with ourselves: I'll study after watching half an hour. Of course, half an hour stretches into forty-five minutes, and that stretches into an hour and a half, and so on. We may try to scare ourselves: If I don't study, I'll fail. We may try to manipulate ourselves: If I study, I can watch television tonight. When, after all this, we are still watching TV two hours later, we may begin to analyze ourselves. Maybe I have a failure complex. Maybe I'm a lazy underachiever.

According to gestalt, in the fully functioning person the organismic self-regulation process would construct the field of experience in such a way that it just *felt* compelling to study. This does not mean that the person would experience studying as "fun," but he would experience it as a pressing incomplete gestalt, that is, he would "want" to do it because of the long-term expectations in his field. According to Simkin and Yontef (1984), the "field will form itself into the best gestalt that global conditions will allow." Self-regulation is seen as a spontaneous integral part of the person, and when the person is functioning optimally, "there is no effort of planning or doing; there is just 'being' " (Van De Reit, Korb, & Gorrell, 1980, p. 11).

Why is it that most people often don't spontaneously choose what is organismically best? According to gestalt theory, optimal functioning requires *full awareness.* All barriers to or breakdowns of full functioning can be attributed to things that interfere with full awareness. Through full awareness change takes place place spontaneously and naturally. The person does not need to "will" change to take place, because the person spontaneously reorganizes his experience in each new situation in the optimal manner. Psychological problems are due to interferences with this natural tendency. In other terms, pathology is an interference with the person's creative problem-solving capacity.

The person functions optimally when he or she is fully present and fully aware in the moment. What creates gestalt formation is *attention,* that is, a person's experience of any situation will be determined in part by what he attends to in it. Depressives, for instance, focus their attention on the negative, and so their experience of situations is organized in terms of negatives. In a conversation, if your attention is focused on whether the person likes you or not, your experience of the conversation will be different from that if your attention is focused on the issue being discussed. In a fully aware person attention is free to flow to the whole field of his experience, thereby altering it and constructing it in the best manner possible.

The issue is one of *availability.* Is what is going on both inside and outside available to awareness? Full awareness does not mean being aware at any given moment of everything going on. Attention will flow back and forth, depending on what gestalts form. At times a person will be in a "contact" mode, and attention will be focused on the situation. At other times attention will flow more to "inner" thoughts and feelings, and the person will be in a "withdrawal" mode. In the fully functioning person there is a continual flow of awareness between these two poles. If the person attends to the present field, that is, if he is present-centered, he will not ruminate over why he didn't do what he should have done or wonder why he can't seem to do what he should do. The individual will not stop the flow of his awareness by excessively dwelling on thoughts about how he is functioning, or his problems. In this respect gestalt is often accused of being both anti-intellectual and anti-"should."

It would not be hard to find what sound like anti-intellectual quotes from Perls. For instance, "Intuition is the intelligence of the organism, and intellect is the whore of intelligence" (Perls, 1969, p. 22). The quote from Perls at the start of this chapter also captures the anti-intellectual flavor of gestalt. Yet it is not exactly true that gestalt is anti-intellectual. It is true that in terms of organismic self-regulation it is opposed to one kind of thinking. It is opposed to abstract, analytic thinking about oneself and one's problems. This does not mean gestalt therapists are opposed to all thinking, all abstracting, and all symbolizing. In fact, it is through symbolization and abstraction that people change themselves.

Abstracting and symbolizing are natural self-regulatory functions, if abstractions and symbols arise from experience. Since experience represents organismic wisdom, abstractions and symbols that arise from experience help organize and integrate experience. Furthermore, the kind of abstraction or symbolizing that is useful is synthetic rather than analytic, integrative rather than dissective, that is, it is creative, synthesizing knowing, rather than the kind of analytic dissection that we usually equate with thinking. For instance, there are two ways to "know" a poem. One way is to try to experience the poem, and then try to capture your experience in words. The other way is to try to dissect and analyze it. What does this symbol mean? What is the author trying to say? What is the structure of the poem? We are usually taught in school to approach poetry analytically, but from a gestalt perspective that kind of knowing is useful neither for the understanding of poetry nor for the understanding of ourselves.

Perls believed that the kind of knowing that is therapeutic is the nonrational, intuitive, experiential knowing of the organism. If the person spontaneously organizes himself in the most efficient and harmonious way possible with each situation, then spontaneously bubbling up into awareness will be symbols of that integration. This is *intuition,* which is simply the wisdom of the whole person. This knowing, even if symbolized, is direct and experiential. Most of us "know" what this kind of knowing is like. We have had the experience of struggling with an idea, suddenly everything just "clicks into place," and we just know we know. While this knowing can be expressed in words, the words are the product of the knowing, not the knowing itself.

The other kind of knowing is not useful for organismic self-regulation and represents a kind of splitting off and disruption of organismic knowing. This is the kind of logical deduction many people engage in when they are having problems. They look for "causes" and try to "fit" them to their behavior. They believe that if they can figure out a cause for their behavior, then somehow they will magically change. But, when people engage in that kind of intellectual dissection, they are not attending to their organismic sense of the situation. Thinking about things removes the person from the immediacy of the here and now.

We have seen that gestalt values full, present-centered awareness, but living in the here and now does not mean pretending that the past did not exist or that the future will not occur. It simply means being fully present in one's awareness of both outer and inner experience. It means to live *in* the moment, but not *for* the moment. One's experience will include relevant aspects of one's past, as well as relevant aspects of one's future goals. If one is fully present, these will all be organismically integrated into one's current field of experience. As we have said previously, if one can achieve this, one will just naturally choose the path that enhances the overall actualization.

Does this sound a bit idealized? Gestalt assumes such functioning is possible, but that most people don't function this way most of the time. People are born with the ability to organismically self-regulate, but they lose it when they learn to split experience up and to categorize rigidly. For instance, it is useful to categorize our experience into "inner" ("inside me") and "outer" ("outside" in the environment). It is useful to categorize part of our experience as "thinking" and part as "feeling." However, these are just categories we use to organize and order our experience. For instance, it can be useful to split experience into "inner" and "outer" or into "thinking" and "feeling."

The problem is that people are taught to think of these categories as real. In other words, they learn to apply their category systems rigidly and do not even recognize that they are category systems. They mistake the "map" for the "territory." Therefore, they believe that self and environment are literally and rigidly separate, that feeling and thinking are separate and different, and so on. To make matters worse, they are also taught to categorize some of their experience as "bad" or "sinful." For instance, we are taught to categorize some of our experience as "impulses" and to see these "impulses" as bad. Because we have so categorized them, we come to believe we must control these "bad impulses." But it is our view of them as impulses that makes them seem uncontrollable. It is our view of them as "bad" that makes us anxious to control them. People also learn to split experience into what they "want" to do and what they "should" do. It is not surprising that they experience themselves as divided and caught between two warring factions.

People are taught to regulate behavior by external rules and to distrust their feeling and intuition. As a result they come to believe that the only "good" way to function is to be intellectual, objective, and rational. Both because of the "shoulds" they learn and the labeling of some experience as "bad," they may completely disown some of their experience. For instance, we may completely disown our angry feelings, because it is "bad" to feel anger.

Our upbringing therefore creates splits in our experience. How do these splits affect functioning? In essence these splits become ongoing principles of gestalt formation. What Freudians call defense mechanisms are organizing principles for gestalt theorists. Take projection as an example. One projects onto others parts of oneself that one has disowned. According to Kaplan and Kaplan (1985), a gestalt way of looking at projection is that the individual organizes her experience of the world so that certain aspects are not included in her concept of "me." But as she organizes her concept and experience of "me," she simultaneously determines how she will organize her experience and concept of others as well. For example, if she denies and disowns her own assertiveness (perhaps because she was punished for it as a child), the person will probably experience and define herself as "weak," "helpless," and "passive." She may simultaneously attribute "strength" and "dominance" to others, because, in relation to her passivity, others will appear especially dominant and assertive. If she denies her own assertiveness, she may further organize her experience of the world so that she believes she must "please" others in order to get along. By splitting up her world, the person then "sees" in others what she expects to be there based on her own rigid way of categorizing her experience. A client may "see" the therapist as rejecting or demanding because she "sees" herself as worthy of rejection or as a passive victim of others.

Another defensive organizing principle is *introjection.* Introjections are rules that are taken whole into how one organizes one's experience, but are not integrated with the rest of one's personal rules and values. Thus they are experienced as external to the self. Usually what the person wants to do is experienced as "me," while what he ought to do is experienced as an external rule or demand. Parental and societal rules and demands are often introjections. The "top dog–underdog" conflict, described a bit later, exemplifies this conflict.

The splitting of experience and denial interfere with the person's spontaneous ability to regulate himself or herself. The person must instead rely on external guidelines rather than on his or her own organismic wisdom. The person thus loses the ability to be self-supporting and self-directing. Put another way, he or she is not able to choose optimal patterns of response in any given situation. Thus he or she is not "response-able." By being "response-able" gestalt theory means taking responsibility for oneself and being present centered. If you have followed the discussion so far you can see how they are related. To be fully aware of one's inner and outer situation *is* to be able to make optimum choices for oneself at any given moment.

The word *responsibility* has several meanings. It is important to keep in mind the gestalt meaning we have just given. Otherwise, the idea of "taking" responsibility for oneself can be misused, and it has been by some humanistic therapists, including Perls himself. To be fully in touch with one's organismic experiencing so that one makes optimal choices is to be self-supporting. However, as Simkin and Yontef (1984) point out, there is a difference between being *self-supporting* and being *self-sufficient.* As we have said, the self-supporting person makes choices so that his behavior is harmonious and congruent with himself and with his environment. His choices create a meaningful and fulfilling life for him. He can decide what he needs to solve his problems. And, what he needs may, in some cases, be help from others. Gestalt holds that maturity is moving from environmental support to self-support. But even the most mature person must rely on others. Clearly, I cannot extract my own teeth, do surgery on myself, or depending on my skills, fix my own car. A self-supporting person is able to know when he needs help from others and able to ask for it.

In the history of gestalt theory self-support was confused with self-sufficiency. Perls himself is the most glaring example of this. He seemed to be preoccupied with maintaining his independence from others, as the story about his death and his gestalt prayer illustrate.

The gestalt prayer presents a noninvolved image of interpersonal relationships. Despite Perls's stated emphasis on the "I-thou" nature of relationships with others, he remained quite distant and uninvolved with his clients. The "I do my thing . . . you do your thing" idea is an image of ships passing in the night, which, if they just happen to be sailing along on the same course, sail along together for a while. But that is not an image of involvement. Rather it is an image of insularity, of two people more interested in protecting their autonomy than in sharing. Further, it suggests that if one person does anything but follow her impulses, if she takes the other's wishes into account, she is somehow taking responsibility for the other. The prayer implies, "I don't want your wishes, demands, desires, to infringe on me in any way. I want to be free to do my own thing, with no responsibility to you."

The odd thing about this image of insularity is that it contradicts gestalt theory which holds that a person is an interactive creature. The essential nature of a relationship is, by gestalt's own view, sharing. If a person is sharing, then the other person's wishes and needs will influence and be important to him. The other's needs may even become figural at times, with the person's own needs receding into the background. For instance, if the person I care for is sick, I may let my own needs temporarily recede into the background. Perls's "do your own thing" idea is actually a violation of gestalt itself, and in the years since his death there has been a movement away from it within gestalt (see Simkin & Yontef, 1984).

In gestalt theory responsibility means the person's ability to choose for himself, at times taking another person's wishes into account. But the word responsibility has other connotations in our society. To say "I am responsible" for something often means

I am to blame for it, it is my fault, or I am the cause of it. In this sense, some depressed individuals take too much responsibility for themselves, rather than too little. They see themselves at fault for just about everything. The meaning of responsibility is sometimes confused by some therapists. A therapist might view a schizophrenic as being responsible for being schizophrenic, as if he caused the condition in some way. There are cases where some therapists have led their clients to believe that to be responsible for oneself means that one has no responsibility to others. In one such case one woman client abandoned her pre-teenage children to go off and "find herself." The client rationalized her action by saying that the children had to "be responsible for themselves." But, of course, these are different meanings of the word responsibility than that of being "response-able."

Therapeutic Approach

The gestalt goal is not to help the client resolve the particular problem that he or she brings to therapy. The gestalt belief is that the presenting complaint is merely a symptom of a style of living that is the true problem. If the therapist helps clear up the presenting complaint without altering that style, other problems will surely arise for the client in the future.

The focus of gestalt therapy is to increase the individual's ability to maintain full contact and awareness with the current situation. Remember that what gestalt means by an "increase in awareness" is not the acquisition of insight. It does not mean "learning truths" about oneself, such as "I have deep underlying hostility" or "I am a passive dependent personality." The goal is to increase one's ability to stay present-centered and be aware in the moment. For this reason, gestalt is a kind of "behavioral existentialism," in that the goal of therapy is to increase the client's "behavior" of maintaining full contact.

As a result gestalt is a highly experiential therapy. Gestalt does not proceed like verbal therapies where the therapist and client sit around and talk about the client and his or her problems. In fact, many gestalt therapists see "talking about" problems as an avoidance of here and now experiencing, and they will often not allow it to take place. It is thought that some talking is a cover-up for experiencing. This does not mean that all talking is banned. It is desirable that clients express their feelings toward the therapist or to group members in a group therapy situation and that they express and formulate their present awareness. However, attempts to sit around and talk about one's childhood or one's family life will often be interrupted.

Not all gestalt therapists prohibit talking about one's problems. Some will engage in "conversation" with the client, as long as the conversation is fresh and alive and is a way of creating contact between therapist and client. Polster (1985), for instance, is interested in the "stories" people develop about themselves. Polster is particularly interested in having his clients "flesh out" their stories with concrete details. Often clients come into therapy only with "titles," such as "I'm a failure." Such a title is an abstract, intellectual global statement, distant from experience. As the client fleshes out the story that goes with this title, he or she gets in touch with the concrete experiences that have led to that global conclusion. Getting in touch with the concrete experiences allows one to change how the story is "evolving," whereas staying with the title leads nowhere. All verbal, interactive therapies, including psychoanalytic, client-centered, and cognitive, can be said to operate in part by getting the client to flesh out their abstract titles with concrete experiences. Cognitive therapy, for instance, works by helping the client to see that the concrete experiences rarely justify an abstract "title," such as "I am a failure."

Some "talking about" that clients engage in is called rehearsing. Often clients will talk about what the future might bring: "What if I am rejected?" "What if I fail the test?" Such rehearsing can be an avoidance of here and now experiencing. Furthermore, it is *catastrophizing.* Rumination about what the future might bring is, in the gestalt view, what causes *anxiety.* If one remains present-centered, one will not experience anxiety. Anxiety is the fear of what might happen and is thus an "escape into the future." Similarly, guilt is "escape into the past." This is one respect in which gestalt differs from other existential approaches, which see the experience of anxiety as basic to living. The gestalt approach holds that the fully functioning, present-centered person simply does not experience anxiety.

Instead of having the clients talk about problems, the gestalt therapist uses exercises to make clients focus on the present experiential process. Many of these exercises are well known, but gestalt therapists do not like to think of gestalt as a technique-oriented therapy. Resnick (1980) said, "If every technique that any gestalt therapist had ever used before were never used again, true gestalt therapists would barely be affected" (p. x). Nevertheless, there are a number of techniques or exercises that are commonly used.

Since the main goal of gestalt therapy is to increase contact in the moment, one of the most basic techniques is to have the client simply report what he or she is now aware of in order to train present-centered attention. This will often demonstrate how difficult it is to stay present centered, as the client will usually stray off into rumination or self-analysis.

Similar to the "now I am aware of" exercise is "stay with" exercise. The client is instructed to stay with a thought or feeling. Remaining attentive to a feeling may lead to the emergence of some incomplete gestalt or issue the client needs to deal with. Both the "now I am aware of . . ." and "stay with . . ." exercises can be seen as directly training present-centered attention.

Other techniques enhance the experiential focus of the client. Gestalt is a holistic approach, and it is believed that often nonverbal expression conveys what one is experiencing more accurately than one's words. The client may be asked to exaggerate a gesture or tone of voice to enhance the actual experience of what the client is saying. For instance, if the client says in a meek tone of voice, "I feel angry," she may be asked to say it louder. If a client is fooling with his wedding ring as he talks about his depressed feelings, the gestalt therapist may have him exaggerate the gesture and to talk from his experience of the gesture: "Now I am slipping my wedding ring on and off my finger. . . . I have a lot of ambivalence about my marriage." If the client is blinking a lot, the therapist may ask him to "role play" his eyes: "I am my eyes. I am blinking as fast as I can to hold the tears in."

Another gestalt technique is to have the client "do the opposite." One of us saw Fritz Perls do a demonstration onstage with a group of students before a large audience. The first student that Perls worked with said he felt anxious with the large audience watching him. Perls instructed the student to walk down into the audience and stare at members of the audience. This was doing the opposite in the sense that the student was doing the watching, instead of feeling he was being watched. After doing this for a few minutes, the student reported feeling less anxious. In Perls's words, the student had "taken back his eyes." What Perls meant was that the student had given the audience the power to judge him. By doing the opposite he "owned the projection"; *he* did the judging. When he "took back his eyes," he became less afraid of their judging him.

Another technique is to have a client substitute the phrase "I won't" for "I can't." Often clients will say, "I can't confront my boss" or "I can't control my sexual feelings." This is a signal that the person is splitting off certain aspects of experience and not being response-able. By saying "I won't confront my boss" or "I won't control my sexual feelings," the individual focuses his attention back to his organismic experiencing. He may decide that he does not want to control his sexual feelings or confront his boss, because that is "organismically wise" for him. However, at least now he is able to be response-able.

Perhaps the most well-known experiential exercise used by gestalt therapists is role playing. For instance, to work with a dream a client will act out parts of the dream. Perls's view was that the parts of a dream, including nonhuman objects such as chairs, cars, or houses, represent different aspects of the self and feelings. One client dreamed of an old road that had fallen out of use when a new superhighway was built nearby. When asked to role play this road he said, "I'm an old, neglected road. For years I was the center of attention, but even then people used me. They used me and broke me down and then they abandoned me. No one cares about me. I'm just falling apart."

One role-playing exercise is called the empty chair (or "two chair") technique. It is used to help clients resolve internal conflicts and their feeling about conflicts with others. The client sits facing an empty chair. If the problem is an internal conflict between different aspects of the self, the client is asked to pretend that one side of the conflict is sitting in the chair opposite him. The client role plays one side. Then the client switches chairs and role plays the opposite side. If, for instance, you are having a conflict over studying one Sunday afternoon, you would be asked to place the side that watches television in the empty chair and to role play the side that wants to study. Then you change chairs and role play the side that wants to watch television. It might go as follows.

SIDE A: It is necessary that I study. I'll never graduate and get a good job if I don't. We must study. You're bad for wanting to watch television. You just want to do nothing but lie around.

SIDE B: But I only wanted to watch the football game. I need time to relax. You can study later. I mean to study later. You demand too much.

The chair-switching continues until some integration between the two sides is achieved.

SIDE A: It's just that I feel so incompetent. I study and study but don't feel I'm getting it. Then I get desperate.

SIDE B: But then I feel like escaping when you feel like that. I don't like feeling incompetent. It's easier to watch TV.

Through the dialogue the feelings of ineptness that are the heart of the conflict emerge. Once you can "own" your feelings, you can deal with them, ultimately freeing you to choose or not to choose to study on any given Sunday afternoon.

The conflict over studying is an example of what Perls called the "top dog–underdog" conflict. The "top dog" is the "should" side, and the "underdog" is the excuse-making side. Perls believed that in everyday life the underdog usually wins. In other words, while our should side yells at us, we actually do what our underdog side wants to do. It is important to note that the goal of gestalt is not to get rid of shoulds, but rather, to own them so that they become "wants": "I want to study because I want to get my degree" ("I want to study" does not mean "I enjoy studying"). Shoulds that do not feel organismically congruent will be dropped.

The same role-playing technique can be used for interpersonal conflicts. If you are having a conflict with your father, you would pretend that your father is sitting in the empty chair opposite you. You would role play your side of the conflict, switch chairs, and role play your father's side. Again, you would continue the dialogue until some integration occurs. But what is achieved by this role playing? After all, no matter how successfully you use the technique in your therapy sessions, your real father might still act as unbending as ever.

Presumably the problem with your father is not *all* your father. Your father can be thought of as a "limit" in your life. He may act in ways you do not like, but then reality does that all the time. But what do you do to contribute to the problem? Perhaps you are in an emotional tangle about your father because you are projecting your expectations onto him. You feel crushed, angry, and depressed when he responds critically to you. Why? It is possible that this is related to your lack of full acceptance of yourself. If you could fully accept and feel congruent with yourself, then you wouldn't need his approval so much and his rejection of you might be disappointing, but it would not be depressing or devastating. When you role play your father in the empty chair technique, you learn about the projections you put on your father. The integration that takes place is within you, and as it occurs it will contribute to the resolution of the conflict with your father. You may be able to say: "I love you and want you to understand. But if you do not, that is you. I will still love you, but I will not feel bad about myself. I will still feel congruent and whole within myself. I would like your approval, but I do not need it."

There are other gestalt techniques and exercises that we will not present here. The important point is that for many gestalt therapists techniques are secondary to maintaining full, present-centered contact with the client. While Perls tended to remain distant and uninvolved, many current gestalt therapists respond openly and interactively to their clients.

TRANSPERSONAL PSYCHOLOGY

Transpersonal approaches generally hold that full personal growth cannot be achieved through a psychological approach alone. They emphasize the necessity for a spiritual or transpersonal transformation as well. While there has always been a tradition of Christian counseling, the transpersonal view was dominated in the late 1960s and 1970s by Eastern mystical traditions. Mystical experience, meditation, and altered states of consciousness were important topics.

Eastern mystical thought tends to see the subject-object dichotomy as an illusion. In other words, the idea that the self observing the world is somehow separate from the world that is observed is an illusion. Further, the idea that the world is made up of separate things, which have fixed identities, is also an illusion. Actually the world is an ever changing "flux" or "dance" (Zukav, 1979). Eastern mystical approaches hope to get the individual to suspend these illusory concepts about the world.

Of particular psychological relevance is the concept of the self. People form a concept of themselves as separate from others and from the world. Because they see themselves as separate from the rest of reality, they believe that when "they" die, they cease to exist. So they fear death. Because people see themselves as separate, they believe they cannot know all of reality and worry that they distort reality. They develop concepts of what they are like, that is, they see themselves as having fixed, stable character structures. They evaluate as good or bad the character traits and character structure that they have attributed to themselves. Then when people do something right, they attribute it to their essential goodness. When they do something wrong, they see it as a reflection of their essential badness. Because they feel small, finite, and vulnerable, people try to protect and maintain their image of themselves, and this leads to distortion and defense. They become selfish and inconsiderate of others, worry that they are being treated unfairly, and set up shoulds to make sure that they act in a way they define as good.

Deikman (1982) has argued that while most therapies work by questioning some of these constructs about the self, none goes far enough in encouraging the client to let go of his investment in his personal self and reach the level of his "observing self." The observing self is that sense of "I" or identity that underlies any concepts a person makes about himself, including the concept that the "I" is separate from "the world."

The main tool of attaining such realizations for many transpersonal psychologists is meditation. There are two kinds of meditation: concentrative and receptive. In concentrative meditation the person attempts to keep his attention focused on one object, usually a word, image, or phrase. In receptive meditation the person attempts to do what appears to be the opposite: to allow consciousness to flow freely and uninterruptedly, to let go and become a pure observer of experience. Washburn (1978) has argued that the seemingly different types of meditation ultimately have similar effects. As internal chatter is suspended, the individual becomes able to become aware of himself as the constructor of his own conscious activity. He becomes aware of the unconscious, automatic thoughts and schemas that he uses to shape and form concepts and perceptions. As these are suspended he moves toward a state of "bare witnessing."

Christian approaches to psychotherapy hold that the accepting of Christ and of a Christian way of life is the ultimate healing act. Christian approaches stress human finiteness and imperfection in comparison to God. Being finite and imperfect, people should be tolerant and forgiving of selves and others. We may ask for God's forgiveness. Forgiveness leads to a kind of living in the here and now. Instead of ruminating over past sins, they focus on how I can improve now. Instead of judging my self, since I and all other human beings are imperfect and will occasionally err, focus on what I can do in the future to live a better life. Christianity also values selflessness and doing away with pride. If one is able to do away with pride, then one will not need to be defensive and to protect one's self-esteem. One will be able to accept one's failings and drawbacks with humility.

EVALUATION OF HUMANISTIC APPROACHES

Effectiveness of Therapy

Smith, Glass, and Miller (1980) found an average effect size of 0.64 for gestalt therapy, which places it around average in effectiveness with most other approaches. Some evidence specifically supports the effectiveness of the gestalt role-playing technique. Bohart (1977) had subjects work on anger conflicts using the empty chair technique. It was found to reduce anger, hostile attitudes, and behavioral aggression more than an emotional catharsis procedure or an intellectual analysis procedure. Studies by Greenberg and colleagues (Greenberg, 1984) also demonstrated the efficacy of the empty chair technique in helping a person resolve conflictual feelings. The technique was also found to get the client experientially involved in the therapy process more quickly and immediately than the Rogerian technique of reflection of feelings.

We are unaware of any empirical data on existential therapy. There is an extensive literature on meditation (De Santis, 1985), but conflicting results and the uneven quality of many of the studies make conclusions tentative. There is some evidence that meditation is an effective therapy technique. However, it does not appear to induce any physiological changes greater than simple relaxation does (Holmes, 1985).

Theoretical Evaluation

The group of existential-humanistic perspectives can be generally criticized in several ways. First, existential-humanistic terminology is vague. Terms like "living in the here and now," "taking responsibility for oneself," "authenticity," and "staying with one's feelings" are open to a wide range of interpretations. Such vagueness not only leads to widely differing applications of the terms (with some resulting abuses), it also makes it extremely difficult to study existential-humanistic approaches empirically. Further, it is confusing to the beginning therapist. What is "living in the here and now"? How do I know if I am being "authentic"?

A second criticism is the complement of our criticism of psychoanalysis. We criticized psychoanalysis for its overemphasis on the impact of early childhood on personality and the resulting views that personality is fixed and there is therefore little growth and change throughout life. A virtue of the existential-humanistic approach is that it sees the personality as constantly changing. However, this results in an almost complete lack of focus on what remains the same in personality. Existential-humanistic approaches have no language for describing personality structure. Existentialists often write as if people are completely free to remake themselves at any moment. Yet most people are painfully aware of how difficult it is to modify long-standing behavior patterns. In contrast, psychoanalysis has a rich vocabulary for describing various constellations of personality and recognizes that it is not easy to modify ingrained patterns of behavior. The idea that one can "choose" to be whatever one wants at any given moment can be highly distressing to a client. Take as an example a client who feels hollow and depressed when he is alone (one of the symptoms of borderline personality). While it may be true in some theoretical sense that the client is "choosing" to feel that way, the client experiences it as out of his control. To have the client say "I won't feel good when I'm alone" instead of "I can't feel good when I'm alone" may make the client feel even more helpless and guilty. The existential-humanistic overemphasis on the fluidity of human personality is the flip side of the psychoanalytic overemphasis on the fixity of personality.

A third criticism of existential-humanistic approaches is their inconsistent and self-contradictory view of the impact of the environment on behavior. Client-centered therapy, existentialism, and gestalt therapy are all self-identified field theories, that is, they hold that the person exists interactively with the environment. This should mean that the person's current situation would be taken seriously as a partial cause of his or her moment-to-moment behavior. Yet the environment is rarely considered as an influence except in a negative sense. Ricks, Wandersman, and Poppen (1976) said, "Humanistic ignorance of the environment has often led to a naive radicalism, in which the environment is simply treated as an obstacle to self-realization, rather than the arena in which the self will either be realized or lost" (pp. 254–255). We previously made this criticism of client-centered therapy, but it is frequently true of existential-humanistic approaches in general.

As a result of this overemphasis on the possibility of change and underestimation of the environment, humanists do not have ways to explain how situations can influence individuals despite their choices. This sometimes leads to a moralistic flavor in humanistic theorizing, where, in effect, the client is "at fault" for his problems. He or she has not had the "courage" to rise above the situation and "create" a meaningful life despite environmental limitations. Frankl (1963), for instance, pointed out that some individuals were able to create meaningful existences even in the most extreme circumstances of being in a Nazi concentration camp. However, if we assume that such individuals represent how we all *ought* to behave, then we have no alternative but to see those who were unable to do this as lacking courage or will or refusing to take responsibility for themselves. In our criticism of psychoanalysis we mentioned some research that finds a correlation between depression in women and adverse circumstances in their life situation (Brown & Harris, 1978). If attributing such depression primarily to early childhood experiences seems overbalanced, it seems equally overbalanced to accuse these women of avoiding choice and not taking responsibility. Humanistic theories don't seem to take into account the fact that some situations are objectively much harder to live in in a creative and actualizing way than others.

Put another way, existential-humanistic approaches see psychological problems as ones of *attitude.* The problem is that one has the "wrong" attitudes toward life. If one will only accept responsibility for oneself, then one can handle life. What is left out of this approach is the possibility that the individual is doing the best he can given his circumstances and his prior learning history. He may be acting in "good faith," rather than in "bad faith." It may simply be that his view of the world, acquired in an "honest" manner from his upbringing, is limiting. It may also be that he never learned good skills for handling certain situations. Perhaps he avoids, not because he lacks courage, but because he lacks skills to cope. Those individuals who handled the concentration camp experience, for instance, may have had the benefit of life experiences (not necessarily favorable ones) that taught them the skills necessary to survive in highly adverse circumstances. Rather than extol them as being "authentic," and by implication blame those who did not cope, we might be better off trying to identify the skills these individuals used to survive. It might be possible to teach these skills to others. Existential and gestalt therapists tend to assume that the problem stops with the acceptance of responsibility. But even if the client accepts that he has the power to change, the client still needs to learn how to do it. This is especially true if the client's life circumstances are particularly unfavorable.

Gestalt therapy specifically can be criticized. Its model of the person as an integrated whole sometimes leads gestalt therapists to talk and practice as if the person were a simple undifferentiated whole. They talk, for instance, about one incomplete gestalt emerging and capturing our attention until it is finished, and then another emerging. But often many figures compete for our attention, and no one seems dominant. It is precisely at such times we have difficulty choosing. Their assumption of the holistic nature of the organism also leads some to assume that body language reflects what the organism is really doing, while words can lie. However, we would argue that the person is a complex system of subsystems and that he or she can do, and usually does, several things at one time (Barker, 1968).

For instance, in a filmed therapy interview Fritz Perls (1965) accuses the client, Gloria, of being "phony" because at the start of the session she says she is nervous, although she is smiling. Perls claims that frightened people don't smile. Yet it is possible for a frightened person to smile simply because a person can do two things at once. She can engage in one behavioral sequence, which we will call "trying to be friendly" and hence smiling, while engaging in another, "being frightened." Furthermore, there seems to be no "rule" that says we must act as a monolithic whole all the time. If I am feeling frightened, my fright does not need to control or dominate all my behavioral systems. For instance, I can feel anxious while taking a test, but I do not sit there and shake. Yet it would be most peculiar to be accused of being phony because part of me is answering test questions while I claim that another part of me is anxious.

We also find the gestalt concept of the fully functioning person a bit "utopian." Gestalt theory holds that the fully functioning person does not have to figure out intellectually, plan, or guess at what's going on and what to do, because the person with present-centered awareness has direct sensory contact with the situation and intuitive knowledge of the most organismically enhancing course of action at any given moment. However, this view seems to contradict gestalt's own emphasis on choice. If the most organismically enhancing course of action will just magically bubble up out of experience, the fully functioning person would never have to choose. After all, what is difficult about choice is that we don't know which is the better course of action or what is likely to be beneficial for us. Yet for gestalt, the present-centered person would not attempt to predict the future and would certainly not try to figure out intellectually what to do. However, the difficulty of choice lies precisely in the fact that true choice usually involves ambiguities and unknowns and is not spontaneous and easy.

Another circumstance to consider is that reality is complex and ambiguous and not easily knowable no matter how present centered we are. People often have to make educated guesses about what is going on in a situation. They develop heuristics and rules of thumb (Nisbett & Ross, 1980) to help them "navigate," but these rules cannot be completely accurate. They make errors and and miscalculations and are not always perfectly congruent in their behavior. But that is not because they are dysfunctionally "split up."

In fact, effortless and spontaneous functioning may occur only in situations where people have well-learned functional scripts that match those situations (Langer, 1978). In the novel *Sophie's Choice* (Styron, 1979), Sophie must choose which of her two children will be executed by the Nazis. If she does not choose one, they will both die. It is hard to imagine that any amount of personal congruence could make this extraordinary choice easy. It can be be argued that people are most often in the position of having to read a complex and ambiguous "text" of reality and that they will only occasionally have a spontaneous, easy, intuitive grasp of the text and of what to do. They often will have to struggle and "think" to decipher the text in order to make complex and difficult decisions.

Part of this problem relates to what many (for example, Corey, 1986) have seen as an anti-intellectual bias in gestalt in particular and other humanistic approaches in general. For Perls and some Eastern mystical approaches, "thinking about," "figuring out," and conceptualizing are the "whores" of intelligence, whereas direct, intuitive, experiential knowing is "real knowing." Presumably it is our concepts that blind us. However, we would argue that there is no such thing as "conceptless" knowing. In meditation one supposedly experiences the oneness of self and reality. This experience is a "knowing" that cannot be put into words. But we believe that that experience depends on the concepts of self, reality, and separateness. One cannot experience oneness between two things unless one previously has had a sense of them as separate. It is likely that such experiences have already been shaped by the concepts of self and reality held previously by the person. Further, just because an experience cannot be put into words does not mean it is free of conceptual organization. Cognitive psychologists like George Mandler (1984) argue that all experience is cognitively constructed, but that only a portion of it is translatable into words.

Furthermore there are times when what "feels right" may be a less accurate guide to actualizing than what the person thinks is right. For example, a colleague of ours had a client who was raised in an abusive, alcoholic family. For her, what "felt right" was to put up passively with abuse, as she was doing in her marriage. She began to realize intellectually how deadly this was and to work to get out of it. But it was her cognitive analysis of the situation that provided the wisdom and dragged her "reluctant body" and feelings along.

The problem is not a matter of either-or; both intellectual thinking and intuitive knowing have their useful purposes. The problem is that we may learn to overemphasize intellectual knowing at the expense of experiential knowing. Also we may learn to treat concepts as more real than the experiences we are using the concepts to describe. The goal is not to eliminate concepts, but rather to realize that concepts are concepts and that one must be open to testing them against experience.

CONTRIBUTIONS OF THE EXISTENTIAL-HUMANISTIC APPROACH

First, existential-humanistic approaches take growth and change seriously. As such they give central attention to the creativity of the person. Second, existential-humanists were among the first to take the idea seriously that the person is to some degree the constructor of his or her world. Following from this is an emphasis on choice and individual responsibility. These emphases can now be found in recent psychoanalytic thinking and in cognitive views. Third, existential-humanists see growth as a process of actualization of self, and this idea is also now popular in psychoanalytic thinking. Fourth, existential-humanistic thinking was among the first systems views of personality, though the implications of this were often neglected by existential-humanistic writers. Fifth, existential-humanists were among the first to emphasize the importance of an authentic encounter between therapist and client, now increasingly recognized by most approaches. Sixth, approaches like gestalt and meditation have contributed useful techniques to the therapist's "kit."

REFERENCES

Barker, R. G. (1968). *Ecological Psychology.* Stanford, CA: Stanford University Press.

Binswanger, L. (1963). *Being-in-the-world: Selected papers of Ludwig Binswanger.* New York: Basic Books.

Bohart, A. (1977). Role playing and interpersonal conflict reduction. *Journal of Counseling Psychology, 24,* 15–24.

Boss, M. (1963). *Psychoanalysis and Daseinanalysis.* New York: Basic Books.

Brown, G. W., & Harris, T. O. (1978). *Social origins of depression.* London: Tavistock; New York: Free Press.

Bugental, J. (1976). *The search for existential identity.* San Francisco: Jossey-Bass.

Corey, G. (1986). *Theory and practice of counseling and psychotherapy* (3rd ed.). Monterey, CA: Brooks/Cole.

Deikman, A. (1982). *The observing self.* Boston: Beacon Press.

De Santis, J. (1985). *Effects of the intensive Zen Buddhist meditation retreat on Rogerian congruence as real-self/ideal-self disparity on the California Q-sort.* Unpublished doctoral dissertation, California School for Professional Psychology, Los Angeles.

Frankl, V. E. (1963). *Man's search for meaning: An introduction to logotherapy.* New York: Washington Square Press.

Frings, Manfred S. (Ed.). (1968). *Heidegger and the quest for truth.* Chicago: Quadrangle.

Gendlin, E. T. (1968). The experiential response. In E. Hammer (Ed.), *Use of interpretation in treatment.* New York: Grune & Stratton.

Greenberg, L. S. (1984). A task analysis of intrapersonal conflict resolution. In L. N. Rice & L. S. Greenberg (Eds.), *Patterns of change.* New York: Guilford.

Heidegger, M. (1959). *Unterwegs zur Sprache.* Pfullingen, West Germany.

Holmes, D. S. (1984). Meditation and somatic arousal reduction: A review of the experimental evidence. *American Psychologist, 39,* 1–10.

Husserl, E. (1964). *Cartesian meditations: An introduction to phenomenology.* The Hague, Netherlands: Martinus Nijhoff.

Kaplan, M. L., & Kaplan, N. R. (1985). The linearity issue and Gestalt therapy's theory of experiential organization. *Psychotherapy, 22,* 5–15.

Kempler, W. (1973). Gestalt therapy. In R. J. Corsini (Ed.), *Current psychotherapies.* Itasca, IL: Peacock.

Kobasa, S. C., & Maddi, S. R. (1983). Existential personality theory. In R. J. Corsini & A. J. Marsella (Eds.), *Personality theories, research, and assessment.* Itasca, IL: Peacock.

Langer, E. (1978). Rethinking the role of thought in social interaction. In J. H. Harvey, W. I.

Ickes, & R. F. Kidd (Eds.), *New directions in attribution research* (Vol. 2). Hillsdale, NJ: Erlbaum.

Lieberman, M. A., Yalom, I. D., & Miles, M. B. (1973). *Encounter groups: First facts.* New York: Basic Books.

Mandler, G. (1984). *Mind and body: Psychological stress and emotion.* New York: Norton.

May, R., Angel, E., & Ellenberger, H. F. (Eds.). 1958. *Existence: A new dimension in psychiatry and psychology.* New York: Basic Books.

May, R., & Yalom, I. (1984). Existential psychotherapy. In R. J. Corsini (Ed.), *Current psychotherapies* (3rd ed.). Itasca, IL: Peacock.

Montemayor, R., & Eisen, M. (1977). The development of self-conceptions from childhood to adolescence. *Developmental Psychology, 13,* 314–319.

Nisbett, R., & Ross, L. (1980). *Human inference: Strategies and shortcomings of social judgment.* Englewood Cliffs, NJ: Prentice-Hall.

Perls, F.S. (1965). *Gestalt therapy* (Film No. 2). In E. Shostrom (Ed.), *Three approaches to psychotherapy* (Three 16 mm motion pictures). Santa Ana, CA: Psychological Films.

Perls, F. S. (1969). *Gestalt therapy verbatim.* Moab, UT: Real People Press.

Polster, E. (1985). *The story line in psychotherapy* (Live demonstration). Presented at the Evolution of Psychotherapy Conference, Phoenix, AZ, December 12, 1985.

Resnick, R. W. (1980). Foreword. In V. Van De Reit, M. P. Korb, & J. J. Gorrell, *Gestalt therapy: An introduction.* New York: Pergamon Press.

Ricks, D. F., Wandersman, A., & Poppen, P. J. (1976). Humanism and behaviorism: Toward new syntheses. Reprinted in M. R. Goldfried (Ed.), *Converging trends in psychotherapy: Trends in psychodynamic, humanistic and behavioral practice.* New York: Springer, 1982.

Rogers, C. R. (1985). Toward a more human science of the person. *Journal of Humanistic Psychology, 25,* 7–24.

Sartre, J.-P. (1956). *Being and nothingness.* New York: Philosophical Library.

Schmitt, R. (1969). *Martin Heidegger on being human: An introduction to Zein und Zeit.* New York: Random House.

Shepard, M. (1975). *Fritz.* New York: Bantam Books.

Simkin, J. S., & Yontef, G. M. (1984). Gestalt therapy. In R. J. Corsini (Ed.), *Current psychotherapies* (3rd ed.). Itasca, IL: Peacock.

Smith, M. L., Glass, G. V., & Miller, T. I. (1980). *The benefits of psychotherapy.* Baltimore: Johns Hopkins University Press.

Styron, W. (1979). *Sophie's choice.* New York: Random House.

Tillich, P. (1952). *The courage to be.* New Haven, CT: Yale University Press.

Van De Riet, V., Korb, M. P., & Gorrell, J. J. (1980). *Gestalt therapy: An introduction.* New York: Pergamon Press.

Washburn, M. (1978). Observations relevant to a unified theory of meditation. *Journal of Transpersonal Psychology, 10,* 45–65.

Yalom, I. (1981). *Existential psychotherapy.* New York: Basic Books.

Zukav, G. (1979). *The dancing Wu Li masters.* New York: Bantam Books.

Chapter 7

Behavioral Approaches to Therapy

> Much confusion about the etiology of neurotic fear emanates from the assumption that it is quite different from that of normal fear. . . . There is in fact no basic difference. Just as some normal (i.e., appropriate) fears develop on the basis of classical conditioning and some on the basis of information (cognitive learning), the same is true of neurotic fears. What differentiates normal and neurotic fears is the character of the stimulus situation to which the conditioning has occurred. If that stimulus situation is objectively either a source of danger or a sign of danger, the fear is appropriate or "adaptive"; if it is neither, the fear is neurotic. (Wolpe, 1982, p. 27)

> A 34-year-old man had a severe fear of being in an automobile. This had started four years previously when his car had been struck from behind while he was waiting for a red light to change. He had been thrust forward so that his head, striking the windshield, had sustained a small laceration. He had not lost consciousness, but a surge of panic had swept over him, brought on by the thought "I am about to die." The fear became connected to the car's interior and spread to all car interiors. During these four years he had been unable to enter a car without great anxiety. Driving was out of the question. That fear was entirely due to classical autonomic conditioning. (Wolpe, 1982, p. 28)

One day you are walking down the hall in the psychology building on campus, when a research assistant beckons to you from a laboratory door. "Want to see something weird?" "OK," you say, following the assistant into the lab.

"See anything unusual about this rat?" she says, reaching into a cage and grabbing a fat, glossy, white rat by the scruff of the neck.

"No, it looks like a normal rat," you conclude after a careful examination of 1.5 seconds.

"Well, watch this." She carries the rat over to a large box with lights and wires attached to it. There is no top on the box and it is divided into two compartments with an opening between them. One compartment is painted all white and the other dark brown.

"What will happen if I put the rat in there?"

"Well," you consider, trying to remember what you know about rats, "the rat will probably explore the compartments, and it will probably stay mostly in the dark compartment," for you suddenly remember that rats prefer darkness to light.

She lowers the rat into the dark side of the box, and almost before its paws can hit the floor, it shoots through the doorway into the white compartment, and there it stays, sniffing around.

"How peculiar," you say, because you are absolutely certain that you recall Professor Lecturn telling the class that rats prefer dark areas. "Maybe it just doesn't know any better," you suggest. "Let's see that again."

Obligingly, the assistant places the rat in the dark compartment again. Again, it rushes to the white side and stays there. She repeats this activity several times, and the rat always runs to the white side without the slightest hesitation. She even inserts a door into the opening between the compartments, which can be opened by a lever in the dark compartment. When she then puts the rat in, it rushes to the lever, pushes it, and scurries through the opened door into the white side. Since you (and Professor Lecturn) could not possibly be wrong about normal rat behavior, there must be something wrong with this particular rat. "Wow," you say, "what an abnormal rat!"

"You think so?" the assistant asks. "What if I told you that there used to be an electric grid on the floor of the dark compartment? This rat received a huge electric shock in there."

"I *see,*" you nod knowingly. "But there's no electric grid in there now, so it's impossible for the rat to get shocked again."

"That's the neurotic paradox. The learned behavior remains even though the conditions for the original learning no longer hold."

"Why doesn't the rat eventually learn that no shock is coming?"

"It would under certain circumstances," she admits, "but there are several theories about why it doesn't under these conditions. One possibility is that when the rat runs into the white side, its fear is reduced, which is highly rewarding, so the behavior of running to the white side is constantly being reinforced by fear reduction."

You nod as if you understand and remark, "So this is a perfectly normal rat after all."

"Yes, when you know its learning history."

Mowrer and his associates did a series of experiments similar to the one described above during the 1940s and 1950s (Mowrer, 1947; Mowrer & Lamoreaux, 1946; Mowrer & Solomon, 1954). At that time behaviorism was the dominant school of thought in academic psychology. Behaviorism took over in the 1920s, in large part because of the influence of John B. Watson's work. Watson is supposed to have attempted the first demonstration that "abnormal" behavior is learned in humans as well as rats.

Watson reported that in an experiment he classically conditioned a fear of white rats in 11-month-old Albert (Watson & Rayner, 1920), although some scholars now question the veracity of the tale of Little Albert (Harris, 1979). Prior to Watson's intervention, Little Albert had enjoyed playing with a white rat. Watson paired a loud, frightening noise with handing Little Albert the rat, and he did this a few times. Soon Little Albert cried at the sight of a rat and tried to crawl away, and he showed the same fear reaction to any white, furry object. Watson had demonstrated that an abnormal behavior like a phobia could be learned. He even wrote, "It is probable that many of the phobias in psychopathology are true conditioned emotional reactions" (Watson & Rayner, 1920, p. 14).

Strict behaviorists, such as B. F. Skinner (1938, 1971), believe that the behavior of all organisms, rat and human alike, can be explained by the principles of learning and conditioning, without any reference whatsoever to what goes on, if anything, in the organism's head. The same laws of learning apply to all behavior, both "normal" and "abnormal." Abnormal behavior is simply the normal, lawful response to abnormal learning conditions. Abnormal behavior can be changed by changing these learning conditions. Before going further, we should perhaps review some of the basic principles of behaviorism.

PRINCIPLES OF LEARNING

There are two basic types of conditioning: *classical* or *respondent conditioning* and *instrumental* or *operant conditioning.* Classical conditioning was first demonstrated by the Russian biologist I. Pavlov in his famous experiments with dogs. Pavlov was actually trying to study digestion when he discovered classical conditioning and then turned to a whole new career in neuropsychology. Each dog was hooked up to a device so that its saliva drained out of a fistula into a beaker to be measured. Pavlov introduced measured amounts of food into a dog's mouth and observed the salivation response, which is the first step in digestion. Soon he noticed that the dogs began to salivate when they saw him approaching with the food, and they even began to salivate at the sight of the experimental harness. While this ruined his digestion research, he became intrigued and began to study this process systematically. He rang a bell immediately before introducing the food into the dog's mouth, and he paired the bell and food several times. Soon the dogs salivated to the sound of the bell, even if no food followed.

In Pavlov's experiment salivation is the *unconditioned response* to the *unconditioned stimulus* of food. Salivation is the natural or automatic response to food. The bell, rung just before food was given, is the *conditioned stimulus,* and salivating to it, instead of to food, is the *conditioned response.* In other words, salivating to a bell is not a natural, automatic response, but is a conditioned, or learned, one. A stimulus must occur close in time, usually just before an unconditioned stimulus for it to become a conditioned stimulus. Any stimulus that occurs around an unconditioned stimulus can become associated to it, as the sight of Pavlov and their experimental harness became associated to food for Pavlov's dogs.

Classical conditioning occurs only with behaviors that are automatic, perhaps even unconscious responses to things, such as reflexes like salivation and emotions like fear. The rat described at the beginning of this chapter was classically conditioned to fear the dark compartment. The automatic or unconditioned response to the unconditioned stimulus of electric shock is fear. The cue of the dark compartment was close in time and place to the rat's perception of the shock, so the dark compartment became the conditioned stimulus to the conditioned response of fear.

The most famous example of *instrumental* or *operant conditioning* is Skinner's bar-pressing rat. In Skinner's experiments rats learn to press a bar, which releases a pellet of rat chow into a food cup. It is called instrumental because the conditioned response of bar pressing is instrumental in obtaining the reward of food. It is called operant because the behavior being conditioned or learned is operant behavior, that is, behavior that is voluntarily put forth by the organism, rather than an automatic response to a stimulus as in classical conditioning. Bar pressing is the *conditioned response,* which *precedes* the *conditioned stimulus* or reward of food. Recall that in classical conditioning, it is the opposite: The conditioned stimulus precedes the conditioned response.

Besides classical and operant conditioning, there is a third type of learning called *extinction.* Extinction occurs when rewards are no longer delivered after the operant response, and the organism learns to stop making the conditioned response. A rat presses its bar and no food falls into the food cup; the rat is said to be *on extinction.* It may give the bar a few more quick presses—still no food. Gradually it gives up pressing the bar altogether. Bar pressing has been *extinguished.* Classically conditioned responses can also be extinguished. If Pavlov rang the bell many times without delivering food, the dogs would gradually stop salivating to the bell. Notice that extinction is an active learning process, not simply forgetting or fading. The rat learns that bar pressing does not result in food. A behavior is said to be *strongly conditioned* and *resistant to extinction* if it takes a long time, or many trials of doing the behavior for no reward, to extinguish.

Social learning theorists such as Bandura (1977b) have argued that in addition to classical conditioning, operant conditioning, and extinction, another type of learning, *imitation* or *observational learning,* is important in humans. Humans and other primates are great copiers of others, and it may be that most human learning is a result of imitation. All that is necessary for this type of learning to occur is for the person to observe someone else engaging in the behavior. In many experiments Bandura (1969) and his colleagues demonstrated that humans will imitate almost anyone, including film and cartoon characters, but they are more likely to imitate models who are warm and nurturant and who have high status and power than to imitate mean, low status models. They are also more likely to imitate models who are rewarded for their behavior than models who are punished for their behavior.

The reinforcement in operant conditioning has been defined several ways. Currently, a *reward* is defined as either the delivery of a positive stimulus, such as food, or the removal of a negative stimulus, such as turning off a loud noise. Delivering a positive stimulus is also called positive reinforcement; removing a negative stimulus, negative reinforcement. A *punishment* can be either the delivery of a negative stimulus, such as an electric shock, or the removal of a positive stimulus, such as docking someone's allowance. However, one question that has puzzled behaviorists is "What constitutes a reward?" (McDowell, 1982). Food is obviously a reward to a hungry rat. But rewards are rarely that obvious in human learning, and much of our behavior does not seem to be followed by any obvious reward.

In humans an important reward seems to be the attention of other human beings. We are a social species. We work with people, we talk to them, we go out to lunch, we play cards, we goof off and hang out together. What is the reward? Just the pleasure of interacting with others seems to be enough. There is evidence that the reward of human attention has drive properties—we need it and are motivated to try to obtain it. In one experiment (Gewirtz & Baer, 1958), children who had been deprived of human attention for 20 minutes worked longer and harder at a subsequent marble-dropping task for the reward of an adult's saying "Mm hmm" and "Fine" than children who got lots of attention before the task. This is similar to a food-deprived rat's working longer and harder at bar pressing for food than a fed rat. We say the rat is hungry—it has a drive or need for food. People may have a similar need for attention.

Furthermore, if people are deprived of attention, they may resort to unpleasant or "abnormal" behavior to get it. Even if the form of attention they receive for abnormal behavior is disapproval or punishment, it appears that they prefer it to being ignored. Most of you can probably remember a really obnoxious kid in your elementary school who made the other children laugh or bothered them and was repeatedly scolded or threatened by the teacher. When that kid did work quietly, probably everyone ignored him. A child who does not seem able to get enough attention by prosocial methods may resort to disturbing or disturbed behavior in order to get it. Such behavior is called *negative attention seeking,* because both the behavior to get attention and the attention it gets are negative.

Many experiments have studied how the timing of rewards affects the speed and strength of conditioning. Rewards can be given after every instance of an operant response, for a 100 percent reinforcement schedule, or after every few operant responses, for a partial reinforcement schedule. In "real life" it is unlikely that rewards ever arrive on a 100 percent reinforcement schedule. In general, 100 percent reinforcement results in faster conditioning than partial reinforcement, but partial reinforcement results in stronger conditioning. The more unpredictable the partial reinforcement schedule, the more resistant to extinction is the behavior. Place a rat who has received food variably for every tenth to twentieth bar press on extinction, and it will take that rat a long time to learn that no food is coming for any bar press.

Human behavior is most often rewarded on some type of variable partial reinforcement schedule, which is probably why it is so difficult to break some bad habits. An hour before dinner, children start whining for snacks. Their parents tell them no, because dinner is almost ready. On the tenth whine, exasperated parents cave in and give the children snacks. Then they wonder why the next night, the children start in whining for snacks before dinner. On a schedule of partial reward whining has been inadvertently and unfortunately strongly conditioned and made resistant to extinction.

After rewarding the tenth whine, parents will have to bear with 20 or 30 whines the next night before the children will give up.

Extensive research has been conducted on many other aspects of learning. One example, already discussed, is the variety of conditions that make learned responses resistant to extinction. Another example is *generalization.* A response learned under one set of conditions may generalize to other situations. A child who whines for snacks before dinner and gets rewarded for it may generalize this learning to whining for snacks before lunch, whining for toys as well as snacks, or whining for things at school as well as at home. However, since this is not a book on learning theory, we will not cover every aspect of learning, but trust that this review is sufficient to make sense of the rest of the chapter.

By now you may be asking, "What has all this got to do with behavior therapy?" Some scholars believe that all mental disturbance can be traced to conditioned responses and reinforced behavior. If so, then the mentally disturbed can be helped with the principles of learning just discussed. So let us now turn to a discussion of how abnormal behavior is learned.

THE DEVELOPMENT OF ABNORMAL OR UNWANTED BEHAVIOR

Behaviorists believe that just the basic principles of learning—classical conditioning, operant conditioning, extinction, and imitation—can account for *all* behavior, both normal and abnormal. Abnormal behavior, bad habits, and other unwanted behaviors are learned in the same way as normal or desired behaviors. Because a behavior that seems odd or abnormal was acquired by the basic learning principles, it will make sense when its learning history is known. And it should be possible to change it by applying those same learning principles.

It is easy to see that phobias might result from experiences like the electric shocking of the rat in the dark compartment. A phobia is a strong fear of something that does not elicit fear in most people. Since most rats prefer dark places, we could say that, compared to other rats, the behavior of the rat that always ran away from the dark looked abnormal. When it is known that the rat had been shocked in the dark compartment, its behavior makes sense. A fear-evoking event may classically condition a phobia in humans as well.

Let us turn to the example of the young woman, described in Box 7.1, who was severely afraid of birds. As a child, she was locked in a hen house and "attacked" by the frightened chickens. She was classically conditioned to fear chickens, harmless birds that do not ordinarily elicit fear in the human heart. In her case the sight of chickens was paired with the experience of being locked in a small enclosure with scratching, squawking, flapping, and pecking chickens, an experience that would naturally be frightening to a small child, if not to all of us. The pecking chickens were the unconditioned stimuli for the unconditioned response of fear. That is, fear is the automatic, reflexive response to these stimuli. The sight of chickens, which was paired with the unconditioned stimuli, became the conditioned stimulus for the conditioned fear response. Furthermore, this response generalized, so that the sight of other birds also frightened the girl. She had developed a bird phobia.

BOX 7.1
One Flew Over . . .

Several years ago a psychologist sat quietly in a staff meeting while two psychoanalytically oriented psychiatrists argued for an hour about the patient they had all seen recently in intake. The patient was an attractive 17-year-old woman who was suffering from anxiety and a severe phobia of birds, which kept her from being able to go out to school or work. One analyst argued strongly that the fear of birds symbolized her fear of heterosexual encounters, since the birds unconsciously represented penises or "cocks." The other analyst argued, equally vociferously, that the fear of birds represented her fear of her latent homosexuality, since at that time and place "bird" was slang for young girl or "chick."

During intake the psychologist had asked the patient why she thought she was so afraid of birds. The patient immediately described an incident when she was 4 years old and visiting her aunt's farm. As punishment for some naughty act, the aunt locked her in the hen house for a few minutes. In her attempts to escape from the hen house, the crying child probably frightened the chickens. She vividly recalled the hens squawking and flying about, hitting her with their wings and scratching her face and arms. She remembered feeling terrified, and she avoided birds ever after.

When the analysts finished arguing, the psychologist ventured to report the client's history. The analysts paused for only a moment before uniting in asserting that the hen house incident was merely a "screen memory" invented to rationalize the phobia. Nevertheless, the psychiatrists agreed to allow the psychologist and her young colleague to try out a new approach to treatment based on the assumption that the fear was a conditioned response and that unconscious childhood memories need not be dealt with.

The treatment (described in Box 7.3) was successful in that the patient's fear was reduced and seemed to generalize to other birds in the environment, and she was able to leave her house and obtain a job. It is not known if the young woman developed new or substitute symptoms for the phobia as would be predicted by psychoanalysis, but she did not come back to the agency in the four years the psychologist worked there.

Why didn't this fear extinguish with time, as the girl grew up? This phenomenon is the so-called *neurotic paradox.* The conditioned fear remains even though the original conditions for learning it are no longer present or relevant. The rat's fear of the dark compartment remains even though the electric grid floor has been removed and the rat is no longer shocked when it is placed in the compartment. In the case of the bird-phobic woman the fear of birds remained even though the fearful event was long in the past and in everyday life birds don't attack or injure people.

There are several explanations for the neurotic paradox. One possibility is that the amount of time it takes to run away from or avoid the feared stimulus is shorter than the amount of time it takes for real fear to build up and be extinguished. The rat runs away from the dark compartment before it has a chance to learn that it won't be shocked. If the rat were to be locked in the dark compartment, its fear would extinguish. Forced to remain in the dark compartment, its fear would build up, no shock would follow, its fear would decrease, and the classically conditioned fear of the dark compartment would eventually be extinguished.

Another explanation for the persistence of phobia is that the operant behavior of running away or avoiding the feared stimulus is repeatedly rewarded with anxiety reduction. When the rat is put in the dark compartment, it starts to feel fear and quickly runs into the white compartment, where it immediately feels better because its fear is reduced. This reward is a so-called negative reinforcement, in that the reduction of the unpleasant fear is rewarding. Thus, the avoidant or phobic behavior repeatedly is rewarded through the reduction of a negative stimulus, fear, and it will therefore persist. For years every time the woman saw a bird, she would feel afraid, walk away from it, and immediately feel better, so that the avoidance of birds was a highly rewarded and well-learned behavior. To summarize then: *A phobia is the result of operantly conditioned avoidance behavior that is rewarded by the reduction of classically conditioned fear.* Behaviorists believe that complex neuroses and other abnormal behaviors may also be operant behaviors rewarded by the reduction of classically conditioned fears.

Let's look at just one more example of how abnormal or unwanted behavior is learned—temper tantrums. Most small children throw one or two temper tantrums at some time or other. The behavior is not abnormal, although it is definitely unwanted. However, some parents inadvertently train their children to throw tantrums. Such parents tend to fail to reward desired behavior and to pay attention only to undesired behavior. We have seen that humans find receiving the attention of other humans highly rewarding. Children will do a lot of things to get their parents' attention: "Look at me! Watch this! See the doggy, mommy!" A stressed parent may ignore these normal and fairly pleasant attempts to get attention. She may also be so relieved when the child plays quietly by himself that she goes off to rest and so fails to reward this type of "good" behavior with any attention. (It could be said that desired behavior is on extinction.) In stressed families the level of reward is often low for all behavior. The child may then throw a tantrum, a behavior that is difficult to ignore, especially if it is done in the middle of the supermarket. The parent is forced to pay attention, even if that attention is scolding or punishing, and the child has learned a guaranteed way to get the parent's attention. The parent has rewarded the child for throwing the tantrum by paying attention. In a low-reward family a child may throw more and more tantrums to get attention, until it is a well-learned behavior. The parent has not planned to train the child to throw tantrums, but failing to reward desired behavior and paying attention to undesired behavior has had that result.

By now you have probably thought of some examples of abnormal behaviors that learning theory cannot explain. Not all children in low-reward families learn to throw temper tantrums. It is possible that not all children locked in a hen house would become bird phobic. Some adults can reason themselves out of early learned fears. Not all survivors of plane crashes develop a fear of flying, but many do. How can learning theory account for such individual differences? How can a behaviorist explain such apparently complicated disorders as schizophrenia, which includes hallucinations and bizarre thinking? How could someone learn such a thing as an anxiety neurosis, when the aversive feeling of anxiety is experienced almost all the time?

There are many such criticisms of the behavioral view of abnormality. Box 7.2 deals with the issue of symptom substitution. A detailed account of these issues is beyond the scope of this book. In general, behaviorists counter the criticisms of their theory by arguing that if we could obtain a sufficiently accurate learning history for each case, we would find appropriate explanations. Also, even if we are not certain precisely how all abnormal behavior is learned, we can nevertheless change it by applying learning principles. If all behavior is learned, it can be unlearned, and new behavior can be learned.

FEATURES COMMON TO ALL BEHAVIOR THERAPIES

Behaviorism was the dominant view in academic psychology for decades before clinical psychology noticed it. Except for Watson's case of Little Albert, behaviorists appeared uninterested in the seemingly obvious opportunity to apply their theories to abnormal behavior. There are several reasons for this odd state of affairs. Academic psychologists were interested in establishing the scientific status of their field, not in applications. Clinical psychologists were working in a field dominated by the medical profession and the psychoanalytic viewpoint. It took an outsider, Joseph Wolpe, to introduce behaviorism to clinical psychology.

Wolpe was a South African psychiatrist trained in psychoanalysis who became interested in Pavlov's research and theories. Pavlov theorized that fields of excitation and inhibition in the brain caused behavior and that certain kinds of excitation could interfere with or inhibit other responses. Wolpe generalized these ideas to the causes and treatment of phobias. He saw that phobias could be explained as classically conditioned fear responses. He believed they could be treated by conditioning a new response to the fear stimulus, a response that would interfere with or inhibit the fear response. It is interesting to speculate whether Wolpe, had he been familiar with American learning theory, would have developed a treatment based simply on extinction, rather than the *reciprocal inhibition* method he developed.

Since Wolpe wanted to condition a new response to the phobic stimulus, he wanted a response that would be incompatible with the fear response, that is, something that could not be done or felt at the same time as fear. He settled on deep muscle relaxation, also known as progressive muscle relaxation (Jacobson, 1938). Sexual arousal, eating, and the response to laughing gas are also incompatible with fear, but he rejected these as unworkable. Wolpe taught his patients to induce deep muscle relaxation in themselves, and then he gradually introduced verbal images of the phobic object, with the aim of replacing the classically conditioned fear response with the classically conditioned relaxation response to the feared stimulus. (This method, also known as *systematic desensitization,* is described below in the section on classical conditioning methods of behavior therapy.)

Wolpe achieved good results with his new treatment method, which he described in his *Psychotherapy by Reciprocal Inhibition* (1958). The method was an immediate hit among clinical psychologists, who then turned to their own rich background of behaviorism with new appreciation. Pragmatic American psychologists realized that at last here was a theory and technology that could challenge psychoanalysis in explanatory and treatment power. This realization coincided with the post-World War II increase in demand for psychological services for people with a wide variety of problems and economic resources. Behavior therapies promised to be a quick, relatively inexpensive, and highly effective way of meeting this increased demand.

BOX 7.2
Symptom Removal or Symptom Substitution?

Since the 1950s the debate between behaviorists and psychoanalysts over psychotherapy theory and practice has focused on the issue of symptom substitution. Psychoanalysts believe that neurotic symptoms are expressions of some unconscious internal conflict and that the conflict must be resolved in treatment. Behaviorists believe that internal conflicts, even if they exist, are unimportant; they believe the symptom is the problem, and it is the symptom that can and should be treated. When behaviorists demonstrated empirically that symptoms could be removed with behavioral methods, psychoanalysts countered that symptom removal would merely be followed by symptom substitution. Since the true cause of the neurosis, the internal conflict, was untreated, it would cause new symptoms to appear if one were removed.

In considering the case of the bird-phobic woman in Box 7.1, the psychoanalysts thought that the phobia was caused by her unconscious fear of heterosexuality or of homosexuality and that treatment should focus on dealing with that unconscious fear, whichever it was. If the bird phobia itself were treated and removed, they argued, she would soon develop another symptom, such as agoraphobia, anxiety attacks, or even sexual acting out or other impulse disorder, because she would still be suffering from her unconscious conflict about sex, which would cause new symptoms to develop.

The controversy over symptom substitution is really about which theoretical and therapeutic approach is correct, and it would seem that the issue could be solved empirically. Does symptom substitution occur? After years of research, the answer is a clear "Maybe, sometimes." The question turns out to be a difficult one to answer.

First of all, there is little agreement about what constitutes a symptom. Second, it is difficult to distinguish between a symptom that is a replacement and one that is a new problem. How long after therapy should it be concluded that a substitute symptom is not going to occur? Most behaviorists follow up cases for six months or a year after treatment, and report few instances of new symptoms, but psychoanalysts argue that it takes longer for symptom substitution to occur. If another symptom does appear after treatment, how is it to be proved that it is caused by the same internal conflict that caused the first one, rather than being a separate problem?

Given these research difficulties, it is probably not surprising that behaviorists continue to report successful symptom removal with little evidence of symptom substitution after six months or a year and psychoanalysts continue to treat unconscious conflicts rather than "mere" symptoms.

There are behavioral treatment methods based on all the learning principles previously discussed. In addition to Wolpe's method of classically conditioning new responses to fear stimuli, there are behavior therapies based on extinction, classical conditioning of aversive responses, operant conditioning with rewards, and imitation, and combinations of these methods. Different forms of behavior therapy have been developed to treat every type of psychological disorder, as well as to modify bad habits, to eliminate unwanted behaviors, and to teach new skills. As you can see, behavior therapy must cover a wide variety of treatment methods, and indeed, there are many different kinds of techniques that get labeled behavior therapy. This chapter will cover only a representative sample of the many behavior therapies currently available.

Behavior therapists agree that there is no commonly agreed upon definition of behavior therapy. The following definition is, nevertheless, endorsed by the American Association of Behavior Therapists.

> Behavior therapy involves primarily the application of principles derived from research in experimental and social psychology for the alleviation of human suffering and the enhancement of human functioning. Behavior therapy emphasizes a systematic evaluation of the effectiveness of these applications. Behavior therapy involves environmental change and social interaction rather than the direct alteration of bodily processes by biological procedures. The aim is primarily educational. The techniques facilitate improved self-control. In the conduct of behavior therapy, a contractual agreement is negotiated, in which mutually agreeable goals and procedures are specified. Responsible practitioners using behavior approaches are guided by generally accepted principles. (Franks & Barbrack, 1983, p. 509)

Although they may not define therapy the same way, most behavior therapies do share certain assumptions.

1. All behavior is learned by the same principles.
2. Behavior can be unlearned and changed.
3. Therapy methods are tied to experimentally verified principles of behavior.
4. Therapy techniques are specified clearly and concretely, so they are testable.
5. The outcome of therapy is evaluated empirically with measurable behavior changes.

You will note that these assumptions include the belief that abnormal behavior is not due to anything that needs to be inferred or cannot be directly observed, such as motives, internal conflicts, or unconscious "parts" of the "personality." The true causes of abnormality are both observable and changeable.

All behavior therapies begin with an interview between therapist and client, in which the nature of the client's problem and its appropriateness for behavioral treatment is assessed. The initial interview may include some of the behavioral assessment techniques described in Chapter 2, such as questionnaires or observations. Although not strictly within the realm of behaviorism, trust and understanding between therapist and client are assumed to be essential for the success of the initial interview(s) and for the success of treatment as well. Thus, behavior therapists recognize the importance of the nature of the relationship between therapist and client and the role of therapist warmth and empathy to enhance that relationship. The behavior therapies described below may *seem* relatively simple and straightforward, but they are not.

Initially, a detailed history of the client's problems is taken, including when and how the problems began, their frequency (or baseline), what the environmental stimulus of the problems is, and what the client has tried to do so far. The therapist tries to clarify with the client precisely what the client hopes to accomplish in therapy. The therapist will also try to cast these goals in behavioral terms: What type of behavioral changes will the client and therapist have to see in order to know that therapy has been successful and the goals have been reached?

Once the problems and therapy goals have been defined, the therapist thoroughly explains the therapeutic procedures and their rationale to the client. The therapist may cite research demonstrating the effectiveness of the method with other clients with similar problems. Only when the client completely understands the steps involved in the behavior therapy can the client consent to it. Only then will behavior therapy begin.

To summarize, most behavior therapies include at least these five steps in their procedures:

1. Assess and evaluate the client's problem.
2. Choose the best therapeutic method for the problem.
3. Educate the client about the method, including exactly what will be done and the likelihood of success.
4. Apply the therapeutic method.
5. Evaluate the success of treatment.

CLASSICAL CONDITIONING METHODS

The assumption behind behavior therapies based on classical conditioning is that abnormal behavior is due to inappropriate, classically conditioned emotions, especially fear and anxiety. These emotions then motivate avoidance and other behaviors that are rewarded by anxiety reduction.

Systematic Desensitization

Originally called reciprocal inhibition, systematic desensitization has already been described as a treatment for phobias, fears, and anxiety, based on classically conditioning a new response that is incompatible with fear and anxiety. The client is trained in deep muscle relaxation, a response that is incompatible with fear. In addition, the therapist and client create an *anxiety hierarchy.* This hierarchy lists aspects of the fear- or anxiety-producing objects, events, or situations from least frightening to most frightening. For example, an anxiety hierarchy for a snake phobia might be a snake in the next county, a snake in the next room, a snake in the same room in an escape-proof cage, a snake on the floor, a snake touching the client. Then the hierarchy and the relaxation are put together to create systematic desensitization. The client is desensitized, that is, made less sensitive, to the previously frightening things.

In deep muscle relaxation the client typically lies on a couch (after all, Wolpe *was* a psychoanalyst!) in a quiet, dimly lit room and proceeds through a series of exercises to induce relaxation in all the muscles of the body. The therapist, speaking quietly and soothingly, guides the client through the exercises. The therapist instructs the client to tense and relax all the major muscle groups in the body, usually starting with the toes or feet and working up to the arms, shoulders, neck, and head, and to note the different physical sensations associated with each state. After this rather boring procedure, the client is deeply relaxed, if not asleep!

However, the therapist interrupts this pleasant state by beginning to introduce items from the anxiety hierarchy. The client is asked to imagine vividly each item on the hierarchy while in the relaxed state. The therapist introduces the least frightening item on the anxiety hierarchy first. The therapist may assist the client in imagining the item by describing it in great detail, but still in a soothing voice. If the client remains relaxed, the next most frightening item on the hierarchy is described and imagined. The therapist may simply ask the client if he or she still feels relaxed or the client may indicate tension by raising a finger. Some therapists use a Subjective Units of Discomfort scale (SUDS) for clients to indicate anxiety, with 1 representing complete relaxation and 10 complete fear. The procedure continues until the client feels a little anxiety or the therapy hour is up. If the client experiences tension, the therapist may repeat the relaxation exercises and return to a less frightening item on the hierarchy. In this way the client is gradually conditioned to experience relaxation rather than fear to the idea of the phobic thing.

Desensitization is accomplished in a few sessions, usually less than 10. It has been successfully used to treat a variety of problems (Wolpe, 1982), including generalized anxiety (anxiety neurosis). In the case of extremely generalized anxiety many hierarchies of frightening things may have to be used and the treatment will necessarily take longer than desensitizing a client for a single phobia. Other problems treated with desensitization, to name just a few, are fear of flying, agoraphobia, fear of injections or other medical procedures, severe social embarrassment and blushing, inability to urinate in public rest rooms, and fears of animals.

In Vivo Desensitization

In vivo (Latin, "in life") desensitization is a logical extension of systematic desensitization, and it is often used to assess the success of that procedure. Since systematic desensitization relies on *imagining* the phobic thing, it is possible that clients could remain relaxed with the *idea* of the phobic thing, but become frightened in its actual presence. *In vivo* procedures gradually place the phobic person in contact with the actual feared object or situation. If a person has undergone systematic desensitization and can approach a previously feared object without much anxiety, then all would agree that the behavior therapy was a success.

Like systematic desensitization, the *in vivo* procedure begins with teaching the client deep muscle relaxation, but rather than imagining that the feared object or situation is closer and closer, the client is required to make closer and closer approaches to it. The *in vivo* portions of the treatment of the bird-phobic woman are described in Box 7.3. The snake-phobic client would first be told that there is a snake in the next room. If the client remains relaxed knowing there is a snake in the next room, the snake is gradually brought closer and closer until the client can touch the snake. Obviously, only gentle nonpoisonous snakes are used. Perhaps even baby snakes are used before bigger ones are introduced.

The possibilities for *in vivo* desensitization in the hands of creative therapists are endless. For example, fear of flying is treated by asking the client to engage in behaviors that gradually approach getting on a airplane, such as phoning for a flight reservation, then driving to the airport. The client may be required to sit in an airplane on the ground and then finally to take a short flight. The client is required to take each next step only when he or she is able to remain relaxed and unafraid through the preceding step.

Implosion (Extinction)

Implosive therapy, also called flooding, is both an extension of the desensitization work and a direct application of academic research on extinction (Stampfl & Levis, 1973). Rather than conditioning a new response, why not just massively extinguish the fear all in one go? Like the rat kept in the dark compartment, people forced to remain in a frightening situation will have to stop feeling afraid after a while. It is physiologically impossible to remain strongly afraid for more than 20 or 30 minutes. So if a person could be induced to stay in the frightening situation, rather than immediately running away and feeling better, then the fear should extinguish, according to learning research.

Implosion involves making the client vividly imagine all aspects of whatever is frightening until he or she becomes relaxed. An *in vivo* version keeps the client in the actual frightening situation until the fear is extinguished and relaxation replaces it. A snake phobia might be treated implosively by helping the client imagine all the vivid details of being trapped in a snake pit with snakes crawling all over his body. An *in vivo* implosion might put the client in a room full of caged snakes for an hour or so. Implosion is a potentially effective, quick form of treatment that should take just one session after the client agrees to it. However, perhaps because there is a risk that it may increase the client's fears, implosion is not a popular form of behavior therapy today.

Aversion Therapy

Aversion therapy involves the use of an unconditioned aversive stimulus to classically condition fear or aversion to a previously attractive stimulus in order to create an avoidance response or to suppress undesirable or unwanted operant behavior. Electric shock is the most commonly used aversive stimulus, although nausea-inducing drugs have also been used. For example, an electric shock is paired with an alcoholic drink in order to reduce drinking. Through classical conditioning the previously attractive stimulus of the drink should become aversive, so that the person will avoid the drink or suppress the operant behavior of drinking.

Note that it is *not* operant behavior that is being punished. In most cases it would not be ethical or desirable to have clients perform unwanted operant behaviors, and there are also ethical questions about administering punishment. (These questions are discussed later.) An obvious example would be child molesting. No one would want the person being treated to approach a child sexually so that the behavior could be punished. Rather, classical conditioning of negative emotions to children by pairing electric shock with showing slides of children may be used to create an avoidance response to children.

Aversion therapy has been used most often to treat alcoholism, homosexuality, the so-called paraphilias such as pedophilia (child molesting) and fetishism, and bad habits such as smoking and overeating. Except in the treatment of bad habits, aversion therapy alone has not been demonstrated to be an effective treatment. It appears that the aversion

BOX 7.3
And One Flew Under . . .

In the systematic desensitization of a phobia the therapist and client first develop a hierarchical list of phobic situations. Together they work up a list progressing from the least to the most anxiety-provoking situation. There must be enough items on the list so that there are only small increases in anxiety associated with each step. The bird-phobic woman in Box 7.1 and her therapist developed the following anxiety hierarchy:

Looking out of the window at the street

Looking out of the window and seeing one bird in a tree

Looking out of the window and seeing many birds

Walking outside with no birds in sight

Walking outside with one bird down the street

Walking outside with several birds in view

A bird flying near to her

A bird hopping toward her

An injured bird at her feet

Picking up the injured bird

Touching a healthy small bird

Touching a large bird

The next step in systematic desensitization is to train the client in deep muscle relaxation. There are several methods of teaching muscle relaxation, including hypnosis and tape-recorded suggestions. The therapist may train relaxation by directing the reclining client to tense and relax the various muscles of her body noting the different sensations, until she can easily relax all the muscles deeply. The physiological response of muscle relaxation is incompatible with the physiological response of anxiety. Therefore, when the items on the anxiety hierarchy are introduced, the relaxation response should prevent the anxiety response. Additionally, a new response, relaxation, is being conditioned to the anxiety-provoking stimuli.

Once the client has mastered relaxation, the therapist begins to describe items on the anxiety hierarchy, starting with the first item. The therapist invites the client to imagine all the details of an item on the list. The therapist describes sensory details to help make the image vivid and stresses the client's positive feelings. For example, for the item "Walking outside with several birds in view," the therapist may say,

> You are walking outside on a beautiful fall day. The sun is shining, you are walking comfortably, and you feel confident and strong. You can hear a breeze rustling the trees, and you can hear the leaves crunch under your feet as you walk. The air smells fresh. You can hear the cheerful chirping of some small birds in the trees. You keep walking, enjoying their songs. You can see some birds on nearby yards. They are hopping around looking for things to eat. They are very pretty with the sun shining on their feathers. You continue walking past the birds, who do not

appear to notice you. You are enjoying your walk in the fresh air, the sunshine, the chirping birds, the beautiful day.

The therapist procedes to cover each item on the anxiety hierarchy, describing the situation in detail, as long as the client remains relaxed. If the client begins to tense her muscles or states that she is experiencing anxious feelings, the therapist may reinstitute muscle relaxation procedures or go back to a less anxiety-provoking item on the hierarchy. It may take several sessions for the client to imagine every item on the anxiety hierarchy while remaining completely relaxed.

The bird-phobic woman was able to complete her anxiety hierarchy in two sessions. *In vivo* desensitization was then used. A bunch of feathers was tied to a clothesline pulley so that she could recline and relax and still pull the feathers closer to her at a speed that was comfortable for her. The therapist helped her remain relaxed by giving relaxation suggestions while she pulled the feathers closer. The therapist also described the feathers vividly as they came closer. When the client felt she could, she touched the feathers, then held them, then brushed them over her arms and face, while the therapist continued to give relaxation suggestions and to describe the feather sensations. Then a caged, tame parakeet was connected to the pulley, and a similar procedure was carried out.

Finally, when the client tolerated the close presence of the caged bird well, the therapist put her hand in the cage and petted the parakeet to model touching a bird. The client was encouraged to do the same, and she was able to do so. The *in vivo* part of the desensitization took three sessions and the client was successfully desensitized to a phobic object.

gradually wears off or extinguishes. However, when used in conjunction with other techniques, it appears to be highly effective in treating smoking and overeating.

Another problem with aversive techniques is that substitute methods of gratification are not taught. What is an alcoholic to do for fun when drinking is made aversive? Some therapy programs that incorporate aversive techniques also include procedures to train new responses and ways to meet clients' needs. A treatment program for alcoholism may include teaching alternative behaviors such as juice drinking and assertion training for the social skills necessary to socialize without alcohol.

Covert Sensitization

Although not exactly a classical conditioning behavior therapy method, covert sensitization is the use of an imagined stimulus in place of an actual aversive stimulus or punishment to create new learning. Almost the opposite of systematic desensitization, covert sensitization may be used to create classically conditioned anxiety to teach an avoidance response. For example, a dieter may be asked to imagine vividly a favorite food with worms all over it (an aversion stimulus), so that disgust or fear will be conditioned to the food and the person will avoid it in the future. Or, the client may be asked to imagine negative consequences (a punishment) to unwanted operant behavior. For example, a kleptomaniac may be asked to imagine what would happen if he shoplifted. The therapist may guide his imagery so that he imagines going home with the stolen object, waiting anxiously in his apartment wondering if he will be caught, having the police arrive at his door and arrest him in front of all the neighbors, going to jail, and so on. The goal is to create anxiety so that the individual will refrain from stealing when tempted to do so. This procedure is similar to the use of punishment, but avoids some of the ethical problems associated with punishment.

OPERANT CONDITIONING METHODS

Behavior therapists who use operant conditioning methods assume that many types of abnormal behavior, such as shyness or even schizophrenic symptoms, are due to a lack of skills or a poor environment or both. Shy individuals lack the social skills to understand and make contact with other people. It follows that the needed skills can be taught. Abnormal behavior may result from an environment that inadvertently rewards that behavior and fails to reward desirable behavior. Again, such an environment can be changed.

Assertion Training (Social Skills Training)

Originally designed to help shy, retiring people become better able to deal with other people, assertion training should now be called social skills training. Assertion therapy includes a variety of training techniques for several social skills and is used with diverse types of clients individually and in groups. It is based on operant conditioning in that operant behaviors that display social skills, such as conversation, asking for dates, and dealing with bosses, are rewarded by praise from the therapist or by success of the behaviors themselves.

For some time the majority of assertion clients were women. Feminists criticized assertion therapy as reinforcing a masculine way of relating to others, a way that emphasizes confrontation and competition, rather than the caring, nonconfrontal way women relate. Defenders of assertion training argue that in a culture that emphasizes passivity, dependence, and nurturance as feminine qualities, women will have difficulty trying to assert their own needs without being labeled aggressive (or "castrating"). Assertion training can be seen as a way of helping women to obtain need satisfaction and independence.

Assertion therapy is widely used to treat shyness. In addition, it has been found useful in teaching mentally retarded adults how to be more effective in a confusing world and how to protect themselves from possible exploitation. It is also used in conjunction with other forms of therapy to train new responses to substitute for abnormal behaviors that are being eliminated.

The social skills taught vary according to what the clients believe they need. Some shy clients wish to learn to make conversation in many social situations. Some clients are not shy, but want to learn to deal more effectively with specific individuals, such as bosses, or in specific situations, such as negotiating a raise at work. Among the skills and situations covered in assertion training are asking for dates, turning down dates, making requests or successfully giving orders to others, refusing requests or orders, starting conversations, making social conversation, negotiation, asking for a raise, dealing with aggressive or difficult coworkers or customers, dealing with sexual harassment, and asserting independence from guilt-inducing parents.

For such social skills to be effective, clients must also learn to understand other people's feelings, to be nonjudgmental and uncritical of others, to curb their anger or aversive behavior, and to increase their awareness of the impact of their behavior on others. They must learn to pay attention to the nonverbal behavior of others and to alter their own nonverbal behavior so that it has the effect they intend. For example, shy clients must learn to have eye contact with people during conversation. They must learn how to detect and to convey understanding and interest in others. Social skills are complex, and they must be broken down into specific parts so they can be taught.

The techniques most frequently used to teach these complex social skills are lecture, demonstration, and role playing. Assertion therapists describe social skills to their clients, explain how they work, and advise clients what to try. They demonstrate social skills by acting them out in front of the client, saying what they want the client to say, pointing out their own nonverbal behavior. They then ask clients to role play. The client may role play the target person, such as a boss or parent, while the therapist plays the client and demonstrates what the client should do. Then the client role plays his or her own role while the therapist role plays the target person, so that the client has a chance to rehearse the demonstrated social skills. In groups clients role play individuals and social situations for each other. For example, the entire group may pretend to be at a cocktail party, and they practice initiating and carrying on social conversations. Or one group member may practice asking another for a date. Then they can switch roles or change to practicing refusing a date.

Shaping and covert practice are also sometimes used by therapists to teach social skills. *Shaping* is making closer and closer approximations to the desired response of the client. Each step closer to the desired behavior is rewarded with praise from the therapist or group. A shy person cannot be expected to go to a party and start several lively conversations right away. The first step may be simply to go to a party. The next step may be saying "Hello" to just one person, then speaking to two people, and so on. *Covert practice* is imagining performing the social skills competently. The shy person is asked to imagine carrying on lively conversations.

An important element in assertion training is feedback. As clients rehearse and role play, the therapist and group members give feedback on the effectiveness of the rehearsed social skills. They point out which aspects of the performance need to be improved and which were done well. The more specific the feedback, the more useful it is. Videotaping the role play is an effective way to give accurate feedback.

The rewarding behaviors of the therapist are an important part of social skills training. Warm praise for successful social skills performance reinforces the behavior. The status, power, warmth, trustworthiness, attractiveness, and other personal attributes of the therapist affect how rewarding the praise will be. Although behaviorists do not emphasize therapist characteristics, this is an example, like the interview situation, of the importance of the therapist-client relationship in the effectiveness of behavior therapy.

Most assertion therapy includes practicing the skills in the real world. Specific homework assignments are often given. A shy man may be required to ask a specified woman for a date before the next therapy meeting. A woman may be assigned to say no to at least one request at work by the following week. Such assignments are clear and precise as to what the client is expected to do, and the behavior is practiced beforehand. Usually the therapist thinks the client has a reasonably good chance at success, but the emphasis is on performing the social skill in the real world, rather than on whether it succeeds or fails. Since the behavior is being done at the direction of the therapist, the therapist will take the blame for failure, but give praise to the client for success.

Contingency Management (Behavior Modification)

A set of behavioral management techniques known as *contingency management* or *behavior modification* utilizes operant conditioning principles. These behavior change methods involve simply the planned use of rewards to increase wanted behavior and of extinction to decrease unwanted behavior. The environment is fixed. Rewards are contingent on desirable behavior and are not given for undesirable behavior. These methods are used in many different settings, including businesses, schools, and prisons. We will describe operant methods used in parent training or child behavior modification, the token economy in mental hospitals, and self-management.

Parent Training Modifying the problem behaviors of children is often accomplished by training the parents to use operant techniques. Therapists teach the parents these techniques in group classes, in couples, or individually with such methods as role playing and videotaping. Basically, parents are taught to reward behavior they want in their children and to remove the rewards for behaviors they don't want. In addition, parents must learn how to communicate clearly to the children what they want done, to be consistent in delivering behavioral consequences, to reduce their own aversive and ineffective parenting behaviors, and to give appropriate rewards. Once again, an operant procedure turns out on examination to require complex behavior changes. Even something as seemingly natural and simple as rewarding a child for being "good" is extremely difficult for some parents to learn. Some parents are opposed to the use of rewards on principle, because they see it as "bribing" the child, who should "want" to be good for goodness's sake. Others have difficulties being warm or affectionate and so cannot deliver effective praise. These kinds of problems must be addressed before operant techniques can be used effectively.

There are many programs to train parents to modify their children's behavior. Patterson's program at Oregon Research Institute (Patterson, 1973; Patterson & Gullion, 1976) is well documented, researched, and evaluated, and it is fairly representative of others. Patterson argues that behavioral disorders in children are a result of parents' reliance on what he calls aversive control, that is, reliance on scolding, punishment, screaming, nagging, and the like to try to control their children. The relatively powerless children engage in disruptive, defiant, or destructive behaviors in an attempt to control their parents and also learn aversive control from their parents through imitation. These parents also tend to use few rewards, either because they don't know how or they don't feel like being rewarding or pleasant because of stress or anger. Because of the low level of rewards, the children may engage in aversive behavior just to get their parents' attention. A vicious circle is set up in which the parents try to control the children with punishment, which makes the children hurt and angry and more likely to be unpleasant or punishing, too, which makes the parent use more punishment, and so on.

Patterson tries to break this circle by teaching the parents to increase their use of rewards and to stop all use of punishments and threats. Instead of punishment, extinction in the form of a procedure called time-out is used. There are several steps in Patterson's program.

The child and the family must be assessed so that an appropriate behavioral program can be designed. Patterson has worked mostly with school-age children with behavior problems of aggressiveness and noncompliance. Similar behavior modification methods have been used to treat temper tantrums, excessive sibling fighting, hyperactivity, disruptive school behavior, stealing and lying, enuresis and encopresis, and any sort of frequent unpleasant behavior used as negative attention seeking.

Once the problem has been defined and assessed, Patterson involves both parents and target child in deciding upon the behavior modification program. What the child must do is discussed, specified clearly, and agreed upon. For example, it might be specified that the child must obey parental requests to do household chores by the second time he is asked. The consequences of behavior are discussed. For example, if the child obeys the first parental request, he will receive a certain reward; if he obeys the second, he will receive a certain other reward; and if he does not comply, he will be placed in five minutes of time-out. Usually, several such concrete behaviors are worked on at once. All of the specified behaviors and consequences may be written down in a behavioral contract, which parents and child sign as an indication of their understanding of the treatment program and their agreement to try it.

The nature of the rewards is open to negotiation. Different children find different things rewarding. Some children prefer monetary rewards, some prefer objects such as toys or bicycles, and others prefer time spent with a parent in an activity of their choice. Parents and children agree upon a formula for the distribution of rewards that takes into account the number of behaviors being modified and the frequency with which they occur. For example, each act of compliance with a parental request may be worth 10 cents, or the child must comply with parental requests 90 percent of the time for six weeks in order to get a bicycle. Charts with points or check marks are used to keep track of performance and rewards. The charts are kept in an accessible place, such as on the refrigerator door, and each and every rewarded behavior is noted carefully. Patterson also tries to teach parents to give social rewards like attention and praise when the points or money or other concrete rewards are given, so that concrete rewards can eventually be eliminated.

Time-out is used to eliminate unwanted behavior or as a consequence for not performing wanted behavior. Unwanted behavior and noncompliance are assumed to be reinforced and maintained by the parental attention they gain. Even if that attention consists of punishment, it seems that some children prefer it to being ignored. So the solution to such problem behavior is to remove the reward in order to extinguish it. Sometimes parents can successfully ignore aversive behavior, but often time-out is more effective.

Time-out is removing children from the rewarding situation to a place where there are no social rewards. A bathroom, a porch, even the child's own room or a corner of the living room can be used for time-out. It should be some relatively uninteresting, but safe place where children will not be getting attention. It must be emphasized that time out is not a punishment, but the removal of the social reward of attention.

Time-out should not be frightening, so children should not be locked up and small children should be able to see their parents. Time-out needs to be only a short time, such as five minutes. For very young children two minutes of time-out is a long time. Children have a different sense of time from adults, and five minutes without human attention can seem very long to them. Some therapists suggest giving children a clock or a timer so they can see how long time-out will take.

Some parents express surprise or even outrage that time-out is so short and seems to be such a mild consequence. They need to be convinced that time-out is not a punishment and that five minutes of the removal of social rewards is sufficient. Even children may say, "Oh, time-out! Big deal! What's five minutes?" The first time children must go into time-out, they may well act nonchalant. However, that first time-out is often more difficult than children or parents anticipate. Parents are instructed that they are to add five additional minutes for every instance of unacceptable behavior during time-out. If the child swears, yells, kicks the door, breaks things, leaves the time-out area, or even calls the parent, then five more minutes must be added. That first time out may well end up being more than 40 minutes long. However, the second time-out is likely to be 20 minutes and subsequent ones only five.

It is essential that parents use time-out consistently for every behavior it was agreed it was to be used for. It is also important that it not be viewed as a punishment, used as a threat, or randomly invoked without prior agreement. Parents are encouraged to apply time-out in a matter-of-fact manner, without criticism or yelling. It is supposed to be merely the elimination of the reward of attention. Most parents who apply time-out correctly and consistently find that it does not have to be used often after the first few times. They also find it to be far more effective than the nagging and yelling and punishments they had tried before.

Evaluation research studies of behavior modification programs like Patterson's find that it is an effective treatment for child behavior disorders. In addition, parents tend to feel happier and more competent after treatment, as do the children. Parents report that they are able to generalize the principles they learn in treatment to other aspects of child raising and family life. Generally, other behaviors of the child improve, as well as the treated behaviors. Another frequently reported result is that the behavior of siblings of the treated children also improves (Forehand & McMahon, 1981; Dangel & Polster, 1984).

Parent training can be combined with attempts to modify children's school behaviors. Teachers may agree to keep behavior charts at school, which can be sent home for the parents to reward. For example, for every half hour that children sit and work quietly, the parents can give praise and points toward an agreed upon reward. Behavior modification principles are sometimes used (and sometimes misused) in classrooms for all the children. Teachers attempt to reward desired child behaviors with praise, gold stars, and prizes. Teachers also try to implement time out for disruptive negative attention seeking. Placing the child in time-out outside the classroom can be an effective technique for eliminating such behavior. Using time-out to shame or punish children, making it too long, or keeping children in the classroom during time-out so that they still receive peer attention are common misuses of time-out. However, research indicates that well-conducted behavior management programs in schools are effective in reducing classroom disruptions and increasing the academic progress of all the students (Klein, Mapkiewicz, & Roden, 1973; Kiraly & McKinnon, 1984; O'Leary & O'Leary, 1977). Such programs are particularly effective in special education classrooms, such as classes for hyperactive, behavior disordered, or mentally retarded children.

Token Economy Token economies are behavior modification programs commonly used in psychiatric wards in hospitals. They are also used in classrooms and institutions for the mentally retarded. Token economies are based on operant procedures, and rewards are given for desired behavior and not for undesired behavior. Since it is difficult to give actual rewards for each desired behavior, tokens are commonly given to patients instead, hence the name of the programs. When sufficient numbers of tokens are collected, patients can exchange them for designated rewards, such as ten tokens for a pack of cigarettes or five for an extra dessert. Undesirable behavior, such as psychotic talk or failure to show up for therapy appointments, may either be ignored or have a consequence such as losing privileges or being docked tokens.

Originally token economies were envisioned as a method to "cure" patients by training them to behave in ways that would allow them to live successfully outside the mental hospital. However, token economies can readily become just a way to manage patient behavior easily while they are in the hospital. That is not necessarily a criticism. The goal of managing mental patient behavior through rewards rather than threats, drugs, or force may be a sufficient justification for the use of token economies.

Positive behaviors commonly rewarded on token economies include getting dressed, shaved, and cleaned up by themselves, arriving at meals on time, engaging in constructive activities, such as socializing or occupational therapy, taking medications without complaining or resisting, cooperating with staff requests, responding nonpsychotically to questions or conversations initiated by staff or fellow patients. It is argued that learning such behaviors as punctuality and self-care will help patients live better outside the hospital, as well as making the ward easier to manage.

One of the pioneers of token economies, Ted Ayllon, originally used food as a reward (Ayllon & Azrin, 1968). He was allowed to try an experimental behavior modification program on a locked ward of very disturbed schizophrenics, many of whom had been there for many years and some of whom did not even get out of bed or feed themselves. Ayllon thought that it was possible that the schizophrenics were rewarded for this behavior by concerned nurses coming to spoon feed them in bed. So Ayllon altered the conditions on the ward so that only patients who showed up at the dining room by a certain time were allowed to eat. Despite staff concerns that the very disturbed patients would starve to death, all patients were eating in the dining room within four days.

Everyone would agree that food is a powerful reward. However, patients' rights advocates have argued that people in mental hospitals have basic rights to care, protection, and treatment, and these rights certainly include the right to eat. So meals are no longer used as rewards in token economies, although some do use special foods or good desserts. The most commonly used reward is cigarettes. Apparently, most mental patients will do quite a lot in order to get cigarettes. It seems to us that the use of health-endangering addictive chemicals like nicotine is just as ethically questionable as the use of food as a reward. Yet cigarette rewards have not been much criticized and are still frequently used.

Some token economies have tried to offer patients choices of rewards, so that they can work for whatever they find most rewarding (Ayllon & Azrin, 1968). Tokens may be exchanged for privileges such as being allowed to go to the movies or for things like candy or sunglasses. When it is available, one of the most popular rewards is a private room. Interestingly enough, when psychotherapy is available as a reward, patients rarely choose it. Rather, they have to be rewarded to go to therapy!

Critics have charged that token economies are manipulative methods of social control, used against helpless mental patients. It is true that the ability to give rewards contingent on desirable behavior rests on the power to control what patients are or are not allowed to do or have. Defenders argue that token economies mimic the real world, in which people go to work for the reward of money. The "real world" argument seems to be substantiated by the fact that on many token economies there is a flourishing black market in tokens. Patients make counterfeit tokens, play poker with them, steal them, trade them with each other for things, and hoard them, just like people do with ordinary money.

In general, evaluation research on token economies suggest that they are effective in making psychiatric wards fairly pleasant and cooperative places (Ayllon & Azrin, 1968). The consequences of behavior are clear, and patients seem to like that. However, it is not clear that patients on token economies are more likely to be released from the hospital or less likely to return to the hospital than patients on regular wards (Kazdin & Bootzin, 1972). In other words, the token economy does not appear to affect the course of the mental illness itself. Some behaviorists believe that this is because the token economy needs to be more carefully designed, so that specific "well" behavior is rewarded and made to generalize to situations outside the mental hospital. Others find that more recent research demonstrates that token economies are more effective than regular wards (Paul & Lentz, 1977). The potential of operant conditioning to help severely disturbed individuals is not fully evident at this time and needs further research.

In addition to further research, alternatives to the token economy should be investigated. It is possible that hospitalized psychotics can respond well to other behavioral methods. Levendusky and his colleagues (1983) reported that behavioral contracting worked as well as a token economy in preliminary research. *Behavioral contracting,* or *contingency contracting,* is the development of an individual behavior modification program for the patient by the patient and therapist. The patient is fully informed and actively involved in deciding on the behaviors and rewards to be covered by the program. This type of patient involvement would appear to reduce the potential for manipulation and coercion.

Self-management As implied in the name self-management, behaviorists can train individuals to use operant techniques to modify their own behaviors. Such behavior modification treatments use self-monitoring and self-reward, as well as methods known variously as problem-solving training, coping, and contingency contracting. Clients set a goal to modify certain behaviors, keep a chart of the frequency and context of the behaviors, and apply appropriate rewards for achieving the goals. It is surprising, but true, that simply recording the frequency of unwanted behaviors often results in their reduction. Perhaps increased awareness of behavior makes it easier to change.

Some smoking reduction programs include self-monitoring and self-reward. Clients keep count of the number of cigarettes smoked. As noted, simply counting may reduce the number. If the number of cigarettes falls below a certain number in a day, clients reward themselves with a dinner out, a movie, or whatever.

Clients are also trained to reward themselves with self-approval for meeting behavioral goals. People who are trying to modify a bad habit are frequently critical of themselves, and they need to learn to attend to and reward their positive behavior, as is done in cognitive behavior therapy (discussed in Chapter 8).

Problem-solving training is not strictly a behavioral method, for it involves logical reasoning and other cognitive skills. Clients are taught, first, to define and assess the problem; second, to recognize their reaction to it, such as anger, which might be part of the problem; third, to generate several alternative solutions or responses to the problem; fourth, to evaluate the solutions and decide to act on one; and, fifth, to assess the effect of the attempted solution.

Coping and coping imagery exercises also incorporate cognition. The therapist and client review possible coping strategies for the client's problem, and the client imagines using them in various situations. In reviewing coping strategies, the therapist may teach coping skills that the client lacks or has not thought of before. In contingency contracting the therapist and client form an agreement or contract about certain consequences of certain acts by the client. For example, a therapist and client may contract that the therapist's fee will be reduced 10 percent when the client loses 5 pounds, or they may contract that the client will be free to buy a new outfit after a specific weight loss.

Punishment

Delivering punishment for operant behavior is rarely used. The same ethical concerns about aversion therapy and punishment as used in classical conditioning are also considered important here. However, punishment has been used to suppress quickly severely psychotic behavior such as self-injury in retarded or autistic children (Lovaas & Simmons, 1969). Defenders of the practice of shocking autistic children for biting or hitting themselves argue that it is preferable to the amount of injury the child would receive if extinction were used. They agree that punishment should be used only when other methods fail. They also point out that eliminating the psychotic behavior allows the child to make use of other forms of psychotherapy.

Self-administered punishment is sometimes used to modify bad habits. For example, a cigarette smoker may put a rubber band around her wrist and use it to give herself a painful snap every time she reaches for a cigarette. Such a technique may be part of a larger self-management program. A 12-year-old girl we know invented a self-management technique that incorporated a form of punishment. To make herself complete reading assignments quickly, she would check the required book out of the library and refuse to return it before she had finished reading it. The threat of (and sometimes the payment of) mounting overdue fines motivated her to finish reading the book.

Some behavior modifiers request clients to deposit a sum of money at the beginning of a program. Donation of the sum to a charity the client dislikes is then used as a threatened form of punishment for failure to comply with the treatment program. For example, a liberal client may be asked to give a deposit of $100 prior to treatment. If he fails to comply with the agreed upon treatment, his money will be given to the John Birch Society. Liberals would agree that this is a punishment!

SOCIAL LEARNING METHODS

Like many behavior therapists, those who use social learning methods assume that it is not necessarily important to know the cause of abnormal behavior. They assume that normal behavior can be learned in its place, whatever its causes, through the normal social learning process of imitation or *modeling*.

Social learning theorists such as Bandura (1977a) have extended their concepts of imitation and observational learning to the treatment of behavior disorders such as phobias. Rather than desensitizing or extinguishing fearful feelings, social learning theorists argue that nonphobic behavior can be learned by watching others. Typically, the therapist models the desired behavior for the client, who will learn to engage in the same type of behavior through imitation. For example, a snake phobia is treated by having the client observe the therapist handling a snake. Then the client is encouraged to copy the behavior. Modeling is probably an important component of assertion training and other forms of therapy. Through demonstration and role playing, the therapist models appropriate assertive behavior. According to social learning theory, the client learns assertion by observing and imitating the therapist. Even in a talking psychotherapy such as psychoanalysis or client-centered therapy, the client may be learning important relationship skills by observing and imitating the therapist as he or she relates to the client.

Covert modeling, similar to covert practice, is imagining the self or another person engaging in the desired behavior. A therapist may tell a child a story about another child who successfully stops fighting with his siblings and learns other ways to get attention. It is assumed that imagining a successful model faciliates learning new behavior that is similar to the model's.

OTHER FORMS OF BEHAVIOR THERAPY

Multimodal behavior therapy is an assessment and therapy framework that encompasses elements of all the above behavioral methods as well as cognitive-behavioral therapy and rational-emotive therapy. It is associated with the work of Lazarus (1976, 1981). Psychological disorders are viewed in terms of seven modalities—behavior, affect, sensation, imagery, cognition, interpersonal relationships, and drug/biological aspect—which result in the acronym BASIC ID. Clients are assessed as to their functioning in each of the modalities, and a specific treatment plan is made for each of the seven. This procedure results in a comprehensive, individualized program for each client. For example, a shy client may show passivity and compliance in behavior, for which assertion training is prescribed; anxiety and fear in affect, for which desensitization is prescribed; images of helplessness and ridicule in imagery, for which coping imagery exercises are taught; perfectionism in cognition, for which cognitive disputation is done; avoidance and withdrawal in interpersonal relations, for which risk-taking assignments are given; and excessive eating and coffee drinking in the drugs/biology aspect, for which diet and exercise are prescribed. (Coping exercises, disputation, and perfectionism are described in Chapter 8.) You can see that multimodal therapy is not strictly a conditioning behavior therapy, but is eclectic.

As already stated, there are many variations of behavior therapy, and this chapter covers only the more usual ones. Behavior therapists tend to be pragmatic and ingenious in adopting new techniques, and it can be difficult to keep up with the latest developments. For example, the technique of *massed practice* is deliberately doing an unwanted behavior repeatedly, as when someone with a tic repeats the tic deliberately many times until it is almost uncomfortable. *Negative practice* is repeatedly doing the opposite of an unwanted behavior, as when someone with bruxism (habit of grinding the teeth) repeatedly relaxes her jaws.

BEHAVIORAL MEDICINE

Recently, behavioral principles, including biofeedback and hypnosis, have been applied to the treatment of medical problems. Also called health psychology, medical psychology, behavioral health, and other names, behavioral medicine is not yet a clearly defined field. It could be said to be the application of psychological principles to problems that have been traditionally labeled medical. In many instances these medical problems seem to involve significant psychological factors, which suggests that psychological techniques may be useful in treating them. Some scholars distinguish between health psychology, as the application of behavioral principles to prevent disease and promote health, and behavioral medicine, as the application of behavioral principles to the diagnosis, treatment, and rehabilitation of disease. For now we will use the term behavioral medicine as the general name for this new field.

Medical science seems to be coming to the conclusion that at present in the United States the major killer of humans is not disease caused by viruses and other pathogens, but rather harm to the body caused by the individual's *behavior.* It is estimated that one-fifth of U.S. deaths are related to cigarette smoking and that in 1986 smoking-related illness, death, and lost work cost between $27 billion and $67 billion (Raloff, 1986). Other leading causes of death, illness, and injury include incorrect eating habits (too much food, too much fat, too much salt), drug and alcohol abuse, and vehicle accidents. All of these health problems are related to the behavior of the individual. And, as Matarazzo (1982) wrote, "Psychology is a discipline with 100 years of experience in the study of individual behavior, including behavior change." It is only logical that psychology should be in the forefront in the treatment of these problems.

In addition, it is generally estimated that 60 percent of patient visits to physicians are for symptoms due to psychosocial factors or to abuses such as smoking and obesity. Many people "somatize" their stress, depression, or anxiety into physical symptoms, for it is still more acceptable to many people to be physically ill than mentally ill. Besides, the U.S. health care delivery system encourages the use of physicians rather than mental health professionals (as discussed further in Chapter 12). If somatization leads to an expensive and inappropriate use of medical care, then physicians need psychologists a great deal.

Behavioral medicine as an identifiable specialty expanded greatly in the late 1960s when it was discovered that biofeedback (discussed below) could be used to help treat some medical disorders. Once biofeedback legitimized psychology's entrance into the medical field, many other behavioral techniques, including hypnosis, were applied to a variety of medical problems.

General Purposes of Behavioral Therapy in Relation to Medical Problems

The various behavior therapy methods that may be considered part of behavioral medicine can be grouped according to three major purposes. First, behavioral techniques are used to change physiological responses or learned symptoms that constitute or contribute to threats to health. Second, behavioral medicine contributes to the improvement of health care delivery. Third, behavioral medicine or health psychology treats known risk factors, that is, behavior that is known to increase risks to health.

Some medical disorders are a result of some sort of physiological response. Tensing the muscles of the head and neck may cause headaches, producing too much stomach acid may produce ulcers, breathing incorrectly intensifies some forms of asthma. The research on biofeedback suggests that people can to a degree control such physiological responses when they become aware of them and so it is possible they may be able alleviate the resulting disorder.

In addition, it is possible that people are rewarded with attention and sympathy for being in pain or for being sick. Called secondary gain, the attention and sympathy people receive for their symptoms may serve as a powerful reward for those symptoms. In that sense, symptoms are *learned.* Furthermore, patients may become "socialized" or "trained" by the medical bureaucracy to fall into "sick roles" that may become chronic. In such cases as these, behavior therapy techniques may help improve the medical problem.

Biofeedback, systematic desensitization, classical conditioning, operant conditioning, hypnosis, contingency management, and other methods have been used alone and in combination to treat migraines, headaches, back pain, alcoholism, drug abuse, hypertension, asthma, insomnia, Raynaud's syndrome, arthritis, gastrointestinal disorders, incontinence, enuresis, encopresis, anorexia, bulimia, irritable bowel syndrome, seizures, ulcers, vomiting, nausea, bruxism, head injuries, scoliosis, hives, and other disorders. In addition, it has been demonstrated experimentally that the immune system itself may be open to suppression or enhancement through classical conditioning, and sleep and diet are clinically modifiable behaviors of importance to immunocompetence. The behavioral treatment of allergies and other immune system disorders (perhaps even AIDS) is a possibility worthy of future research.

Not everyone is enthusiastic about the possibilities for using behavioral methods to treat medical disorders. Critics charge that the effectiveness of behavioral methods in this context is not proven and that insufficiently researched techniques are rushed into application. Applying unproven techniques to medical problems may be especially risky and ethically questionable. Without doubt, more research on this aspect of behavioral medicine is needed.

Behaviorists can assist in the improvement of health care delivery in two major ways: (1) increasing patient compliance with medical regimens and (2) helping patients cope with medical procedures. Patient compliance is an interesting problem for medicine. All the diagnostic tests and medical advances in the world won't help if patients don't follow doctors' orders. Some surveys suggest that over half of patients do not take prescribed medicines correctly—they take them too much, not enough, or not at all. Patients often fail to keep follow-up appointments.

Certain disorders involve difficult regimens to follow. The best example is diabetes, which may require a special diet and a strict regimen of medications for all of the patient's life. Teenagers are especially resistant to the treatment necessary for diabetes. Education, group therapy, contingency management, and other techniques are used to increase patient compliance.

Behavioral medicine can help patients cope with medical procedures, some of which are frightening, painful, or nauseating. Education, modeling, and role playing can prepare patients for procedures. Simply knowing exactly what is going to happen to them can reduce patients' anxiety. Explanations, discussions, slide shows, and demonstrations help adults. Some therapists use special dolls and puppets to demonstrate surgical and treatment procedures for children. The children's fears and questions can be addressed though playing out a doctor-patient scene. Some therapists use modeling through films showing children undergoing the same medical procedure as the patient.

Behavioral techniques can help patients control their pain when they must have painful diagnostic tests or treatments. Dental treatments, spinal taps, angiograms and the like are often painful. Systematic desensitization, relaxation, guided imagery, hypnosis, and other techniques can help patients reduce or at least control their response to the pain. The same techniques can help patients reduce or control the nausea and vomiting that are the side effect of some chemotherapy for cancer.

Certain behaviors, such as smoking and overeating, have been demonstrated by research to increase the risk of fatal diseases such as lung cancer, emphysema, and cardiovascular disorders. It follows that modification of these behaviors would decrease the health risks. A quick glance at the titles of articles in recent clinical psychology journals will show that obesity is the single disorder most frequently mentioned, with smoking a close second. The treatment of these two risk factors is a rapidly growing field.

Smoking and overeating are habits that are extremely difficult for some people to modify. Failure and relapse rates have in the past been unacceptably high. Behavioral medicine has entered the fray. A combination of behavioral techniques, including aversion therapy, relaxation, identification of signaling stimuli, negative practice, imagery, self-reward, contingency management, group therapy, exercise, hypnosis, and whatever else creative therapists think of seem to be equally or somewhat more effective in modifying smoking and eating behavior than traditional methods of stopping these behaviors.

Besides the modification of smoking and eating behaviors, other known risk factors targeted by behavioral medicine include the so-called Type A personality, stress, and lack of education regarding the prevention and early detection of diseases. The traditional Type A or coronary-prone personality consists of a set of behaviors that include competitiveness, driving ambition, and the inability to relax. Hypnosis and behavioral techniques are used to reduce competitiveness and increase relaxation, assuming that this in turn will reduce the likelihood of having a heart attack in the future.

Stress management programs continue to grow in popularity. It is assumed that if people can learn to control their stress, they will reduce the likelihood of developing stress-related diseases, such as hypertension, ulcers, headaches, and heart disease. Behavioral techniques are used to teach individuals to recognize the signs of stress, learn to relax, alter their priorities, and organize their time better. In addition to relaxation training, hypnosis, guided imagery, desensitization, exercise, group therapy, assertion training, and role playing, biofeedback is often used to teach people how to relax their muscles, lower their blood pressure, lower their heart rate, or induce certain kinds of relaxing brain waves.

Behaviorists are involved in educating the public regarding the prevention and early detection of disease. They teach the importance of self-examinations of the breasts and testicles in order to detect cancer in its earliest, most curable stages. The importance of proper diet, exercise, and rest in preventing disease is taught, along with specific techniques to increase the likelihood that individuals will begin and continue to engage in exercise or good diets. Teaching people to announce their plans to exercise or diet publicly, to enlist the support of friends, to reward themselves for meeting their goals, and to structure their environment to support their goals are some of the ways that behaviorists can help people with disease prevention.

Biofeedback

Biofeedback was first developed by academic psychologists researching questions of learning. Biofeedback is a system of recording information about individuals' ongoing physiological responses and displaying the information so they can see second-by-second changes in their functioning. It makes ordinarily nonconscious, automatic bodily responses evident by the electronic display of information taken from mechanical or electrical sensors. For example, ordinarily your heart beats at a certain rate or changes its rate automatically and without your awareness. When you are hooked up to an EKG machine, your heart rate becomes available to your conscious awareness. You can watch and listen to the tracing and bleeps that represent your heartbeats. You are given visual and auditory feedback about the biological activity, hence the name biofeedback.

Research psychologists such as Neal Miller (1985) were astonished to find that people could learn to raise or lower their heart rate when they got biofeedback about the rate. They also found that many other nonconscious, automatic physiological responses, such as blood pressure, muscle tension, and brain waves, appear to be modifiable by *learning.* Rather than wait several decades as they did with other academic behavioral discoveries, clinical psychologists immediately saw that if such physiological responses could be modified, then perhaps patients could learn to control health-threatening responses. Biofeedback technology has been used to treat several types of medical disorders. Biofeedback of blood pressure has been used to treat hypertension and migraine headaches; biofeedback of muscle tension to treat headaches, backache, vaginismus, and stress; biofeedback of brain waves to treat stress and teach relaxation; and biofeedback of heart rate to treat anxiety and cardiac rate disorders.

Biofeedback was discovered by psychologists studying learning, and at first it appeared to result in true learning curves and the acquisition of a new response. Subsequent research has suggested that this is incorrect and that biofeedback enhances a person's ability to make relatively small voluntary changes in physiological responses through increased awareness alone. Furthermore, it now appears that in many cases biofeedback alone results in a degree of permanent change in the physiological response, such as blood pressure, that is too small to be clinically significant in controlling the condition, such as hypertension (Blanchard & Young, 1974). Roberts (1985) concluded that the research does not justify the use of biofeedback alone in therapy; it must be accompanied by other techniques.

Nevertheless, patients and professional psychologists alike report that biofeedback, when used in combination with other behavioral methods, is effective in the treatment of many disorders. If so, how does it work? Some scholars believe that the positive effects of biofeedback, if any, are mediated through a generalized relaxation effect and through cognitive factors. Biofeedback may simply enhance people's ability to relax, and relaxation itself improves their health and well-being. Several cognitive processes are hypothesized to be an important part of biofeedback. It may increase individuals' sense of self-efficacy, that is, they become more confident that they can have an effect on their disorder, and so they do. Once people believe they have control over their problems, they feel less anxious and stressed.

Hypnosis

Hypnosis has wavered in and out of respectability over the years, and even today the word has connotations of the bizarre and the manipulative. While hypnotic techniques have been used for centuries, the formal use of hypnosis in medical treatments began in the last century when it was popularized by Mesmer. Then known as mesmerism, hypnosis was used in obstetrics as early as 1831 (Chertok, 1981). Freud originally used hypnosis in psychoanalysis, but dropped it in favor of his own technique of free association. Mesmer eventually fell into disrepute, and his methods were forgotten by the medical community for many decades. In recent years hypnosis, as used in dentistry, medicine, psychotherapy, and especially behavioral medicine, has again gained respectability and popularity.

One possible reason for the questionable status of hypnosis is that it is extremely difficult to define, to measure, and to investigate. After many years of research and controversy, there is still little agreement as to what hypnosis is. Whether it is an altered state of consciousness, a trance, or simply deep relaxation is not known for certain. Most writers in the field of hypnosis settle for defining it simply as a heightened state of suggestibility.

How is that state of heightened suggestibility achieved? The techniques for inducing hypnosis and those used once the client is hypnotized vary tremendously, and therapists invent new ones every day. Hypnotic inductions may be direct or indirect, administered by a therapist or self-administered by the client. They may take a few moments or a half an hour. Induction may involve a quiet room, sitting comfortably, the hypnotist's soothing voice, and suggestions to relax and concentrate. It is believed that when clients successfully follow a series of suggestions to close their eyes, breathe deeply, and concentrate on the therapist's voice and their own bodily sensations, they are then more open to following other therapeutic suggestions given by the therapist.

Hypotheses to explain how hypnotism works range from the view that its effects are due solely to relaxation to the idea that people feel less threatened by and therefore less resistant to therapeutic suggestions when they cognitively attribute their obedience to the hypnosis and not to simply obeying someone else's advice. It appears that some individuals are more suggestible than others, and hypnosis is more effective with them. However, it does not appear that hypnosis can make people do things against their will, and neither does hypnosis appear to induce amnesia in most cases.

Hypnosis is used for many therapeutic purposes, from pain control in minor surgery, childbirth, and dentistry to habit control and stress reduction. Like behavior therapy, hypnosis has helped remove a variety of symptoms, including phobias, tics, anxiety, chronic pain, enuresis, and bruxism.

Similar to systematic desensitization, the hypnosis treatment for phobias, for example, includes suggesting that the client will not feel fear when near the feared object or situation and suggesting an alternative feeling. After hypnotizing a bird-phobic client, the therapist may say,

> You are sitting in the peaceful meadow we talked about before. You see a bird, a beautiful red bird, singing sweetly in the sunshine, and you look at it calmly, you feel happy listening to its song, you enjoy watching its beauty. When you leave my office, you will see many birds, and they will remind you of the beautiful red bird, and you will feel glad to see them, glad that there are singing birds in the world.

Perhaps you can see the similarity of this approach to systematic desensitization as described in Box 7.3.

Hypnosis has been used to treat the symptom of chronic pain when other forms of medical treatment do not help. The relaxation may help control the pain, and new reactions to pain are suggested. If the pain cannot be removed, it can sometimes be moved to a less debilitating spot or reduced. Under hypnosis the client is taught to experience chronic back pain, for example, as a pink spot that can be moved to the head or to the lower arm, where it does not hurt as much.

Besides symptom removal, hypnosis helps change or control problem behaviors such as smoking, overeating, drug abuse, or gambling. Interventions may include direct commands to stop the offending behavior, the use of guided imagery for increasing desired behavior, and suggestions that the client will not feel like doing the offending behavior any more, that he will be able to control himself easily by doing specific suggested behaviors or thoughts, that he will do some alternative behavior. As an example, the treatment of overeating may involve a direct command to not feel hungry, the suggestion that the sight of food will lessen the urge to eat or make the client feel like doing something else such as drinking water, or the use of guided imagery to change the client's image of himself as a pig to one of himself as a greyhound as a metaphor for the goal of therapy. The same techniques can be used to change bad habits such as procrastination or nail biting. The similarity of this approach to cognitive behavior therapy will be evident in Chapter 8.

Hypnosis appears to be useful in teaching relaxation and stress management. Hypnotic induction itself relaxes the client, and once the client learns how to use hypnotic techniques to relax, she can use them whenever needed. Besides directly teaching relaxation, hypnosis helps clients manage stress by suggesting alternative behaviors, thoughts, or emotions to experience when under stress. Rather than feeling rage in a traffic jam on the freeway or at work, the client may be taught to retrieve the image of a peaceful place, such as a beach or meadow, at stressful times and to substitute the peaceful feeling the scene induces for the anger or anxiety being felt. Pain is a form of stress, and hypnosis is also used to teach people to control their responses to painful dental or medical treatments. Again, rather than feeling pain and fear when undergoing a painful cancer treatment, the patient can be hypnotized during the treatment or taught under hypnosis how to substitute another response for pain.

Hypnosis is also used in conjunction with other types of psychotherapy, and part or even all of the therapy is conducted with the client under hypnosis in order to enhance the effectiveness of the therapy. However, the success of treatment is not attributed to the hypnosis, but rather to the theoretical principles of whatever type of therapy is being done. If a phobia is being treated with systematic desensitization and hypnosis is used to speed up the learning of deep muscle relaxation, the effectiveness of the treatment depends on the correct application of the behavior modification principles of systematic desensitization, not the hypnosis. Hypnosis has been used as an additional technique in almost all types of therapy, from psychoanalysis to the family systems approach.

Despite years of research hypnosis remains a fascinating enigma. Clear evidence of dramatic cures tempts many therapists and clients to try hypnosis, but hypnosis is not for everyone. Not all clients are sufficiently cooperative or suggestible to enter hypnosis, and hypnosis is clearly not appropriate for some, such as psychotics. Not all therapists are equally comfortable or competent with hypnotic techniques. However, it appears that hypnosis, like biofeedback, has achieved sufficient clinical success, especially in behavioral medicine, that it is once again a respected therapeutic technique.

EVALUATION OF BEHAVIOR THERAPY

Criticisms of Behavior Therapy

Many criticisms of behavior therapy center on theoretical disagreements between different schools of thought. Critics claim that because their theory is the correct one, behavior therapy is wrong, not "deep enough," or just misses the point. For example, psychoanalysts criticize behavior therapy for not treating the underlying unconscious conflict, but just the superficial symptoms. Client-centered therapists criticize behaviorists for ignoring the therapeutic conditions of therapist characteristics and the therapist-client relationship.

Some forms of behavior therapy are criticized as not being behavioral at all. Systematic desensitization is especially criticized as relying on cognitions and "imagining" the phobic stimulus. Some strict behaviorists deny the existence or the importance of such cognitive activity (Skinner, 1938). However, other behaviorists have shifted in recent years toward including cognitive factors in their behavior therapies.

Another criticism is that behavioral technology is applied too quickly, too enthusiastically, and with too many modifications, so that it frequently loses its ties to empirically verified behavioral principles. Precisely how is a technique like role playing asking for a date based on behavioral principles? Pairing all the stimuli surrounding lighting up a cigarette with electric shock seems a clear case of classical conditioning and aversive therapy. However, what kind of behavioral technique is making the client chain-smoke many cigarettes fast until exhausted and nauseous? Does giving it the name massed practice make it a behavioral method? Can it be considered a technique of aversion therapy? Or is it an example of reverse psychology? It may be that practitioners generalize or modify behavioral techniques without considering their theoretical or empirical rationale, until some methods do not appear to be related to the known principles of learning.

Behavior therapy is criticized for being open to incorrect applications and deliberate misuse. The principles of behavior therapy seem clear and easy to understand, but inexperienced individuals unfamiliar with the empirical foundation of behaviorism may try to apply the principles in inappropriate ways or to inappropriate problems. Attempting to extinguish depression would be an obvious example of misapplication, and we mentioned earlier how time out is sometimes used incorrectly in schools.

Since behavior modification involves the deliberate manipulation of reward contingencies so that desirable behavior is increased and undesirable behavior is decreased, critics contend that it is or can be misused to serve merely a social control function or to manipulate or even oppress people. Behavior therapy is accused of being coercive and manipulative, promoting social conformity, and limiting freedom of choice. Critics are concerned with who decides what is desirable behavior to be rewarded and what is undesirable behavior, since value judgments are inherent in such decisions. They also point out that behavior modification methods are often used with relatively powerless groups, such as children or mental hospital patients. Defenders of behavior modification point out that any procedure can be misused and that care must be taken to serve the best interests of the clients. Furthermore, they say, rewards are being given out in all social situations, and children and mental patients are being managed and manipulated all the time anyway. With behavior modification, the value judgments as to which behaviors to reward and which not to reward are made explicit and therefore open to criticism and change. In other words, defenders argue, behavior modification is just ordinary social behavior made conscious and deliberate and out in the open. Finally, they conclude, proper contingency management techniques are highly effective for helping individuals change in directions they themselves wish to go.

A similar criticism is made by Blechman (1984), who argues that behavior therapy may be used in support of the majority culture without considering the possibly negative consequences to certain groups, such as women. For example, parent training, although called parent training, is given almost only to mothers. Women do most of the parenting in our culture even today, and they are the ones most likely to be able to attend therapy sessions. It is possible that parent training has unintended negative consequences for women by making them feel to blame for their children's problems, lowering their self-esteem, and giving them more activities to be responsible for and to organize. In research journals the most commonly studied problem is obesity, and many more women than men are treated for obesity. It is possible that there are unintended negative consequences for women in behavior therapy that emphasizes the cultural value of female thinness.

Behavior therapy is charged with being mechanistic and impersonal. Critics say that behavior therapists ignore the importance of the relationship between client and therapist in helping clients change. Again, in the hands of inexperienced persons, behavior therapy may be administered in a mechanical or impersonal way. However, we have already pointed out that behavioral therapists recognize the importance of rapport and the need for the therapist to be rewarding and trustworthy.

Aversion therapy is especially criticized, for ethical reasons. Aversion is seen as mechanistic and dehumanizing. Like the aversive procedures in the film *Clockwork Orange,* it is also associated with coercive enforcement of social conformity. The use of it to treat homosexuality is especially criticized, since homosexuality is no longer seen as a disorder or abnormality. Defenders argue that aversion therapy is given only to homosexuals who *want* to change their sexual preference. Critics counter that perhaps those homosexuals who "want" to change are merely giving in to social pressure. Behavior therapists may be helping them conform without adequately questioning the rightness of such conformity.

The level of punishment required for aversion therapy to be effective may be greater than many therapists would be comfortable with. One of us worked on an experimental treatment for alcoholism at the Veterans Administration. The treatment involved placing electrodes on the rugged old veterans' tattooed arms and giving shocks either before or after a sip of an alcoholic drink. The veterans were asked to set the level of shock themselves to something that they experienced as moderately uncomfortable. After the treatment, when we research assistants removed the electrodes, we often found that they had burned deep into the men's skin. It apparently took a lot to make these veterans admit to being moderately uncomfortable! It certainly made us uncomfortable to pull the electrodes out of the bloody holes in their arms. Many people find the use of aversive stimuli unethical.

New applications and new forms of behavior therapy are being developed every day. Some critics believe that behavior therapy is developed and implemented without adequate preliminary empirical research. They also argue that there is insufficient follow-up and evaluation research. Some psychologists believe that *all* therapies, including behavior therapy, should be empirically demonstrated to be effective before they are ever offered to the public. However, given American pragmatism and the demand for quick, inexpensive psychological treatments, the ideal of empirically evaluating every behavior therapy method is unlikely to be met.

Strengths of Behavior Therapy

A large body of research demonstrates that behavior therapy is at least as effective as other forms of therapy and possibly the most effective treatment. (Much of this research is covered in Chapter 10, including reviews of studies that do not support this conclusion.) Behavior therapy is probably the most cost-effective form of treatment, an aspect that becomes increasingly valued in our society, as discussed in Chapter 12. Even though behaviorists do not meet the ideal of empirically evaluating every treatment before it is implemented, behavior therapists subject their methods to empirical research far more frequently than any other group, except client-centered therapists. And this research tends to support the effectiveness of behavior therapy (Wilson, 1980; Kazdin & Wilson, 1978).

From a values orientation, a strength of behavior therapy may be that it is essentially equalitarian. Although criticized as potential social control agents, behavior therapists see themselves as "giving away" their knowledge to clients. They fully explain their procedures and their theoretical and empirical rationales. They describe the empirically verified effectiveness of their methods. They do not "interpret" their clients' questions about their methods as "resistance," but respect their clients' right to know by answering their questions fully. Once clients have their therapists' knowledge, they can use it to achieve any goal they desire. Behaviorists claim that they refrain from making value judgments about what is best for the client by allowing clients to choose their own therapy goals.

We have already discussed various instances when behavior therapists acknowledge the importance of the relationship between client and therapist. In addition, a large research study found that compared to other therapists, behavior therapists were equally high in warmth, empathy, and genuineness, even slightly more so (Sloane et al., 1975). Behaviorist therapists recognize the importance of being rewarding and being warm and empathic increases their ability to be rewarding. Trustworthiness and their equalitarian approach also make them more rewarding.

Although not all behaviorists are equalitarian and even though it can be argued that children and mental patients do not freely choose their own therapy goals, behavior therapy is essentially a cooperative enterprise between therapist and client. The client defines the treatment goals, and the therapist describes and explains the methods to reach them. They mutually agree upon a clear plan of action, and then they work together to implement the treatment plan. This equalitarian approach undoubtedly contributes to a good relationship between therapist and client. It may be an essential ingredient for behavior therapy's effectiveness.

REFERENCES

Achterberg-Lawlis, J. (1982). The psychological dimensions of arthritis. *Journal of Consulting and Clinical Psychology, 50,* 984–992.

Agras, W. S. (1982). Behavioral medicine in the 1980s: Nonrandom connections. *Journal of Consulting and Clinical Psychology, 50,* 797–803.

Anderson, K. O., & Masur, F. T. (1983). Psychological preparation for invasive medical and dental procedures. *Journal of Behavioral Medicine, 6,* 1–40.

Andrasik, F., Blanchard, E. B., Neff, D. F., & Rodichok, L. D. (1984). Biofeedback and relaxation training for chronic headache: A controlled comparison of booster treatments and regular contacts for long-term maintenance. *Journal of Consulting and Clinical Psychology, 52,* 609–615.

Atkins, C., Kaplan, R., Timms, B., Reinsch, S., & Lofback, K. (1984). Behavioral exercise programs in the management of chronic obstructive pulmonary disease. *Journal of Consulting and Clinical Psychology, 52,* 591–603.

Ayllon, T., & Azrin, N. H. (1968). *The token economy: A motivational system for therapy and rehabilitation.* New York: Appleton-Century-Crofts.

Azrin, N., & Nunn, R. (1977). *Habit control in a day.* New York: Simon & Schuster.

Bandura, A. (1969). *Principles of behavior modification.* New York: Holt, Rinehart and Winston.

Bandura, A. (1977a). Self-efficacy: Toward a unifying theory of behavior change. *Psychological Review, 84,* 191–215.

Bandura, A. (1977b). *Social learning theory.* Englewood Cliffs, NJ: Prentice-Hall.

Barber, T. (1969). *Hypnosis: A scientific approach.* New York: Van Nostrand.

Bellack, A., & Hersen, M. (1985). *Dictionary of behavior therapy techniques.* New York: Pergamon Press.

Berglas, S., & Levendusky, P. G. (1985). The Therapeutic Contract Program: An individual-oriented psychological treatment community. *Psychotherapy, 22,* 366–345.

Black, D., & Scherba, D. S. (1983). Contracting to problem solve versus contracting to practice behavioral weight loss skills. *Behavior Therapy, 14,* 100–109.

Blanchard, E., & Andrasik, F. (1982). Psychological assessment and treatment of headache: Recent developments and emerging issues. *Journal of Consulting and Clinical Psychology, 50,* 859–879.

Blanchard, E., & Young, L. (1974). Clinical applications of biofeedback training: A review of evidence. *Archives of General Psychiatry, 30,* 573–579.

Blechman, E. (1984). *Behavior modification with women.* New York: Guilford.

Bookbinder, L. (1962). Simple conditioning versus the dynamic approach to symptoms and symptom substitution: A reply to Yates. *Psychological Reports, 10,* 71–77.

Borkovec, T. (1982). Insomnia. *Journal of Consulting and Clinical Psychology, 50,* 880–895.

Brownell, K. (1982). Obesity: Understanding and treating a serious, prevalent, and refractory disorder. *Journal of Consulting and Clinical Psychology, 50,* 820–840.

Carney, R., Schechter, K., & Davis, T. (1983). Improving adherence to blood glucose testing in insulin-dependent diabetic children. *Behavior Therapy, 14,* 247–254.

Chertok, L. (1981). *Sense and nonsense in psychotherapy: The challenge of hypnosis.* New York: Pergamon Press.

Coe, W., & Ryken, K. (1979). Hypnosis and risk to human subjects. *American Psychologist, 34,* 673–681.

Cohen, L. (1985). What's in a name: Clinical psychology, medical psychology, health psychology . . . ? *American Psychologist, 38,* 29–32.

Curran, J., & Monti, P. (1982). *Social skills training: A practical handbook for assessment and treatment.* New York: Guilford.

Dangel, R., & Polster, R. (1984). *Parent training: Foundation of research and practice.* New York: Guilford.

Davison, G., & Stuart, R. (1975). Behavior therapy and civil liberties. *American Psychologist, 30,* 755–763.

Epstein, L., & Cluss, P. (1982). A behavioral medicine perspective on adherence to long-term medical regimens. *Journal of Consulting and Clinical Psychology, 50,* 950–971.

Erickson, M., & Rossi, E. (1976). Two level communication and the microdynamics of trance and suggestion. *American Journal of Clinical Hypnosis, 18,* 153–171.

Erickson, M., & Rossie, E. (1979). *Hypnotherapy: An exploratory casebook.* New York: Irvington.

Finesmith, B. (1979). An historic and systematic overview of behavior management guidelines. *The Behavior Therapist, 2,* 2–6.

Finney, J., Rapoff, M., Hall, C., & Christophersen, E. (1983). Replication and social validation of habit reversal treatment for tics. *Behavior Therapy, 14,* 116–126.

Fisher, E., Delamater, A., Bertelson, A., & Kirkley, B. (1982). Psychological factors in diabetes and its treatment. *Journal of Consulting and Clinical Psychology, 50,* 993–1003.

Fordyce, W. (1982). A behavioral perspective on chronic pain. *British Journal of Clinical Psychology, 21,* 313–320.

Forehand, R., & McMahon, R. (1981). *Helping the noncompliant child: A clinician's guide to parent training.* New York: Guilford.

Franks, C. (1969). Behavior therapy and its Pavlovian origins: Review and perspectives. In C. M. Franks (Ed.), *Behavior therapy: Appraisal and status.* New York: McGraw-Hill.

Franks, C., & Barbrack, C. (1983). Behavior therapy with adults: An integrative perspective. In M. Hersen, A. Kazdin, & A. Bellack (Eds.), *The clinical psychology handbook.* New York: Pergamon Press.

Gentry, W. (1984). *Handbook of behavior medicine.* New York: Guilford.

Gewirtz, J., & Baer, D. (1958). Deprivation and satiation of social reinforcers as drive conditions. *Journal of Abnormal and Social Psychology, 57,* 165–172.

Goisman, R. (1983). Therapeutic approaches to phobia: A comparison. *American Journal of Psychotherapy, 37,* 227–234.

Griest, D., & Wells, K. (1983). Behavioral family therapy with conduct disorders in children. *Behavior Therapy, 14,* 37–53.

Harris, B. (1979). Whatever happened to Little Albert? *American Psychologist, 34,* 151–160.

Havens, R. (1985). *The wisdom of Milton H. Erickson.* New York: Irvington.

Heiby, E., Ozaki, M., & Campos, P. (1984). The effects of training in self-reinforcement and reward: Implications for depression. *Behavior Therapy, 15,* 544–549.

Henton, W., & Iversen, I. (1978). *Classical conditioning and operant conditioning: A response pattern analysis.* New York: Springer-Verlag.

Jacobson, E. (1938). *Progressive relaxation.* Chicago: University of Chicago Press.

Johnston, D. (1982). Behavioral treatment in the reduction of coronary risk factors: Type A behavior and blood pressure. *British Journal of Clinical Psychology, 21,* 281–294.

Kazdin, A. (1978). *History of behavior modification: Experimental foundations of contemporary research.* Baltimore, MD: University Park Press.

Kazdin, A. (1982). Symptom substitution, generalization, and response covariation: Implications for psychotherapy outcome. *Psychological Bulletin, 91,* 349–365.

Kazdin, A., & Bootzin, R. (1972). The token economy: An evaluative review. *Journal of Applied Behavioral Analysis, 5,* 343–372.

Kazdin, A., & Wilson, G. (1978). *Evaluation of behavior therapy: Issues, evidence and research strategies.* Cambridge, MA: Ballinger.

Keefe, F. (1982). Behavioral assessment and treatment of chronic pain: Current status and future directions. *Journal of Consulting and Clinical Psychology, 50,* 896–911.

Kelly, J. (1982). *Social-skills training: A practical guide for interventions.* New York: Springer-Verlag.

Kiraly, J., & McKinnon, A. (1984). *Pupil behavior, self-control, and social skills in the classroom.* Springfield, IL: C. C Thomas.

Klein, R., Hapkiewicz, W., & Roden, A. (1973). *Behavioral modification in educational settings.* Springfield, IL: C. C Thomas.

Lashley, J., & Elder, S. (1982). Selected case studies in clinical biofeedback. *Journal of Clinical Psychology, 38,* 530–540.

Latimer, P. (1982). External contingency management for chronic pain: Critical review of the evidence. *American Journal of Psychiatry, 139,* 1308–1312.

Lazarus, A. (1976). *Multimodal behavior therapy.* New York: Springer-Verlag.

Lazarus, A. (1981). *The practice of multimodal therapy.* New York: McGraw-Hill.

Levendusky, P., Berglas, S., Dooley, C., & Landau, R. (1983). Therapeutic contract program: Preliminary report on a behavioral alternative to the token economy. *Behavior Research and Therapy, 21,* 137–142.

Lichtenstein, E. (1982). The smoking problem: A behavioral perspective. *Journal of Consulting and Clinical Psychology, 50,* 804–819.

Linton, S. (1982). A critical review of behavioral treatments for chronic benign pain other than headache. *British Journal of Clinical Psychology, 21,* 321–337.

Lovaas, O., & Simmons, J. (1969). Manipulation of self-destruction in three retarded children. *Journal of Applied Behavioral Analysis, 2,* 143–157.

Mahoney, M. (1972). Research issues in self-management. *Behavior Therapy, 3,* 45–63.

Mahoney, M., & Thoresen, C. (1974). *Self-control: Power to the person.* Monterey, CA: Brooks/Cole.

Martin, J., & Dubbert, P. (1982). Exercise applications and promotion in behavioral medicine: Current status and future directions. *Journal of Consulting and Clinical Psychology, 50,* 1004–1007.

Matarazzo, J. (1982). Behavioral health's challenge to academic, scientific, and professional psychology. *American Psychologist, 37,* 1–14.

Mathews, A., Gelder, M., & Johnston, D. (1981). *Agoraphobia: Nature and treatment.* New York: Guilford.

Mazur, J., & Logue, A. (1978). Choice in a "self-control" paradigm: Effects of a fading procedure. *Journal of the Experimental Analysis of Behavior, 30,* 11–17.

McDowell, J. (1982). The importance of Herrnstein's mathematical statement of the law of effect for behavior therapy. *American Psychologist, 37,* 771–779.

McMahon, R., Tiedemann, G., Forehand, R., & Griest, D. (1984). Parental satisfaction with parent training to modify child noncompliance. *Behavior Therapy, 15,* 295–303.

Melamed, B., & Siegel, L. (1980). *Behavioral medicine: Practical application in health care.* New York: Springer.

Meyers, A., Thackwray, D., Johnson, C., & Schleser, R. (1983). A comparison of prompting strategies for improving appointment compliance of hypertensive individuals. *Behavior Therapy, 14,* 267–274.

Miller, N. (1985). Rx: Biofeedback. *Psychology Today, 19* (2) 54–56.

Millon, T., Green, C., & Meagher R. (Eds.). (1982). *Handbook of clinical health psychology.* New York: Plenum.

Morrow, G. (1984) Appropriateness of taped versus live relaxation in the systematic desensitization of anticipatory nausea and vomiting in cancer patients. *Journal of Consulting and Clinical Psychology, 52,* 1098–1099.

Mostofsky, D., & Piedmont, R. (1985). *Therapeutic practice in behavioral medicine.* San Francisco: Jossey-Bass.

Mowrer, O. (1947). On the dual nature of learning—A reinterpretation of "conditioning" and "problem-solving." *Harvard Educational Review, 17,* 102–148.

Mowrer, O., & Lamoreaux, R. (1946). Fear as an intervening variable in avoidance conditioning. *Journal of Comparative Psychology, 39,* 29–50.

Mowrer, O., & Solomon, L. (1954). Contiguity vs. drive-reduction in conditioned fear: The proximity and abruptness of drive-reduction. *American Journal of Psychology, 67,* 15–25.

O'Leary, K., & O'Leary, S. (1977). *Classroom management.* New York: Pergamon Press.

Patterson, G. (1973). Reprogramming the families of aggressive boys. In C. Thoresen (Ed.), *Behavior modification in education.* Chicago: University of Chicago Press.

Patterson, G., & Gullion, M. (1976). *Living with children: New methods for parents and teachers.* Champaign, IL: Research Press.

Paul, G., & Lentz, R. (1977). *Psychosocial treatment of chronic mental patients: Milieu vs. social learning programs.* Cambridge, MA: Harvard University Press.

Pomerleau, O. (1982). A discourse on behavioral medicine: Current status and future trends. *Journal of Consulting and Clinical Psychology, 50,* 1030–1039.

Poser, L. (1977). *Behavior therapy in clinical practice.* Springfield, IL: C. C Thomas.

Premack, D. (1965). Reinforcement theory. In D. Levine (Ed.), *Nebraska symposium on motivation: 1965.* Lincoln: University of Nebraska Press.

Raloff, J. (1986). An economic case for banning smoking? *Science News, 129,* 40.

Redd, W., & Andrykowski, M. (1982). Behavioral intervention in cancer treatment: Controlling aversion reactions to chemotherapy. *Journal of Consulting and Clinical Psychology, 50,* 1018–1029.

Roberts, A. (1985). Biofeedback: Research, training, and clinical roles. *American Psychologist, 40,* 938–941.

Rosen, J., & Solomon, L. (Eds.). (1985). *Prevention in health psychology.* Hanover, NH: University Press of New England.

Sanders, S. (1983). Component analysis of a behavioral treatment program for chronic low-back pain. *Behavior Therapy, 14,* 697–705.

Schafer, L., Glasgow, R., & McCaul, K. (1982). Increasing the adherence of diabetic adolescents. *Journal of Behavioral Medicine, 5,* 353–362.

Shapiro, D., & Goldstein, I. (1982). Biobehavioral perspectives on hypertension. *Journal of Consulting and Clinical Psychology, 50,* 841–858.

Shure, M. (1981). Social competence as a problem-solving skill. In J. D. Wine & M. D. Smye (Eds.), *Social competence.* New York: Guilford.

Skinner, B. (1938). *The behavior of organisms.* New York: Appleton-Century.

Skinner, B. (1971). *Beyond freedom and dignity.* New York: Knopf.

Sloane, R., Staples, F., Cristol, A., Yorkston, N., & Whipple, K. (1975). *Psychotherapy versus behavior therapy.* Cambridge, MA: Harvard University Press.

Spivack, G., Platt, J., & Shure, M. (1976). *The problem solving approach to adjustment.* San Francisco: Jossey-Bass.

Stampfl, T., & Levis, D. (1973). *Implosive therapy: Theory and technique.* Morristown, NJ: General Learning Press.

Suinn, R. (1982). Intervention with Type A behaviors. *Journal of Consulting and Clinical Psychology, 50,* 933–949.

Surwit, R., Feinglos, M., & Scovern, A. (1983). Diabetes and behavior: A paradigm for health psychology. *American Psychologist, 38,* 255–262.

Sweet, A. (1984). The therapeutic relationship in behavior therapy. *Clinical Psychology Review, 4,* 253–272.

Turk, D., Meichenbaum, D., & Genest, M. (1983). *Pain and behavior medicine: A cognitive-behavioral perspective.* New York: Guilford.

Wachtel, P. (1977). *Psychoanalysis and behavior therapy.* New York: Basic Books.

Wadden, T., Luborsky, L., Greer, S., & Crits-Christoph, P. (1984). The behavioral treatment of essential hypertension: An update and comparison with pharmacological treatment. *Clinical Psychology Review, 4,* 403–429.

Watson, J. (1913). Psychology as the behaviorist views it. *Psychological Review, 20,* 158–177.

Watson, J., & Rayner, R. (1920). Conditioned emotional reactions. *Journal of Experimental Psychology, 3,* 1–14.

White, L., & Tursky, B. (1982). *Clinical biofeedback: Efficacy and mechanisms.* New York: Guilford.

Whitehead, W., & Bosmajian, L. (1982). Behavioral medicine approaches to gastrointestinal disorders. *Journal of Consulting and Clinical Psychology, 50,* 972–983.

Wilson, G. (1980). Current status of treatment approaches to obesity. In W. R. Miller (Ed.),

The addictive behaviors: Treatment of alcoholism, drug abuse, smoking and obesity. New York: Pergamon Press.

Wilson, G. (1982). Psychotherapy process and procedure: The behavioral mandate. *Behavior Therapy, 13,* 291–312.

Wilson, G., & Franks, C. (1982). *Contemporary behavior therapy: Conceptual and empirical foundations.* New York: Guilford.

Wilson, G., & O'Leary, K. (1980) *Principles of behavior therapy.* Englewood Cliffs, NJ: Prentice-Hall.

Wolpe, J. (1958). *Psychotherapy by reciprocal inhibition.* Stanford, CA: Stanford University Press.

Wolpe, J. (1982). *The practice of behavior therapy* (3rd ed.). New York: Pergamon Press.

Woolfolk, R., & Lehrer, P. (1984). *Principles and practice of stress management.* New York: Guilford.

Woolfolk, R., & Richardson, F. (1984). Behavior therapy and the ideology of modernity. *American Psychologist, 39,* 777–786.

Yates, A. (1958). Symptoms and symptom substitution. *Psychological Review, 65,* 175–182.

Yates, B. (1980). *Improving effectiveness and reducing costs in mental health.* Springfield, IL: C. C Thomas.

Zahara, D., & Cuvo, A. (1984). Behavioral applications to the rehabilitation of traumatically head injured persons. *Clinical Psychology Review, 4,* 477–491.

Chapter 8

Cognitive Approaches to Psychopathology and Psychotherapy

> We take the stand that there are always some alternative constructions available to choose among in dealing with the world. No one needs to paint himself into a corner; no one needs to be completely hemmed in by circumstances; no one needs to be the victim of his biography. (Kelly, 1955, p. 15)

> Change is mediated through cognitive processes, but the cognitive events are induced and altered most readily by experiences of mastery arising from successful performance. (Bandura, 1977a, p. 79)

Suppose a parent tells his young child that he is not allowed to draw on the walls of his room with his crayons. Later the parent discovers the child drawing on the living room walls. The parent becomes angry and spanks the child. Asked why he became angry, he says, "He knew better. He was drawing on the walls because he was deliberately being naughty." Asked why he chose spanking as a method of discipline, he replies, "I spanked him because if you spare the rod, you spoil the child. It'll probably whip some sense into him."

How would a cognitive psychologist explain this anger at the child and the choice of spanking as a method of discipline? First, the cognitive psychologist would assume that the anger is based on the parent's perception and interpretation of the situation. From a cognitive perspective anger is a response to the perception that the other person could have controlled his actions (Weiner, 1982). Thus, the feeling of anger is based on the interpretation that the child was "deliberately being naughty" and that he "knew better." But perhaps he didn't. Little children often are quite literal, and they do not necessarily interpret things as we do. So the child may not have known that he was doing anything wrong, believing that he had been told only not to draw on his own walls. If the parent had interpreted the situation this way, he probably would not have felt quite as angry.

The action of spanking was also based on the parent's interpretation of the situation. Believing the child's actions were deliberately naughty, he concluded that severe measures were called for. He may have said to himself: "He must not be allowed to act defiantly that way. That is an awful way to act." His choice of spanking came out of his beliefs about appropriate methods of discipline, and these beliefs were probably based on his own experience as a child. The choice may also have been influenced by his perceptions of *efficacy,* that is, effectiveness in a situation. He may have perceived himself as unable to influence the child's behavior in other ways, for instance, through dialogue. In sum, a person's actions in a situation are determined by his perceptions of the situation, his ideas about the best way to handle the situation, and his perceptions about his own skills and competencies in the situation. In addition, interpretations and cognitions influence how a person feels about the situation.

Generalizing this to abnormal behavior, the cognitive perspective sees cognition as mediating or causing both psychopathological feeling states and behavior. Psychotherapy becomes, directly or indirectly, the attempt to modify these cognitions. Cognition includes our perceptions and interpretations of situations, our behavior schemes for handling situations, our values and beliefs, and our perceptions of ourselves and of our own competencies. As we shall see, cognitions do not necessarily have to be conscious, and some perspectives give cognition a place of more central importance than others. For instance, social learning theory does not see the direct modification of cognition through verbal communication as a particularly effective therapeutic strategy. In contrast, both Beck's cognitive therapy and Ellis's rational-emotive therapy rely extensively on verbal communication as a therapeutic approach.

We will first look at the work of George Kelly. Kelly was a pioneer in applying cognitive ideas to understanding personality and to psychotherapy. Because he died before the "cognitive revolution" took place, his work is less influential than it deserves to be. We will then consider social learning theory, attribution theory, Aaron Beck's cognitive therapy for depression and anxiety, Albert Ellis's rational-emotive therapy, and Donald Meichenbaum's cognitive-behavioral therapy.

KELLY'S CONSTRUCT THEORY

George Kelly was a clinical psychologist and college professor. He also coached the college drama club. As a clinician interested in behavior change, Kelly noticed that some drama students would permanently change their behaviors as a result of playing certain roles in plays. Kelly decided to apply role playing as a therapeutic method with students who sought counseling. To account for the changes he observed using this method, Kelly developed the first comprehensive cognitive theory of personality and therapy. He also developed an assessment device, called the repertory grid, to detect individuals' cognitive structures. Kelly published his ideas in 1955, then died a few years later. His work did not become well known in the United States. However, his theory has become popular in Britain, where Bannister, Fransella, and others continue to use some of his ideas.

Kelly's theory of personality begins with his fundamental postulate: A person's processes are psychologically "channelized" by the ways in which he anticipates events. The construction corollary is that a person anticipates events by construing their replications. What these statements mean is that a person makes sense of the world by developing cognitive categories which he can then use to try to predict, that is, anticipate, events. Furthermore, these cognitive constructions of the world determine behavior, or, in Kelly's words, "psychologically channelize" the person's "processes." For example, the young child is confronted with complexity and chaos when he first notices the world around him. However, certain events repeat themselves; there are regularities even in the complexity of reality. Children may notice that there are big people and little people. Big people smile, say goo-goo, and give food and help; little people play, yell, hit, or grab things. It becomes useful for survival and comfort to notice this difference between big people and little people. Children develop a cognitive category of adult versus peer. They can then use this category to anticipate help from adults and no help from peers. They will then behave in help-seeking ways toward adults and not toward peers. Their behavior is "channelized" or determined by the way they construe events.

Kelly elaborates an entire personality theory about these cognitive constructs. There are individual differences. People will construe the same events differently, and they will develop different numbers and types of cognitive constructs, which can be organized in different ways. A person's construct system is organized with some all-embracing categories such as "good" versus "bad" and some subordinate categories such as "morally good," "esthetically good," "sensately good," and so on. While the cognitive construct system is always organized, it may be well organized or poorly organized (or fragmented), with some constructs incompatible with others. It may also be permeable (open to change) or impermeable (rigid). People are motivated to extend and define their cognitive systems. They are motivated to elaborate the system they use to make sense out of the world in order to be better able to predict and control what happens to them.

As implied above, some cognitive construct systems are better than others at helping people cope with reality. Several characteristics of cognitive constructs lead to behavior problems or mental disturbance. A simplistic system, with few cognitive constructs, will lead to trouble, because the person will constantly be confronted with new data that cannot be understood or anticipated with the system. For example, a person who sees the world in simplistic black-and-white or good-versus-evil terms will have difficulty dealing with the multitude of grays in life. There are just too many events that are not clearly good or evil. Similarly, a cognitive system that is too rigid will cause difficulties when it cannot account for everything. A paranoid person who rigidly sees everyone as untrustworthy will not be able to determine who to relate to or who can be trusted. On the other hand, a system that is too permeable will not help the person make sense out of the world at all. Psychosis, with its intruding and confusing thoughts and its lack of contact with reality, is an example of too permeable a cognitive system of constructs.

Kelly developed the repertory grid to assess what an individual's cognitive constructs are and how they are organized. The repertory grid consists of the names of people important to the individual with spaces for descriptions of these people. The examiner asks the client to describe these people and then to compare pairs of them, asking how they are alike and how they are not alike. The examiner gradually elicits the cognitive constructs the client uses to make sense out of the behavior of the people around him. By analyzing these responses the examiner can determine what in the client's construct system is causing problems. For instance, a young man having difficulty relating to women may discover that his construct system divides people into kind and frightening, and trustworthy and untrustworthy, with females always seen as frightening and untrustworthy. To relate to women, this young man will have to change his construct system so that the male-female dimension is independent of his other categories.

Kelly prescribes a form of behavior therapy in order to change such troublesome cognitive construct systems. He believed that the individual develops a particular construct system because his particular life experiences make these constructs useful. In the case of the young man, perhaps his mother and other important female figures were unkind, withholding, and unreliable. However, now his cognitive constructs get him into trouble. If he anticipates that women are going to be unkind to him, he will behave toward them as he would toward any unkind, frightening people: defensively and perhaps hostilely. This behavior may then induce women (who may or may not be kind, but who won't understand his hostility) to be unkind and hostile in return. Then his cognitive constructs will be validated, and he will continue to avoid or be hostile to women. Kelly would try to get this young man to behave in such a way that his old cognitive constructs will be invalidated by new data; new experiences will force him to develop new cognitions.

Kelly's technique was to write out a role for a client to play in his everyday life for a couple of weeks. He emphasized that it was "just role *playing,*" just an experiment, so the client wouldn't become anxious over performing correctly or failing. He made the role just slightly different from the way the client usually acted. The role could not be so different that the client wouldn't be able to do it or to make sense out of the new data it generated. However, it had to be different enough so that others would perceive the client's behavior as different and behave differently toward him than they had in the past. This would provide invalidating experiences for the old construct system and force the development of new constructs. The client is supposed to play the role with everyone for a couple of weeks. Specific behaviors in specific situations may also be assigned as homework from time to time. The client then discussed the resulting experiences with Kelly, who helped the client integrate the new data and the old cognitions.

Let us use the young man as an example. Kelly might have written a role like this for him: "You are a strong, self-confident, but gentle man, especially protective and kind to women. You help women in conversations by asking them questions about their interests, listening carefully to their answers, and showing concern for their difficulties.

You also like to have fun, and can occasionally tell a joke. . . ." If this young man even partially succeeds with this approach to women, he will elicit warm and kindly behavior from them, rather than the hostile and defensive behavior he provoked before. These new experiences provide new data that do not fit his old constructs of women being unkind and mean. He will be forced to construe women differently, which will change his behavior toward them.

Kelly's approach was novel for its time and anticipated many of the recent developments in cognitive therapy and such behavioral techniques as assertion training. He reported great success with it among his young, changeable college student population. Research in England suggests that the repertory grid is a useful assessment procedure in clinical and research settings and that variations of Kelly's therapy are suitable for many types of problems.

SOCIAL LEARNING THEORY

Perhaps the best way to introduce social learning theory is to compare it to behaviorism. Behaviorism assumes that learning is the automatic association of a stimulus with a response. Such an automatic association is "strengthened" by reinforcement, and behavior is a function of the consequences. In order for learning to occur a behavior must be performed and reinforced. Learning is essentially trial-and-error learning, in which an organism emits a variety of behaviors until one is reinforced.

Bandura (1986) takes this view to task. He asserts that all learning is cognitively mediated. A stimulus comes to be associated with a response because it comes to have predictive value. If a shock is repeatedly paired with a light, a person avoids the light, but not because the light itself has become aversive, but because it has become predictive of shock and pain. Thus, what people learn are *expectancies.* They do not develop conditioned responses to stimuli unless they are aware of the relationship between the stimulus and response, that is, unless they are aware that the stimulus predicts the onset of reinforcement or punishment.

Furthermore, Bandura argues that the idea that reinforcement "strengthens" associations between stimulus and response is a metaphor and not literally true. He suggests that reinforcement leads to learning because reinforcers are information givers and incentives. For instance, many social reinforcers, such as good grades on tests or teachers' approval, are reinforcing in part because they give the information that the student is on the right track. In addition, good grades are associated with other rewards and opportunities, so they have some incentive value. If a person is told that shock is a signal for a correct response, shock will function as a positive reinforcer (see, for instance, Dulany, 1968). In general, Bandura says that behavior is more a function of its *anticipated* consequences than of its immediate, real consequences.

Bandura goes on to point out that most important human learning is *vicarious learning.* People do not learn most of the important skills in life by performing trial-and-error responses until one is reinforced. They would not be likely to survive long if that was the way they learned. It would be a highly inefficient way to train surgeons or automobile builders, for instance, if they had to do things by trial and error until they finally got them right. Instead, most important learning is through observation and instruction. People learn through watching others' behavior, reading books or gathering information from other media, and receiving instructions.

People learn both how to interpret situations and what to do in a given situation. For instance, Bandura was one of the first investigators to note the relationship between being abused as a child and becoming a child abuser as an adult (Bandura & Walters, 1959). An abused child might learn that when a person with more power gets angry at a transgression by a person with less power, the person with more power has the right and obligation to use the infliction of physical pain as a punishment. No one explicitly verbalizes this as a rule, but it is modeled by the parent's actions. When the abused child becomes an adult, she may enact this same pattern of behavior. If he becomes a leader of a country, he may use it as a principle of national policy.

Situational Specificity of Behavior

A key concept of social learning theory is that of the *situational specificity of behavior.* Traditional views of the person, such as psychoanalysis, believe that each individual has an enduring personality structure made up of an organized pattern of character *traits.* A person might be described, for instance, as having the traits of cleanliness, friendliness, conscientiousness, optimism, extroversion, and assertiveness. Such a view assumes that this person's behavior is primarily determined by his character traits, that is, he is generally be expected to be friendly, assertive, extroverted, and clean.

However, social learning theorists believe that behavior is *situation-specific.* Behavior is guided by the expectancies in a specific situation. If a person acts assertively in some situation, it is not because she has an internal trait of assertiveness, but because she has learned to expect that assertiveness is effective in that situation. Because her behavior is guided by what she has learned to expect in different situations, she might act quite differently in a different situation. If she had learned to expect that quiet deference is the most effective behavior in that situation, she would probably act deferentially.

Therefore, social learning theorists do not believe that people will necessarily exhibit consistency of behavior in different situations. Bandura, for instance, describes an autistic child who was calm, well-behaved, considerate, and cooperative when the child's father was home, but at other times was destructive and undisciplined (Moser, 1965, as reported in Bandura, 1977a, p. 86). Now, which is the "real" child? According to social learning theory, both are, because the child's behavior is different in different situations.

But this example is a child. Surely most adults exhibit more consistency than this. Walter Mischel (Mischel, 1968; Mischel & Peake, 1982) has argued that there is little evidence for *cross*-situational consistency in behavior in general. Mischel and Peake studied the traits of conscientiousness and friendliness in college students and generally found that individuals who acted one way in terms of these traits in one situation were not particularly likely to exhibit similar behavior in different situations. For example, just because a person characteristically is friendly in class with classmates does not mean he will be similarly friendly in home or work situations.

Why then do people believe in consistency in their personality and behavior? Mischel argues that they do act consistently within situations and they observe apparent consistency in others. For instance, if I act in a friendly way in class, I am likely to act that way consistently in similar classroom situations. This creates the impression of consistency in my behavior, and people who know me only in class come to believe that friendliness is part of my character. They then expect that I would be friendly in most or all situations. Yet, as we have seen, such consistency does not appear to be characteristic of humans, and inconsistency may, in fact, be the rule.

Most people are aware of this, but tend to overlook it to believe in stability in personality. They are aware that the teacher who seems friendly in class may be distant outside of class, the man who is beloved at work may be a tyrant at home, the child who is a "little angel" at home may be a demon at school, the person who seems distant and unfriendly at a party may be warm and caring in a one-to-one conversation. Yet because of people's beliefs in the stability of personality, they tend to discount these examples as exceptions.

This can also explain why psychologists, psychiatrists, and other mental health professionals seem to be so poor at predicting violent behavior. Often they are asked to predict if an individual in a prison or mental hospital is likely to be violent if released. Typically, such predictions are based on the idea of personality character structure: Does this individual still exhibit character traits of a violent nature or not? The numerous examples of violent crime committed within days of release by someone who was judged nonviolent by professionals support the idea that the situational specificity of behavior is often more important than the individual's personality structure in predicting what they will do.

Therefore, most social learning theorists are skeptical of "internal" explanations of behavior that rely on concepts like personality trait and character structure. Social learning theorists such as Bandura would argue that a so-called borderline personality does not have a fixed character structure that includes traits like "fear of being alone." If one were to observe that person over the course of several days, one would probably find that he is afraid of being alone only in certain situations, for instance, only on a Saturday night, but not when he is working during the day in his office. There are, however, theorists who adopt social learning ideas who do believe that there are ingrained pervasive patterns to personality such as traits. Millon's (1981) "biosocial-learning" approach is one example. Millon is one of the foremost theorists of personality disorders. He believes that there are characteristic "types," such as "dependent" or "narcissistic," personalities. He argues that such enduring kinds of personality organizations develop largely through processes described by social learning theorists, such as extensive patterns of modeling and reinforcement in childhood.

Self-efficacy

Perhaps one of the best examples of situational specificity is Bandura's concept of self-efficacy. Self-efficacy is like self-esteem in some respects, but it is specific to situations. Self-efficacy is a person's self-perception of competence to enact a behavior. For example, some of you may have a sense of self-efficacy as an auto mechanic and others may not. In our example of the parent who spanked his son for writing on the walls, we suggested that he may have chosen spanking because he felt he could not influence his son through dialogue. If this was because he perceived himself as not good at verbal persuasion, then we would say he had a perception of low self-efficacy as a communicator.

Bandura has argued that an increase in self-efficacy is the common underlying dimension of effectiveness of psychotherapy (1977b). A perception of low self-efficacy has a number of negative consequences. It leads to avoidance. People are likely to avoid situations in which they feel incompetent. Thus, if you believe that if you go outdoors you will be overwhelmed by a panic attack that you cannot manage, you will stay indoors. Defensive behavior, then, is a response to perceived low efficacy. One acts defensively when one believes one cannot handle something. In essence, then, defensiveness is the converse of a feeling of mastery.

Along with avoidance, low self-efficacy leads to a tendency to give up too soon. As a result, a person does not persist long enough to find out if he or she can master a situation. In addition, low self-efficacy leads to a tendency to self-monitor in a self-destructive manner. The person observes her own efforts to cope with a situation and engages in negative self-evaluation. Such self-conscious rumination has a tendency to further disrupt behavior. A person who is absorbed in thoughts about how badly she is performing is no longer focusing on the situation and therefore cannot respond to it adequately. For example, if you feel sexually inadequate, you may focus on how well you are doing, not on your partner or the stimuli that make sex pleasurable. As a result you may do things mechanically, and you are not likely to respond adequately to your own or your partner's sensations and reactions. Low self-efficacy can be seen to relate to a variety of disorders including phobias, substance abuse, depression, and anxiety disorders. We will further consider the impact of negative self-monitoring below.

Related to the idea of low self-efficacy is the idea that behavior problems may be based on a lack of skills to handle situations. If one does not have adequate assertion skills, the feeling of being "stepped on" by employers or intimates may generate depression or anxiety. Someone who lacks effective stress management skills may engage in dysfunctional stress reduction procedures, such as the use of alcohol or drugs. A person who does not have effective communication skills may be unable to establish and maintain nurturing interpersonal relationships. Someone lacking effective parenting skills may have to resort to anger outbursts and child abuse to try to control children's behavior. Consequently, many social learning theorists have been interested in social skills training (already discussed briefly in Chapter 7).

Social skills training (Wine & Smye, 1981) is based on the idea that if psychopathology is a result of a lack of skills, training good social skills is therapeutic. Aside from assertion training, there are communication skills programs (Egan, 1984), stress management programs, and comprehensive programs that include a whole range of skills (Goldstein, Gershaw, & Sprafkin, 1984). One study (Paul, 1981) found that a social skills training program was considerably more effective in helping hospitalized patients than typical hospital regimens, such as group or milieu therapy.

Contributions to Psychotherapy

Bandura has argued that raising the level of perception of self-efficacy is the most potent therapeutic change event and that verbal persuasion is probably the least effective way to do this. He states quite forcefully that "performance-based" therapeutic interventions are more effective than verbal ones. While verbal persuasion can be useful in modifying fears that have not been reinforced by direct experience and that are primarily a matter of misinformation, it is relatively ineffective in modifying fears that have been learned through direct experience or that have been heavily reinforced. Basically, Bandura is arguing that direct experience is a much more potent teacher than words delivered in a therapeutic setting. For this reason he believes therapy must include situations where individuals actually engage in successful mastery experiences, and the therapist must arrange therapeutic tasks so that mastery experiences occur. This can be done with the aid of therapist guidance and modeling or through the use of carefully graduated steps. Sex therapy, for instance, often includes what could be called graduated mastery experiences. The client starts out learning to enjoy sensual play without attempting intercourse. As the client learns to respond to sensual experience, he or she gradually engages in behaviors more directly related to intercourse and orgasm. By the time he or she attempts intercourse, the client has usually acquired a sense of competency and mastery at being sexually responsive.

Bandura states that a potent way of learning in addition to direct experience is observation. Both direct performance and observation are considerably more experiential than verbal persuasion. Most of us can sense the difference between being told "Snakes aren't dangerous" and seeing someone like us learn to overcome his or her fear of snakes. Bandura has demonstrated that observing someone else overcoming fears helps the client overcome his own fears.

ATTRIBUTIONAL APPROACHES

Primarily a social psychological theory, attribution theory (Jones, Kanouse, Kelley, Nisbett, Valins, & Weiner, 1972) is based on the assumption that humans are "naive scientists." In order for people to predict and control what happens to them, they must figure out the causes of the behavior of others and their own behavior. The causes they perceive partially influence how they act. For example, if you have repeatedly failed to live up to your obligations to me, I may doubt the next promise you make. I may *attribute* your making that promise to a momentary desire to please me, rather than to a sincere desire to live up to your obligations. On the other hand, if I attribute your prior failures to meet your obligations to unfortunate circumstances, then I may be willing to believe you the next time you make a promise.

Since people cannot directly perceive other people's feelings, thoughts, motives, or character traits, they infer them from their behavior. Many attribution theorists assume that people do not have direct internal knowledge of the causes of their own behavior, thoughts, and feelings and therefore make similar inferences about themselves. Character traits, for instance, are inferences from patterns of behavior. I can have no direct internal knowledge of a trait of "friendliness." Instead I attribute this trait to myself if I observe myself frequently acting in friendly manner or if I am told by others that I am "friendly."

If people attribute negative traits to themselves and negative causes of their own behavior, then they may become self-destructive. One of the contributions of attribution theory to understanding psychopathology is the insight that individuals sometimes interpret their own behavior in negative ways (Valins & Nisbett, 1972). For instance, Weiner and his associates (Weiner, Frieze, Kukla, Reed, Rest, & Rosenbaum, 1972) have found that certain individuals act in self-defeating ways in achievement situations. When they succeed on a task, they attribute the cause of their success to either luck or to the ease of the task. When they fail, however, they attribute their failure to their own lack of ability. In contrast, people who perform well in achievement situations attribute success to their own efforts or to their ability, and attribute their failures to a lack of effort or the difficulty of the task. Those who act in self-defeating ways see the causes of their own success or failure in such a way that they are defeated before they start. If they succeed, it is not because they have any ability. If they fail, it is because they lack ability. Such a pattern is liable to lead to a lack of trying, which will in turn lead to a further lack of success.

Weiner's views have been incorporated into a model of depression by Martin Seligman and his associates (Abramson, Seligman, & Teasdale, 1978). They hypothesize that depression is caused by seeing oneself as the cause of something negative in one's life and then extending that perception to making a global negative attribution to one's whole character. In other words, the depressive sees himself at fault for his difficulties and in addition believes that he is at fault because of some fundamental flaw in his character. Therefore, he not only sees himself at fault for his difficulties, but also feels helpless to do anything to change or control the negative events.

Several therapeutic approaches have been based on attributional ideas. Försterling (1985) has reviewed several programs designed to retrain people who are self-defeating in achievement situations in how they make attributions. The programs appear promising in getting such individuals to make less self-defeating attributions.

A group of approaches, called *misattribution procedures,* are based on the idea that individuals make negative attributions to themselves, and then these attributions cause anxiety, which disrupts behavior. For example, a person who sees himself as shy may particularly notice his pounding heart and high pulse rate in a new social situation and say to himself, "Oh no! I'm getting scared again!" This negative self-perception then increases feelings of fear and actually leads to shy behavior. In a study by Brodt and Zimbardo (1981) based on this assumption, some extremely shy individuals were told that they would be bombarded with loud noise and that the noise would be the cause of their pounding heart and increasing pulse rate. The hypothesis was that since shy individuals would now *mis*attribute the cause of their symptoms to the loud noise, instead of to their shyness, they would not worry so much about their shyness and would be able to act in a more socially appropriate manner. In fact, such subjects did act in an essentially "normal" fashion in a new social situation, while shy subjects who had not been given this misattribution treatment acted in a noticeably shy manner.

Misattribution is based on the idea that individuals observe themselves exhibiting behavior they do not like (a pounding heart) and then make negative attributions to themselves ("Oh gad! Here I go acting shyly again!"). We have already discussed how perceptions of low self-efficacy can lead to such negative self-monitoring. If a person feels incompetent in a particular situation, he may begin to observe himself critically, looking for signs of dysfunction, and because he is no longer focused on the situation acts less competently. Wicklund and Frey (1980) suggested that such "objective self awareness" or self-focused attention makes one more likely to engage in self-evaluation. Buss (1980) suggested that such self-focused attention can intensify negative mood states (such as anxiety or depression) and may be more likely to lead to attributing negative character traits to oneself in certain situations.

Zelen (in press) has suggested that such critical self-observation can become pathological. When a person is doing something (acting), it is necessary for a part of her to self-monitor and observe herself. However, if the "observer" part gets too big, if she is too aware of herself and how she is doing, she will disrupt her own behavior. Most of us are aware of how such self-consciousness can be dysfunctional. It is difficult to be spontaneous if we are constantly critically observing ourselves.

Bandura (1986) suggested that there are ways to use self-monitoring effectively. Effective self-monitoring does not focus on what momentary success or failure means in terms of personality, self, or future. Rather it focuses on the situation and task: "What does this situation demand?" "What did I just do? Did it work? If not, why not?" "What resources do I need for my next task?" As we shall see, Meichenbaum's cognitive-behavioral therapy is an attempt to replace disruptive self-monitoring processes with more effective ones. Sex therapy also does this by trying to deflect the client's attention from self-evaluation to enjoyment of the activity. Attempts to modify dysfunctional self-focused attention are also parts of Ellis's and Beck's cognitive approaches.

BECK'S COGNITIVE THERAPY

Some people, we say, look at the world through "rose-colored glasses." Aaron Beck's (Beck, Rush, Shaw, & Emery, 1979) cognitive view of depression assumes that the depressive's glasses are of a somewhat more dusky hue. Beck holds that the symptoms of both depression and anxiety are a result of the client's cognitions about the world. Beck's approach, originally formulated for work with depression, has been expanded to a wide range of disorders (Emery, Hollon, & Bedrosian, 1981) and is currently one of the most popular approaches to therapy. We will focus on Beck's view of depression first.

Cognitive Therapy for Depression

A cognitive triad characterizes the depressive's thinking: a negative view of himself (low self-esteem), a negative view of his personal future, and a negative view of his current experiences. For instance, one young woman client of one of us was convinced that things would "never get any better" for her. That was because she was "all screwed up as a person." If she was asked how her week was she would say, "Terrible."

Depressives also exhibit basic errors in information processing that contribute to their negative perceptions. They tend to magnify negative things and minimize positive things. For instance, every week one client would begin her session by reporting that her week had been "terrible," She would then be asked to review her week day by day. It was invariably discovered that she had had both negative and positive experiences that week. When she said her week had been "terrible," what she had done was magnify the negative and minimize the positive. One week the big "negative" was that her mother had insulted her, while the positive experience, which had not even been mentioned at first, was that she had been promoted on her job.

Depressives also overgeneralize. For example, if your relationship breaks up, you may conclude if you are good at depressive thinking that "No one will ever love me." Still another depressive error is selective abstraction, in which a detail is taken out of context and then overgeneralized. Thus, in a whole conversation with someone there is perhaps one moment where things don't go well. A depressive will focus on that moment, take it out of the context of the rest of the conversation, and conclude that she made a fool out of herself and that the conversation went badly.

A predisposition toward depressive thinking is learned in early childhood. Beck assumes that children think in global, absolute, either/or ways and that in depressives these primitive ways of thinking are carried forward into adulthood. In particular they are maintained in the form of primitive simplistic schemas learned in early childhood, such as "In order to be happy, I have to be successful in whatever I undertake," "To be happy, I must be accepted by all people at all times," "If I make a mistake, it means that I am inept," "I can't live without you" (Beck, Rush, Shaw, & Emery, 1979, p. 246)

Therapeutic Goals Cognitive therapy is a systematic, structured problem-solving approach. It is generally time limited and rarely exceeds 30 sessions. Each therapy session has an agenda, in contrast to the free format of psychoanalysis or client-centered therapy. Beck believes the therapist should be warm, empathic, and genuine, as does Carl Rogers (see Chapter 5). However, in contrast to Rogers, he does not see these conditions as sufficient for therapy to take place. Rather, the therapeutic relationship is important because it is the source of learning. Among other things, the therapist is a model of what he or she is trying to teach. If the therapist is judgmental or moralizing, that will merely reinforce the primitive judgmental thoughts of the client.

The ultimate goal of cognitive therapy is to identify dysfunctional cognitions, see how they trigger and generate depressive feelings and behavior, and learn to modify them. It is important to note that Beck is not as interested in what the client thinks as in how he thinks. Beck even admits that on occasion a depressive cognition may be accurate (for instance, somebody may ignore you because they really don't like you). Beck is not interested in teaching "positive thinking." He sees positive thinking as potentially as destructive as negative thinking. The issue is not whether the client likes or dislikes himself. The issue is whether he thinks in a mode of either "I am good" or "I am bad" depending on what happens. If he is stuck in this mode of thinking then when things go right he will say, "I am good." But of course that just sets him up for "I am bad" when he makes a mistake or things go wrong. It's better for him not to think in terms of "I am good or I am bad," depending on what happens, but rather to focus on what he does: "Did I do this well, or not?"

Similarly, life, for Beck, is not the pursuit of happiness. Happiness is a by-product of activity. Though Beck has been accused of being a "positive thinker" (Hazleton, 1981), we can see that this is inaccurate. Beck does not think it is better to see a glass as "half full" than as "half empty." Instead, it is better to see it as containing four ounces of water (Beck, Rush, Shaw, & Emery, 1979).

Beck does not want to get clients to think positively, but to teach them to test hypotheses. Even though occasional depressive cognitions may be accurate, depressives generate their depression through their dysfunctional errors in information processing and the cognitive triad. Beck attempts to teach clients to treat these ideas as hypotheses rather than as facts and then to test them against the evidence. The development of this hypothesis-testing attitude will lead to a much more flexible, nonjudgmental cognitive system that can handle an occasional negative cognition that is supported by the evidence.

In initial sessions Beck explores the client's difficulties and formulates a plan of action. The link between thoughts and feelings is demonstrated to the client, with examples. Then, two general lines of attack are used to combat dysfunctional cognitions. They are behavioral techniques and cognitive techniques.

Behavioral Techniques Behavioral techniques are used first with more severely depressed clients. Severely depressed clients may have difficulty processing ideas and information. Therefore, cognitive interventions are often ineffective with them. For example, one client one of us worked with could barely say more than "This is stupid. I've got to get over this and get back to work." Trying to get her to explore her feelings and thoughts was unsuccessful. She would elaborate slightly, but then lapse back into "This is stupid. I've got to get over this and get back to work."

For such clients behavioral interventions are used to help lift the depression. Getting the client to act counters cognitions such as "I can't do anything" or "I'm a vegetable." In addition, the therapist can get the client to begin to test his dysfunctional cognitions while engaging in the behavioral activities. As these interventions gradually help lift the depression, the client becomes open to cognitive interventions.

Beck does not believe that behavioral interventions can cure depression by themselves. The underlying negative cognitions that generated the depression need to be attacked as well or the depression will return. Nevertheless, *doing something* is a good "cure" to lift the depression temporarily.

Behavioral interventions utilized by Beck include having the client keep a daily record of activities, the mastery and pleasure technique, scheduling a graduated series of activities to attempt, cognitive rehearsal, and role playing. The daily activity schedule is an hourly record kept by the client of all his activities, no matter how trivial. It helps counter the dysfunctional cognition that "I never do anything." In addition, the client is often asked to rate each activity for the amount of pleasure and the amount of "mastery" it gives him. The amount of mastery is the sense of accomplishment one gets from doing something. This also often gives the therapist insight into the client's dysfunctional cognitions. For instance, one client's daily activity record (Beck, Rush, Shaw, & Emery, 1979, p. 130) rated wallpapering the kitchen zero for mastery and pleasure and rated getting up, getting dressed, and eating one. How could wallpapering provide even less of a sense of mastery than getting up? The answer lies in this depressed client's distorted, perfectionist perceptions of his achievement (see Box 8.1), which the therapist was able to explore with the help of the mastery-pleasure ratings.

Another behavioral intervention Beck uses with depressed clients is a series of graduated task assignments. For example, a client for whom getting out of bed is an accomplishment may be assigned the task of brushing his teeth and shaving. After he has mastered that, he may be assigned the task of fixing himself breakfast and going for a walk. The next week the assignment may include reading the paper and looking at the want ads. The strategy is to pick activities that slowly and gradually return the depressed client to full functioning. However, it is important to pick tasks that are within the client's grasp. To say to a seriously depressed client who can barely get out of bed, "You'll feel better if you go look for a job," will probably contribute to his

BOX 8.1
Cognitions Involved in Mastery and Pleasure Ratings

Below is a sample of a dialogue between a depressed man who had rated his achievement in wallpapering a kitchen as providing no sense of mastery or pleasure. Note Beck's questioning technique to first uncover and then attack the dysfunctional cognitions involved.

THERAPIST: Why didn't you rate wallpapering the kitchen as a mastery experience?
PATIENT: Because the flowers didn't line up.
T: Your kitchen?
P: No. I helped a neighbor do his kitchen.
T: Did he do most of the work?
P: No. I really did almost all of it. He hadn't wallpapered before.
T: Did anything else go wrong? Did you spill the paste all over? Ruin a lot of wallpaper? Leave a big mess?
P: No, no, the only problem was that the flowers did not line up.
T: So, since it was not perfect, you get no credit at all.
P: Well . . . yes.
T: Just how far off was the alignment of the flowers?
P: *(Holds out fingers about an eighth of an inch apart)* About that much.
T: On each strip of paper?
P: No . . . on two or three pieces.
T: Out of how many?
P: About 20 to 25.
T: Did anyone else notice it?
P: No. In fact, my neighbor thought it was great.
T: Did your wife see it?
P: Yeh, she admired the job.
T: Could you see the defect when you stood back and looked at the whole wall?
P: Well . . . not really.
T: So you've selectively attended to a real but very small flaw in your effort to wallpaper. Is it logical that such a small defect should entirely cancel the credit you deserve?
P: Well, it wasn't as good as it should have been.
T: If your neighbor had done the same quality job in your kitchen, what would you say?
P: . . . Pretty good job! (Beck, Rush, Shaw, & Emery, 1979, pp. 130–131)

depression rather than help it. It is too big a leap to go from getting out of bed to looking for a job. In addition, Beck stresses that the goal of the activity is the *doing* of it, rather than the accomplishing of it. The client is told that no one accomplishes everything he or she sets out to do and that the important thing is to treat the activity as a learning experience.

Another behavioral technique is cognitive rehearsal. Severely depressed clients often cannot handle a complex task assignment, because they have difficulty in concentrating and thinking. As a result, they will "self destruct." They will forget directions or they will fail to anticipate crucial prerequisites to getting the task accomplished. For instance, a client whose task assignment is to go look for a job may forget to get clothes washed the day before, or may forget to arrange for transportation. These things may only dawn on the client at the moment when the client is preparing to leave. Without clothes or transportation the client cannot carry out the task assignment and the experience becomes another failure, confirming the client's self-perception of incompetence. To counter this, the therapist has the client rehearse the task, that is, to go through the task step by step to discover what he will need to do to accomplish it. Such pitfalls are then discovered in advance, and the client can take steps to overcome them. In addition, the therapist can give the client suggestions as to how to handle unexpected pitfalls.

Another technique used by the cognitive therapist is role playing. For example, Beck found that depressed clients are often more critical of themselves than of others in the same situation (Beck, Rush, Shaw, & Emery, 1979, p. 138). He has clients role play what they would say to someone else who had their problem. In the example in Box 8.1, Beck does this when he asks the client how he would feel about his wallpapering job if someone else had done it for him. One of us used this technique with a religious young man who felt guilty about masturbating. He had given it up and had been absolved by the elders of his church, who told him that the important thing was not to dwell on his past transgressions, but to try to do better in the future. Yet he still felt guilty and anxious. In therapy he was asked to pretend to counsel another young man with the same problem. He was much more forgiving toward this imaginary man than he was toward himself. When he realized this, his guilt and anxiety subsided.

Cognitive Techniques Once the depression has lifted sufficiently, the therapist can begin to concentrate on cognitive techniques. The first thing necessary is to make the client aware of the connection between his thoughts and his feelings. In order to do this the client is given the assignment of keeping a daily record of automatic thoughts. Every time the client notices himself feeling depressed, he is to attempt to recover the thoughts that immediately preceded the onset of the depressed feelings. He is to record the objective situation, the thoughts he had, and the feelings they led to. For example, you are sitting in class and you suddenly begin to feel depressed. You realize that you had just noticed the attractive person near you who acts as if you don't exist. You record the situation: sitting in class, noticing the attractive person. You also record your thoughts: "That person acts as if I don't exist. I'll never get a date." And you record your mood.

Initially people often report that the depressed mood came on them without any thoughts. Beck believes that in these cases there were thoughts present, but they occurred so quickly the client was unaware of them. These are called *automatic thoughts,* and they are the cognitive therapist's equivalent of the unconscious (Meichenbaum & Gilmore, 1984). Automatic thoughts are thoughts that have become so habitual that when they are triggered by some situation they flit through the client's mind too rapidly for him to notice. Yet they stimulate depressive feelings. The daily record helps clients become aware of the automatic thoughts that precede their depressive feelings and can be used by the therapist to help clients modify their dysfunctional thinking pattern.

An assignment in addition to the daily record of dysfunctional thoughts is often made. Along with recording the situation, thoughts, and feelings, the client is asked to write down alternative, less dysfunctional ways of perceiving the situation. This has the effect of helping the client realize that he or she has been locked into one way of seeing the situation and that there are other ways. Generating alternative views of the situation encourages the hypothesis-testing attitude that Beck is trying to teach.

The main cognitive technique used by the therapist is questioning. Questions are designed to help the client explore and test dysfunctional cognitions. Note in the dialogue about wallpapering in Box 8.1 that the therapist explores the possibility that the client's perception of failure as a wallpaperer might have a real basis—he made a mess, wasted wallpaper, and so on. It is clear in this example that the client's perception of failure is based instead on his perfectionist attitude. The therapist helps the client realize this through questioning. However, even if the client had made a mess, the cognitive therapist could then have explored the dysfunctional cognitions based on that situation, such as "I never do anything right," "I'm inept," and so on. Cognitive therapists use three general kinds of questions (Beck, Emery, & Greenberg, 1985): "What's the evidence?" "What's another way of looking at the situation?" and "So what if it happens?"

It is important to point out that Beck uses questions rather than attempting to argue the client out of dysfunctional cognitions. Why doesn't he try to logically persuade the client that the client's beliefs are incorrect? People often react to depressives in everyday life by saying, "You did fine! I'm sure your neighbor didn't care about the misaligned flowers. Don't be so hard on yourself. Everyone likes you. Why just the other day we were all talking about what a nice guy you are! You have to have more confidence in yourself!"

The depressive might respond with a short-lived good feeling or argue back, "But you don't really know me. Maybe the misaligned flowers aren't so bad in themselves, but they're just a symptom of the generally sloppy careless way I live my life. Besides, you like me. You're just trying to cheer me up." After a few rounds of this the "friend" will go away feeling angry and frustrated. The friend may go say to another friend, "Oh, he just likes to be depressed. He wants everyone to feel sorry for him." Anyone who has argued with a depressive has probably come away with such feelings. The perception that the depressive likes being depressed then becomes a further problem for the depressive, who begins to be rejected by the people around him, who no longer want to listen to him complain or to attempt to lift his depression. In yet another way depression becomes a vicious circle.

Trying to argue someone out of a deeply entrenched point of view is usually quite fruitless. Some research (Nisbett & Ross, 1980) has shown that people with deeply committed beliefs simply explain away or assimilate information contradictory to their belief system and paradoxically end up believing in it more than ever. Even if depression is based on a dysfunctional belief system, presenting contradictory evidence will still have little effect. This is true for all of us, whenever we have a deeply committed belief, be it religious, political, or psychological. Imagine trying to use logical argument and evidence to convince Ronald Reagan to be a liberal, or Edward Kennedy to be a conservative! Because it is difficult to argue a person committed to a belief system out of it, it is inaccurate to accuse depressives of "wanting to be depressed" when arguments fail. Beck holds that depressives would love to get out of the binds they're in if they could. They do not counter arguments because they want to stay depressed; they counter them because they are locked into a depressive belief system that they would be only too happy to escape from if they saw a way.

Beck uses a questioning technique to get the depressed person to challenge her own depressive cognitions. In Plato's *Dialogues,* Plato's philosophy is articulated through the main character of Socrates. Socrates does not expound or argue. What Socrates does is ask skillful questions to make the person he is talking to think it out until he arrives at Socrates's perspective. Arguing leads to defensiveness. People will often hang on to a point of view in an argument just to justify themselves and defend their own autonomy. The therapist who argues with a depressive may put him in the position of having to defend and justify his negative perspective. This can be circumvented by using the Socratic method—by asking questions to get the client to think it out so that he arrives at a less depressive view. In addition, it mobilizes the patient's cognitive resources and trains the patient in a method that he can use at other times.

Beck's questioning technique, then, mobilizes the depressive to challenge his own cognitions. Even so, the challenges must be repeated over a period of time before they "sink in." One disconfirmation of a dysfunctional belief is rarely enough to change it. The insight must be acquired over and over again before the belief system will finally change.

In addition, Beck gives homework assignments so that dysfunctional cognitions can be tested against direct experience. A client may be instructed to test out the belief "My boss will never give me a raise" by asking for a raise. (If the boss does not give the client a raise, then the dysfunctional cognitions generated by the client from that will be dealt with, and so the experience will be a productive learning one either way.)

Cognitive Therapy for Anxiety

Beck, Emery, and Greenberg (1985) have applied the cognitive approach to the treatment of anxiety disorders such as generalized anxiety disorder, panic disorder, phobias, and various kinds of performance and social anxiety states. While the core of the cognitive approach remains the same, there are some additions and modifications specific to anxiety.

For Beck anxiety is a normal defensive reaction to threat or danger. When one is feeling threatened, anxiety leads to a focusing of conscious attention on the dangerous stimuli. While this is adaptive in a truly threatening situation, it is maladaptive if the individual remains perpetually in this state. In anxiety disorders the individual remains defensive long after the danger has passed. The narrowing of attention under conditions of anxiety leads to biased scanning of the environment. Threatening stimuli may be exaggerated, and symptoms associated with anxiety may be magnified. The symptoms of anxiety disorders are occasionally experienced by everyone, according to Beck. One of these symptoms, for instance, is experiencing a sense of unreality. For most people they are fleeting. The anxiety-disordered individual, however, focuses on them and attributes undue significance to them.

One of the paradoxes of anxiety disorders is that individuals often bring about the very thing they are afraid of. A person who is afraid of making a fool of himself in a public speaking situation becomes so anxious he freezes up. Beck argues that at the core of anxiety disorders is a feeling of vulnerability and that this feeling of vulnerability is based on the perception that the person lacks the basic skills necessary to cope with a particular threat (low self-efficacy). In a situation of threat people appraise the danger and compare it to their coping skills. If they are confident of their skills, they then can focus on the threat and problem solve to cope with it. If they feel they lack skills, they become more focused on protecting themselves or escaping. Attention shifts from the problem situation to themselves and performance is disrupted. Beck argues that people feel most threatened in areas of vital interests, such as achievement, socializing, and health.

Cognitive therapy for anxiety includes many of the techniques used for depression. As a general statement about therapy, Beck (Beck, Emery, & Greenberg, 1985) suggests that one of the most important learnings to occur in therapy is "learning how to learn" by overcoming the human tendency to repeat the same self-destructive patterns of behavior. He also suggests that some of the tacit assumptions mentioned above may form a basic core of assumptions that are defensively protected. In addition, since anxiety is a defensive reaction and anxiety-disordered clients will sometimes attempt to deny or fight off their anxiety feelings, therapy for anxiety is modified to pay more attention to denial and resistance.

In order to cope with denial and resistance the client is encouraged to simply allow his feelings to be, that is, to accept them and to adopt a nonjudgmental distancing attitude toward them. As Beck et al. say, "The therapist should thus make it clear that acceptance is allowing what exists at the moment to be as it is. Acceptance is acknowledging the existence of an event without placing a judgement or label on it" (Beck, Emery, & Greenberg, 1985, p. 233). The client is encouraged to note the existence of fearful feelings and thoughts and then let them go: "The more you try to not think about something, the more you think about it" (p. 193); "There's another fearful thought . . . I'll just count it and let it go" (p. 196).

The anxious client must learn to "own" his feelings and to replace statements like "It made me anxious" with "I was making myself anxious." This also counters resistance and denial.

The client is encouraged to replace why questions with how questions. Instead of asking herself why she is anxious, which simply elicits more thinking, judging, and analyzing, she might ask how she is making herself anxious, which elicits observing her feelings and the situations in which they occur rather than judging and labeling them. Such nonjudgmental observing serves by itself to widen the scope of awareness.

The client is encouraged to focus on the positive aspects of some of her symptoms and not to dwell on the negative. For instance, a symptom of one client was homesickness. She was told that the experience of feeling homesick could be used to help her learn how to accept change, how to tolerate frustration, and so on. This "reframing" of the symptom (see Chapter 10) focuses the client's attention away from the dangerous, catastrophic aspects of the anxiety.

One final set of techniques stressed especially in the work with anxiety disorders is exploration of the question "So what if it happened?" Clients may be asked to use imagery and fantasy to explore possible negative outcomes and then to practice ways of handling these negative outcomes.

Since Beck has suggested that the cause of anxiety disorders is being stuck in the defensive mode, any technique that encourages the client to defocus his attention on the threatening outcomes and negative symptoms automatically counters the cause of the anxiety. Accepting and not judging, owning feeling, asking how instead of why questions, and reframing experience by focusing on positive aspects all have the effect of widening awareness beyond the defensive focus on danger and threat.

ELLIS'S RATIONAL-EMOTIVE THERAPY

We have seen that one depression-causing cognition begins "I'll NEVER . . ." So when your third or fourth relationship doesn't work out, you say, "I'll never have a good relationship." You might even go further and say, "I'll never have a good relationship because I'm unlovable." We have seen how Beck would treat this. He would get the client to evaluate the evidence for these propositions and encourage the client to see that even though he had had a series of failures, that does not prove that it will never work out. It is also obvious that it would be difficult to find evidence proving that he is unlovable.

But there is another way to proceed. For Albert Ellis, founder of rational-emotive therapy, the important question is "So what if you never did have a good relationship?" (We have seen that Beck stresses this question in therapy for anxiety.) For Ellis, a client's answer to the question can be something depressing to him only if he makes it mean something depressing. For example, most people answer the question "What if I never have a good relationship" by insisting "I must have a good relationship in order to be happy." In other words, if they didn't set such an absolute philosophical condition on their life, then the thought that they might never have a good relationship would not be threatening or depressing.

Ellis claims that this kind of "musturbatory" thinking, that is, this setting of an absolute standard for behavior and life, is at the basis of most personal difficulty. Ellis (1979a, pp. 3–4) lists three groups of such ideas that "virtually all humans hold to some degree but which disturbed individuals hold more intensely, extensively, and rigidly."

1. I must be competent, adequate, and achieving, and I *must* win the approval of virtually all the significant people in my life. It is awful when I don't. I can't stand failing in these all-important respects. I am a rotten person when I don't do what I must do to act competently and to win others' approval.
2. Others must treat me kindly, fairly, and properly when I want them to do so. It is terrible when they don't. I can't bear their acting obnoxiously toward me. They are damnable, worthless people when they don't do what they must do to treat me satisfactorily.
3. I need and must have the things I really want. The conditions under which I live and the world around me must be well ordered, positive, certain—just the way I want them to be. I must gratify my desires easily and immediately, without having to deal with too many difficulties or hassles. It is horrible when conditions are not this way. I can't tolerate their being uncomfortable, frus-

> trating, or merely not ideal. The world is a rotten place and life is hardly worth living when things are not as they should be in this respect.

These ideas are what Ellis calls *irrational beliefs.* They are absolute, rigid, intolerant, and demanding. But they are beliefs. Ellis is fond of quoting Shakespeare's *Hamlet:* "There's nothing either good or bad, but thinking makes it so." Ellis is especially interested in what people think they must have in order to be happy, how they must act in order to be a good person, what the world should be like, and how others ought to be. When Ellis holds that beliefs are irrational, he means that they cannot be empirically or scientifically verified. He says, "They can all be easily exposed and demolished by any scientist worth his salt; and the rational-emotive therapist is exactly that: an exposing and nonsense-annihilating scientist" (Ellis, 1973, p. 173).

Where do irrational cognitions come from? Ellis believes that all people are born with tendencies toward rational and irrational thinking as well as self-actualization. We all have them, even educated academics and intellectuals. The two main kinds of irrational thinking are a tendency toward "musturbatory" thinking and a tendency to make non sequiturs, or to believe conclusions that do not follow from the evidence or from the premises.

Ellis (1979b) gives examples of what he considers to be irrational tendencies. People complain that they are being treated unfairly because they don't get something they think they deserve, but they don't say anything about the positive things they have gotten. People express concern about dangers to their existence, drive carefully, dress warmly, and wash their hands before eating, but they overeat, don't exercise, and drink or smoke. People resist unlearning old things, even when they are dysfunctional and self-destructive. They often believe things for which there is virtually no objective evidence, such as astrology, magic, health fads and cures, but ignore or resist factual evidence showing associations between smoking and cancer, consumption of fat and poor health, poverty and crime. People are born with a tendency to learn self-defeating behavior more easily than life-enhancing behavior, to remain attached to beliefs that do not work in various ways, to need to prove themselves superior to others, to demand rather than to want, to be overcautious, to be lazy, to be undisciplined, to have low frustration tolerance, to prefer the easiest way out of situations, and to be shortsighted. Ellis also says we are born with "an exceptionally strong tendency to want and to insist that everything happens for the best in (one's) life and to roundly condemn (1) [oneself], (2) others, and (3) the world when [one] does not immediately get what [one] wants" (Ellis, 1973, p. 176).

Though general tendencies to think irrationally may be inborn, the specific irrational thoughts are learned from the culture. Even if they are learned in early childhood, however, they are kept alive because people continually reindoctrinate themselves all the time.

According to Ellis, it is a person's cognitions about events that determine behavior, not the events themselves. He quotes Adler:

> No experience is a cause of success or failure. We do not suffer from the shock of our experiences—the so-called trauma—but we make out of them just what suits our purposes. We are self determined by the meaning we give to our experiences; and

> there is probably something of a mistake always involved when we take particular experiences as the basis of our future life. Meanings are not determined by situations, but we determine ourselves by the meanings we give to situations." (Adler, 1931, as quoted in Ellis, 1973, p. 167)

The effect of cognition on behavior is represented by Ellis's famous A-B-C model. A is the objective event, B is the person's interpretation of the event, and C is the person's emotional or behavioral reaction. Most people tend to think that A causes C, but Ellis believes that while A contributes to C, B is the most important determinant of reactions. For instance, borderline personality disordered clients feel they "cannot stand" being alone. But is it really true that they "can't stand" being alone? Or is that merely a self-perception on their part? Their perception is that A ("I am alone") leads to C (feelings of depression or panic). Ellis would suggest that this happens only because of intervening cognitions: "I do not like being alone," "I must NOT be alone," "I CAN'T STAND being alone." It is this set of intervening cognitions that causes the borderline's reactions of depression or panic, not being alone itself. Ellis suggests that the borderline person has made a non sequitur. He has followed a rational (sane) sentence, "I do not like being alone," with an irrational (insane) inference, "I must not be alone," leading to the perception "I cannot stand being alone" and feelings of depression.

Ellis also says people create problems by turning preferences into needs. There is a difference between the rational statements that I prefer to have a good income, to have a good relationship, to be attractive and well liked, and the irrational beliefs that I must have a good income, I can't stand to be without a loving fulfilling relationship, I MUST be attractive, and I deserve to be well-liked. To prefer to do things well or to be a good person is not the same feeling that one must do everything well and never make a mistake or that one must never be inconsiderate or not perfectly honest. For instance, the belief that just because I was mistreated by my parents I am now permanently maimed for life is based in part on the irrational belief I held as a child (and also hold now) that I must have caring loving treatment in order to grow up well.

Ellis generally does not believe that "shoulds" and "musts" exist in nature and that people would behave much more sanely and rationally if they stayed at the level of their wants and preferences. Sounding very existential, he holds that the world just "is" and that people would be better off to accept that, rather than to make demands that the world be fair or just according to their perceptions. This is also true of the self. Ellis has argued that self-evaluation is probably the major cause of personal distress. Positive self-esteem is just as bad as negative self-esteem. It is better not to judge or evaluate the self at all. In this he agrees with Beck that it is rational to evaluate actions, but not the self.

Ellis illustrates the destructive consequences of self-evaluation, rather than behavioral evaluation, in the case of Myra, a woman who came to therapy feeling inadequate because she was unable to have an orgasm. He asks Myra to recount what she is thinking as she tries to achieve orgasm. It turns out that not only is she trying to have an orgasm, but she is also thinking that if she doesn't have an orgasm "wouldn't that be terrible, what a lousy sex partner I'd be . . . all that effort for nothing . . . how awful . . . how unfair . . . while so many other women have one so easily, with no effort at all!" (Ellis, 1979d, p. 71). A person dwelling on such thoughts cannot possibly be focusing on the pleasurable aspects of sex. Thus the self-evaluation becomes a self-fulfilling prophecy. Ellis also talks about "disturbance about disturbance" (1979c, p. 48), which is thinking less of oneself for having problems. In addition to Myra's contributing to her own lack of orgasmic responsiveness, she also criticized herself and felt guilty for not being able to have an orgasm: "I MUST get orgasms like other women do, and I don't get them; that's awful! I can't stand it! I must be something of a turd for being so inferior to most other women!" (1979d p. 69).

Basically Ellis believes that humans are hedonistic. Though he sees hedonism as a choice rather than a necessity, he sees most people as primarily motivated by the pursuit of happiness. With this in mind he lists the following as criteria of healthy functioning: self-interest, social interest, self-direction, tolerance, flexibility, acceptance of uncertainty, committment, scientific thinking, self-acceptance, risk-taking, and nonutopianism (not believing in perfection) (1979c).

In terms of therapeutic practice, rational-emotive therapy is relatively short term (usually not over 50 sessions) and utilizes techniques from a wide range of approaches. Rational-emotive therapists will use operant conditioning techniques, desensitization, assertion training, role playing, interpersonal skills training, modeling, imagery, shame-attacking exercises (see below), and bibliotherapy (the use of reading material).

However, its central technique is *disputing.* As the name implies, disputing is the logical challenging of irrational beliefs. Ellis believes that he can identify and begin attacking a client's irrational cognitions within the first few minutes of the first session. An example of his technique is given in Box 8.2. Ellis describes this method thus:

> The rational-emotive practitioner mainly employs a fairly rapid-fire active-directive-persuasive-philosophic methodology. In most instances, he quickly pins the client down to a few basic irrational ideas which motivate much of his disturbed behavior; he challenges the client to validate these ideas; he shows them that they are extralogical premises which cannot be validated; he logically analyzes these ideas and makes mincemeat of them; he vigorously and vehemently shows why they can't work and will almost inevitably lead to renewed disturbed symptomatology; he reduces these ideas to absurdity, sometimes in a highly humorous manner; he explains how they can be replaced with more rational, empirically based theses; he teaches the client how to think scientifically. . . . (Ellis, 1973, p. 185)

Ellis has noted, however, that disputing alone is frequently insufficient for psychotherapeutic change to occur. Most clients also require active, experiential exercises in order to test out their irrational cognitions. Because of the biological tendency to think irrationally it is difficult to correct irrational habits. One "insight" into irrationality will not suffice to change such an ingrained pattern of thinking.

Because of the name rational-emotive therapy, one might expect that the rational-emotive therapist attacks clients' value systems and shows them to be irrational. Ellis (1979c) states that the rational-emotive therapist respects the client's value system and does not impose his value system on the client. It is not the values themselves that are attacked, but rather their absolute, musturbatory quality. For instance, if a client does something contrary to his own values, he will feel depressed, anxious, or guilty only

BOX 8.2
Ellis Disputes

This is the first part of an initial interview with a 25-year-old female client complaining of guilt, unworthiness, depression, and insecurity, among other things.

T: All right, what would you want to start on first?
C: I don't know. I'm petrified at the moment!
T: You're petrified—of what?
C: Of you!
T: Because of what I am going to do to you?
C: Right! You are threatening me, I guess.
T: But how? What am I doing? Obviously, I'm not going to take a knife and stab you. Now, in what way am I threatening you?
C: I guess I'm afraid, perhaps, of what I'm going to find out—about me.
T: Well, so let's suppose you find out something dreadful about you—that you're thinking foolishly or something. Now why would that be awful?
C: Because I . . . I guess I'm the most important thing to me at the moment.
T: No, I don't think that's the answer. It's, I believe, the opposite! You're really the least important thing to you. You are prepared to beat yourself over the head if I tell you that you're acting foolishly. If you were not a self-blamer, then you wouldn't care what I said. It would be important to you—but you'd just go around correcting it. But if I tell you something really negative about you, you're going to beat yourself mercilessly. Aren't you? (Ellis, 1984, pp. 215–216)

if he believes that he is "an awful person" because of what he did. A more rational way of responding would be "I would prefer not to act that way. I'll try to do better next time." The rational-emotive therapist would not attack the person's values, but his rigid way of using his values.

It is important to note that Ellis's therapy involves an attitude of unconditional acceptance toward the client. The therapist does not judge the client as a person, even though he may vigorously attack some of the client's behavior and ideas. Ellis points out that his client Myra occasionally irritated him: "Not that I wasn't tempted, on several occasions, to really tell her off. But, with the use of RET [rational-emotive therapy], I kept reminding myself that she was not a louse even though her behavior was quite lousy. And I actually got myself to believe this and to convey my belief to her!" (1979d, p. 83).

In addition to disputing in therapy sessions, the therapist often gives the client the homework assignment of disputing his or her own beliefs. For instance, Myra worked at disputing the beliefs that she must have sex enjoyment easily and quickly and that she *should* have orgasms as other women do. She realized that although it would be highly desirable if she could, there was no evidence that she should. She also disputed the idea that it would be awful if she never had a sexual climax and realized there are many other pleasures in life, including sexual ones. She also realized that having more difficulty in reaching orgasm than other women did not make her a bad person.

Many of the techniques that rational-emotive therapists will use, such as the behavioral techniques, are discussed elsewhere in this book. We will briefly mention two others here. The first is the *shame-attacking exercise.* Because Ellis believes that shame is the essence of many disorders, he has clients attack this feeling. In these exercises the clients deliberately make fools of themselves. Myra, for instance, was given the assignment of walking a banana down the street on a leash. Despite feeling foolish at first, she soon realized that nothing bad happened to her, and she actually began to enjoy the experience.

The use of *imagery* is another technique. It is based on the work of Maultsby (1971). Myra, for instance, was to imagine a scene of sexual failure. She was to imagine trying hard to have an orgasm, failing, and her husband's being critical of her. As she imagined these things she experienced shame and depression. Her assignment was to imagine these scenes repeatedly, but to practice feeling the more rational feelings of sadness and disappointment. Gradually she learned that she could feel these feelings instead. She need not feel bad about herself if she "failed" sexually. She did not have to feel bad about herself even if her husband was critical of her.

Comparison of Ellis and Beck

You may have noticed that the approaches of Beck and Ellis are similar. Although Ellis considers his therapeutic approach to be scientific, we believe that Beck places more emphasis on a scientific attitude than Ellis, and Ellis places greater emphasis on philosophical analysis. Both believe that clients make logical errors that lead to dysfunctional conclusions. However, Beck emphasizes testing hypotheses. Are the client's ideas true or false? Are they overgeneralizations? Can they be backed up by evidence? If the client says, "I will never have a relationship," the main thrust of Beck's approach is to demonstrate that this conclusion does not have any evidence to back it up. Ellis may do this also, but his main emphasis is on what the client believes to be the consequences of the statement, whether it is verifiable or not: "Even if it were true, does that mean you cannot enjoy life?"

As therapists their methods differ also. Beck is certainly active in asking questions, structuring the therapy hour, and suggesting assignments and techniques, but he is relatively nondirective in his approach to the client's cognitions and beliefs. Beck never tells the client his beliefs are irrational or which beliefs to modify. Rather he ultimately lets the client draw his own conclusions. Ellis is much more directive. He tells the client which beliefs are irrational and need modification. The technique of disputing by its very name implies this more confrontational approach.

MEICHENBAUM'S COGNITIVE BEHAVIOR MODIFICATION

Do you talk to yourself? If you do, you probably do it privately and might be embarrassed to be caught at it. You might even wonder if you were a little crazy. According to Donald Meichenbaum (1977), however, you not only have nothing to worry about, but how you talk to yourself is crucial in determining how you behave and feel. Meichenbaum points out that children talk to themselves all the time as they play and practice new skills. It is through such self-guiding speech that people learn to direct and control much of their behavior. For example, when you first learned how to drive, you most likely guided your first attempts with self-speech. Others guided your behavior at first with their instructional speech, but you then began to guide yourself, silently or out loud, saying, "Now, first put the clutch in—no—step on the brake and release the emergency brake. Start the car. Now put the clutch in. Put it in gear. Now let the clutch out—not too fast. . . ." Talking to yourself is actually quite adaptive, if you say the right things. And that is the crux of Meichenbaum's cognitive-behavioral therapeutic approach.

Self-speech can be maladaptive and contribute to psychological problems in two ways. First, some individuals engage in dysfunctional self-speech. They say things to themselves that are disruptive and distress producing. Someone who says "I can never do anything right. What's the use?" may give up on tasks or engage in dysfunctional behavior, such as drinking, to avoid the task. Second, the absence of adaptive self-speech makes dysfunctional behavior more likely. If a person does not have effective self-guiding strategies for handling a situation, then she is likely to employ ineffective, maladaptive coping methods.

Self-guiding speech is initially learned through internalizing what others say and by conscious practice, but eventually it becomes automatic and nonconscious. After a while you no longer say to yourself: "Now put in the clutch . . ." when you go driving. Beck defines automatic thoughts as habitual thoughts that occur so rapidly that one is not even aware of having thought them. Meichenbaum says that they are thoughts that occur with very "low intensity" and so are not easily noticed.

Meichenbaum's general therapeutic strategy is to retrain how clients talk to themselves. The retraining attempts to eliminate dysfunctional self-speech and to increase adaptive self-speech. First, the therapist models the kind of self-speech the client is to learn to use. This, as with each of the succeeding steps, may be done several times. The client then practices the self-speech aloud, then whispering, and finally silently. The practice is repeated until the desired type of self-speech becomes habitual.

This general model of self-instructional training, modified appropriately to fit each particular disorder, has been used to treat many kinds of problems, including hyperactivity in children, anxiety, schizophrenia, and anger control. It has also been used to teach creativity and stress management.

Meichenbaum's early work was with hyperactive, impulsive children. Following is an example of self-speech the therapist models for a child.

> "Okay, what is it I have to do? You want me to copy the pictures with the different lines. I have to go slowly and carefully. Okay, draw the line down, down, good; then to the right, that's it; now down some more and to the left. Good, I'm doing fine so far. Remember, go slowly. Now back up again. No, I was supposed to go down. That's okay. Just erase the line carefully. . . . Good. Even if I make an error I can go on slowly and carefully. I have to go down now. Finished. I did it!" (Meichenbaum & Goodman, 1971, p. 117)

The speech models the skills necessary to solve the task. More importantly, however, the speech models self-reinforcement ("Good, I'm doing fine so far") and what to do if a mistake is made (*not* "I goofed! That's terrible! I'll NEVER get this right!"). Thus three skills are being learned: the task skills themselves, self-reinforcement skills, and "coping with failure" skills.

This same general strategy has been used to train creativity.

> "I want to think of something no one else will think of, something unique. Be free-wheeling, no hangups. I don't care what anyone thinks; just suspend judgement. I'm not sure what I'll come up with; it will be a surprise. The ideas can just flow through me. Okay, what is it I have to do? Think of ways to improve a toy monkey. Toy monkey. Let me close my eyes and relax. Just picture a monkey. I see a monkey; now let my mind wander; let one idea flow into another. I'll use analogies. Let me picture myself inside the monkey . . . Now let me do the task as if I were someone else." (Meichenbaum, 1975, as quoted in Meichenbaum, 1977, p. 62)

An extensive body of research by Meichenbaum and others (reviewed in Meichenbaum, 1977) supports the efficacy of this strategy. For example, Meyers, Mercatoris, and Sirota (1976) were able to reduce the incidence of psychotic speech from 65 percent to 8 percent in one psychotic client using a self-instructional training. It must be emphasized that it is effective only when the self-speech is practiced enough to become habitual. No magical results can be achieved with only a few rehearsals. If you go and try this after reading this chapter, you will not find that you can magically make your anxiety go away because it has not become a *habit* for you.

The need for such repetition of the model may give the impression that Meichenbaum's training requires almost robotlike behavior. However, this is not the case. Meichenbaum emphasizes flexibility during training. He says, "In using self-instructional procedures, it is important to insure that the child does not say the self-statements in a relatively mechanical, rote fashion without the accompanying meanings and inflection" (Meichenbaum, 1977, p. 89). In addition, the therapist attempts to vary the self-statements when he models them. The goal is to have a person learn not a rigid, mechanical set of self-statements, but a flexible set of coping strategies to guide behavior.

Meichenbaum (1977) suggests that in a general sense the process of observing and altering self-speech is an important component of all psychotherapy. The client must first engage in self-observation to monitor thoughts, feelings, and behaviors. This will often involve getting in touch with dysfunctional self-speech, which the therapy will then attempt to alter. Some therapies do this by *translating* the self-speech. For example, psychoanalytic therapy would translate "I'm afraid of authority" into "I'm unconsciously afraid of my father." Such translation leads to the generating of self-statements incompatible with the previous dysfunctional ones. Instead of saying, "I have to go see my boss. I'm afraid of him. I know I'll get anxious and make a fool out of myself!" the client might say, "Now remember, I'm not really afraid of my boss. I'm just transferring feelings onto him from my father. There's really nothing to be afraid of. Don't overreact. Try to see him as he really is." Meichenbaum does not assert that the internal dialogues resulting from different therapy approaches are all necessarily equally effective. The point is that they all may work in roughly the same way, that is, by inducing self-observation, translating internal self-speech, and generating self-speech that is more effective in coping.

Some therapies generate new cognitions to accompany behavior change. For instance, behavioral therapies encourage clients to engage in new behaviors, which may lead to new cognitions, which then feed back to support behavior change. Meichenbaum suggests that behavioral interventions will be effective to the extent that they generate new more effective self-speech or to the extent that more effective self-speech is learned along with them.

Recent Theoretical Advances

One of the most exciting things about the thought of cognitive behaviorists such as Meichenbaum and Michael Mahoney is that their theoretical flexibility may allow them to integrate insights from a variety of approaches. (We will consider some of Mahoney's ideas in Chapter 11.) While Meichenbaum's therapy focuses on the relatively specific acquisition and modification of self-statements, both Meichenbaum and Mahoney consider the modification of meaning as the most important therapeutic event. Meichenbaum and Gilmore's (1984) cognitive model takes into account insights of many approaches. For instance, they talk about the possibility that "core organizing principles" are learned in early childhood. These may be the basic principles with which people structure and organize meaning in their lives. They, along with other schemas, often operate at an implicit, or unconscious, level and influence how people appraise the situations they encounter. Fundamentally, each person lives in a world of his own creation, at least to some extent. Cognitive schemas and core organizing principles tend to resist "counterschematic input." Put another way, they tend to resist information that is incompatible with them. This, then, is a cognitive view of resistance in therapy. It occurs not so much because the person is afraid to know something about himself, but because cognitive systems and interpretation schemes, once in place, tend to screen out information that is incompatible with them.

In our discussion of Beck we have seen how any deeply entrenched belief system appears to be relatively impervious to information that doesn't fit with it. Meichenbaum and Gilmore (1984) mention the work of Thomas Kuhn, who sees exactly the same pattern in scientific belief. In *The Structure of Scientific Revolutions,* Kuhn (1970) argues that discrepant information is first dealt with in science by trying to assimilate it to existing theory. Scientists resist overthrowing a well-entrenched, well-worked out theory simply because there is some discrepant evidence. Only after repeated efforts to assimilate the information into the accepted theory fail may the theory itself come into question and eventually be replaced. Such a view can explain resistance in therapy also. Clients come in with a world view, but almost all therapies insist they learn a new view, be it psychoanalytic, existential, cognitive, or rational-emotive. The reason insight does not magically change behavior is that the underlying cognitive system, being well entrenched and well organized, resists change. For instance, in psychoanalysis a client may resist the information that "castration anxiety" is at the basis of his fear of success, not because that information is so painful, but because it is so incompatible with his current view of the world. It may take a long time before the client can modify his world view sufficiently to accept such an "insight."

Because behavior is organized by cognitive schemas and core organizing principles, common themes may show up in a variety of situations in the client's life. In a manner reminiscent of recent developments in brief psychoanalytic psychotherapy (see Chapter 4), Meichenbaum and Gilmore (1984) give the example of a client who repeatedly became overly upset at life's daily hassles. A common emotional theme was identified in the various situations in which this occurred. The client became upset when he perceived himself or others as being treated unfairly. This theme was related to childhood experiences of seeing his father, an immigrant, being humiliated. He had constructed an implicit, nonconscious rule that he would never allow others to treat him unfairly. This became, in Meichenbaum and Gilmore's language, a "readiness set" or "cognitive template" for appraising situations in his life. This template was held rigidly and was not open to disconfirmatory data. The general compatibility between this view and a psychoanalytic view (though they differ in their particulars) is obvious. At the same time the cognitive-behavioral view is more flexible in terms of treatment, for Meichenbaum and Gilmore argue that the "full armamentarium" of behavioral therapeutic techniques would be used to change this cognitive schema.

EVALUATION OF COGNITIVE APPROACHES

Effectiveness of Psychotherapy

In general the evidence for the effectiveness of cognitive approaches to therapy is quite positive. DiGiuseppe, Miller, and Trexler (1979) review a number of studies that generally support rational-emotive therapy as an effective approach. For instance, Molesky and Tosi (1976) compared RET to systematic desensitization in the treatment of adult stutterers and found it to be superior in reducing both stuttering and the accompanying anxiety. Smith, Glass, and Miller (1980) found an effect size of 0.68 for RET, which places it with psychodynamic, gestalt, and client-centered approaches in terms of effectiveness.

The evidence for Beck's cognitive therapy of depression has been encouraging. Some recent research shows it to be as effective as drug treatment for depression (Bower, 1986). A review of 10 studies, 6 with student populations and 4 with clinical populations, also supports the effectiveness of this approach (Beck, Rush, Shaw, & Emery, 1979).

Smith, Glass, and Miller (1980) report effect sizes of 1.13 and 2.38 for other cognitive-behavioral approaches. These are the largest effect sizes found, along with that for hypnotherapy.

Theoretical Evaluation

To what extent is it true that cognitions cause psychopathology? We will look at the approaches of Beck and Seligman to depression, because of the extensive amount of work done in that area. Seligman (Abramson, Seligman, & Teasdale, 1978) hypothesized that depression is a result of learned helplessness and, more particularly, of blaming oneself (making an internal attribution) for the negative aspects of one's life situation. He associated depression not just with internal attributions, but with attributions to stable aspects of the self, such as lack of ability. However, Hammen (1985) concludes that the research has failed to support the idea that depression is associated with either internal or stable attributions. What this means is that not all depressives blame themselves for their problems. Hammen does find some evidence that depressives make global attributions ("My life is rotten," "I am no good"), but the evidence does not indicate whether global attributions are a cause of depression or whether depression causes global attributions.

Hammen (1985) has similiar pessimistic conclusions about Beck's model of depression. For one thing, it is not clear that depressives distort reality and nondepressives don't. A number of studies in recent years have found that depressives and people with low self-esteem do indeed focus on negative evidence. However, several studies in which depressives are compared to nondepressives have found that it is nondepressives who distort, not depressives. Nondepressives have been found to overestimate their control of situations, while depressives more accurately perceive the amount of control they have. Nondepressives overestimate how positively they are seen by others, while depressives are more accurate.

Another difficulty is that the cognitive hypothesis of both Beck and Ellis that cognitions cause emotions may not be true. Recent evidence (Bower, 1981) suggests that mood can cause or influence cognition. Thus, if one is feeling depressed, depressive thoughts and memories become more available to consciousness. While these depressive thoughts and memories may feed back and reinforce the depressive mood, they do not originally cause the depressive mood. Hammen has suggested that while the two interact, it is more likely that depression causes depressive cognitions than vice versa. Depressive cognitions may function primarily to maintain a depression once it is started, rather than to cause it.

Finally, Hammen reviews other evidence that provides little support for the idea that depressive cognitions or depressive cognitive styles precede the development of depressive states. Instead, depressive cognitions seem to develop along with depressive states.

None of this means that cognition plays no role in the development of depression. However, neither the depressed distorted cognitions of Beck and Ellis nor the negative attributions of Seligman may be associated with the development of depression. Instead, Hammen mentions that depression may be associated with one's perception of whether or not one can cope with a negative situation (Bandura's self-efficacy, for example). In addition, depression may be associated with what are called one's "self-schemas" (Markus, 1980). Hammen mentions some evidence suggesting that people with dependent self-schemas (those who define themselves in terms of their dependency on others) are likely to become depressed when they suffer a negative interpersonal event, but not when they suffer a negative achievement event. Individuals with self-critical self-schemas (those who define themselves in terms of how successful they are) are likely to become depressed when they suffer a negative experience related to achievement.

One of the most important criticisms of cognitive approaches has been made by Sampson (1981). Basically Sampson argues that cognitive approaches try to adjust the individual to fit in with social reality. The cognitive approach assumes that a client's problems are, so to speak, all in his or her head. If an individual is depressed, it is because he or she is distorting or engaging in musturbatory thinking. The possibility that his or her situation is objectively depressing is not taken seriously. Thus, cognitive therapists have little to say about unjust or oppressive social conditions that may cause abnormal behavior. The client needs to adjust his or her cognitions, and then everything will be fine.

The dangers in this seem to be obvious. If all one's problems lie in how one conceives of events, then all that is necessary is for us to think differently about things. Recently, one of us heard an example of this kind of thinking. A fellow psychologist was discussing how he had worked at a job that he hated. He discussed how he realized that it was his perception of his job as boring and hateful that made him feel that way, and when he chose to see things differently he was able to find things in the job situation to make it interesting and exciting.

Can people, at their discretion, change their cognitions to suit their convenience? And should people change their cognitions in such a way that they will be happy? If I am a guard in a Nazi concentration camp, feeling guilty every time I put another person into the oven, can I change my cognitions in such a way that I not only no longer feel guilty, but find my work interesting and enjoyable? This is an extreme example, but the point should not be dismissed because of that. Perhaps depression, for instance, is a legitimate reaction to certain situations. Neither Beck nor Ellis appear to grant this as a possibility. A lower-class black woman, with few job skills, trying to support a family by herself, has reason to become depressed. The belief that she might never get out from under racism and poverty may not be distorting. The belief that she needs more money, not just that she would *prefer* to have more money, is not a distortion either. The point is that cognitive approaches, in assuming that everything is in how people construct reality, leave no basis for making judgments. If "there is nothing good nor bad but thinking makes it so," why shouldn't we only think what will make us happy? How can we decide?

We would particularly like to discuss this and related difficulties in regard to Ellis's rational-emotive therapy. We think Ellis's approach is quite important and insightful. However, he is somewhat imprecise in his definition of rationality. In a 1973 article, as we have seen, he defines irrational beliefs as ones that cannot be empirically verified. In a 1979 article, however, he says that "RET posits no absolutistic or invariant criteria of rationality" (Ellis, 1979, p. 40c). For most people the word rational carries the connotation of "objective correctness," while irrational carries the connotation of "error," "craziness," or "stupidity." Therefore, we feel uncomfortable with an approach that uses these two words, but isn't able to define what they mean.

Ellis's criterion that a belief is irrational if it cannot be empirically verified is particularly disturbing. We believe, along with Meehl (1981), that Ellis himself commits a logical error by assuming that "musts" and "shoulds" can be shown to be irrational because they cannot be supported by empirical evidence. The problem is one that dogged a philosophical movement called logical positivism in the early part of this century. Meehl essentially accuses Ellis of thinking like a positivist. This movement held that unless you could gather data to prove or disprove the truth or falsity of an idea, the idea was simply a meaningless one. The problem was that it was eventually realized that many of our human values could not be empirically verified by data. How can one prove that murder is bad, robbery is wrong, charity is good, and so on, using the scientific method? Many philosophers continue to believe that there is no empirical way to prove that values are right or wrong. Ironically enough, this fact ultimately backfired on the positivist movement itself. After all, the belief that "If something cannot be empirically verified, it is meaningless" is itself a value statement. And it itself cannot be empirically verified (how would one gather data to prove or disprove this statement?). Ellis seems to commit the same mistake when he labels as irrational any belief that cannot be empirically verified. We see no way Ellis could empirically verify his statement that such statements are irrational. The point is that value statements, at least in many crucial respects, are not matters of empirical validation.

As Meehl points out also, some of our most advanced disciplines, such as mathematics, rest on propositions that cannot be empirically verified. It is clear that Ellis's earlier criterion of irrationality as being something that cannot be empirically supported would lead to a characterization of mathematics as "irrational."

Ellis believes it is more rational to say, "I prefer to be a success" than it is to say "I must be a success." We agree that the former is certainly a statement that makes life more easily lived than the latter. But is it more "rational"? We would argue that this is not true. We believe that Ellis is proposing a value system. As a value system it is neither rational nor irrational (at least in the strict sense of these words). To say "I must be a success" is to make a value statement. To say "I prefer to be a success" is to make a different value statement. It may well be that in most instances values stated in terms of preference lead to a more flexible, adaptive way of living than values stated in terms of musts and shoulds. But they are not more rational. For instance, we can think of a number of must statements that do not strike us as so "irrational": "I can't stand what Hitler did to the Jews," "I can't stand racial prejudice," "I will not tolerate child abuse," "People must not enslave other people." Stating these as preferences does not capture the absolute, strong nature of the value: "I would have preferred it if Hitler hadn't murdered 6 million Jews," "I would prefer it if you didn't sexually abuse your child." Ellis (1981) has recently claimed, in answer to a similiar criticism by Meehl (1981), that he is not opposed to all shoulds, but just to those associated with neurotic beliefs. But this seems to beg the question. What is a neurotic belief? It seems to us that it is a belief that Ellis has previously defined in terms of its musturbatory quality.

The problem with believing that certain values can be said to be rational or irrational is that it can lead to labeling values you don't agree with as irrational. Ellis claims that in therapy he never tells a client that the client's values are irrational. He does point out the negative consequences of holding absolute beliefs. However, elsewhere Ellis labels certain values as irrational. For instance, while a variety of religions hold sexual celibacy to be one valid way of living, Ellis says, "But voluntary abstinence remains an unnecessary evil. Accept that misery and you seem off your rocker. You'd better see a psychologist, fast, than keep afflicting yourself with that kind of nonsense" (Ellis, 1976, p. 35). He says, "Here we are, in the Western world . . . allowing ourselves to love intensely only one member of the other sex at a time. . . . Pretty crazy, eh?" (Ellis, 1979b, p. 17).

Ellis, along with many others, attacks "shouldism." Humanistic therapies are also often interpreted as being "anti-should." Ellis says that shoulds are not found in nature. Nature just "is," therefore shoulds are irrational. The implication seems to be that the healthy person lives in accord with reality and does not demand anything of it. This is supported by the contention that the neurotic is someone who demands that the world be fair, when in fact it is neither fair nor unfair. But "should" we do away with shoulds? It seems to us that one of the qualities of being human is the ability to stand outside of one's life situation and imagine it otherwise. It is our suspicion that this is what leads to shoulds. The concept of should is a kind of imperative to correct "real life" to our image of what might or could be. Involved in our image of what might be are our concepts of justice and right and wrong. Thus, we can look at children and say they should not be subjected to sexual abuse. To do away entirely with shoulds would be to accept whatever is, but we can certainly wonder if that is desirable. A should, then, seems to us to be a comparison of a real state of affairs to a more desirable, imagined or possible state of affairs. It would seem to be our unique human capacity to be able to imagine better states of affairs and to work toward actualizing those images. To do away entirely with shoulds would be to do away with a human capacity that has many positive aspects and to accept things no matter how bad or unjust they may be.

CONTRIBUTIONS OF COGNITIVE THERAPY

In general, cognitive therapies have the following virtues. They have provided therapists with powerful, effective, and fast-acting methodologies. Their constructs are much more easily understood by people without professional training than the rather esoteric concepts of psychoanalysis and humanistic approaches. This means that the therapist is able to explain the therapeutic approach and goals to the client more thoroughly and quickly.

Cognitive therapies, like the behavioral approaches, have the virtue of being systematic, planned, and structured, but they are more flexible than the behavioral approaches. In this respect they may provide one of the most fruitful grounds for future integration of all therapies. Both Beck and Ellis are eclectic in their use of techniques in therapy. In addition, theorists such as Meichenbaum and Mahoney are providing theoretical models that may help integrate the contributions of many approaches.

Finally, despite our criticisms of some aspects of the cognitive model, it seems clear that absolute preconceptions are often involved in dysfunctional personal functioning. Cognitive therapists encourage the client to look for evidence and to try not to force his or her life into the narrow bounds of a rigid world view.

REFERENCES

Abramson, L. Y., Seligman, M. E. P., & Teasdale, J. D. (1978). Learned helplessness in humans: Critique and reformulation. *Journal of Abnormal Psychology, 87,* 49–74.

Adler, A. (1931). *What life should mean to you.* New York: Blue Ribbon Books.

Bandura, A. (1977a). *Social learning theory.* Englewood Cliffs, NJ: Prentice-Hall.

Bandura, A. (1977b). Self-efficacy: Toward a unifying theory of behavioral change. *Psychological Review, 84,* 191–215.

Bandura, A. (1986). *Social foundations of thought and action: A social cognitive theory.* Englewood Cliffs, NJ: Prentice-Hall.

Bandura, A., & Walters, R. H. (1959). *Adolescent aggression.* New York: Ronald Press.

Beck, A. T., Emery, G., & Greenberg, R. L. (1985). *Anxiety disorders and phobias: A cognitive perspective.* New York: Basic Books.

Beck, A. T., Rush, A. J., Shaw, B. F., & Emery, G. (1979). *Cognitive therapy of depression.* New York: Guilford.

Bower, B. (1986). Treating depression: Can we talk? *Science News, 129* (21), 321–336.

Bower, G. H. (1981). Emotional mood and memory. *American Psychologist, 36,* 129–148.

Brodt, S. E., & Zimbardo, P. G. (1981). Modifying shyness-related social behavior through symptom misattribution. *Journal of Personality and Social Psychology, 41,* 437–449.

Buss, A. H. (1980). *Self-consciousness and social anxiety.* San Francisco: Freeman.

DiGiuseppe, R. A., Miller, N. J., & Trexler, L. D. (1979). A review of rational-emotive psychotherapy outcome studies. In A. Ellis & J. M. Whiteley (Eds.), *Theoretical and empirical foundations of rational-emotive therapy.* Monterey, CA: Brooks/Cole.

Dulany, D. E. (1968). Awareness, rules, and propositional control: A confrontation with S-R behavior theory. In T. R. Dixon & D. L. Horton (Eds.), *Verbal behavior and general behavior theory.* Englewood Cliffs, NJ: Erlbaum.

Egan, G. (1984). Skilled helping: A problem-management framework for helping and helper training. In D. Larson (Ed.), *Teaching psychological skills: Models for giving psychology away.* Monterey, CA: Brooks/Cole.

Ellis, A. (1973). Rational-emotive therapy. In R. Corsini (Ed.), *Current Psychotherapies.* Itasca, IL: Peacock.

Ellis, A. (1976). *Sex and the liberated man.* Secaucus, NJ: Stuart.

Ellis, A. (1979a). Rational-emotive therapy as a new theory of personality and therapy. In A. Ellis & J. M. Whitely (Eds.), *Theoretical and empirical foundations of rational-emotive therapy.* Monterey, CA: Brooks/Cole.

Ellis, A. (1979b). Toward a new theory of personality. In A. Ellis & J. M. Whiteley (Eds.), *Theoretical and empirical foundations of rational-emotive therapy.* Monterey, CA: Brooks/Cole.

Ellis, A. (1979c). The theory of rational-emotive therapy. In A. Ellis & J. M. Whiteley (Eds.), *Theoretical and empirical foundations of rational-emotive therapy.* Monterey, CA: Brooks/Cole.

Ellis, A. (1979d). The practice of rational-emotive therapy. In A. Ellis & J. M. Whiteley (Eds.), *Theoretical and empirical foundations of rational-emotive therapy.* Monterey, CA: Brooks/Cole.

Ellis, A. (1981). Is RET ethically untenable or inconsistent? A reply to Paul E. Meehl. *Rational Living, 16,* 11, 38–42.

Ellis, A. (1984). Rational-emotive therapy. In R. Corsini (Ed.), *Current psychotherapies* (3rd ed.). Itasca, IL: Peacock.

Emery, G., Hollon, S. D., & Bedrosian, R. C. (Eds.). (1981). *New directions in cognitive therapy.* New York: Guilford.

Försterling, F. (1985). Attributional retraining: A review. *Psychological Bulletin, 98,* 495–512.

Goldstein, A. P., Gershaw, N. J., & Sprafkin, R. P. (1984). Structured learning therapy: Background, procedures, and evaluation. In D. Larson (Ed.), *Teaching psychological skills: Models for giving psychology away.* Monterey, CA: Brooks/Cole.

Hammen, C. L. (1985). Predicting depression: A cognitive-behavioral perspective. *Advances in cognitive-behavioral research and therapy* (Vol. 4). New York: Academic Press.

Hazleton, L. (1984). *The right to feel bad.* New York: Ballantine.

Jones, E. E., Kanouse, D. E., Kelley, H. H., Nisbett, R. E., Valins, S., & Weiner, B. (Eds.) (1972). *Attribution: Perceiving the causes of behavior.* Morristown, NJ: General Learning Press.

Kelly, G. A. (1955). *The psychology of personal constructs: A theory of personality* (2 vols.). New York: Norton.

Kuhn, T. S. (1970). *The structure of scientific revolutions* (2nd ed.). Chicago: University of Chicago Press.

Markus, H. (1980). The self in thought and memory. In D. M. Wegner & R. R. Vallacher (Eds.), *The self in social psychology.* New York: Oxford University Press.

Maultsby, M. C. (1975). *Help yourself to happiness.* New York: Institute for Rational-Emotive Therapy.

Meehl, P. E. (1981). Ethical criticism in value clarification: Correcting cognitive errors within the client's—not the therapist's framework. *Rational Living, 16,* 3–9.

Meichenbaum, D. (1974). *Cognitive behavior modification.* Morristown, NJ: General Learning Press.

Meichenbaum, D. (1975). Enhancing creativity by modifying what subjects say to themselves. *American Educational Research Journal, 12,* 129–145.

Meichenbaum, D. (1977). *Cognitive behavior modification: An integrative approach.* New York: Plenum Press.

Meichenbaum, D., & Gilmore, J. B. (1984). The nature of unconscious processes: A cognitive-behavioral perspective. In K. S. Bowers & D. Meichenbaum (Eds.), *The unconscious reconsidered.* New York: Wiley.

Meichenbaum, D., & Goodman, S. (1971). Training impulsive children to talk to themselves: A means of developing self-control. *Journal of Abnormal Psychology, 77,* 115–126.

Meyers, A., Mercatoris, M., & Sirota, A. (1976). Use of covert self-instruction for the elimination of psychotic speech. *Journal of Consulting and Clinical Psychology, 44,* 480–483.

Millon, T. (1981). *Disorders of personality.* New York: Wiley.

Mischel, W. (1968). *Personality and assessment.* New York: Wiley.

Mischel, W., & Peake, P. K. (1982). Beyond *déjà vu* in the search for cross-situational consistency. *Psychological Review, 89,* 730–755.

Molesky, R., & Tosi, D. (1976). Comparative psychotherapy: Rational-emotive psychotherapy versus systematic desensitization in the treatment of stuttering. *Journal of Consulting and Clinical Psychology, 44,* 309–311.

Moser, D. (1965, May 7). Screams, slaps, and love. *Life,* pp. 90a–101.

Nisbett, R. E., & Ross, L. (1980). *Human inference: Strategies and shortcomings of social judgment.* Englewood Cliffs, NJ: Prentice-Hall.

Paul, G. L. (1981). Social competence and the institutionalized mental patient. In J. D. Wine & M. D. Smye (Eds.), *Social competence.* New York: Guilford.

Sampson, E. E. (1981). Cognitive psychology as ideology. *American Psychologist, 36,* 730–743.

Smith, M. L., Glass, G. V., & Miller, T. I. (1980). *The benefits of psychotherapy.* Baltimore, MD: Johns Hopkins University Press.

Valins, S., & Nisbett, R. E. (1972). Attribution processes in the development and treatment of emotional disorders. In E. E. Jones, D. E. Kanouse, H. H. Kelley, R. E. Nisbett, S. Valins, & B. Weiner (Eds.), *Attribution: Perceiving the causes of behavior.* Morristown, NJ: General Learning Press.

Weiner, B. (1982). The emotional consequences of causal attributions. In M. S. Clark & S. T. Fiske (Eds.), *Affect and cognition: The Seventeenth Annual Carnegie Symposium on Cognition.* Hillsdale, NJ: Erlbaum.

Weiner, B., Frieze, I., Kukla, A., Reed, L., Rest, S., & Rosenbaum, R. M. (1972). Perceiving the causes of success and failure. In E. E. Jones, D. E. Kanouse, H. H. Kelley, R. E. Nisbett, S. Valins, & B. Weiner (Eds.), *Attribution: Perceiving the causes of behavior.* Morristown, NJ: General Learning Press.

Wicklund, R. A., & Frey, D. (1980). Self-awareness theory: When the self makes a difference. In D. M. Wegner & R. R. Vallacher (Eds.), *The self in social psychology.* New York: Oxford University Press.

Wine, J. D., & Smye, M. D. (1981). *Social competence.* New York: Guilford.

Zelen, S. L. (In press). Actor-observer perspective, balance and reversal: An attributional model of pathology. *Journal of social and clinical psychology.*

Chapter 9

Group and Relational Approaches to Treatment

Suppose a client brings the following symptoms to a therapist. For a while he has been unable to respond sexually to his spouse. He has begun to feel depressed, and he feels the depression is out of control. He is not sure what caused what. Did the sex problem cause his depression or did depression cause the sex problem? The therapist may think that these problems are better treated in some kind of group context than in individual therapy. She points out that what she means by a "group" is that he will not be treated alone, but along with at least one other person. She discusses four general alternative modes of "group" counseling with him.

First there is group therapy. The client might attend a group on a weekly basis. The other members of the group would be other individuals who also are trying to solve personal problems. They might have problems similar to the client's or they might all have different kinds of problems. It is most likely that the members would not know one another before therapy starts. Group therapy operates on the general assumption that individual problems are best treated through interaction with others.

The second possible treatment approach is sex therapy. Since sexual difficulties involve individual psychological problems, but also may reflect problems in a relationship, couples often participate in the treatment program and are seen together by the therapist.

A third possible treatment approach is marital (or couples) therapy. This approach assumes that individual problems in one form or another are tied up with marital (or relationship) problems. Perhaps problems between the client and his wife have created the client's sex and depression problems. On the other hand, perhaps sex problems have contributed to marital problems, which in turn have contributed to the depression. Or, perhaps the client's individual problems are causing marital problems. In any case, the client's problems will be treated in the context of his relationship with his partner.

A fourth possibility is family counseling. The client's whole family participates in the treatment program. The family approach assumes that an individual's problems are intricately related to his or her family in general. Individual and group therapy approaches assume that the individual's problem lies within the individual. In contrast, most family approaches assume that the individual who presents the problem is expressing a problem that involves the whole family system. The client who seeks counseling is sometimes called the "identified patient," implying that the whole family is really the one with the problem, though one individual manifests it.

We are going to take a look at each of these approaches. Although they are discussed together in a chapter stressing group or couple situations in therapy, the techniques and approaches can be used with individuals or in combination with other approaches. For example, many of the techniques used in sex therapy and family therapy can be used with individuals. A client in a group can also be in individual therapy. Sex therapy is frequently coupled with marital therapy.

GROUP THERAPY

Group therapy is "a psychosocial process wherein a specially trained professional . . . utilizes the emotional interaction in small, carefully constructed groups to effect amelioration of personality dysfunctions in individuals" (Scheidlinger, 1984). Almost every form of individual psychotherapy has its parallel group approach. The aim of the therapy is the same in both. Since both assume that the cause of psychopathology is to be found within the individual, treatment focuses on changing something within the individual's personality. The difference is that treatment is done in groups. However, even these groups focus intensively on interactions in the group to achieve these aims (Yalom, 1985).

Group psychotherapy as we know it today actually began in the psychoanalytic tradition. Group analysis was seen as a way to treat greater numbers of patients. Some consider only psychoanalytic groups to be real group psychotherapy, categorizing all other types as merely "therapeutic groups," that is, groups "oriented toward providing emotional support, developing self-esteem and social skills" (Scheidlinger, 1984).

Group analysis may be combined with individual analysis for some patients. Since the disturbance in the individual's internal functioning leads to difficulties relating to others, analysis in groups may foster more or faster insights. Psychoanalysts assume that groups develop a transference relationship with the therapist and a sibling transference with group members. The therapist interprets both transference relationships. Patients free associate to each other and report dreams, with both therapist and group members interpreting the dreams and the resistances. Group members reinforce the analyst's interpretations of individuals by agreeing with the interpretation and citing examples of it from the group's interactions.

Another early form of group therapy is psychodrama, developed by J. L. Moreno (1934). Clients act out scenes of conflict from their childhood or present life. Group members help each other by acting the necessary parts in an individual's scene. Thus, if our depressed client had had trouble with his mother, another member of the group plays his mother. Coaches or "alter egos" stand behind the actors and suggest what to say and do. The members may switch roles, or the alter egos may play out a scene. As in gestalt, the client may be asked to play the role of the person with whom he had the conflict. However, in contrast to gestalt, the client's role would then be taken by another group member. This way the client can gain insight into how he appears to others. Psychodrama stresses insight and catharsis through the acting process.

There are client-centered, behavioral, gestalt, and other group therapies. The group therapists use similar interventions as they do with individuals. Client-centered group therapists are nondirective and mirror the feelings of the group members. Behavioral group therapists conduct desensitization or assertion training in front of the group.

As among individual therapies, there is little consensus in the group therapy field as to theory and practice. However, group therapies share certain features. Most groups meet once a week, sometimes twice a week in the case of group psychoanalysis. Group sessions tend to be an hour and a half to two hours long. There are six to twelve group members, with eight to ten generally considered best. Some group therapists believe a carefully constructed group of equal numbers of men and women with different, but complementary problems is best, while others prefer groups composed of people all with the same problem or characteristics. A lot of talking goes on in most group therapies. There may be one or two leaders.

Recently, some group therapists have begun to consider how group dynamics affect the members (Yalom, 1985). They see the group as a system in its own right, rather than as merely the setting in which they work with individuals. Interactions among the members are used as a particularly potent source of learning, and therapists help the group understand how various forces and pressures in the group itself influence behavior. Yalom (1985), for instance, believes that all problems outside the group, with bosses, spouses, and family, can be dealt with inside the group by focusing on how the group member interacts with other group members. He lists a set of "curative factors" that seem to be common to all effective group therapies, despite apparent differences.

1. Imparting information. Group members give each other advice and other information.
2. Instilling hope. The fact that some group members have learned to deal with their problems gives hope to others.
3. Universality. Group members learn that they are not alone in thinking and feeling the way they do. They lose their "pluralistic ignorance"—the idea that they are the only person who feels insecure or whatever.
4. Altruism. Being helpful to other group members increases a person's feeling of confidence, competence, and self-worth.
5. Interpersonal learning. Group members have an opportunity to interact with others in deep, open, and honest ways.

6. Corrective recapitulation of the primary family. In the supportive, intimate, emotionally intense "family" of the group, members learn new ways of viewing and relating to their family members and to others.
7. Catharsis. Expressing emotion helps group members feel better. It also helps develop trust, closeness, and honest communication.
8. Group cohesiveness. Developing closeness to the group enhances feelings of self-worth through group acceptance.
9. Development of socializing techniques. Groups provide opportunities for learning social skills.
10. Imitative behavior. Individuals learn through behaviors modeled by other group members, including the leader.
11. Existential factors. Individuals recognize that life is sometimes unfair, they have to face the fact of death and of their ultimate aloneness, and they have to take responsibility for themselves.

Group therapy may be one of the waves of the future. Some psychologists believe it simply makes sense. Most psychological problems are interpersonal, not just intrapsychic, so group therapy may be a superior form of treatment. It is clearly more economical than individual therapy. Greater numbers of people can be treated in less time with fewer therapists. The present and future emphasis on cost-effectiveness by institutions that pay for psychological treatment (the government and private health insurance) almost certainly ensures the increasing use of group therapy. Furthermore, some research (Kaul & Bednar, 1986) supports its general effectiveness, though there is little specific data on what approaches help what clients in what ways. Data also generally favor the conclusion that group approaches are at least as effective as individual approaches.

TRANSACTIONAL ANALYSIS

Eric Berne (1964, 1966) developed transactional analysis, or TA, in the 1950s. As the name implies, this form of therapy has a strong interpersonal flavor. Although it is also used with individual clients, it is frequently done in group settings. TA analyzes the transactions between people rather than the inner conflicts of the individual. While social in emphasis, it takes from psychoanalysis the ideas of a tripartite division of the personality and the importance of early experience in forming the personality. The therapist interprets the client's way of interacting with other people in order to clarify these early experiences and the effect they have on current relationships. TA is also instructive; clients are taught how the personality is formed and how relationships work.

Berne named his three ego-states or parts of the personality the Child, the Adult, and the Parent. Each ego-state represents conscious and unconscious ways of feeling about and behaving toward others, and each has both positive and negative qualities that are learned in childhood. The Child is similar to the id, and it contains the childish and childlike impulses and ways of behaving. The Child is immature, dependent, demanding, and helpless (childish), but it is also playful, creative, and genuine (childlike). The Adult, similar to the ego, is rational, independent, and responsible, but also unfeeling and perhaps not much fun. The Parent, similar to the superego, can be nurturant, caring, and helpful, but also domineering, guilt inducing, critical, and controlling.

Each ego-state is appropriate to certain types of relationships. For example, it is appropriate for a parent to operate in the Parent ego-state toward a child. Such a way of relating usually works, and the relationship goes fairly smoothly. Problems enter when the ego-state is not appropriate to the relationship. If an individual operates in the Parent state toward his or her spouse, when the Adult is more appropriate, problems arise. The spouse may be induced to behave in the Child state, which may appear to make the relationship work. However, such a relationship will eventually create dissatisfaction, especially if the Child spouse tries to act like an Adult, or if the Parent spouse wants to give up the burdens of that role.

While people may play a fairly permanent role in relation to others, most often they move back and forth among ego-states as they communicate. They may begin a rational conversation as Adult, make a joke as Child, then start an argument as Parent. The other person may respond to the Adult conversation with a flippant Child disagreement, to the Child joke with a Parent criticism, and to the Parent argument with a reasonable Adult answer. Therapists interpret such social transactions for the client, pointing out the ego-state that is operating in each transaction and the effect it has on others. Therapist and client may also role play certain ego-states to analyze their effect on the transaction.

Like the psychoanalyst, the TA therapist interprets how the client behaves toward him or her but in terms of the client's transactions in the Child, Adult, and Parent ego-states. In addition to helping clients with relationships, TA tries to increase the client's acceptance of all the internal ego-states so the client can relate more appropriately and flexibly to others. A disowned (unconscious) Child will cause trouble, and the client is taught that it is acceptable and appropriate to be a Child sometimes.

Berne also discussed the concept of *games.* Games are orderly transactions with rules that conceal ulterior motives. They generally serve as a way of avoiding getting close to people. Berne gave descriptive names to the games he observed. For example, "Yes, But" involves playing helpless and eliciting advice from others, but always having a reason why that advice won't work or can't be done. "Yes, I should be firmer with my kids, but that always makes them angrier." In group therapy players of "Yes, But" can keep the attention of others for hours without ever having to risk being genuinely vulnerable. Berne (1966) described the rules of several such games and the ways therapists can intervene with game players.

The life script is another TA concept. Berne believed that based on early life experiences, people "unconsciously" write a script for themselves to play all their lives. Abused children see themselves as victims and compose a life script with themselves in the permanent role of victim. Because destructive relationships in which they are victimized fit their script, they may "unconsciously" seek them out. Berne believed that if clients became aware of their scripts and roles, they could rewrite them. He also believed that people's favorite fairy tale from childhood was an indication of their life script.

Transactional analysis has found wide application in education and business. It is also used in marriage, family, and group therapy. Its popularity may be due to its vivid, easy-to-understand terminology and its optimistic view of relationships. It gives people a handy frame of reference for dealing with each other. A wife can deal with a critical husband by saying, "That's your Parent talking," and it is likely to have a more beneficial effect than many other possible responses, such as anger, whining, or counterattack. TA's nonjudgmental attitude ("I'm O.K.—You're O.K," Harris, 1969) may be one of the factors that makes it popular.

SEX THERAPY

Sex therapy as it is practiced today is a relatively recent development. For a long time it was assumed that sexual problems were symptoms of deeper personality disturbances, and they were treated with in-depth psychotherapy. However, with the work of Masters and Johnson (1970) in the late 1950s and 1960s, treatment of the sexual dysfunctions themselves was developed. This is not to say that sex therapists ignore the possibilities that a person's sexual problems may reflect underlying personality difficulties and that they may be secondary to problems in a relationship. These may be taken into account. However, there are now treatment procedures specifically for the sexual dysfunctions themselves. In this respect sex therapy more resembles a behavioral approach to therapy than a psychoanalytic or humanistic approach.

In most cases treated with sex therapy, one member of a couple has an identifiable sexual dysfunction, such as erectile dysfunction, premature ejaculation, orgasmic dysfunction, or vaginismus (painful involuntary muscle spasms when intercourse is attempted). Though we are including sex therapy in a chapter that deals with therapy with more than one individual, an individual may seek sex therapy even though he or she is not a member of a couple.

After education about normal sexual functioning, a first step in sex therapy with couples is to take the burden of blame from the identified patient and to define the sexual dysfunction as a couple problem. A second step is to forbid sexual intercourse until the therapist gives permission, an order that some theorists see as a "paradoxical intervention," which we shall discuss later in this chapter. Masters and Johnson claim this restriction reduces "performance pressure." According to their theory, sexually dysfunctional people are so anxious about their performance and their possible failure that the anxiety interferes with their ability to perform or enjoy sex. Such individuals also engage in "spectatoring" (watching and judging their own sexual performance) so they lose touch with their "sensate focus" (what actually feels good sexually). Many of the exercises in sex therapy are supposed to teach people to regain their sensate focus.

The assigned exercises and homework in sex therapy are similar to a gradual desensitization procedure. Ethical sex therapists do not touch their clients sexually or observe their clients' sexual behavior. Exercises are always done in private with the partner, or possibly with a "sexual surrogate." The first exercises may be to touch, hug, and kiss with their clothes on. The next day (in Masters and Johnson's program) or the next week (in weekly, outpatient sex therapy) the couple reviews what happened with the therapist. If the exercise went well and did not elicit much anxiety, the next assignment may be touching and fondling with clothes above the waist removed. Part of the touching may involve a sensate focus exercise in which partners take turns massaging each other while the person being massaged directs the massager on what to do. The receiver of the massage also says what feels good where. This is educational for both partners and also increases communication. The next assignment may be touching with all clothes off. Subsequent exercises are specific to the type of dysfunction being treated. While erotic activities are encouraged during sex therapy, sexual intercourse is specifically prohibited until the therapist gives permission. If it is successful, the therapy has worked. However, if the couple is not successful at intercourse, the therapist accepts responsibility for failure, and they go back to earlier exercises.

If the problem is erectile dysfunction and it has been determined that the problem is largely or exclusively psychological, the exercises are designed to help the man obtain and sustain an erection, and intercourse is gradually introduced. If the problem is premature ejaculation, a stop-start technique may be used. The couple start intercourse, and when the man feels he may ejaculate, he stops until he feels he has regained control. Or the squeeze technique, in which the penis is squeezed, may be used. If the problem is psychological orgasmic dysfunction in the woman, she is taught to have orgasms through manual stimulation, and then intercourse is gradually introduced. If the problem is vaginismus, she is induced to have orgasms with nothing in the vagina. Then a small object like a finger is inserted, working gradually up to orgasm with a penis in the vagina.

Though sex therapy is most frequently done with couples, there are methods for working with individuals alone. Zilbergeld (1978) presents methods that can be used by a male to cope with erectile dysfunction or premature ejaculation. One of Zilbergeld's most important contributions is helping the client be aware of his "conditions for good sex" and of myths about male sexuality (for instance, "Sex equals intercourse," "Sex requires an erection," "A man always wants and is ready to have sex"). Similarly, Barbach (1975) presents exercises women can do by themselves to become orgasmic. She also discusses the many conflicting and contradictory messages about sex that a woman in our culture receives. For example, she is taught to turn off sexual feelings all through adolescence, and then, when she is married, she is suddenly expected to "emerge as a turned on passionate woman" (p. 39).

Sex therapy has been criticized for being so limited in focus that it can be effective only for couples whose problem is solely sexual and who have a good relationship otherwise. However, most sex therapists are not so naive as to concentrate exclusively on the sexual dysfunction without making some attempt to assess its relation to other individual or relationship problems and to include those problems in the therapy if necessary.

Sex therapy has also been criticized by feminists on the grounds that it is used to enforce cultural norms of the right way to have sex, and these cultural norms are usually masculine. For example, the goal of women's attaining orgasm through intercourse may meet men's expectations and desires, but it may not be practical for women. Some research indicates that women attain orgasm more easily through oral or manual stimulation than through intercourse, and, indeed, it may be difficult for many women to attain orgasm through intercourse, even with sex therapy.

MARITAL COUNSELING AND THERAPY

A marital counselor's initial assumption is that problems of the individuals in the couple are caused by the malfunctioning of the couple as a unit, rather than solely by emotions or personality structures within either or both individuals. A couples therapist makes a point of defining clients' difficulties as a couple dysfunction, even if the couple enters therapy because of the disorder of one partner.

In other words, most marital counselors assume that psychological problems lie between individuals, rather than solely *within* one or the other partner, though the couple's problems may manifest in the individual symptoms of one of the partners. Many theorists therefore view marital therapy as a subset of family therapy, and many of the ideas discussed in this section are similar to those of the family therapists discussed below.

Most marriage therapists focus on the communication between the spouses. It is assumed that part of the couple's dysfunction is their inability to communicate clearly what they think, feel, and want to each other. There are several reasons: Their parents may not have taught them how to communicate, their childhood experiences may have taught them to ignore or repress certain dangerous feelings or issues, they may fear the spouse's reaction if they reveal their real feelings. Because they don't communicate what they want, they don't get what they want, and the resultant hurt and anger contribute further to their problems. As long as important feelings and beliefs are kept hidden or communicated indirectly, the couple will not be able to solve their conflicts and misunderstandings.

Here is a typical example. The wife wants the husband to take out the trash. In her childhood family the man took out the trash, and it was a part of how he showed he cared for his wife. When her husband fails to take out the trash, she feels hurt and rejected. Perhaps she is unaware of these feelings, or perhaps she is afraid or ashamed to reveal them, but she does get hurt and then angry when he does not take out the trash.

In the husband's childhood family perhaps the woman took out the trash or perhaps there was a constant battle over the trash and the loser had to take it out. When his wife asks him to take it out, he feels pressured and threatened, and he experiences the request as an unreasonable demand, demeaning of his role as head of the family. However, he is also unaware or afraid or ashamed of these feelings, and he just feels angry.

How does this situation affect their communication? She, feeling hurt and let down, says, "Why didn't you take out the trash?" He, feeling nagged by this unanswerable question, says, "I didn't see it." She, feeling frustrated and further enraged at this evasion of her real message, shouts, "Are you blind? It's right by the back door where you left it all week!" He, feeling attacked, screams, "Are you crippled? Take it out yourself!" It goes on. She yells, "You never help, you worthless bum," and he returns, "Shut up, you bitch," or worse, "There's no need to get so irrational." You can see they won't be able to solve the conflict this way.

Couples therapy involves techniques to help clarify communication. They focus on the precise nature of the problem and its accompanying experience. In therapy the wife may cry, "He never contributes. He never helps." The therapist tries to narrow this blanket condemnation down to a specific example of nonhelping. Perhaps the wife remembers that he didn't take out the trash the night before. The therapist tries to elicit her version of what happened and how she experienced it: What was she thinking and feeling at each point? Her underlying feelings of hurt and rejection may be brought out. The therapist elicits the husband's version and his experience, with his underlying feelings of hurt and criticism. The spouses are usually surprised to learn what the other one really thought and was trying, however indirectly, to say. The therapist's next task may be to teach or elicit alternative ways of communicating about this issue.

Much of marital therapy involves teaching the couple social skills. The therapist tries to model clear, direct, nonjudgmental, effective communication when talking to the couple and also employs specific techniques to teach communication skills. One such technique is sometimes called *mirroring.* The husband is asked to tell his version of a conflict, and the wife is directed to listen carefully. She is then asked to say as precisely as possible what she heard her spouse say. He is asked if she got what he was trying to say and, if not, to say it again. It is surprising how frequently spouses cannot do this task. Even when they are given the specific assignment of listening carefully so they can repeat the message, they get caught up in thinking of a defense to what the spouse is saying or hear an attack when none is intended or simply are unable to hear anything other than their own projections or expectations. In other cases, the communicating spouses do not say clearly what they want to. If they can be made aware of their spouses' misunderstanding, they may be able to restate or explain what they want and gradually learn to communicate more directly and clearly.

When a couple's communication skills are improved by these methods, their difficulties often seem to disappear, or they are able to solve their problems on their own with their new ways of communicating. Sometimes the therapy must continue to help the couple. Even with clear and honest communication, some conflicts are difficult to resolve. There may be profound differences in sexual desire or values about religion or child rearing. Compromises can be negotiated or tolerance for each other's differences taught.

Finally, some couples decide to divorce when the nature of their conflict is clarified. Whether marital therapists should always work to save a marriage or accept divorce as a reasonable alternative solution is a controversy we will avoid. Also, it should be unnecessary to note that the principles of marital therapy apply to all intimate couples, married or not, heterosexual or not.

Behavioral Marital Therapy

One particular form of couples counseling is behavioral marital therapy (Jacobson & Margolin, 1979). As with behavioral interventions in general, behavioral marital counseling has two aims: to reduce or eliminate problem behaviors and to increase positive and effective behaviors.

Usually the goal of increasing positive behaviors is considered first. Partners are asked to list all the positive behaviors they would like the other person to perform. They are told to exclude initially positive behaviors they would like the other to perform, but which are a source of conflict. Then the partners work on increasing the frequency of these behaviors. For instance, they may have "caring days": one spouse tries to maximize the positive experience of the other, and spouses are encouraged to surprise one another with positive experiences.

A key part of this is training and encouraging partners to show their appreciation for the positive behaviors of the other. In addition, the partners monitor the rates of pleasing events and keep records of daily levels of satisfaction.

The second part of counseling is aimed at reducing problems. This is attacked by teaching the partners effective problem solving. Problem solving breaks down into two phases: problem definition and problem resolution. To define their problems clients are taught to state their complaints in brief, specific, nonblaming ways. They are also taught to state their feelings, to admit their own role in the problem, and to paraphrase the other person's viewpoint, even if it is not consistent with their own. An example of an effective problem definition, which includes a statement of feelings, is "When you let a week go by without initiating sex, I feel rejected." (Jacobson & Margolin, 1979, p. 230).

To resolve problems clients are encouraged first to brainstorm, to come up with as many possible solutions as they can. They are to suspend judgment of the various options until as many have been generated as possible. Then they consider and evaluate each option. Finally, they are taught to negotiate and compromise until a solution is arrived at. This solution is recorded in writing.

Sometimes a *contract* is included. A contract may be set up with specific reinforcers or consequences associated with the performance or nonperformance of the behaviors involved. Thus if one partner wants more sex and the other wants more affection, the provision of these may be made contingent on the performance of other behaviors that each desires in the other person, such as taking out the trash or not nagging so much. However, there is some controversy over the use of contracts and reward contingencies with marital problems (Christensen, 1983), and they are not used in all cases.

A general goal of the behavioral approach is to teach these problem-solving skills so that the couple can use them on their own. Couples are encouraged to set aside certain specified times to engage in problem solving and to refrain from attempting problem solving when they are in the midst of an emotional conflict itself.

FAMILY COUNSELING AND THERAPY

A logical extension of couples counseling is to include the whole family. The client may be seen not only with his spouse, but also with his children. Some family approaches go so far as to include the "families of origin," that is, the spouses' parents and siblings.

Family approaches to therapy assume that any individual's problem is a function of something within the family itself. Let us return to the example of the husband who comes to therapy complaining of depression. He may believe that there are no problems with his family; he may *believe* that the problem is strictly his. Yet family systems approaches assume that the identified patient's complaint is a symptom of a disorder in the whole family structure.

The husband's depression results from an interaction of forces in the family, serves some function in the family, or is maintained by the family system. For instance, the husband's depression may result from a feeling of not being needed in the family. Perhaps the children are growing up successfully. The wife is working and self-sufficient. The husband may never pinpoint it, but he may begin to feel unneeded and therefore depressed. Perhaps not feeling needed robs him of a feeling of manliness and potency and results also in his sexual difficulties, which then further contribute to his depression.

Another possibility is that his depression actively serves some function in the family. Perhaps, for instance, it is in some way keeping the family together. Perhaps a child is about to leave home, and if the child leaves there would be less reason for the wife to stay. The child may decide to stay at home to help tend the depressed father. The presence of the child, along with the husband's depression, may keep the mother in attendance.

Or the depression may have originally occurred because of the husband's individual problems (perhaps he is experiencing a midlife crisis), but the family develops an equilibrium around his depression in such a way as to maintain it. Perhaps the wife begins to pay more attention to him and inadvertently reinforces his depression.

There are many different approaches to family therapy. There are psychoanalytic, client-centered, gestalt, transactional analytic, and behavioral versions of family therapy. Because they are largely extensions of the ideas and principles used in individual contexts, we will not cover these approaches. Instead we will look at approaches that make other contributions to the understanding and treatment of behavioral difficulties.

Common to all these approaches is a view of the family as a system. We have already discussed the idea of a system in the chapter on gestalt psychotherapy. Basically, a system is a pattern of interrelationships among elements, such that each element of the system both determines and is determined by the other elements in the system. More specifically, the behavior of any part of a system reflects the overall organization of the system and feeds back into the system itself. Furthermore, systems evolve toward a state of equilibrium, or "homeostatic balance."

An example is an ecological system. In any given region of the earth a delicate balance evolves that includes the atmosphere and weather conditions, the soil, geography and geology, and the plant and animal life. The system becomes balanced so that predators survive by eating the animals that can live on the vegetation that can grow in the region. The number of predators is controlled by the number of vegetation-eating animals present. They in turn are controlled both by the amount of vegetation present and by the predators. Each life form plays a part in the operation of the system. For instance, in a system with coyotes and rabbits, the coyotes eat the rabbits, which keeps the rabbit population from overexpanding. The number of rabbits available for eating determines the size of the coyote population. Both the number of coyotes and the amount of vegetation determines the size of the rabbit population. Any disturbance may destroy the balance of the system. For example, if large numbers of coyotes are killed, the numbers of rabbits may increase to the extent that they strip the terrain of vegetation, and then the rabbit population will plummet because its food supply has disappeared.

We shall now consider some of the differing family systems views. In this section we will examine the work of Virginia Satir, Salvador Minuchen, and Murray Bowen. In the next section we will look at the strategic approaches of Milton Erickson, Jay Haley and Cloé Madanes, Paul Watzlawick, and Steven de Shazer.

Virginia Satir and Dysfunctional Communication

Satir (1967) assumes that dysfunctional communication is a large part of families' problems. Dysfunctional communication results from the way the marital partners were raised as children and from their unrealistic, unspoken expectations of what the spouse will do for them.

Satir believes that every individual grows up with unspoken assumptions and rules learned from parents about the way families should work and how family life should run. In disturbed families the spouses grew up with low self-esteem and chose their marital partners in the hope that the partner would supply the esteem they lack. Of course, a partner cannot do that, so these insecure people are doomed to disappointment. Furthermore, they tend to view differences with a partner as threats, as evidence that the other does not love them. However, differences are inevitable, because they come from different families with different unspoken rules. Since the rules are unspoken, disagreements about them are difficult to resolve. All of this leads to severely disturbed communication and disturbed family functioning.

Let us look at a typical case. The wife comes from a large family in which the men waited on the women. Since it was a large family, one had to be assertive and expressive to gain attention. The husband is an only child from a family in which the women waited on the men, and the men were quiet and unexpressive. When the couple first met, they were immediately attracted to one another. He, being quiet and unassertive, saw her as a fascinating, lively mysterious creature who will love him and take care of him. She saw him as a strong, stable person who will love her and take care of her (wait on her). As the inevitable disappointment sets in, she comes to see him as a boring stick-in-the-mud, and he comes to see her as irrational, bossy, and overemotional. (It is not uncommon that the quality in a spouse that most aggravates a partner is the very quality that first attracted the partner.)

In addition to the disappointment of unrealistic expectations, this couple's low self-esteem makes them perceive differences between them as threatening to their relationship. When the husband does not talk to her or wait on her, the wife takes it as evidence that he does not love her. When she talks all the time and fails to wait on him, the husband concludes the same thing. Both their lack of confidence and the fact that they may not even be aware of their unspoken rules about family life prohibit them from discussing these rules. They are in pain, but they cannot talk about that either. Their younger child develops symptoms: poor grades and noncompliance. The child's problems keep the family from falling apart and give the parents an issue they can agree to focus on. It is the child's symptoms that bring the family into therapy.

In weekly family therapy sessions Satir tries to make the couple aware of all these processes. She takes a family history from each spouse and points out how differently they were raised. She tries to elicit their unspoken assumptions and their feelings about behavior that differs from these assumptions. She helps them communicate more clearly and directly by reflecting their feelings and raising their intended meanings. She may ask the clients to mirror one another's statements. Satir also interprets the family's behavior as it occurs in front of her. Frequently, when the parents start to talk about a meaningful issue, the child with problems engages in distracting or symptomatic behavior. She may break things, start talking loudly about something else, twitch and squirm hyperactively, or throw a temper tantrum. Satir interprets this behavior as the child's attempt to protect the parents from having to deal with the pain of their low self-esteem and their marital disappointments. The role of the child's symptoms in the family is thus made clear to all.

Satir describes five roles or basic modes of communication in families: placating, blaming, superreasonable, irrelevant, and congruent. In this disturbed family the father is always superreasonable, never showing his true feelings; the mother placates him all the time, never showing her true feelings; the older child blames everything on everyone else; and the symptomatic child responds with irrelevant annoying habits and silly talk. Only congruent communication—messages that reflect a person's genuine feelings and intentions—can help solve family conflict. Satir tries to model and teach congruent communication.

Once the family has gained insight into the role the child's symptomatic behavior is playing in the family, the behavior is useless to protect the parents or to maintain family homeostasis, and it will be given up. In this respect, Satir is one family therapist who values the acquisition of insight. In addition, as the parents learn to communicate more effectively, their sense of competence and feelings of esteem improve. They are better able to tolerate each other's differences and to explore the meaning of those differences. The child learns a new role in the family, and they all learn communications and problem-solving skills. The entire family system functions better.

One significant difference between Satir's approach and other family approaches that emphasize communication is that Satir places a greater emphasis on feelings. Communication is not merely the communication of ideas and perspectives, but of feelings. Therefore, in addition to gaining access to unspoken family rules and assumptions, her approach focuses on becoming more aware of feelings, which are the intended meanings of most messages.

Minuchin and the Structural Approach

Salvador Minuchin (1974) is one of the founders of the family systems view of personal problems. His therapy, called *structural family therapy,* is based on a view of the family as a hierarchically organized system. That means that the system has various levels and subsystems. For instance, there is the spousal subsystem (husband and wife relating to one another), the parental subsystem (husband and wife relating to one another in terms of the children and relating to the children), and a sibling subsystem. There may be other subsystems, such as ones that include grandparents or in-laws or subsystems organized by sex (female and male subsystems). These subsystems overlap, interact, and separate as the family goes about its daily functioning.

What goes wrong in disturbed families has to do with the characteristics of the subsystems. Difficulties can develop around *boundary* problems. In a well-organized family there are clear, but not rigid, boundaries between various subsystems. For instance, there is a clear distinction between the parental and the child subsystems. In a disturbed family that distinction may be blurred, as in a family in which there is an alliance of a mother and child against a father, or in totally child-focused families, in which the spouses have no relationship, or in immature families, in which no one takes the role of parents or where children have too much authority. In a well-organized family the sibling subsystem is organized in a hierarchical manner appropriate to age, that is, children are given responsibilities and privileges commensurate with age. In a poorly organized family, older children may be treated like younger children, or younger children may be given responsibilities and privileges more appropriate to older children. In the well-organized system distinctions are not too rigidly drawn. For instance, the parental subsystem is not so rigid that parents *always* act like parents and always put themselves in the role of authority.

There are two major types of dysfunctional family systems. In the *disengaged family* the subsystem boundaries are excessively rigid, and family members are disconnected from one another. This type of family is conducive to the development of antisocial personality in children. In the *enmeshed family* the boundaries are weak or unstable, and individuality is difficult to maintain. A disorder typical of this type of family is anorexia, which Minuchin sees as an attempt to assert autonomy and gain control over the self.

Minuchin's goal is to help families restructure their subsystems and to establish appropriate boundaries. He uses a variety of methods and takes an active and directive part in the therapeutic process. Some compare him to a freedom fighter trying to liberate the family from its destructive rules and roles. He learns the family's language and rules and joins the family system for a while. Once the therapist joins the family, it is a different system already. Minuchin may take sides in family arguments if he perceives that a family member has no appropriate allies. Sometimes he speaks for family members, putting their unspoken thoughts into words. He tries to provoke weak couples into strengthening their spousal subsystem. He may define a child as inappropriately parental and by doing so challenge the parents to ally with each other and to exert their authority. Minuchin directs family members to behave certain ways in homework assignments. He might put a weak father in charge of a symptomatic son for a week and tell the overcontrolling mother not to interfere. He sometimes exaggerates family patterns, for instance, by yelling in a family that yells too much.

One interesting aspect of Minuchin's method is his use of the family's seating arrangement in therapy sessions. He arranges the room so that family members have a choice of where to sit as they enter the room for the first session. How they sit is often a gauge of how the family interacts. Minuchin will actively rearrange seating to change the interaction. For instance, if overprotective mother and dysfunctional son sit together and father sits off to the side, son and father may be made to sit next to one another.

Murray Bowen and Personal Differentiation

For Murray Bowen (1978), who was one of the first to designate his approach a family systems approach, the key issue in psychopathology is the *degree of personal differentiation* of each person from his or her family of origin. Therefore, even though Bowen is a systems theorist, his approach has also been heavily influenced by psychoanalysis. For Bowen differentiation consists of the ability to remain emotionally controlled while in the context of one's family and the ability to have a clear sense of one's own values, beliefs, and reactions separate from others. A truly differentiated person is able to think objectively about a situation and not be overwhelmed by emotion and to assert and own his or her values and beliefs without attacking or dismissing the values and beliefs of others.

For most people there are areas in their relationships to their families where they remain undifferentiated. People remain *fused,* or emotionally entangled, with their families in various ways. The degree of lack of differentiation is an index of the emotional disturbance of an individual. Bowen believes in a *multigenerational transmission process* for lack of differentiation. Lack of differentiation in the parents is transmitted to the children. An anxious mother, for instance, who is not sufficiently differentiated herself, will project her anxiety onto a child. Bowen argues that this process may lead to progressively lower levels of differentiation generation by generation, ultimately resulting in the production of a psychotic child.

Lack of differentiation leads either to an inability to keep oneself separate from another or to a pathological, defensive separateness. Unresolved attachments to parents may be "resolved" by cutting off emotions. Thus someone may yearn for emotional closeness, but defend against it. Either an inability to maintain separateness or a defensive separateness will lead to an unstable situation with a spouse. You will either be demanding things you feel you are not getting from your spouse or you will feel demands from your spouse.

In order to deal with the tension and instability, couples usually form a *triangle* with a third person. This means that a third person is drawn into the emotional system in order to provide a kind of stability. For instance, a wife who cannot feel close to her husband may devote herself to her child and distance herself from her husband. In states of relative calm most triangles include two members who are relatively close to one another and one member who is an outsider, as in our example of the wife and child. Triangulation can occur because of an intergenerational instability. For instance, a son who has been overly close to his mother may marry in order to create some distance between himself and her. In states of high tension more and more people may be included in triangles. Other siblings, relatives, and even neighbors may be included. Thus a husband and wife who have been unable to deal with their tension by including one child may include more children. There may be a husband-wife-son triangle and a husband-wife-daughter triangle and perhaps even a wife-daughter-son triangle. One example of including members outside the family in a triangle is the affair.

Even though Bowen believes that fusion and lack of differentiation are passed down through generations and that ultimately an individual's problems have to do with lack of differentiation from the family of origin, Bowen does not necessarily work with the whole family. He believes the therapist can work with individual members of the family, but he prefers to work with the marital subsystem.

One technique Bowen uses is constructing a *genogram* of the family. This is a diagram that shows the relationships of the husband and wife to their families of origin. Relationships are diagramed in terms of fusion and emotional cutoff. Bowen may show the genogram to the family as a way of helping them gain insight into their difficulties.

The primary goal of Bowen's family therapy is to develop the autonomy of each family member. Part of this process is helping the spouses to become aware how their relationships to their families of origin affect their relationships to each other and to their children. Thus, Bowen, like Satir, values insight as a growth-producing mechanism. Bowen attempts to provide an atmosphere where such learning can occur, modeling differentiation himself. For instance, husband and wife will attempt to triangle Bowen into their problems by trying to get him to take sides in an argument. Bowen attempts to avoid this by making sure that any statements he makes are identified as his own and by not being judgmental.

Bowen also tries to model and teach *observation* of the family system. In other words, he attempts to model separating objective observation of what is going on from overly subjective emotional reactions. His belief is that emotional reactions of anger, blame, sadness, anxiety, and so forth result from lack of differentiation. Therefore, by keeping the emotional climate of therapy toned down and by encouraging observation, he is facilitating differentiation. This approach differs from Satir's emphasis on feelings.

Bowen provides an atmosphere that facilitates differentiation also by having each spouse talk to him rather than to each other. As the husband, for instance, talks to Bowen, the wife listens. Afterwards, Bowen may ask the wife for her reactions to what she heard. Bowen might then ask the husband for his reactions. This mechanism facilitates differentiation because it keeps the spouses from falling into old undifferentiated patterns of argument, blame, criticism, and so forth, in which emotions run high. It puts one spouse in the role of observer as the other talks. Again, Bowen differs from Satir who encourages spouses to talk to each other.

STRATEGIC APPROACHES

In the early 1960s the Mental Research Institute in Palo Alto, California, was a hotbed of innovation. Some of the biggest names in family therapy were there—Virginia Satir, Don Jackson, Jay Haley, and Paul Watzlawik. Virginia Satir developed her communication approach. Don Jackson also emphasized communication (we shall not discuss his work). Jay Haley and Paul Watzlawik went on to formulate their own, fundamentally different approaches to family therapy.

Haley and Watzlawik are two of the foremost names in what is generally called the strategic approach, but there are others. We will also mention the work of de Shazer. Another influential form of strategic therapy was developed in Milan, Italy (Selvini Palazzoli, Cecchin, Prata, & Boscola, 1978). What is common to all of these approaches is denoted by the term *strategic.* The goal of these approaches is to design a strategy to change the problem behavior in either a family or an individual client. The goal of therapy is to remedy the problem behavior, not to gain insight, get in touch with feelings, assume responsibility, or challenge dysfunctional cognitions. Watzlawick (1978) argues that cognitive insight is not only therapeutically useless, but may be counterproductive. Thus, each strategic intervention is individually tailored to a particular client's or family's problem. The strategic therapists are content to remove the problem behavior or symptom, without worrying about the dynamics supposedly underlying them. In this regard these approaches are similar to behavior therapy.

Another important commonality is that the approaches all derive much of their therapeutic strategy from the work of Milton Erickson. Although some therapists think that Erickson's influence equals Freud's (Dowd & Milne, 1986), he is not well known among nonprofessionals. Therefore, before we discuss strategic approaches to family therapy, we will introduce Erickson's work.

Milton Erickson

We shall use a story to introduce Milton Erickson's work (Feldman, 1985). A woman spent some time studying with him and then returned to her home city. She subsequently wrote Erickson complaining about her lack of results in trying to work the way he did. In the same letter she incidentally asked for a recipe for cinnamon pie, which she had had at his home. In his reply Erickson did not address her concerns about her work. Instead, he merely gave her the recipe for cinnamon pie, with the comment, "Of course, every good cook must adjust the seasoning to suit their own particular taste" (Dammann, cited in Zeig, 1980, p. 200).

This story illustrates the indirect and subtle way that Erickson worked. The woman was not directly told, "You need to adapt what you learned from me to your personal style," but the message was implied. Erickson was one of the most colorful therapists. The things he did were often startling, uncommon, and delightful. Perhaps what is most impressive about his work is that he was a pioneer. Now, several years after his death (he died in 1980), he is becoming a highly influential figure. Yet while he was alive, he worked in relative obscurity, engaging in a kind of therapy that fit no models popular at the time, for it was not Freudian, client centered, or behavioral.

Erickson did not believe in the importance of insight or awareness for inducing personality change. Instead, he believed that the unconscious was a source of wisdom, and his therapy was designed to draw on that. In addition, Erickson believed that major change could be induced by first inducing smaller changes. Like a snowball rolling downhill, a small change could change the overall system of the personality or the family for the better.

Erickson is primarily known as a hypnotist, and that was one of his major tools. He believed that all therapy worked by suggestion. However, he devised many techniques to utilize the power of suggestion without the use of hypnosis. Reframing and the use of paradox are two of the techniques that have been adopted by modern strategic therapists.

Reframing is reinterpreting a behavior that a client sees as pathological in a positive way. For instance, de Shazer (1985) relates the case of a young woman whose problem was that she was unable to speak up around her fiance. Instead of treating this as a problem, the therapist congratulated her on having learned the most important lesson in communication—how to listen. *Her* perception of her silence as pathological was reframed as something positive. In addition, she was told that she now had to learn another skill. She had to pay attention to her fiance and try to detect when he was ready to listen.

Paradox or *paradoxical intervention* is prescribing the symptom, in one form or another. The therapist instructs the client to perform the symptom behavior, although not neccessarily exactly as it occurs spontaneously. The paradox is, of course, that the therapist asks the client to perform the behavior the client is trying to get rid of. In one of Erickson's most well-known cases, a husband and wife who both wet the bed were instructed to deliberately wet the bed each night before they went to bed. Watzlawick (1985b) relates the case of a man who was constantly arguing with his wife. He was instructed to go out on the weekend and pick arguments with others. After trying to follow this instruction, he stopped arguing with his wife.

While reframing and paradox are perhaps the best known Ericksonian interventions, there are others. One thing Erickson did was to give the client an apparent choice, but actually the message left no choice. In addition, the message carried an indirect suggestion that the client would stop the symptom. For instance, Erickson might say,

"When are you going to stop the arguing—on Wednesday or on Thursday?" Such a message apparently presents the client with a choice, but takes it for granted that the client will stop the symptom.

Another Ericksonian technique was the use of *teaching stories,* stories that convey a message metaphorically. This technique has been adopted by a recently developed therapeutic approach called neurolinguistic programming. Cameron-Bandler (1978), for instance, used it to treat a young man for premature ejaculation. First, the man was told that nothing can be done about his problem. Later, he was placed in a hypnotic trance and told a story. The essence of the story was that one could go on a "vacation" in one of two ways. One could either rush to the destination or take the slow route, enjoying the sights along the way. The message implied should be clear, and this teaching story appeared to cure the young man's difficulties.

An example of Erickson's belief that a small change could lead to much larger changes is given in Feldman (1985). The client was a depressed, angry woman, who complained of hating Phoenix, but was reluctant to go on a vacation. While she was in a hypnotic trance, Erickson suggested to her that while on vacation she would be curious about seeing an unexpected "flash of color." This mobilized her to look for the unexpected, and of course she did eventually see an unexpected flash of color in the form of a redheaded woodpecker flying past a tree. After seeing this, she continued to search for "color" in her life, and she eventually became someone who enjoyed traveling and was not depressed.

Erickson believed that one could use a client's symptom as part of the solution to his problem. In other words, instead of working against the client's symptom, he worked with it and turned it to the client's favor. Actually, this is the strategy that underlies his other techniques, such as reframing and paradoxical intervention. However, we will give an example in which the technique is used directly. A hospitalized patient believed himself to be Jesus. Many therapists would presume the belief is a defense and try to remove it by helping the client acquire insight into its defensive nature. These therapists would be working against the symptom. Erickson's approach was to mobilize the symptom positively. He said to the man, "I understand that you have experience as a carpenter." Thus, part of the symptom of believing himself to be Jesus was used therapeutically. Erickson was able to get the client involved in doing productive work, thereby lessening the need for the symptom in the first place.

Modern Strategic Therapists

We will consider the work of three "teams" of modern strategic therapists: Jay Haley and his colleague Cloe Madanes (Haley, 1976; Madanes, 1984), Paul Watzlawick and his colleagues (Watzlawick, Weakland, & Fisch, 1974), and Steven de Shazer (1985). All are similar (though not identical) in their therapeutic strategies, and all draw on Erickson's work. They differ most in their theory of psychopathology and personality.

Jay Haley and Cloé Madanas For Jay Haley, all behavior is communication. Humans cannot *not* communicate. Even remaining silent conveys a message: "I don't want to talk." Communication occurs on more than one level at once. For instance, if you ask me for advice, I may answer by saying "You should do so and so." What I suggest you do is the *content* of the communication. For Haley, in addition to conveying content, communication serves to define a relationship in terms of who has power. He sees power, "who's in charge," as a basic issue in all human relationships.

Haley analyzes interpersonal relationships in terms of power arrangements and sees psychological symptoms as metaphorical communications through which the power relationships in a family system are expressed. For instance, a wife who wishes her husband to stay home with her may develop anxiety attacks. She is not consciously in control of the anxiety attacks, but at the same time her husband must stay home in case she has one. Therefore, the message "Stay home with me" is conveyed metaphorically in the symptom of the attacks, and the symptom also serves the purpose of exerting power over the husband.

In a family system a pathological behavior is some metaphorical communication about the family. For Haley, as well as for Watzlawick, the question of why pathological behavior occurs is not as productive as the question of what purpose does it serve. Haley and many other theorists who take a "functionalist" view, believe that pathological behaviors serve functions in the family (Bogdan, 1986). The functions are unconsciously generated, that is, families are largely unaware of how the symptoms function in the family. Madanes (1984) has argued that individuals may unconsciously plan ahead in developing their dysfunctional behavior in order to solve some family problem.

While Haley sees the process of symptom formation as largely unconscious, he does not believe that insight and awareness are important therapeutic goals. Instead, he advocates direct manipulation of behavior as it functions within the family system. The therapist must take charge and intervene in the family in such a way as to change the dysfunctional family system. Haley, Madanes, and others have developed a large set of techniques to be applied to individual cases.

Before we describe the strategies we wish to mention how such strategies are arrived at. First, these therapists often work with a "one-way mirror." One therapist sees the family, while a group of other therapists observe through a one-way mirror. The intervention strategy used is devised by the whole team. In designing a strategy, Haley (1985) points out that great care must be taken to design a strategy that the clients will comply with. Therefore, as with many of the other therapeutic interventions described in this book, it takes a great deal of skill to successfully design a strategic intervention that both will be followed by the clients and will be effective. So, if you're having problems with your husband or wife, or children, or parents, it would be better for you to try something besides reframings, paradoxes, or other strategies discussed here.

In designing the strategy, the therapists make certain assumptions about the purpose the problem behavior is serving in the underlying family system. They continue to observe the family to see how their intervention works. A failure of an intervention is taken as further information about what may be going on in the family, and revisions are made accordingly.

One set of strategies used by these therapists involves restructuring the family. In one form of restructuring other members of the family are asked to share the symptom. For example, one family came to therapy because the middle daughter was exhibiting problem behavior. Her siblings were "model" children. The family was told that it was unfair that the middle daughter carry the burden of being the troublemaker for the whole family. The family appeared to need a troublemaker, but the burden should be shared. Each of the other children was given the assignment of being the troublemaker for a period of time. This eliminated the middle daughter's problem behavior (Madanes, 1985a).

In another type of restructuring the normal power structure in the family is reversed. If a parent is acting irresponsibly, a child may be put in charge of that parent or of that parent's happiness. In one case, a mother was accused of physically abusing her children, who were generally unruly and uncooperative. One of the most uncooperative children (who, among other things, set fires) was put in charge of making his mother's life easier. This appeared to bring out the love and caring the child felt for the mother, and her abuse of the children stopped, as did the son's disruptive behavior (Madanes, 1984).

These therapists also use reframing and paradoxical interventions. For example, a young adult male was gambling so much he was seriously in debt and was draining off family funds. His gambling was being supported by his mother and aunt, who would give him money to help get him out of debt. The therapist, rather than telling him to stop gambling, instructed him to gamble. However, the structure under which he gambled was altered. His mother and aunt had to go with him to the race track, tell him which horses to bet on, and then stand in line with him while he placed his bets, warding off any friends or acquaintances that might approach. In addition, the family was to hold nightly poker games in which the mother and aunt were to coach the young man on how to play. Though the mother and aunt did not know anything about gambling, they enthusiastically agreed to learn so they could play their parts. After rehearsing these procedures in therapy sessions, the young man disgustedly told the therapist that she did not know anything about gambling, but that it did not matter, because he was going to give up gambling, get a job, and pay his debts anyway. This is what he proceeded to do.

In the paradoxical intervention in the gambler's case, the behavior prescribed differed quite a bit from the spontaneous symptom. In some cases the change is more subtle. For instance, if a husband and wife tend to argue in one room in their home, they will be instructed to argue deliberately, but in a different room. Or the timing of the arguments might be changed. The husband and wife might be instructed to set aside 20 minutes each day to argue.

Related to the use of paradox is an intervention in which the therapist talks about all the possible negative things that might occur if the problem is solved. The therapist implies that the family could not tolerate the elimination of the problem or even that it would be disastrous for the family to eliminate the problem and that they are at the best level of adjustment they can hope for. This intervention is thought to work by mobilizing the family's resistance. In order to prove the therapist wrong, they must change for the better. (See Box 9.1)

Finally we will mention the use of therapeutic *ordeals,* another technique borrowed from Milton Erickson. Basically the strategy is to make the symptom too costly to maintain. For example, one client was a housewife who was a compulsive cleaner (Madanes, 1984). If someone used a towel in the middle of the night, she had to get

BOX 9.1 The Function of Disruption

The therapist ushered the family into the therapy room, where an angry mother and her two oldest teenage daughters immediately sat together on a sofa and the youngest, the identified patient, sat in the farthest away chair. The mother reported that Wendy was being truant from junior high, failing several classes, lying, and stealing. As a single mother who worked full time and went to college at night, she just "couldn't take" any more disruption from her always difficult child.

Most of the therapy hour was spent eliciting each person's version of the family's difficulties with the therapist empathizing with each individual's feelings and perceptions. The mother and two oldest daughters insisted that everything would be just fine if it weren't for Wendy. Her truancy was the final straw because the mother had to miss work to go to Wendy's school for a parent conference. Since Wendy sat far away, huddled sullenly in her chair, refusing to speak or look at anyone, the therapist empathized with how difficult it must be for her to talk with everyone against her and how distressed, embarrassed, hurt, and angry she must feel. Having made contact with each family member by validating her viewpoint, the therapist made her paradoxical intervention.

The therapist delivered this speech slowly and seriously:

> As you know, I believe the reason one member of a family shows problem behavior is because the entire family is in pain. And this family certainly is in pain. Everyone is busy, stretched to the limit, and stressed out. Mrs. G works, goes to college, raises a family alone. Each daughter goes to school, helps run the household, does chores and homework, tries to have a social life. It's just too much. But only Wendy acts out the family pain by doing bad things. She saves the rest of you from having to look at the kind of stress and pain you live under by being the bad one. In fact, she is sacrificing herself to save you, her loved ones, from having to experience your own pain. And she *is* sacrificing herself, because after all she's the one who will have to pay. She must really love all of you a lot.
>
> But I don't want you to change too fast. If Wendy suddenly started being good, you'd all have to face your own pain, and you might not like that. So Wendy, during the next week, I want you to be truant as much as possible and continue lying. In fact, tell at least three really good lies. I want you to continue to sacrifice yourself and protect the rest of your family. OK, I'll see you all next week at this time.

The effect of this intervention on the family was electric. They all immediately sat straight and listened carefully. Wendy sat up, leaned forward, and looked at the therapist as if she were crazy. The others looked between Wendy and the therapist in confusion. The mother started to protest that she didn't want Wendy to sacrifice herself in that way, but the therapist ushered them out of the room with promises to see them next week.

The next week quite a different family entered the therapy room. Three cheerful daughters sat comfortably on the sofa together, and a beaming mother sat in a chair beside them. They reported that they couldn't understand it, but they'd had a great week together. For some reason Wendy went to school and did not lie or steal. They all got along well together and even had some fun together. No one could explain it. The therapist said that she was glad to see the family handling their issues so well and that they could call her in the future if they needed to. The family did not request another appointment for over a year.

up and immediately put it in the washing machine. She had had five years of psychoanalysis, behavior modification, and several encounter group experiences, without any results. It was postulated, based on a family interview, that the wife spent her time cleaning in order to avoid being with her husband, who seemed somewhat obnoxious. It was hypothesized that if things were reversed (if the consequence of compulsive cleaning was that she would have to spend time with him), the symptom would abate. Therefore, to summarize the set of interventions used, when the wife cleaned more than a reasonable amount, she had to either spend time watching television with her husband in bed or go out to dinner with him. This eliminated the problem. At a nine-month follow-up the wife was still not engaging in compulsive cleaning, though she insisted that the therapy had nothing to do with it.

Paul Watzlawick Paul Watzlawick is one of the foremost spokespersons for the viewpoint of *constructivism* (Watzlawick, 1984). Briefly put, constructivism holds that there is no "one true objective reality"; rather, each individual constructs his own reality and there are therefore multiple possible constructions of reality. Individuals' concepts of reality are like maps. Maps are representations of reality, but no map reproduces reality. Furthermore, different maps of the same territory can be drawn, and each may be useful in its own way. A geological map of an area will not look identical to a road map.

Does this mean that any construction of reality is equally acceptable? No. While we might not be able to say that any one view is the true one, we can say that some constructions work better than others. Watzlawick (1984) gives the example of a boat captain navigating a channel at night. There may be multiple "correct" routes that will get him through the channel. However, there are also clearly wrong routes that will lead to shipwreck. Watzlawick argues the same is true of people's views of their world.

For Watzlawick, therefore, we can never talk about the *validity* of an idea about reality, we can only talk about its *viability.* This is a view echoed by Michael Mahoney:

> Mental representations are not to be judged by their validity (which is technically unknowable) or their power to control, but by their capacity to afford adaptation and development. . . . Knowing and learning do not entail absolute levels of objectivity and certainty. Put in other terms, we do not survive and develop because our mental representations of self-world relationships are progressively more *valid,* but because they are more *viable. . . . Validity* presumes that knowledge is correct, true, accurate, and enduring. . . . The constructive developmentalists, on the other hand, believe that all knowing organisms are embodied, self-developing "theories" of relationships. (In press, pp. 25–26, 30)

For Watzlawick psychological problems are actually attempts at *solutions* to life problems. Psychological problems occur when people attempt to solve new life problems with a solution that worked in the past or for old problems, but that does not work now. Often, when the old solution strategy does not work, they try "upping the dosage." Finally, they may even "break down."

Watzlawick (1985b) gives the example of army ants, who have evolved a pattern of marching in a column. This strategy allows the colony of ants much greater flexibility in adaptation and survival than any one ant would have on its own. Yet, this life-enhancing strategy can become their downfall. If by some accident of terrain the lead ant starts to march in a circle and catches up to the last ant in the column, the ants will continue to march in a circle until they die. The strategy that evolved because of its survival value becomes a problem under the wrong conditions. The ants are "stuck."

Wile (1981), writing from a psychodynamic perspective, also embraces the idea that psychopathology involves being "stuck." He points out that traditional psychoanalysis, some family views, some behaviorial views, and some humanistic views hold that a person acts psychopathologically because in some way he or she is gaining gratification from the pathological behavior. For instance, a depressive may be seen as trying to gain attention through her depression. Or perhaps her depression is a way of protecting herself against unconscious anger, thereby providing gratification through a feeling of safety. Wile, like Beck, Rogers, and the constructivists, holds that the depressive remains depressed because she is "stuck." The solutions she is using simply get her mired still deeper. We can think of someone in quicksand, whose "solution" is to struggle, which makes things worse. Depressives react to a failure by setting higher standards for themselves, as if they are trying to motivate themselves to succeed. However, this solution is actually dysfunctional, since it only increases the chance of failure, which is followed by increased depression (Simon, 1979, in Bandura, 1986, p. 360).

Therapy for those who believe pathology is maintained by gratification involves either making the client aware of how his or her symptoms are providing unconscious gratification or removing the gratifications. Therapy for those who believe the client is repeating unproductive solutions because he or she does not know better involves helping the client get "unstuck."

How does Watzlawick propose to get a client unstuck? How would you help the ants? Would you put the lead ant on a couch and help it gain insight into its past? Would you have it focus in on its feelings or felt meanings? Would you wonder what dysfunctional cognitions the ant has? Or would you simply place a stick strategically so that the circular pattern is broken up, allowing the ants to march forward once again?

For Watzlawick, therapy is a matter of using some intervention to break up the circle in which the client is stuck. He (1985a) argues that insight is irrelevant to change and that change occurs all the time in everyday life without insight. If the old system is broken up, new, forward-moving behavior will take its place, and engaging in a new behavior can change a whole personal system for construing reality. This is a crucial point because Watzlawick believes that a simple change can result in a major, pervasive, personal change. In contrast, psychoanalysis, for instance, believes that changing one's personal construct system takes years of review of its roots in early childhood.

One of Watzlawik's key ideas is the distinction between first order and second order change. People get stuck because they operate out of unquestioned assumptions about the nature of reality and, in particular, about the nature of the problem situation they are dealing with. For some "traditional" husbands, it is practically "bred in the bone" that the husband is supposed to be dominant; the wife is supposed to stay at home and not work. All people have these unquestioned assumptions. They form part of their *first order reality.* When individuals attempt to solve problems, they operate out of those assumptions, without realizing they are assumptions. Then, when things go wrong, they do not question the assumptions underlying their actions, goals, and perceptions, but simply try to refine their strategies or actions in accord with those same old assumptions. For instance, someone sinking in quicksand may not question his assumption that some kind of vigorous action is needed to get out. So even when thrashing about does not help, he shifts to another kind of vigorous action (perhaps trying to swim and kick with one's feet), rather than questioning his assumption that vigorous activity is an appropriate solution.

Watzlawick argues that what is needed is not a *first order change* in which one simply tries new ways to solve the problem from the same old assumptions. It is a *second order change* in which the assumptions themselves are overthrown. The person has to be able to step outside of the old "frame" he or she puts on situations, to see them in a new way. A simple illustration of this is given in Figures 9.1 and 9.2.

The therapist's task, then, is to induce second order change. This will get the system "unstuck" and moving again. Let us consider an example of someone who attempts to solve a problem by instituting first order changes. One of us knows of a family in which the wife, because of her own traumatic family background, is overprotective toward her teenage daughter. Because the woman was somewhat wild as a child, she is concerned about her daughter's becoming wild. So she is highly restrictive concerning her daughter's curfew time and her daughter's friends. If you think in terms of a system, you can imagine what might happen next. Such overprotectiveness generates rebellion in the daughter. She begins to exhibit some of the very behaviors the mother has been so worried about: cutting school, hanging around with people the mother dislikes, and acting rebellious at home. This convinces the mother that she was on the right track all along—the daughter *is* in danger of going down the wrong path. The mother therefore *redoubles* her efforts to control the daughter and becomes even more restrictive. Thus, her solution is to do "more of the same." This is the first order change she attempts. The basic premise underlying all her attempts to control her daughter is never questioned.

How does Watzlawick propose to initiate second order change? Watzlawick argues that there are two languages. The verbal, logical, analytic language of the left brain and the language of image, metaphor, synthesis, and totality of the right brain. According to Watzlawick, "This language [of the right brain] does not explain; it creates, it evokes" (1978, p. 58), and it is in this language that therapists must speak. This is the language of strategic interventions, the language of concrete imagery, indirect suggestion, metaphorical communication, paradox, and jokes. It is this language that can create second order change.

Watzlawick's approach to therapy is quite brief, with the average being about six sessions per client (Watzlawick, 1985b). The Watzlawick group uses many of the techniques we have already encountered (Watzlawick, Weakland, & Fisch, 1974).

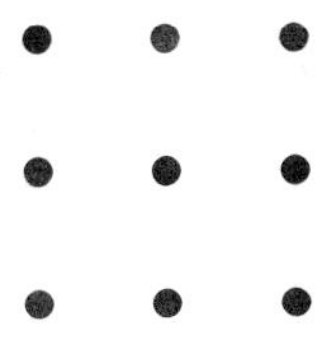

● ● ●

● ● ●

● ● ●

Figure 9.1 The problem is to connect all nine dots by drawing four lines *without* lifting the pencil from the page. See Figure 9.2 for the solution.

Among others mentioned by Watzlawick (1985b) is the therapeutic double bind. The client is given an instruction that puts her in a paradoxical position. A woman client who said she "couldn't say no" was instructed to go around to each person in the room and say no to them. She said, "No! I can't do that!" Of course, by saying no to the intervention she was saying no.

Watzlawick uses the technique of expressing pessimism about the client's chances of change. (This obviously must be done with great care and skill. It would not be appropriate with depressed or suicidal clients.) Thus a client might be told that his current level of adjustment is the best that can be hoped for and that any sudden changes might be disastrous. Similarly, when a client *does* show positive gains after the first session or two, it is standard practice for many strategic therapists to predict that there will be relapse. Paradoxically, this induces clients to change.

Watzlawick phrases his communications in such a way as to make "every success theirs" and "every failure ours." After a successful change the client might be told, "Amazing! You must have done something different. What did you do to make it a success?"

Steven de Shazer De Shazer (1985) shares the idea that problems are most often the outcomes of attempts at solution, and he would agree with Watzlawick (1985a) that pathology is a system that has run out of ways of dealing with a problem. On the development of the causes of the problem, the de Shazer position is compatible with other theoretical perspectives covered in this book. For instance, it could be that a problem has complex roots in the past. However, de Shazer believes that just because a problem is complex does not mean that it demands a complex solution. One could think of the story of Alexander the Great and the Gordian Knot, which no one could untie. Alexander's solution was to take his sword and cut it apart. There may well be solutions to problems that are quite simple, though the problem itself is quite complex.

De Shazer does not believe that the solution must exactly match the problem. As a skeleton key can be used to unlock a variety of locks, therapeutic solutions can unlock a variety of problems or complaints. In this respect therapeutic solutions work by "unsticking" the client. They break up the old system, and de Shazer believes, as with Milton Erickson, that the clients actually then resolve the problem with new creative solutions the therapist could never have anticipated or planned.

A key theoretical point of de Shazer's is a rejection of the traditional concept of clients' unconscious resistance to change. He says,

> I became more and more convinced that clients really do want to change. Certainly some of them found that the ideas about *how* to change did not fit very well. However,

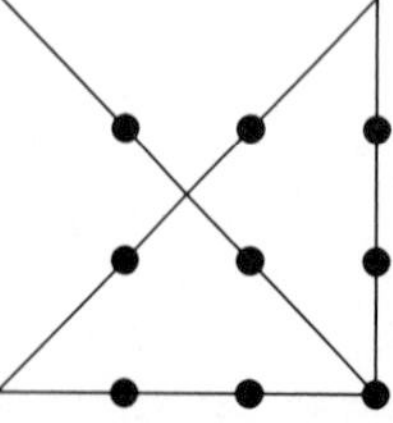

Figure 9.2 People have trouble with this problem because they see the nine dots as a square. They have to change that assumption and see the dots in a different way to solve the problem.

> I found it difficult to label this as "resistance" when it seemed to be a message the clients were sending in an effort to help the therapist help them. . . . Over and over I found people sent to me by other therapists . . . to be both desperate for change and highly cooperative. (1985, p. 15)

The implication is that resistance may be as much a function of the therapist's interventions as it is a function of the client. Perhaps clients resist intervention techniques that do not fit them well. The de Shazer group works to minimize resistance and elicit the client's cooperation by complimenting the clients on what they are already doing to try to solve their problem.

Many of the interventions used by the de Shazer group are based on Milton Erickson and are shared by other strategic therapists. We will mention some we have not previously covered. De Shazer respects the reality of each client. If two clients give differing views of the problem, the therapist stays neutral and does not take sides. Rather, the therapist may mirror the conflict. However, it may be done in such a way as to put the couple in a "positive double bind," as Watzlawick does. In one example a husband and wife were treated for cocaine abuse. They also were concerned about problems in the marriage. One partner believed the real problem was not the drug abuse, but their fights and arguments. The other thought it was the drugs that were causing the marital problems. The intervention given by the de Shazer group to the couple is as follows. We will not reproduce the rather complex theoretical logic for this intervention here (De Shazer, 1985, pp. 50–57), but it is based on the fact that each member of the couple was seeing the problem in either-or terms.

> You've got a problem. It seems to us, Ralph, that your marital problems are being exacerbated by the drugs, or fogged over by the drugs, or perhaps even created by the drugs. Perhaps you need to, stop the drugs, just to see what is going on. But, on the other hand, we agree with you, Jane, that if you two were to stop the drugs, then there might be nothing there. And, you might not have time to create anything before the marriage broke up. In short, we don't know what the fuck you are going to do.
>
> I suggest you think about what I just said, and decide what actions you are going to take . . . first. (De Shazer, 1985, p. 52)

The interesting thing is that this intervention resulted in a two-thirds reduction of drug use by the next session and complete elimination of drug use by two weeks later, along with the development of new, positive marital activities. Follow-ups at six months and one year indicated no further drug use and infrequent arguments. In other words, a substance abuse problem *and* a marital problem appeared to be "cured" in two sessions!

Another intervention, similar to one used by the Watzlawick group, is to have the clients concretely and specifically define what they would like changed. Most clients come in and say things like "We want our marriage improved" or "I want to get over being depressed" or "I want to stop being anxious so much." These are global, vague goals. Clients are asked to try to imagine concrete behavioral differences that could be used as an index of change for the better. For instance, for the people who want their marriage "improved" it might be "spending one night together sharing a pleasant activity without fighting." For the depressive it might be "feeling calm and content while sitting at home on a Saturday night watching TV." For the anxious person it might be "stepping outside the door and feeling calm." The interesting thing is that the simple act of developing and defining such concrete goals is therapeutic. Clients find ways of bringing them about that are unique, creative, and not predictable by the therapist.

De Shazer, following along with Erickson, believes that change is not only possible, it is "inevitable," and this attitude is conveyed to the client. For example, the client may be asked "What will you do when you have changed" or "When do you think you will be over this problem—by next week or the week after?" A specific intervention is to tell a client to "pay attention to what you do when you overcome the urge to . . ." (1985, p. 132). This may be used, for instance, with overeating. The client is told to pay attention to what he or she does when he or she overcomes the urge to eat. There are two parts to this intervention. First, it implies that the client can change, that is, she can overcome the urge to eat. Second, it focuses the client's attention on the positive moments when he or she succeeds and counteracts either-or thinking. De Shazer points out that things in life are rarely "always" or "never" and that always-never thinking is an example of the either-or thinking that is often involved in dysfunctional behavior. Overeaters often say "I always overeat" or "I never can control my appetite," yet this is rarely true. Most dieters do overcome their urges to eat, frequently. They may fail at other times, but they do not always fail.

One final technique of de Shazer we will mention is "do something different." In some sense this could be thought of as the generic strategic strategy, since its goal is to do something different from the old ways. De Shazer gives the example of parents who had been unable to control their son's temper tantrums, even with the use of behavioral techniques such as time-out. The husband and wife were told "Do something different next time Josh throws a tantrum, no matter how strange, or weird, or off-the-wall it might seem. The only important thing is that whatever you decide to do, you need to do something different" (1985, p. 126). The next time Josh threw a tantrum, the father gave him a cookie without saying a word. The time after that the mother danced circles around him. This eliminated the tantrums, both at home and at school.

Summary of Strategic Approaches

Despite their differing theoretical orientations, the strategic therapists we have examined all share a belief that the therapist's task is to intervene in such a way that the old, dysfunctional system is disrupted, freeing the system to develop and move forward in positive ways. They all believe that small, seemingly irrelevant changes can have a ripple effect, resulting in major and lasting changes within the individual client or the family system. They believe that instead of pitting themselves against the client's or family's problems, which could mobilize resistance, they should work with the symptoms in some way. Therefore, interventions frequently do not proscribe the symptom, but rather place it in a different context. They also agree that insight into the causes of the symptoms is not necessary or important for change.

EVALUATION OF MARITAL AND FAMILY THERAPIES

Gurman and Kniskern (1978) reviewed research on marital and family therapy and drew the following conclusions. First, nonbehaviorial marital and family therapies are effective and produce beneficial outcomes in two-thirds of cases. Second, marital therapy is more likely to be successful when both spouses are treated than when only one spouse is treated. Third, the positive benefits of both behavioral and nonbehavioral approaches can usually be achieved in less than 20 sessions. Fourth, family and marital approaches appear to work better than individual therapy in treating family-related problems.

Weakland, Fisch, Watzlawick, and Bodin (1974) reported complete relief or significant improvement in 72 percent of their cases using the Watzlawick brief therapy approach. A follow-up on many of these, as well as other cases, found similar results (62 percent improvement), indicating that the changes wrought by this approach persist for some time after treatment. There was some evidence that there were positive changes in areas other than the specific presenting problems. However, their data do not meet stringent research standards. Success rates are largely based on clients' subjective reports, and no control groups were used. The de Shazer group tends to follow up their clients for six months to a year, and they report a similar figure of 72 percent. However, their results are subject to the same criticisms.

Several reports support the effectiveness of Minuchin's approach. Rosman, Minuchin, Liebman, and Baker (1978, as reported in Prochaska, 1984) report results on the treatment of 53 anorectics; they found that 86 percent of them achieved normal eating patterns. These writers also report successful outcomes for 17 chronic asthmatics and for the reduction of stress effects on children with diabetes. As with the research noted above, there were no control groups, however. The one study that utilized a control group, Stanton and Todd (1979), reported equivocal results on Minuchin's approach with drug problems.

Finally, Gurman, Kniskern, and Pinsoff (1986) reviewed research on different approaches to family therapy and drew conclusions based on an evaluation of the quality of the data available. They conclude that it is too early to dismiss any approach and that there is some evidence for the effectiveness of several different approaches. The strongest evidence exists for behavioral approaches, but there is also evidence for Minuchin's approach, strategic approaches, and psychodynamic approaches, among others. In sum, the research is supportive of the effectiveness of marital, family, and strategic approaches. However, much of the data are not scientifically rigorous and must be treated with caution.

Because the marital, family, and strategic approaches constitute a diverse collection, we will not evaluate them as a whole. However, there are criticisms that have been leveled specifically at the strategic approaches that need to be considered. Many systems theorists believe that an individual client's symptom serves some *functional* significance in the family. In other words, the symptom is an unconscious strategy for dealing with some family issue. There is some evidence that the identified patient may in some cases be playing just such a role in the family (Christensen & Margolin, 1985). However, criticisms of such a view can be made (Bogdan, 1986). First, it is no more than an assumption or an indirect inference that the presenting complaints of the identified patient are meeting some family need. This is not directly observable.

Second, there are certain inconsistencies in the idea. For example, an adolescent's school problems might be assumed to serve to bring father and mother, who have intimacy problems, closer together. But if we assume that *all* family problems are an attempt to resolve some family imbalance, then what imbalance is the parents' intimacy problems attempting to resolve? This leads to an infinite regress.

Third, this viewpoint can be questioned from an ecological view of systems. In an ecological system it is true that changes in the behavior of one member of the system lead to adjustments in other parts. But to argue that one element of the system changes in order to keep the system in balance would be like arguing that coyotes eat rabbits in order to keep the ecological system in balance. But that is not why coyotes eat rabbits. They eat rabbits because they are hungry, and their eating rabbits keeps the system in balance because the whole system interactively evolved in that way. Bogdan (1986) prefers an ecological metaphor and argues that family systems often evolve problems accidentally. Arguing from the work of Watzlawick and his colleagues, Bogdan suggests that problems evolve because "ordinary life difficulties are mishandled. And they persist because no one realizes that it is the mishandling that perpetuates the problem" (p. 35).

In a similar manner the functionalist perspective can be criticized for minimizing the role of individual psychological variables. The assumption is that pathological behavior is always the result of the family system and not the result of any individual process. This perspective was originally developed in family theories of schizophrenia, in which it was argued that schizophrenics were actually the identified patients in pathological families. Case histories were given suggesting that families of schizophrenics were more disturbed in many ways than normal families. However, the functionalist perspective overlooks an alternative possibility. It is possible that having a disturbed family member, such as a schizophrenic, disturbs the family. Patterns of disturbance similar to those found in families of schizophrenics have also been found in families of children with other serious illnesses, such as leukemia. It would be most peculiar to argue that a child developed leukemia in order to bring his mother and father closer together. An ecological system point of view could handle the fact that an individual member of the system could be disturbed, and that disturbance could then disturb the rest of the system. This could then become an accidental dysfunctional feedback loop.

Let us give a concrete example. There is now research (Chess & Thomas, 1984) suggesting that some children are more difficult to raise from birth than others. Suppose there is a family who has had an "easy child" first. This child is now 6 years old, and everything has gone smoothly. Now they have a second child, and from birth this child is "difficult." The parents do not realize that difficult children take more active and different parenting strategies than easy children. They apply the same techniques to this child as they did to the older child, but they do not work. The child grows up to be a problem child. The parents, who were successful with the first child, blame this on the second child and redouble their efforts. Perhaps in the interim they pay less attention to the older child, who begins to feel resentful and rebellious. Now the parents have two problem children and begin to blame each other. Their marriage is in trouble, but they stay together in order to try to help the children. In this scenario the family system has created both the problems in the older child and between the parents, and in some sense in the younger, difficult child, by virtue of the parents' inability to shift parenting styles. Yet none of the problems can be said to have evolved to serve some function in the family.

Furthermore, the systems idea depends on the idea that each element of the system has some identity of its own independent (at least partially) of its place in the system. A system with coyotes and rabbits will be different from a system with sheep and raccoons. Some systems theorists seem to discount the idea that each individual in the family system has his or her own personality, which plays its role in the overall family system. To really understand a family system one has to take into account the individual characteristics of the members of that system, just as one must know that an ecological system has rabbits and coyotes in it instead of sheep and raccoons. There is nothing fundamentally incompatible between the ideas that family members have their individual personalities (and problems) and that they are part of an interactive system.

Another major criticism of strategic approaches has to do with their manipulativeness. Strategic therapists do not value insight. They do not believe that change occurs by making clients aware of their own problems so that the clients can consciously initiate and control their own changes. Instead, it could be said that the therapists institute change by playing tricks on the client.

The therapists might reply that all therapy interventions are manipulations, so why not do them consciously and deliberately? This is an argument that behaviorists used to make in response to criticisms that they were manipulative. Haley, who has been openly assertive about the therapist's using manipulation to help the client, has made fun of the idea that if a therapist does something without deliberately trying to manipulate and it works, that is somehow all right, while if the same thing is consciously done as a manipulation, it is not (Haley, 1985). Furthermore, it could be argued that these manipulations work. People are better off afterwards and with a lot less investment of time and trouble than with so-called insight therapies.

An argument against manipulative intervention is that it does not empower people. One of the important current movements in psychology is the idea of "giving psychology away" (Larson, 1984). The idea is to develop techniques that people can use to manage their own lives. Strategic therapy may eliminate symptoms, but it does not empower individuals to change their lives on their own if further problems arise. It seems to imply that people must be "operated on" when they are stuck, rather than unstick themselves. Psychoanalytic and humanistic approaches do not merely wish to get the client unstuck, to get rid of symptoms, but to develop the client's own self-management skills. It may be that that is why they take longer.

While all strategic therapists plan their interventions and use paradoxical techniques, not all of them accept the manipulative model of theorists like Jay Haley. They use the techniques not to manipulate the client into some specific outcome, but to free the client to solve the problem creatively. De Shazer points out that the actual solutions clients come up with to their problems are that unique, developed by the clients themselves, and not predictable by the therapist.

Another criticism is leveled at the range and permanence of strategic approaches. Advocates of psychoanalytic and humanistic approaches sometimes question whether changes brought about in such a brief time, using such noninsight methods, can have any enduring quality. They argue that in such a short time these approaches cannot cause change that persists and that they will not work with enduring characterological problems, such as addictions and personality disorders. In response Watzlawick (1985b) has pointed out that even if it were true that a client might eventually have to return to treatment with a new problem or a recurrence of the old, that does not invalidate the treatment's success. He notes that no one expects medical doctors to effect cures of infections so that the patient will never get another infection. Furthermore, there is no evidence that the changes wrought by analytic or humanistic approaches are any more permanent. In fact, not only does analysis take years, but people frequently return to it with recurrent or new problems. Finally, strategic therapists point to cases of supposedly chronic characterological problems that they have helped, such as bulimia, substance abuse, and antisocial behavior in adolescents. However, individual case histories do not prove that the strategic approach is generally effective with such problems, and strategic therapists do not present any systematic evidence showing that it is.

CONTRIBUTIONS OF GROUP, MARITAL, AND FAMILY APPROACHES

Group therapy has made several important contributions. First, therapy in groups allows more individuals to be treated in less time and with fewer therapists than therapy on an individual basis. Typically, an individual has to pay less for group therapy per session than for individual therapy. Therefore it may be more cost-effective than other forms of therapy.

A more important advantage is that it allows for learning to occur that would be more difficult to obtain in individual therapy. A client can obtain concrete information on how he or she interacts with others. The client can get feedback from others, as well as explore his or her perceptions about others.

Before Masters and Johnson, most sex therapy was nonspecific. Specific sexual problems, such as impotence, were treated by nonspecific exploration of the client's unconscious or life style on the assumption that sex problems reflected underlying problems. The main contribution of sex therapy has been the development of specific techniques that can be used to enhance sexual experience, whether or not therapy also deals with other underlying issues.

The major contributions of marital and family therapies have been the development of an effective treatment approach and a model of psychopathology and psychotherapy that provides an alternative to the psychoanalytic, humanistic, and cognitive-behavioral theoretical perspectives.

Strategic therapy has contributed the idea that treatment may be simple even if the causes and structure of a problem are complex, which is a distinction that had not been made before. This view makes it possible to imagine cases in which a psychoanalytic view of the causes is the best explanation for why the disorder occurs, but family or strategic approaches provide the best treatment of the disorder.

REFERENCES

Bandura, A. (1986). *Social foundations of thought and action: A social cognitive theory.* Englewood Cliffs, NJ: Prentice-Hall.

Barbach, L. G. (1975). *For yourself: The fulfillment of female sexuality.* New York: Signet.

Berne, E. (1964). *Games people play.* New York: Grove Press.

Berne, E. (1966). *Principles of group treatment.* New York: Oxford University Press.

Bogdan, J. (1986). Do families really need problems? *The Family Therapy Networker, 10,* 30–35, 67–69.

Bowen, M. (1978). *Family therapy in clinical practice.* New York: Aronson.

Cameron-Bandler, L. (1978). *They lived happily ever after.* Cupertino, CA: Meta.

Chess, S., & Thomas, A. (1984). *Origins and evolution of behavior disorders: From infancy to early adult life.* New York: Brunner/Mazel.

Christensen, A. (1983). Intervention. In H. H. Kelley, E. Berscheid, A. Christensen, J. H. Harvey, T. L. Huston, G. Levinger, E. McClintock, L. A. Peplau, & D. R. Peterson (Eds.), *Close relationships.* New York: Freeman.

Christensen, A., & Margolin, G. (1985). *Correlational and sequential analyses of marital and child problems.* Unpublished manuscript, University of California Los Angeles.

Dammann, C. (1980). Family therapy: Erickson's contribution. In J. Zeig (Ed.), *Ericksonian approaches to hypnosis and psychotherapy.* New York: Brunner/Mazel.

De Shazer, S. (1985). *Keys to solution in brief therapy.* New York: Norton.

Dowd, E. T., & Milne, C. R. (1986). Paradoxical interventions in counseling psychology. *The Counseling Psychologist, 14,* 237–282.

Feldman, J. B. (1985). The work of Milton Erickson: A multisystem model of eclectic therapy. *Psychotherapy, 22,* 154–162.

Gurman, A. S., & Kniskern, D. P. (1978). Research on marital and family therapy: Progress, perspective and prospect. In S. Garfield & A. Bergin (Eds.), *Handbook of psychotherapy and behavior change: An empirical analysis* (2nd ed.). New York: Wiley.

Gurman, A. S., Kniskern, D. P., & Pinsoff, W. M. (1986). Research on marital and family therapies. In S. L. Garfield & A. E. Bergin (Eds.), *Handbook of psychotherapy and behavior change* (3rd ed.). New York: Wiley.

Haley, J. (1976). *Problem-solving therapy: New strategies for effective family therapy.* San Francisco: Jossey-Bass.

Haley, J. (1985). *Strategic family therapy* (Video and discussion). Presented at the Evolution of Psychotherapy Conference, Phoenix, AZ, December 11, 1985.

Harris, T. A. (1969). *I'm ok—you're ok.* New York: Harper & Row.

Jacobson, N. S., & Margolin, G. (1979). *Marital therapy: Strategies based on social learning and behavior exchange principles.* New York: Brunner/Mazel.

Kaul, T. J., & Bednar, R. L. (1986). Research on group and related therapies. In S. L. Garfield & A. E. Bergin (Eds.), *Handbook of psychotherapy and behavior change* (3rd ed.). New York: Wiley.

Larson, D. (Ed.). (1984). *Teaching psychological skills: Models for giving psychology away.* Monterey, CA: Brooks/Cole.

Madanes, C. (1984). *Behind the one-way mirror: Advances in the practice of strategic therapy.* San Francisco: Jossey-Bass.

Madanes, C. (1985a). *Strategic therapy* (Video and discussion). Presented at the Evolution of Psychotherapy Conference, Phoenix, AZ, December 13, 1985.

Madanes, C. (1985b). *Strategic family therapy.* Paper presented at the Evolution of Psychotherapy Conference, Phoenix, AZ, December 14, 1985.

Mahoney, M. (In press). *Human change processes: Notes on the facilitation of personal development.* New York: Basic Books.

Masters, W., & Johnson, V. (1970). *Human sexual inadequacy.* Boston: Little, Brown.

Minuchin, S. (1974). *Families and family therapy.* Cambridge, MA: Harvard University Press.

Moreno, J. L. (1934). *Who shall survive?* New York: Nervous and Mental Disease Publishing.

Selvini Palazzoli, M., Cecchin, G., Prata, G., & Boscolo, L. (1978). *Paradox and counterparadox.* New York: Aronson.

Prochaska, J. O. (1984). *Systems of psychotherapy.* Homewood, IL: Dorsey Press.

Rosman, B., Minuchin, S., Liebman, R., & Baker, L. (1978). *Family therapy for psychosomatic children.* Paper presented at the annual meeting of the American Academy of Psychosomatic Medicine, Atlanta, GA, November, 1978.

Satir, V. (1967). *Conjoint family therapy.* Palo Alto, CA: Science and Behavior Books.

Scheidlinger, S. (1984). Group psychotherapy in the 1980's: Problems and prospects. *American Journal of Psychotherapy, 38,* 494–504.

Simon, K. M. (1979). *Effects of self comparison, social comparison, and depression on goal setting and self-evaluative reactions.* Unpublished manuscript, Stanford University, Stanford, CA.

Stanton, M., & Todd, T. (1979). Structural family therapy with drug addicts. In E. Kaufman & P. Kaufman (Eds.), *The family therapy of drug and alcohol abuse.* New York: Gardner Press.

Watzlawick, P. (1978). *The language of change: Elements of therapeutic communication.* New York: Basic Books.

Watzlawick, P. (Ed.) (1984). *The invented reality: How do we know what we believe we know? (Contributions to constructivism).* New York: Norton.

Watzlawick, P. (1985a). *If you desire to see, learn how to act.* Paper presented at the Evolution of Psychotherapy Conference, Phoenix, AZ, December 12, 1985.

Watzlawick, P. (1985b). *Brief therapeutic interventions.* Paper presented at the Evolution of Psychotherapy Conference, Phoenix, AZ: December 13, 1985.

Watzlawick, Pa., Weakland, J., & Fisch, R. (1974). *Change: Principles of problem formation and problem resolution.* New York: Norton.

Weakland, J., Fisch, R., Watzlawick, P., & Bodin, A. (1974). Brief therapy: Focused problem resolution. *Family Process, 13,* 141–168.

Wile, D. B. (1981). *Couples therapy.* New York: Wiley.

Yalom, I. D. (1985). *The theory and practice of group psychotherapy* (3rd ed.). New York: Basic Books.

Zilbergeld, B. (1978). *Male sexuality.* New York: Bantam Books.

Chapter 10

Research in Psychotherapy

EXPERIENCE IN THERAPY AND DETERMINING "TRUTH"

You're about to work with your first client. He enters your office, complaining of chronic and pervasive anxiety. You've decided from reading this book that a short-term psychoanalytic approach to therapy makes sense to you. You look for a recurring relationship theme related to events in his early childhood. You discover that he was criticized a lot as a child by his father. You see that he now chronically expects criticism. Underlying that is a lot of unconscious resentment and hostility. You help him become aware of this pattern. As you do this he gets in touch with his anger and resentment toward his father. After several sessions he reports that he feels better, and soon the anxiety seems to have diminished to a manageable level. You are amazed at the efficacy of your method, you stand a picture of Freud on your mantle, and put fresh flowers before it daily.

Or you prefer the behavioral approach. You help your client examine his life and find that he becomes anxious in situations where he must assert himself, though he had not previously noted the connection. Since he is a traffic policeman, you realize that he is likely to feel anxious frequently. You create a series of hierarchies of situations in which he feels anxious. You teach him deep relaxation. You have him imagine these situations in a state of relaxation and also practice assertion skills with him. After 10 to 20 sessions the client happily reports that he rarely feels anxious. You are highly impressed with your behavioral approach and begin to carry a picture of Joseph Wolpe in your wallet.

Or you've been most impressed with the approach of Carl Rogers. Empathically you reflect your client's feelings. At first he says, "I don't know why I'm anxious." You say, "And that probably scares you even more. You're anxious and you don't know why." And he says, "Yeah! I hate not being in control." And you say, "It sounds like you've felt in control most of your life, and now you're not, and you wonder what's happening to you." And he says, "Yeah! I've always been the kind to have complete command of myself. I've always acted logically and rationally. I've never let my emotions get out of hand! And now they are!" And you say, "You have trouble trusting your emotional side. I bet you feel vulnerable, and maybe a little weak, if you allow yourself to feel feelings." And he says, "Yeah! I put up such a front! I feel I need to be so strong!" You continue like this for several sessions. Gradually the client learns to listen to himself. He discovers that he has a soft side that he's never allowed or trusted. He begins to accept himself without feeling he has to be unemotional and in control all the time. He reports that the anxiety has decreased remarkably. You can't get over how effective helping someone get in touch with feeling is, and you go around to motels and leave copies of Carl Rogers's works in the rooms.

Or you are particularly taken with the cognitive-behavioral approach. You use Meichenbaum's stress management program. You have your client practice saying things to himself that help soothe and manage the anxiety. For instance, "I don't need to get anxious here. That person cannot really hurt me. Even if I do get anxious, I don't need to fall apart. I can just take a deep breath and relax." You also have your client keep track of his automatic thoughts. You discover that before each experience of anxiety he was saying things to himself like "What if I lose control?" "What if I can't manage the situation?" "What if I freak out and make a fool of myself?" You use Ellis's RET to attack the ideas that "I must always be competent," "I must never be disliked," "It would be awful if I allowed traffic to slow down." After a few sessions of these treatments your client reports his anxiety has almost gone. You are so impressed with cognitive-behavioral methods that you get your editions of Meichenbaum, Beck, and Ellis bound in leather. You set them out in your lobby in a glass case and each day keep them open to a new page.

Whichever approach you have chosen, you have become a committed believer in its effectiveness. After all, seeing is believing, isn't it? It is often on the basis of such experience that people become firm believers in a particular theoretical approach to therapy. Psychoanalysts become convinced that problems are based on repressed feelings from early childhood. Behaviorists become convinced that problems are a matter of conditioning. Humanists become convinced that problems stem from a lack of self-acceptance and the fragmentation of the person into intellectual and emotional sides. And cognitive-behaviorists become convinced that problems depend on what clients think to themselves.

The experience of seeing an apparent cure may be so vivid that the therapist believes that what he has seen verifies the "truth" of his theory. For instance, one psychoanalyst has asserted that the view that later psychological difficulties are caused by events in early childhood "is not a theory; it is an empirical finding confirmed in every psychoanalysis" (Arlow, 1984, p. 24). Guntrip, another analyst, said, "I have stated that much of Freud's clinical observation of psychic experiences as verifiable matters of fact, turning up again and again in the widest variety of persons, has proved to be of permanent validity . . ." (Guntrip, 1973, p. 7). From a gestalt perspective, Fritz Perls said, "We present nothing that you cannot verify for yourself in terms of your own behavior . . ." (Perls, Hefferline, & Goodman, 1951, p. 7).

How valid and trustworthy is experience in therapy for supporting the truthfulness of particular theoretical beliefs? Not very valid at all! In fact, none of the conclusions in the previous paragraph or in our earlier case examples is warranted! It is one of the purposes of this chapter to make you aware of how deceptive "seeing is believing" can be in drawing conclusions about psychotherapy. We will also look at attempts to find reliable evidence on questions related to the effectiveness of psychotherapy.

There has been a continuing debate over research on psychotherapy. In the 1950s, Hans Eysenck published an article that suggested that there was no evidence that psychotherapy worked. Because of the difficulty of the task, many practitioners have dismissed attempts to study the effectiveness of psychotherapy scientifically. Guntrip (1973) makes one typical argument. He says that psychotherapy is so individualized that it is difficult, if not impossible, to study it using normal experimental methods. Similarly, Simkin and Yontef (1984) said, "Gestalt therapists are singularly unimpressed with . . . nomothetic research methodology. No statistical approach can tell the individual patient or therapist what works for him" (p. 306). They go on to say that each gestalt session is an experiment, and so constant research is being done on each individual client. Yet Guntrip is willing to draw conclusions about the "permanent validity" of many of Freud's ideas, because they have turned up "again and again." And gestalt certainly has drawn its own set of general conclusions about psychotherapy and the change process.

You may already have seen the problem in claiming that "facts" about personality and psychotherapy can be learned from therapy sessions. If many of Freud's observations are "facts," why are they repeatedly confirmed in psychoanalytic sessions, but not in gestalt sessions? If the gestalt view is correct, why is it not confirmed in psychoanalytic sessions? Both psychoanalysts and gestalt therapists sometimes argue that anyone who doubts the truth of their viewpoint will discover the truth if he undergoes analysis or gestalt therapy. The basis of this type of argument is that you can learn "truths" from direct experience that you cannot gain from books or empirical research. Yet Carl Rogers, Joseph Wolpe, Albert Ellis, Aaron Beck, Carl Jung, Alfred Adler, and Fritz Perls all started out doing psychoanalytically oriented psychotherapy, but later developed theories that have little in common with psychoanalysis. Farrelly (Farrelly & Brandsma, 1974) started out as a client-centered therapist and now does something called "provocative therapy," which is quite different. Lazarus (1984) found conventional behavior therapy too narrow.

It should be obvious that the kinds of experiences therapists and clients have in therapy, no matter how vivid and compelling, do not provide a scientifically reliable basis for knowledge. People may have a tendency to place more confidence in and generalize from highly vivid experiences than is warranted (Nisbett & Ross, 1980). Seeing may be believing, but neither seeing nor believing is necessarily knowing.

Why are conclusions drawn from the therapy experience not scientifically reliable? One reason is that people tend to "see" what they expect to see. There is reason to believe that Freud had already developed a belief in the sexual basis of neurosis before he began to "see" it in his clients. Freud developed the idea that problems are based on early childhood, and analyst after analyst carried that idea into therapy with them. Theorists carrying different preconceptions did not "see" the things that Freudians claim are empirical truths. Analysts encourage their clients to talk about early childhood and then when change occurs, attribute the change to reviewing early childhood. Cognitive therapists have their clients talk about their dysfunctional cognitions and then attribute change to that. Client-centered therapists focus on clients' feelings, so assume it is something about that process that creates change.

Therapist preconceptions also probably shape the kind of material that the client brings out. There is some evidence (Truax, 1966) that Carl Rogers reinforced client statements that were in accord with his point of view by responding more empathically when such statements were made. And it is likely that all therapists do this. Analysts prick up their ears when the word *mother* creeps into the conversation, Beck focuses on the words *always* and *never,* and gestalt therapists are highly sensitive to the word *can't.* It has been argued (Hobbs, 1968) that Freudian clients get Freudian insights, Jungian clients get Jungian insights, and so on. Over the course of many sessions, a good deal of material compatible with the therapist's point of view will be highlighted and discussed. It is not surprising that both the therapist and client become convinced that what they have discovered is the "truth."

But what about the client? Change experiences, when you gain an insight and suddenly feel transformed, are very powerful and experiences that include a lot of emotion are also very compelling. If there is a great deal of emotion, people tend to believe that somehow something important must be happening. Yet these experiences are not reliable scientifically. Let us take an example from psychoanalysis. Guntrip (1973, pp. 176–177) reports a case of a client who came to therapy for treatment of depression. In addition he had a chronic sinus condition. Through the analysis process he remembered that he had been left alone to nurse his dying mother, but the day of her death remained a total blank. One night the forgotten memory of her death burst into his consciousness. He remembered that she had gone mad at the end and had died cursing him. This memory had been so horrible he had repressed it. When the memory was recovered his sinuses opened, and the fluid poured out.

Such an experience is quite dramatic. Both therapist and client are likely to conclude that the repression of the memory "caused" the sinus condition and the recovery of the memory "cured" it. But is that true? There is no obvious connection between his blocked sinuses and his mother's madness. But even if there were (suppose she had yelled at him, "You're so stuffy!"), would that have proved that the repressed memory caused the sinus condition? Would the clearing up of the sinus condition after recovery of the memory prove that recovering the memory was the cure of the sinus condition? The answer to both is no.

Any highly emotional experience, in the proper context, might have a direct impact on the body. The specific content of the memory may have had nothing to do with the physical effect, except to make it seem more plausible. What may have been important was the emotional impact of recovering the memory. Intense emotional experiences are often associated with change, regardless of the belief system they are associated with. It is not implausible to imagine that this same man goes to a Christian evangelist, has a highly emotional conversion experience, is told by the preacher that his sinuses will open, and, lo and behold, they do. Or he goes to a primal therapist, "recovers" some primal pain from early childhood, and his sinuses open.

Still another possibility is the power of suggestion. The client recovers this emotionally charged memory and says to himself, "This must be it!" Unconsciously he convinces himself that this was the cause, and the power of suggestion causes his sinuses to open.

We are not saying that these alternatives (and there are many others) are the correct ones. We simply want you to see that you cannot conclude that it was specifically the recovery of the particular repressed memory that was therapeutic. (Again, we are using psychoanalysis to illustrate a point that applies to any belief system.) In addition, we do not even know for sure that it was the therapy that caused the memory to surface into consciousness. Perhaps some random event happened that day to bring the memory to consciousness. So we may not conclude that the therapy was responsible for the sinuses opening.

Further, you cannot conclude that the repressed memory caused the problem, either. Suppose there is an apparent connection between the memory and the clogged sinuses; the mother did say, "You're so stuffy!" There is certainly a similarity between this experience and the client's symptom of a stuffy nose. But because two things are similar does not mean that one caused the other. Nisbett and Ross (1980) have pointed out that such reasoning underlies voodoo and other magical beliefs. (For instance, make a doll that is similar to another person. Then stick pins in it and the person will die.) It is easy to find past experiences that "fit" current problems in retrospect. Probably all of us can find some experience in our childhood that is like some problem we are having now. But that does not mean that those experiences caused the problems. It is tempting to conclude that I dislike myself now because my father was overly demanding, but there is no inevitable connection between the two. Many people who had an overdemanding father do not dislike themselves as adults.

The fact that it is easy to search one's past and find things that "explain" one's present was demonstrated in one research study (Ross, Lepper, Strack, & Steinmetz, 1977). Students were given a history of a person. Some were told that he went on to have a career as a politician, while others were told that he went on to commit suicide. Neither group had any difficulty in finding things in the history that "explained" the eventual outcome, though both groups were working with identical past histories for the person.

It is possible that what is therapeutic about an insight or explanation in therapy has nothing to do with the truthfulness of that insight or explanation. Jerome Frank (1974, 1982) suggests that therapy operates by combating demoralization. Insights and explanations help if they make the client's experience seem sensible. An insight or explanation need not be true if it gives a person some hope and if it suggests some things the person can do to manage his or her life. Suppose you "learn" in therapy that your low self-esteem was "caused" by your father's constant put-downs. It does not even matter if this is true. If you believe it is true, you may decide, "Well, I don't have to put myself down just because he did." Or, "That was his opinion, and he was pretty screwed up himself." In other words, the explanation may be therapeutic anyway. Spence (1982), a psychoanalyst, has recently argued that psychoanalytic interpretations are therapeutic because of their coherence-making qualities, not because of their truth. Kelly (1963) found that plausible-sounding interpretations, based on no theory, were often therapeutic. So, just because an interpretation is therapeutic does not mean it is true, and just because it isn't true does not mean it won't be therapeutic.

We hope by now you see that you cannot draw conclusions from experience in therapy about whether or not therapy works, what in therapy works, or what the causes of psychological problems are. Therapy sessions are an important source of ideas, but do not provide empirically validated *truth.*

We emphasize this point because we so strongly disagree with therapists who say they have directly experienced the truth of their theories in therapy and dismiss attempts to examine their therapy scientifically. While there are great difficulties in doing scientific research on psychotherapy, that does not justify comfortably accepting one's experiences in therapy as "true." In fact, such an attitude, in our opinion, is dangerous. We believe that good therapists do not have dogmatic faith in their theories, but realize they are almost certainly inadequate in some ways. They are willing to modify their theories to fit the client, rather than try to force the client into their theory. Understanding why one's direct experience in therapy is such an untrustworthy guide to "truth" is a first step in this direction. To further reinforce this we will consider the enormous difficulties in doing valid scientific research on therapy.

METHODOLOGICAL ISSUES IN PSYCHOTHERAPY RESEARCH

We believe it is important for prospective therapists to understand the issues involved in examining psychotherapy scientifically. Understanding scientific methodology is really understanding what it is to truly know something or, more importantly, recognizing when you don't know something with certainty. Being aware of the limitations of his or her knowledge should help the therapist keep an open mind. Since we believe that therapy is often a matter of trying things until one finds what works for a particular client, maintaining an open attitude is an essential part of being a good therapist. For this reason we give a brief overview of methodological issues in doing psychotherapy research.

Controls

We have seen that we cannot attribute the "cure" of the man with the sinus condition to the type of psychotherapy he was undergoing, and it is possible that he might have recovered the memory of his mother's death or been cured of his symptom, even without therapy. In order to say that a particular therapy works, a therapist must be able to demonstrate that it was that treatment that caused change. However, it is possible that something else going on in client's life caused the change, not the therapy. A client may improve when he gets a job or when his wife recovers her passion for him. Many of the changes in children are simply due to the maturation process. It is even possible that certain disorders have their own natural course, like a cold or the flu, and the client would eventually get better without therapy. There is some evidence this is true for depression (Rosenhan & Seligman, 1984).

The most common way of demonstrating that it is a form of therapy that is the agent of change is to use a *control group.* A group of clients receives the treatment, and a group (the control) does not receive that treatment or any other. A bare outline of the procedure is to have, for example, 40 depressed patients, with 20 randomly assigned to the treatment group and 20 to the control group. Change in the individuals in both groups is measured at the end of treatment. If the clients in the treatment group have changed more than those in the control group, it is concluded that something about the treatment procedure caused the change.

The procedure is not as simple as the outline sounds. First, there are ethical problems in putting people in a control group because they are being denied treatment that they may need. Second, it may be difficult to get a group of patients who are similar in diagnosis, age, sex, and other variables. There are ways to handle this, which we will not go into here, but such matching methods make the research design more complicated. Third, control groups often do not remain untreated. Individuals who are not receiving the therapy being researched may go to some other therapist or talk to a friend, doctor, or minister (some of whom have had counseling training).

One of the ways devised to handle some of these problems is the *waiting list* control group. Since there are waiting lists at many clinics anyway, there is nothing unethical about placing some clients in the waiting list control group. Clients are randomly assigned either to available therapists or to the waiting list control. After the research treatment period, people on the waiting list are given treatment. People on waiting lists may be less likely to seek treatment elsewhere, so the waiting list control group may remain somewhat more "pure." One problem with the waiting list is that clients will not wait indefinitely. It cannot be used, for instance, in studies of a two- or three-year psychoanalysis. The treatment studied must be relatively brief.

Even if it is found that the treatment group does improve more than the control group, can it be concluded that it was really the therapy that did it? No. It could be that simply the attention given the clients or the power of suggestion or their belief that they would get better was the agent of change.

One way some psychologists have attempted to compensate for the effect of client expectations is to try to use *placebos.* In recent years the issue of placebos has received extensive attention in both medicine and psychotherapy (Shapiro & Morris, 1978). In medicine placebos are regularly used in research. In testing a new drug, for example, some patients are given the drug and others are given an inactive sugar pill, but are told they are being given the drug. In many studies placebos have been found to cause some improvement. In studying a therapy, a placebo control group would be a group that receives a "pseudo-treatment," a treatment that really does nothing, but looks like it would. However, how can a placebo group for doing therapy research be designed when we are not sure what ingredients make therapy work? Some have even argued that the powerful ingredients in therapy *are* the placebo effects: the power of suggestion and of hope.

Recently there has been controversy over whether placebos are meaningful or necessary for psychotherapy research (Critelli & Neumann, 1984; Parloff, 1986). An alternative to a placebo design is a *comparative design* (Basham, 1986; Parloff, 1986).

In a comparative design, known treatments are compared to one another. Basham argues that this may be preferable even to the use of control groups. These arguments rest partly on the state of our current knowledge about how effective psychotherapies are. We will return to this point later after discussing research on effectiveness.

Meaning and Measurement of Change

Defining Change Suppose you have an untreated control group and a placebo or comparison group. Now you have to decide how you are going to measure change. To do that you have to decide what you mean by change. And this turns out to be perhaps even more complex than the issue of controls.

What is change in therapy? How could you tell if your client had improved? Perhaps the most obvious answer is an improvement in the client's presenting complaint. If a client came to therapy because he was drinking too much, change might be if he is no longer drinking, that is, if there is *symptom removal.*

However, most therapies have more grandiose goals for their clients than the clients themselves have (Bergin & Lambert, 1978). They want to "reorganize the personality" or "get the client to trust his feelings, take responsibility," and "think rationally." Most therapies assume that symptoms are the result of a more pervasive underlying disorder. Substance abuse may reflect difficulties with self-esteem or interpersonal relationships. Anxiety may reflect a distorted cognitive style or a denial of one's potential. Conversion disorders may represent attempts to manage fear. Most psychological disorders, such as schizophrenia, personality disorders, conversion disorder, substance abuse disorders, and so on, are generally thought to represent organized patterns of symptoms, not collections of isolated symptoms (only the behavioral view has systematically questioned this). If symptoms are believed to represent some underlying disorder, therapists will not be interested in symptom improvement, but in changes in personality traits, emotional experiencing and self-esteem, and cognition.

Another difficulty with looking at change in terms of symptom removal is that often there is no simple, clear symptom. There may be multiple symptoms, and therapy may help some but not others. For instance, the borderline personality syndrome consists of several symptoms including impulsiveness, difficulty being alone, boredom, identity problems, anger, and depression. Or the presenting complaint may not be a clear-cut symptom, such as "drinking" or "fear of going out of the house." For example, a client may complain of being depressed, feeling that life is meaningless, or having difficulties in managing children, relating to a spouse, or relating to superiors at work.

One of the consequences of this is that what therapists see as change depends on their theoretical point of view. A behaviorist will focus on symptom removal and behavior change, a humanist on increased self-acceptance, responsibility taking, and emotional experiencing, a cognitive-behaviorist on progress toward a flexible, differentiated cognitive system.

In addition, what is considered a positive change varies. Generally, the therapist has a set of values about change derived from his or her theory of therapy. The client may have another. And relatives and friends of the client may have still another.

But you as a therapist are not only interested in change per se; you are also interested in positive change. And what you define as positive change depends in part on your values. Therefore, it is possible that people with different values will see change differently. Your client is a depressed, middle-aged woman who has spent her adult life being a housewife and mother, and starts therapy complaining of depression. Her children are now leaving home, and her life feels empty. Through therapy she begins to feel that she has spent her life living for others and that she wants to do something in the way of a career herself. As she begins to make these realizations, her depression lifts. Both she and the therapist see these changes as positive, but will her traditional husband who believes that a woman's place is in the home? Or a 17-year-old boy is referred to therapy because his parents are worried that he does not show proper interest in girls. The therapist discovers that he is gay, and therapy consists of helping him accept this side of himself. This may or may not sit well with the parents. In the extreme we have the point of view of R. D. Laing, who argues that schizophrenia is not an illness to be cured, but a growth experience to be accepted. Instead of trying to stop or suppress schizophrenic symptoms, Laing might possibly even encourage them.

It has generally been accepted that change in therapy is multidimensional (Bergin & Lambert, 1978). Different therapies concentrate on different types of change in the personality or behavior, and change looks different from different vantage points in the person's life. In fact, Stiles, Shapiro, and Elliot (1986) have argued that psychological normality is heterogeneous, in contrast to physical health. Different therapies have differing definitions of psychological health, and they may all be right for different individuals.

Measuring Change In the days when psychoanalysis ruled the roost in psychotherapy, change was usually defined in terms of change in personality structure. Thus someone who wished to demonstrate that therapy worked would use various personality tests to measure change. Since client-centered therapy emphasizes self-acceptance, research on therapy conducted by client-centered therapists used measures of self-acceptance, such as self-esteem scales or the "Q-sort." With the ascendancy of the behavioral perspective in the 1960s an increasing emphasis was placed on behavioral measures. It was argued that changes in personality structure and self-acceptance were meaningless unless they manifested themselves in observable behavior change, and so behavorial measures were favored over personality measures (Lambert, 1983).

Behavioral measures, self-acceptance measures, and personality tests are ways of measuring change. For instance, one way to measure change is to use a client's self-report before and after therapy. The client may be asked to rate the degree to which he has improved on the target symptoms that brought him to therapy. Or he may rate his behavior in various areas, such as in functioning socially and at work. Or he may rate himself on self-acceptance or on various personality traits. There are simple personality inventories in which the client checks off adjectives that he believes describe him. The Q-sort is another self-report measure (Stephenson, 1953). It consists of statements that the client sorts into series from "most like me" to "least like me." He may also do this for an ideal self, or how he would like to be. A moderate discrepancy between a perceived self-concept and an ideal self-concept is thought to be healthy.

If the client provides one source of measurement of change, the professional psychologist provides another. In research studies it is common to have the therapist rate the client's progress, often making the same kinds of ratings the client might be asked to make on himself. Or a professional psychologist assesses the client's personality from tests such as the MMPI, Rorschach, and TAT administered before and after therapy. They interpret results of the projective tests (for example, to see if ego strength has increased or tendencies toward denial and repression have declined) and look at changes in scores on objective test scales. For instance, Rogers, Gendlin, Keisler, and Truax (1967) found that clients with therapists high in warmth, empathy, and genuineness showed reductions on the "schizophrenia" scale of the MMPI.

A professional psychologist or psychiatrist may be used as a neutral observer. A common practice now in psychotherapy research is to have the client undergo a structured interview with a neutral psychologist or psychiatrist who preferably does not know whether the client was in therapy or in a control group. This neutral observer rates the client on a number of scales, for instance, how much anxiety or depression the client is exhibiting.

Another source of measurement of change is an informant's report, that is, a rating of the client made by some person in the client's life. For example, a client's wife may be asked to rate his personality or behavior before and after therapy.

Still another measurement of change involves attempts to assess behavior change directly. These may include ratings of behavior by others and more "objective" measures of behavior. We have already discussed behavioral measures in Chapter 2, but will briefly review them in their use in psychotherapy research. An example of an objective measure of behavior change is one that has been used in research on fears of snakes (Lang, Lazovik, & Reynolds, 1965). Before treatment with systematic desensitization, clients with fears of snakes were asked to approach a cage with a snake as close as they could. Some were so afraid of snakes they were not even able to enter the room in which the cage was placed. After treatment the same procedure was used. Most clients were able to approach the cage and look at the snakes, and some were even able to pick one up.

Most behavioral measures involve direct or indirect observation of behavior. A relative may keep track of the number of times the client loses his temper or drinks or engages in whatever target behavior is being modified. In hospitals nurses and attendants usually do the observing. They keep track of the target behaviors on some kind of behavior rating form. An indirect way of observing behavior is the use of tape recorders. For example, if family interaction patterns are the target, the family may be asked to keep cassette tape recorders going. This allows direct recording of arguments and other verbal patterns of interaction. Still another behavioral observation technique is to set up role-playing situations. These are less desirable than observing behavior in real life, but sometimes observing behavior in real life can be difficult. A role-playing situation may be set up, for instance, in which a client asks his boss for a raise. The effectiveness and appropriateness of his assertive behaviors can be rated.

Behaviorists do not rate traits, such as "aggressiveness," but observe the specific situations in which the client acts aggressively and how the client acts aggressively in those situations. After therapy, ideally the person is observed in the same kinds of situations to see if the behavior has indeed been modified. Therapy researchers in general now favor measurement of situation-specific behaviors as indexes of therapy effectiveness, if they can be obtained (Lambert, 1983).

We have not previously mentioned the *single subject research design* used by behaviorists. This strategy avoids the necessity of having many subjects to serve as treatment and control groups. Behaviorists sometimes use an individual subject as her own control. Before therapy begins the target behaviors are observed in the situations in which they occur and a baseline of the frequency is established. For instance, before treatment starts it is observed that on the playground a boy commits an average of four aggressive acts per 15-minute observation period. Behavioral observations are made again after treatment is initiated. If it has worked, the rate will have changed, in this case, perhaps it drops to one incident every 15 minutes. The effect of the treatment can be further studied by withdrawing or reversing it. Suppose the treatment for the aggressive boy was reinforcing positive behavior and ignoring negative behavior. Suppose also that before treatment it had been observed that the child was ignored when he acted positively and received a lot of attention (in the form of criticism and punishment) when he acted up. Upon the return to those responses to his behavior, the rate rose again to four incidents per 15 minutes. When the therapeutic strategy is resumed, once again the rate drops to one incident per 15 minutes. This demonstrates that it is the therapeutic strategy that has caused the improvement, without the use of control groups. Unfortunately, such a design is most appropriate to behavioral treatments and is far less applicable to approaches such as psychoanalysis or gestalt (how would you reverse the treatment of "insight into the past"?).

Objective records can be used as a measurement of change in psychotherapy. Some studies, for instance, use grade point average in school, and several studies have found increases in the average as a result of therapy. Other objective indexes that have been used include hospitalization rates, rates of incarceration in jail, and number of clients receiving therapy who are unemployed versus control subjects unemployed.

A particularly important subgroup of objective indexes for some disorders are physiological measures, such as blood pressure, heart rate, galvanic skin response (which reflects anxiety), penile tumescence (when sexual dysfunction is the target symptom), and brain wave response. These measures are usually used when the disorder being treated involves stress or anxiety or when the treatment used includes relaxation, meditation, or biofeedback methods. Weight loss or weight gain are obvious biologically based measures when the problem being treated is either obesity or anorexia.

Since each of the many ways to measure change has its limitations, it is now usually recommended that multiple measures, utilizing different sources of information, be used (Lambert, 1983). For instance, a battery of measuring devices recommended by a group of psychotherapy researchers (Waskow & Parloff, 1975) includes several client self-reports, one report filled out by the therapist, one assessment done by an independent mental health professional, two reports filled out by other people in the client's life, and one objective personality test. Most of the reports filled out by client, therapist, and independent assessor are ratings of target complaints and symptoms of psychopathology. The particular measures recommended by Waskow and Parloff have been debated (see various articles in Lambert, Christensen, & DeJulio, 1983), but the idea of multiple measures is generally accepted.

A number of research studies (see Lambert, 1983) have shown that different measures of change do not correlate with one another. For example, several studies have found that therapy attempts to reduce specific fears may reduce behavioral avoidance of the feared object without modifying the client's self-reported level of fear (Lambert, 1983, p. 19). Other studies support this. Thus therapist, client, significant others, independent assessors, and personality tests may all give different answers on how much change, if any, has occurred. Also, behavioral measures may not correlate with any of these other measures.

Behaviorists have criticized client self-reports of how much they have changed, therapist ratings, ratings by independent assessors, and personality test measures, because they do not measure behavior change directly. On the other hand, behavioral measures are difficult to obtain on many client problems. For instance, Frank (1974) has argued that therapy primarily works by countering demoralization. How would one use a behavioral measure to decide if demoralization has been countered? Perhaps one could follow the person around and note that she smiles more, but this does not seem very workable.

The issue of behavior change versus self-reported change deserves a bit more comment. We believe that objective measures of behavior, when possible, are highly desirable, but we also believe that some kinds of changes in therapy do not lend themselves to such measures. For instance, a client who says he wants to be able to "handle situations more adaptively" may want to be flexible rather than reacting in stereotyped ways to specific situations. It is difficult to imagine any manageable behavioral measure of this, short of following the person around for several days. It would seem to us that the client's self-report may be the most workable index of change on such a goal. Or suppose the goal of therapy is self-acceptance. The behavior change associated with self-acceptance may be quite subtle. Suppose a client comes to therapy complaining of shyness. There are at least two ways to treat shyness. One may be to use assertion training. If this is the method, then we can use the criterion of behavior change to see if the therapy worked: Does the client act less shy in social situations? But suppose the goal is self-acceptance (as it might be for client-centered therapy). Suppose the client comes to prize and value being introverted and not outgoing, but wants to feel better about holding this value. Overt behavior change may not be a meaningful criterion, because the client's behavior will be virtually identical before and after therapy. Increased self-acceptance would manifest itself in changes in the client's feelings, such as not feeling anxious about being shy, but they may be quite difficult to observe and measure.

Client self-reports have their own problems. Clients may have a desire to please the therapist and so may say that therapy has helped whether it has or not. Or clients may have a need to believe that it has helped (especially at $90 an hour). Ratings by therapists and independent assessors also have problems. Behavior is often situation specific. Therefore, how someone acts in the therapy hour or in a one-hour interview with an assessor may not have much to do with how the client behaves in real life. In addition, therapists have their own motives for perceiving the client as having changed for the better. Indeed, while therapists do not always overestimate how much their clients change (Newman, 1983), several studies have found that they sometimes do. For instance, Lieberman, Yalom and Miles (1973), in their study on encounter groups, found that therapists vastly overestimated how many of their clients benefited from the group experiences. Therapists estimated 89 percent; more objective measures of change placed the figure at 34 percent.

Analogue Designs

We will mention one way psychotherapy researchers attempt to cope with some of the above complexities. This is the use of *analogue research designs.* An analogue design attempts to scale down real therapy to a few variables that can be studied in a laboratory setting. What is gained over doing research on real therapy is precision. For instance, a technique may be studied independently of how it is actually used in a real therapy context. Studies of the gestalt empty-chair technique (reviewed in Chapter 6) are examples. In each study a subject attempts to resolve conflict feelings by using the empty-chair technique. In contrast to a real therapy context, this is the only technique used, it is done only for a short time, and it is done only once. The problem of control groups is simplified because it is easy to have some subjects do nothing for an hour and serve as a control. It is also easy to design a placebo control. One might, for example, have subjects merely discuss their problem or read articles about it for an hour. Measurement problems are also simplified. Usually specific, immediate change is measured, and issues of how the person will behave in real life are avoided. Behavioral measures that can be taken in the laboratory, physiological measures of anxiety, or paper-and-pencil attitude measures may be used. Analogue studies on fears of snakes, for instance, may measure how much closer the subject will approach a snake after treatment. In the empty-chair studies various ratings of conflict resolution were taken. One study (Bohart, 1977) found that subjects were less likely to be punitive toward other subjects on a learning task after the empty-chair technique.

Analogue studies can help to understand relationships between the time-limited use of specific therapeutic interventions and certain specific changes that can be immediately measured in a laboratory situation. The problem is that analogue situations are rarely similar to real therapy situations. Clients are often college undergraduates rather than "real" clients. Only one specific technique is usually used, in contrast to actual therapy in which a variety of things may happen over several sessions. One may question if analogue situations tell us much about how real therapy works. On the other hand, there is no guarantee that analogues don't tell us about what goes on in real therapy (Kazdin, 1980). Furthermore, they can be helpful in understanding specific therapy processes. Ideally both analogue studies and studies of actual therapy can converge to help us understand how therapy works.

Other Research Problems

We have only scratched the surface of the many problems associated with doing research on psychotherapy. Follow-up is another problem: How long after therapy should clients be followed to see if change has been maintained? Following clients for any length of time is difficult; clients move, die, or otherwise become unavailable.

Or suppose you want to compare psychoanalysis to behavior therapy. You should probably have several psychoanalysts and several behavior therapists in your study. But do all psychoanalysts or behavior therapists proceed identically? What if different kinds of persons become psychoanalysts and behavior therapists? Suppose some personality characteristic differs between these kinds of persons and suppose that affects the outcome of therapy?

By now we hope you realize it is exceedingly difficult to provide an answer to the question: "Does the so-and-so approach to psychotherapy work?" For similar reasons it is quite difficult to know why a therapy works in certain cases. Is it the personality of the therapist or the ingredients in the therapy that the particular theory claims are important? Is it factors that no one is aware of? We also hope by now that you see that believing you can tell whether therapy works by personal experience, either as therapist or client, is quite simplistic. By returning to our examples at the start of the chapter you can ask yourself: Would the client have changed without the therapy? Has the client changed? If change has occurred, is it because of insight, getting in touch with feelings, combating dysfunctional cognitions, or desensitization? Could it have been that any of those techniques would have worked because they all gave the client a sense of hope? Could it have been that the therapist was a supportive, encouraging person? Are the therapist's perceptions of change accurate? How permanent and stable are the changes?

THE EFFECTIVENESS OF PSYCHOTHERAPY

Despite all the problems, a good deal of research has been done on psychotherapy. There are two general kinds of psychotherapy research: *process research* and *outcome research.* Outcome research deals with the effectiveness of psychotherapy. Process research deals with the processes that go on in therapy interactions. An example of process research is a study by Brunnink and Schroeder (1979), in which they compared the verbal behavior of psychoanalytic, gestalt, and behavior therapists. As expected, there were several differences. For instance, gestalt therapists were more active in providing direct guidance and used more self-disclosure than psychoanalysts.

Process and outcome research can be linked; a study can attempt to relate differences in therapy process to therapy effectiveness. For instance, researchers could see if the differences between gestalt and psychoanalytic therapists in verbal behavior relate to differences in effectiveness. Our review of psychotherapy research below will focus primarily on outcome research.

If we arbitrarily date the existence of psychotherapy as a formal discipline to Freud's work, then psychotherapy has been around for almost 100 years. Yet aside from a few early efforts, among them some early work by Carl Rogers (see Rogers & Dymond, 1954), it has only been in the last 30 years that intensive efforts have been made to study the question of psychotherapy's effectiveness scientifically. Perhaps the event that triggered these efforts was a report by Hans Eysenck published in 1952. Eysenck searched the literature for published reports of success rates for different psychotherapies and for different psychotherapy institutes. He collated these rates for neurotic patients and found a success rate of 44 percent for psychoanalysis and 64 percent for various other approaches. In order to know if these rates meant that therapy worked or not, Eysenck attempted to find a recovery rate for neurotic patients who did not receive psychotherapy. He discovered data on two such groups of patients and calculated that they had a spontaneous recovery rate of 72 percent. The discouraging conclusion from Eysenck's data was that at best there was no evidence that therapy worked, and at worst the less therapy one had the better!

For many years Eysenck's conclusion remained unchallenged. From 1970 on, however, things have changed. Bergin (1971) did a thorough analysis of Eysenck's original data and came to different conclusions. He suggested that Eysenck had made a number of debatable decisions in calculating his success rates. For instance, he thought that Eysenck's criteria for success were considerably more rigorous for the psychoanalytic data than for the untreated control patients. Making alternative decisions, which Bergin admitted are no more defensible than Eysenck's, Bergin calculated an 89 percent success rate for psychoanalysis.

Reviews of Evidence

A number of different reviewers have claimed to have found large amounts of data supporting the effectiveness of psychotherapy. Meltzoff and Kornreich (1970), Bergin (1971), Bergin and Lambert (1978), and Luborsky, Singer, and Luborsky (1975) have all concluded that the evidence generally supports its effectiveness. Parloff (1979), for instance, stated that "A review of controlled studies permits the conclusion that psychodynamic therapies, client-centered psychotherapy, cognitive therapies, and behavioral therapies have achieved results that are superior to no-treatment procedures" (p. 298). In addition most of these reviewers conclude that at this point it cannot be said that any one approach is significantly superior to any of the others.

Meta-analysis

We have repeatedly referred to the meta-analysis of Smith, Glass, and Miller (1980). Meta-analysis is a statistical procedure that is applied to the results of all available studies on a certain topic. From the procedure an effect size is calculated. For those of you who know something about statistics, an effect size is something like a standard deviation. It is a way of calculating how much the average effect due to a particular treatment is above the mean or average effect of those who are not given the treatment. The numbers given for effect sizes are not easily interpretable by themselves, but we can give you an approximate idea of what they mean. Smith, Glass, and Miller (1980) located 475 studies in which some kind of therapy was compared to some kind of control group. The overall effect size for psychotherapy was 0.85. This means that the average person who received therapy was better off than 80 percent of the persons who did not. For comparison's sake, the effect size for nine months of instruction in reading in elementary school in improving reading scores is 0.67 (Smith, Glass, & Miller, 1980, p. 88). The effect size for cigarette smoking's increasing the probability of getting lung cancer is 0.60 (APA Commission on Psychotherapies, 1982, p. 137).

In terms of specific treatments cognitive therapies, hypnotherapy, and systematic desensitization appeared to be the most effective. Psychodynamic, client-centered, gestalt, rational-emotive, transactional analysis, behavior modification, and various eclectic behavioral treatments were around the average in effectiveness. Despite the apparent superiority of some of the cognitive-behavioral therapies, Smith, Glass, and

Miller conclude that on closer analysis there is no evidence that behavioral therapies in general are superior to verbal therapies in general. They reach this conclusion for a variety of reasons, including the fact that behavioral treatments used different kinds of measures of effectiveness than verbal therapies and in studies where the two were pitted against one another directly there was no clear superiority.

Other conclusions from the Smith, Glass, and Miller meta-analysis are as follows. There was no evidence of differences in effectiveness between group and individual therapy, nor did the duration of treatment make a difference. Psychologists were more effective than psychiatrists, who in turn were more effective than educational counselors. However, Smith, Glass, and Miller believe that the data do not support a conclusion that one professional group is indeed more effective than another, since many variables enter in. As has often been found, a significant contributor to the effectiveness of psychotherapy was the client. Depressed and phobic clients, more intelligent clients, and female clients appeared to benefit most from therapy.

In general, reviews of studies of effectiveness find evidence supporting the effectiveness of all the established "brands" of therapy (psychodynamic, gestalt, client-centered, cognitive, cognitive-behavioral, and behavioral). All of these therapies appear to cause client improvement superior to clients in both untreated and placebo control groups. There is no evidence that any one of these therapies is generally superior to the others. However, in both the Luborsky, Singer, and Luborsky (1975) review and the Smith, Glass, and Miller (1980) meta-analysis, behavioral therapies appear to have a slight edge over the others, accompanied by cognitive therapy in the Smith, Glass, and Miller analysis, as well as hypnotherapy.

We will briefly review one particular research study that exemplifies the above conclusions. The study by Sloane, Staples, Cristol, Yorkston, and Whipple (1975), comparing psychoanalytically oriented psychotherapy to behavior therapy, is generally considered to be one of the best ever done on comparative effectiveness of psychotherapies (Smith, Glass, & Miller, 1980; Bergin & Lambert, 1978). A group of patients with diagnoses of either personality disorder or neurotic disorder were randomly assigned to psychoanalytically oriented treatment, behavioral treatment, or a waiting list control group. Three psychoanaytic therapists and three behavioral therapists were used. Attempts were made to get experienced, outstanding representatives of each approach (two of the three behavior therapists were Joseph Wolpe and Arnold Lazarus). Patients were treated for four months. Attempts were made to define what would be included as behavior therapy and as psychoanalytic therapy. Patients were assessed right after the end of treatment, and again a year after beginning treatment. Assessment of therapeutic outcome included several personality inventories, ratings by patients, therapists, and informants, assessment by an independent assessor, and analysis of target symptoms.

On target symptoms both therapy groups improved more than the control group. On assessments of more global improvement the two therapies were again rated as generally equal, though there were some instances in which behavior therapy appeared to be superior. No specific patient characteristics appeared to relate generally to therapeutic outcome, but there was some evidence that "acting-out" patients did better in behavior therapy.

Findings on Some Specific Issues

We will touch briefly on some other issues and findings about psychotherapy. One such issue is the *spontaneous recovery rate.* Eysenck (1952) estimated that about two-thirds (72 percent) of untreated neurotic patients improved spontaneously over a two-year period. Bergin (1971) and Bergin and Lambert (1978) contested this view. Their argument is essentially that there is no such thing as "one" spontaneous recovery rate. Studies have found different spontaneous recovery rates for different disorders, in different settings, using different criteria of outcome. Bergin and Lambert (1978) say the average of available figures is closer to 43 percent than to Eysenck's 67 percent. However, they believe even this figure is misleading, because the rate varies. They also point out that it is difficult to obtain a pure figure, because individuals denied therapy in the study often go elsewhere and are not truly "untreated." Rachman (1973) has defended Eysenck's figure, but the Bergin and Lambert view is generally accepted (for instance, see Parloff, 1979).

Another issue raised by Bergin and Lambert (1978) is that of *therapy-caused deterioration.* Is it possible that therapy could hurt some clients? On the basis of their review of the research literature Bergin and Lambert's answer is yes. For instance, Lieberman, Yalom and Miles (1973) studied the impact of 30 hours of encounter group experience and found that 8 percent of the participants could be judged to have been actively hurt by the experience. The researchers concluded that certain kinds of clients are susceptible to deterioration, mainly those with lower self-esteem, lower interpersonal skills, and more unrealistic expectations about the group experience. Certain types of therapist styles are also associated with participant deterioration. Particularly destructive are aggressive, confrontive therapy styles. Gurman (1975) also concluded that there was evidence to support an 8 percent deterioration rate in marital and family therapy as well.

Because of the difficulty in determining whether therapy causes some clients to deteriorate (perhaps they would have with or without therapy), others do not think that the deterioration effect has been reliably established (APA Commission on Psychotherapies, 1982). Although Smith, Glass, and Miller (1980) found that 9 percent of the effect sizes they calculated were negative, they did not feel that they had established convincing evidence of deterioration (p. 88). While deterioration has not been unequivocally demonstrated, in our opinion the evidence that destructive effects may occur is sufficient for therapists to take seriously the possibility that their treatments may occasionally harm people as well as help them.

There have been some findings on the applicability of different approaches for specific disorders. To quote the American Psychiatric Association Commission on Psychotherapies:

> The general trend has been for the more recent and more comprehensive reviews to conclude that psychotherapy is effective for a variety of symptomatic and behavioral problems: these include chronic moderate anxiety states, simple phobias, depressive symptoms, sexual dysfunctions, adjustment disorders, family conflicts, and communication difficulties. . . . Research on schizophrenia has demonstrated that traditional psychotherapies contribute little additional benefit to pharmacother-

> apy. . . . the effects of psychotherapy plus drugs are basically additive in treatment of depression. . . . studies of psychotherapy for medically ill patients suggest that psychotherapy plus medical regimen is more effective in certain medical illnesses than is medical treatment alone. (p. 233)

According to Parloff (1979) systematic desensitization is particularly effective with simple phobias. Smith, Glass, and Miller (1980) found that cognitive and cognitive-behavioral approaches are effective with anxiety problems. Beck's cognitive therapy has been demonstrated to be effective with depression; it has recently been reported that it is as effective as the use of antidepressant medication (Bower, 1986). Smith, Glass, and Miller found that verbal therapies are especially effective in dealing with problems of self-esteem. It is generally conceded that behavior modification approaches are particularly effective with problems such as bed-wetting, tics, and other such specific symptoms. There is little evidence that psychotherapy helps antisocial disorders, alcoholism, and drug abuse (Parloff, 1979).

CURRENT STATUS AND THE FUTURE OF PSYCHOTHERAPY RESEARCH

We have seen that many reviewers concluded that psychotherapy is effective and that there are no significant differences among the varying approaches. However, not all reviewers have accepted this conclusion. There are still those who dispute the idea that all therapies are approximately equivalent. By and large these are behaviorists, who claim that their analyses of the data support the superiority of behavior therapy and that the supposed effectiveness of other approaches is based on faulty data (Eysenck, 1978; Heimberg & Becker, 1984; Rachman & Wilson, 1980; Wolpe, 1982). However, the general consensus is that the evidence is ambiguous and does not currently justify saying that any one approach is superior (Kazdin, 1986; Stiles, Shapiro, & Elliot, 1986).

With the general acceptance of "equivalence," psychotherapy research appears to be ready to move on to other issues. VandenBos (1986), introducing a special issue of the *American Psychologist* on psychotherapy research, says, "By about 1980 a consensus of sorts was reached that psychotherapy, as a generic treatment process, was demonstrably more effective than no treatment. . . . It now appears that single-focus 'outcome' (or efficacy) research should be a 'thing of the past' " (p. 111). In addition, because of its emphasis on questions of whether psychotherapy works and which approach works best, most psychotherapy research in the past has not generally been useful to practicing clinical psychologists (Morrow-Bradley & Elliot, 1986). It is likely that psychotherapy research in the future will focus on more specific questions of effectiveness, such as effects of particular interventions, different aspects of the therapy process, client variables, and effects on different disorders.

One example of this new direction is the "events" approach of Rice and Greenberg (1984). They analyze reports by researchers of different theoretical persuasions (predominantly gestalt, psychoanalytic, and client-centered) in which specific events in psychotherapy are studied. The goal is to do a fine-grained analysis of what actually occurs in a therapy intervention. For example, Greenberg (1984) analyzes the gestalt empty chair technique as follows. The client attempts to work out a conflict by "splitting" herself into an "experiencing" part and a "critical" part. The "critic" starts out focusing externally ("you should"). It is also lower on a measure of experiential involvement than the "experiencing" part (meaning that it is more distant and "intellectual" in the way it communicates). As the dialogue continues, both sides move toward compromise, but in particular, the critic becomes more experientially involved, begins to explore from an internal frame of reference more, and becomes more accepting of the other side. These changes are associated with the person's finding a resolution between the two sides.

This kind of research focuses on specific processes in therapy that may affect positive or negative outcome. Another related research area of current interest is the "therapeutic alliance." Going back to the emphasis of client-centered therapy on the importance of the relationship of the therapist and client (see Chapter 4), there has been a good deal of research on the qualities the therapist presents to the client. Henry, Schacht, and Strupp (1986) have done a more fine-grained analysis of the therapist-client relationship. They found that greater levels of "helping and protecting" and "affirming and understanding" were associated with positive therapeutic outcome. Patient behaviors of "disclosing and expressing" were related to these qualities, while the behaviors of "walling off and avoiding" were more associated with negative and hostile therapist behaviors. The most intriguing finding of this study was that the same therapist, using the same techniques, could come across with one client as "affirming and understanding" and with another as "blaming and belittling." This suggests that the presence of helpful behaviors in the therapist is partially dependent on the behavior of the client.

Research from the events paradigm and on the therapeutic alliance seem to offer concrete, helpful information for practicing therapists. Global comparisons between differing approaches will undoubtedly continue to be done, but it appears that therapy research in the future will be more oriented toward determining the effects of specific aspects of therapy.

REFERENCES

APA Commission on Psychotherapies. (1982). *Psychotherapy research: Methodological and efficacy issues.* Washington, DC: American Psychiatric Association.

Arlow, J. A. (1984). Psychoanalysis. In R. Corsini (Ed.), *Current psychotherapies* (3rd ed.). Itasca, IL: Peacock.

Basham, R. B. (1986). Scientific and practical advantages of comparative design in psychotherapy outcome research. *Journal of Consulting and Clinical Psychology, 54,* 88–94.

Bergin, A. E. (1971). The evaluation of therapeutic outcomes. In A. E. Bergin & S. L. Garfield (Eds.), *Handbook of psychotherapy and behavior change.* New York: Wiley.

Bergin, A. E., & Lambert, M. J. (1978). The evaluation of therapeutic outcomes. In S. L. Garfield & A. E. Bergin (Eds.), *Handbook of psychotherapy and behavior change: An empirical analysis* (2nd ed.). New York: Wiley.

Bohart, A. C. (1977). Role playing and interpersonal-conflict reduction. *Journal of Counseling Psychology, 24,* 15–24.

Bower, B. (1986). Treating depression: Can we talk? *Science News, 129,* 324.

Brunnink S., & Schroeder, H. (1979). Verbal therapeutic behavior of expert psychoanalytically oriented, Gestalt and behavior therapists. *Journal of Consulting and Clinical Psychology, 47,* 567–574.

Critelli, J., & Neumann, K. (1984). The placebo: Conceptual analysis of a construct in transition. *American Psychologist, 39,* 32–39.

Eysenck, H. J. (1952). The effects of psychotherapy: An evaluation. *Journal of Consulting Psychology, 16,* 319–324.

Eysenck, H. J. (1978). An exercise in meta-silliness. *American Psychologist, 33,* 517.

Farrelly, F., & Brandsma, J. (1974). *Provocative therapy.* Cupertino, CA: Meta.

Frank, J. D. (1974). Psychotherapy: The restoration of morale. *American Journal of Psychiatry, 131,* 271–274.

Frank, J. D. (1982). Therapeutic components shared by all psychotherapies. In J. H. Harvey & M. M. Parks (Eds.), *Psychotherapy research and behavior change.* Washington DC: American Psychological Association.

Greenberg, L. (1984). A task analysis of intrapersonal conflict resolution. In L. Rice & L. Greenberg (Eds.), *Patterns of change: Intensive analysis of psychotherapy process.* New York: Guilford.

Guntrip, H. (1973). *Psychoanalytic theory, therapy, and the self.* New York: Basic Books.

Gurman, A. S. (1975). Evaluating the outcomes of marital therapy. In A. S. Gurman, (Chair), *Research in marital and family therapy.* Workshop presented at the Sixth Annual Meeting of the Society for Psychotherapy Research, San Diego, CA, June, 1976.

Heimberg, R. G., & Becker, R. E. (1984). Comparative outcome research. In M. Hersen, L. Michelson, & A. S. Bellack (Eds.), *Issues in psychotherapy research.* New York: Plenum.

Henry, W. P., Schacht, T. E., & Strupp, H. H. (1986). Structural analysis of social behavior: Application to a study of interpersonal process in differential psychotherapeutic outcome. *Journal of Consulting and Clinical Psychology, 54,* 27–31.

Hobbs, N. (1968). Sources of gain in psychotherapy. In E. Hammer (Ed.), *Use of interpretation in treatment.* New York: Grune & Stratton.

Kazdin, A. E. (1980). *Research design in clinical psychology.* New York: Harper & Row.

Kazdin, A. E. (1986). Comparative outcome studies of psychotherapy: Methodological issues and strategies. *Journal of Consulting and Clinical Psychology, 54,* 95–105.

Kelly, G. A. (1963). *A theory of personality.* New York: Norton.

Lambert, M. J. (1983). Introduction to assessment of psychotherapy outcome: Historical perspective and current issues. In M. J. Lambert, E. R. Christensen, & S. S. DeJulio (Eds.), *The assessment of psychotherapy outcome.* New York: Wiley.

Lambert, M. J., Christensen, E. R., & DeJulio, S. S. (Eds.). (1983). *The assessment of psychotherapy outcome.* New York: Wiley.

Lang, P. J., Lazovik, A. D., & Reynolds, D. J. (1965). Desensitization, suggestibility, and pseudotherapy. *Journal of Abnormal Psychology, 70,* 395–402.

Lazarus, A. A. (1984). Multimodal therapy. In R. Corsini (Ed.), *Current psychotherapies* (3rd ed.). Itasca, IL: Peacock.

Lieberman, M. A., Yalom, I. E., & Miles, M. B. (1973). *Encounter groups: First facts.* New York: Basic Books.

Luborsky, L., Singer, B., & Luborsky, L. (1975). Comparative studies of psychotherapies: Is it true that everyone has won and all must have prizes? *Archives of General Psychiatry, 32,* 995–1008.

Meltzoff, J., & Kornreich, M. (1970). *Research in psychotherapy.* New York: Atherton Press.

Morrow-Bradley, C., & Elliot, R. (1986). Utilization of psychotherapy research by practicing psychotherapists. *American Psychologist, 41,* 188–197.

Newman, F. E. (1983). Therapist's evaluation of psychotherapy. In M. J. Lambert, E. R. Christensen, & S. S. DeJulio (Eds.), *The assessment of psychotherapy outcome.* New York: Wiley.

Nisbett, R. E., & Ross, L. (1980). *Human inference: Strategies and shortcomings of social judgment.* Englewood Cliffs, NJ: Prentice-Hall.

Parloff, M. (1979). Can psychotherapy research guide the policymaker? A little knowledge may be dangerous. *American Psychologist, 34,* 296–306.

Parloff, M. (1986). Placebo controls in psychotherapy research: A *sine qua non* or a placebo for research problems? *Journal of Consulting and Clinical Psychology, 54,* 79–87.

Perls, F. S., Hefferline, R. F., & Goodman, P. (1951). *Gestalt therapy.* New York: Julian Press.

Rachman, S. (1973). The effects of psychological treatment. In H. Eysenck (Ed.), *Handbook of abnormal psychology.* New York: Basic Books.

Rachman, S., & Wilson, G. T. (1980). *The effects of psychological therapy* (2nd enlarged ed.). New York: Pergamon Press.

Rice, L. N., & Greenberg, L. S. (Eds.). (1984). *Patterns of change: Intensive analysis of psychotherapy process.* New York: Guilford.

Rogers, C. R., & Dymond, R. F. (Eds.). (1954). *Psychotherapy and personality change.* Chicago: University of Chicago Press.

Rogers, C. R., Gendlin, E. T., Kiesler, D., & Truax, C. B. (1967). *The therapeutic relationship and its impact: A study of psychotherapy with schizophrenics.* Madison: University of Wisconsin Press.

Ross, L., Lepper, M. R., Strack, F., & Steinmetz, J. L. (1977). Social explanation and social expectation: The effects of real and hypothetical explanations upon subjective likelihood. *Journal of Personality and Social Psychology, 35,* 817–829.

Shapiro, A. K., & Morris, L. A. (1978). The placebo effect in medical and psychological therapies. In S. L. Garfield & A. E. Bergin (Eds.), *Handbook of psychotherapy and behavior change: An empirical analysis* (2nd ed.). New York: Wiley.

Simkin, J. S., & Yontef, G. M. (1984). Gestalt therapy. In R. Corsini (Ed.), *Current psychotherapies* (3rd ed.). Itasca, IL: Peacock.

Sloane, R. B., Staples, F. R., Cristol, A. H., Yorkston, N. J., & Whipple, K. (1975). *Psychotherapy versus behavior therapy.* Cambridge, MA: Harvard University Press.

Smith, M. L., Glass, G. V., & Miller, T. I. (1980). *The benefits of psychotherapy.* Baltimore, MD: Johns Hopkins University Press.

Spence, D. P. (1982). *Narrative truth and historical truth: Meaning and interpretation in psychoanalysis.* New York: Norton.

Stephenson, W. (1953). *The study of behavior: Q-technique and its methodology.* Chicago: University of Chicago Press.

Stiles, W. B., Shapiro, D. A., Elliot, R. (1986). Are all psychotherapies equivalent? *American Psychologist, 41,* 165–180.

Truax, C. B. (1966). Reinforcement and non-reinforcement in Rogerian psychotherapy. *Journal of Abnormal Psychology, 71,* 1–9.

VandenBos, G. (1986). Psychotherapy research: A special issue. *American Psychologist, 41,* 111–112.

Waskow, I. E., & Parloff, M. B. (Eds.). (1975). *Psychotherapy change measures.* Washington, DC: Department of Health and Human Services.

Wolpe, J. (1982). *The practice of behavior therapy* (3rd ed.). New York: Pergamon Press.

Chapter 11

Convergence of Approaches to Psychotherapy

The era when most therapists were strict adherents of one approach to psychotherapy or another may be passing. Recent surveys have found that the majority of practicing clinical psychologists perceive themselves as eclectic (Garfield & Kurtz, 1976; Norcross & Prochaska, 1982; Prochaska & Norcross, 1983), that is, they use techniques and concepts from a variety of theoretical sources. This is true even of those identified with major theoretical approaches. For instance, both James Masterson, an object relations theorist, and Aaron Beck, one of the major cognitive therapists, will use family therapy if appropriate (Beck, 1985; Masterson, 1985). This trend has resulted in several systematic eclectic approaches (see Norcross, 1986).

Along with the tendency toward eclecticism in practice, there has been a growing interest in finding commonalities among differing approaches and ways of integrating them. Prior to the 1970s there had been sporadic efforts in this direction. Dollard and Miller (1950) attempted to translate Freudian concepts into behavioral terminology. Gendlin's theory of experiencing (Gendlin, 1968, 1969) proposed that there was a common underlying therapeutic process among differing approaches. Frank (1961) was among the first to propose that there may be nonspecific factors common to the effectiveness of the various approaches.

Recent interest in integrating approaches has taken several directions. One approach is to incorporate ideas and techniques from other approaches into a theoretical base derived from one particular perspective. For instance, Wachtel (1977) attempts to integrate behavioral ideas into a contemporary ego-psychoanalytic framework. Several other authors suggest ways behavioral techniques can be utilized in a psychoanalytic framework (see Goldfried, 1982; Arkowitz & Messer, 1984). Johnson (1985) proposes that a wide range of therapeutic approaches, including gestalt therapy, behavior modification, neurolinguistic programming, and family systems theory, can be used to treat characterological disturbances. While his approach is eclectic at the level of therapeutic technique, it is based on a contemporary psychoanalytic theoretical model.

Similarly, Swensen (1980) provides a scheme for using a range of therapy approaches based on where the client falls on a model of ego development (Loevinger, 1976). Ellis sees his rational-emotive therapeutic approach as providing a base for eclectic use of techniques. Client-centered therapists also see their approach as an underlying philosophy that can be compatible with a wide range of therapeutic techniques from different orientations. Eclectic models of therapy based on the Rogerian therapeutic conditions have been developed (Carkhuff & Berenson, 1967; Egan, 1982). Finally, Lazarus's multimodal therapy is eclectic in its use of techniques, but is founded on a social learning theory.

A separate approach has been to look for common elements among theoretical perspectives and practices. Frank (1982) has suggested that one underlying dimension of all therapies is that they combat demoralization. In addition they provide an emotionally charged, confiding relationship; a healing setting (such as, hospital, clinic, office); a rationale or conceptual scheme to help the client make sense out of his or her experiences; and a ritual to restore health that both client and therapist believe in. These function to provide a therapeutic relationship that combats alienation and demoralization, expectations of help, new learning experiences, arousal of emotions, enhancement of the client's sense of self-efficacy or mastery, and opportunities to practice new learning.

Goldfried (1980a) has noted the following common features: a facilitative therapeutic relationship, creation of client expectancy of help, encouragement of reality testing of client ideas and perceptions, provision of corrective experiences through which faulty ideas and behaviors may be modified, and provision of an external or objective perspective on things.

Marmor (1985) has suggested that most therapies provide a facilitative relationship, opportunities for release of emotional tension in an atmosphere of expectation and hope, cognitive learning, repeated reality testing and practice, and corrective emotional experiences. Furthermore, most therapies rely on operant conditioning, reinforcing some behaviors and not others, even if only by talking about them in therapy. Also, whether they explicitly acknowledge it or not, most therapies provide opportunities for identifying with and modeling after the therapist. Finally, all therapies work partially through suggestion and persuasion, again, even if this is not explicitly acknowledged.

In an issue of the journal *Cognitive Therapy and Research* (Goldfried, 1980b), therapists of differing orientations were asked for their opinions on the importance of various elements of the therapy experience. Almost all agreed on the importance of a good therapeutic relationship, the provision of new, corrective experiences, the provision of direct feedback on thinking, emotion, and behavior, and the utilization of cognition and awareness.

A third approach has been to suggest an integrative model for doing therapy that is not based on any one theoretical perspective. For example, Prochaska (1984) suggests problems can be primarily within the person (self-esteem, anxiety), between people (sex, communication, hostility), between the individual and society (impulse control, conformity versus self-actualization), or concerning values and life's meaning (self-actualization, personal fulfillment). Prochaska suggests there are five basic therapeutic processes: consciousness raising, emotional catharsis and corrective emotional experiences, exploration of choice and responsibility, alteration of responses to conditional stimuli, and reinforcement and contingency management. A good eclectic therapist would be willing to use any or all of these if relevant to treating a particular client's problem.

There are also approaches to commonality and integration on the theoretical level. Meichenbaum suggests that all therapies may operate in part by disrupting patterns of dysfunctional self-speech (Chapter 8). Mahoney (1985) believes that the problem of meaning underlies many psychological difficulties and makes a number of general theoretical suggestions about processes of human change. (We will refer to this article in our discussion of commonalities below.) Bohart (1982) suggests several theoretical goals common to cognitive and humanistic approaches. He also points out that when cognitive therapists disrupt global abstract dysfunctional thought patterns, they may be inadvertently disrupting what humanists call intellectualizing. This may lead to clients' attending to the immediacy of their experiencing, a humanistic goal. Conversely, when humanists encourage clients to attend to immediate experiencing, they may be inadvertently disrupting cognitive patterns viewed as dysfunctional by cognitive therapists.

Finally, Mahoney (in press) has proposed an integrative *developmental cognitive model.* He assumes that reality is relative and that each individual constructs his or her reality. This is compatible with Carl Rogers's multiple realities and constructivist ideas. There is no "one" objective reality that can be said to be the correct one. Therefore, one cannot talk about the rationality or irrationality or the truthfulness or falsity of constructions. One can only talk about whether or not a person's construction of reality works or is viable. This also implies that ideas about reality are never perfect or finished, but continue to be modified with experience. Learning and development involve elaborating, differentiating, and refining ideas about the world. These ideas or constructions exist to a large extent at a tacit or nonconscious level. Some of these constructions may have been developed early in life. People resist rapid change in their core constructs because they strive to protect the integrity and coherence of their world views.

In contrast to some cognitive theorists, Mahoney emphasizes the importance of affect or emotion. He sees emotions as powerful, primitive knowing processes. He also emphasizes the unity of thought, feeling, and action.

For Mahoney, psychological difficulties represent discrepancies between challenges and capacities. In other words, difficulties arise when coping skills cannot match the challenges of reality. Furthermore, pathological responses often represent behavior patterns that were adaptive in some prior life situations. Therapy for Mahoney includes utilizing cognitive insight, exploring affective responses, utilizing behavioral methods, working with rather than against resistance, and providing a safe, caring therapeutic relationship as a context that facilitates change.

Mahoney's approach draws on psychodynamic, humanistic, cognitive, behavioral, and systems perspectives. In this respect it represents one of the first truly eclectic theoretical attempts at integration.

Not all theorists welcome attempts at integration. Landsman (1982) suggests that behaviorism and humanism have much to learn from one another while preserving their separate identities. Franks (1984) believes that behavior therapy and psychoanalysis are conceptually incompatible and that integration even at the level of clinical practice has drawbacks. Kendall (1982) presents several arguments against integration, although his general stance is cautiously open to it.

We believe there is a convergence in various areas and that in the not too distant future someone may be able to propose a unifying theory that preserves and integrates the most important insights of each perspective. Below we will give our view of similarities among differing approaches, as a tentative step in that direction.

We often have heard graduate and undergraduate students say, "All the therapies are talking about the same thing, only in different language!" For instance, they might note similarities between Carl Rogers and Heinz Kohut (and, in fact, Kahn, 1985, and Rogers and Sanford, 1984, have also noted similarities). Both Rogers and Kohut talk about the development of the self and the importance of empathy, yet we know of some psychoanalytic theorists who have said that these concepts of self and development are not the same at all. So, whereas individuals not identified with a particular approach may see similarities between it and other approaches, those working within the approach will often see it as quite different.

Who is correct? We believe both are. Those who look at two different approaches and see similarities are usually focusing on dimensions that the two approaches have in common, while those who see differences are focusing on dimensions on which the approaches differ. Are an apple and an orange "the same" or not? From the perspective of a grocer, they are "the same" in that they are both fruits. The apple, however, might react quite indignantly to the suggestion that it is "the same" as an orange.

To say an apple and an orange are "the same" is to say they share some common characteristics (they are both fruits). This does not deny that they are crucially different in many other aspects. We believe this is also true in comparing approaches. At a general, abstract level, we are impressed by the fact that a variety of therapies have common features. For instance, we think it is interesting that psychoanalytic and humanistic theories both see the development of the self as important. Both approaches seem to focus on a roughly similar area of functioning as important and to come up with concepts in that area that roughly resemble one another in some general ways. At the same time the differences between the psychoanalytic and humanistic concepts of the self are also important. The psychoanalytic self is not the humanistic self.

Once similarities and differences have been identified, theorists of psychotherapy can begin to ask questions that may lead to future integration. Based on research we may ultimately decide that one view of the self is more adequate than another. Or we may find that one perspective best explains some clients, but another best explains others. We might then be able to find a unified concept that preserves what is useful among the individual views. Finally, it might turn out that all the theories are wrong in focusing on a particular area of functioning.

Our first suggestion will be that all therapies are based on an attempt to solve a common underlying problem. We will look at their differing conceptualizations of that problem, and their procedures for circumventing it. Then we will look at commonalities among their views of what is psychopathological and what changes will lead to more effective functioning. Finally we will look at the therapeutic procedures that are supposed lead to changes.

THE BASIS OF ALL THERAPIES: THE PROBLEM OF ACCESS

In a sense all therapies exist because people's attempts to control their own or others' behavior and feelings by rational argument, persuasion, command, and analyzing frequently fail (see Rachman, 1981, for a similar suggestion). Suppose you have a friend named Sue. Sue is involved with Bill, but Bill constantly mistreats her. He goes out on her, is inconsiderate and self-centered, and has even hit her on occasion. All of Sue's friends tell her that Bill is no good for her. She even will say that she knows that he is no good for her. Yet this knowledge seems to have no impact on her feelings. She loves him nevertheless.

At the same time there is Ron. Ron is kind, considerate, faithful, and reliable. Everyone tells Sue that Ron would be perfect for her. Intellectually, Sue believes this also. But knowing that Ron is right for her seems to have no impact on how she feels. She just doesn't feel attracted to him.

We will give one other example. You are about to go on a job interview. You begin to feel anxious. You tell yourself there is nothing to fear. You may even try rationally to argue with yourself: "It is in my better interest to be relaxed at the job interview." Yet, perversely, against your own better interest, you find your pulse racing, you're sweating, and your voice may be quavering as your enter the interview room.

People may know intellectually what they should do, what would be best for them, but find themselves unable to act or feel accordingly. When they dislike some way they are behaving or feeling, they may try different intellectual means to change. They may self-engineer (Gendlin, 1964), that is, decide how they should behave and command themselves to act accordingly. They may argue rationally with themselves, marshaling evidence for why they ought to change their behavior. Or, they may hunt for reasons why they aren't acting the way they believe they ought—they speculate that there may be underlying reasons for their behavior. They play detective and marshal clues for various possibilities. Maybe they are staying in a dysfunctional relationship because they have an underlying need for security. Or perhaps they eat too much because they are compensating for dissatisfaction in their love life. Or maybe they have an underlying need to fail. But such deductions do no good. They still don't change. Thus, it could be said that they try to cognitively control their behavior either through rational argument, command and persuasion, or through attempts at self-analysis. Underlying these attempts to change behavior are usually expectations of how they think they should be in order to be happy.

People use similar methods to try to control or change others' behavior. Parents say, "Eat your spinach. It's good for you." They warn adolescents of the dangers of drug abuse. They present a friend with rational arguments in favor of leaving a destructive relationship.

From Freud on, therapists have been aware of the impotence of cognitive knowledge alone to cause behavior change. For instance, Beck (1979), working with a client, suggests the following insight: "Do you see any connection then between your trying to make things go well with the men and your futile attempts to make things go with your mother?" And the client replies, "Yes, I can see it. . . . I understand it in my head but somehow I haven't been able to digest it emotionally and get to the point where I can not involve myself in these negative relationships."

If behavior and feeling states could be controlled consistently through conscious, rational means, we would not need therapists. People would simply explain to themselves and others logically why they should act or feel in such and such a way and they would do it. But people come to therapy when such efforts fail. They come when they are unable to persuade themselves not to be depressed or that there is nothing to fear if they go outdoors. They come because they cannot control their drinking or change the pattern of arguing in their marriage. They come because they have physical illnesses that are inexplicable and do not respond to medical treatment. They are sent by parents or the legal system, who have failed to persuade them to comply with society's norms.

The problem of access is: Why does direct rational, intellectual information fail to gain access to the system of the person and facilitate change? For instance, why doesn't it work when a person says to herself, "I can control my impulses to eat if I try," but it does work when a therapist, utilizing Erickson's techniques, says, "Pay attention to what you do this week when you control your urge to eat." The message "I can control my impulses to eat" is implied in both, but the less direct communication somehow gains access and works, while the more direct communication does not get through.

Different therapies have different theories of why direct, conscious, rational communications do not have an immediate impact on the person. Different therapies also have their own ways of gaining access. In fact, most therapy techniques could be viewed as different methods of communicating or generating information so that it gets through and facilitates change. We will first look at general strategies for facilitating access and then at each major perspective and how it deals both theoretically and practically with this problem.

STRATEGIES FOR FACILITATING ACCESS

Experiential Methods

Cognitive learning and consciousness raising have been postulated as common underlying dimensions in psychotherapy, yet, as we have repeatedly pointed out, no approach relies on cognitive learning alone. All, in one way or another, include an experiential component to increase the effectiveness of cognitive learning. The importance of experiential learning has also been cited as a common dimension (Goldfried, 1980a). However, we wish to point out the interrelatedness of cognitive and experiential learning. That is, sheer cognitive learning alone seems to be ineffective. Therefore, an experiential component to therapy appears to be one of the ways of gaining access. There are at least three different, but overlapping, ways it is utilized to facilitate access: direct experience, experiential articulation, and experiential evocation.

Direct Experience Many approaches rely on direct experiential learning. Behavioral approaches are perhaps the best example of this. Behavior modifiers reinforce or extinguish behavior at the moment it is occurring. Meichenbaum and Bandura provide direct modeling of individuals learning how to cope with various problem situations and then encourage practice of the behaviors involved. Assertion training and social skills training programs involve direct behavior rehearsal. Conditioning techniques, such as systematic desensitization, attempt to modify directly emotional reactions to real or imagined stimuli.

The cognitive-behavioral approaches of Beck and Ellis include homework assignments in which clients are instructed to test their cognitions directly against experience. Beck also believes that the therapeutic relationship itself is an important source of learning. The client can learn from watching the therapist how to challenge dysfunctional cognitions.

From a client-centered perspective Gendlin (1967) has argued that direct experiential interaction in the therapeutic relationship is a potent source of learning. Clients learn how to be self-accepting, how to listen to themselves, and how to be genuine through interaction with an accepting, empathic, genuine therapist.

Recent psychoanalytic approaches, such as those of Kohut and object relations theory, see the therapeutic relationship as a situation in which the client can directly experience the distorting aspects of primitive childhood constructions of reality. Change takes place through a corrective emotional experience as much as through cognitive insight.

Strategic therapists also use exercises involving direct experience. For instance, a client may be coached in how to woo his wife (Madanes, 1985). Other techniques encourage the client to engage in certain behaviors in the hopes that they will break up the client's old system. Once the system is broken up, new, more adaptive behaviors may be creatively discovered through action, without the necessity of cognitive learning or insight.

Finally, gestalt therapy also relies on direct experiential learning. Rather than talk about conflict resolution, gestalt therapists will have clients role play the various sides of the conflict to experience direct learning (Greenberg, 1984).

Experiential Articulation Many approaches value the acquisition of some kind of insight, or the generation of new, useful self-knowledge. In psychoanalysis insights may be acquired by the client's own processes of introspection or may be given by the therapist. In client-centered therapy the process of finding just the right words to formulate what is implicitly known or sensed at the experiential level "carries forward" the growth process (Gendlin, 1964). In both cases the formulation of this new knowledge in words is not therapeutic unless it articulates or matches the client's experiential state.

Psychoanalytic interpretations are effective only if the proper affective context has been established, that is, the relevant concrete memories and feelings must be close to consciousness. It is like discussing a movie: One is most likely to "gain insight" into the movie when it is "fresh" in one's mind. Similarly, insights only work when the problem is "hot," "present," or "alive," rather than "cold." At that point an insight can articulate or connect with a host of bodily aspects of the problem: vivid memories, feelings, or bodily reactions. In the words of one of our colleagues, therapy may connect "feelingless words" with the experiential feeling and "wordless feelings" with meanings (Beverly Palmer, personal communication).

Client-centered reflections or experiential responses are also attempts to articulate what is currently being felt at the experiential level. Gendlin (1964, 1969) says that words are therapeutic if they come from the client's experiential sense of the problem, rather than being cognitively generated and applied *to* experiential sense. Thus, a client may say, "I feel really bothered with my wife," and a client-centered therapist may articulate that sense of being bothered more fully, "You feel like she never lets you alone."

Something like experiential articulation also plays a role in Beck's cognitive therapy. For instance, a cognitive therapist could say to a depressed client, "You generate your own depression by interpreting events in a negative way." Such an abstract cognitive insight would probably have little effect on the depressive. What Beck has the client do is to keep a daily record of dysfunctional thoughts. At the moment the client is experiencing depression associated with some dysfunctional thought, he attempts to capture that thought in words and write it down, along with an objective description of the situation. The abstract cognition that the client generates his own depression through his cognitions is now matched to a vivid, concrete experiential example.

Finally, de Shazer (1985), a strategic therapist, also uses a variety of experiential articulation. A client who is having trouble dieting may say, "I never can control my eating." De Shazer points out that clients often phrase their complaints in terms of "always" or "never," but things are rarely "always" or "never." However, it would be useless to tell the client, "Oh no. It's not true that you never control your eating. Sometimes you do." It is more effective to instruct the client to "pay attention to what you do when you control your urge to eat," because there almost always will be times that the client does control the urge. The client thus learns concretely and experientially that it is not a matter of "always" or "never." We will have other occasions to consider this intervention, as there is more to it than the client's matching of cognitive insight to experience.

All this suggests that cognitive articulation can be useful if it is done in relation to the relevant, directly felt experience. While Beck has his clients keep daily records of dysfunctional thoughts primarily for data-gathering purposes for later discussion and evaluation, psychoanalysis and client-centered therapy believe there is an immediate, direct benefit of experiential articulation. For psychoanalysis such articulation is an emotionally experienced insight that leads to change. For client-centered therapy experiential articulation leads to a directly felt change in the problem, a sense of integration, clarification, and closure.

It is possible that formulation or articulation of one's experience at the moment it is "fresh" consolidates or facilitates learning from it. We have already considered the example of talking over a movie when it is fresh. As one attempts to put one's reactions into words, one clarifies, integrates, and consolidates one's impressions of it. Another example might be recording one's impressions of a situation as one observes it. One's articulation of what one observes will help organize and consolidate learning from the observations (see, for instance, Bandura, 1986). Trying to articulate one's impressions later when the situation is not "fresh," is more difficult and will probably have less of an impact on learning.

There is a question whether experiential articulation creates change or merely consolidates it. Psychoanalysis assumes that gaining insight causes change. Gendlin (1964) has argued that insight actually follows change. For example, by the time a person can articulate his anger toward his father, a change has already taken place to make that anger consciously available. Repression has already been overcome. The formulation of the anger in words may serve only to consolidate and integrate this change into the personality structure.

Experiential Evocation in Therapy In order for new meanings to be developed and learned in an experiential context, therapy may have to evoke the relevant experiential reactions. This can be done through the use of words, images, or exercises. Techniques may be used to evoke vivid memories, images, relevant feelings, "felt meanings" (Gendlin, 1964), or other whole body experiences associated with a problem situation. Or there may be a specific focus on the evocation of strong emotional reactions.

Evocation of experiential reactions There are various ways therapists attempt to evoke experiential reactions in therapy. One way is to use vivid, concrete language instead of abstract language or jargon. Concrete, everyday language is more likely to evoke an experiential reaction than abstract jargon. Some research (Nisbett & Ross, 1980) has suggested that we are more influenced by vivid information than by "pallid" abstract information. Most therapy orientations advocate the use of concrete, vivid language.

To make information vivid and concrete, therapists of many schools attempt to get clients to "flesh out" vague, abstract characterizations of their problems with concrete details. Polster (1985), from a gestalt perspective, has suggested that clients often come into therapy only with "titles" of their stories ("My wife and I don't get along"), and the job of therapy is to supply the concrete details. Fleshing out abstractions is also an integral part of Beck's cognitive therapy.

Fleshing out abstractions partially allows hypothesis testing. The client is able to see if generalizations such as "I can never control my hunger" or "I always fail" are accurate. In addition, however, recalling a concrete example of when the client failed or when he had difficulty controlling his hunger will be more likely to evoke the bodily feelings and experiences associated with the abstract statement. This is an explicit part of Rice's reformulation of empathic and experiential responding in client-centered therapy (Rice, 1974; Rice & Saperia, 1984). The client is asked to imagine himself in the specific situation in which the problem is experienced. Then exploration takes place with that specific situation as a constant referent. The gestalt role-playing technique also reevokes the concrete experiential components of a problem.

Exercises designed to be experientially evocative are a part of many encounter groups. Participants may engage in a "blind walk," in which they are blindfolded and led around by another participant. The issue of trust is not merely talked about, but actively experienced. Guided imagery or guided fantasy exercises are also used. Presumably imagery and fantasy evoke more of the full body response to a situation than mere words. For instance, one might imagine how it would feel to be a "lost lonely child in the woods."

Body-oriented approaches, such as bioenergetics, manipulate the body. Their belief is that buried memories and conflicts are directly represented in muscle tightness and body posture. Exercises designed to loosen the body will then "release" a flood of feelings, memories, and experiences.

Imagery is also used in the cognitive therapies of Beck and Ellis, and therapy approaches based on Erickson's work, such as strategic therapy and neurolinguistic programming, often use stories or metaphors. Such stories probably work both because they convey the meaning in an experientially evocative context and because their indirect nature bypasses the "negative self-monitor" (see below).

Arousal of emotion Some approaches to therapy, such as primal therapy, focus explicitly on the arousal of strong emotion. The belief is that certain emotions, usually anger or sadness, are so repressed by society and thus by the individual that they "build up" like fluids inside the person, causing psychological problems. This is often called the "hydraulic model" of emotions. These approaches attempt to evoke these emotions and to cause them to be discharged through expression, called "emotional catharsis."

While catharsis therapies and techniques may often be effective, the idea that emotions are like fluids that need to be vented and discharged is debatable. Gendlin (1984), for instance, has pointed out that merely "feeling the feeling" is not by itself therapeutic. People often fully experience and express their anger without undergoing any change or resolution of their problems. Beck (Beck, Rush, Shaw, & Emery, 1979) has noted that crying and the expression of sadness in cognitive therapy sometimes makes clients feel better, but often does not.

Bohart (1980), summarizing research literature on anger, has concluded that the hydraulic model of emotions does not fit the data and that catharsis or expression of feelings alone is not therapeutic. Sometimes anger expression makes people feel more angry rather than less, and while crying sometimes makes people feel better, frequently it does not. He suggests that what is therapeutic about approaches that stress emotional arousal and expression is that such approaches provide experiential opportunities for cognitive insight or working through. Without such an insight or working through process, the sheer expression of feelings will not be therapeutic. In other words, to relate it to our current topic, it is likely that emotional arousal and expression evokes the whole range of bodily experiences and memories associated with a conflict situation. It is not merely the emotional expression itself that happens. In addition, the whole experiential context of the problem is made available for cognitive reworking. (See Box 11.1.)

Beck (1985) has said that cognitive therapy works better when affect is aroused. It is easier to work on a client's anxiety or depression when the client is experiencing these feelings. But this is not because the emotions are being expressed and drained off, but because when the client is feeling anxious or depressed, the associated dysfunctional cognitions are more available and more readily modified.

One other reason for the therapeutic efficacy of emotional arousal has been suggested by Frank, Hoehm-Same, Imber, Liberman, and Stone (1978). They suggest, on the basis of some research findings, that emotional arousal makes the client more likely to adopt the suggestions and cognitive framework being advocated by the therapist.

BOX 11.1
Are Emotions Like Fluids to Be Discharged?

You are angry at your professor because you feel you were unfairly graded on a test. Is your anger like a fluid that can be drained off through expression? It may depend on where and how you express it. If you talk over your feelings with an empathic friend, you may indeed feel better. If you express your anger to the professor, and he admits his mistake and changes your grade, you will feel still better. But is it the expression of the feelings in these two cases that would make you feel better or the communication with someone who helped you work through the issues involved with your anger?

Bohart (1980) suggests it is more likely to be the latter. Instead of talking to a friend or a responsive professor, suppose you scream in the middle of a field. Do you think your anger would be drained away and you would no longer feel angry about how unfairly you were treated? Or suppose your professor is unresponsive to your feelings? Do you think your expression would drain off the anger in that case? It would be quite unadaptive if we could eliminate feelings of anger regarding some injustice by simple expression without doing anything to modify the unfair situation.

If emotions are like fluids, and we can drain them away through expression, what about love and happiness? Do we reduce our level of love by expressing it? Do we become less happy if we shout for joy?

Sheer emotional expression by itself is not necessarily beneficial. It needs to be accompanied by some sort of cognitive working through process (see also Nichols & Efran, 1985).

Experiential Components in Therapy All these various uses of an experiential component in therapy suggest that therapy must ultimately have an impact at the bodily or experiential level. Sheer cognitive insight, especially if couched in abstract terms, seems to have little impact at the bodily or experiential level. Therefore, some therapists attempt to work directly at that level. They reinforce behavior changes. These behavior changes presumably include the bodily cues and schemas that direct and control the behavior. Or they attempt to teach new behavior schemes or to directly condition emotional responses.

Other approaches attempt to modify these bodily reactions and schemes through cognitive reconstruction. They may help the client to gain insight, or they may convey a new way of looking at something in a story. In either case such cognitive insights are useless unless the relevant bodily, experiential cues are present. There must be a matching between bodily experience and cognition for the cognition to influence or consolidate behavior change. Experiential evocation, then, may make bodily cues available for reworking and reprocessing. Cognitively talking about and articulating one's experience as one is experiencing it may possibly create change at the bodily level. In a similar manner, observing someone do something is a direct visual experience, and learning may be facilitated if one articulates to oneself the relevant factors being demonstrated.

This would explain why abstract, cognitive insight is frequently useless. Such abstract cognitive insights by themselves do not evoke the relevant concrete bodily reactions. If they are to be useful at all, they need to be timed to when such cues are present.

Some social psychological research is relevant. At least under some conditions (see Collins, 1970) attitude change is facilitated by having people role play the attitude one would like to have them adopt. For instance, a person may be instructed to write an essay in favor of a certain position. To write an essay one needs to think, remember, and rehearse, and any bit of experience relevant to the position being argued may be dredged up. Under some conditions (and what conditions these are continues to be controversial) such role playing does indeed cause attitude change.

It should also be pointed out that the relevant variable is the presence of experiential cues, not necessarily emotional cues. Many therapies have focused on emotion or affect. But emotion is actually a subset, or one kind, of experience. It is likely that emotional focus in therapy is helpful because it evokes experiential reactions. When a client gets in touch with his childhood anger toward his father, this usually also evokes vivid visual memories and other bodily reactions. The therapeutic learning probably involves all the bodily components of the experiential reaction, not just the emotional ones, just as learning to drive a car evokes and involves experiential reactions that are not necessarily emotional.

We will conclude this section with a relevant story of a friend we know. When this friend was a young woman she was in a play. Her role was of a pregnant woman considering an abortion. Until our friend played this role she had never really "worked out" her own feelings about abortion. Oh sure, she had heard pro and con arguments. But, as we have seen, most such arguments tend to be abstract, and they often do not have an impact on people because they are not "meaningful" or "relevant" at the time. How often do you hear people say: "They were just words until it happened to me." In terms of what we have been saying, the arguments do not have an impact, they are "just words" because the person is not having the relevant bodily experience. For our friend, arguments pro and con abortion had been just words until she played the role of someone struggling with the issue. She found that through playing this role, the issue became much more "concrete and real" to her, and she had to work through her own feelings about it. When, sometime later, she accidently became pregnant and had to face the issue for herself, she found that her prior experience in the play had helped her clarify her choices. She was able to decide fairly confidently on the right thing to do for her.

The Use of Habit

Aside from an experiential component, there are two other general therapeutic solutions to the problem of access. We turn to that of "habit" next.

We have suggested that abstract cognitive knowledge by itself often fails to have a bodily impact. However, this may be true only if we are talking about single instances of insight. Repeating the insight over and over may eventually have an impact on both behavior and feeling. This is a key component of the cognitive approaches of Beck and Ellis.

There are at least two reasons for this. The first is evidential, that is, people are not going to give up a belief system simply because of one or two disconfirmations of it. Even though Beck could demonstrate that a client's failure at wallpapering wasn't really a failure (see Chapter 8), the client will need repeated demonstrations before he is willing to give up his general belief that he is incompetent. People want good, stable evidence before they are willing to change their beliefs.

A second possible reason why insights may need to be repeated before they have any effect relates to the experiential component in therapy. Suppose you are learning to drive and your instructor gives you directions: "Let out the clutch slowly as you step on the accelerator." While this may seem fairly specific, it is actually an imprecise, abstract description of what you are to do. How slowly? How much do you step on the accelerator? When do you coordinate the two events? You jarringly find out that the instruction is only a rough guide to what you are to do as you lurch forward wildly or stall the car. The words of the instruction are abstract because they do not precisely tell you (nor could they) the specific bodily movements and events involved. You have to use the words as a rough guide and then practice. Eventually, you learn at the bodily level the specific reactions and movements involved and no longer need to guide yourself with the imprecise words. When you finally "get it right," you may even find that the vague and abstract words now make concrete bodily sense. "Oh, I see! Let the clutch out as I step on the accelerator!"

Practice with any cognitive abstraction may eventually cause bodily change. The abstract generalizations guide the learning of specific bodily skills. Suppose I challenge myself every time I catastrophize: "It's not awful that I didn't get an A on the test, although I would have preferred an A." I may eventually change the bodily schemas associated with the catastrophizing in a manner similar to my learning to work a clutch. Eventually I may no longer need to verbalize to myself. Suddenly I may find that the words make more sense to me: "Oh, I see! I would have preferred to get an A, but it isn't awful that I didn't!"

We have given examples of habit as a method of creating access for certain cognitive insights. Of course, habit is also a key component of behavioral approaches, in which repeated practice facilitates direct experiential learning.

Neutralizing the Effects of Negative Self-monitoring

One of the most important abilities that human beings have is to monitor their own actions, thoughts, and feelings. They not only respond to stimuli, perform behaviors, think, and feel, but watch themselves do these things and use their observations to change if they are not responding adaptively. It has been argued that virtually all dysfunctional behavior involves dysfunctions in self-monitoring (Bohart, 1987). An integrative approach to psychotherapy by Ryle (1982) is based on a similar idea. All of us have mistaken ideas about reality from time to time and occasionally behave in ways that are not adaptive. However, most of the time we are able to correct this behavior, while in cases of dysfunctional behavior the person fails to correct or modify mistaken ideas or maladaptive responses.

In psychotherapy we suggest that there are various ways clients have of monitoring themselves and others that contribute to the access problem. Information can result in change only if it is fully and accurately heard. However, this does not always occur in therapy because people tend not to *listen* to the information being given, but instead evaluate it in ways that seem to interfere with its therapeutic function. We call this "negative self-monitoring." For instance, clients may find ways of discounting or misusing the information they receive. They may hear feedback as criticism and use it to further devalue themselves. Clients may discount positive feedback because they believe the therapist is being paid to "say nice things," or they may resist input because they perceive it as a threat to their autonomy or to unconscious maintenance of repression. Or, as part of how they monitor themselves, they may use their perceptions of what is wrong to implement dysfunctional methods of fixing things. For example, they may try to fix a sexual arousal problem by trying to become aroused, which may instead make matters worse. Two methods that therapies use to solve the problem of negative self-monitoring are the adoption of the phenomenological attitude and the use of indirect communication.

Phenomenological Attitude Many therapies attempt to get the client to suspend critical evaluation. For instance, psychoanalysis encourages the client to free associate. In normal social conversation a person evaluates the thoughts that pop into his mind. Those that are seen as irrelevant or morally or socially inappropriate are censored by the person and not verbalized. With free association the client is to report whatever comes to mind.

Psychoanalysis believes there is an unconscious censor that critically evaluates both internal and external information. It screens out of consciousness forbidden wishes, impulses, and thoughts. It also leads the person to distort, deny, or otherwise misuse information from outside, such as communications by the therapist. Getting the client to at least consciously suspend the censor and simply listen to whatever comes to mind nonevaluatively gradually allows forbidden material to appear. As this happens more and more the client's conscious "observing" ego becomes strengthened, and the client has less and less need to evaluate and screen out or distort information. In some sense the goal of psychoanalysis is to enable the client to listen nonevaluatively to all his thoughts, feelings, and fantasies, no matter how primitive.

Client-centered therapists similarly encourage a nonevaluative attitude. They do this through their own nonjudgmental acceptance of the client and through attempts to intuit a human, understandable motive behind behavior, even if the behavior is dysfunctional or repugnant. Gendlin (1964) emphasizes that attempts at self-monitoring and self-regulation "from above" are untherapeutic and that the client needs instead to wait and listen to his experiential self. A person cannot therapeutically hear what is in his experiencing if he is critically evaluating what ought to be there.

Gestalt therapists have argued that "pure awareness" is therapeutic. They encourage attempts to simply observe and be aware of what is, without either analysis of what it means or judgments of how it ought to be or whether it is good or bad, appropriate or inappropriate, adaptive or maladaptive.

We call this the use of the "phenomenological method" in therapy. The phenomenological method was originally a philosophical approach developed by Edmund Husserl (1964). The goal of the phenomenological method is to "get back to pure experience" by suspending preconceptions. Therapeutically, this means the client should try to simply observe something without attempting to figure out what it "means" at an underlying level, or without judging it or evaluating it as good, bad, adaptive, inadaptive, appropriate or inappropriate. This also means that the client suspends the way he already views and interprets the world and his experience. Only by doing this can new learning occur.

The phenomenological method is used in its purest form in meditation. Washburn describes receptive meditation as "the practice of open, nonreactive attention. Experience is witnessed nonselectively and without interference or interpretation . . ." (1978, p. 46). Variants also appear in both cognitive and behavior therapy. Behavioral approaches to habit control include the client's keeping of a diary of when and where he or she engages in the habitual behavior. Keeping such a record makes the client observe his or her own behavior and reactions and the situations that seem to elicit them. Reinforcement procedures can be utilized to modify the behavior. However it has been found (Goldfried, 1982) that simply keeping the diary itself is often helpful, perhaps because of the client's increased awareness.

Beck's cognitive treatment for depression includes keeping records of when and where depression occurs and the dysfunctional cognitions present. This employs the phenomenological method because the client is learning to separate the situation itself from his analysis and evaluations of it. Beck has clients practice writing alternative interpretations of the situation. This further reinforces the client's learning to perceive a situation independently of his or her preconceptions. Ellis's A-B-C model, in which A is the situation, B the interpretation, and C the emotional or behavioral reaction, also encourages the client to observe nonevaluatively.

Finally, de Shazer (1985), a strategic therapist, also uses a variant of the phenomenological method. As we have seen, a client with a dieting problem may be encouraged "pay attention to what he does when he resists the urge to eat." The intervention is to simply pay attention to these things, not to try to make them happen.

Adopting the phenomenological attitude encourages the client's "gaining distance" from his or her problem. Mahoney (1985) lists "distanced manifestation" as one method of problem resolution. He says it "entails a joint effort to allow the problem to manifest itself fully while one simultaneously disidentifies from it" (p. 30). This can be seen to operate in various therapeutic approaches. For instance, psychoanalytic free association allows parts of the problem to become "fully manifest" and the client learns to "disidentify" with the unconscious impulses: "I am not identical with my primitive incestuous desires. There is more to me than that."

From a client-centered perspective, Gendlin (1982) has described what happens as one learns to listen nonevaluatively and focus on one's felt meanings: "In learning to put problems down one learns a specific relation to problems: sensing them but not being in them. . . . That distance enables one to relate to the problem as a whole, *from a spot a little outside it*" (p. 27, italics Gendlin's). From a cognitive perspective, Beck, Rush, Shaw, and Emery (1979) say, "As situations and cognitions are recorded, the patient gains some distance from their effect. The therapist's goal is to increase the patient's objectivity about his cognitions . . ." (p. 164).

Indirect Circumvention These techniques are used primarily by therapists who have been influenced by Milton Erickson. They include indirect suggestion, communication through metaphorical stories, reframing, and paradoxical interventions (see Chapter 9). The intervention we have considered several times previously is an example of indirect suggestion. A client who wants to diet is not directly told "You can control your eating." Instead, the message is indirectly suggested: "Pay attention to what you do when you control your urge to eat."

Paradoxical interventions and reframing apparently encourage the persistence of symptoms and problem behaviors. A contentious client may be told to deliberately get in arguments. A couple who continually fight may be told that their fighting is a sign of how much they love one another. They may even be told that to stop fighting would be disastrous for their marriage. How do such paradoxical interventions work?

There are a variety of theories as to why they do work (Riebel, 1984). We suggest that one reason is that they circumvent or turn off critical self-monitoring. The activity of criticizing oneself for problem behavior such as arguing is disrupted if one is told to do it, or if one is told that it would be disastrous if one stopped it. Similarly, the activity of trying to self-engineer, control, and demand that one act differently is also disrupted.

Therapeutic Value of Suspending Self-monitoring But why is it therapeutic to turn off these activities? Why is it therapeutic to cease self-criticism, conscious intellectual self-analysis, and self-engineering? Why is it therapeutic to observe and listen nonevaluatively?

We have suggested that critical self-monitoring can get in the way of therapy. Gendlin (1984) has pointed out that we often try to solve our own problems by playing therapist with ourselves. "Our usual conscious self is the therapist, often a crudely directive one who gets in the way. . . . That therapist frequently attacks in a hostile way . . . claims to be smarter . . . takes up time with distant inferences and interpretations" (p. 83). Similarly, Rice and Saperia (1984) suggest that what often gets in the therapist's way is "the tendency of clients to react to their own reaction and focus on how irrational or undesirable it had been, expanding on their own childishness or irrationality or on the undesirable consequences" (p. 40).

One positive result of suspending one's critical, analytic, and evaluative monitoring is that new information can "get through" and facilitate change. For instance, if I am continually evaluating my behavior and feelings in terms of shoulds and oughts, I may distort them. If I think I should not be behaving in a certain way, I may either deny the existence of this behavior or misrepresent it. I may "repress," "deny," or "split off" my feelings or other parts of myself. I may also misrepresent or distort messages from outside. Information then fails to have an impact and facilitate change.

Similarly, if clients' existing ways of interpreting the world are inadequate, then any self-analysis they engage in will reflect these inadequacies and merely perpetuate the problem. Depressive thinking is a good example. Even information that most people see as positive fails to change a depressive, because it is evaluated in terms of the depressive's existing negative conceptions. Similarly, a depressive critically monitors his own behavior and sees it as inappropriate, bad, or maladaptive. He does not merely receive information, but interprets it to conform to his view of the world and himself. Because of this monitoring any internal or external communication loses its therapeutic potential.

Social psychological research on attitude change (Collins, 1970) shows that information will best facilitate attitude change if monitoring activity can be neutralized. For instance, people are more likely to be influenced by a speaker who presents both sides of the argument, not just the side he is advocating. Their "critical monitor" says, "He is trying to be fair," and they allow themselves to trust the information more. Similarly, people are more likely to be influenced by something they overhear than by the same thing said directly to them. The critical monitor says, "He doesn't know I'm listening, so he's not trying to impress or please me, so he must really mean it." The fact that overheard communications "get through" better than communications made directly to the person recalls the use of indirect suggestion and related therapeutic techniques.

Critical self-monitoring may interfere with information processing because it mobilizes resistance. People resist being influenced by others, even if it is to their disadvantage to resist. Brehm (1966) has suggested that people sometimes resist attempts to influence them to protect and demonstrate their freedom and independence. For instance, if they comply with a suggestion made directly to them, they may feel as though they are compromising their autonomy.

People also resist internal behavioral and emotional prescriptions. If I critically tell myself I ought to diet, I may experience my freedom as being restricted and rebel. This may be particularly true if I perceive dieting as a demand internalized from my parents and society. It is for this reason that gestalt and client-centered approaches are so interested in getting clients to choose their shoulds and oughts as their own or discard them.

There are other reasons for resistance. The critical monitor may evaluate information as a threat to repression and therefore distort or deny it. Similarly, information that is evaluated as a threat to existing ways of viewing the world and the self may be interpreted and modified to be compatible with the existing schemes (Nisbett & Ross, 1980; Kuhn, 1970). The information's potential for causing change is therefore neutralized.

Another way self-monitoring may interfere therapeutically is that there appear to be times when one is more likely to change if one does not try, rather than try. Perhaps the best example is modifying sexual behavior. If a client is busy trying to change behavior, he or she is less available to experiencing the pleasurable, self-corrective aspects of the activity. In this case monitoring behavior and trying to self-engineer become part of the problem and interfere with natural self-regulatory processes. De Shazer (1985) and Watzlawick (1985) point out that a person's attempts at solution often perpetuate or magnify the problem. This is particularly true if one's attempts grow out of one's way of viewing the problem and the world, and these views are dysfunctional.

For instance, suppose a husband and wife both believe that "If you love me, you will make no demands on me. You will be sensitive to my needs." The husband comes home from work and does not want to talk. The wife, who has been at home with only a 3-year-old to talk to all day, wishes to talk. She interprets the husband's wish not to talk as a sign he doesn't care about her. Her solution to this is to criticize and accuse him of not caring about her. Similarly, he feels that if she cared about him, she would not demand that he talk. His solution is to criticize her. Then they both see the arguing as a further sign of the other's lack of caring. So both become increasingly guarded and defensive, looking for further signs of lack of caring and responding with further criticism. In other words, they try to solve the problem by criticizing each other, but the attempt at solution becomes itself a part of the problem.

Disrupting the clients' attempts to try to solve the problem, then, may facilitate solution ("Don't just do something. Stand there!"). If arguments are reframed as "showing love," then people will not worry so much if an argument occurs. They will not interpret the argument as a sign of difficulty. They will then not get so defensive and be so vigilant for further signs of lack of caring or "insensitivity" or whatever. And the relationship will become less of a battleground.

Paradoxical interventions also suspend trying. Suppose our couple is assigned the task of noticing and responding to anything that appears to be a slight. They have been assigned to try to do what they have apparently already been doing. But actually, what they had previously been trying to do was fix up the marriage by noticing apparent slights and challenging them. Now they have been assigned to try to be critical and defensive, rather than to try to save the marriage. Thus the paradoxical intervention suspends their attempts to save the marriage. This may interfere with their interpreting apparent slights as threats to the marriage. If they are busily on the lookout for slights because they are supposed to notice them and defend themselves, they are less likely to be thinking that a slight means "My spouse doesn't love me." As they no longer worry so much about whether they love each other, the tension may ease. Put another way, the paradoxical intervention may disconnect the occurrence of an argument from the interpretation that "This means that you don't love me." The cessation of trying leads to an increase in acceptance, and as we have seen, many therapies advocate acceptance, especially self-acceptance, as a therapeutic goal.

Mahoney (1985) has said, "Contemporary western ideologies continue to reflect an impatient preoccupation with increasing the boundaries of personal causation. . . . We long to control our feelings, our actions, and our lives. . . . The net message . . . is to try harder. Little wonder, then, that we appear to lead the world in dysphoria and stress-related diseases" (p. 31). Oddly enough, ceasing to try seems to contradict the injunction of many therapies to "take responsibility for oneself." We will discuss this contradiction in our final section on empowerment.

Finally, we believe that both methods of dealing with negative self-monitoring partially work by shifting the client's *attentional focus;* that is, by either *defocusing* or *refocusing* the client's attention. Clients partly create their problems by dysfunctionally focusing attention on aspects of their own behavior and the environment, which feed back and maintain their problematic reactions. For instance, according to Beck's cognitive theory, depressives overfocus on aspects of their experience that are negative. At the same time they neglect positive aspects. All that a person might see in a particular situation is its potential for failure, rather than noticing the potential available for success. Psychoanalytically, someone who has failed to develop a stable sense of separation and individuation as a child will overfocus on aspects of relationships that involve autonomy or dependency. Such a person might focus *only* on a prospective romantic partner's apparent ability to provide a merging experience, and therefore may neglect to focus on other things relevant to a good relationship. Encouraging clients to adopt the phenomenological attitude encourages them to *defocus* their attention. Instead of paying attention to only selected aspects of their experience, they are encouraged to "stand back." This may lead to their noticing previously neglected aspects, and may by itself cause a shift in the way they view things.

Indirect methods also appear to work in part by shifting attentional focus. For instance, reframings shift the focus of the client's attention away from the failure aspects of an experience to more positive ones. If the client is not overfocusing on failure aspects, he or she may be free to now notice aspects of the situation that can lead to new, positive behavior or to solutions. Paradoxes may also do this. Suppose a husband and wife who argue are ordered to argue at 5:00 P.M. every day. Knowing they are going to argue at that time, they may find their attention free to flow to other aspects of their relationship at other times, rather than continually looking out for potential conflicts between them. They may begin to focus on positive aspects and find ways of compromising so that by 5:00 P.M. they have nothing to argue about.

THEORETICAL REASONS FOR THE ACCESS PROBLEM

Now that we have considered the various ways therapies attempt to deal with the access problem, we will look at some theoretical explanations for its existence. In one way or another they all involve the idea that a lack of conscious awareness is involved.

Our whole consideration of the problem of access was based on the observation that people usually cannot change problem behavior or feeling through abstract cognitive self-commands or self-analysis. Nor are such commands and information from others particularly useful by themselves. In considering different therapeutic solutions to this problem we have encountered a variety of therapeutic techniques in which cognitive formulation of insight is irrelevant. Behavioral approaches may work whether or not the client formulates a cognitive, verbal insight about what is going on. Metaphorical stories may convey meaning and initiate change even though the individual cannot consciously state how he has been changed. Similarly, paradoxical techniques may instigate change without the client's being consciously aware of how the change has occurred. Watzlawick (1985) has said that change occurs all the time in everyday life without insight.

Thus, it is not clear that in order to change the client needs to be able to formulate the problem or its presumed cause or what needs to be done. Yet the issue of awareness or its lack is involved in each theoretical perspective on the access problem. These theories either assume that the reason conscious, rational self-direction doesn't work is because of a lack of awareness of the relevant factors involved or that the human is built in such a way that cognition is simply impotent to modify behavior.

For psychoanalysis, conscious, rational self-control is normally impotent because the real causes of behavior have been repressed and are unconscious. In therapy conscious insights work only if they are timed to coincide with the availability to awareness of the relevant previously repressed concrete memories and affects. For client-centered therapy conscious, rational self-control often does not work because it consists of shoulds and oughts learned from society and directed at the person. The result is that the individual's experiential organismic wisdom is ignored or denied. In therapy verbally formulated self-knowledge can be therapeutic if it arises from listening to the experiential, organismically wise bodily level, rather than simply being cognitively derived. For gestalt conscious, rational self-control frequently fails because it has been split off from ongoing organismic awareness. Words and symbolizations can create behavior change if they arise from the ongoing stream of organismic awareness. Cognitive behavioral approaches assume that behavior is often controlled by automatic thoughts of which the client is unaware or by cognitions that are conscious, but that are not recognized as dysfunctional or irrational.

Each of the above approaches assumes that lack of awareness—of repressed material, experiential bodily wisdom, automatic thoughts, or dysfunctional cognitions—plays a role in dysfunctional behavior and is why one cannot consciously control such behavior. In various ways they suggest that cognitive awareness, under the proper circumstances, can effect change. Many other approaches also see a lack of awareness as important in causing dysfunctional behavior, but are skeptical that cognitive awareness under any conditions is therapeutic. Behavior therapy is one example. Most problem responses are seen as being learned at a subcortical level and are therefore simply not modifiable by conscious, cognitive activity. Many family systems theorists believe that problems arise from the dynamics of the family system, and family members are not aware of these dynamics. Even family therapists may not have direct knowledge of these dynamics, but may have to infer them. Furthermore, many such therapists do not believe that increasing awareness of these dynamics is particularly therapeutic. They believe that therapeutic interventions must work to change the system directly. Increased awareness is irrelevant.

What is common to practically all the theoretical perspectives is the suggestion that psychopathological behavior is at least partially created by a lack of awareness. Put another way, behavior is at least partially controlled by factors that lie outside of conscious awareness.

To what extent is behavior nonconsciously determined? Modern cognitive psychologists believe that the answer is a large portion. George Mandler, a leading cognitive psychologist, has stated that "most of mind is unavailable to introspection" (1984, p. 53). He also says that the part of the mental organization that we usually think of as consciousness is only "a very small cross section, constrained by the vast number of organizations and structures that are not represented in consciousness" (p. 52). Mandler believes that "[conscious] ideas do not cause actions. Both ideas and actions are products of underlying representations and processes," (p. 11) which are themselves unconscious.

The idea that extensive information processing happens nonconsciously is now commonly accepted. Nisbett and Ross (1980) have argued that while people have conscious awareness of their thoughts, they are not aware of the processes that generate them. Similarly, while people may be aware of their emotions, they are often not aware of their causes (Maslach, 1979). Shevrin and Dickman (1980), after reviewing a variety of models of consciousness, suggest that all information processing is first at the nonconscious level and only later and secondarily do some aspects show up as conscious ideation. Fischer and Pipp (1984) have even argued that consciousness is a construction in the sense that knowledge is at first unconscious and people "become conscious" in certain areas only when knowledge in that area becomes sufficiently developed and complex.

Information can be detected and processed nonconsciously (Shevrin & Dickman, 1980; Lewicki, 1986). Therefore, theories that suggest that people are unconsciously influenced by family dynamics and therapy techniques that rely on indirect communication seem plausible. That people may pick up and process information without being aware that they are doing so was demonstrated by Maier (1931). Maier asked subjects to tie together two ropes hanging from the ceiling. The ropes were too far apart to be grasped at the same time while the subjects were standing on the floor. The solution was to tie a weight to one rope, get it swinging, catch it near the other rope, and tie them together while standing on a box. None of the subjects thought of the solution until Maier walked into the room and "casually" flicked a rope to get it swinging. Most subjects solved the problem shortly thereafter, but did not recall noticing Maier's action. They said, "The solution just came to me."

The extensiveness of the control of behavior, thoughts, and feelings by nonconscious processes raises questions as to what the unconscious is like. Is it Freud's unconscious, full of primitive repressed wishes and fantasies? Modern cognitive psychologists do not rule out the possibility that repression plays a role in keeping some things nonconscious. However, the majority believe that much of what is unavailable to conscious awareness is unavailable simply because that is the way people are built (see Bowers, 1984, for an argument that the ultimate causes of behavior are necessarily nonconscious). The unconscious may or may not contain repressed desires and fantasies. However, many nonconscious processes are not repressed. Some are simply "scripts" (Langer, 1978) people learn. These scripts become habitual and guide behavior nonconsciously.

Shevrin and Dickman (1980) have suggested that nonconscious information processing is holistic, associationistic, and nonlinear, as compared to conscious cognitive activity. Even if there are primitive, repressed aspects to nonconscious processes, there is also reason to believe that aspects of nonconscious information-processing processes may be considerably more complex than conscious processes. Gendlin (1984) has argued that one reason people sometimes have problems putting feelings into words is that nonconscious, preconceptual experience is more finely ordered and more complex than the rather crude words can handle. Mahoney (1985), based on the work of Hayek (1978), has argued that nonconscious processes may actually be too complex for consciousness and that is why they are unavailable to consciousness.

With respect to this, Polyani (1966) has stated that people "know more than we can say." Recent evidence (Bowers, 1984; Reber, 1976) suggests that people can "know" things intuitively. Sometimes they even do better trying to solve a problem intuitively than in a strictly cognitive, analytic way. Similarly, Shweder, Turiel, and Much (1981) have done research demonstrating that children have greater intuitive moral understanding than they can verbalize in words.

We will give two examples of "knowing more than we can say." It is often reported that Einstein said that he was "guided by a feeling" in his pursuit of resolving the problems that ultimately led to the development of relativity theory. Apparently his ideas originated in visual imagery, and it was only from that that he was able to derive the words and mathematical expressions needed to develop the theory (Gardner, 1983). More recently, it has been pointed out that no one understands how outfielders in baseball catch fly balls (Shirley, 1984). How does an outfielder "know" to turn his back and run to where the fly ball is coming? He only has an instant after the ball is hit to make his appraisal and then act. Not even physicists seem to be able to understand how this is done.

In reference to feelings and affect, Zajonc (1980) has argued that feelings are generated by processes that lie outside of conscious awareness. Zajonc's argument has been influential (and is now being referred to by theorists of psychotherapy) and controversial (Lazarus, 1982). He proposes that there are two parallel, partially independent mental systems: the affective and the cognitive. Zajonc locates the affective system in the right hemisphere of the brain, which is spatial, visual, holistic, and nonverbal in its functioning. He points out that affective judgments are basic. People have like and dislike reactions quickly and immediately in many situations before they are able to figure out reasons for the reactions. Affective reactions are not subject to conscious, cognitive control, and they may persist long after the evidential base for them is discredited. Also affective judgments are difficult to verbalize and are often encoded in visceral or muscular symbols. Therefore, they are acquired, organized, categorized, represented, and retrieved differently than factual, cognitive knowledge. Finally, Zajonc refers to Paivio's (1978) views that information in affective judgments is more closely associated with the image system than the verbal system. This fits in with Zajonc's contention that affective information is coded nonverbally in the right hemisphere of the brain. Zajonc concludes by characterizing the affective system as relatively quick in its responsiveness but stereotyped, while the cognitive system is slow but flexible.

Zajonc's views are compatible with the observations that abstract, cognitive knowledge is often impotent in effecting change at the affective, feeling level. Furthermore, his views are compatible with the idea that therapy must have its impact at the bodily, experiential level. If affective reactions are indeed stored in the right brain, then it makes sense that therapeutic communications in the form of vivid language or metaphors involving visual imagery may work better than abstract verbal interventions.

Others have argued that feelings are "intuitive appraisals," or meaningful reactions (Greenberg, 1984), and therefore feelings may be a road into the individual's implicit nonconscious ways of interpreting and construing reality. Zajonc's contention that feeling and cognition are separate is not universally accepted. Recently, Greenberg and Safran (1984) have proposed an integrative model. Feelings are generated by nonconscious information-processing processes, in which perceptions of the environment are combined with memories and cognitions. The product of this combination is a feeling, which appears in consciousness. Greenberg and Safran argue that cognitions can change feelings, if the appropriate bodily data are present at the right time.

Much is unknown about nonconscious processes and feelings. However, recent research and theorizing by experimental psychologists appear to be compatible with many of the observations of clinical psychologists.

THE IMPORTANCE OF SELF-ACCEPTANCE

The problem of access is a common theme in recent approaches to psychotherapy. Another common element is their concern with self-acceptance. In previous chapters and in the discussion of negative self-monitoring we pointed out some negative effects of low self-evaluation. Individuals with feelings of low self-efficacy may pay so much attention to evaluating themselves that they pay less attention to the demands of the task and as a result perform less well than they could have. Similarly, focusing on the self may magnify negative feelings and lead to attributing negative character traits to the self.

Theorists like Ellis, Rogers, and Beck have pointed out the dysfunctional aspects of making negative self-attributions. They suggest that while it may be functional to make process evaluations of how one is performing on a task ("Is this behavior that I am engaging in working or not?"), it is not functional to generalize from specific behavioral failures to one's whole self. It is one thing to say, "I am not understanding this material" and another to conclude, "Therefore I am stupid and no good."

Originally client-centered therapy seemed to hold that a positive view of the self was healthy and a negative view unhealthy. More recently, Rogers's view that fully functioning people do not have a fixed self-concept implies that fully functioning persons nonevaluatively accept themselves, that is, they don't evaluate themselves either positively or negatively, though they may evaluate their behavior. Ellis and Beck also suggest that nonevaluative acceptance is healthier than either positive or negative self-evaluation. Ellis has perhaps been most forceful of all in arguing that one simply would be better off never making generalizations about one's whole self from one's behavior.

It should be pointed out that self-evaluation per se is not bad (Bandura, 1986). Rather, it is self-evaluation in which people take their behavior to represent their overall ability or worth that is dysfunctional. We have already seen that receptive, listening, nonevaluative observation of the self is useful. Evaluation of how one's specific behaviors are meeting task demands is also useful. But this evaluation is done not to judge overall self-competence, but as a guide to changing performance in order to meet the demands of the task better.

A common goal of psychoanalytic, humanistic, and cognitive approaches is client self-acceptance. Each attempts to get the client to believe that "I am not an overall bad person because I have primitive incestuous wishes and fantasies" (psychoanalysis), "I have certain thoughts, feelings, or perspectives that do not agree with the 'shoulds' I have been taught" (humanistic), or "I have not behaved perfectly or my life does not match my perfectionistic, rigid either/or schemas" (cognitive approaches).

RIGID SCHEMAS AS A MAJOR CAUSE OF PSYCHOPATHOLOGY

The idea that it is people's interpretations of events that cause problems, rather than the events themselves, is a common theme in psychoanaltyic, humanistic, and cognitive therapies. Virginia Satir, a humanistically oriented family therapist, says, "I think if I have one message . . . it would be that the event does not determine how to respond to the event" (Krier, 1986).

More particularly, these diverse theoretical approaches see psychopathology as the result of rigid, repetitive constructions or world views that are imposed on reality. For psychoanalysis, the diversity of the real world is reduced by the client to a repetitive reliving of perceptions and interpretations developed in early childhood. For instance, a client may perceive any person in authority not in the present as an individual, but only in terms of the client's past conflict with his father. Thus, the client is not able to respond to what is new and different about this authority figure.

For humanistic therapies, the client boxes reality into rigid shoulds and oughts learned in childhood. Feelings that do not fit the boxes may be disowned or ignored. Gestalt suggests that the client splits experience into rigid categories, such as "good and evil," "mind and body," and then treats these rigid categories as more real than the reality they were meant to describe.

Beck's cognitive therapy is based on the assumption that both depression and anxiety are in part the result of dysfunctional cognitive interpretations of reality. These interpretations are based on schemas learned in early childhood and are treated as real. Ellis holds that psychopathology is the result of irrational cognitions. In his A-B-C model the person's reaction (C) is caused more by the interpretation (B) than by the event (A).

Finally, many family systems therapists (Watzlawik, 1985; de Shazer, 1985) hold that problems are caused by the individual's perception and construction of events. They argue that therefore what is needed in therapy is a second order change, in which the individual's way of construing the world is fundamentally reorganized.

Solving a problem from within an established way of construing the world is a first order change. Second order change would seem to be the goal of most therapies. For instance, psychoanalysis is not interested in helping you cope from within your rigid childhood-based way of construing the world. Instead it hopes to cause a fundamental reorganization in this system, so that new, more flexible and accurate solutions to one's problems appear.

Rigid schemas have a primitive either-or quality. De Shazer (1985) has said that construing problems in either-or terms is itself part of the problem. For psychoanalysis, the primitive construct systems developed in early childhood include a number of simplistic, either-or ways of construing things: "Mommy loves either me OR daddy, but not both," "Mommy is either all good OR all bad." Some constructions are so primitive that, according to object relations theory, the child does not separate itself from the mother.

Client-centered therapists have also focused on the rigid, global nature of clients' personal construct systems. Gestalt believes it is the splitting up of the world into polarities that is a major source of problems. Both Beck and Ellis see global, either-or ways of construing things at the root of psychopathology. For instance, if I do something wrong, then all of me is bad and unworthy of respect.

THERAPY AS THE DEVELOPMENT OF A HYPOTHESIS-TESTING ATTITUDE

If psychopathology is based on the rigid application of a primitive interpretation of reality, then therapy must involve an attempt to change this interpretation. But most therapies are not interested in merely changing the client's existing way of interpreting reality. They are also interested in developing a hypothesis-testing attitude toward reality. In other words, they do not want the client to recognize his interpretation as limited and simply replace it with another interpretation that is applied the same way. They want the client to realize that any interpretation of the world is a construction, or hypothesis, and that it should be subjected to continual and lifelong evaluation. Carl Rogers said a goal of therapy is to get the client to "hold his constructs tentatively." Beck teaches his clients the method of empirically testing and evaluating cognitions. Similarly, Ellis wants his clients to dispute their irrational cognitions. Finally, Schafer (1978) has argued that a key event in psychoanalytic therapy is not merely learning that one has been interpreting the world through primitive childhood constructions, but that such interpretations are constructions and therefore are modifiable.

MEANING SYSTEMS AND THE SELF

Therapy, therefore, is the reorganization of the client's personal meaning system (Mahoney, 1985). In particular, therapy can be seen as including the differentiation and integration of meaning (Wexler, 1974; Rice & Saperia, 1984). A good example would be object relations theory. Object relations theory holds that borderline personalities construe people in rigid ways as either "all good" or "all bad." Part of therapy is learning to develop a more differentiated view of people, that there are gradations of good and evil and that a person may be a combination of both. This leads to the person developing a more integrated view, that people are complex creatures containing both good and bad qualities. Then, if someone does something "bad," the person does do not see him as "all bad." Client-centered, gestalt, and cognitive therapies similarly attempt to create more differentiated and integrated ways of construing the world.

Mahoney (1985) has argued that therapy often works, not by eliminating a problem behavior, but by consolidating it into the personality into a more functional way. Something that is currently maladaptive is integrated into the personality in such a way that it loses its destructive qualities and may even come to possess functional qualities. For instance, rebelliousness that may be causing a person difficulty at a job may be "tamed" or integrated into the personality in such a way that it comes to have adaptive uses. When the person learns when, where, and how to express her rebelliousness, it may become useful in fighting injustice or in challenging rigid, conformist ways of doing things.

Similarly, a client who is "oversensitive" to signs of rejection may not eliminate that oversensitivity, that is, he may still notice the subtle cues that he previously interpreted as rejection. But he may learn that his interpretations are not necessarily correct and become able to engage in reality testing. His oversensitivity may become adaptive in that he notices subtle cues others don't, and this quality may make him more effective with other people.

Reframing may work in part by facilitating consolidation and integration (see Chapter 9). The ultimate in reframing is R. D. Laing's view of schizophrenia as a growth process instead of a disease. Regardless of whether or not schizophrenia is a disease, reframing it as a growth experience may be therapeutic. First of all, it will encourage the schizophrenic to no longer view part of herself as bad or socially undesirable. Therefore, it should raise her self-esteem. This should lead to a reduction in anxiety and an increase in effective functioning. In addition, it should encourage the schizophrenic to "use" her schizophrenic experiences in adaptive, prosocial ways. For instance, one may learn to "tame" them and use them artistically. Reframing the experience of being paralyzed in an automobile accident in such a way as to find some meaning may help patients cope. This has been called the use of "interpretive secondary control" (Fiske & Taylor, 1984), in which a person "controls" an event by extracting meaning from it. The person may then reorganize the priorities in his life.

Insights into the past also are ultimately therapeutic only if they can be consolidated and reframed. To know that you are the way you are because your father mistreated you may be of little help if all that does is leave you feeling angry. However, if you can reframe the experience, for example, learn to forgive him or see him as an imperfect human being, too, then the experience can be consolidated into your personality. As you forgive him, you forgive yourself and others, so you take a more flexible, differentiated view of others. You may even be able to use your own experience of being mistreated to empathize with others or to gain a sense that you can triumph over tragedy.

A particularly important structure of meaning for an individual is the self. For humanists, the self is an organized system that is constantly shifting and changing. Therefore, it has fluid boundaries and does not have "thing-like" properties. A healthy self is characterized not so much by stability but by differentiation, integration, and flexibility to change and evolve from moment to moment. The healthy self for recent psychoanalytic theorists also is characterized by differentiation and integration, but is talked about in structural terms. In other words, it is described in terms of stability and clear boundaries between self and other.

In either case the self includes the identity function, that sense of organization of various wants, goals, and experiences as all belonging to "me." The important function of the self is the integration and coordination of conflicting aims, desires, and goals (Eagle, 1984). Eagle sees the self as a hierarchical organizing structure. Mahoney (1985) sees therapy as involving the creation of hierarchical organizing structures that consolidate and integrate meaning. From a cognitive perspective Beck's concept of a master control system is similar to these views.

SELF-EMPOWERMENT

Another common theme among the various therapy approaches is that they all try to give the client a sense of control or "empowerment," a sense of "I can . . ." or "I am able . . ." We have chosen the term empowerment as an umbrella term for several related concepts: overcoming a sense of helplessness, gaining a sense of self-efficacy, taking responsibility for oneself, becoming able to choose, becoming autonomous. While empowerment is a goal of several approaches, they differ somewhat in how it is to be achieved.

In psychoanalytic theory a sense of empowerment develops as a result of reowning disowned parts of the self. As people are able to acknowledge what has been repressed, they become able to control, coordinate, and integrate their own functioning. Bettelheim's (1982) retranslation of Freud states it well: "Where 'it' was shall 'I' be." In other words, something that felt separate from the person and not controllable ("it") becomes part of the self ("I") and under control. A similar goal is found in client-centered therapy, gestalt, and other humanistic approaches in their emphasis on owning, choosing, or becoming response-able.

In social learning theory and social skills training the goal is expressed as increasing feelings of self-efficacy. Self-efficacy is the perception that one is able to enact certain behaviors, and it usually increases as one learns effective skills.

One of Ellis's goals of therapy is for the client to take responsibility for choices. This occurs as the client learns to challenge his or her rigid, absolute, musturbatory tendencies.

Research has shown that those who have an "internal locus of control," that is, feel able to control what happens to them, generally exhibit greater adaptive behavior than those who have an "external locus of control," who feel their fate is not in their hands, though there are complications and exceptions to this picture (Phares, 1976). Seligman (1975) cites evidence suggesting that feeling one lacks control, or feeling "helpless," is associated with various maladaptive psychological and physical responses. Langer and Rodin (1976) found that having a sense of responsibility for themselves was physically beneficial to people in an old-age home.

In a similar vein we have seen that Frank (1982) argues that one of the main things therapy does is overcome feelings of demoralization. And Bandura (1977) thinks that the ultimate outcome of all therapies is to increase feelings of self-efficacy. Both overcoming demoralization and increasing feelings of self-efficacy lead to a sense of hope. And research on the placebo effect suggests that believing one has a chance of improving increases one's likelihood of improving (Shapiro & Morris, 1978).

We have also seen that trying to control oneself is at times counterproductive. There are times when receptive acceptance seems to be more therapeutic than attempts at control. However, this may be because active attempts at control do not work, whereas receptive acceptance is the best way to control the situation. Precisely this point has been argued by Rothbaum, Weisz, and Snyder (1982), who have suggested that giving up attempts at control is sometimes more adaptive than continued attempts to control. They call this "secondary control," and we have mentioned this in our discussion of therapy as differentiation and integration of meaning.

Mahoney (1985) comments on our culture's overemphasis on personal control.

> Embedded in our desperate quest for control is a metatheory of personal and public freedom. And much of that freedom is libertarian in flavor—it seeks *freedom from* its contexts rather than *freedom within* them . . . the net message . . . is to try harder. . . . The eastern alternative to effort is "surrender," a kind of passive intentionality that attempts to integrate and utilize the contrasting powers of internal and external influence. . . . The practical implications of the effort/surrender issue merit our close attention. To me, its relevance seems most apparent in disorders that involve sympathetic/parasympathetic conflicts—anxiety, insomnia, and several sexual dysfunctions. Here it is clear that there are times when effort seems to get in the way of progress. Here I am comfortable encouraging patience, gentleness, and some kind of self-trust. (pp. 31–32)

Beck, Emery, and Greenberg (1985) prescribe acceptance of anxiety as part of their treatment program for anxiety disorders. The old maxim that wisdom is controlling what can be controlled, accepting what cannot be controlled, and knowing the difference seems relevant.

A cautionary note is sounded by Brickman, Rabinowitz, Karuza, Coates, Cohn, and Kidder (1982). They present four models of helping, three of which we will briefly mention here. The four models are based on seeing a client as either responsible or not responsible for having a problem and either responsible or not responsible for resolving the problem. The traditional medical model sees the patient as not responsible for having the problem (it is caused by a disease process) and not responsible for the solution (the doctor prescribes).

The moral and compensatory models are most directly relevant to psychotherapy. Both hold the client responsible for helping to resolve the problem. However, the moral model also holds the client responsible for having the problem. We have seen that existential-humanistic approaches see the person as having chosen his or her life path. This sometimes leads therapists of this persuasion to hold the client responsible for his or her problem. In the extreme clients have been held responsible for having diseases such as leukemia or for having been raped. As Brickman and his colleagues point out, such a belief is based on the idea that the world is just (Lerner, 1970) and that nothing happens to people that they in some way or the other do not deserve or have not brought on themselves.

The problem with this view is that it sometimes ends up "blaming the victim." A client who is told he "chose" to have leukemia will now not only feel anxious about having the disease, but feel guilty as well. We know of clients who were told they "chose" to be schizophrenic, to be depressed, or to have anxiety attacks. The clients have no awareness of having made such choices and do not experience themselves as being able to choose otherwise. The effect is to make the clients feel bad about themselves. It creates what Seligman and his colleagues have described as a depression-causing situation. Clients feel responsible for the negative situation they are in, but feel unable to control it or do anything about it. Such interpretations made to the clients may function more as accusations and blame than as therapeutic information.

The compensatory model holds that the client "came by her problems legitimately" (to quote one of our supervisors when we were in graduate school). While she may have made a variety of choices that ultimately led to having a problem, she did not knowingly do this. However, once she becomes aware of the problem, she is responsible for working to resolve it, and the goal of many therapies is to help her feel able (empowered) to solve it.

REFERENCES

Arkowitz, H., & Messer, S. B. (Eds.). (1984). *Psychoanalytic and behavior therapy: Is integration possible?* New York: Plenum.

Bandura, A. (1977). Self-efficacy: Toward a unifying theory of behavioral change. *Psychological Review, 84,* 191–215.

Bandura, A. (1986). *Social foundations of thought and action: A social cognitive theory.* Englewood Cliffs, NJ: Prentice-Hall.

Beck, A. T. (1979). *Cognitive therapy of depression* (Live demonstration of interview procedures). New York: BMA Audio Cassettes, Guilford.

Beck, A. T. (1985). *Cognitive therapy of depression.* Workshop presented at the Evolution of Psychotherapy Conference, Phoenix, AZ, December 14, 1985.

Beck, A. T., Emery, G., with Greenberg, R. L. (1985). *Anxiety disorders and phobias: A cognitive perspective.* New York: Basic Books.

Beck, A. T., Rush, A. J., Shaw, B. F., & Emery, G. (1979). *Cognitive therapy of depression.* New York: Guilford.

Bettelheim, B. (1982). *Freud and man's soul.* New York: Vintage.

Bohart, A. (1980). Toward a cognitive theory of catharsis. *Psychotherapy: Theory, Research and Practice, 17,* 192–201.

Bohart, A. (1982). Similarities between cognitive and humanistic approaches to psychotherapy. *Cognitive Therapy and Research, 6,* 245–250.

Bohart, A. C. (1987). Converging aspects of psychotherapy: Overview, similarities in goals, the access problem, and experiential learning. *Invited Symposium on Integrative Aspects of*

Psychotherapy, 67th Annual Convention of the Western Psychological Association, Long Beach, CA, April 25, 1987.

Bowers, K. S. (1984). On being unconsciously influenced and informed. In K. S. Bowers & D. Meichenbaum (Eds.), *The unconscious reconsidered.* New York: Wiley.

Brehm, J. W. (1966). *Response to loss of freedom: A theory of psychological reactance.* New York: Academic Press.

Brickman, P., Rabinowitz, V. C., Karuza, J., Jr., Coates, D., Cohn, E., & Kidder, L. (1982). Models of helping and coping. *American Psychologist, 37,* 368–384.

Cameron-Bandler, L. (1978). *They lived happily ever after.* Cupertino, CA: Meta.

Carkhuff, R. R., & Berenson, B. G. (1967). *Beyond counseling and therapy.* New York: Holt, Rinehart and Winston.

Collins, B. (1970). *Social psychology.* Reading, MA: Addison-Wesley.

De Shazer, S. (1985). *Keys to solution in brief therapy.* New York: Norton.

Dollard, J., & Miller, N. E. (1950). *Personality and psychotherapy.* New York: McGraw-Hill.

Eagle, M. N. (1984). *Recent developments in psychoanalysis.* New York: McGraw-Hill.

Egan, G. (1982). *The skilled helper* (2nd ed.). Monterey, CA: Brooks/Cole.

Fischer, K. W., & Pipp, S. L. (1984). Development of the structures of unconscious thought. In K. S. Bowers & D. Meichenbaum (Eds.), *The unconscious reconsidered.* New York: Wiley.

Fiske, S. T., & Taylor, S. E. (1984). *Social cognition.* Reading, MA: Addison-Wesley.

Flavell, J. H. (1981). Monitoring social cognitive enterprises: Something else that may develop in the area of social cognition. In J. H. Flavell & L. Ross (Eds.), *Social cognitive development: Frontiers and possible futures.* Cambridge: Cambridge University Press.

Frank, J. D. (1961). *Persuasion and healing.* Baltimore, MD: Johns Hopkins University Press.

Frank, J. D. (1982). Therapeutic components shared by all psychotherapies. In J. H. Harvey & M. M. Parks (Eds.), *Psychotherapy research and behavior change.* Washington, DC: American Psychological Association.

Frank, J. D., Hoehn-Saric, R., Imber, S. D., Liberman, B. L., & Stone, A. R. (1978). *Effective ingredients of successful psychotherapy.* New York: Brunner/Mazel.

Franks, C. M. (1984). On conceptual and technical integrity in psychoanalysis and behavior therapy: Two fundamentally incompatible systems. In H. Arkowitz & S. B. Messer (Eds.), *Psychoanalytic therapy and behavior therapy: Is integration possible?* New York: Plenum.

Gardner, H. (1983) *Frames of mind: The theory of multiple intelligences.* New York: Basic Books.

Garfield, S. L., & Kurtz, R. (1976). Clinical psychologists in the 1970's. *American Psychologist, 31,* 1–9.

Gendlin, E. T. (1964). A theory of personality change. In P. Worchel & D. Byrne (Eds.), *Personality change.* New York: Wiley.

Gendlin, E. T. (1967). Therapeutic procedures in dealing with schizophrenics. In C. R. Rogers, E. T. Gendlin, D. J. Kiesler, & C. B. Truax (Eds.), *The therapeutic relationship and its impact: A study of psychotherapy with schizophrenics.* Madison: University of Wisconsin Press.

Gendlin, E. T. (1968). The experiential response. In E. F. Hammer (Ed.), *Use of interpretation in treatment.* New York: Grune & Stratton.

Gendlin, E. T. (1969). Focusing. *Psychotherapy: Theory, Research and Practice, 6,* 4–15.

Gendlin, E. T. (1982). An introduction to the new developments in focusing. *The Focusing Folio, 2,* 24–35.

Gendlin, E. T. (1984). The client's client: The edge of awareness. In R. F. Levant & J. M. Shlien (Eds.), *Client-centered therapy and the person-centered approach: New directions in theory, research, and practice.* New York: Praeger.

Goldfried, M. R. (1980a). Toward the delineation of therapeutic change principles. *American Psychologist, 35,* 991–999.

Goldfried, M. R. (Ed.). (1980b). Special issue: Psychotherapy process. *Cognitive Therapy and Research, 4,* 271–306.

Goldfried, M. R. (Ed.). (1982). *Converging themes in psychotherapy: Trends in psychodynamic, humanistic, and behavioral practice.* New York: Springer.

Greenberg, L. S. (1984). A task analysis of intrapersonal conflict resolution. In L. N. Rice & L. S. Greenberg (Eds.), *Patterns of change.* New York: Guilford.

Greenberg, L. S., & Safran, J. D. (1984). Integrating affect and cognition: A perspective on the process of therapeutic change. *Cognitive Therapy and Research, 8,* 559–578.

Haley, J. (1985). *Strategic family therapy* (Video and discussion). Presented at the Evolution of Psychotherapy Conference, Phoenix, AZ, December 11, 1985.

Hayek, F. A. (1978). *New studies in philosophy, politics, economics, and the history of ideas.* Chicago: University of Chicago Press.

Husserl, E. (1964). *Cartesian meditations: An introduction to phenomenology.* The Hague: Martinus Nijhoff.

Johnson, S. M. (1985). *Characterological transformation: The hard work miracle.* New York: Norton.

Kahn, E. (1985). Heinz Kohut and Carl Rogers: A timely comparison. *American Psychologist, 40,* 893–904.

Kendall, P. C. (1982). Integration: Behavior therapy and other schools of thought. *Behavior Therapy, 13,* 559–571.

Krier, B. A. (1986, February 12). Viginia Satir: Making psychological connections. *Los Angeles Times,* Section V, pp. 1, 12–13.

Kuhn, T. S. (1970). *The structure of scientific revolutions* (2nd ed.). Chicago: University of Chicago Press.

Landsman, T. (1982). Not an adversity but a welcome diversity. Reprinted in M. R. Goldfried (Ed.), *Converging themes in psychotherapy: Trends in Psychodynamic, humanistic, and behavioral practice.* (1982). New York: Springer.

Langer, E. J. (1978). Rethinking the role of thought in social interaction. In J. H. Harvey, W. I. Ickes, & R. F. Kidd (Eds.), *New directions in attribution research* (Vol. 2). Hillsdale, NJ: Erlbaum.

Langer, E. J., & Rodin, J. (1976). The effects of choice and enhanced personal responsibility for the aged: A field experiment in an institutional setting. *Journal of Personality and Social Psychology, 34,* 191–198.

Lazarus, R. S. (1982). Thoughts on the relations between emotion and cognition. *American Psychologist, 37,* 1019–1024.

Lerner, M. J. (1970). The desire for justice and reactions to victims. In J. McCauley & L. Berkowitz (Eds.), *Altruism and helping behavior.* New York: Academic Press.

Lewicki, P. (1986). *Nonconscious social information processing.* New York: Academic Press.

Loevinger, J. (1976). *Ego development.* San Francisco: Jossey-Bass.

Madanes, C. (1985). *Advances in strategic family therapy.* Paper presented at the Evolution of Psychotherapy Conference, Phoenix, AZ, December 12, 1985.

Mahoney, M. J. (1985). Psychotherapy and human change processes. In M. J. Mahoney & A. Freeman (Eds.), *Cognition and psychotherapy.* New York: Plenum.

Mahoney, M. J. (In press). *Human change processes: Notes on the facilitation of personal development.* New York: Basic Books.

Maier, N. R. F. (1931). Reasoning in humans: II. The solution of a problem and its appearance in consciousness. *Journal of Comparative Psychology, 12,* 181–194.

Mandler, G. (1984). *Mind and body: Psychological stress and emotion.* New York: Norton.

Marmor, J. (1985). *The nature of the psychotherapeutic process.* Paper presented at the Evolution of Psychotherapy Conference, Phoenix, AZ, December 14, 1985.

Maslach, C. (1979). Negative emotional biasing of unexplained arousal. *Journal of Personality and Social Psychology, 37,* 953–969.

Masterson, J. F. (1985). *Conversation hour.* Discussion at the Evolution of Psychotherapy Conference, Phoenix, AZ, December 14, 1985.

Nichols, M. P., & Efran, J. S. (1985). Catharsis in psychotherapy: A new perspective. *Psychotherapy, 22,* 46–58.

Nisbett, R. E., & Ross, L. (1980). *Human inference: Strategies and shortcomings of social judgment.* Englewood Cliffs, NJ: Prentice-Hall.

Norcross, J. C. (Ed.). (1986). *Handbook of eclectic psychotherapy.* New York: Brunner/Mazel.

Norcross, J. C., & Prochaska, J. O. (1982). A national survey of clinical psychologists: Affiliations and orientations. *The Clinical Psychologist, 35,* 1, 4–6.

Paivio, A. (1978). Dual coding: Theoretical issues and empirical evidence. In J. M. Scandura & C. J. Brainerd (Eds.), *Structural/process models of complex human behavior.* Leiden, The Netherlands: Nordhoff.

Phares, E. J. (1976). *Locus of control in personality.* Morristown, NJ: General Learning Press.

Polster, E. (1985). *The storyline in psychotherapy* (Live demonstration). Presented at the Evolution of Psychotherapy Conference, Phoenix, AZ, December 12, 1985.

Polyani, M. (1966). *The tacit dimension.* New York: Doubleday.

Prochaska, J. O. (1984). *Systems of psychotherapy.* Homewood, IL: Dorsey Press.

Prochaska, J. O., & Norcross, J. C. (1983). Contemporary psychotherapists: A national survey of characteristics, practices, orientations, and attitudes. *Psychotherapy: Theory, Research and Practice, 20,* 161–173.

Rachman, S. (1981). The primary of affect: Some theoretical implications. *Behavior Research and Therapy, 19,* 279–290.

Reber, A. S. (1976). Implicit learning of synthetic languages: The role of instructional set. *Journal of Experimental Psychology: Human Learning and Memory, 2,* 88–94.

Rice, L. N. (1974). The evocative function of the therapist. In D. A. Wexler & L. N. Rice (Eds.), *Innovations in client-centered therapy.* New York: Wiley.

Rice, L. N., & Saperia, E. (1984). Task analysis of the resolution of problematic reactions. In L. N. Rice & L. S. Greenberg (Eds.), *Patterns of change: Intensive analysis of psychotherapy process.* New York: Guilford.

Riebel, L. (1984). Paradoxical intention strategies: A review of rationales. *Psychotherapy, 21,* 260–272.

Rogers, C. R., & Sanford, R. C. (1984). Client-centered psychotherapy. In H. I. Kaplan & B. J. Sadock (Eds.), *Comprehensive textbook of psychiatry* (Vol. 4). Baltimore, MD: Williams & Wilkins.

Rothbaum, F., Weisz, J. R., & Snyder, S. S. (1982). Changing the world and changing the self: A two-process model of perceived control. *Journal of Personality and Social Psychology, 42,* 5–37.

Ryle, A. (1982). *Psychotherapy: A cognitive integration of theory and practice.* New York: Grune & Stratton.

Schafer, R. (1978). *Language and insight.* New Haven, CT: Yale University Press.

Seligman, M. E. P. (1975). *Helplessness.* San Francisco: Freeman.

Shapiro, A. K., & Morris, L. A. (1978). Placebo effects in medical and psychological therapies. In S. L. Garfield & A. E. Bergin (Eds.), *Handbook of psychotherapy and behavior change: An empirical analysis* (2nd ed.). New York: Wiley.

Shevrin, H., & Dickman, S. (1980). The psychological unconscious: A necessary assumption for all psychological theory? *American Psychologist, 35,* 421–434.

Shirley, B. (1984, August 7). Judging fly balls puzzles fielders, physicists. *Los Angeles Times,* Section III, p. 4.

Shweder, R. A., Turiel, E., & Much, N. C. (1981). The moral intuitions of the child. In J. H. Flavell & L. Ross (Eds.), *Social cognitive development: Frontiers and possible futures.* Cambridge: Cambridge University Press.

Swensen, C. H. (1980). Ego development and a general model for counseling and psychotherapy. *Personnel and Guidance Journal, 58,* 382–388.

Wachtel, P. L. (1977). *Psychoanalysis and behavior therapy: Toward an integration.* New York: Basic Books.

Washburn, M. (1978). Observations relevant to a unified theory of meditation. *Journal of Transpersonal Psychology, 10,* 45–65.

Watzlawick, P. (1985). *If you desire to see, learn how to act.* Paper presented at the Evolution of Psychotherapy Conference, Phoenix, AZ, December 12, 1985.

Wexler, D. A. (1974). A cognitive theory of experiencing, self-actualization, and therapeutic process. In D. A. Wexler & L. N. Rice (Eds.), *Innovations in client-centered therapy.* New York: Wiley.

Zajonc, R. B. (1980). Feeling and thinking: Preferences need no inferences. *American Psychologist, 35,* 151–175.

Chapter 12

Professional Psychology: Current Concerns and the Future

Does clinical psychology *have* a future? George Albee was saying it was uncertain at best as early as 1970. Why does psychology ask such questions of itself at all? As we saw in Chapter 1, clinical psychology as an independent profession is relatively young, only about 30 years old. Social and professional forces are bringing about changes that virtually guarantee that all the mental health professions will change dramatically in the next few years. In this chapter we will examine some of these forces and attempt to predict how psychology will change.

First, however, we will examine professional issues that have concerned psychology since its beginning and that will undoubtedly continue to be important into the future. Some of these issues reflect clinical psychology's attempt to establish itself as an independent profession. Others reflect its response to the forces of social change. Most of these issues are interesting because they show how clinical psychology and the mental health professions interact with society as they try to define and solve social problems.

PROFESSIONAL ISSUES

This section examines issues that are important to psychology as a profession that offers helping services to the public. Many of them are relevant to other helping professions as well. Present and future practice of clinical psychology and laws affecting it reflect its efforts to define itself as an independent profession in the face of opposition and competition from medicine, psychiatry, and other groups. Controversies over the definition and diagnosis of mental disorder, causes of psychopathology, effectiveness of psychotherapy, and the like mask political struggles over professional territory and the right to practice. Often these conflicts are couched in "scientific" terms, posed as efforts to "discover the truth" in order to avoid facing the underlying political issues of territoriality.

Ethics and the Law

As an independent profession, psychology, like medicine and law, developed a set of ethical principles to guide its own practice and internal methods to police and discipline its members, rather than being regulated by government or any other external agency. It is argued by these professions that only fellow professionals understand the field well enough to judge the correctness of other professionals' practices. In many states the ethical principles of psychologists have been incorporated into civil law as part of licensing laws, and failure to abide by them is a basis for losing the license to practice.

Legal constraints on the practice of clinical psychology and other mental health professions come from two sources: government legislation and court decisions in lawsuits brought by individuals against therapists. The law from both these sources is constantly changing. Civil lawsuits for malpractice and negligence have resulted in rulings that have affected how therapists implement confidentiality. Some laws have been passed as a result of lobbying by psychologists; these include licensing laws and freedom-of-choice legislation, which allows people to choose any therapist they wish. Some laws have been passed to end licensing laws. We will cover how such court rulings and legislation affect the practice of psychology in detail below.

Another important factor in determining the nature of psychology as a profession is the policy of health insurance companies. What types of therapy insurance companies will pay for, how many sessions are covered, and what types of therapists will be reimbursed are issues that have had a tremendous impact on all the mental health professions, as we shall see.

Ethical Standards of Psychologists Early in the development of psychology, the American Psychological Association established a set of ethical principles to guide psychologists, including professors, researchers, and clinical psychologists. The 1981 revision of APA's ethical standards of psychologists is summarized in Box 12.1. Another revision is planned possibly by 1988. The principles are all based on a concern for human rights and human welfare. The welfare of the consumer of psychological services is paramount, and the principles, such as confidentiality and competence, are designed to ensure that welfare. "Consumers" include students and research subjects (including animals) as well as therapy clients. Although always considered unethical, sexual relations between psychologist and consumer are specifically labeled unethical and harmful to the consumer in the 1981 ethics as a section of Principle 6. Dual relations (such as agreeing to be someone's therapist while also that person's friend or professor) are also considered unethical under Principle 6.

These ethical principles seem almost obvious and commonsensical. Of course,

BOX 12.1
Ethical Principles of Psychologists

PREAMBLE

Psychologists respect the dignity and worth of the individual and strive for the preservation and protection of fundamental human rights. They are committed to increasing knowledge of human behavior and of people's understanding of themselves and others and to the utilization of such knowledge for the promotion of human welfare. While pursuing these objectives, they make every effort to protect the welfare of those who seek their services and of the research participants that may be the objects of study. They use their skills only for purposes consistent with these values and do not knowingly permit their misuse by others. While demanding for themselves freedom of inquiry and communication, psychologists accept the responsibility this freedom requires: competence, objectivity in the application of skills, and concern for the best interests of clients, colleagues, students, research participants, and society. In the pursuit of these ideals, psychologists subscribe to principles in the following areas: . . .

PRINCIPLE 1. RESPONSIBILITY

In providing services, psychologists maintain the highest standards of their profession. They accept responsibility for the consequences of their acts and make every effort to ensure that their services are used appropriately.

PRINCIPLE 2. COMPETENCE

The maintenance of high standards of competence is a responsibility shared by all psychologists in the interest of the public and the profession as a whole. Psychologists recognize the boundaries of their competence and the limitations of their techniques. They only provide services and only use techniques for which they are qualified by training and experience. In those areas in which recognized standards do not yet exist, psychologists take whatever precautions are necessary to protect the welfare of their clients. They maintain knowledge of current scientific and professional information related to the services they render.

PRINCIPLE 3. MORAL AND LEGAL STANDARDS

Psychologists' moral and ethical standards of behavior are a personal matter to the same degree as they are for any other citizen, except as these may compromise the fulfillment of their professional responsibilities or reduce the public trust in psychology and psychologists. Regarding their own behavior, psychologists are sensitive to prevailing community standards and to the possible impact that conformity to or deviation from these standards may have upon the quality of their performance as psychologists. Psychologists are also aware of the possible impact of their public behavior upon the ability of colleagues to perform their professional duties.

PRINCIPLE 4. PUBLIC STATEMENTS

Public statements, announcements of services, advertising, and promotional activities of psychologists serve the purpose of helping the public make informed judgments and choices. Psychologists represent accurately and objectively their professional qualifications, affiliations, and functions, as well as those of the institutions or organizations with which they or the statements may be associated. In public statements providing psychological information or professional opinions or providing information about the availability of psychological products, publications, and services, psychologists base their statements on scientifically acceptable psychological findings and techniques with full recognition of the limits and uncertainties of such evidence.

PRINCIPLE 5. CONFIDENTIALITY

Psychologists have a primary obligation to respect the confidentiality of information obtained from persons in the course of their work as psychologists. They reveal such information to others only with the consent of the person or the person's legal representative, except in those unusual circumstances in which not to do so would result in clear danger to the person or to others. Where appropriate, psychologists inform their clients of the legal limits of confidentiality.

PRINCIPLE 6. WELFARE OF THE CONSUMER

Psychologists respect the integrity and protect the welfare of the people and groups with whom they work. When conflicts of interest arise between clients and psychologists' employing institutions, psychologists clarify the nature and direction of their loyalties and responsibilities and keep all parties informed of their commitments. Psychologists fully inform consumers as to the purpose and nature of an evaluative, treatment, educational, or training procedure, and they freely acknowledge that clients, students, or participants in research have freedom of choice with regard to participation.

PRINCIPLE 7. PROFESSIONAL RELATIONSHIPS

Psychologists act with due regard for the needs, special competencies, and obligations of their colleagues in psychology and other professions. They respect the prerogatives and obligations of the institutions or organizations with which these other colleagues are associated.

PRINCIPLE 8. ASSESSMENT TECHNIQUES

In the development, publication, and utilization of psychological assessment techniques, psychologists make every effort to promote the welfare and best interests of the client. They guard against the misuse of assessment results. They respect the client's right to know the results, the interpretations made, and the bases for their conclusions and recommendations. Psychologists make every effort to maintain the security of tests and other assessment techniques within limits of legal mandates. They strive to ensure the appropriate use of assessment techniques by others.

PRINCIPLE 9. RESEARCH WITH HUMAN PARTICIPANTS

The decision to undertake research rests upon a considered judgment by the individual psychologist about how best to contribute to psychological science and human welfare.

Having made the decision to conduct research, the psychologist considers alternative directions in which research energies and resources might be invested. On the basis of this consideration, the psychologist carries out the investigation with respect and concern for the dignity and welfare of the people who participate and with cognizance of federal and state regulations and professional standards governing the conduct of research with human participants.

PRINCIPLE 10. CARE AND USE OF ANIMALS

An investigator of animal behavior strives to advance understanding of basic behavioral principles and/or to contribute to the improvement of human health and welfare. In seeking these ends, the investigator ensures the welfare of animals and treats them humanely. Laws and regulations notwithstanding, an animal's immediate protection depends upon the scientist's own conscience.

Source: American Psychologist, 36, 633–638.

psychologists should put the welfare of the consumer first, keep information confidential, and practice only within their area of expertise and competence! The problems arise when it is not clear who the "consumer" is and when there are conflicting rights and obligations. For example, most psychological services are paid for by third-party payers. Who is the consumer—the person in treatment or the person paying for the treatment?

The necessity for laws and ethical principles to protect the welfare of the public rests on the assumption that there is a disparity in power and expertise between psychologists and consumers. People seeking psychotherapy are assumed to be vulnerable and liable to be harmed by improper practices. Therapists are assumed to be more knowledgeable than clients and to hold a position of authority over them. The weaker and less knowledgeable clients, then, must have the additional protection of laws and ethics. Some psychologists object to these assumptions, arguing that the public should be educated to have as much knowledge as the psychologists do ("giving psychology away") and that therapy should be based on an equalitarian relationship.

Confidentiality and Privilege Confidentiality is the responsibility of mental health professionals to safeguard information they receive in the course of their practice. Privilege is a legal right of consumers of medical, legal, and therapy services to control whether or not information about themselves is revealed. Both the ethic of confidentiality and the legislated right of privilege are based on two assumptions: (1) that successful treatment of consumers of medical or therapy services rests on the full disclosure by the client of potentially embarrassing or harmful information and (2) that consumers will not dislose this important information unless they are assured it will not be revealed. Both of these assumptions are open to empirical verification, which has not been done, and are not necessarily true. However, they guide ethical practice and legislation.

Privilege is a concept that has evolved over the centuries for priests, lawyers, and doctors, and it is now legislated in the criminal codes of most states to apply to the mental health professions. It is a legal right held by the consumers of these services. In the case of children or incompetents, it is a legal right held by their parents or guardians, although in some cases it devolves to the therapist. The holder of the privilege chooses whether information is revealed to others, such as the court or other professionals. The therapist may advise the client and assist in the decision, but only the holder of the privilege may decide to release the information, and the therapist may release information only with the written permission of the holder of the privilege.

There are several exceptions to confidentiality and privilege. In most states privilege does not apply in certain cases, such as a child who is a victim of a crime (such as physical or sexual abuse) or a person who seeks counseling in order to commit a crime or tort. California law specifies that certain minor children over the age of 12 may receive psychological services without parental consent under certain circumstances. In these special cases the therapist holds the privilege, not the child, although some children's rights advocates argue that the child should hold the privilege.

Another important exception to confidentiality is embodied in the 1971 *Tarasoff* decision of the California Supreme Court. The court ruled in favor of parents who sought damages against a psychologist for failing to warn them that the psychologist's client was intending to (and did) kill their daughter. In its famous statement the Court said that "Private privilege ends where public peril begins." This ruling has been interpreted to mean that therapists of homicidal patients and possibly other dangerous or suicidal patients are obliged to break confidentiality and inform the police and the intended victim(s) of their patients' intentions.

Some have argued that the *Tarasoff* case and similar court rulings place an unreasonable burden on therapists in terms of assessing and predicting dangerousness. Empirical studies have repeatedly demonstrated that it is not possible to predict dangerousness based on psychological assessment alone. Yet because psychologists and psychiatrists claim to be able to predict other things, such as the course of a mental disorder, the public expects them to predict dangerousness and becomes angry when they fail to do so. The best predictor of dangerousness is past dangerous acts, yet the police and prisons are not held liable when they release dangerous individuals without warning the public. Other critics of these court rulings argue that any breach of confidentiality threatens the therapeutic process and that dangerous people will be deterred from seeking the treatment they need, thus increasing the danger to the public.

A recent survey (Givelber, Bowers, & Blitch, 1985) found that *Tarasoff* has not greatly affected psychological practices. After all, dangerous clients are fairly rare. However, such court rulings demonstrate how the mental health professions and society are still in the process of working out the ethical obligations of therapists.

The ethical and legal obligations of therapists with suicidal clients are not always clear-cut. *Tarasoff* and the ethical obligation to prevent suicide would appear to indicate that confidentiality may be broken when a client expresses suicidal intentions. Family members or close friends (if there are no family members nearby) should be informed so that they can provide extra support to the client and be alert to indications of suicidal behavior. The suicidal client should be informed of the therapist's intention to so inform others. Issues of trust and the therapeutic relationship will, of course, be raised by this breaking of confidentiality. Some argue that breaking confidentiality may heighten the possibility of suicide by reducing the effectiveness of therapy or making the client less trusting of the therapist. Others respond that preventing the suicide takes precedence over all other considerations.

Informed Consent The necessity for and what constitutes informed consent are concepts that have been developed in recent years. It is argued that people cannot really consent to something unless they have been fully informed as to exactly what they are consenting to. It is well established that patients submitting to a medical procedure must be fully informed of what is to be done and all the possible side effects before they consent to it. Regulations and practices regarding informed consent arose because patients would consent to a procedure, then something would go wrong, and they would sue the doctor, claiming if they had known that that particular thing could go wrong, they would not have consented to it. To obtain sterilization, for example, patients must read, initial every paragraph, and sign a three-page document listing, in very small print, every known risk of the procedure and then wait two weeks to allow for a change of mind, which they certainly consider after reading all that!

Psychologists have worked toward developing a good informed consent procedure for psychotherapy. Most agree that before clients consent to psychotherapy, they should be informed of how much it will cost, how often therapy appointments are to be held, what happens if they miss appointments, and the qualifications and competence of the therapist. Some psychologists believe that clients should also be informed of what type of therapy is being offered, including a brief description of what is expected of the client and what the therapist will do. Some state that this should include the possible risks and benefits of therapy. Some even believe that clients should be told how likely the form of therapy is to work (based on empirical studies of similar cases) and how long it will take to work.

One important aspect of informed consent includes telling clients of the limits of confidentiality. Therapists who do not inform clients of the limits and who later because of *Tarasoff* must disclose a client's dangerous intentions are liable to be sued for malpractice (if they don't disclose, of course, they are liable to be sued for negligence). However, it may be frightening to clients to hear right away that confidentiality does not hold if they become homicidal or suicidal, or it may lead them to be distrustful of the therapist. A full disclosure of the limits of confidentiality right away may deter the very people who need therapy from obtaining it. These issues have not been resolved, so informed consent procedures for psychotherapy still vary greatly from one therapist or agency to another.

Malpractice Even the best therapists are human, and humans make mistakes. Therapists carry malpractice insurance so that if they make a mistake, the victim of that mistake will be adequately compensated for the harm they have suffered. Malpractice insurance also protects clients if therapists knowingly do something wrong, such as practicing outside of their area of competence.

In general, malpractice of therapists is difficult to prove, partly because there is so little agreement as to what constitutes "good practice" and partly because malpractice suits come down to the word of a mentally disturbed patient against that of a professional therapist. In fact, malpractice suits against psychologists are quite uncommon (Wright, 1981).

In 1985 the malpractice insurance carriers for both the American Psychiatric Association and the American Psychological Association announced that they would not cover therapists who had sexual relations with their clients. Some people see this announcement as progress, in that the insurance companies are taking a strong stand against therapist-client sexual relations. However, others see it as a way for the insurance companies to cut costs at the expense of the victims. Certainly a therapist's having sex with a client is definitely malpractice—it is unethical, it is a mistake, it harms the client. Yet the insurance companies are singling out this particular type of malpractice as not covered. If a client sues a therapist over the malpractice of sexual contact and if the therapist is found not guilty, then the insurance companies will pay the legal expenses of defending the case. If, however, the therapist is found guilty (did have sex with the client, did harm the client), then the companies will not pay the therapist's legal fees or compensate the victim! Sexually abused therapy clients have always been reluctant to bring suit and now they will be even more so, because if it is proved that they were abused, they will not be compensated.

Therapist-Client Matching and Multicultural Counseling Should clients and therapists be matched on important characteristics such as gender or ethnic group? Is therapy with a matched therapist more effective? Is it true that only therapists from the same background as the client can truly understand and help the client? While these would be appear to be questions that are empirically answerable, they remain controversial. Some argue that ethical practice necessitates therapist-client matching, and others counter that good therapy touches universal themes meaningful to all groups.

Most would agree that therapists who treat members of groups other than the therapist's own are ethically obliged to learn as much as possible about the values and social norms of those groups. Since many people needing help are female and from ethnic minorities and since the majority of therapists remain both white and male, the field of cross-cultural or multicultural counseling is a growing one. The disparity between the ethnicity of therapists and clients is only going to increase. For example, it is projected that by the year 2000 people of Hispanic origin will be 25 percent of the U.S. population. Furthermore, prejudice, poverty, and oppression puts minority group members at risk for developing psychological disorders. Yet the number of ethnic minority students in psychology graduate programs remains small.

It appears that therapists need multicultural training. Therapists working with different ethnic groups are encouraged to examine their own values in relation to those of clients, to value client differences and learn from them, to learn specific communication skills effective in working with different groups, and to refrain from blaming the victim, that is, seeing natural responses to racism and oppression as evidence of individual psychopathology. Multicultural therapists avoid stereotyping and encourage clients to explore their full potential, while realistically acknowledging social barriers to their aspirations.

Psychology as an Independent Profession

Clinical psychology's status as an independent mental health profession is both historically recent and continually tenuous. It has been a struggle, mostly with medicine and psychiatry, to become an independent profession. Until World War II, only psychiatrists were allowed to perform psychotherapy with adults. In spite of the pressure of the need for therapists to treat the returning veterans, the American Medical Association continued into the 1950s to claim that psychotherapy was a medical procedure to be done only by medical doctors. The increased number of trained clinical psychologists and the increased funding for mental health in the 1960s allowed clinical psychology to establish itself as an independent profession. However, in recent years competition for "control of the booming $17 billion a year mental health business" (Cattell, 1983) has increased, and there have been several attempts once again to constrain the practice of clinical psychology and other mental health professions. Controversies over the definition of mental illness, the necessary education and training of therapists, licensing and certification, insurance reimbursement, and hospital privileges are all part of the struggle for clinical psychology to retain its identity.

As we have pointed out, in actual practice clinical psychologists and psychiatrists and other mental health care professionals frequently cooperate and work well together in private practice and in hospitals and mental health agencies. Many psychologists and psychiatrists call for an end to the competition and point out that the two professions need each other, that their respective expertises are complementary (Berg, 1986), and that the resources spent on competition would be better spent on a cooperative approach to the mental health problems facing our society (Cattell, 1983).

However, the alliance between clinical psychology and psychiatry remains uneasy. At its annual meeting in 1984 the AMA passed a resolution in which it pledged "to fight incursions of nurse midwives, podiatrists, nurse practitioners, physician's assistants, psychologists, nurse anesthetists and optometrists into medical practice via prescribing privileges, independent practice, mandated third-party reimbursement or other expansion of their scope of practice." The AMA agreed to provide staff to help state medical societies resist new legislation that expands the independent practice of psychologists and others and also to support amendments to current law in order to restrict that expansion. A recent article concerned about psychiatry's future alleged that one of the factors threatening the existence of psychiatry is "dominance of psychotherapy by nonmedical psychotherapists" (Lesse, 1986). With its tremendous economic resources the AMA may succeed in reversing some of the gains clinical psychology and other mental health professions have made as independent professions.

Definitions of Mental Illness Originally an attempt to reduce the stigma of mental disorder (it seemed better to be ill than sinful or possessed), the definition of mental disorder can also be viewed as a way to establish professional territoriality. If psychological problems are viewed as biological illnesses, then they should be treated by medical doctors in clinics and hospitals with medication and prescribed treatments. By this definition, clinical psychologists are not qualified to treat the mentally ill. However, if mental disorders are defined as psychological or behavioral in nature, then psychologists and other therapists would be qualified to treat them. The problem, of course, is that mental disorders are probably both physical and psychological.

The Diagnostic and Statistics Manual of Mental Disorders, Third Edition (DSM-III) was written by medical doctors, although other mental health professionals were consulted. In spite of its careful avoidance of the term mental illness, the words diagnosis, prognosis, illness, and disease appear throughout DSM-III, reflecting its medical assumptions. Since third-party payers require DSM-III diagnoses, all mental health professionals must use it, reinforcing the medical definitions of psychological disorders. Controversies over definitions of mental problems and the implicit struggle over professional territoriality have not been resolved, but have become more subtle than before.

Professional Competence What is the proper training for people who offer helping services to the public? To make the question more precise, what is the proper training for people who offer what type of help for what type of problems? It should be possible to obtain an empirical answer to the question, yet it remains controversial, partly because issues over training and competence have to do with the competition between psychiatry and clinical psychology and other mental health professions.

As part of their attempt to attain professional parity with psychiatry, clinical psychology determined that the Ph.D. degree was a necessary part of training, as were so many hours of supervised practice. In fact, the Ph.D. in clinical psychology may take more years to complete than medical school, and the amount of training in treatment and psychopathology is probably greater than that for psychiatrists. Nevertheless, psychiatry still argues that psychologists are not competent to treat certain groups of people, because they are not trained in medicine and pharmacology. Even within psychology there are controversies over training, as we saw in Chapter 1, regarding the scientist-practitioner model versus the professional model. Most graduate programs continue to emphasize individual psychotherapy in their training, and, as we shall see, it is likely that in future professional psychologists will need training in several different areas.

Chapter 1 noted that individuals may obtain psychoanalytic training only if they hold an M.D. degree. Psychologists argue that this requirement is unnecessary except for the purpose of restricting who may become psychoanalysts. Their training qualifies them for psychoanalytic training as well as that of psychiatrists. Currently, a group of psychologists are suing some psychoanalytic institutes over this requirement as constituting restraint of trade, that is, restraint of their right to practice their profession.

Supervision and continuing education are also important issues related to professional competence. Psychologists, counselors, and social workers are supervised in their practice while they are in graduate school and while they obtain the hours of experience necessary for licensure. Should they also seek supervision whenever they try something new or confront a case they do not feel expert in? How can they obtain good supervision when they want to extend their competence? How much supervision is necessary? Some believe that specific continuing education should be required by law for the maintenance of the license. Others believe that the need for additional supervision or continuing education should be left to the judgment of the individual professional.

Licensing, Certification, and Registration Licensing and certification of psychologists and other therapists were established amid controversy in the 1950s and 1960s, as noted in Chapter 1, and continue to be controversial today. Both the desire to protect the public from untrained and incompetent practitioners and the need to establish an independent professional identity prompted organized psychology to pressure state legislatures to pass laws to license psychologists.

A license is issued by a state to professionals who have demonstrated competence in their field by academic achievement and by passing certain kinds of tests or requirements set by the licensing board. The license is supposed to protect the public by ensuring that only qualified and competent persons may offer their services to the public. The laws regarding the license are usually explicit as to just what activities the licensee may engage in and what services the licensee may offer to the public. Laws regarding ethical and competent practice are enforced with the threat of the revocation of the license and the loss of the right to practice.

Certification is generally seen as a weaker form of control than licensure. The state merely certifies that the professional has completed the education or experience requirements for that profession. The certificate does not imply competence, while the license is supposed to do so. The certificate may or may not prescribe the activities engaged in by the holder and there may be little enforcement of what the professional does after certification.

Registration of therapists is the minimum way to regulate the mental health professions, in that therapists merely inform the state that they are practicing.

In most states licensure was preferred to certification or registration because it offered greater control of psychological practices and therefore greater protection to the public. It was also preferred because it was regarded as being more legitimate and equal to the requirements for medical practice.

In recent years the practice of licensing psychologists and other therapists has come under attack as failing to protect the public and merely serving a guild function to protect the professions. Critics argue that licensing keeps the cost of psychological services high by limiting the number of practitioners and reducing competition. Some states have threatened to pass "sunset laws" that would abolish licensing boards automatically every five years unless they were first evaluated regarding effectiveness with public hearings and then specifically reenacted. In the late 1970s several states passed sunset legislation, and in Alaska, Florida, and South Dakota the practice of psychology was unlicensed and unregulated for a period of time. The APA and state psychological organizations lobbied these states, and psychology is once again regulated in all states. It can be seen from these events that the professional status of clinical psychology remains tenuous. No one has ever seriously suggested abolishing the licensing of physicians.

When it was uncertain whether state governments would pass appropriate licensing laws for psychologists, the American Psychological Association decided to establish an independent, national, professional body to recognize competent psychologists. The American Board of Professional Psychology (ABPP) awards a special diploma of recognition to experienced, qualified psychologists. To become an ABPP diplomate, a psychologist must have five years of professional experience, be a member of the APA, hold a Ph.D. from an APA-approved program, submit copies of his or her work, see an unknown patient under observation, and pass an oral examination. Being a diplomate of ABPP implies additional competence and professional status for the clinical psychologist. If licensing were abolished, some experienced psychologists could use their ABPP diplomas to establish their right to practice.

The National Register of Health Service Providers in Psychology was established in the 1970s in response to some of these issues. If licensing were abolished, membership in the National Register could substitute. In anticipation of national health insurance, the register is also supposed to serve as a guide to insurance companies as to who is a licensed psychologist, that is, whose fees to pay. Membership in the APA and state licensure or certification are required to join the National Register, which lists all members' degrees, addresses, phone numbers, states in which they hold licenses, and areas of expertise.

Third-Party Payers The questionable professional status of clinical psychology is reflected in current struggles over the reimbursement policies of insurance companies. In the United States today few people pay directly for their own medical care, only the very poor or the very rich. Almost 90 percent of all civilian Americans possess health insurance (DeLeon, VandenBos, & Kraut, 1984) in the form of government insurance, private insurance, or membership in health maintenance organizations or other corporate health care systems. Thus, most medical services are paid for by these third-party payers.

Government and corporate health care and insurance companies wield tremendous power in determining the nature of health care in the United States and the practice of the mental health professions. See Box 12.2 for details.

Whether these insurance programs will pay for psychotherapy and under what circumstances will directly affect the ability of providers of psychotherapy services to earn a living. Currently, most government health insurance programs have severe restrictions on the amount and type of psychotherapy they will pay for, and corporate health insurance rarely provides more coverage than the government. Almost all will pay for the services of a psychiatrist, especially when the client is hospitalized. Some will pay for the services of clinical psychologists, some will not, some used to and will no longer, and some will only if the patient has been referred to the psychologist by a psychiatrist. It is apparent that if insurers pay for patients to see psychiatrists and do not pay for them to see clinical psychologists, then psychologists are at a distinct disadvantage in their ability to attract clients and earn a living. The same is true for other mental health professionals.

Psychologists have struggled for years to force health insurance programs to recognize their expertise and status as independent practitioners and to cover or reimburse their fees. They have argued that in light of the fact that there is no evidence that in the practice of psychotherapy psychiatrists are any more effective than psychologists (see Chapter 10 for this research), the policy of insurers to cover only the fees of medical doctors infringes on the right of patients to choose their own doctors and their own forms of treatment.

Many states have passed freedom-of-choice (FOC) legislation as a result of lobbying by both consumer groups and mental health professionals other than psychiatrists. FOC laws are supposed to guarantee patients the right to choose their own therapists

BOX 12.2
Psychology and the U.S. Health Care Delivery System

The way health care is delivered in the United States has changed dramatically over the last two centuries. In the eighteenth century health care was a matter of informal cooperation between family and community members. If someone in the community became known as good at delivering babies, pulling teeth, sawing off limbs, or whatever, then that person was consulted when the need arose. Payment, if any, was in the form of goods or returned favors, and the person performing the health service did not earn his or her living that way.

By the middle of the nineteenth century sufficient numbers of individuals earned their living providing healing services that an identifiable profession of physicians developed, and the American Medical Association was formed in order to establish an identity and formal qualifications for the profession of medicine. By the turn of the century other types of healers, such as community members, midwives, and others, were almost eliminated. Physicians established and owned hospitals and clinics, which also employed doctors, and many were in private practice or partnerships. Most physicians charged a fee for each visit or service they performed, and this fee-for-service method of payment financed the system of health care delivery until about the middle of this century.

By the 1950s several factors combined to make continuing the fee-for-service system of payment for health care almost economically impossible. Population increases and medical technology advances increased both costs and demand dramatically. Some physicians responded by forming health insurance companies, and business followed suit. Health insurance spreads the costs of the health care delivery system more evenly throughout the population, because those covered by the insurance directly or indirectly (through premiums or through decreased pay when employers provide insurance) for the system, but only a few people use it a great deal. With insurance our health care system is financed in a way that is similar to taxation (everyone pays something), but since physicians and corporations own the insurance companies, they control the health care delivery system rather than consumers or citizens.

At present the U.S. health care delivery system is undergoing another revolutionary change, apparently with little notice by the general public. Health insurance basically preserved the fee-for-service system while making its cost bearable by spreading it out among many people. Currently, for-profit corporations are developing and marketing many types of health care organizations to replace the system of independent practitioners supported by health insurance payments.

The "alphabet soup" of new health care systems includes the health maintenance organization (HMO), the preferred provider organization (PPO), the independent practitioner association (IPA), the employee assistance program (EAP), and others. Health care professionals join together to form HMOs as corporations offering complete health care to patients who pay monthly or annual fees to remain members of the HMO. Theoretically, HMOs should stress prevention and health maintenance over acute care after health has deteriorated, because they make more money if their members stay well. PPOs and IPAs are similar. Large corporations and businesses form EAPs or contract out for them to offer disturbed employees therapy and other services at the place of employment, so they will become less disturbed and more productive, thus saving the company the costs of firing, hiring, and training a new employee.

In addition to these organizations, for-profit hospitals and specialty hospitals (for example, hospitals that treat only AIDS or Alzheimer's) are being established, and soon chains of for-profit hospitals owned by large corporations may be the only type of hospital available.

Another trend, started by Medicare and some prepaid medical plans, is the use of diagnosis-related groups (DRGs) to cut costs. Hospitals and health care professionals are paid a flat fee based on the average cost of care for a patient's diagnosis, whether that actual patient's case is treated quickly or develops complications. It is especially difficult to predict the course of a mental disorder, and the use of DRGs may lead to inappropriate discharge of patients and financial risks to those who treat more severe cases.

The potential for conflict between the interests of for-profit corporations and those of consumers and citizens is great. Corporations are interested in profits, and not all forms of health care are profitable, but may still be needed. Some mental health professionals and some physicians are concerned about the possibility that soon the corporate world will take over the role of gatekeepers and watchdogs of national mental and physical health. By owning the majority of the health care delivery system, corporations may tell employees and citizens where to go for what limited health services. Private practitioners of all health professions will become increasingly rare. So will patients who freely choose their doctors and therapists and the type and extent of health care they want. It is also possible that a two-tiered medical system will become common, with expensive modern treatments available to the wealthy and cost-saving services available to everyone else.

The corporate model of prepaid health care is basically an extension of the medical model with cost containment features. This system is not responsive to the special characteristics of people needing psychological help or to the mental health professions other than psychiatry with its emphasis on biological causes and drug treatments. The changes in the health care delivery system directly threaten the hard-won gains of psychology to be recognized as an independent profession.

Health care is the third largest industry in the United States, every year the amount of money spent on it increases, and some psychologists are arguing that psychology should be part of it, as well as physicians and corporations. Furthermore, they contend that the mental health professions must drastically change the way they operate, or they will end up the poorly paid employees of large corporations. They must create new services and market them aggressively. For example, clinical psychologists could form their own special organizations to market specific services, such as stop smoking clinics, and they could market them to individuals, HMOs, and insurance companies. Psychologists could address the problem of somatization, that over half of visits to doctors are for nonphysical reasons. They could move more persuasively into the field of health psychology (discussed in Chapter 7) and emphasize wellness, prevention, and social action. Psychologists could move aggressively into medicine's traditional territory, for some believe that clinical psychologists are competent to prescribe psychotropic medication (DeLeon, 1986).

There is enough business to go around. The need for care of the physically ill and mentally disordered is universal to all times and cultures. What is less clear is which professions will provide the needed services and who will own the institutions that profit by their delivery. Only by attending carefully to the changes in the health care system and responding promptly and creatively to them will psychology remain a viable, if very different profession.

by requiring health insurance programs to provide equal coverage of psychotherapy services by psychologists and psychiatrists (and sometimes social workers and other therapists as well). These laws are supposed to reduce consumer costs by increasing competition. They also help ensure the right of psychologists to practice independently.

A recent threat to psychologists was ERISA, the Employee Retirement Income Security Act (1980). This federal act was designed to improve all employee benefits, but it does not require health insurance to cover mental health benefits or to provide employees freedom of choice of doctors. Most state laws do require employee benefit programs to cover mental health and to guarantee freedom of choice, but does ERISA preempt state laws? Chrysler Corporation announced in late 1984 that it would no longer pay for the services of a psychologist for any of its employees nationwide, citing ERISA as preempting state law. On June 3, 1985, the U.S. Supreme Court ruled that state laws take precedence over ERISA, that is, that states can require insurance coverage exceeding that required by federal law. Thus, another potential threat to the practice of clinical psychology as an independent profession was averted. However, now many big companies self-insure, and then state laws mandating freedom-of-choice and mental health benefits do not apply.

In recent years, beset by mounting medical costs, health insurance programs have sought to cut expenses by restricting the coverage of treatment of psychological disorders. One way of doing this is to cut out payment for certain types of practitioners or certain types of treatment. So once again many health insurance programs no longer cover the services of psychologists. A challenge for clinical psychology in the future, as discussed below, will be to demonstrate that their services save money for the insurance companies by enhancing insurees' mental and physical health (Cummings, 1986).

Insurance companies tend to pay for treatment for mental disorders more liberally if the patient is hospitalized than if the patient is seen as an outpatient. This practice increases costs by encouraging the use of hospitalization in treatment when in fact it may be the least effective form of treatment (Miller & Hester, 1986). It also discriminates against the nonpsychiatric mental health professionals, who may not hospitalize their clients in most cases. As can be seen, the mental health professions and society are still in the process of working out how therapists may practice and who will pay for their services.

JCAH and Hospital Privileges Until 1984 only psychiatrists and medical doctors were allowed hospital privileges and the right to hospitalize their clients. The Joint Commission on Accreditation of Hospitals (JCAH) accredited only hospitals that allowed only psychiatrists and medical doctors to admit their private patients and to treat hospitalized patients. Due to pressure in the form of antitrust suits brought by the psychological community, in 1984 the JCAH agreed to accredit hospitals that extend hospital privileges to licensed psychologists, although physicians will still determine patient care. However, it is entirely up to individual hospitals whether to include psychologists, and since hospitals are governed almost exclusively by medical doctors, few hospitals have extended staff privileges to psychologists. It is obvious that if only psychiatrists may hospitalize and treat hospitalized clients, the ability of other mental health professionals to treat clients and to earn a living is severely curtailed. This problem is exacerbated by the fact that insurance companies pay more for the care of hospitalized clients than for outpatients.

Related to this issue is the fact that psychologists may not commit patients to mental hospitals or psychiatric wards. A 1978 national survey of state laws (Drude, 1978) found that only 24 out of 50 states include psychologists in their commitment statutes, and inclusion is generally of an optional type, that is, psychologists *may* be substituted for one of two physicians. The conclusion of the survey is that clinical psychologists "remain in many ways unrecognized as qualified mental health professionals competent to judge the appropriateness of hospitalization of mentally ill persons" (Drude, 1978, p. 499). While committing patients may not account for much of any therapist's practice, this situation is an example of the continual struggle facing clinical psychology to be recognized as an independent profession equal in competence and qualifications to psychiatry.

Peer Review, Accountability, and Cost-Effectiveness As a result of research that demonstrated that psychotherapy was not always effective and of the pressure of third-party payers, there have been calls to make the mental health professions more accountable for their claims and services. In order to continue to receive funding from government programs and payment from private health insurance, providers of psychotherapy must now demonstrate that their services accomplish what they claim. Any program designed to treat a certain problem, provide a certain service, or prevent a certain disorder must evaluate itself and demonstrate that it has been effective, or else it will receive no more funds or payment.

Peer review is a way for clinical psychology to become accountable while retaining the professional independence to judge its own performance. Peer review is the examination of an individual psychologist's cases by other psychologists to see if the treatment provided is appropriate, competent, and necessary. It is a little like supervision, and done correctly, it should help therapists with their difficult cases. Many mental health agencies instituted their own peer review programs in the 1970s before it was required by their funding sources. Now many insurance companies require peer review of certain cases before they pay for the costs of the treatment.

Along with general accountability, there have been increased demands that psychology demonstrate that its services are cost-effective, that its services or solutions to problems both work *and* cost less than other methods of treatment or doing nothing. Many studies demonstrate that psychological services can be very cost-effective. Providing certain patients with psychotherapy can reduce overall health costs by decreasing utilization of other, more expensive medical services. Alcoholism treatment programs save companies more money than they cost by reducing lost work days and the costs of training new employees. Relatively inexpensive stop smoking programs save enormous amounts of money that would otherwise be spent on expensive cancer treatments or wasted on lost work days and reduced productivity due to illness.

It takes a certain amount of creativity to assess cost-effectiveness. With their training in research methods and statistics, clinical psychologists are qualified to conduct empirical studies of cost-effectiveness. But it also takes educating the public and third-party payers as to what should go into measuring cost-effectiveness of psychotherapy. The costs of psychotherapy are relatively easy to determine, but how do you measure its benefits? How do you put a price on improved human functioning, reduction of lost work days, increased productivity, decreased use of other, more expensive services? These are all benefits that are related to psychotherapy outcomes.

People must be convinced that psychotherapy is worth it. Some psychologists believe that psychology does not adequately trumpet its successes. They believe there should be organized, active efforts to educate the public (the taxpayers and buyers of insurance) regarding the empirical evidence of the cost-effectiveness of psychological services. Not just education is needed, however. It is well known that treating mental disorders is more expensive in the hospital than out, yet insurance companies continue to pay for treatment in such a way that encourages hospitalization. They continue to act against their apparent self-interests partly because of habit, partly because of their bias toward the medical model, and partly because cutting outpatient services saves money in the short run. So, forceful and persuasive education is needed.

The increased unwillingness of taxpayers to fund mental health programs and the ever-present desire of insurance companies to cut their costs and increase their profits mean that demonstrating and convincing the public of the cost-effectiveness of psychological services will be essential to the survival of professional psychology. All of this sounds terribly money-grubbing. Whatever happened to helping people in distress, to the sense of community responsibility for the less fortunate members of society, to the desire to enhance human functioning and improve our society? These American ideals can probably be elicited, especially if it is shown that it saves money to act on them.

The Profession and Society

What is the relation between psychology and society at large? What should that relation be? Psychologists and other therapists are citizens and members of their society, and their professions exist in a certain historical and social context. Clinical psychology came into being in the United States at a time when science and individualism were highly valued. Should clinical psychology try to remain neutral, accept society as it exists, encourage society to change, or work actively to bring about social change? If being an agent of change is an acceptable role, what social changes should be worked toward?

Clinical psychology is in the business of changing people, yet it is often accused of preserving the status quo. Like any established profession or interest group, it tends to resist change and to see its self-interest in keeping the advantages it has. If a profession makes its living by "treating" certain types of people, it will resist anything that redefines those people or that reduces their numbers (i.e., prevention). And like any science, psychology must view the world through its own cultural values.

Change Versus Adjustment Continuing controversy occurs over the individual-versus-situation issue of whether people should change to adjust to society or society should change to fit the needs of individuals. Many critics have argued that the goal of most psychotherapy is to make people fit into what exists, so they don't rock the boat. We even refer to how "adjusted" people are. These critics contend that it is the situation (the way society is organized) that is the problem, not the "maladjusted" individuals (Albee, 1986). If society is organized in an unhealthy or inhumane way, then people will naturally become disturbed. It is both immoral and futile to help these people adjust without changing the conditions that lead to maladjustment. Helping people "adjust" is just another way of shoring up the status quo.

Feminist critics regard much of the practice of psychotherapy as incorporating the sexism and stereotypes of the current society. Mostly men therapists try to get mostly women clients to "adjust" to their gender role, their stereotype, their oppression. A woman who dislikes the female role and its lack of power may not be suffering from "penis envy" or a gender identity disturbance. She may simply be realistic about her role in society. By helping women "adjust" to unjust conditions, therapists are both preserving the status quo and perpetuating the oppression of women. Psychology has been responsive to these criticisms, for the American Psychological Association has established guidelines for therapy with women (APA, 1978) that encourage therapists to locate the cause of women's distress in their situation, not as something wrong with them.

Many writers have recognized the social control functions of the mental health professions and criticized them for serving as the "soft police." Some behaviors have been defined differently over the years, so that different social control agents have been brought to bear on them. Excessive drinking behavior was once a sin, railed against by preachers and temperance organizations. Then for a few years, it was a crime, and excessive drinkers were arrested and imprisoned. Recently, excessive drinking behavior has become a disease, treated by doctors and therapeutic programs. In this sense alcoholism doctors and counselors are now the soft police—the social control agents for excessive drinking behavior. Some critics contend that the mental health professions are the soft police for all nonconforming and politically disruptive behavior. This view casts the mental health professions firmly on the side of the status quo.

Political Misuses of Mental Health Concepts The most widely criticized misuse of mental health concepts is the so-called insanity defense. Hinckley's attempt to assassinate President Reagan and his subsequent acquittal due to insanity enraged many people and brought the issue to the public's attention. Szasz has been arguing against the insanity defense since 1961. Szasz (1961) has documented how the insanity defense results in miscarriages of justice, usually with those being adjudged "innocent by reason of insanity" serving longer periods of incarceration in mental hospitals than they would have if sentenced to prison. Szasz writes that since "mental illness" is a myth and therefore professionals often disagree on whether a defendant was insane at the time of the offense or not, trials should be conducted solely on the basis of whether the person committed the act he or she is accused of or not. Defenders of the insanity defense contend that abolishing it would also result in grave injustice, for each case must be assessed individually and the accused's state of mind, intentions, and capability of making rational decisions must be taken into account.

Other misuses of mental health concepts are not as apparent, although certainly just as debatable, as the insanity defense. Two examples come to mind. Recently a stress management program for blue-collar workers was being advertised in Oakland. The billboard shouted "Stress at work? Powerlessness is bad for your health." Was this an innovative program showing workers how to gain power at work? No, it was a call for workers to seek counseling. Through stress management workers would be taught to adjust to aversive working conditions, rather than organizing and demanding that their working conditions be improved (this holds for stress management programs for executives as well). No longer do employers and corporations have to worry about disruptive employees or providing appropriate working conditions—they just teach the workers to adjust to them. The source of employee distress is placed in the employee, not on the way business and work are currently organized.

Our second example has to do with a study recently funded by the Department of Energy. The DOE paid a psychiatrist to determine the causes and cures of "nuclear phobia." Several psychologists attacked this study because of its methodological flaws and because of its obvious pronuclear bias. The critics claimed the study was a political use of mental illness jargon to label concerned citizens as having a phobia. Concerned citizens who disagree with the government's pronuclear energy stand and who may engage in political activities against nuclear power and nuclear weapons are "crazy"—they've got "nuclear phobia"! Potentially, the DOE could next fund a study to "cure" nuclear phobia. Psychological methods could be used to manipulate the public for pronuclear purposes under the guise of "treating" a "mental illness." Regardless of the merits of nuclear power, most people would agree that introducing a "mental disorder" like "nuclear phobia" into the controversy confuses the issue and renders reasonable discussion difficult. And many would agree that it is a misuse of mental health concepts.

It is not only the politically conservative who misuse mental health concepts. Some liberal therapists argue that all anxiety and mental disorder are due to the ever-present threat of nuclear war and that the only way to treat them is to eliminate that threat. The point we are trying to make is that in our present society social values get "medicalized." We then argue about the nature and payment of "treatment," rather than confronting fundamental differences in our values.

Politics and the Mentally Disordered Sufferers of mental disorders are also victims of political processes. In the 1960s the progressive Community Mental Health Act encouraged states to replace hospital-based treatment with community-based treatment of the mentally disturbed. Many states changed laws and regulations so that the population of the mental hospitals was severely decreased. However, neither the state nor the federal government sufficiently funded community alternatives to hospitalization, and with the cutting of mental health funding in the 1970s many mentally disordered individuals had nowhere to go. Many of them became the media-defined "homeless" of the 1980s. Many others have ended up in prison or in nursing homes.

Another aspect of this problem is a result of the civil liberties movement in the 1960s, which believed involuntary commitment to a mental hopsital constituted a violation of a person's civil rights in many cases. There were many documented instances of abuse of the commitment procedures. Disturbing people were committed for long periods of time when they did not really belong in the mental hospital. One of us recalls a middle-aged man committed for some years to a locked ward. His major "symptom" appeared to be that he spent the family fotune too freely for his relatives' tastes. True, he was abrasive and he was odd—he had a bullet hole in the middle of his forehead, slurred his speech, walked in a funny way, and liked to argue politics, play the harmonica, and spend money on wine, women, and song. However, he was not suffering from psychosis, depression, or any other mental disorder. Nor was he a danger to himself or others or gravely disabled (the criteria for commitment in most states). Nevertheless, there he stayed until California's Lanterman-Petris-Short Act set him free in 1969.

Civil libertarians argued that in our country, which values individual freedom so much that it is written into the Constitution, people should not be involuntarily incarcerated just because they are different, nonconforming, or difficult for others or even just because they are psychotic. Court decisions on lawsuits initiated by patients or their advocates agreed that some commitments were an unconstitutional deprivation of liberty and civil rights. In addition, many states passed laws making involuntary commitment much more difficult. Today it may be almost impossible to commit clearly psychotic individuals, because they are not a danger to themselves or others. And since they can manage to survive eating out of garbage cans and sleeping on the street, they are not gravely disabled either. So they have the "freedom" to hallucinate, avoid people, do nothing all day, and live a barren existence on the street. It appears that our society has decided that the value of individual freedom is worth the risk of a few lost souls. And how can one say for certain that they would be better off in a mental hospital? In short, the severely mentally disordered have been shifted around, and their problems have not been adequately addressed, as a result of a number of complex political processes.

Community Psychology As the arm of professional psychology most concerned with psychology's role in society, community psychology assumes that the causes of psychological disorder are to be found in society. The stress of poverty, for instance, interacts with poor child-rearing practices or biological weakness to cause schizophrenia, psychosomatic illnesses, or other disorders. Poverty, which contributes significantly to these disorders, is a result of how our society is organized. Intervention at the level of the disordered individual is seen as less effective in the long run than intervening so as to change the social causes of disorder. Taken to its logical conclusion, community psychology is revolutionary—the entire organization of society must be changed in order to eliminate the conditions that foster individual disorders and to help disturbed individuals.

Community psychology stresses changing social institutions with the goal of preventing the development of individual psychological disorders and social problems as well. Institutions, which are originally created to serve the community, develop a tendency to serve their own needs for self-maintenance and control over people, and they end up not only failing to serve the community, but in many cases contributing to the problems in the community. Since individual and social problems arise as a result of the interaction between people and institutions, community psychology intervenes at both points. As a consultant to a group of people or a community experiencing difficulties, the community psychologist helps the group define and assess its problems, encourages the group to develop its own objectives and solutions based on alternatives generated by the assessment and consultation, helps implement the programs the group chooses, and may assess the effectiveness of the programs. Community psychologists tend to utilize existing community resources, such as training indigenous nonprofessional counselors, to focus on increasing the strengths already present in a system, to value and enhance social diversity, and to stress the prevention, rather than the treatment, of psychological disorders.

Although there is some degree of professional controversy over how to define prevention (Forgays, 1983), most writers describe three types of prevention. *Primary prevention* focuses on trying to reduce the incidence of psychological disorder in a community by changing the social causes of psychological disorder before they affect anyone, before disorders can develop. Programs to educate the populace on the risks of smoking, to reduce prejudice against the elderly, and to teach all school children social competence are examples of primary prevention efforts. *Secondary prevention* tries to reduce the duration of psychological disorders or to help groups at risk of certain disorders before they develop severe pathology. Programs to provide crisis counseling (discussed below), to provide Big Brothers for predelinquent boys, and to counsel adolescents stopped by the police for minor violations are examples of secondary prevention. Most of the efforts of the mental health professions are directed toward *tertiary prevention,* which stresses reducing the impairment of psycholgical disorders once they have developed.

An important part of community psychology is the practice of crisis intervention. A crisis is any event that threatens individuals' *homeostasis*—their equilibrium or usual ability to function and cope. A crisis can be maturational, as is the identity crisis at adolescence, or situational, as is divorce or a natural disaster. If persons in crisis receive immediate help from family, friends, or social institutions such as the church or the community mental health center, their equilibrium and functioning can be fairly quickly restored. The social skills and sense of competence learned from coping adequately with a crisis will help individuals in future crises. If help is not obtained, crisis behavior can develop into chronic incompetence or psychological disorder. Thus, it is essential for community psychologists to intervene early in crisis situations as a form of secondary prevention.

Caplan (1964) argued that crisis intervention is the best and the most cost-effective form of therapy. By intervening precisely when the client is vulnerable and disorganized, the active therapist can have the greatest impact. Rather than conducting months or even years of therapy when the client may well be coping fairly adequately, the crisis counselor intervenes just when the client is most likely to change, either for better or for worse. Therapy and support during the crisis not only help the client survive the crisis, but also aid in the development of confidence and skills for other life problems, while failing to obtain help during the crisis may lead to deterioration and chronic incompetence.

In addition to crisis counseling, community psychologists are involved in walk-in clinics, hot lines, cross-cultural counseling, and other community programs. Their roles in these activities include program development, consultation, grant writing and fund raising, training of nonprofessional counselors and hot line workers, supervision, and evaluation of program effectiveness, as well as the provision of direct services to clients.

Community psychology is criticized for serving a social control function rather than making meaningful changes in society. Despite its potentially revolutionary theory, community programs tend to provide just enough help to damp the dissatisfaction and potential disruptiveness of certain segments of society. In that sense such programs sustain the oppressive social system by quieting its casualties. The reply to these criticisms is that it is inhumane and ethically unacceptable to leave people in misery until they become disruptive enough to force social change. Helping people in our present society and working toward a better society should not be mutually exclusive goals. Some psychologists, particularly George Albee (1986), explicitly argue that the only genuine way to prevent psychopathology and human misery is to increase social justice by redistributing power and wealth.

Community psychology is also criticized for failing to deliver on its promises. In spite of extensive funding for many community programs, we still have unacceptably high rates of psychological disorders, and some argue that prevention has not worked. Others criticize community psychologists for abandoning the goal of primary prevention and focusing too much on tertiary prevention. Defenders of community psychology reply that inadequate funding has undermined many otherwise effective programs and that the government has become unwilling to fund primary prevention programs. Reviews of research on community psychology (Cowan, 1980; Long, 1986; Goldston, 1986; Albee & Joffe, 1977) conclude that we now have a good knowledge base of the social causes of disorder and how to intervene, that primary prevention has been demonstrated to be both effective and cost-effective in many cases, and that community psychologists may have to turn to political action in order to obtain the funding to implement their goals.

THE FUTURE

What are the social, economic, political, and demographic trends that will affect the future of professional psychology? Some have already been mentioned, and others are easily discerned from the daily news. The population of the United States is shifting. Ethnic minorities are increasing their proportion of the population. The aged are also increasing their percentage of the population, and this trend can only continue, since the baby-boomers are hitting middle age. Although no one seems certain of the direction, it is apparent that the socioeconomic organization of the United States is in the throes of profound change, shifting from industrial production to services and information. Such drastic social changes increase people's stress and consequently the demand for psychological, medical, and psychiatric services.

One important trend is the decreased availability of money to pay for training, research, and services in mental health. The tremendous deficit spending by the federal government in the 1980s coupled with constant demands for a balanced budget and lower taxes guarantee reduced spending by the federal government for mental health and other programs for decades to come. States and private charities will try with varied (mostly limited) success to make up for the loss in federal funds. Less and less money for mental health appears certain for many years.

With the government funding far fewer mental health programs, the costs of whatever psychotherapy and treatment services are available will be increasingly borne by the third-party payers. The power of the corporate world through insurance companies to regulate who gets paid for what, to determine the nature of both medical and psychological practice, will increase. And their major goal is not to improve the quality of life for all Americans, but to increase their profits and cut costs, in most cases, to increase profits and cut costs in the short run. The potential for conflict between the goals of the corporate world and the goals of mental health professionals and even the citizens is great. The citizens may believe that psychotics should receive extensive psychotherapy, just because it is right, but if it's not profitable, the insurance companies may try to avoid paying for it. However, it is possible that improving the quality of life for all Americans can be shown to contribute to the profits of insurers, especially in the long run.

Where do insurance companies get their money? Directly and indirectly from almost every citizen. As we said about 90 percent of people in the United States are covered by some form of government or private health insurance. Taxpayers pay for government insurance. And taxpayers pay for the private insurance, too. They pay premiums or their employers pay premiums and pay them less (an indirect cost to the employee). So virtually every citizen pays for the health care system in the United States. Yet, because in our country private companies provide this service rather than the government (as in countries with "socialized medicine" such as Great Britain), the citizens have little power to determine how the health care system is run and a lot of their health care money goes for profit. Decisions about the health care system, which affect all of us and which all of us pay for, will be increasingly made by the corporate owners of insurance companies and health care companies.

What does all of this augur? To say that therapists should consider alternatives to the traditional private practice and seeing clients in individual psychotherapy is an understatement. Even work in psychological clinics and mental health agencies is likely to change drastically. It is imperative that the mental health professions develop new roles and services. It is probably equally imperative that they empirically demonstrate the effectiveness and the cost-effectiveness of these new roles and services, and then learn to market them as well (Cummings, 1986).

What changes can be expected in the practice of psychology? It is easy to guess that there will be increasing use of group therapy and brief psychotherapy. The demand for bilingual and multicultural therapists will increase. More specialists in aging, disability, and handicaps will be needed. With the predicted increase in AIDS, experts in immunocompetence, death and dying, and grief counseling will be needed, too. Traditional employment opportunities for psychologists in government-funded mental hospitals, mental health agencies, and private practice will decrease, and employment will be sought in business and industry and new systems of health care delivery.

Many psychologists argue that psychology as a profession must give up its traditional role of treating psychologically disordered individuals. Not only are insurance companies and taxpayers becoming disenchanted with that role, but it can also be said that clinical psychologists are wasting their behavioral and research skills in that role. Their skills would be of greater benefit to society if used in dramatically different contexts, including public education and social action. So let us turn to an examination of some of the new roles proposed for professional psychology.

Future Roles for Psychologists

In order for clinical psychology to move into new roles, training and education of psychologists must change, and new definitions of the competencies required of psychologists must be developed. An example of one obviously needed change in training is to shift the emphasis from learning individual psychotherapy to learning to apply behavioral and psychological principles to a wide variety of problems and situations, such as brief psychotherapy, behavioral toxicology, and prevention of illness.

The emphasis on accountability and cost-effectiveness means that clinical psychologists interested in research will turn to evaluation research. They will be increasingly involved in the assessment of the effectiveness of mental health and other programs. Private foundations and government agencies that grant money to groups to carry out various treatment programs increasingly demand that an evaluation research component be built into the program. Third-party payers also demand empirical demonstration of the effectiveness of treatments before they pay for them. Clinical psychologists are qualified with their research skills and clinical experience to conduct such evaluation studies.

George Albee (1968, 1970, 1982, 1985, 1986) has long argued that professional psychology should be working to put itself out of business by focusing on the prevention of psychological disorders. He believes psychologists should stop wasting their expertise providing inefficient and costly psychotherapy to a few individuals. Prevention has been demonstrated to be more cost-effective than treatment, and further studies on this point should be done. In addition, psychology should forcefully make the case for prevention to the public and to third-party payers. If the cost-effectiveness of prevention can be gotten across, then many new roles for psychologists would open up, including education, community programs, and social action.

Part of prevention and "giving psychology away" may involve increasing use of nonprofessional counselors. One study (Strupp & Hadley, 1979) on nonprofessional counselors concluded that nonprofessional counselors are equally effective as professionals in many cases. The use of nonprofessional counselors increases the number of counselors available and decreases costs, in addition to providing counselors similar to the clients. Leaving individual therapy to nonprofessionals, professional psychologists in future may become more involved in the provision of other services, including the training and supervision of the nonprofessional counselors.

Another aspect of "giving psychology away" is teaching the public how to help themselves. This goal may include educating existing helping institutions to be more effective, as well as teaching the public self-help skills. Some psychologists (Katz & Rolde, 1981) believe psychology should research the relative effectiveness of other forms of help available in the community, with the goal of educating consumers as to how to make the best use of the helping alternatives available. Albee (1985) argues that rather than spending time and energy making theoretical distinctions and creating professional lines of demarcation, psychology should spend its resources wisely by joining forces with effective groups that share the goal of ameliorating human suffering and enhancing human potential. The California Self-Help Center, described in Box 12.3, provides a model for the effective utilization of both psychologists' expertise and community resources so that help reaches many people at a relatively low cost.

Levy (1984) has recommended that clinical psychology become human services psychology, with psychologists serving a resource collaborative role. Human services psychology would be concerned with "the promotion of human well-being through the acquisition and application of psychological knowledge about the treatment and prevention of psychological and physical disorders." It would be comprehensive, using a

BOX 12.3
The California Self-Help Center

A unique collaboration of professional psychologists and community resources is to be found in the California Self-Help Center, funded by the California Department of Mental Health and housed in the psychology department at the University of California at Los Angeles. Directed by two UCLA psychologists, Dr. Marion Jacobs and Dr. Gerald Goodman, the Center is designed to promote the appropriate use of self-help. Dr. Jacobs says,

> When you're coping with stressful problems, such as a serious illness, loss of a loved one, alcohol abuse, being overweight, retirement, or a parent who's growing senile, it really helps to have the support of other people who truly understand your situation. . . . [Although] a self-help group is not necessarily the right choice for every person, I really believe that often a self-help group provides the best available help anywhere." (Bazrod, 1986)

The Center is a statewide computerized network of self-help groups, and it refers people who call its toll-free number (800-222-LINK) to the most appropriate self-help group or helping organization available in their own communities. If the form of help requested does not exist, the Center helps the people form a group from like-minded people in their community. In addition to referring individuals to the well-known self-help groups such as Alcoholics Anonymous and Gamblers Anonymous, the Center lists hundreds of available organizations to help with problems ranging from stuttering, compulsive spending, and hair loss to rare diseases, divorce, and losing a loved one to murder. Although some groups charge a small fee (up to $6 per meeting), most are free.

The Center provides other services as well. A psychologist may consult with existing self-help and other groups to help them be more effective. Drs. Jacobs and Goodman have developed a series of tape-recorded instructions for leaderless groups, called the Common Concern Program, which teaches communication and group management skills. These tapes are loaned free to people throughout the state. Consultants to the Center often write new audiotapes for special audiences, such as one covering specific issues common to adults who were abused as children and one for divorced women.

The Center advertises its services to the public, conducts community workshops, holds conferences, and engages in research. Recently it held two training workshops for child abuse prevention specialists in which they received instruction in starting self-help groups for abuse prevention. Participants were asked to commit themselves to starting at least one self-help group in their communities. The Center sponsors an annual conference for medical and mental health professionals and self-helpers, with workshops, films, exhibits, and panel discussions to increase fruitful collaboration between professionals and self-helpers. One of the Center's research projects is a study of self-help groups for middle-aged divorced women, which involves developing a method for coding group process, a method for measuring outcome, and a way to link process with outcome.

The Center's effective use of psychologists' expertise and community resources means that help reaches many people at a relatively low cost. The federal Department of Health and Human Services predicts that the self-help movement will double its 1985 membership by 1990. This trend suggests that the potential partnership between mental health professionals and self-help groups is an important possibility for the future. The California Self-Help Center is leading the way.

biopsychosocial model of human behavior, and collaborative with other helping professions. Weiss (1983) urges psychology to move into the field of behavioral toxicology and environmental health science, including research, assessment, treatment, and prevention related to environmental hazards that affect behavior. Shifting the emphasis from "disorder" to "well-being" would lead to many new applications of psychological skills and new roles for psychologists.

Psychological Skills and Social Problems

Many psychologists urge their profession to use behavioral skills to treat expensive social problems. Many individual behaviors lead to problems that are costly to all of us. Often these behaviors appear to be matters of individual choice and personal freedom, and the fact that they constitute social problems that cost us all lots of money is not obvious. People cannot be forced to alter these behaviors, but the application of psychological principles can help alter them without threatening individual freedom.

Whether people want to wear their seat belts or not would appear to be a matter of individual choice. Some people may be more willing to take risks than others, but the choice doesn't seem to be anybody's business but the individual driver's. However, it is well documented that not wearing seat belts dramatically increases the probability of death and serious injury when automobile accidents occur. And that makes it everybody's business. We all bear the costs of an individual's serious injuries through the costs of health insurance. If everyone wore seat belts, there would be fewer serious injuries, and medical and insurance costs would go down for the entire society. The truth of this argument has led some states to pass laws requiring all drivers to wear seat belts (not a very effective way to increase seat belt use).

The same argument could be made for many other behaviors. It is not just the individual smoker's business when he gets cancer, emphysema, or heart disease. Each and every one of us pays directly and indirectly for the expensive treatments for these diseases, which are largely preventable. In late 1985 the U.S. Surgeon General, C. Everett Koop, in his annual report noted that smokers use the health care system 50 percent more than nonsmokers do. Koop said, "A smoking employee is a more expensive employee than a nonsmoking employee." As businesses recognize this fact, they increasingly refuse to hire smokers, and as experts in behavior change, clinical psychologists may be called upon to help alter or prevent such "individualistic" behaviors.

Another individual problem is obesity. The United States stands out in the extent of its problem of overeating. The high risks to health of being overweight are well documented, but overeating is a behavior that seems to be very resistant to change. Psychologists have developed methods successful in reducing overeating, and they could be involved in education and prevention of obesity as well.

Psychologists could increase compliance with safety procedures in many situations. They have the skills to increase individuals' use of seat belts, safety helmets, and other safety devices. They could also consult with communities and businesses as to how to increase the safety of the environment. Some changes can reduce physical hazards and the likehood of accidents. Other changes—certain kinds of lighting, certain ways of situating buildings, certain layouts of streets—are known to reduce the likelihood of crime such as vandalism and gang activity.

Alcohol and drug abuse are pervasive behaviors that are difficult to change and are extremely expensive to the individuals, their families, and society. Psychologists have the skills to discover and apply principles to reduce and prevent these behaviors.

Environmental toxicology is a new field psychologists could enter. The environment is increasingly polluted with dangerous chemicals that affect health, the brain, and behavior. Psychologists could research the behavioral and neurological effects of toxins and develop methods of treating those effects. They are also capable of designing programs to educate the public about toxins, how they can avoid them, and how pollution can be prevented. They could also be involved in modifying the behavior of the polluters.

Psychologists have a great deal to contribute to the social problem of crime and its victims. They have researched the causes of crime and have something to say about how it could be prevented by altering the social conditions that lead to it. Since altering social conditions like poverty and racism is both expensive and unlikely, Siegel (1983) has suggested that society and psychology shift their attention from crime to the victims. Treating and compensating the victims of crime may be more humane and cost-effective than building more prisons and increasing the punishments for crime. Psychologists could also be involved in demonstrating the effectiveness of and implementing alternatives to prison for those who commit crimes.

Chronic pain costs a great deal in terms of lost work days, lost productivity, inappropriate and excessive use of medical services, and loss of a normal life for the victims and their families. Behavioral medicine psychologists can research and treat pain, teaching clients how to reduce it, ignore it, or control it.

Family mediation is a relatively new and growing field. Family mediation is seen as an alternative to the adversarial courts to handle divorce, an increasingly common event. Family mediators help divorcing families clarify their goals, develop a workable divorce agreement, and solve problems that arise after the divorce. The goal of family mediation is to reduce the unnecessary trauma of divorce and to help parents meet the children's needs as much as possible. At present there are no professional requirements for family mediators, although most have training in the law and psychotherapy. The clinical psychologist's skills in communication, family processes, contracting and negotiation, and behavior modification would be helpful in family mediation.

There are many other possibilities. It is incumbent on psychologists to demonstrate that their methods of dealing with these socially expensive individual problems are cost-effective, humane, and good for society and to lobby politically for recognition and payment for their professional skills. By dropping their old roles and creatively developing new ones, psychologists will both improve society and enhance the prospects for the profession. (See Box 12.4.)

Employment Prospects in Psychology

Students who wish to pursue a career in professional psychology may be either overwhelmed or encouraged by what we have said about the future. In fact, the services provided by the mental health professions have been and always will be needed and valuable. At present psychology is a fluid field in a rapidly changing society. The traditional advantage of clinical psychology for someone entering the field was its

Box 12.4
How to Choose a Therapist

After learning about the many types of therapies and therapists available, you may wish for some more practical information about how to choose a therapist for a family member, a friend, or yourself. The plethora of possibilities is perhaps confusing. However, there are two basic pieces of advice: ask others and pay attention to what your own feelings tell you about any therapist you see.

Asking friends, relatives, and other health care professionals for a recommendation for a therapist is a good strategy. You may already have an idea of what type of therapist is needed. If someone is depressed, possibly suicidal, and possibly in need of hospitalization, a psychiatrist would be best. You may already know whether a sex therapist, hypnotist, psychoanalyst, feminist, or behaviorist is needed or preferred. In that case, you can ask state and local professional organizations for therapist referrals. For example, you may telephone the county mental health association, the state psychological association, a psychoanalytic institute in a large city, United Way, or other groups. Get enough recommendations so there are several therapists to choose from.

The next step is to call the therapists to ask about their services and perhaps to make an appointment. Do not hesitate to ask questions about fees, therapist training and qualifications, and therapeutic methods over the telephone. A concerned and ethical therapist will be willing to talk about such issues. Furthermore, therapists should be willing to discuss your problem and to make some statement about whether it is within their area of expertise. If you wish to know that the therapist is licensed, you may call the appropriate state licensing board. (You would also call it if you ever wanted to make a complaint against a therapist.)

After getting an idea of the therapists available and getting some information from them, you may decide to make an appointment with one or two. An initial appointment does not mean a commitment to that therapist. Many therapists encourage people who are in the process of deciding to begin therapy to "shop around," to visit other therapists, and to be sure they are comfortable with one before they decide to go into therapy. Again, you should feel free to ask the therapist anything you need to know in order to make your decision. The therapist will also ask you questions in order to assess the nature of your problem and what sort of treatment it requires.

Your own reactions to the therapist and to the therapy hour are your best guides to choosing a therapist. Did you feel comfortable? Do you now feel hopeful? Did the therapist seem competent? Do you feel some degree of trust and confidence in the therapist? Do the methods the therapist intends to use appeal to you? While it is likely that a person trying to choose a therapist feels vulnerable and confused, and while that person's problem may be inability to trust or judge others, nevertheless a person should be able to give some thought to these sorts of questions. And certainly any strongly negative reactions would indicate that another therapist should be chosen.

You may not develop clear feelings about a therapist until you have seen him or her several times. If after an initially positive reaction, you begin to have doubts or negative feelings, you should raise these feelings for discussion in therapy. Admittedly, this may be difficult. It is possible that these feelings are important for your therapy and they can be worked on. It is also possible that you may decide to change therapists. Most likely, however, if you have obtained several referrals from good sources and paid attention to your feelings while you interviewed several therapists, you will feel comfortable with your therapist and benefit greatly from therapy.

diversity. The psychologist could go into research, teach at colleges and universities, do private practice, or obtain employment in a variety of clinical settings.

Professional psychology will increase in diversity and provide even more different career opportunities. However, it will probably become the student's responsibility to seek out a variety of education and training experiences. Graduate training has been slow to change in the past, and there is no reason to expect it to offer many new forms of training, especially since it is not clear where the field is heading. So students will have to seek out special education, supervisors, and training experiences on their own. They should explore several options and develop a special skill. In addition, an expertise in evaluation research, a second language, multicultural counseling, aging, and, of course, computers will enhance employment prospects. Grant-writing and business administration skills are also valuable.

Professional psychology is exciting precisely because it is a changing field. As it always has, it is responding to important social forces in the midst of social change. Clinical psychology interacts at many levels with individuals and society to attempt to solve the crucial issues of our time and place. That makes it a fascinating field and a rewarding career.

REFERENCES

Albee, G. (1968). Conceptual models and manpower requirements in psychology. *American Psychologist, 23,* 317–320.

Albee, G. (1970). The uncertain future of clinical psychology. *American Psychologist, 25,* 1071–1080.

Albee, G. (1982). Preventing psychopathology and promoting human potential. *American Psychologist, 37,* 1043–1050.

Albee, G. (1985). The answer is prevention. *Psychology Today, 19(2),* 60–65.

Albee, G. (1986). Toward a just society: Lessons from observation on the primary prevention of psychopathology. *American Psychologist, 41,* 891–898.

Albee, G., & Joffe, J. (1977). *Primary prevention of psychopathology. Vol. I: The issues.* Hanover, NH: University Press of New England.

American Psychological Association. (1981). Ethical principles of psychologists. *American Psychologist, 36,* 633–638.

Banta, H., & Sax, L. (1983). Reimbursement for psychotherapy: Linking efficacy research and public policymaking. *American Psychologist, 38,* 918–923.

Bazrod, S. (1986, Oct. 16). Here's how to find self-help groups. *Los Angeles Times,* Part V, p. 10.

Berg, M. (1986). Toward a diagnostic alliance between psychiatrist and psychologist. *American Psychologist, 41,* 52–59.

Bersoff, D. (1983). Hospital privileges and the antitrust laws. *American Psychologist, 38,* 1238–1242.

Binner, P. (1986). DRGs and the administration of mental health services. *American Psychologist, 441,* 64–79.

Birren, J. (1983). Aging in America: Roles for psychology. *American Psychologist, 38,* 298–299.

Boll, T. (1985). Graduate education in psychology: Time for a change? *American Psychologist, 40,* 1029–1020.

Brownell, K. (1982). Obesity: Understanding and treating a serious, prevalent, and refractory disorder. *Journal of Consulting and Clinical Psychology, 50,* 820–840.

Caplan, G. (1964). *Principles of preventive psychiatry.* New York: Basic Books.

Cattell, R. (1983). Let's end the duel. *American Psychologist, 38,* 769–776.

Cheifetz, D., & Salloway, J. (1984). Patterns of mental health services provided by HMOs. *American Psychologist, 39,* 495–502.

Conrad, P., & Schneider, J. (1980). *Deviance and medicalization.* St. Louis: Mosby.

Cowan, E. (1980). The wooing of primary prevention. *American Journal of Community Psychology, 8,* 258–284.

Cummings, N. (1986). The dismantling of our health system. *American Psychologist, 41,* 426–431.

Cunningham, S. (1985). The public and nuclear power: Scientists attack DOE attempt to reduce 'phobia.' *APA Monitor, 16,* 1, 18.

DeKraai, M., & Sales, B. (1981). *Privileged communications of psychologists* (Report for APA's Ad Hoc Committee on Legal Issues). Washington, DC: American Psychological Association.

DeLeon, P. (1986). Increasing the societal contribution of organized psychology. *American Psychologist, 41,* 466–474.

DeLeon, P., & Pallak, M. (1982). Public health and psychology: An important, expanding interaction. *American Psychologist, 37,* 934–935.

DeLeon, P., Uyeda, M., & Welch, B. (1985). Psychology and HMOs: New partnership or new adversary? *American Psychologist, 40,* 1122–1124.

DeLeon, P., VandenBos, G., & Cummings, N. (1983). Psychotherapy—Is it safe, effective, and appropriate? The beginning of an evolutionary dialog. *American Psychologist, 38,* 907–911.

DeLeon, P., VandenBos, G., & Kraut, A. (1984). Federal legislation recognizing psychology. *American Psychologist, 39,* 933–946.

Drude, K. (1978). Psychologists and civil commitment: A review of state statutes. *Professional Psychologist, 10,* 499–506.

English, J. (1986). Diagnosis-related groups and general hospital psychiatry: The APA Study. *American Journal of Psychiatry, 143,* 131–139.

Ewing, C. (1978). *Crisis intervention as psychotherapy.* New York: Oxford University Press.

Fisher, K. (1984). CHAMPUS changes: Good and bad news. *APA Monitor, 15,* 2.

Forgays, D. (1983). Primary prevention of psychopathology. In M. Hersen, A. Kazdin, & A. Bellack. (Eds.), *The clinical psychology handbook.* New York: Pergamon Press.

France, K. (1982). *Crisis intervention: A handbook of immediate person-to-person help.* Springfield, IL: C. C Thomas.

Givelber, D., Bowers, W., & Blitch, C. (1985). *The* Tarasoff *controversy: A summary of findings from an empirical study of legal, ethical, and clinical issues* (NIMH Summary Report). Washington, D.C.: NIMH.

Goldston, S. (1986). Primary prevention: Historical perspectives and a blueprint for action. *American Psychologist, 41,* 453–460.

Gorenstein, E. (1984). Debating mental illness: Implications for science, medicine, and social policy. *American Psychologist, 39,* 50–56.

Hager, P. (1985, June 4) State power to mandate health benefits upheld. *Los Angeles Times,* p. 1.

Hattie, J., Sharpley, C., & Rogers, H. (1984). Comparative effectiveness of professionals and paraprofessional helpers. *Psychological Bulletin, 95,* 534–541.

Kaplan, R. (1984). The connection between clinical health promotion and health status. *American Psychologist, 39,* 755–765.

Katz, R., & Rolde, E. (1981). Community alternatives to psychotherapy. *Psychotherapy: Theory, Research and Practice, 18,* 365–374.

Kilburg, R., & Ginsberg, M. (1983). Sunset and psychology or how we learned to love a crisis. *American Psychologist, 38,* 1227–1231.

Klerman, G. (1983). The efficacy of psychotherapy as a basis for public policy. *American Psychologist, 38,* 929–934.

Lesse, S. (1986). The uncertain future of clinical psychiatry. *American Journal of Psychotherapy, 40,* 4–16.

Levy, L. (1984). The metamorphosis of clinical psychology: Toward a new charter as human services psychology. *American Psychologist, 39,* 486–494.

Lichtenstein, E. (1982). The smoking problem: A behavioral perspective. *Journal of Consulting and Clinical Psychology, 50,* 804–819.

Long, B. (1986). The prevention of mental-emotional disabilities: A report from a National Mental Health Association commission. *American Psychologist, 41,* 825–829.

McCall, N., & Rice, T. (1983). A summary of the Colorado clinical psychology/expanded mental health benefits experiment. *American Psychologist, 38,* 1279–1291.

McGuire, T., & Frisman, L. (1983). Reimbursement policy and cost-effective mental health care. *American Psychologist, 38,* 935–940.

Michael, J. (1982). The second revolution in health: Health promotion and its environmental base. *American Psychologist, 37,* 936–941.

Miller, W., & Hester, R. (1986). Inpatient alcoholism treatment: Who benefits? *American Psychologist, 41,* 794–805.

Pion, G., & Lipsey, M. (1984). Psychology and society: The challenge of change. *American Psychologist, 39,* 739–754.

Quayle, D. (1983) American productivity: The devastating effect of alcoholism and drug abuse. *American Psychologist, 38,* 454–458.

Resnick, R. (1985). The case against the Blues: The Virginia challenge. *American Psychologist, 40,* 975–983.

Rodriguez, A. (1983). Psychological and psychiatric peer review at CHAMPUS. *American Psychologist, 38,* 941–947.

Schacht, T. (1985). DSM-III and the politics of truth. *American Psychologist, 40,* 513–521.

Siegel, M. (1983). Crime and violence in America: The victims. *American Psychologist, 38,* 1267–1273.

Silver, L., & Segal, J. (1984). Psychology and mental health: An enduring partnership. *American Psychologist, 39,* 804–809.

Strupp, H., & Hadley, S. (1979). Specific versus nonspecific factors in psychotherapy: A controlled study of outcome. *Archives of General Psychiatry, 36,* 1125–1136.

Szasz, T. (1961). *The myth of mental illness: Foundations of a theory of personal conduct.* New York: Harper & Row.

Tanney, F. (1983). Hospital privileges for psychologists: A legislative model. *American Psychologist, 38,* 1232–1237.

Taube, C., Burns, B., & Kessler, L. (1984). Patients of psychiatrists and psychologists in office-based practice: 1980. *American Psychologist, 39,* 1435–1447.

Teplin, L. (1984). Criminalizing mental disorder: The comparative arrest rate of the mentally ill. *American Psychologist, 39,* 794–803.

Theaman, M. (1984). The impact of peer review on professional practice. *American Psychologist, 39,* 406–414.

Tulkin, S., & Frank, G. (1985). The changing role of psychologists in health maintenance organizations. *American Psychologist, 40,* 1125–1130.

Turkington, C. (1985). For-profit hospitals: Are they for psychologists? *APA Monitor, 16,* 1, 26–27.

Turkington, C. (1985). Analysts sued for barring non-MDs. *APA Monitor, 16,* 2.

Turkington, C. (1985). Automakers halt Ohio coverage. *APA Monitor, 16,* 30.

Tyler, F., Pargament, K., & Gatz, M. (1983). The resource collaborator role: A model for interaction involving psychologists. *American Psychologist, 38,* 388–398.

VandenBos, G., & Stapp, J. (1983). Service providers in psychology: Results of the 1982 APA human resources survey. *American Psychologist, 38,* 1330–1352.

Weiss, B. (1983). Behavioral toxicology and environmental health science: Opportunity and challenge for psychology. *American Psychologist, 38,* 1174–1187.

Widiger, T., & Rorer, L. (1984). The responsible psychotherapist. *American Psychologist, 39,* 503–515.

Widiger, T., & Trull, T. (1985). The empty debate over the existence of mental illness: Comments on Gorenstein. *American Psychologist, 40,* 468–470.

Wolkon, G., Peterson, C., & Gongla, P. (1982). University-based continuing education and mental health systems change. *American Psychologist, 37,* 966–970.

Woolfolk, R. (1985) What's at stake in the mental illness controversy. *American Psychologist, 40,* 468.

Wright, R. (1981). Psychologists and professional liability (malpractice) insurance: A retrospective review. *American Psychologist, 36,* 1485–1493.

Zaro, J., Batchelor, W., Ginsberg, M., & Pallak, M. (1982). Psychology and the JCAH: Reflections on a decade of struggle. *American Psychologist, 37,* 1342–1349.

Name Index

Subject Index